INTERNATIONAL CONFLICT RESOLUTION: CONSENSUAL ADR PROCESSES

By

Jacqueline Nolan–Haley
Professor of Law
Fordham University School of Law

Harold Abramson
Professor of Law
Touro College Fuchsberg Law Center

Pat K. Chew
Professor of Law
University of Pittsburgh School of Law

AMERICAN CASEBOOK SERIES®

Mat #40134168

American Casebook Series and West Group are trademarks
registered in the U.S. Patent and Trademark Office.

© 2005 Thomson/West
    610 Opperman Drive
    P.O. Box 64526
    St. Paul, MN 55164–0526
    1–800–328–9352

Printed in the United States of America

ISBN 0–314–14588–5

 TEXT IS PRINTED ON 10% POST CONSUMER RECYCLED PAPER

To Jamie, problem-solver par excellence

J.N.H.

To my family, thanks for the lifelong lessons

H.I.A.

To Robert, Lauren, and Luke
Who have taught me so much about both
culture and conflict

P.K.C.

*

Introduction

This book addresses a growing phenomenon in the twenty-first century, namely that we are a global society deeply afflicted with conflict. Whether arising in the form of transborder legal disputes between individual parties or at a broader social and political level among nation-states, groups and communities, conflict is pervasive. The traditional and Western response to managing and resolving conflict, as reflected in the *Restatement (Third) of Foreign Relations Law*, focuses on international law—that set of "rules and principles of general application dealing with the conduct of states and of international organizations and with their relations *inter se*, as well as with some of their relations with persons, whether natural or juridical."[1] Traditional analysis considers the extent to which international law may be binding and the factors that lead states to comply with it.

Over the last decade, as global conflict has intensified, the significance of law as a response to conflict has diminished in favor of approaches that honor international cooperation and conflict prevention. This focus calls for early intervention in the life cycle of a conflict to prevent further escalation with all its attendant, and sometimes deadly, consequences. While conflict prevention has been a major global concern over the last several years, it is a concept that raises what Abram Chayes labels a "significant paradox" for the international community:

> On the one hand, the need for conflict prevention arises because the parties cannot or will not settle the conflicts or issues between them on their own. On the other hand, a settlement cannot, in the nature of things, be imposed from the outside. And, even short of imposition, outside intervention is almost universally opposed, resisted and manipulated by parties involved in a conflict. It is almost inevitable that our institutions, as well-intentioned as they are, cannot know or understand enough about the intimate details of the conflict. Moreover, our international institutions tend to be clumsy, ponderous, bureaucratic and remote-at the other end of a long, long telephone line from the action-and compelled by the inadequacy of the resources made available to them to allocate those resources thinly. . . . The central paradox is that a clash among parties calls for some "intervention" to help resolve it because the parties cannot do so, while the form of intervention available is almost necessarily not knowledgeable enough, flexible enough or close enough to the problem. . . .[2]

---

1. Restatement (Third) of Foreign Relations Law § 101 (1987).

2. George E. Morris, *Conflict Prevention for a New Century*, 88 Am. Soc'y Int'l L. Proc. 142 (1994).

The message presented in this paradox is increasingly clear—consent is a value that matters when parties are in conflict situations, whether the conflict is legal, political or social in nature. Thus, in preparing for the practice of law in the 21st century, students must think beyond the boundaries of "international law" per se, enforced through traditional adjudicatory processes, and gain a greater appreciation of the extent to which consensual processes such as negotiation and mediation may have a more significant impact on the management and resolution of conflict. This challenge requires an understanding of the extent to which cultural considerations affect conflict. It is important to keep in mind that while the contemporary regime of international law is based largely on the Western European model of the nation-state, great and ancient empires such as those in Africa, China, and Japan, existed long before Western Europe. The materials in this text will expose you to the experience of handling conflict in non-western cultures.

Objectives

This book focuses on consensual approaches to resolving international conflicts and disputes. By consensual processes, we refer to the range of methodologies and strategies through which parties affected by conflict participate in its resolution. For purposes of this text, the critical distinction between consensual and non-consensual processes is the degree of autonomy in decisionmaking that disputing parties retain. In consensual processes, decisionmaking belongs to the parties affected by the conflict or dispute, and the third-party intervener is not empowered to impose a result. To the extent that an understanding of adjudicatory processes is helpful to round out the study of consensual processes, adjudicatory processes are presented in an abbreviated fashion in the text.

There are three overarching themes in this book. The first theme introduces you to the significance of culture in the analysis and resolution of public and private sector conflicts. Chapter 3 which presents the foundation for the rest of the book, affirms the importance and persuasiveness of culture in conflict and conflict resolution. Moreover, it teaches practical tools: caveats to considering culture, constructs for comparing cultural approaches, and finally, ways to reconcile cultural conflicts.

The second theme explores the interrelationships among the fragmented field of international conflict resolution. It considers how the consensual processes used in private, commercial consensual dispute resolution differ in the public context. Concepts such as informed consent and neutrality, important in domestic versions of ADR and conflict resolution, may be understood quite differently in the international arena, and even within private and public international practice.

The third theme considers how consensual processes, which introduce a civilized way to resolve disputes and conflicts, can be essential internationally because of the limitations of domestic judicial processes and the lack of a binding international public process. It examines how consensual processes can fill gaps in the international landscape for resolving private and public disputes.

Many of the materials and case studies in this text provide you with what cultural theorists refer to as "thick descriptions" of events. These thick descriptions give you a detailed, contextual understanding of particular conflicts. They help you to understand some of the factors that differentiate groups in conflict, and challenge you to think creatively about how to respond to specific conflict situations. As you read these materials we hope that you will gain greater appreciation of the lawyer's role as peacemaker and problem-solver in responding to contemporary public and private international conflicts.

The text is divided into three parts with Part I providing the background, context and cultural foundation of the book. Parts II and III, dealing with private and public sector processes, reflect formal international law discourse that distinguishes between private and public international law. The latter relates to the activities of governments while the former refers to activities of corporations and individuals that engage in transborder activities.

The materials in Part I begin with an understanding of the meaning of conflict and a description of basic terms and approaches to conflict resolution, including the adjudication process. These definitional understandings are then applied to a wider transborder setting which enables students to consider a broad array of possible solutions to all manner of international conflict. The final section exploring the role of culture in conflict, establishes the foundational underpinnings of this book.

Part II explores a range of issues that arise in the practice of private negotiation and mediation in the international arena. It considers the suitability of specific disputes for mediation, discusses some distinctive issues in international negotiation and mediation and explores the new subject of client representation in international mediation. Ways to combine private processes and draft clauses are also included. The final section examines how Internet-based facilities can be used to supplement, or replace, traditional processes for resolving private disputes.

Part III introduces you to international negotiation and mediation practice in the public sector. It acknowledges that these two processes occupy a central position in international conflict resolution as an alternative to the use of force in resolving conflicts between nations and ethnic groups. Part III expands the definitional sections in Part I with coverage of processes focused specifically on addressing ethnic conflicts and also recognizes the growing role of international organizations and NGOs in the work of conflict resolution. The final section highlights the influence of the human rights movement in contemporary conflict resolution efforts.

As you read through these materials, think about the following questions:

1. How *has* the international community responded to conflict in the latter half of the twentieth century? How have cultural considerations affected such decisionmaking?

2. How *should* the international community respond to conflict? What is the proper role of outside actors in shaping the future of political communities? In this regard, what is the meaning and scope of self-determination?

3. How has the human rights movement challenged traditional notions of sovereignty?

4. What do we have to offer parties living in protracted conflict? How can justice and healing take place for people within conflict and after severe conflict situations?

5. How can parties who are separated by culture and distance productively resolve disputes in a world of rapidly increasing interaction and interdependence?

6. What are the significant differences between domestic and international negotiation and mediation practice? How do cultural considerations affect both?

Acknowledgments

The authors would like to thank Patricia Harrington Wysor for her excellent editing assistance, Elizabeth Frayer, Nycole Thompson, Nicole Stryker and Dennis Yai at Fordham, Noel Munier and Joseph Wilson at Touro for their excellent research assistance, and Kathleen Ruggiero at Fordham and Salome Geronimio at Touro for their excellent secretarial support. We would also like to thank Fordham University Law School, Touro College, Jacob D. Fuchsberg Law Center and the University of Pittsburgh Law School for financial support and the Documents Technology Center at the University of Pittsburgh School of Law for outstanding technical support.

Permissions

The following authors and publishers gave us permission to reprint excerpts from copyrighted material; we gratefully acknowledge their assistance.

Introduction

George E. Morris, *Conflict Prevention for New Century*, 88 Am. Soc'y Int'l L. Proc. 142 (1994). Copyright © 1994 by the American Society of International Law; George E. Morris. Reprinted with permission of the American Society of International Law.

Chapter 1

Jan Eliasson, *Perspectives on Managing Intractable Conflict*, Negotiation Journal 371, 373–74 (October 2002). Copyright 2002 Kluwer Academic/Plenum Publishers. Reprinted with permission from the author.

Dominic Bryan, *Parading Protestants and Consenting Catholics in Northern Ireland: Communal Conflict, Contested Public Space, and Group Rights*, 5 Chicago Journal of International Law 233, 234–37, 241–42 (2004). Copyright 2004 Chicago Journal of International Law. Reprinted with permission of the publisher and copyright holder Chicago Journal of International Law.

Chapter 2

Robert H Mnookin, *Why Negotiations Fail: An Exploration of Barriers to the Resolution of Conflict*, 8 Ohio State Journal on Dispute Resolution 235 (1993). Reprinted with the permission of Professor Robert H. Mnookin and the Ohio State Journal on Dispute Resolution. Originally published at 8 Ohio State Journal on Dispute Resolution 235 (1993).

Jacqueline M. Nolan-Haley, *Informed Consent in Mediation: A Guiding Principle for Truly Educated Decisionmaking*, 74 Notre Dame Law Review 775 (1999). Reprinted with the permission of the author.

Stephen J. Burton, *Combining Conciliation With Arbitration of International Commercial Disputes,* 18 Hastings Int'l & Comp. L. Rev. 637 (1995). ©1995 by the University of California, Hastings College of the Law. Reprinted from Hastings International and Comparative Law Review, Volume 18, Number 4, Summer 1995, 637, by permission.

John D. Feerick, *The Peace-Making Role of a Mediator*, 19 Ohio State Journal on Dispute Resolution 229 (2003). Reprinted with the permission of the Ohio State Journal on Dispute Resolution.

Linda C. Reif, *Conciliation as a Mechanism for the Resolution of International Economic and Business Disputes,* 14 Fordham Int'l L. J. 578 (1990/1991). Copyright 1991 by the Fordham University School of Law; Linda C. Reif. Reprinted with permission of the author and the Fordham International Law Journal.

Richard B. Bilder, *International Third Party Dispute Settlement*, 17 Denver Journal of International Law and Policy 471 (1989). Reprinted with the permission of the Denver Journal of International Law & Policy.

Chapter 3

Kevin Avurch & Peter W. Black, *Conflict Resolution in Intercultural Settings: Problems and Prospects*, in Dennis J. Sandole & Hugo van der Merwe eds. CONFLICT RESOLUTION THEORY AND PRACTICE: INTEGRATION AND APPLICATION 131–40 (1993). Reprinted with permission from the authors.

Pat K. Chew, *The Pervasiveness of Culture*, 54 Journal of Legal Education 60, 66–69 (2004). Reprinted with permission from the author.

Alison Dundes Rentelyn, *Cross-Cultural Dispute Resolution: The Consequences of Conflicting Interpretations of Norms*, Willamette Journal International Law & Dispute Resolution 103, 113–115 (2002). Reprinted with permission of the Willamette Journal of International Law & Dispute Resolution.

James K. Sebenius, *Caveats for Cross-Border Negotiation*, Negotiation Journal 121, 122–31 (April 2002). Reprinted with permission of

Hazel Rose Markus & Leah R. Lin, *Conflictways: Cultural Diversity in the Meanings and Practices of Conflict* in Deborah A. Prenctice & Dale T. Miller eds. CULTURAL DIVIDES 302, 313–27 (1999).

Harold Abramson, *International Dispute Resolution: Cross-Cultural Dimensions and Structuring Appropriate Processes*, in Alan Rau, Edward Sherman & Scott Peppet, PROCESSES OF DISPUTE RESOLUTION 918–21 (3rd ed. 2002). Reprinted with permission of the author.

Pat K. Chew, *The Rule of Law: China's Skepticism and the Rule of People*, 20 Ohio State Journal on Dispute Resolution   (200). Reprinted with permission of the author.

Chapter 4

Walter G. Gans, *Saving Time and Money in Cross-Border Commercial Disputes,* Dispute Resolution Journal, 52–54 (January 1997). Permission given by the American Arbitration Association.

Harold I. Abramson, MEDIATION REPRESENTATION-ADVOCATING IN A PROBLEM-SOLVING PROCESS 1–6, 104–108 (NITA © 2004). Reproduced with permission from the National Institute for Trial Advocacy. Further reproduction is prohibited.

Jeanne M. Brett, NEGOTIATING GLOBALLY: HOW TO NEGOTIATE DEALS, RESOLVE DISPUTES, AND MAKE DECISIONS ACROSS CULTURAL BOUNDARIES 16, 61–72 (John Wiley & Sons © 2001). Reprinted with permission of John Wiley & Sons, Inc.

John L. Graham and N. Mark Lam, *The Chinese Negotiation*, Harvard Business Review. 82, 84–89 (Oct. 2003). Adapted and reprinted by permission of *Harvard Business Review*. Copyright © 2003 by Harvard Business School Publishing Corporation; all rights reserved.

Ann Black, *Alternative Dispute Resolution in Brunei Darussalam: The Blending of Imported and Traditional Process*, 13 Bond Law Review (Dec. 2001) at pg. 21, Table Only "Comparison of Features of Western and Traditional Mediation."

Harold Abramson, *Problem-Solving Advocacy in Mediations: A Model of Client Representation*, 10 Harvard Negotiation Law Review 103 (2005).

Harold Abramson, *Mining Mediation Rules for Representation Opportunities and Obstacles,* 1 Journal of International Dispute Resolution 40 (Jan. 2004) (European Law Publishers and Verlag Rechht und Wirtschaft Heidelberg, Germany, January 2004) and 15 American Review of International Arbitration 103 (2005).

Donna L. Pavlick, *Apology and Mediation: The Horse and the Carriage of the Twenty-First Century,* 18 Ohio State Journal on Dispute Resolution 829, 843–847 (2003).

Hiroshi Wagatsuma and Arthur Rosett, T*he Implications of Apology: Law and Culture in Japan and the United States,* 20 Law and Society Review 461–62, 466–69, 471–74, 475–76, 478–79, 492–493 (Blackwell Publishing, 1986).

Jennifer K. Robbennolt, *Apologies and Legal Settlement: An Empirical Examination,* 102 Michigan Law Review 460, 506–507 (2003).

Max Edison, How TO HAGGLE—PROFESSIONAL TRICKS FOR SAVING MONEY ON JUST ABOUT ANYTHING 11–13, 29–39 (2001). Used by permission of Paladin Press (www.paladin-press.com).

Prosando v. High-Tech Dispute. Prepared by the CPR Institute for Dispute Resolution (formerly known as the Center for Public Resources/CPR Legal Program), 366 Madison Avenue, New York, NY 10017, www.cpradr.org. (Permission granted to change Prosando party to an Italian-Chinese joint venture.) © 1994. Reprinted with permission. All rights reserved.

Michael T. Colatrella, *Court-Performed Mediation in the People's Republic of China: A Proposed Model to Improve the United States Federal District Courts' Mediation Programs*, 15 Ohio State Journal on Dispute Resolution 391, 395–400, 404–406 (2000).

Robert Perkovich, *A Comparative Analysis of Community Mediation in the United States and the People's Republic of China*, 10 Temple International and Comparative Law Journal 313–327 (1996).

China Council for the Promotion of International Trade (CCPIT) and China Chamber of International Commerce (CCOIC), Conciliation Rules (Selected Rules) 2000. Revised Conciliation Rules are expected to be issued in 2005.

Chapter 5

Christian Buhring-Uhle, ARBITRATION AND MEDIATION IN INTERNATIONAL BUSINESS 141–143, 389–391 (1996). Reprinted with permission from Kluwer Law International (www.kluwerlaw.com).

Lucy F. Reed, *Drafting Arbitration Clauses* in INTERNATIONAL BUSINESS LITIGATION & ARBITRATION 2000 624 PLI/Lit 563, 565–577 (Practicing Law Institute, February 2000, PLI Order No. H0–005R) (Copyright © 2000 Practicing Law Institute). Reprinted with permission from the author.

Kathleen M. Scanlon, *Multi-Step Dispute Resolution Clauses in Business-Business Agreements* SJO34 ALI-ABA, 6–15 (Mediation and Other ADR-Dispute Resolution for the 21st Century, American Law Institute-American Bar Association Continuing Legal Education, September 18–19, 2003) (Copyright © 2003 Kathleen M. Scanlon, Special Counsel, Heller Ehrman White & McAuliffe. All Rights Reserved.) Reprinted with permission from the author.

Robert H. Mnookin, *Creating Value Through Process Design*, 11 Journal of International Arbitration 125, 126–130 (1994). Reprinted with permission from the author.

Harold Abramson, *Protocols for International Arbitrators Who Dare to Settle Cases* 10 American Review of International Arbitration 1–2, 7–15 (1999).

Chapter 6

Melissa Conley Tyler & Di Bretherton, SEVENTY-SIX AND COUNTING: AN ANALYSIS OF ODR SITES, A REPORT OF RESEARCH CONDUCTED FOR THE DEPARTMENT OF JUSTICE, VICTORIA, AUSTRALIA, Proceedings of the UNECE Forum on ODR 2003, www.odr.infro/unece2003. This study is being updated to one hundred and fifteen sites and counting. Reprinted with permission from the author.

Llewellyn J. Gibbons, Robin M. Kennedy, and John M. Gibbs, *Cyber-Mediation: Computer-Mediated Communications Medium Massaging the Message,* 32 New Mexico Law Review 27, 35–37, 37–39, 43–54, 62–65, 136–37, 140–41 (2002).

Lucille M. Ponte, *The Michigan Cyber Court: A Bold Experiment in the Development of the First Public Virtual Courthouse,* 4 North Carolina Journal of Law & Technology 51, 55–56, 62–65 (2002).

Ethan Katsh and Janet Rifkin, ONLINE DISPUTE RESOLUTION 9–10, 73–90, 136–37, 140–41 (John Wiley & Sons © 2001). Reprinted with permission of John Wiley & Sons, Inc.

Benjamin G. Davis, *Disciplining ODR Prototypes: True Trust Through True Independence*, Proceedings of the UNECE Forum on ODR 2003, http://www.odr.info/unece2003. Reprinted with permission from the author.

James C. Melamed, *Mediating on the Internet Today and Tomorrow,* 1 Pepperdine Dispute Resolution Law Journal 11, 20–24 (2000). Reprinted with permission from the author and Mediate.com.

Karen Stewart & Joseph Matthews, *Online Arbitration of Cross-Border, Business to Consumer Disputes,* 56 University of Miami Law Review 1111, 1130–36 (2002).

Chapter 7

Robert H. Mnookin, *When Not To Negotiate: A Negotiation Imperialist Reflects on Appropriate Limits*, 74 University of Colorado Law Review 1077 (2003). Reprinted with permission of the University of Colorado Law Review and the author.

Jacqueline Nolan-Haley & Bronagh Hinds, *Problem-Solving Negotiation: Northern Ireland's Experience with the Women's Coalition,* Journal of Dispute Resolution 394 (2003). Reprinted with permission of the authors and the Journal of Dispute Resolution, University of Missouri-Columbia, Center for the Study of Dispute Resolution, 206 Hulston Hall, Columbia, Mo 65211.

David M. Rothenberg, *Negotiation and Dispute Resolution in the Sri Lankan Context: Lessons from the 1994–95 Peace Talks,* 22 Fordham International Law Journal 505 (1998). Reprinted with permission of the author.

Jacob Bercovitch, ed. STUDIES IN INTERNATIONAL MEDIATION 5 (2002). Reprinted with permission of the publisher, Palgrave Macmillan.

Melanie Greenberg, *Mediating Massacres: When "Neutral, Low-Power" Models of Mediation Cannot and Should Not Work,* 19 Ohio State Journal on Dispute Resolution 185 (2003). Reprinted with permission of Melanie Greenberg and the Ohio State Journal on Dispute Resolution. Originally published at 19 Ohio St. J. On Disp. Resol. 185 (2003).

I. William Zartman, *Cowardly Lions: Missed Opportunities for Dispute Settlement,* 18 Ohio State Journal on Dispute Resolution 1 (2002). Reprinted with permission of the Ohio State Journal on Dispute Resolution and the author.

John D. Feerick, *The Peace-Making Role of a Mediator*, 19 Ohio State Journal on Dispute Resolution 229 (2003). Reprinted with permission of the Ohio State Journal on Dispute Resolution.

Dale E. Spencer & Honggang Yang, *Lessons from the Field of Intra-National Conflict Resolution*, Volume 67, Number 5, Notre Dame Law Review (1992) 1495–1511. Reprinted with permission. © by Notre Dame Law Review, University of Notre Dame. The publisher bears responsibility for any errors which have occurred in reprinting or editing.

Chapter 8

Harold H. Saunders, *Sustained Dialogue in Managing Intractable Conflict*, Negotiation Journal 85 (January 2003). Reprinted with permission of the Negotiation Journal, Kluwer Academic/Plenum Publishers and the author.

Elena A. Baylis, *Beyond Rights: Legal Process and Ethnic Conflicts,* 25 Michigan Journal of International Law 529 (2004). Reprinted with permission of Michigan Journal of International Law.

Arthur Lenk, *Fact-Finding as Peace Negotiation Tool—The Mitchell Report and the Israeli-Palestinian Peace Process,* 24 Loyola of Los Angeles International & Comparative Law Review 289 (2002). Reprinted with permission of the Loyola of Los Angeles International and Comparative Law Review.

Philip C. Aka, *Nigeria: The Need for An Effective Policy of Ethnic Reconciliation in the New Century*, 14 Temple International & Comparative Law Journal 327 (2000). Reprinted with permission of the Temple International & Comparative Law Journal.

Eugene Weiner, *Coexistence Work: A New Profession* in Eugene Weiner, ed., THE HANDBOOK OF INTERETHNIC COEXISTENCE 13–17, 19–21 (1998). © 1998 by the Abraham Fund. Reprinted with permission of the Continuum International Publishing Company.

Carla S. Copeland, *The Use of Arbitration to Settle Territorial Disputes,* 67 Fordham Law Review 3073 (1999). Reprinted with permission of the Fordham Law Review.

Chapter 9

Robert Kirsch, *The Peacemaker: An Interview with UN Under-Secretary-General Alvaro de Soto,* 26 Fletcher Forum of World Affairs 83 (2002). Reprinted with permission of the Fletcher Forum of World Affairs.

Ruth Wedgwood, *United Nations Peacekeeping Operations and the Use of Force*, 5 Washington University Journal of Law & Policy 69 (2001). Reprinted with permission of the Washington University Journal of Law & Policy and the author.

P. Mweti Munya, *The Organization of African Unity and its Role in Regional Conflict Resolution and Dispute Settlement: A Critical Evaluation,* 19 Boston College Third World Journal 537 (1999). Reprinted with permission of the Boston College Third World Journal.

Diane F. Orentlicher, *Separation Anxiety: International Responses to Ethno-Separatist Claims,* 23 Yale Journal of International Law 1 (1998). Reprinted with permission of the Yale Journal of International Law.

T. Modibo Ocran, *The Doctrine of Humanitarian Intervention in Light of Robust Peacekeeping,* 25 Boston College International and Comparative Law Review, 1 (2002). Reprinted with permission of the Boston College International & Comparative Law Review.

Edward N. Luttwak, *Give War A Chance,* 78 Foreign Affairs 36 (1999). Reprinted by permission of Foreign Affairs, Vol. 78, No. 4 (July/August 1999). © 1999 by the Council on Foreign Relations.

Paul R. Williams, *The Role of Justice in Peace Negotiations* in POST-CONFLICT JUSTICE 122–23 (M. Cherif Bassiouni ed., 2002). Reprinted with permission of Transnational Publishers.

Gillian Martin Sorenson, *The Roles A Civil Society Can Play in International Dispute Resolution,* 18 Negotiation Journal 355 (2002). Reprinted with permission.

Richard J. Goldstone, *Justice as a Tool for Peace-Making: Truth Commissions and International Criminal Tribunals,* 28 New York University Journal of International Law and Policy 485 (1996). Reprinted with permission of the author.

Jose E. Alvarez, *Rush to Closure: Lessons of the Tadic Judgment,* 96 Michigan Law Review 2031 (1998), originally published by the Michigan Law Review. Reprinted with permission of the Michigan Law Review and the author.

Jason S. Abrams & Priscilla Hayner, *Documenting, Acknowledging and Publicizing the Truth* in POST-CONFLICT JUSTICE 283 (M. Cherif Bassiouni ed., 2002). Reprinted with permission of Transnational Publishers.

Dominic Bryan, *Parading Protestants and Consenting Catholics in Northern Ireland: Communal Conflict, Contested Public Space, and Group Rights,* 5 Chicago Journal of International Law 233 (2004). Reprinted with permission of the Chicago Journal of International Law.

Ellen L. Lutz, Eileen F. Babbitt & Hurst Hannum, *Human Rights and Conflict Resolution from the Practitioner's Perspective,* 27 Fletcher Forum of World Affairs 173 (2003). Reprinted with permission of the Fletcher Forum of World Affairs.

*

Summary of Contents

Table of Contents

Table of References

References are to Pages

Chapter 1

David J. Bederman, INTERNATIONAL LAW FRAMEWORKS (2001), 8.

Dominic Bryan, *Parading Protestants and Consenting Catholics in Northern Ireland: Communal Conflict, Contested Public Space, and Group Rights*, 5 Chicago Journal of International Law 233, 234–37, 241–42 (2004), 6–8, 15–16.

Guy Burgess and Heidi Burgess, *Constructive Confrontation: A Transformative Approach to Intractable Conflicts,* 13 MEDIATION QUARTERLY 305 (1996), 3.

John W. Burton, *Conflict-Dispute Distinction*, 2 in CONFLICT: RESOLUTION AND PREVENTION (1990), 9.

Walker Connor, *A Few Cautionary Notes on the History and Future of Ethnonational Conflicts,* in FACING ETHNIC CONFLICTS: TOWARD A NEW REALISM (Eds., Andreas Wimmer, Richard J. Goldstone, Donald L. Horowitz, Ulrike Joras, Conrad Schetter (2004), 6.

Jan Eliasson, *Perspectives on Managing Intractable Conflict*, Negotiation Journal 371, 373–74 (October 2002), 4–5.

Louis Kreisberg, CONSTRUCTIVE CONFLICT: FROM ESCALATION TO RESOLUTION (1998), 2.

Mavrommatis Palestine Concessions (Greece v. U.K.), 1924 P.C.I.J. ser. A No. 2, (Judgment of Aug. 13), 8.

MCC-Marble Ceramic Center, Inc. v. Ceramica Nuova D'Agostino, S.P.A., 144 F.3d 1384 (11th Cir.1998), 9.

Richard Miller & Austin Sarat, *Grievances, Claims, and Disputes: Assessing the Adversary Culture,* 15 Law & Soc'y Rev. 525 (1980–81), 9.

George E. Morris, *Conflict Prevention For A New Century*, 88 Am. Soc'y Int'l L. Proc. 142 (1994) (Remarks of Professor Abram Chayes), 2.

Dean G. Pruitt and Jeffrey Z. Rubin, SOCIAL CONFLICT: ESCALATION, STALEMATE AND SETTLEMENT (1986), 2.

Andreas Wimmer, "Introduction: Facing Ethnic Conflicts" in FACING ETHNIC CONFLICTS: TOWARD A NEW REALISM (Eds., Andreas Wimmer, Richard J. Goldstone, Donald L. Horowitz, Ulrike Joras, Conrad Schetter (2004), 3.

Chapter 2

Jerold S. Auerbach, JUSTICE WITHOUT LAW? (1983), 17.

David J. Bederman, INTERNATIONAL LAW FRAMEWORKS (2001), 36.

Jacob Bercovitch, *Mediation in International Conflict*, *in* I. W. Zartman & L. Rasmussen, eds., PEACEMAKING IN INTERNATIONAL CONFLICT (U.S. Institute of Peace 1997), 31.

Jacob Bercovitch, ed., STUDIES IN INTERNATIONAL MEDIATION (2002), 18.

Richard B. Bilder, *International Third Party Dispute Settlement*, 17 Denver Journal of International Law and Policy 471 (1989), 38–41, 44–46.

Stephen J. Burton, *Combining Conciliation With Arbitration of International Commercial Disputes,* 18 Hastings Int'l & Comp. L. Rev. 637 (1995), 47–48.

Antonia Chayes and Martha Minow, eds., IMAGINE COEXISTENCE: RESTORING HUMANITY AFTER VIOLENT CONFLICT (2003), 18.

Commission of the European Communities, Green Paper on Alternative Dispute Resolution in Civil and Commercial Law (COM(2002)196 Final) (Brussels April 19, 2002), 19.

Chester A. Crocker, Fen Osler Hampson and Pamela Aall, eds., HERDING CATS: MULTIPARTY MEDIATION IN A COMPLEX WORLD (U.S. Institute of Peace 1999), 18.

William J. Davey, *The World Trade Organization's Dispute Settlement System*, 42 S. TEX. L. REV. 1199 (2001), 34.

Dogger Bank Incident (Great Britain v. Russia), Hague Ct. Rep. (Scott) 403 (Comm'n Inquiry 1905), 35.

John D. Feerick, *The Peace-Making Role of a Mediator*, 19 Ohio State Journal on Dispute Resolution 229 (2003), 33–34.

Ronald J. Fisher, *Interactive Conflict Resolution*, *in* PEACEMAKING IN INTERNATIONAL CONFLICT: METHODS & TECHNIQUES 39, 61 (William Zartman & J. Lewis Rasmussen, eds. 1997), 21.

Roger Fisher, William Ury, & Bruce Patton, GETTING TO YES: NEGOTIATING AGREEMENT WITHOUT GIVING IN (2d ed. 1991), 23.

Lon Fuller, *Mediation—Its Forms and Functions*, 44 SO. CAL. L. REV. 305 (1971), 18.

Lon Fuller, *The Forms and Limits of Adjudication*, 92 HARV. L. REV. 353 (1978), 18.

J. Gold, *Prior Consultation in International Law*, 24 VA. J. INT'L L. 729 (1983–84), 34.

P .H. Gulliver: DISPUTES AND NEGOTIATIONS: A CROSS CULTURAL PERSPECTIVE (1979), 18.

HANDBOOK ON THE PEACEFUL SETTLEMENT OF DISPUTES BETWEEN STATES (UN Office of Legal Affairs 1992), 34.

P. Terrance Hopmann, *Two Paradigms of Negotiating: Bargaining and Problem-Solving*, ANNALS, AAPSS, 542 (Nov. 1995), 18.

F.L. Kirgis, PRIOR CONSULTATION IN INTERNATIONAL LAW (Charlottesville 1983), 34.

Russell Korobkin, NEGOTIATION THEORY AND STRATEGY (2002), 22.

Victor A. Kremenyuk, INTERNATIONAL NEGOTIATION (2d ed. 2002), 23.

Louis Kriesberg, *The Development of the Conflict Resolution Field*, in PEACEMAKING IN INTERNATIONAL CONFLICT: METHODS & TECHNIQUES 51, 60 (I. William Zartman & J. Lewis Rasmussen, eds. 1997), 21.

David Lax & James Sebenius, THE MANAGER AS NEGOTIATOR: BARGAINING FOR COOPERATION AND COMPETITIVE GAIN (1986), 23.

Peter Malanczuk, AKEHURST'S MODERN INTRODUCTION TO INTERNATIONAL LAW (7th ed. 1997), 35.

J. G. Merrills, INTERNATIONAL DISPUTE SETTLEMENT (3d ed. 1998), 34.

Robert H Mnookin, *Why Negotiations Fail: An Exploration of Barriers to the Resolution of Conflict,* 8 Ohio State Journal on Dispute Resolution 235 (1993), 24–31.

Robert H. Mnookin, Scott R. Peppet, Andrew S. Tulumello, BEYOND WINNING: NEGOTIATING TO CREATE VALUE IN DEALS AND DISPUTES 24 (2000), 23.

Laura Nader & Harry Todd, THE DISPUTING PROCESS: LAW IN TEN SOCIETIES (1978), 18.

Philip M. Nichols, *Two Snowflakes Are Alike: Assumptions Made in the Debate Over Standing Before the World Trade Organization Dispute Settlement Board,* 24 Fordham Int'l L. J. 427 (2000), 43.

Jacqueline Nolan-Haley, *Court Mediation and the Search for Justice Through Law*, 74 WASH. U.L.Q. 47 (1996), 31.

Jacqueline M. Nolan-Haley, *Informed Consent in Mediation: A Guiding Principle for Truly Educated Decisionmaking*, 74 Notre Dame Law Review 775 (1999), 32–33.

Linda C. Reif, *Conciliation as a Mechanism for the Resolution of International Economic and Business Disputes,* 14 Fordham Int'l L. J. 578 (1990/1991), 36.

RESTATEMENT (THIRD) OF FOREIGN RELATIONS, § 902, Reporters Notes, n. 4, p. 20.

Simon Roberts, *Institutionalized Settlement in England: A Contemporary Panorama*, 10 WILLIAMETTE J. INT'L L. & DISP. RES. 17 (2002), 19.

Valerie A. Sanchez, *Back to the Future of ADR: Negotiating Justice and Human Needs*, OHIO ST. J. DISP. RES. 669 (2002–03), 18.

Frank Sander, *Varieties of Dispute Resolution*, 70 F.R.D. 111 (1976), 19.

Harold Saunders, *We Need a Larger Theory of Negotiation: The Importance of Prenegotiating Phases*, in NEGOTIATION THEORY AND PRACTICE 57–70 (J. William Breslin & Jeffrey Z. Rubin, eds. Harvard Law School, Program on Negotiation 1991), 22.

Cynthia A. Savage, *Culture and Mediation: A Red Herring,* 5 Am. U. J. Gender & L. 269 (1996), 48.

Andrea Schneider, *Getting Along: The Evolution of Dispute Resolution Regimes in International Trade Organizations*, 20 Mich. J. Int'l L. 697 (1999), 43.

Marcia J. Staff & Christine W. Lewis, *Arbitration Under NAFTA Chapter 11: Past, Present and Future*, 25 Hous. J. Int'l L. 301 (2003), 43.

Kim Van der Borgt, *The Review of the WTO Understanding on Dispute Settlement: Some Reflections on the Current Debate*, 14 AM. U. INT'L L. REV. 1223 (1999), 34.

William Zartman, *Prenegotiation: Phases and Functions*, *in* GETTING TO THE TABLE: THE PROCESS OF INTERNATIONAL PRENEGOTIATION 1–17 (Janice Gross Stein, ed. 1989), 22.

Chapter 3

Harold Abramson, *International Dispute Resolution: Cross-Cultural Dimensions and Structuring Appropriate Processes*, in Alan Rau, Edward Sherman & Scott Peppet, PROCESSES OF DISPUTE RESOLUTION 918–21 (3rd ed. 2002), 82–84.

Ryunosuke Akutagawa, IN A GROVE, RASHOMON AND OTHER STORIES (Takashi Kojima trans.) (1952), 68.

Kevin Avurch & Peter W. Black, *Conflict Resolution in Intercultural Settings: Problems and Prospects*, in Dennis J. Sandole & Hugo van der Merwe eds. CONFLICT RESOLUTION THEORY AND PRACTICE: INTEGRATION AND APPLICATION 131–40 (1993), 50–57.

Pat K. Chew, *The Pervasiveness of Culture*, 54 Journal of Legal Education 60, 66–69 (2004), 57–60.

Pat K. Chew, *The Rule of Law: China's Skepticism and the Rule of People*, 20 Ohio State Journal on Dispute Resolution (200), 84–89.

Sara Cobb & Janet Riskin, *Practice and Paradoxes: Deconstructing Neutrality in Mediation,* 16 Law and Social Inquiry 53 (1991), 68.

Doriane Lambelet Coleman, *Individualizing Justice Through Multiculturalism*, 96 Colum. L. Rev. 1093 (1996), 81.

Thomas Donaldson, *Values in Tension: Ethics Away from Home*, Harv. Bus. Rev. 3–12 (Sept.–Oct. 1996), 81.

Tracy E. Higgins, *Anti-Essentialism, Relativism, and Human Rights*, 19 Harv. Women's L. J. 89 (1996), 80.

Michelle LeBaron, Erin McCandless, and Stephen Garon, CONFLICT AND CULTURE: A LITERATURE REVIEW AND BIBLIOGRAPHY (1998), 61, 62.

John Paul Lederach, PREPARING FOR PEACE: CONFLICT TRANSFORMATION ACROSS CULTURES (1995), 67, 68.

Hazel Rose Markus & Leah R. Lin, *Conflictways: Cultural Diversity in the Meanings and Practices of Conflict* in Deborah A. Prenctice & Dale T. Miller eds. CULTURAL DIVIDES 302, 313–27 (1999), 72–78.

Richard E. Nisbett, THE GEOGRAPHY OF THOUGHT: HOW ASIANS AND WESTERNERS THINK DIFFERENTLY... AND WHY (2003), 82.

Alison Dundes Rentelyn, *Cross-Cultural Dispute Resolution: The Consequences of Conflicting Interpretations of Norms*, Willamette Journal International Law & Dispute Resolution 103, 113–115 (2002), 62–63.

Kay Schaffer & Sidonie Smith, HUMAN RIGHTS AND NARRATED LIVES (2004), 69.

James K. Sebenius, *Caveats for Cross-Border Negotiation*, Negotiation Journal 121, 122–31 (April 2002), 63–67.

Stella Ting-Toomey, *Toward a Theory of Conflict and Culture*, W. Gudykuns, L.P. Steward, and S. Ting-Toomey, eds. COMMUNICATION, CULTURE, AND ORGANIZATIONAL PROCESSES 71, 75–82 (1985), 71.

Karen G. Turner, *Introduction: The Problem of Paradigms,* Karen G. Turner, James V. Feinerman & R. Kent Guy eds., THE LIMITS OF THE RULE OF LAW IN CHINA (2000), 85.

Chapter 4

Harold I. Abramson in *International Dispute Resolution: Cross-Cultural Dimensions and Structuring Appropriate Processes* in Alan S. Rau, Edward F. Sherman, and Scott R. Peppet, PROCESSES OF DISPUTE RESOLUTION: THE ROLE OF LAWYERS Ch. VI (3d ed. 2002), 103, 153, 177, 196.

Harold I. Abramson, MEDIATION REPRESENTATION-ADVOCATING IN A PROBLEM-SOLVING PROCESS 1–6, 104–108 (2004), 103, 105, 114, 128, 129, 155, 157, 159, 174.

Harold Abramson, *Mining Mediation Rules for Representation Opportunities and Obstacles,* 1 Journal of International Dispute Resolution 40 (Jan. 2004) (European Law Publishers and Verlag Rechht und Wirtschaft Heidelberg, Germany, January 2004) and 15 American Review of International Arbitration 103 (2005), 150.

Harold Abramson, *Problem-Solving Advocacy in Mediations: A Model of Client Representation*, 10 Harvard Negotiation Law Review 103 (2005), 141.

Amr Adballa, *Principles of Islamic Interpersonal Conflict Resolution: A Search Within Islam and Western Literature,* 15 Journal of Law and Religion 151 (2000–2001), 107.

Nadja Alexander, *What's Law Got to Do with It? Mapping Modern Mediation Movements in Civil and Common Law Jurisdictions,* 13 Bond Law Review 16 (Dec. 2001), 131.

Salah Al-Hejailan, *Mediation as a Means for Amicable Settlement of Disputes in Arab Countries* presented to the WIPO Conference on Mediation, Geneva, Switzerland (Mar. 29, 1996), 134.

American Arbitration Association, International Dispute Resolution Procedures (July 1, 2003), 129, 199, 208.

A Voluntary European Code of Conduct for Mediators (adopted on July 2, 2004 in Brussels), 146, 148.

William K. Bartels, *The Stormy Seas of Apologies: California Evidence Code Section 1160 Provides a Safe Harbor for Apologies Made After Accidents*, 28 Wayne State University Law Review 141 (2000–01), 169.

Ann Black, *Alternative Dispute Resolution in Brunei Darussalam: The Blending of Imported and Traditional Process*, 13 Bond Law Review (Dec. 2001), 113, 132, 133.

Max Bolstad, *Learning From Japan: The Case for Increased Use of Apology in Mediation*, 48 Cleveland State Law Review 545 (2000), 169.

William Bradford, *'With a Very Great Blame on Our Hearts': Reparations, Reconciliation, and an American Indian Plea for Peace with Justice,* 27 American Indian Law Review 1 (2002–03), 169.

Jeanne M. Brett, NEGOTIATING GLOBALLY: HOW TO NEGOTIATE DEALS, RESOLVE DISPUTES, AND MAKE DECISIONS ACROSS CULTURAL BOUNDARIES 16, 61–72 (2001), 112, 117, 123, 160.

Brown, *The Role of Apology in Negotiation*, 87 Marquette Law Review 665 (2004), 169.

Christian Buhring-Uhle, Arbitration and Mediation in International Business (1996), 138, 140, 196.

Robert A. Baruch Bush & Joseph P. Folger, THE PROMISE OF MEDIATION—RESPONDING TO CONFLICT THROUGH EMPOWERMENT AND RECOGNITION (1994), 128.

Charles R. Calleros, *Conflict, Apology, and Reconciliation at Arizona State University: A Second Case Study in Hateful Speech*, 27 Cumberland Law Review 91 (1996–97), 169.

CEDR Model Mediation Procedure and Agreement (October 2002), 143.

Ho-Beng Chia, Joo Eng Lee-Partridge, and Chee-Leong Chong, *Traditional Mediation Practices: Are We Throwing the Baby out with the Bath Water,* 21 Conflict Resolution Quarterly 451 (Summer 2004), 144, 161.

China Council for the Promotion of International Trade (CCPIT) and China Chamber of International Commerce (CCOIC), Conciliation Rules 2000, pp. 135, 151.

Kenneth Cloke, *Politics and Values in Mediation: The Chinese Experience,* 17 Med. Quarterly 69, 74 (Fall 1987), 135.

Jonathan R. Cohen, *Advising Clients to Apologize*, 72 Southern California Law Review 1009 (1999), 169, 170, 172.

Jonathan R. Cohen, *Legislating Apology: The Pros and Cons*, 70 U. Cincinnati Law Review 819 (2002), 169.

Michael T. Colatrella, *Court-Performed Mediation in the People's Republic of China: A Proposed Model to Improve the United States Federal District Courts' Mediation Programs*, 15 Ohio State Journal on Dispute Resolution 391 (2000), 134.

Charles B. Craver, EFFECTIVE LEGAL NEGOTIATION AND SETTLEMENT (4th ed. 2001), 174.

Daini Tokyo Bar Association's Rules of Procedure for Arbitration and Mediation (June 9, 2000), 139, 143.

Giuseppe De Palo, *Crisis of Courts and the Italian Mediation Debate*, International Journal of Dispute Resolution 14 (Germany, 2003), 131.

Donahey, *Seeking Harmony: Is the Asian Concept of the Conciliator/Arbitrator Applicable to the West?*, 50 Dispute Resolution Journal 74 (April 1995), 138.

Max Edison, How to Haggle—Professional Tricks for Saving Money on Just About Anything (2001), 174.

European Commission's Green Paper on Alternative Dispute Resolution in Civil and Commercial Law (April, 2002), 148.

Roger Fisher and William Ury, Getting to Yes (2d edition with Bruce Patton, 1991), 109, 111, 112.

Taryn Fuchs-Burnett, *Mass Public Corporate Apology*, Dispute Resolution Journal 27 (July 2002), 169.

Walter G. Gans, *Saving Time and Money in Cross-Border Commercial Disputes*, Dispute Resolution Journal, 52–54 (January 1997), 99.

German Institution of Arbitration, DIS Mediation/Conciliation Rules (January 1, 2002), 151.

Eric Glassman, *The Function of Mediation in China: Examining the Impact of Regulations Governing the People's Mediation Committees,* 10 UCLA Pacific Basin Law Journal 460 (1992), 134, 183.

Bee Chen Goh, *Remedies in Chinese Dispute Resolution*, 13 Bond Law Review 4 (Dec. 2001), 161.

John L. Graham and N. Mark Lam, *The Chinese Negotiation*, Harvard Business Review. 82, 84–89 (Oct. 2003), 121, 161.

Tang Houzhi, *The Use of Conciliation in Arbitration,* presented to WIPO Conference on Mediation, Geneva, Switzerland (March 29, 1996) at http://arbiter.wipo.int/events/conferences/1996/tang.html, 140.

ICC ADR Rules (July 1, 2001) and Guide to ICC ADR (June 2001) at http://www.iccwbo.org., 147, 199, 211.

Introduction, Section XV. Combination of Arbitration and Conciliation, at www.cietac.org, 139.

George Irani, *Islamic Mediation Techniques for Middle East Conflicts,* 3 Middle East Review of International Affairs 4 (Jan. 1997), 132, 155.

Kozan and Ergin, *Preference for Third Party Help in Conflict Management in the United States and Turkey-An Experimental Study*, 29 Journal of Cross-Cultural Psychology 525 (1998), 161.

Elizabeth Latif, *Apologetic Justice: Evaluating Apologies Tailored Toward Legal Solutions*, 81 Boston University Law Review 289 (2001), 169.

Deborah L. Levi, *The Role of Apology in Mediation*, 72 New York University Law Review 1165 (1997), 170.

Song Lianbin, Zhao Jian, and Li Hong, *Approaches to the Revision of the 1994 Arbitration Act of the People's Republic of China,* 20 Journal of International Arbitration 169 (2003), 139.

Mitsubishi Motors Corp. v. Soler Chrysler-Plymouth, 473 U.S. 614 (1985), 92.

Model Law on International Commercial Conciliation of the United Nations Commission on International Trade Law (2003), 129, 151, 154.

Model Standards of Conduct for Mediators (American Arbitration Association, the Litigation and Dispute Resolution Sections of the American Bar Association, and The Society of Professionals in Dispute Resolution, 1992–1994), 125.

Christopher Moore, THE MEDIATION PROCESS—PACTICAL STRATEGIES FOR RESOLVING CONFLICT (2nd ed. 1996), 124.

J. S. Murray, *The Cairo Stories: Some Reflections on Conflict Resolution in Egypt,* Negotiation Journal 39 (Jan. 1997), 132, 152.

Melissa L Nelken, UNDERSTANDING NEGOTIATION (2001), 174.

Jacqueline Nolan-Haley, *Informed Consent in Mediation: A Guiding Principle for Truly Educated Decisionmaking,* 74 Notre Dame Law Review 775 (1999), 148.

Erin Ann O'Hara & Douglas Yarn, *On Apology and Consilience,* 77 Washington Law Review 1121 (2002), 170.

Norimitsu Onishi, *Freed From Captivity in Iraq, Japanese Return to More Pain,* New York Times, April 23, 2004 (Section A; Column 1), 162.

Order of the Ministry of Justice of the People's Republic of China People's Mediation Committee (No. 75), adopted at the working meeting of Ministers of the Ministry of Justice on September 11, 2002 and promulgated to be effective as of November 1, 2002, p. 135.

Aviva Orenstein, *Apology Excepted: Incorporating a Feminist Analysis into Evidence Policy Where You Would Least Expect It,* 28 Southwestern University Law Review 221 (1999), 170.

Oslo Chamber of Commerce, Rules of the Arbitration and Dispute Resolution Institute of the Oslo Chamber of Commerce (2003), 146.

Donna L. Pavlick, *Apology and Mediation: The Horse and the Carriage of the Twenty-First Century,* 18 Ohio State Journal on Dispute Resolution 829 (2003), 163, 170

Robert Perkovich, *A Comparative Analysis of Community Mediation in the United States and the People's Republic of China,* 10 Temple International and Comparative Law Journal 313 (1996), 134.

Prosando v. High-Tech Dispute. Prepared by the CPR Institute for Dispute Resolution (1994), 180.

Alan Rau & Edward Sherman, *Tradition and Innovation in International Arbitration Procedure,* 30 Texan International Law Journal 89, 105 (1995), 97, 140, 202.

Regulations Governing the Organization of People's Mediation Committees, Promulgated by the State Council on 17 June, 1989, p. 135.

Leonard L. Riskin, *Decisionmaking in Mediation: The New Old Grid and the New New Grid System,* 79 Notre Dame Law Review 1 (2003), 130.

Leonard Riskin, *Understanding Mediators' Orientation, Strategies, and Techniques: A Grid for the Perplexed,* 1 Harvard Negotiation Law Review 7 (1996), 109, 149.

Jennifer K. Robbennolt, *Apologies and Legal Settlement: An Empirical Examination,* 102 Michigan Law Review 460 (2003), 170.

Jeswald W. Salacuse, MAKING GLOBAL DEALS (1991), 155.

Stockholm Chamber of Commerce, Rules of the Mediation Institute (April 1, 1999), 178.

Lee Taft, *Apology Subverted: The Commodification of Apology,* 109 Yale Law Journal 1135 (2000), 170.

Chapter 5

Yves Dezalay and Bryant G. Garth, DEALING IN VIRTUE–INTERNATIONAL COMMERCIAL ARBITRATION AND THE CONSTRUCTION OF A TRANSNATIONAL LEGAL ORDER (1996), 202.

Dan B. Dobbs, DOBBS LAW OF REMEDIES (Vol. 1, 2nd Edition, 1993), 211.

Neil Kaplan, *New Developments on Written Form* in NEW YORK CONVENTION DAY—June 10, 1998, A/CN.9/1998/INF.1 pp. 5-6 (UN, 20 May 1998), 206.

London Court of International Arbitration: Procedure and Costs (June 24, 2002), 198.

Andreas F. Lowenfeld, *The Party-Appointed Arbitrator in International Controversies: Some Reflections,* 20 Texas International Law Journal 59 (1995), 209.

Robert H. Mnookin, *Creating Value Through Process Design*, 11 Journal of International Arbitration 125 (1994), 219.

Lawrence W. Newman and Michael Burrows, *Proposed Hague Convention on Judgments,* 220 New York Law Journal 3 & 29 (December 30, 1998), 137.

William W. Park, *Duty and Discretion in International Arbitration*, 93 American Journal of International Law 805 (1999), 206.

Jan Paulsson, *Awards Set Aside at Place of Arbitration* in NEW YORK CONVENTION DAY—June 10, 1998, A/CN.9/1998/INF.1 p. 10 (UN, 20 May 1998), 206.

Lawrence Perlman and Steven C. Nelson, *New Approaches to the Resolution of International Commercial Disputes,* 17 International Lawyer 215 (1983), 196.

James T. Peter, *Med-Arb in International Arbitration*, 8 THE AMERICAN REVIEW OF INTERNATIONAL ARBITRATION 83 (1997), 211.

Alan Scott Rau, *Integrity in Private Judging*, 38 South Texas Law Review 485 (1997), 208.

Lucy F. Reed, *Drafting Arbitration Clauses* in INTERNATIONAL BUSINESS LITIGATION & ARBITRATION 2000 624 PLI/Lit 563, 565–577 (Practicing Law Institute, February 2000), 203.

Kathleen M. Scanlon, *Multi-Step Dispute Resolution Clauses in Business-Business Agreements* SJO34 ALI-ABA, 6–15 (Mediation and Other ADR-Dispute Resolution for the 21st Century, American Law Institute-American Bar Association Continuing Legal Education, September 18–19, 2003) (Copyright © 2003 Kathleen M. Scanlon), 212.

UNCITRAL Notes on Organizing Arbitral Proceedings, U.N. Doc. V.96-84935, p. 228.

V.V. Veeder, *Provisional and Conservatory Measures* in NEW YORK CONVENTION DAY—June 10, 1998, A/CN.9/1998/INF.1 p. 8 (UN, 20 May 1998), 206.

Chapter 6

Addressing Disputes in Electronic Commerce: Final Recommendations and Report, 58 Business Law 415 (November 2002), 248.

Alternative Dispute Resolution in the Context of Electronic Commerce, Doc. No. Econ 12–00 (February 2000, www.tacd.org), 250.

American Arbitration Association Supplementary Procedures for Online Arbitration, (January 1, 2001), 241.

John Cooley, MEDIATION ADVOCACY (2nd ed. 2002), 232, 270.

John Cooley and Steven Lubet, ARBITRATION ADVOCACY (2nd ed. 2003), 270.

Benjamin G. Davis, *Disciplining ODR Prototypes: True Trust Through True Independence*, Proceedings of the UNECE Forum on ODR 2003, http://www.odr.info/unece2003, p. 263.

Llewellyn J. Gibbons, Robin M. Kennedy, and John M. Gibbs, *Cyber-Mediation: Computer-Mediated Communications Medium Massaging the Message*, 32 New Mexico Law Review 27 (2002), 232, 237, 252, 272.

Hornle, *Online Dispute Resolution—More Than The Emperor's New Clothes*, Proceedings of the UNECE Forum on ODR 2003 http://www.odr.info/unece2003, p. 273.

Ethan Katsh and Janet Rifkin, ONLINE DISPUTE RESOLUTION (2001), 230, 241, 243, 261.

Lever Bros. Co. v. United States, 299 U.S.App.D.C. 128, 981 F.2d 1330 (1993), 270.

James C. Melamed, *Mediating on the Internet Today and Tomorrow*, 1 Pepperdine Dispute Resolution Law Journal 11, 20–24 (2000), 267.

New York Recommendations, Summit 2003 (Global Business Dialogue on Electronic Commerce, 2003, www.gbde.org), 249.

Lucille M. Ponte, *The Michigan Cyber Court: A Bold Experiment in the Development of the First Public Virtual Courthouse*, 4 North Carolina Journal of Law & Technology 51 (2002), 241.

Karen Stewart & Joseph Matthews, *Online Arbitration of Cross-Border, Business to Consumer Disputes*, 56 University of Miami Law Review 1111 (2002), 273.

Melissa Conley Tyler & Di Bretherton, SEVENTY-SIX AND COUNTING: AN ANALYSIS OF ODR SITES, A REPORT OF RESEARCH CONDUCTED FOR THE DEPARTMENT OF JUSTICE, VICTORIA, AUSTRALIA, Proceedings of the UNECE Forum on ODR 2003, www.odr.infro/unece2003, p. 234.

www.cybersettle.com., 230, 235.

www.smartsettle.com., 236.

Chapter 7

Cecilia Albin, JUSTICE AND FAIRNESS IN INTERNATIONAL NEGOTIATION (2001), 302.

Jacob Bercovitch, ed. STUDIES IN INTERNATIONAL MEDIATION 5 (2002), 304–305.

Jacob Bercovitch, *The Structure and Diversity of Mediation 6 in* INTERNATIONAL RELATIONS: MULTIPLE APPROACHES TO CONFLICT MANAGEMENT (Jacob Bercovich and Jeffrey Rubin, ed. 1992), 306.

Boutros Boutros-Ghali, *An Agenda for Peace* (1992) (rev.ed. 1995), 279.

Peter J. Carnevale & Sharon Arad, *Bias and Impartiality in International Mediation*, in RESOLVING INTERNATIONAL CONFLICTS: THE THEORY AND PRACTICE OF MEDIATION, 39 (Jacob Bercovitch, ed. 1996), 307.

Chester A. Crocker, Fen Osler Hampson & Pamela R. Aall, *Two's Company But Is Three a Crowd? Some Hypotheses about Multiparty Mediation*, in STUDIES IN INTERNATIONAL MEDIATION 228 (Jacob Bercovitch, ed. 2002), 305, 307.

Christopher Dupont & Guy-Olivier Faure, *The Negotiation Process*, in INTERNATIONAL NEGOTIATION: ANALYSIS, APPROACHES, ISSUES (Victor A. Kremenyuk, ed., 2002), 286.

Jan Egeland, *The Oslo Accord: Multiparty Facilitation through the Norwegian Channel*, in Chester A. Crocker, Fen Osler Hampson, and Pamela Aall, HERDING CATS: MULTIPARTY MEDIATION IN A COMPLEX WORLD 544 (1999), 331.

John D. Feerick, *The Peace-Making Role of a Mediator*, 19 Ohio State Journal on Dispute Resolution 229 (2003), 318–322.

Melanie Greenberg, *Mediating Massacres: When "Neutral, Low-Power" Models of Mediation Cannot and Should Not Work,* 19 Ohio State Journal on Dispute Resolution 185 (2003), 307–310, 327–331.

Melanie C. Greenberg, John H. Barton and Margaret E. McGuinness, eds., WORDS OVER WAR: MEDIATION AND ARBITRATION TO PREVENT DEADLY CONFLICT (2000), 305.

David A. Hamburg, NO MORE KILLING FIELDS: PREVENTING DEADLY CONFLICT (2002), 279, 280.

Marieke Kleiboer, *Great Power Mediation: Using Leverage to Make Peace*, in STUDIES IN INTERNATIONAL MEDIATION 127 (Jacob Bercovitch, ed. 2002), 306.

David A. Lax & James K. Sebenius, THE MANAGER AS NEGOTIATOR (1986), 287.

John Paul Lederach, *Cultivating Peace: A Practitioner's View of Deadly Conflict and Negotiation, in* CONTEMPORARY PEACEMAKING: CONFLICT, VIOLENCE, AND PEACE PROCESSES (John Darby & Roger MacGinty eds., 2003), 317.

Robert H. Mnookin, *When Not To Negotiate: A Negotiation Imperialist Reflects on Appropriate Limits*, 74 University of Colorado Law Review 1077 (2003), 280–286.

Jacqueline Nolan-Haley & Bronagh Hinds, *Problem-Solving Negotiation: Northern Ireland's Experience with the Women's Coalition,* Journal of Dispute Resolution 394 (2003), 287–290.

Dean Pruitt, *Mediator Behavior and Success in Mediation*, in STUDIES IN INTERNATIONAL MEDIATION (Jacob Bercovitch, ed. 2002), 310.

Dean G. Pruitt, *Strategy in Negotiation*, in INTERNATIONAL NEGOTIATION: ANALYSIS, APPROACHES, ISSUES 86 (Victor A. Kremenyuk, ed., 2002), 287.

David M. Rothenberg, *Negotiation and Dispute Resolution in the Sri Lankan Context: Lessons from the 1994–95 Peace Talks,* 22 Fordham International Law Journal 505 (1998), 290–302.

Jeffrey Z. Rubin, *The Actors in Negotiation, in* INTERNATIONAL NEGO-TIATION: ANALYSIS, APPROACHES, ISSUES 104 (Victor A. Kremenyuk, ed. 2002), 279, 286.

Dale E. Spencer & Honggang Yang, *Lessons from the Field of Intra-National Conflict Resolution*, 67 Notre Dame Law Review 1495 (1992), 322–326.

STANDARD II, JOINT CODE, STANDARDS OF CONDUCT FOR MEDIATORS, ADOPTED BY THE AMERICAN BAR ASSOCIATION, AMERICAN ARBITRATION ASSO-CIATION, AND THE SOCIETY OF PROFESSIONALS IN DISPUTE RESOLUTION (1994), 306.

H. Touzard, LA MEDIATION ET LA RESOLUTION DES CONFLITS [Mediation and the Resolution of Conflicts] (Paris: PUF, 1977), 286.

Michael Watkins & Susan Rosegrant, BREAKTHROUGH INTERNATIONAL NEGOTIATION: HOW GREAT NEGOTIATORS TRANSFORMED THE WORLD'S TOUGHEST POST-COLD WAR CONFLICTS (2001), 279.

I. William Zartman, *Cowardly Lions: Missed Opportunities for Dispute Settlement,* 18 Ohio State Journal on Dispute Resolution 1 (2002), 311–317.

I. William Zartman, ed., PREVENTIVE NEGOTIATION: AVOIDING CONFLICT ESCALATION (Carnegie Commission on Preventing Deadly Conflict, 2001), 279, 280, 302.

I. William Zartman, RIPE FOR RESOLUTION: CONFLICT AND INTERVEN-TION IN AFRICA (1989), 310.

I. William Zartman & Saadia Touval, *International Mediation in the Post-Cold War Era, in* MANAGING GLOBAL CHAOS: SOURCES OF AND RESPONSES TO INTERNATIONAL CONFLICT 455 (Chester A. Crocker *et al.,* eds. U.S. Institute of Peace 1996), 307.

Chapter 8

Philip C. Aka, *Nigeria: The Need for An Effective Policy of Ethnic Reconciliation in the New Century*, 14 Temple International & Comparative Law Journal 327 (2000), 379–384.

Elena A. Baylis, *Beyond Rights: Legal Process and Ethnic Conflicts,* 25 Michigan Journal of International Law 529 (2004), 342–361.

Peter N. Bouckaert, *The Negotiated Revolution: South Africa's Transition to a Multiracial Democracy,* 33 STAN. J. INT'L L. 375 (1997), 334.

Gennady I. Chufrin & Harold M. Saunders, *A Public Peace Process,* 9 NEGOTIATION J. 155 (1993), 334.

Carla S. Copeland, *The Use of Arbitration to Settle Territorial Disputes,* 67 Fordham Law Review 3073 (1999), 391–397.

Mica Estrada-Hollenbeck, *The Attainment of Justice through Restoration, Not Litigation: The Subjective Road to Reconciliation,* in RECONCILI-ATION, JUSTICE, AND COEXISTENCE: THEORY AND PRACTICE 74 (Mohammed Abu-Nimer, ed. 2001), 378.

Michael Ignatieff, *Afterward: Reflections on Coexistence,* in Antonia Chayes & Martha Minow, eds., IMAGINE COEXISTENCE: RESTORING HUMANI-TY AFTER VIOLENT ETHNIC CONFLICT 326 (2003), 385.

Douglas Johnston, ed., FAITH-BASED DIPLOMACY: TRUMPING REALPOLITIK (2003), 378.

Herbert C. Kelman, *Informal Mediation by the Scholar/Practitioner, in* MEDIATION IN INTERNATIONAL RELATIONS: MULTIPLE APPROACHES TO CONFLICT MANAGEMENT 64 (Jacob Bercovitch & Jeffrey Z. Rubin, eds. 1992), 334.

Herbert C. Kelman, *Interactive Problem-Solving: Informal Mediation by the Scholar-Practitioner, in* STUDIES IN INTERNATIONAL MEDIATION 167 (Jacob Bercovitch, ed. 2002), 334.

Louis Kriesberg, *Changing Forms of Coexistence, in* RECONCILIATION, JUSTICE, AND COEXISTENCE: THEORY AND PRACTICE 61 (Mohammed Abu-Nimer, ed. 2001), 385.

John Paul Lederach, PREPARING FOR PEACE: CONFLICT TRANSFORMATION ACROSS CULTURES (1995), 391.

Arthur Lenk, *Fact-Finding as Peace Negotiation Tool—The Mitchell Report and the Israeli-Palestinian Peace Process,* 24 Loyola of Los Angeles International & Comparative Law Review 289 (2002), 361–377.

Jacqueline Nolan-Haley, *The Intersection of Religion, Race, Class, and Ethnicity in Community Conflict,* Negotiation J. 351 (October 2002), 390.

Harold H. Saunders, *Sustained Dialogue in Managing Intractable Conflict,* Negotiation Journal 85 (January 2003), 335–341.

Archbishop Desmond M. Tuto, Foreward, in FOREGIVENESS AND RECONCILIATION: RELIGION, PUBLIC POLICY, AND CONFLICT TRANSFORMATION (Raymond G. Helmick, S.J. & Rodney L. Petersen, eds. 2001), 378.

Eugene Weiner, *Coexistence Work: A New Profession* in Eugene Weiner, ed., THE HANDBOOK OF INTERETHNIC COEXISTENCE 13–17, 19–21 (1998), 385–390.

Chapter 9

Pamela Aall, *Nongovernmental Organizations and Peacemaking, in* Chester Crocker & Fen Osler Hampson with Pamela Aall, MANAGING GLOBAL CHAOS: SOURCES OF AND RESPONSES TO INTERNATIONAL CONFLICT 433 (U.S. Institute of Peace 1996), 440.

Jason S. Abrams & Priscilla Hayner, *Documenting, Acknowledging and Publicizing the Truth* in POST-CONFLICT JUSTICE 283 (M. Cherif Bassiouni ed., 2002), 460–470.

Agenda for Peace: Preventive Diplomacy, Peacemaking and Peacekeeping, UN Doc. A/47/277–S24111 (1992), 406.

Jose E. Alvarez, *Rush to Closure: Lessons of the Tadic Judgment,* 96 Michigan Law Review 2031 (1998), 449–458.

Mary B. Anderson, *Humanitarian NGOs in Conflict Intervention,* in Chester A. Crocker & Fen Osler Hampson with Pamela Aall, eds., MANAGING GLOBAL CHAOS: SOURCES OF AND RESPONSES TO INTERNATIONAL CONFLICT 343 (1996), 441.

Andrea Bartoli, *Mediating Peace in Mozambique: The Role of the Community of Sant' Egidio, in* Chester A. Crocker, Fen Osler Hampson and Pamela Aall, eds., HERDING CATS: MULTIPARTY MEDIATION IN A COMPLEX WORLD 247 (1999), 440.

M. Cherif Bassiouni, *Accountability for Violations of International Humanitarian Law and Other Serious Violations of Human Rights, in* M. Cherif Bassiouni, ed., POST-CONFLICT JUSTICE 4 (2002), 446.

Dominic Bryan, *Parading Protestants and Consenting Catholics in Northern Ireland: Communal Conflict, Contested Public Space, and Group Rights*, 5 Chicago Journal of International Law 233 (2004), 471–472.

William W. Burke-White, *Regionalization of International Criminal Law Enforcement: A Preliminary Exploration*, 38 TEX. INT'L L.J. 729 (2003), 449.

Audrey R. Chapman, *Truth Commissions as Instruments of Forgiveness and Reconciliation, in* Raymond G. Helmick, S.J. & Rodney L. Petersen, eds., FORGIVENESS AND RECONCILIATION (2001), 459.

Elizabeth M. Cousens & Chetan Kumar, eds. with Karin Wermester, PEACEBUILDING AS POLITICS: CULTIVATING PEACE IN FRAGILE SOCIETIES (2001), 406.

Chester A. Crocker, Fen Osler Hampson & Pamela Aall, TAMING INTRACTABLE CONFLICT (2004), 439.

Larry A. Dunn & Louis Kriesberg, *Mediating Intermediaries: Expanding Roles of Transnational Organizations, in* STUDIES IN INTERNATIONAL MEDIATION 194 (Jacob Bercovitch ed. 2002), 441.

Carrie J. Niebur Eisnaugle, *An International "Truth Commission": Utilizing Restorative Justice as an Alternative to Retribution*, 36 VAND. J. TRANSNAT'L L. 209 (2003), 459.

Judith Fretter, International *Organizations and Conflict Management: The United Nations and the Mediation of International Conflicts in* STUDIES IN INTERNATIONAL MEDIATION 98 (Jacob Bercovitch ed. 2002), 399.

Richard J. Goldstone, *Justice as a Tool for Peace-Making: Truth Commissions and International Criminal Tribunals*, 28 New York University Journal of International Law and Policy 485 (1996), 446–448.

HANDBOOK ON THE PEACEFUL SETTLEMENT OF DISPUTES BETWEEN STATES (1992), 400.

Fabienne Hara, *Burundi: A Case of Parallel Diplomacy, in* Chester A. Crocker, Fen Osler Hampson and Pamela Aall, eds., HERDING CATS: MULTIPARTY MEDIATION IN A COMPLEX WORLD 139 (1999), 442.

Robert Kirsch, *The Peacemaker: An Interview with UN Under-Secretary-General Alvaro de Soto*, 26 Fletcher Forum of World Affairs 83 (2002), 400–405.

Elizabeth Kiss, *Moral Ambition Within and Beyond Political Constraints: Reflections on Restorative Justice, in* Robert I. Rotberg & Dennis Thompson, eds., TRUTH V. JUSTICE 68 (1999), 459.

Owen Philip Lefkon, *Culture Shock: Obstacles to Bringing Conflict Prevention under the Wing of U.N. Development...and Vice Versa,* 35 N. Y. U. J. Int'l L. & Pol'y 671 (2003), 406.

Jennifer J. Llewellyn & Robert Howse, *Institutions for Restorative Justice: The South African Truth and Reconciliation Commission,* 49 U. Toronto L.J. 355 (1999), 459.

Edward N. Luttwak, *Give War A Chance,* 78 Foreign Affairs 36 (1999), 432–438.

Ellen L. Lutz, Eileen F. Babbitt & Hurst Hannum, *Human Rights and Conflict Resolution from the Practitioner's Perspective,* 27 Fletcher Forum of World Affairs 173 (2003), 473–481.

Peter Malanczuk, Akehurst's Modern Introduction to International Law (7th rev. ed. 1997), 440.

Martha Minow, Between Vengeance and Foregiveness: Facing History after Genocicde and Mass Violence (1998), 459.

P. Mweti Munya, *The Organization of African Unity and its Role in Regional Conflict Resolution and Dispute Settlement: A Critical Evaluation,* 19 Boston College Third World Journal 537 (1999), 420–425.

T. Modibo Ocran, *The Doctrine of Humanitarian Intervention in Light of Robust Peacekeeping,* 25 Boston College International and Comparative Law Review, 1 (2002), 431–432.

Diane F. Orentlicher, *Separation Anxiety: International Responses to Ethno-Separatist Claims,* 23 Yale Journal of International Law 1 (1998), 426–430.

Jelena Pejic, *The Yugoslav Truth and Reconciliation Commission: A Shaky Start,* 25 Fordham Intl L. J. 1 (2001), 459, 460.

Eric A. Posner & Adrian Vermeule, *Transitional Justice As Ordinary Justice,* 117 Harv. L. Rev. 762 (2004), 446.

Prevention of Armed Conflict: Report of the Secretary-General, U.N. GAOR/SCOR, 55th Sess. Agenda Item 10, UN Docs A/55/985-S/2001/574 (2001), 406.

Soliman M. Santos Jr., *The Muslim Dispute in the Southern Philippines: A Case of Islamic Conference Mediation* [2001] Aus. Int'l L. J. 35, p. 419.

Oscar Schachter, *United Nations Law,* 88 Am. J. Int'l L. 1 (1994), 399.

William R. Slomanson, Fundamental Perspectives on International Law (4th ed. 2003), 400.

Gillian Martin Sorenson, *The Roles A Civil Society Can Play in International Dispute Resolution,* 18 Negotiation Journal 355 (2002), 443–445.

Carsten Stahn, *Accommodating Individual Criminal Responsibility and National Reconcilation: The UN Truth Commission for East Timor,* 95 Am. J. Int'l L. 965 (2001), 449.

Lily R. Sucharipa-Behrmann & Thomas M. Frank, *Preventive Measures,* 30 N. Y. U. J. Int'l L. & Pol'y 485 (1998), 405.

Max Van der Stoel, *The Role of the OSCE High Commissioner in Conflict Prevention in* Chester A. Crocker, Fen Osler Hampson and Pamela Aall, eds., HERDING CATS: MULTIPARTY MEDIATION IN A COMPLEX WORLD 65 (1999), 419.

Ruth Wedgwood, *United Nations Peacekeeping Operations and the Use of Force*, 5 Washington University Journal of Law & Policy 69 (2001), 407–417.

Ruth Wedgwood, Harold K. Jacobson & Allan Gerson, *Peace Building: The Private Sector's Role*, 96 Am. J. Int'l L. 102 (2001), 406.

Paul R. Williams, *The Role of Justice in Peace Negotiations* in POST-CONFLICT JUSTICE 122–23 (M. Cherif Bassiouni ed., 2002), 441–442.

I. William Zartman, *Mediation by Regional Organizations: The OAU in Chad and Congo 95, in* Bercovitch, ed. INTERNATIONAL MEDIATION (2002), 419.

*

INTERNATIONAL CONFLICT RESOLUTION: CONSENSUAL ADR PROCESSES

*

Part I

INTERNATIONAL CONTEXT

Chapter 1

UNDERSTANDING CONFLICT

A. DEFINING CONFLICT

Before exploring the variety of consensual ADR processes used to resolve and manage international conflicts, it is useful to understand the nature of a conflict and how it differs from a dispute. The readings in this chapter explore the differences between conflicts and disputes and examine the role of perceptions in contributing to conflict. Because of the overwhelming number of ethnonationalist conflicts in this century and the challenges posed by their continuation, we pay special attention to ethnic and intractable conflicts.

1. GENERAL CONSIDERATIONS OF CONFLICT

Conflict is a natural part of the human condition as well as an important means of securing justice. It does not necessarily require suppression. As one international scholar has observed about the nature of conflict, "It is something like anger—we shouldn't repress all of it. We should let some of it out, because otherwise it might come out in a more serious or violent form."[1] The history of the twentieth century's destructive wars suggests that too much conflict has been repressed.

For definitional purposes, conflict can be categorized in numerous ways depending upon the entities and issues involved. Referring to social conflict, Pruitt and Rubin define conflict as a "... perceived divergence of interest, or a belief that the parties' current aspirations cannot be achieved simultaneously."[2] At a very basic and human level, conflict that exists between individuals acting in an adversarial relationship to each other can be conceived of as social in nature. Kriesberg defines social conflict as existing "when two or more persons or groups manifest the belief that they have incompatible objectives."[3]

---

1. George E. Morris, *Conflict Prevention For A New Century*, 88 Am. Soc'y Int'l L. Proc. 142 (1994) (Remarks of Professor Abram Chayes).

2. Dean G. Pruitt & Jeffrey Z. Rubin, Social Conflict: Escalation, Stalemate and

Settlement 4 (1986) [hereinafter Pruitt & Rubin].

3. Louis Kriesberg, Constructive Conflict: From Escalation to Resolution 2 (1998).

2

Conflict should be viewed as a process of multiple human interactions, rather than as a single, identifying event. It is from within this perspective that negotiation theorists have identified at least three stages in the life cycle of a conflict: an early contentious stage or escalation, stalemate, and problem-solving or settlement.[4] The point at which external interveners enter into the life cycle of a conflict may make a significant difference in the outcome of the conflict. In later chapters we will examine the effectiveness of third party interveners, such as mediators, at various stages of this life cycle, and consider the relevance of the concept of ripeness.

2. INTRACTABLE CONFLICT

Interactions among people with different objectives can result naturally in conflict. There are, however, species of conflicts that distort harmonious relations between parties, are harmful to societies, and that imperil the human condition. One example of a destructive conflict is a conflict related to identity. With the end of the Cold War, the collapse of communism in Eastern Europe and the Soviet Union, and the growing political crises in Africa as a result of de-colonization, the world has witnessed the spread of ethnic conflict in epic proportions. Not all participants in ethnic conflict would view the phenomenon as negative. As one scholar has observed about the post-Cold War era: "Ethnic conflicts became a testing ground for a new morality of promoting peace, stability, and human rights across the globe."[5]

The proliferation of conflicts over ethnic identity has generated a greater awareness of the intractable nature of some conflicts that have persisted despite multiple efforts at peacemaking. Intractable conflicts are deep-rooted, intense, and persist over long periods of time, often for generations. Scholars have suggested that it may be unrealistic to think that intractable conflict can be completely resolved, given its adversarial and zero-sum nature. They suggest that, instead of focusing on the concept of resolution, studies should be directed toward developing processes that can manage this conflict while at the same time minimizing the negative costs.[6]

A great deal of scholarship has been devoted to understanding how ethnic and intractable conflicts spread beyond national borders and how they can be contained. Complex questions abound. What is the significance of ethnicity in contributing to violent conflict? What is the relationship between territory and ethnic conflict? What are some processes that respond effectively to managing ethnic and intractable conflict? What are some ways of preventing intractable conflict? Many of the

---

4. PRUITT & RUBIN, *supra* note 2, at 137.

5. Andreas Wimmer, *Introduction: Facing Ethnic Conflicts, in* FACING ETHNIC CONFLICTS: TOWARD A NEW REALISM (Andreas Wimmer, Richard J. Goldstone, Donald L. Horowitz, Ulrike Joras & Conrad Schetter, eds.) (2004) [hereinafter Wimmer et al.].

6. Guy Burgess & Heidi Burgess, *Constructive Confrontation: A Transformative Approach to Intractable Conflicts*, 13 MEDIATION Q. 305–22 (1996). *See also* www.beyondintractability.org.

materials in this book, dealing with various forms of third-party interventions, are designed to help you consider some thoughtful responses to
these questions. The following article previews the discussion of mediating public disputes in Chapter 7 of this text and raises questions about
how intractable conflict might be prevented. In this excerpt, Sweden's
former ambassador to the United Nations discusses some of the ingredients for successful mediation and offers reflections on the stages of
international conflict.

JAN ELIASSON, PERSPECTIVES ON MANAGING INTRACTABLE CONFLICT

Negotiation Journal 371, 373–74 (October 2002).

My perspective on managing intractable conflict is that of a negotiator who has worked on international efforts to halt hostilities in the
Iran and Iraq and Nagorno–Karabakh wars. I am also strongly influenced by my negotiation experience as humanitarian coordinator for the
U.N. in Somalia and Sudan.

The interplay between the various actors in the area of conflict
resolution raises two sets of questions for me. The first deals with the
relationship between short-term intervention and long-term resolution-
addressing the root causes of the problem but, at the same time,
realizing that we must stop conflicts that are already going on. The
second focuses on the effectiveness of the mediation and negotiation
tools that we use. Article 33 of the U.N. Charter provides a long list of
these options—I call it the "Christmas Eve" list for a diplomat. It is
indeed a wonderful list of the potential measures that can be taken to
resolve conflict. But do we use these tools? And how well do we use
them?

* * *

I have been looking back at my experience, and I would like to make
some observations on what is important to be successful in mediation,
and to live up to Article 33.

First, the parties themselves—not just the conflict—must be "ripe."
The parties must be receptive to peace processes. I have sometimes
turned down a request when Sweden has been approached to serve as a
mediator because real interest in getting a solution was lacking. If one or
both sides fail to have sufficient interest or commitment, it is extremely
difficult for a mediator to play a resolution role.

Also, I have come to the conclusion that you really start a process of
negotiation when the parties are either *equally strong* or *equally weak*.
Unfortunately, it is easier when they are equally weak. I saw that in a
tragic way in the Iran–Iraq war. It seemed as if both nations fell down
like two bloody bodies in the 15th round of a boxing match, after losing
700,000 people and creating three million refugees. And we knew the
"solution" all the time. The solution we proposed in 1980 was, more or

less, the same solution that was suggested in 1988, eight years later. The difference is that 700,000 people died.

In addition to ripeness and equality (in strength or weakness), the *timing* of proposals is important. More examples of coming in with proposals *too early* exist than do proposals that arrive too late. Normally, one would think that coming in with a proposal too late would be the problem. But I have seen far too many examples where the most workable proposals have been offered too early, so that the ideas are already consumed, denied, and rejected—and then, the parties do not come back to them.

Also, the element of personal trust in mediation and arbitration is extremely important. Personal relationships among the parties really matter. So too does the realization on the part of the mediator to look deeper at cultural and religious backgrounds, and learn more about other cultures. This is absolutely crucial if you want to be successful at negotiation.

Lastly, one should try to achieve more concreteness in talks about negotiation, well beyond the general observations I have just made. I think one should try to think about steps that can be taken *before* a conflict erupts. My sole contribution to the academic literature on prevention is a framework I have called a "ladder of prevention" in international conflict. Six or seven rungs, or stages, exist on this ladder before conflict erupts. They include:

1. early warning, and a system to make the early warning work;
2. the possibility of a fact-finding mission: send out groups early, so that there are international eyes and ears gathering reliable information about a potential conflict;
3. all the elements of Article 33—negotiation, arbitration, judicial settlements, and so forth;
4. the actual peace-keeping—but also preventive peace-keeping;
5. the use of sanctions; and
6. if the other steps have failed, the use of force under Chapter Seven of the U.N. Charter—and the threatened use of force before the actual use of force.

---

3. ROLE OF PERCEPTIONS IN CONTRIBUTING TO CONFLICT

As we have seen from the various definitions discussed above, conflict does not necessarily lie in objective reality, but in how adversaries view a particular situation. How parties think about themselves in relation to others and how they imagine power to be distributed are often critical elements in the creation and perpetuation of conflict. Perceptions play a particularly significant role in the perpetuation of ethnic conflict. One scholar has observed that the resolution of ethnic conflict requires "... an appreciation of the distinction between reality and ethnically filtered reality. Probing these matters requires not knowledge of 'facts' but of commonly held perceptions of facts."[7]

Imagine how the Israeli Jewish population sees itself in relation to the Arab world or how during the time of Northern Ireland's Troubles, the Catholic population in Northern Ireland saw itself in relation to Great Britain. Consider how the South African white population saw itself in relation to the black South African population during the era of apartheid and how each group views itself in the post-apartheid era. Think about how the Iraqi people see themselves in relation to American and other foreign soldiers in their country. Who feels exploited? Who feels threatened? Who feels empowered? It is only when adjustments are made in groups' polarized perceptions, that it may be possible to ameliorate conflict.

In the following excerpt, the author describes how individuals living within the same geographic community and speaking the same language are divided by one group's view of itself as "British" and another group's view of itself as "Irish."

DOMINIC BRYAN, PARADING PROTESTANTS AND CONSENTING CATHOLICS IN NORTHERN IRELAND: COMMUNAL CONFLICT, CONTESTED PUBLIC SPACE, AND GROUP RIGHTS

5 Chicago Journal of International Law 233, 234–37 (2004).

* * *

Northern Ireland is a complex and modern Western European society with large disparities in class and wealth. It suffers from many of the same social and economic problems as other Western European and North American countries. It is ethnically divided between people who belong to the Protestant community and view themselves as British, wishing to remain part of the United Kingdom, and those from the Catholic community who see themselves as Irish, wishing to be part of a politically united Ireland. Whilst culturally these two groups are very similar, share many values and social practices, and are similarly divided by economic class, they are distinct from each other on questions of national allegiance and, at least to a degree, over their Christian religious belief. Around 60 percent of the population is Protestant and has been represented by the Ulster Unionist Party ("UUP"), which controlled a local Parliament from 1921 to 1972. Various forms of discrimination against the Catholic minority during that period led, in 1967, to the development of a civil rights movement. This political conflict in turn led to increased communal violence in the form of rioting, house burning, and sectarian attacks and then to a growing paramilitary campaign

7. Walker Connor, *A Few Cautionary Notes on the History and Future of Ethno-* *national Conflicts, in* Wimmer et al., *supra* note 5, at 32.

by the Irish Republican Army ("IRA") and two unionist/loyalist groups, the Ulster Volunteer Force ("UVF") and Ulster Defence Association ("UDA"). The UK government first introduced the British Army to undertake policing duties in 1969 and then, in 1972, introduced direct government from London. Since then the Democratic Unionist Party ("DUP") under the more fundamentalist Reverend Ian Paisley has grown to rival the UUP as a representative of Protestant and Unionist interests whilst the Catholic community is primarily represented by the Social Democratic Labour Party ("SDLP") and Sinn Féin (the political wing of the IRA).

At the start of the 1990s, a peace process developed which resulted in a cessation of violence from the IRA, the UVF, and the UDA. In 1998, a Multi–Party Agreement (also known as the Good Friday Agreement or the Belfast Agreement) brought some degree of local democracy back to Northern Ireland. Since then there have been numerous difficulties and, at the time of this writing, the operations of the new Northern Ireland Assembly have been suspended over the issue of decommissioning of paramilitary weapons. Above all, whilst there is presently a more peaceful environment in Northern Ireland, there are many victims in both communities and an enormous residue of fear and resentment.

Over the years, communal divisions in Northern Ireland have manifested in many different contexts, including discriminatory practices in employment and a divided system of education. They have also resulted in territorial separation so that in both urban and rural areas, housing and public space is often defined as "Protestant" or "Catholic." In Belfast, the fear of attacks from the other community and sporadic violence has led to the building of "peace walls" between "interface" areas separating "Protestant" and "Catholic" territories. In rural areas towns and villages are often viewed as being "Protestant" or "Catholic" and objects like war memorials and churches become ethnic markers.

It is important to stress that the categories of "Protestant" and "Catholic" in Northern Ireland are ethnic demarcations broader and more complex than the religious groups to which they generally refer. So, for example, a person could be deemed to come from one community or another without necessarily having any strong religious belief. The category of "Protestant" in Northern Ireland implies that someone is likely to be Unionist and British, as the category of "Catholic" implies that someone is Nationalist and Irish. Religion plays an important role in these identifications, but it is not the central point of difference. For example, within the Protestant community there are a wide range of churches and theological beliefs. To put it at its most basic, when one teenage boy throws a stone at others, it is usually because they represent "the other community"; he does not do it because of disagreements over theological issues such as transubstantiation. This point is particularly important when we come to view disputes over parades because there is not even clear agreement amongst those taking part, let alone those opposing it, as to what extent they are distinctly religious events.

The relationships between Protestant and Catholic communities are complex. Whilst there is a range of practices that serves to divide these groups, there is also a range of cross-cutting ties that mean we cannot depict them as having two different cultures or as being two distinct societies. In everyday interaction people can use their social knowledge to tell which community the people they meet are from. In the main they do so not necessarily to avoid "the other" but to attempt to behave in an acceptable manner such as not starting conversations about religion and politics that might prove divisive. Ironically, the friendliness or politeness of the people of Northern Ireland is, in part, a function of the conflict. People will often shop in one area rather than another, visit amenities in particular areas, catch particular buses, or use a particular taxi firm dependent upon their knowledge of territorial divisions. On the other hand, some middle-class areas are mixed, and many pastimes and associations also lead to social mixing.

Northern Ireland, like most other societies throughout the world, is a mix of separateness and cohesion, conflict and accommodation. Managing this mix becomes a central problem in building a working political system. Fundamental to this problem is the way in which groups are treated by the law, particularly minority groups. Does social cohesion demand a common set of principles by which all citizens must abide, or do we allow for abrogations from this in the name of diversity and the protection of minorities? In Northern Ireland these questions have given rise to a debate about whether we give rights to groups. The 1998 Multi–Party Agreement is consociational and has within it political institutions naming the existence of two groups, "Unionists" and "Nationalists," and giving those groups specific voting rights in the new assembly. A new Bill of Rights is to be proposed that will, in all likelihood, recognize the "two traditions." Other possible groups that may suffer a variety of forms of social exclusion—for example, the economically deprived, women, and smaller ethnic groups—will not be given such a profile.

B.   DEFINING DISPUTES

1.   BASIC TERMINOLOGY

Although the terms "conflict" and "dispute" are used interchangeably, the concept of "dispute" is narrowly construed in the context of international law.[8] The Permanent Court of International Justice has defined a dispute as "a disagreement on a point of law or fact, a conflict of legal views or interests between two persons."[9] Within the framework of international law, the concept of dispute suggests that there is a valid disagreement between countries that has become serious enough to

---

8. David J. Bederman, International Law Frameworks 234 (2001).

9. *Mavrommatis Palestine Concessions* (Greece v. U.K.), 1924 P.C.I.J. ser. A No. 2, at 11 (Judgment of Aug. 13).

require peaceful adjustment. As we shall see in Chapter 2, Article 33 of the U.N. Charter lists a variety of consensual and non-consensual processes for the resolution of such international disputes.

Scholars have differentiated between conflicts and disputes based on more temporal considerations. Disputes are perceived commonly as short-term disagreements that may be resolved by reference to external norms such as laws, treaties, customs or values. A conflict on the other hand, is deep-rooted and implies a more long-lasting situation that may or may not be susceptible to resolution in any negotiated context.[10]

2. EVOLUTION OF A DISPUTE

The evolution of a dispute has been conceptualized as a three-stage developmental process. Disputes begin with a grievance, where one believes that one is entitled to some property held by another. The aggrieved person or state then makes a claim for the property, and if the claim is denied, a dispute arises.[11] The following materials offer examples of grievances and claims in both public and private settings. The first excerpt considers the competing claims giving rise to a private dispute that involved the international sale of goods between a United States and Italian corporation.

MCC-MARBLE CERAMIC CENTER, INC. v. CERAMICA NUOVA D'AGOSTINO, S.P.A.

144 F.3d 1384 (11th Cir.1998).

* * *

The plaintiff-appellant, MCC–Marble Ceramic, Inc. ("MCC"), is a Florida corporation engaged in the retail sale of tiles, and the defendant-appellee, Ceramica Nuova d'Agostino S.p.A. ("D'Agostino") is an Italian corporation engaged in the manufacture of ceramic tiles. In October 1990, MCC's president, Juan Carlos Mozon, met representatives of D'Agostino at a trade fair in Bologna, Italy and negotiated an agreement to purchase ceramic tiles from D'Agostino based on samples he examined at the trade fair. Monzon, who spoke no Italian, communicated with Gianni Silingardi, then D'Agostino's commercial director, through a translator, Gianfranco Copelli, who was himself an agent of D'Agostino. The parties apparently arrived at an oral agreement on the crucial terms of price, quality, quantity, delivery and payment. The parties then recorded these terms on one of D'Agostino's standard, pre-printed order forms and Monzon signed the contract on MCC's behalf. According to MCC, the parties also entered into a requirements contract in February 1991, subject to which D'Agostino agreed to supply MCC with high grade

10. John W. Burton, *Conflict-Dispute Distinction*, 2 in Conflict: Resolution and Prevention (1990).

11. Richard Miller & Austin Sarat, *Grievances, Claims, and Disputes: Assessing the Adversary Culture*, 15 Law & Soc'y Rev. 525 (1980–81).

ceramic tile at specific discounts as long as MCC purchased sufficient quantities of tile. MCC completed a number of additional order forms requesting tile deliveries pursuant to that agreement.

MCC brought suit against D'Agostino claiming a breach of the February 1991 requirements contract when D'Agostino failed to satisfy orders in April, May, and August of 1991. In addition to other defenses, D'Agostino responded that it was under no obligation to fill MCC's orders because MCC had defaulted on payment for previous shipments. In support of its position, D'Agostino relied on the pre-printed terms of the contracts that MCC had executed. The executed forms were printed in Italian and contained terms and conditions on both the front and reverse. According to an English translation of the October 1990 contract, the front of the order form contained the following language directly beneath Monzon's signature:

> [T]he buyer hereby states that he is aware of the sales conditions stated on the reverse and that he expressly approves of them with special reference to those numbered 1–2–3–4–5–6–7–8.

R2–126, Exh. 3 ¶ 5 ("Maselli Aff."). Clause 6(b), printed on the back of the form states:

> [D]efault or delay in payment within the time agreed upon gives D'Agostino the right to ... suspend or cancel the contract itself and to cancel possible other pending contracts and the buyer does not have the right to indemnification or damages.

Id. ¶ 6.

D'Agostino also brought a number of counterclaims against MCC, seeking damages for MCC's alleged nonpayment for deliveries of tile that D'Agostino had made between February 28, 1991 and July 4, 1991. MCC responded that the tile it had received was of a lower quality than contracted for, and that, pursuant to the CISG, MCC was entitled to reduce payment in proportion to the defects. D'Agostino, however, noted that clause 4 on the reverse of the contract states, in pertinent part:

> Possible complaints for defects of the merchandise must be made in writing by means of a certified letter within and not later than 10 days after receipt of the merchandise....

Maselli Aff. ¶ 6. Although there is evidence to support MCC's claims that it complained about the quality of the deliveries it received, MCC never submitted any written complaints.

MCC did not dispute these underlying facts before the district court, but argued that the parties never intended the terms and conditions printed on the reverse of the order form to apply to their agreements. As evidence for this assertion, MCC submitted Monzon's affidavit, which claims that MCC had no subjective intent to be bound by those terms and that D'Agostino was aware of this intent. MCC also filed affidavits from Silingardi and Copelli, D'Agostino's representatives at the trade fair, which support Monzon's claim that the parties subjectively intended not to be bound by the terms on the reverse of the order form. The magistrate judge held that the affidavits, even if true, did not raise an issue of material fact regarding the interpretation or applicability of the terms of the written contracts and the district court accepted his recommendation to award summary judgment in D'Agostino's favor. MCC then filed this timely appeal.

DISCUSSION

We review a district court's grant of summary judgment *de novo* and apply the same standards as the district court. * * * Summary judgment is appropriate when the pleadings, depositions, and affidavits reveal that no genuine issue of material fact exists and the moving party is entitled to judgment as a matter of law. * * *

The parties to this case agree that the CISG governs their dispute because the United States, where MCC has its place of business, and Italy, where D'Agostino has its place of business, are both States Party to the Convention. *See* CISG, art. 1. Article 8 of the CISG governs the interpretation of international contracts for the sale of goods and forms the basis of MCC's appeal from the district court's grant of summary judgment in D'Agostino's favor. MCC argues that the magistrate judge and the district court improperly ignored evidence that MCC submitted regarding the parties' subjective intent when they memorialized the terms of their agreement on D'Agostino's pre-printed form contract, and that the magistrate judge erred by applying the parol evidence rule in derogation of the CISG.

I. *Subjective Intent Under the CISG*

Contrary to what is familiar practice in United States courts, the CISG appears to permit a substantial inquiry into the parties' subjective intent, even if the parties did not engage in any objectively ascertainable means of registering this intent. Article 8(1) of the CISG instructs courts to interpret the "statements ... and other conduct of a party ... according to his intent" as long as the other party "knew or could not have been unaware" of that intent. The plain language of the Convention, therefore, requires an inquiry into a party's subjective intent as long as the other party to the contract was aware of that intent.

In this case, MCC has submitted three affidavits that discuss the purported subjective intent of the parties to the initial agreement concluded between MCC and D'Agostino in October 1990. All three affidavits discuss the preliminary negotiations and report that the parties arrived at an oral agreement for D'Agostino to supply quantities of a specific grade of ceramic tile to MCC at an agreed upon price. The affidavits state that the "oral agreement established the essential terms of quality, quantity, description of goods, delivery, price and payment." * * * The affidavits also note that the parties memorialized the terms of their oral agreement on a standard D'Agostino order form, but all three affiants contend that the parties *subjectively* intended not to be bound by the terms on the reverse of that form despite a provision directly below the signature line that expressly and specifically incorporated those terms.

The terms on the reverse of the contract give D'Agostino the right to suspend or cancel all contracts in the event of a buyer's non-payment and require a buyer to make a written report of all defects within ten days. As the magistrate judge's report and recommendation makes clear, if these terms applied to the agreements between MCC and D'Agostino, summary judgment would be appropriate because MCC failed to make any written complaints about the quality of tile it received and D'Agostino has established MCC's non-payment of a number of invoices amounting to $108,389.40 and 102,053,846.00 Italian lira.

Article 8(1) of the CISG requires a court to consider this evidence of the parties' subjective intent. Contrary to the magistrate judge's report, which the district court endorsed and adopted, article 8(1) does not focus on interpreting the parties' statements alone. Although we agree with the magistrate judge's conclusion that no "interpretation" of the contract's *terms* could support MCC's position, article 8(1) also requires a court to consider subjective intent while interpreting the *conduct* of the parties. The CISG's language, therefore, requires courts to consider evidence of a party's subjective intent when signing a contract if the other party to the contract was aware of that intent at the time. This is precisely the type of evidence that MCC has provided through the Silingardi, Copelli, and Monzon affidavits, which discuss not only Monzon's intent as MCC's representative but also discuss the intent of D'Agostino's representatives and their knowledge that Monzon did not intend to agree to the terms on the reverse of the form contract. This acknowledgment that D'Agostino's representatives were aware of Monzon's subjective intent puts this case squarely within article 8(1) of the CISG, and therefore requires the court to consider MCC's evidence as it interprets the parties' conduct.

II. *Parol Evidence and the CISG*

Given our determination that the magistrate judge and the district court should have considered MCC's affidavits regarding the parties' subjective intentions, we must address a question of first impression in this circuit: whether the parol evidence rule, which bars evidence of an earlier oral contract that contradicts or varies the terms of a subsequent or contemporaneous written contract, plays any role in cases involving the CISG. We begin by observing that the parol evidence rule, contrary to its title, is a substantive rule of law, not a rule of evidence. *See* II E. ALLEN FARNSWORTH, FARNSWORTH ON CONTRACTS, § 7.2 at 194 (1990). The rule does not purport to exclude a particular type of evidence as an "untrustworthy or undesirable" way of proving a fact, but prevents a litigant from attempting to show "the fact itself—the fact that the terms of the agreement are other than those in the writing." *Id.* As such, a federal district court cannot simply apply the parol evidence rule as a procedural matter—as it might if excluding a particular type of evidence under the Federal Rules of Evidence, which apply in federal court regardless of the source of the substantive rule of decision.* * *

The CISG itself contains no express statement on the role of parol evidence.* * * It is clear, however, that the drafters of the CISG were comfortable with the concept of permitting parties to rely on oral contracts because they eschewed any statutes of fraud provision and expressly provided for the enforcement of oral contracts. *Compare* CISG, art. 11 (a contract of sale need not be concluded or evidenced in writing) *with* U.C.C. § 2–201 (precluding the enforcement of oral contracts for the sale of goods involving more than $500). Moreover, article 8(3) of the CISG expressly directs courts to give "due consideration ... to all relevant circumstances of the case including the negotiations ..." to determine the intent of the parties. Given article 8(1)'s directive to use the intent of the parties to interpret their statements and conduct, article 8(3) is a clear instruction to admit and consider parol evidence regarding the negotiations to the extent they reveal the parties' subjective intent.

* * *

Our reading of article 8(3) as a rejection of the parol evidence rule, however, is in accordance with the great weight of academic commentary on the issue.

* * *

This is not to say that parties to an international contract for the sale of goods cannot depend on written contracts or that parol evidence regarding subjective contractual intent need always prevent a party relying on a written agreement from securing summary judgment. To the contrary, most cases will not present a situation (as exists in this case) in which both parties to the contract acknowledge a subjective intent not to be bound by the terms of a pre-printed writing. In most cases, therefore, article 8(2) of the CISG will apply, and objective evidence will provide the basis for the court's decision. *See* HONNOLD, UNIFORM LAW § 107 at 164–65. Consequently, a party to a contract governed by the CISG will not be able to avoid the terms of a contract and force a jury trial simply by submitting an affidavit which states that he or she did not have the subjective intent to be bound by the contract's terms. * * * Moreover, to the extent parties wish to avoid parol evidence problems they can do so by including a merger clause in their agreement that extinguishes any and all prior agreements and understandings not expressed in the writing.

Considering MCC's affidavits in this case, however, we conclude that the magistrate judge and the district court improperly granted summary judgment in favor of D'Agostino. Although the affidavits are, as D'Agostino observes, relatively conclusory and unsupported by facts that would *objectively* establish MCC's intent not to be bound by the conditions on the reverse of the form, article 8(1) requires a court to consider evidence of a party's subjective intent when the other party was aware of it, and the Silingardi and Copelli affidavits provide that evidence. This is not to say that the affidavits are conclusive proof of what the parties intended. A reasonable finder of fact, for example, could disregard testimony that purportedly sophisticated international merchants signed a contract without intending to be bound as simply too incredible to believe and hold MCC to the conditions printed on the reverse of the contract. Nevertheless, the affidavits raise an issue of material fact regarding the parties' intent to incorporate the provisions on the reverse of the form contract. If the finder of fact determines that the parties did not intend to rely on those provisions, then the more general provisions of the CISG will govern the outcome of the dispute.

MCC's affidavits, however, do not discuss all of the transactions and orders that MCC placed with D'Agostino. Each of the affidavits discusses the parties' subjective intent surrounding the initial order MCC placed with D'Agostino in October 1990. The Copelli affidavit also discusses a February 1991 requirements contract between the parties and reports that the parties subjectively did not intend the terms on the reverse of the D'Agostino order form to apply to that contract either. *See* Copelli Aff. ¶ 12. D'Agostino, however, submitted the affidavit of its chairman, Vincenzo Maselli, which describes at least three other orders from MCC on form contracts dated January 15, 1991, April 27, 1991, and May 4, 1991, in addition to the October 1990 contract. *See* Maselli Aff. ¶ 2, 25. MCC's affidavits do not discuss the subjective intent of the parties to be bound by language in those contracts, and D'Agostino, therefore, argues that we should affirm summary judgment to the extent damages can be traced to those order forms. It is unclear from the record, however, whether all of these contracts contained the terms that appeared in the October 1990 contract. Moreover, because article 8 requires a court to consider any "practices which the parties have established between themselves, usages and any subsequent conduct of the parties" in interpreting contracts, CISG, art. 8(3), whether the parties intended to adhere to the ten day limit for complaints, as stated on the reverse of the initial contract, will have an impact on whether MCC was bound to adhere to the limit on subsequent deliveries. Since material issues of fact remain regarding the interpretation of the remaining contracts between MCC and D'Agostino, we cannot affirm any portion of the district court's summary judgment in D'Agostino's favor.

CONCLUSION

MCC asks us to reverse the district court's grant of summary judgment in favor of D'Agostino. The district court's decision rests on pre-printed contractual terms and conditions incorporated on the reverse of a standard order form that MCC's president signed on the company's behalf. Nevertheless, we conclude that the CISG, which governs international contracts for the sale of goods, precludes summary judgment in this case because MCC has raised an issue of material fact concerning the parties' subjective intent to be bound by the terms on the reverse of the pre-printed contract. The CISG also precludes the application of the parol evidence rule, which would otherwise bar the consideration of evidence concerning a prior or contemporaneously negotiated oral agreement. Accordingly, we REVERSE the district court's grant of summary judgment and REMAND this case for further proceedings consistent with this opinion.

The following excerpt describes a grievance between two groups in a sectarian community that led to a major controversy in the context of the Northern Ireland "Troubles."

DOMINIC BRYAN, PARADING PROTESTANTS AND CONSENTING CATHOLICS IN NORTHERN IRELAND: COMMUNAL CONFLICT, CONTESTED PUBLIC SPACE, AND GROUP RIGHTS

5 Chicago Journal of International Law 233, 241–42 (2004).

* * *

The dispute is this: The Orangemen claim they should be able to hold their parades in the areas they wish. They make this claim on the basis that parading is a cultural tradition within the Protestant community going back hundreds of years, that some of these parades are part of religious services, that they should have access to "the Queens Highway," and that the denial of the right is an attack upon the Protestant community. They point out that many parades, such as the Drumcree Church parade, would take no more than fifteen minutes to pass along the disputed part of the route. They also point out that many of the residents groups that oppose their parades have spokespeople with connections to the Republican movement with a number of key individuals being ex-prisoners. The residents groups point to the sectarian nature of the Orange Order, the relationship between the Orange Order and the UUP through periods of discrimination against Catholics, ongoing sectarian attacks upon Catholics in areas like Portadown, and the existence of alternative routes that the Orangemen could take. They argue that the parades are therefore "coat trailing exercises" of "triumphalism" designed to keep Catholics in their place. Significantly, both parties claim to represent the views of the Protestant/Unionist or Catholic/Nationalist communities.

In the first couple of years of these disputes, 1995 and 1996, the arguments used by the disputing parties and by the police were not those first and foremost based on a claim to rights or rights legislation, at least not directly. The Orange Order used the claim of "tradition," that is, legitimacy derived from historical precedence, to demand that they should be able to use "the Queen's Highway." An attack upon their tradition was therefore depicted as an attack upon the Protestant people. The residents, on the other hand, used an argument based loosely on a claim to local democracy, demanding that their "consent" should be sought, and presumably given, before a parade should be given access to "their" area. This argument was also problematic as it was just such an argument that Unionists used to claim legitimacy for the existence and nature of Northern Ireland. What is important to note is that both of these arguments are highly communitarian in nature, making a claim on the basis of membership of the collective rather than simply as an individual. Nor did the police make claims to human rights; instead they drew upon their legal duty to maintain public order and depicted themselves as being caught in the middle of two factions. In many respects this reflected the UK legal tradition of public order policing and, unlike what might happen in the United States, there was little exploration of the issue as one of freedom of speech. For example, the legal debate and process was very different from that which took place over the case for the National Socialists' right to march in Skokie, Illinois in 1977.

Notes and Questions

1.   Does the author's discussion of the Northern Ireland parades controversy fit the description of a conflict or a dispute? In what respect does the distinction make a difference?

2.   Describe the ethnic divide in Northern Ireland. Can you think of similar ethnic conflicts in the United States?

3.   How do the perceptions of Protestants and Catholics contribute to the continuation of the conflict cycle in Northern Ireland? To what extent does fear play a role?

4.   Assume you were appointed by the Parades Commission in Northern Ireland as a conflict consultant. How would you begin to reconcile the Orange Order's claim to march based on cultural tradition with the Catholic residents' argument based on a claim to local democracy?

5.   Identify the grievances held by each party in *MCC-Marble Ceramic Center, Inc. v. Ceramica Nuova D'Agostino, S.p.A.* Can you trace the evolution of the dispute in this case?

6.   What competing norms were invoked by the parties in an effort to resolve the competing claims in *MCC-Marble Ceramic Center, Inc. v. Ceramica Nuova D'Agostino, S.P.A?* What norms were acknowledged and relied upon by the court? To what extent did the parties' perceptions contribute to this dispute?

7.   Can you think of any litigated cases that you have studied in law school where the parties might have been able to resolve their disputes if they had been able to manage the perception of what was at stake?

8.   With respect to intractable conflict, can you think of any other steps you might add to the "ladder of prevention" offered by former Ambassador Jan Elisasson?

Chapter 2

INTERNATIONAL CONFLICT RESOLUTION PROCESSES

A. INTRODUCTION

The study of modern international conflict resolution is informed by the convergence of several fields including international relations, social psychology, labor relations, anthropology, law, alternative dispute resolution (ADR), and, most recently, information technology. Today, process choices for the management and resolution of international disputes and conflicts are as broad as the extent of human creativity. From traditional bilateral negotiations to cyberspace transactions with on-line dispute resolution (ODR), the possibilities for the adjustment of disputes and management and resolution of conflicts are substantial.

This chapter describes the emerging field of modern international conflict resolution and locates within that field the Alternative Dispute Resolution (ADR) movement. It offers definitional understandings of traditional conflict resolution processes, particularly negotiation and mediation as well as newer ADR processes to provide you with a structural framework within which you can explore the following chapters on public and private processes of international conflict resolution. While the emphasis of this book is on consensual conflict resolution processes, we discuss adjudication alternatives to give you a more comprehensive understanding of the range of available choices for international conflict resolution and management.

1. U.S. HISTORICAL PERSPECTIVE

The use of multiple dispute resolution remedies has an established history in the United States,[1] but it was not until the industrial and labor relations reforms of the New Deal Era that a new enthusiasm was generated for further developing such processes. Visionary reformers, such as Mary Parker Follett, encouraged integrative bargaining approaches as an alternative to the distributive, competitive behaviors that characterized labor-management disputes. Follett's vision of bargaining

---

1. *See, e.g.,* JEROLD S. AUERBACH, JUSTICE WITHOUT LAW? (1983).

emphasized both the competitive and cooperative aspects of conflict resolution.[2] Scholars in the field of social psychology followed Follett's lead and began to examine both cooperative and competitive processes of dispute resolution and urged cooperative processes to avoid destructive outcomes. Negotiation scholars continued the inquiry by applying game theory to competitive and cooperative modes of conflict resolution.[3]

Beginning in the late 1970s, social anthropologists conducted ethnographic studies on disputing practices in a wide range of cultures.[4] P.H. Gulliver's studies of the African moot with the use of the wise elder helped to locate an understanding of the mediation process in a wider cultural context.[5] Legal scholars, most notably Lon Fuller, enriched the conversation by systematically analyzing both the philosophical underpinnings and process aspects of mediation and adjudication.[6]

Further development occurred when scholar practitioners began experimenting with third-party consultation efforts such as problem-solving workshops and public peace processes. Other scholars explored the application of mediation to multiparty situations in which numerous third parties intervened to facilitate peace negotiations.[7] Finally, the study of international dispute resolution resulted in the exploration of a rich array of new processes: coalition-building, dialogue groups, and coexistence efforts.[8]

2. THE ALTERNATIVE DISPUTE RESOLUTION MOVEMENT

Within the field of modern conflict resolution, the acronym, ADR, is understood as either "appropriate dispute resolution" or "alternatives" to the court adjudication of disputes. The primary ADR processes are negotiation, mediation, and arbitration. While there is nothing new about these processes, which date back to ancient times and cultures, what is new are efforts to combine them and create new and hybrid processes thereby effecting major changes in the legal culture of conflict resolution. This is what occurred with the advent of the ADR movement.

Modern ADR began in the United States as a law reform movement in the early 1970s and has had a significant impact on the study and practice of U.S. and international dispute resolution processes. Serious concern about a "litigation explosion" and lack of access to justice led to a search for alternatives to the judicial adjudication of disputes. In 1976,

2. Valerie A. Sanchez, *Back to the Future of ADR: Negotiating Justice and Human Needs*, 18 Ohio St. J. Disp. Res. 669, 684–687 (2003).

3. *See* P. Terrance Hopmann, *Two Paradigms of Negotiating: Bargaining and Problem–Solving*, ANNALS, AAPSS, 542 (Nov. 1995).

4. *See, e.g.,* Laura Nader & Harry Todd, The Disputing Process: Law in Ten Societies (1978).

5. P.H. Gulliver: Disputes and Negotiations: A Cross Cultural Perspective (1979).

6. Lon Fuller, *Mediation—Its Forms and Functions*, 44 So. Cal. L. Rev. 305 (1971); *ibid., The Forms and Limits of Adjudication*, 92 Harv. L. Rev. 353 (1978).

7. Chester A. Crocker et al., Herding Cats: Multiparty Mediation in a Complex World (1999); Studies in International Mediation (Jacob Bercovitch ed., 2002).

8. Imagine Coexistence: Restoring Humanity After Violent Conflict (Antonia Chayes & Martha Minow eds., 2003); The Handbook of Interethnic Co-Existence (Eugene Weiner ed., 1998).

former Chief Justice Warren Burger convened the Roscoe E. Pound Conference on the Causes of Popular Dissatisfaction with the Administration of Justice (Pound Conference) in Saint Paul, Minnesota. Professors, judges, and lawyers gathered to consider non-judicial methods of resolving disputes and the "alternative dispute resolution" movement was born. One of the major papers that resulted from the conference, Professor Frank Sander's classic "Varieties of Dispute Resolution," established the foundation upon which the institutionalization of ADR would take place in the courts and the legal profession.[9] Sander focused upon negotiation, mediation, and arbitration as the basic forms of alternative dispute resolution. In time, med-arb, early neutral evaluation, mini-trials, and summary jury trials appeared in the landscape.

Over the next quarter of a century, the culture of ADR permeated the legal profession, gaining credibility in academic circles, law firms, and corporations. Although it was originally conceived of as providing out-of-court dispute resolution, the common forms of ADR, such as mediation and arbitration, found a permanent home in the U.S. court system—beginning with the passage of the Civil Justice Reform Act of 1990 and—in federal agencies—with the passage of the Negotiated Rule–Making and Administrative Dispute Resolution Acts of 1990. More recently, with the passage of the Alternative Dispute Resolution Act of 1998, all federal courts have adopted at least one form of ADR, making ADR an institutionalized feature of the U.S. civil justice system.

Following its exponential development in the United States, the ADR movement was exported to many parts of the world.[10] National courts in Europe, stymied by the volume of transborder litigation, have been attracted to ADR. Members of the European Union see ADR as a way to facilitate access to justice, a fundamental right contained in Article 6 of the European Convention for the Protection of Human Rights and Fundamental Freedoms. Growing interest in ADR in the European Union has also resulted in a Green Paper proposing greater use of alternative processes in civil and commercial matters,[11] and efforts are currently underway to develop a European Code of Conduct on mediation.[12]

The development of e-commerce also increased the need for ADR. Given the difficulties of processing e-commerce disputes in a global e-marketplace, on-line dispute resolution has become an attractive alternative, particularly in small disputes. When ADR processes, such as mediation and arbitration, occur in the on-line environment, it is often referred to as online dispute resolution (ODR).

9. Frank Sander, *Varieties of Dispute Resolution*, 70 F.R.D. 111 (1976).

10. Simon Roberts, *Institutionalized Settlement in England: A Contemporary Panorama*, 10 WILLAMETTE J. INT'L L. & DISP. RES. 17 (2002).

11. Commission of the European Communities, Green Paper on Alternative Dispute Resolution in Civil and Commercial Law (COM(2002) 196 Final) (Brussels Apr. 19, 2002).

12. See http://europa.eu.int/comm/justice.

In the context of civil disputes, ADR processes, such as negotiation and mediation, introduce a civilized way to resolve international conflicts. They were designed to overcome the limitations and failures of domestic judicial processes and the lack of a binding international public process.

3. THE TRADITIONAL SYSTEM: A GLOBAL PERSPECTIVE

The traditional dispute resolution procedures available under international law are enumerated in Article 33 of the United Nations Charter:

(1) The parties to any dispute, the continuance of which is likely to endanger the maintenance of international peace and security, shall, first of all, seek a solution by negotiation, enquiry, mediation, conciliation, arbitration, judicial settlement, resort to regional agencies or arrangements, or other peaceful means of their own choice.

(2) The Security Council shall, when it deems necessary, call upon the parties to settle their disputes by such means.

Negotiation is generally acknowledged as the most fundamental of these processes. The most common processes for international dispute settlement, however, are the diplomatic or consensual methods—mediation and good offices, enquiry, and conciliation.[13] The consultation process, although not mentioned in Article 33 of the U.N. Charter, is a species of negotiation that should be considered as part of the traditional package of processes for the resolution of international disputes. Together with pre-negotiation and pre-mediation activities, such as public peace processes, coalition-building, dialogue groups, and co-existence practices, these processes offer a panoply of choices for dispute and conflict resolution practitioners.

4. THE EMERGING SYSTEM OF PUBLIC INTERNATIONAL CONFLICT RESOLUTION

In the wake of the Cold War, religious-based and ethnic conflicts dominated the international political landscape, occurring with greater frequency than the classical types of interstate conflicts. The resulting fragility of international peace and human security motivated institutions to search for better ways to achieve peaceful co-existence. As a result, third-party initiatives often play a more significant role today than the unilateral or bilateral efforts of individual States. Frequently, these third-party activities take place under the auspices of international, regional, and transnational organizations. The search for peaceful co-existence has also resulted in collaborative efforts to develop a culture of conflict prevention through the combined use of traditional methods of international dispute settlement with ADR processes. The convergence of traditional methods of international conflict resolution with ADR methods has resulted in a new system of international conflict resolution that expands the use of ADR processes beyond the commercial and

---

13. Restatement (Third) of Foreign Relations § 902, Reporters Notes n.4.

family law areas into fields as broad as interethnic conflict and post-conflict peace-building. Finally, with the collapse of the Soviet Union in the early 1990s and the demise of colonialism, there has been a genuine interest by emerging States in using ADR to facilitate democratic governance.

Traditionally, international conflict resolution was conducted by official State representatives as part of *Track I Diplomacy*.[14] Over the last two decades, a parallel regime of *Track II Diplomacy* has developed, consisting of individuals or non-governmental organizations (NGOs) that engage in informal efforts to facilitate the peaceful resolution of conflicts and disputes.[15] One of the growing challenges in the field is the coordination of Track I and Track II efforts.

5. THE SYSTEM OF PRIVATE INTERNATIONAL CONFLICT RESOLUTION

The increase in private commercial international transactions has generated an interest in using alternatives to litigation and arbitration for the resolution of cross border disputes. As a result, international commercial mediation is a rapidly developing practice. The extraordinary growth of the Internet as a vehicle for communication and business has also had a significant impact upon international conflict resolution. While the Internet has enormous potential as a problem-solving device, it has generated its own sets of problems and disputes, including public policy, cultural, and consumer issues. Transactions on the Internet often involve individuals from different States and no particular national or international law governs the Internet or its use.

B. DEFINITIONAL CONSIDERATIONS

The following section provides general definitions of the traditional processes of international conflict resolution and the principal ADR alternatives. The distinction between these processes is not always clear. As noted by the *Restatement (Third) of Foreign Relations Law*, while definitions may identify theoretical differences, in practice, these processes are often combined. For example, the terms "conciliation" and "mediation" and the terms "enquiry" and "fact-finding" are often considered interchangeable.

You should be aware that there are controversies even about basic definitional matters. This is particularly true in the case of mediation practice. Therefore, the definitions that follow provide a general understanding of the basic processes. Refinements and variations are contained in the specific chapters that follow.

14. Louis Kriesberg, *The Development of the Conflict Resolution Field, in* Peacemaking in International Conflict: Methods & Techniques 51, 60 (I. William Zartman & J. Lewis Rasmussen eds., 1997) [hereinafter Zartman & Rasmussen].

15. Ronald J. Fisher, *Interactive Conflict Resolution, in* Zartman & Rasmussen, *supra* note 14, at 39, 61.

1. NEGOTIATION

Negotiation represents the most common form of dispute resolution. It is a joint decision-making process in which two or more parties attempt to achieve together what they could not achieve unilaterally. To realize their goal, negotiators engage in specific types of strategies and behaviors to maximize individual or joint gain. There are many different concepts of negotiation.

(a) Structure of Negotiation

Negotiation generally consists of five stages, each of which involves multiple considerations and each of which can itself be considered to be negotiation. For descriptive purposes, these stages are listed chronologically. In reality, negotiation is a fluid process and negotiators may engage in several stages concurrently:

(i) Pre–Negotiation

(ii) Planning

(iii) Information Exchange and Bargaining

(iv) Agreement

(v) Implementation of Agreement

The first three stages merit particular attention. The primary task in the pre-negotiation stage is to determine whether agreement is possible, *i.e.*, whether a bargaining zone exists,[16] and then getting the parties to the table. Several pre-bargaining activities occur after at least one party makes a decision to consider negotiation as a conflict resolution mechanism.[17] The pre-negotiation phase takes on increased significance in the circumstances of political conflicts in which some parties may not be interested in participating in the negotiation process or in which a conflict is not yet ripe for intervention.[18]

The planning stage focuses on process design, a critical foundational step without which negotiation may be doomed. Primary planning tasks include determining goals and objectives and considering strategies and tactics that support those goals and objectives. Among the most important planning tasks are: (a) determining that all relevant parties will be represented at the bargaining table; (b) setting the agenda; and (c) identifying issues and interests.

Where negotiation involves a single issue, the bargaining paradigm is described frequently as distributive in nature. Negotiators attempt to maximize individual gain by engaging in competitive, adversarial behav-

---

16. *See* Russell Korobkin, Negotiation Theory and Strategy 7 (2002).

17. I. William Zartman, *Prenegotiation: Phases and Functions, in* Getting to the Table: The Process of International Prenegotiation 1–17 (Janice Gross Stein ed., 1989).

18. Harold Saunders, *We Need a Larger Theory of Negotiation: The Importance of Prenegotiating Phases, in* Negotiation Theory and Practice 57–70 (J. William Breslin & Jeffrey Z. Rubin eds., Harvard Law School, Program on Negotiation 1991).

iors. Where multiple issues are involved, negotiators have value-creating opportunities and engage in trade-offs. This presents a greater opportunity for integrative bargaining situations in which negotiators cooperate to achieve joint gains.

The information exchange and bargaining stage can be labeled as a value-claiming or value-creating activity.[19] The traditional approach to negotiation is based on an adversarial value-claiming model which focuses on positional bargaining. Negotiators combine conflict and cooperation, taking and arguing for positions, offering concessions and reaching compromise solutions. Sometimes referred to as the Prisoner's Dilemma model by negotiation theorists,[20] the adversarial model typically involves hard-bargaining behaviors and tactics through which opposing negotiators challenge each other. Mnookin, Peppet, and Tulmello's research has identified ten of the most common tactics in this model:[21]

1. Extreme demands followed by small concessions

2. Commitment tactics

3. Take-it-or-leave-it offers

4. Inviting unreciprocated offers

5. Flinch

6. Personal insults and feather ruffling

7. Bluffing, puffing, and lying

8. Threats and warnings

9. Belittling the other party's alternatives

10. Good cop, bad cop.

In contrast to the positional-based approach of adversarial bargaining, the problem-solving value creating approach focuses upon identifying the parties' underlying needs and interests, and creating solutions that meet those needs. While the practice of problem-solving is not new to diplomacy and international negotiation,[22] it was popularized in recent times by Fisher & Ury's landmark book, *Getting to Yes*.[23] The book's prescriptive model of "principled" negotiation focused upon understanding parties' needs and interests rather than responding to their positions, using objective criteria, and having knowledge of a "Best Alternative To A Negotiated Agreement" or "BATNA." Problem-solving negotiators attempt to create value and search for mutually beneficial solutions. Information sharing is critical to a problem-solving approach.

19. David Lax & James Sebenius, The Manager as Negotiator: Bargaining for Cooperation and Competitive Gain (1986).

20. Victor A. Kremenyuk, International Negotiation 28 (2d ed. 2002) [hereinafter V. Kremenyuk].

21. Robert H. Mnookin, Scott R. Peppet & Andrew S. Tulumello, Beyond Winning:

Negotiating to Create Value in Deals and Disputes 24 (2000).

22. V. Kremenyuk, *supra* note 20, at 30.

23. Roger Fisher, William Ury & Bruce Patton, Getting to Yes: Negotiating Agreement Without Giving In (2d ed. 1991).

(b) Barriers to Negotiation

Not all negotiations are successful, and it is helpful to distill the impediments to successful negotiation. To a large extent, the barriers to negotiated resolution of disputes are culturally shaped. Two examples illustrate. First, Western cultures typically presume that resolution of a conflict is positive. Some other cultures such as Middle Eastern cultures instead question whether resolution is necessarily desirable. As political scientist Paul Salem has explained, for these cultures, the process of conflict and struggle may serve important societal and religious purposes while resolution of the conflict may have substantial costs. Second, as the following excerpt below notes, there are cognitive barriers to the resolution of conflict. Individuals from Asian cultures, however, may have distinguishing cognitive processes when negotiating a solution. Cultural psychologist Richard Nisbett argues, for instance, that these cultures have a more holistic view of events than Western cultures, taking into account the perspectives of other people and the broader context in which the conflict arises and is resolved.

ROBERT H. MNOOKIN, WHY NEGOTIATIONS FAIL: AN EXPLORATION OF BARRIERS TO THE RESOLUTION OF CONFLICT

8 Ohio State Journal on Dispute Resolution 235 (1993).

* * *

I. INTRODUCTION

Conflict is inevitable, but efficient and fair resolution is not. Conflicts can persist even though there may be any number of possible resolutions that would better serve the interests of the parties—the recent history of ethnic and religious strife in Lebanon, Israel, Cyprus, and Yugoslavia serves as a reminder of this. In our everyday personal and professional lives, we have all witnessed disputes where the absence of a resolution imposes substantial and avoidable costs on all parties. Moreover, many resolutions that are achieved—whether through negotiation or imposition—conspicuously fail to satisfy the economist's criterion of Pareto efficiency.

* * *

A. Strategic Barriers

The first barrier to the negotiated resolution of conflict is inherent in a central characteristic of negotiation. Negotiation can be metaphorically compared to making a pie and then dividing it up. The process of conflict resolution affects both the size of the pie, and who gets what size slice.

* * *

The disputants' behavior may affect the size of the pie in a variety of ways. On the one hand, spending on avoidable legal fees and other process costs shrinks the pie. On the other hand, negotiators can together "create value" and make the pie bigger by discovering resolutions in which each party contributes special complementary skills that can be combined in a synergistic way, or by exploiting differences in relative preferences that permit trades that make both parties better off. Books like "Getting to Yes" and proponents of "win-win negotiation" emphasize the potential benefits of collaborative problem-solving approaches to negotiation which allow parties to maximize the size of the pie.

Negotiation also involves issues concerning the distribution of benefits, and, with respect to pure distribution, both parties cannot be made better off at the same time. Given a pie of fixed size, a larger slice for you means a smaller one for me.

Because bargaining typically entails both efficiency issues (that is, how big the pie can be made) and distributive issues (that is, who gets what size slice), negotiation involves an inherent tension—one that David Lax and James Sebenius have dubbed the "negotiator's dilemma." In order to create value, it is critically important that options be created in light of both parties' underlying interests and preferences. This suggests the importance of openness and disclosure, so that a variety of options can be analyzed and compared from the perspectives of all concerned. However, when it comes to the distributive aspects of bargaining, full disclosure—particularly if unreciprocated by the other side—can often lead to outcomes in which the more open party receives a comparatively smaller slice. To put it another way, unreciprocated approaches to creating value leave their maker vulnerable to claiming tactics. On the other hand, focusing on the distributive aspects of bargaining can often lead to unnecessary deadlocks and, more fundamentally, a failure to discover options or alternatives that make both sides better off.

* * *

Strategic behavior—which may be rational for a self-interested party concerned with maximizing the size of his or her own slice—can often lead to inefficient outcomes. Those subjected to claiming tactics often respond in kind, and the net result typically is to push up the cost of the dispute resolution process. (*Buchwald v. Paramount Pictures Corp.*, is a good example of a case in which the economic costs of hardball litigation obviously and substantially shrunk the pie.) Parties may be tempted to engage in strategic behavior, hoping to get more. Often all they do is shrink the size of the pie. Those experienced in the civil litigation process see this all the time. One or both sides often attempt to use pre-trial discovery as leverage to force the other side into agreeing to a more favorable settlement. Often the net result, however, is simply that both sides spend unnecessary money on the dispute resolution process.

B. The Principal/Agent Problem

The second barrier is suggested by recent work relating to transaction cost economics, and is sometimes called the "principal/agent" problem. Notwithstanding the jargon, the basic idea is familiar to everyone in this room. The basic problem is that the incentives for an agent (whether it be a lawyer, employee, or officer) negotiating on behalf of a party to a dispute may induce behavior that fails to serve the interests of the principal itself. The relevant research suggests that it is no simple matter—whether by contract or custom—to align perfectly the incentives for an agent with the interests of the principal. This divergence may act as a barrier to efficient resolution of conflict.

Litigation is fraught with principal/agent problems. In civil litigation, for example—particularly where the lawyers on both sides are being paid by the hour—there is very little incentive for the opposing lawyers to cooperate, particularly if the clients have the capacity to pay for trench warfare and are angry to boot. Commentators have suggested that this is one reason many cases settle on the courthouse steps, and not before: for the lawyers, a late settlement may avoid the possible embarrassment of an extreme outcome, while at the same time providing substantial fees.

The Texaco/Pennzoil dispute may have involved a principal/agent problem of a different sort. My colleague Bob Wilson and I have argued that the interests of the Texaco officers and directors diverged from those of the Texaco shareholders in ways that may well have affected the conduct of that litigation. Although the shareholders would have benefited from an earlier settlement, the litigation was controlled by the directors, officers, and lawyers whose interests differed in important respects. A close examination of the incentives for the management of Texaco in particular suggests an explanation for the delay in settlement.

The directors and officers of Texaco were themselves defendants in fourteen lawsuits, eleven of them derivative shareholder actions, brought after the original multi-billion dollar Pennzoil verdict in the Texas trial court. These lawsuits essentially claimed that Texaco's directors and officers had violated their duty of care to the corporation by causing Texaco to acquire Getty Oil in a manner that led to the multi-billion dollar Texas judgment. After this verdict, and for the next several years, the Texaco management rationally might have preferred to appeal the Pennzoil judgment and seek complete vindication, even though a speedy settlement for the expected value of the litigation might have better served their shareholders. Because they faced the risk of personal liability, the directors and officers of Texaco acted in such a way as to suggest they would prefer to risk pursuing the case to the bitter end (with some slight chance of complete exoneration) rather than accept a negotiated resolution, even though in so doing they risked subjecting the corporation to a ten billion dollar judgment. The case ultimately did settle, but only through a bankruptcy proceeding in which the bankruptcy court eliminated the risk of personal liability for Texaco's officers and directors.

C. Cognitive Barriers

The third barrier is a by-product of the way the human mind processes information, deals with risks and uncertainties, and makes inferences and judgments. Research by cognitive psychologists during the last fifteen years suggests several ways in which human reasoning often departs from that suggested by theories of rational judgment and decision making. Daniel Kahneman and Amos Tversky have done research on a number of cognitive biases that are relevant to negotiation. . . . I would like to focus on two aspects of their work: those relating to loss aversion and framing effects.

Suppose everyone attending this evening's lecture is offered the following happy choice: At the end of my lecture you can exit at the north end of the hall or the south end. If you choose the north exit, you will be handed an envelope in which there will be a crisp new twenty dollar bill. Instead, if you choose the south exit, you will be given a sealed envelope randomly pulled from a bin. One quarter of these envelopes contain a $100 bill, but three quarters are empty. In other words, you can have a sure gain of $20 if you go out the north door, or you can instead gamble by choosing the south door where you will have a 25% chance of winning $100 and a 75% chance of winning nothing. Which would you choose? A great deal of experimental work suggests that the overwhelming majority of you would choose the sure gain of $20, even though the "expected value" of the second alternative, $25, is slightly more. This is a well known phenomenon called "risk aversion." The principle is that most people will take a sure thing over a gamble, even where the gamble may have a somewhat higher "expected" payoff.

Daniel Kahneman and Amos Tversky have advanced our understanding of behavior under uncertainty with a remarkable discovery. They suggest that, in order to avoid what would otherwise be a sure loss, many people will gamble, even if the expected loss from the gamble is larger. Their basic idea can be illustrated by changing my hypothetical. Although you didn't know this when you were invited to this lecture, it is not free. At the end of the lecture, the doors are going to be locked. If you go out the north door, you'll be required to *pay* $20 as an exit fee. If you go out the south door, you'll participate in a lottery by drawing an envelope. Three quarters of the time you're going to be let out for free, but one quarter of the time you're going to be required to pay $100. Rest assured all the money is going to the Dean's fund—a very good cause. What do you choose? There's a great deal of empirical research, based on the initial work of Kahneman and Tversky, suggesting that the majority of this audience would choose the south exit—*i.e.*, most of you would gamble to avoid having to lose $20 for sure. Kahneman and Tversky call this "loss aversion."

Now think of these two example together. Risk aversion suggests that most of you would not gamble for a gain, even though the expected value of $25 exceeds the sure thing of $20. On the other hand, most of you would gamble to avoid a sure loss, even though, on the average, the loss of going out the south door is higher. Experimental evidence suggests that the proportion of people who will gamble to avoid a loss is much greater than those who would gamble to realize a gain.

Loss aversion can act as a cognitive barrier to the negotiated resolution of conflict for a variety of reasons. For example, both sides may fight on in a dispute in the hope that they may avoid any losses, even though the continuation of the dispute involves a gamble in which the loss may end up being far greater. Loss aversion may explain Lyndon Johnson's decision, in 1965, to commit additional troops to Vietnam as an attempt to avoid the sure loss attendant to withdrawal, and as a gamble that there might be some way in the future to avoid any loss at all. Similarly, negotiators may, in some circumstances, be adverse to offering a concession in circumstances where they view the concession as a sure loss. Indeed, the notion of rights or entitlements may be associated with a more extreme form of loss aversion that Kahneman and Tversky call "enhanced loss aversion," because losses "compounded by outrage are much less acceptable than losses that are caused by misfortune or by legitimate action of others."

One of the most striking features of loss aversion is that whether something is viewed as a gain or loss—and what kind of gain or loss it is considered—depends upon a reference point, and the choice of a reference point is sometimes manipulable.

* * *

D. "Reactive Devaluation" of Compromises and Concessions

The final barrier I wish to discuss is "reactive devaluation," and is an example of a social/psychological barrier that arises from the dynamics of the negotiation process and the inferences that negotiators draw from their interactions. My Stanford colleague, psychology Professor Lee Ross, and his students have done experimental work to suggest that, especially between adversaries, when one side offers a particular concession or proposes a particular exchange of compromises, the other side may diminish the attractiveness of that offer or proposed exchange simply because it originated with a perceived opponent. The basic notion is a familiar one, especially for lawyers. How often have you had a client indicate to you in the midst of litigation, "If only we could settle this case for $7,000. I'd love to put this whole matter behind me." Lo and behold, the next day, the other side's attorney calls and offers to settle for $7,000. You excitedly call your client and say, "Guess what—the other side has just offered to settle this case for $7,000." You expect to hear jubilation on the other end of the phone, but instead there is silence. Finally, your client says, "Obviously they must know something we don't know. If $7,000 is a good settlement for them, it can't be a good settlement for us."

Both in laboratory and field settings, Ross and his colleagues have marshaled interesting evidence for "reactive devaluation." They have demonstrated both that a given compromise proposal is rated less positively when proposed by someone on the other side than when proposed by a neutral or an ally. They also demonstrated that a concession that is actually offered is rated lower than a concession that is withheld, and that a compromise is rated less highly after it has been put on the table by the other side than it was beforehand.

An example which should provide the flavor of this research is the work of Ross and his colleagues. One study took place in the context of a campus-wide controversy at Stanford over university investment policy concerning companies that did business with South Africa. Ross and his colleagues asked Stanford students to consider two compromise proposals. One proposal, termed the "specific divestment plan," entailed immediate Stanford divestment from corporations doing business with the South African military or police. The other, so-called "deadline plan," proposed to create a committee of students and trustees to monitor investment responsibility, with the promise of total divestment two years down the road if the committee was not satisfied with the rate of progress shown in dismantling the apartheid system in South Africa.

The experiment went as follows: one group of randomly assigned students was told that the University planned to undertake specific divestment, another group was told that the University planned to undertake the deadline plan, the remainder were given no specific reason to believe that the university was considering the immediate adoption of either alternative. The students were asked which plan they preferred. Students tended to denigrate whichever of the two compromise proposals the trustees had been said to offer, and to prefer the alternative proposal. When told that Stanford was allegedly ready to implement the deadline plan, 85% of the respondents ranked specific divestment as the preferred move. By contrast, when the university purportedly was going to pursue specific divestment, 60% rated that plan worse than the deadline plan.

Ross has described a range of cognitive and motivational processes that may account for the reactive devaluation phenomenon. Whatever its roots, reactive devaluation certainly can act as a barrier to the efficient resolution of conflict. It suggests that the exchange of proposed concessions and compromises between adversaries can be very problematic. When one side unilaterally offers a concession that it believes the other side should value and the other side reacts by devaluing the offer, this can obviously make resolution difficult. The recipient of a unilateral concession is apt to believe that her adversary has given up nothing of real value and may therefore resist any notion that she should offer something of real value in exchange. On the other hand, the failure to respond may simply confirm the suspicions of the original offer or, who will believe that her adversary is proceeding in bad faith and is being strategic.

III. Overcoming Strategic Barriers: The Roles Of Negotiators And Mediators

The study of barriers can do more than simply help us understand why negotiations sometimes fail when they should not. It can also contribute to our understanding of how to overcome these barriers. Let me illustrate this by using the preceding analysis of four barriers briefly to explore the role of mediators, and to suggest why neutrals can often facilitate the efficient resolution of disputes by overcoming these specific barriers.

First, let us consider the strategic barrier. To the extent that a neutral third party is trusted by both sides, the neutral may be able to induce the parties to reveal information about their underlying interests, needs, priorities, and aspirations that they would not disclose to their adversary. This information may permit a trusted mediator to help the parties enlarge the pie in circumstances where the parties acing alone could not. Moreover, a mediator can foster a problem-solving atmosphere and lessen the temptation on the part of each side to engage in strategic behavior. A skilled mediator can often get parties to move beyond political posturing and recriminations about past wrongs and to instead consider possible gains from a fair resolution of the dispute.

A mediator also can help overcome barriers posed by principal/agent problems. A mediator may bring clients themselves to the table, and help them understand their shared interest in minimizing legal fees and costs in circumstances where the lawyers themselves might not be doing so. In circumstances where a middle manager is acting to prevent a settlement that might benefit the company, but might be harmful to the manager's own career, an astute mediator can sometimes bring another company representative to the table who does not have a personal stake in the outcome.

A mediator can also promote dispute resolution by helping overcome cognitive barriers. Through a variety of processes, a mediator can often help each side understand the power of the case from the other side's perspective. Moreover, by reframing the dispute and suggesting a resolution that avoids blame and stresses the positive aspects of a resolution, a mediator may be able to lessen the effects of loss aversion. My colleague Tversky thinks that cognitive barriers are like optical illusions—knowing that an illusion exists does not necessarily enable us to see things differently. Nevertheless, I believe that astute mediators can dampen loss aversion through reframing, by helping a disputant reconceptualize the resolution. By emphasizing the potential gains to both sides of the resolution and de-emphasizing the losses that the resolution is going to entail, mediators (and lawyers) often facilitate resolution.

With respect to the fourth barrier, reactive devaluation, mediators can play an important and quite obvious role. Reactive devaluation can often be sidestepped if the source of a proposal is a neutral—not one of the parties. Indeed, one of the trade secrets of mediators is that after talking separately to each side about what might or might not be acceptable, the mediator takes responsibility for making a proposal. This helps both parties avoid reactive devaluation by allowing them to accept as sensible a proposal that they might have rejected if it had come directly from their adversary.

2. MEDIATION

Mediation is an extension of the negotiation process in which a third-party intervenes to help resolve disputes or manage conflicts. There are numerous definitions of mediation. The domestic concept of mediation contemplates an informal, consensual process in which a neutral third-party, without power to impose a settlement, "assists disputing parties in reaching a mutually satisfactory resolution." Lon Fuller's classic formulation reminds us of mediation's "capacity to reorient the parties toward each other, not by imposing rules on them, but by helping them to achieve a new and shared perception of their relationship, a perception that will redirect their attitudes and dispositions toward one another." In the international context, Bercovitch defines mediation as "a process of conflict management, related to but distinct from the parties' own negotiations, where those in conflict seek the assistance, or accept an offer of help from an outsider (who may be an individual, an organization, a group, or a state), to change their perceptions of behavior, and to do so without resorting to physical force or invoking the authority of the law."[24]

(a) Role of the Mediator

The differing views of mediation have generated an equal number of opinions about the appropriate role of the mediator and the permissible range of mediator activities in assisting the parties through the negotiation process. The label "mediation" is attached to a wide variety of practices beginning with court conferences in which mediators sometimes strongly suggest settlement to exercises in moral development in which mediators assist parties in achieving a self-transformation.[25] Whether mediators should limit their activities to facilitating the negotiation process or whether they may engage in more evaluative behaviors, such as communicating their opinion of the case to the parties, is a matter of much debate.

24. J. Bercovitch, *Mediation in International Conflict, in* Zartman & Rasmussen, *supra* note 14.

25. Jacqueline Nolan–Haley, *Court Mediation and the Search for Justice Through Law*, 74 Wash. U. L.Q. 47 (1996).

(b) Governing Principles

The cardinal attributes of domestic mediation are self-determination, autonomy, empowerment, transformation, and efficiency. Mediation enhances the parties' capability to self-determine because it permits them to structure and consent to the outcome of the bargaining process. Unlike decision-making by a neutral third-party in a process such as adjudication, decision-making in mediation rests solely with the disputing parties. They retain control of the outcome.

Informed consent is the foundational value of the mediation process. Parties must understand the mediation process and consent both to participating in it and to shaping its outcome. Without informed consent, the lasting character of any mediated agreement is threatened.

In the following excerpt, the author discusses the fundamental values associated with the principle of informed consent in mediation.

JACQUELINE M. NOLAN–HALEY, INFORMED CONSENT IN MEDIATION: A GUIDING PRINCIPLE FOR TRULY EDUCATED DECISIONMAKING

74 Notre Dame Law Review 775, 781. 787–88, 791–92 (1999).

* * *

Informed consent is an ethical, moral, and legal concept that is deeply ingrained in American culture. In those transactions where informed consent is required, the legal doctrine requires that individuals who give consent be competent, informed about the particular intervention, and consent voluntarily. Informed consent is the foundational moral and ethical principle that promotes respect for individual self-determination and honors human dignity.

* * *

In mediation practice, the principle of informed consent is not an end in itself but is a means of achieving the fundamental goal of fairness. Fairness requires that parties know what they are doing when they decide to participate in mediation, that they understand all aspects of the decisionmaking process, including their right to withdraw consent and discontinue negotiations, and that they understand the outcome reached in mediation. Toward this end, the principle of informed consent in mediation protects the psychological and legal interests associated with the values of autonomy, human dignity, and efficiency.

* * *

The principle of informed consent promotes respect for the fundamental value of human dignity in several aspects of mediation decisionmaking. First, the value of dignity is most frequently associated with the right to participate in decisionmaking. When disputing parties can participate directly in the bargaining process, their perceptions of procedural fairness are enhanced. Second, the principle of informed consent guards against unwanted intrusions into highly personal aspects of parties' lives.

* * *

Third, the principle of informed consent promotes understanding and alleviates the fears associated with lack of information. When parties come to mediation without sufficient knowledge of what is occurring, there is greater likelihood that they will consciously or unconsciously resist mediation and thus never fully give consent to mediation.

(c) American Style Mediation

As discussed earlier, mediation is a process rooted in ancient practice. Adapted by the ADR movement, however, it has acquired a set of labels such as directive or non-directive, facilitative or evaluative, to describe a mediator's practice style and, in some cases, rigid protocols. In western mediation practice, concepts such as neutrality and impartiality are considered key attributes of the mediator. As you will see in later chapters, however, these attributes may not be valued similarly in other cultures. Some scholars have criticized the importation of western mediation models into developing countries. What is the western model? Is it a uniquely American model of mediation? The following excerpt provides some guidance on these questions.

JOHN D. FEERICK, THE PEACE–MAKING ROLE OF A MEDIATOR

19 Ohio State Journal on Dispute Resolution 229, 230 (2003).

* * *

Perhaps is it provocative to ask whether there is an American style of mediation. I would begin by noting that there are many styles in helping parties reach agreement. One approach is that of a facilitative role, helping parties communicate with each other, identifying their interests, and exploring with them options for resolving their dispute. Another method used by mediators involves defining the problem broadly, looking at all the interests of the parties, and engaging them in a problem-solving, collaborative process. A third approach relies on evaluations-providing information and offering views, opinions and proposals on the subject of the dispute. Yet another approach combines all of the above approaches, in different, or even in the same mediation, depending on the wishes of the parties and sometimes at the initiative of the mediator in the particular dispute.

Despite style differences, there is certainly wide agreement among mediation practitioners on the importance of a mediator being neutral and impartial. There is also agreement on the importance of the process being fair and party-oriented. To assure neutrality, mediators make disclosures of possible conflicts, avoid conduct that may give the appearance of partiality toward one of the parties, and respect the right of a party to reach a voluntary, uncoerced agreement. To assure fairness, mediators keep the secrets and confidences of the parties and make commitments to diligence and procedural fairness. There is also consensus on the need for mediators to be able to meet the reasonable expectations of the parties—to be competent in serving as an intermediary in helping them find a solution. However, the widest of agreement is on the importance of the mediator having the qualities essential for inspiring confidence and trust. Even-handedness, commitment, independence, and good judgment are among these, as well as such qualities as being patient, calm, humble, and a good listener. An example of a mediator who embodies such qualities is George Mitchell, a former United States Senator, who chaired the peace talks in Northern Ireland. In his book describing the peace process, George Mitchell observed, "[f]or the two years of negotiations, I listened and listened, and then I listened some more. At times it was interesting, at times entertaining; it was also often repetitive, frustrating, and deliberately quarrelsome." He added, "I believe in letting people have their say. It was important, I told them, not to cut anyone off at this stage. When the right time comes, I said, I'll bring this to a conclusion."

3. THIRD–PARTY CONSULTATION

Consultation is a preliminary form of negotiation in which parties discuss issues and exchange views.[26] Professional writings increasingly recognize consultation as a process for resolving disputes relating to the interpretation of treaties or as a pre-negotiation phase in the settlement of disputes.[27] Most recently, the use of consultation has increased with the growth of international trade. For example, the four-part Dispute Settlement System of the World Trade Organization (WTO) begins with a flexible consultation process conducted by the parties. The purpose of consultation is to help the parties resolve their dispute by giving them a better understanding of the conflict and the legal claims on both sides. WTO statistics show that more than half of the cases are either resolved, settled, or abandoned at the consultation phase.[28]

Effective consultation requires the parties' voluntary good faith cooperation. When disputing parties use consultation as a mere formality or in bad faith, the process lacks integrity and it will not achieve effective results.[29]

26. F.L. KIRGIS, PRIOR CONSULTATION IN INTERNATIONAL LAW (1983); J. Gold, *Prior Consultation in International Law*, 24 VA. J. INT'L L. 729 (1983–84); J.G. MERRILLS, INTERNATIONAL DISPUTE SETTLEMENT 3–6, 201–02 (3d ed. 1998).

27. HANDBOOK ON THE PEACEFUL SETTLEMENT OF DISPUTES BETWEEN STATES 10 (1992).

28. William J. Davey, *The World Trade Organization's Dispute Settlement System*, 42 S. TEX. L. REV. 1199 (2001).

29. Kim Van der Borgt, *The Review of the WTO Understanding on Dispute Settle-*

4. GOOD OFFICES

The traditional understanding of "good offices" refers to the use of third-parties—such as States, international organizations, or individuals—to assist two conflicting countries in negotiating a resolution of their dispute. The use of "good offices" is a traditional method of diplomatic assistance with longstanding historical roots. Its legitimacy was affirmed in the Hague Convention for the Pacific Settlement of International Disputes (1907) which provides that "strangers to the dispute have the right to offer good offices or mediation even during the course of hostilities" (Art. 3, para. 2). Acting under the auspices of "good offices," individuals use a variety of means to facilitate the resolution of disputes and conflicts, including informal contacts, friendly suggestions, or mediation. More recently, the use of good offices has been expanded to include the intervention of international organizations, particularly the Secretary General of the United Nations, to end human rights violations.

5. FACT–FINDING AND ENQUIRY

These terms are generally used interchangeably to describe a bilateral fact-finding process in which one or more impartial persons conducts an independent investigation of disputed facts and establishes an independent finding of facts.[30] While the fact-finders' report is not necessarily binding, it prepares the way for parties to negotiate a resolution of their dispute. The process was originally described as "enquiry commissions" in the 1899 Hague Convention for the Pacific Settlement of Disputes and was limited to disputes involving "neither honor nor essential interests." The 1907 Hague Convention further developed the concept of enquiry commissions.

In some cases, fact-finders are empowered by the parties to make recommendations for settlement. The *Dogger Bank Case* is one of the most well-known historical examples of the use of a combined fact-finding and mediation process. The dispute was precipitated by the Russian Baltic fleet firing on British fishing vessels in the Dogger Bank area of the North Sea in 1904. The Russian fleet claimed that Japanese submarine activity caused them to fire. A commission of enquiry composed of senior naval officers from five countries, including Russia and Britain, was authorized by the disputing parties not only to make findings of fact, but also to determine responsibility. As a result of the commission's findings, Britain withdrew its demand for punishment and Russia agreed to pay compensation.[31]

While this process has been successful in specialized areas such as maritime cases, it has been used infrequently in part because States are reluctant to permit encroachments on their sovereignty. More recently,

ment: Some Reflections on the Current Debate, 14 AM. U. INT'L L. REV. 1223 (1999).

30. PETER MALANCZUK, AKEHURST'S MODERN INTRODUCTION TO INTERNATIONAL LAW 277–78 (7th ed. 1997).

31. Dogger Bank Incident (Great Britain v. Russia), Hague Ct. Rep. (Scott) 403 (Comm'n Inquiry 1905).

fact-finding has been attempted as a means of facilitating the resolution of political conflicts.[32]

6. CONCILIATION COMMISSIONS

Conciliation is a non-binding method of dispute resolution in which a third-party or parties, as in the case of a commission, who are trusted by parties to the dispute, examine the facts of a dispute. The original understanding of conciliation was based on its use in the State-to-State context. Conciliation commissions originated with the Bryan Treaties of 1914–21, named after Secretary of State William Jennings Bryan. Under the basic procedure, commissioners are chosen from States that are not involved in the dispute to make recommendations to the parties to assist them in arriving at a settlement.[33] Unlike arbitrators or other adjudicators, the commissioners have no power to impose recommendations.

7. CONCILIATION

Conciliation is recognized today as a viable method of resolving international economic and business disputes. While the term conciliation is used interchangeably in some contexts with mediation, the concept of conciliation has independent significance. Professor Linda Reif elaborates upon the differences between mediation and conciliation:

> . . . the concept of conciliation stemmed from and resembles mediation, with both methods using a third party to facilitate a nonbinding result through the medium of communication with the disputants. Indeed, the two terms are occasionally used interchangeably. In the transnational system, a distinction between the two can be made in the degree of formality and level of initiative imposed on the third party. A mediation is more informal and the mediator, when making proposals, is expected to construct them based purely on the information provided by the parties. Comparatively, a conciliation is more formal in structure and procedure, yet retains a non-adversarial environment. The central objective of the conciliator is to facilitate an amicable settlement of the conflict by communicating with the parties, typically through structured conciliation proceedings, and by submitting written proposals for a resolution of the dispute.[34]

Hybrid ADR Processes

8. EARLY NEUTRAL EVALUATION (ENE)

Early Neutral Evaluation involves early case assessment by an experienced neutral, usually an attorney specialized in the substantive area of the dispute. The parties make brief presentations and exchange detailed information. The rules of evidence do not apply, and there is no

---

32. See Chapter 8, *infra*.

33. DAVID J. BEDERMAN, INTERNATIONAL LAW FRAMEWORKS, ch. 21, at 234 (2001).

34. Linda C. Reif, *Conciliation as a Mechanism for the Resolution of International Economic and Business Disputes*, 14 FORDHAM INT'L L.J. 578, 584 (1990–91).

formal examination or cross-examination of witnesses. All communications at the evaluation session are protected from disclosure. The ENE process originated in the U.S. District Court for Northern California in 1985 and has been adopted by many other jurisdictions. Some scholars have found similarities between ENE and rights-based mediation in which mediators focus on legal rights and offer evaluations to the parties.

9.   MED–ARB

Med–Arb combines mediation and arbitration in a sequential process. The third-party neutral acts in the first instance as a mediator and attempts to help the parties achieve a resolution of their dispute. If the mediation does not result in settlement, the mediator assumes the role of an arbitrator and renders a binding decision. In effect, the third-party neutral functions as a catalyst for the settlement process because the presence of the neutral, who may ultimately have to render a decision in the case, gives the parties a realistic incentive to settle. In some variations of the med-arb process, the mediator simply acts as an advisory arbitrator.

10.   MINI–TRIAL

The Mini–Trial, used primarily in business disputes, is a structured settlement process that blends components of negotiation and mediation. Attorneys for both sides make concise, summary presentations to a panel consisting of a neutral advisor and senior executives with full settlement authority. Following the presentations, the executives attempt to resolve the dispute. If the parties are unable to settle the case during the post-hearing settlement talks, they can agree that the neutral advisor will act as a mediator or render an advisory opinion regarding the likely outcome if the case were litigated.

11.   OMBUDS

The classical model of "ombudsman" derived from the Scandinavian countries, refers to an official appointed by the government to listen to complaints made by citizens against the government and attempt to respond to them. In the United States, the ombuds role has evolved in the private sector where organizations employ ombuds as in-house neutrals to respond to employment-related disputes using such processes as mediation, fact-finding and counseling. In many corporations, hospitals and universities, for example, the ombuds office is the first department to receive employee grievances. In some cases ombuds offices have been criticized for their lack of independence and limited powers to resolve disputes.

12.   SUMMARY JURY TRIAL

The Summary Jury Trial (SJT), developed by Judge Thomas Lambros of the U.S. District Court for the Northern District of Ohio, facilitates the settlement of disputes by giving parties a possible assessment of what a jury might do in a given case. Essentially an adaptation of the mini-trial in a court setting, it is a non-binding process in which lawyers make a summary presentation of their case to a jury. The presentations are usually based on information that has been the subject of discovery. The jury deliberates and renders a non-binding, advisory verdict, and the lawyers are then allowed to question the jurors about their verdict. Following the questioning session, lawyers and their clients engage in settlement discussions. If a settlement is not reached, the parties are entitled to a full trial and the SJT verdict is inadmissible.

C. THE ADJUDICATION ALTERNATIVE

Although the focus of this text is on the varieties of consensual approaches used to resolve conflicts, it is also important to understand the adjudication alternative, particularly in the context of counseling clients about their available options. The critical difference between adjudicative and consensual approaches to conflict resolution is that ultimate decision-making belongs to a third party in the adjudication process. While parties may "consent" to participate in adjudication by agreeing to arbitrate in a national or international forum, or to litigate in court, they do not have the power to decide the outcome of their dispute.

International adjudication, one of several processes for the pacific settlement of disputes listed in Article 33 of the U.N. Charter, involves the referral of disputes to a judicial or arbitral tribunal for a binding decision that is generally based on legal norms. Historically, States have been reluctant to commit in advance to binding adjudication when important political interests are at stake. The following excerpt discusses the advantages and disadvantages of the adjudicatory process.

RICHARD B. BILDER, INTERNATIONAL THIRD PARTY DISPUTE SETTLEMENT

17 Denver Journal of International Law and Policy 471, 484–97 (1989).

* * *

As is the case with respect to any method of dispute settlement, in deciding whether to use adjudication, the parties to a dispute will weigh its potential advantages against its disadvantages. Among the potential advantages of adjudication, are: (i) it is dispositive, ideally, at least putting an end to the dispute; (ii) it is impersonal, permitting the parties to pass responsibility for unfavorable outcomes to the tribunal; (iii) it is principled and impartial, ostensibly deciding the matter by neutral principles rather than power, bias or whim; (iv) it is serious and demonstrates that the state instituting suit really believes in its claim; (v) it is orderly and can be useful in resolving complex factual and technical disputes; (vi) it can sometimes "depoliticize" a dispute, reducing tensions or buying time; (vii) it can provide rules socially useful for guiding conduct and resolving disputes more broadly; (viii) it can reflect, and educate the community as to social values and interests of the international community more broadly, apart from those of the parties alone, and; (ix) it can be system-re-enforcing, supporting respect for and the development of international law.

But, there are also a number of potential disadvantages of adjudication: (i) it involves the possibility of losing; (ii) adjudicative settlement may be illusory or superficial, deciding the "legal" but not the "real" issues in dispute; (iii) it can be inflexible, resulting in a "win-lose" rather than a compromise decision; (iv) it can be judgmental, labeling one party as a "lawbreaker," rather than providing for a shared acceptance of responsibility as a facesaving way out of a conflictual situation; (v) it looks primarily to the past rather than to the future, possibly jeopardizing the maintenance of a useful ongoing relationship; (vi) it is conservative; (vii) its results are unpredictable; (viii) it may not be impartial; (ix) an adjudicative settlement is imposed on the parties; (x) it is adversarial and may escalate the dispute or conflict; (xi) it may freeze the parties' options and discourage settlement; (xii) it can be complex and costly, and; (xiii) there is no assurance that an adjudicative decision will be enforceable.

As previously noted, adjudication has generally played only a rather limited role in the settlement of international disputes. While nations often pay lip-service to the ideal of judicial settlement, in practice they have entrusted relatively few significant disputes to international tribunals. During the period of 1946 through 1985, the International Court of Justice had only 72 cases submitted to it; it rendered 45 judgements in contentions cases and 17 advisory opinions. Moreover, countries have been particularly reluctant to obligate themselves in advance to compulsory binding adjudication of their potential disputes with other countries—particularly disputes concerning issues that may involve what they consider "vital" national interests. In general, they have been willing to do so, at most, only when their commitment to such compulsory jurisdiction is restricted in terms of subject matter or otherwise carefully circumscribed.

* * *

While adjudication may not be the best way of resolving every dispute, there are clearly a number of situations in which adjudication, or at least the availability of adjudication, can perform a very useful dispute settlement function. In practice, most disputes do not involve issues of significant or "vital" national concerns. In these cases, while each party may prefer to win the dispute, the stakes involved are limited and each can afford to lose. Adjudication is one good way in which the parties can achieve their most important objective in these situations—disposing of the dispute. Indeed, to the extent that states can be assured that a commitment to adjudication will be restricted to less vital issues, they will be more willing to agree, even in advance, to adjudication.

* * *

Among the types of disputes in which adjudication is likely to be particularly useful are: (a) disputes in which governments are indifferent to outcome, but for internal political or other reasons are unable to concede or even compromise the issue in negotiations (i.e., minor boundary disputes or substantively unimportant but emotionally volatile issues of title to small or insignificant areas of territory); (b) disputes involving difficult factual or technical questions in which the parties may be prepared for a compromise solution but where, either because of the complexity of the situation or internal political pressures, they cannot evolve a basis for developing a viable compromise (i.e., again certain complex boundary or maritime, continental shelf, or fishery resource zone delimitation issues); and (c) some particularly awkward or dangerous disputes, in which resort to judicial settlement may be a politically acceptable way of buying time and containing a volatile situation while solutions are sought over time.

* * *

It is also important to note that, for many people throughout the world, international adjudication symbolizes civilized and ordered behavior and the rule of law in international affairs. Whatever the truth may be as to how the international legal system actually works, public judgments as to the relevance and effectiveness of international law are at least in part based on whether the public sees international courts, and particularly the International Court of Justice, as playing a significant role in international dispute settlement. If many states (particularly the important ones) are willing to submit their disputes to impartial settlement and show respect for the International Court, this will be taken by the public as meaning that international law is in itself relevant and worthy of respect, and the public will believe in and support international law. If, on the other hand, important states show indifference or contempt for international adjudication and the Court, the public is likely to conclude that international law is meaningless and withdraw their belief and support. Indeed, these public attitudes may in turn over time reflect back on official and bureaucratic attitudes towards and respect for international law. Consequently, if a state believes that its national interest will be furthered by wider global respect for international law, it will arguably also have an interest in doing what it can to strengthen and support the role of international adjudication.

Finally, even if the role of international adjudication is limited and there is no international court with general compulsory jurisdiction, there can still be effective dispute settlement and a workable international legal order. The international legal order is different in many respects from national legal orders, and need not operate in exactly the same way. Moreover, we are coming to realize that, even in the domestic legal system, adjudication plays a largely supplementary or "back up" role, and that much of the work national courts do is in effect mediation or conciliation.

In sum, since adjudication can be a particularly useful tool in our tool-box of dispute settlement techniques, it is important that it be kept ready at hand, easily available and employed to the fullest whenever its use is warranted. Even if adjudication is not a panacea for problems of world order, it makes sense to do all that we can to strengthen and encourage the greater use of judicial institutions, and to improve their ability to respond in flexible ways to nations' dispute settlement needs.

1. ARBITRATION

Arbitration, a form of private adjudication, is the most formalized and traditional alternative to the court adjudication of disputes. It is a voluntary process in which disputing parties present their case to a neutral third party who has the power to render a binding decision. Unlike court adjudication, the arbitration process is typically more informal and flexible. The rules of evidence are relaxed, and the arbitrator determines the extent of pre-trial discovery.

Practice varies with respect to arbitrators issuing written opinions. In commercial arbitration, arbitrators usually issue awards without written rationale for their decisions. In international and labor arbitration, however, arbitrators do issue reasoned decisions. There are several potential advantages of arbitration over judicial adjudication. Arbitration is a creature of contract and disputing parties have the ability to choose their own decision-maker to conduct a private proceeding. Parties decide what procedural rules will govern and simplified procedures can result in lower costs. The difficulty of appealing an arbitrator's decision lends finality to the result.

One of the best known examples of an international arbitral tribunal is the Permanent Court of Arbitration located in the Peace Palace at The Hague. It was established through the Convention for the Pacific Settlement of International Disputes at The Hague in 1899 during the first Hague Peace Conference.

2. JUDICIAL ADJUDICATION

The judicial adjudication process involves the presentation of arguments to a neutral third party which would apply legal norms in rendering a decision. Two well-known examples of international tribunals are the International Court of Justice and the International Criminal Court.

(a) International Court of Justice

The International Court of Justice is the principal judicial organ of the U.N. It was established in 1945 under the U.N. Charter. The ICJ, which sits at The Hague, hears legal disputes between States. It has no criminal jurisdiction and no means of coercively enforcing its judgments.

It is composed of fifteen judges and may not include more than one judge of any nationality. The Court's decisions and advisory opinions are issued in accordance with treaties and conventions, international custom, and general principles of law.

Since 1946, the ICJ has delivered judgments on a wide range of disputes concerning issues related to land frontiers and maritime boundaries, territorial sovereignty, the non-use of force, non-interference in the internal affairs of States, diplomatic relations, hostage-taking, the right of asylum, nationality, guardianship, rights of passage, and economic rights. Also, since that time, the ICJ has produced numerous advisory opinions concerning, *inter alia*, admission to U.N. membership, reparation for injuries suffered in the service of the U.N., territorial status of South–West Africa and Western Sahara, judgments rendered by international administrative tribunals, expenses of certain U.N. operations, applicability of the U.N. Headquarters Agreement, the status of human rights rapporteurs and, most recently, the legality of the threat or use of nuclear weapons.

(b) International Criminal Court

The International Criminal Court (ICC), is a permanent, independent, treaty-based entity based in The Hague that was established to promote the rule of law. Composed of eighteen elected judges and an elected prosecutor, it has jurisdiction to adjudicate the gravest offenses affecting the international community: genocide, crimes against humanity, and war crimes. Only countries who have ratified the treaty establishing the ICC can vote to elect judges.

On July 17, 1998, one hundred and twenty nations participating in the "United Nations Diplomatic Conference of Plenipotentiaries on the Establishment of an International Criminal Court" adopted the Rome Statute of the International Criminal Court. The Statute entered into force on July 1, 2002. Thereafter, anyone who commits any of the crimes under the Statute will be liable for prosecution by the ICC.

(c) Transborder Litigation

Domestic courts can also be a forum for the adjudication of international disputes, especially private ones. When a domestic court has jurisdiction over a dispute and the foreign party, the domestic court can compel the foreign party to appear in court and be subject to its adjudicatory process and local enforcement of any resulting judgment. The MCC case discussed in Chapter 1 is an example of the operation of this principle.

D. HYBRID INSTITUTIONS FOR COMMERCIAL DISPUTES

Many regional treaties have established dispute resolution mechanisms for dealing with cross-border disputes. Regional and international organizations have also developed dispute settlement mechanisms to resolve issues related to international trade.[35] Often combining elements of negotiation and adjudication, these regimes can be considered hybrid adjudication systems. Two significant examples are the World Trade Organization (WTO) and the North American Free Trade Agreement (NAFTA).

The World Trade Organization (WTO) evolved from the 1947 General Agreement on Tariffs and Trade (GATT). Its core interests deal with trade in goods and services. Functioning as the modern foundation of the multilateral trading system, it has a mandatory, legalized dispute resolution system that promotes settlement. The process operates through its Dispute Settlement Body (DSB) which is composed of all the members of the WTO. Combining elements of negotiation and adjudication, the dispute resolution process begins with a complaint and consultation. If the case is not resolved through the consultation process, the complaining party may request that a three person panel be established to consider the issues. The panel determines the facts and issues a report which can be appealed to the Appellate Body. Decisions of the Appellate Body are automatically adopted by the DSB unless rejected unanimously by its members. The WTO has authority to impose sanctions, including retaliation for noncompliance with the terms of the report. Because trade sanctions can have a powerful economic impact, if there are claims of excessive retaliation, they may be subject to review in arbitration. Given the significant impact of the WTO's dispute settlement mechanism, many questions have arisen over who has standing to appear before its dispute settlement panels.[36]

The North American Free Trade Agreement (NAFTA) is an intergovernmental organization that creates a free trade area in North American with the United States, Mexico and Canada. The purpose of NAFTA is to promote economic activity by eliminating trade barriers, promoting fair competition, and increasing investment opportunities. Chapter 19 of NAFTA establishes a binding dispute resolution process for challenging antidumping and countervailing duties. This process may be initiated by private parties. Chapter 20 creates a non-binding process for dealing with most other disputes under the treaty and this process can only be initiated by governments at the federal level. There are several stages to the Chapter 20 dispute resolution process including consultation, negotiation and the issuance of a report by a five member arbitral panel. Chapter 11, one of the more controversial aspects of NAFTA, allows foreign investors to use binding arbitration against another signatory state that violates the investment provisions of NAFTA.[37]

35. *See* Andrea K. Schneider, *Getting Along: The Evolution of Dispute Resolution Regimes in International Trade Organizations*, 20 MICH. J. INT'L L. 697 (1999).

36. *See, e.g.*, Philip M. Nichols, *Two Snowflakes Are Alike: Assumptions Made in the Debate Over Standing Before the World*

Trade Organization Dispute Settlement Board, 24 FORDHAM INT'L L.J. 427 (2000).

37. See Marcia J. Staff & Christine W. Lewis, *Arbitration Under NAFTA Chapter 11: Past, Present, and Future*, 25 HOUS. J. INT'L L. 301 (2003).

E. FACTORS TO CONSIDER WHEN USING THIRD–PARTIES TO RESOLVE INTERNATIONAL DISPUTES

When parties are unable to achieve a settlement or resolution, third-party intervention, either by individuals or organizations, is often necessary to help them move forward. While several of the foregoing methods of conflict and dispute resolution are species of the negotiation process, they still involve the intervention of a third-party. It is important then to consider how third-parties actually affect the dynamics of conflict, and in what ways and in what processes they can be helpful. As you will see from many of the materials throughout this text, the use of third parties in conflict resolution efforts is a topic with considerable cultural nuances.

RICHARD B. BILDER, INTERNATIONAL THIRD PARTY DISPUTE SETTLEMENT

17 Denver Journal of International Law and Policy 471, 484–97 (1989).

* * *

[I]n the case of advisory and non-binding techniques such as good offices, mediation, fact-finding and conciliation, the third party's role is usually limited to helping the parties to negotiate their own settlement of their dispute. In contrast, in the case of directive and binding techniques such as arbitration and judicial settlement, responsibility for settlement of all or part of the issues in dispute is removed from the parties' direct control and the third-party is authorized to decide the matter for them. In each case, of course, the actual—or even potential—presence and activities of a third party may have various effects upon the dynamics of the disputing process and the disputing parties' relationships, some helpful, but some, perhaps not.

How can third parties help the disputants achieve a settlement themselves? A good deal of research has been done to identify the general functions that mediators and other non-directive third parties can perform and the specific kinds of things they can do that are likely to be most useful.

Pruitt and Rubin, for example, describe the type of negotiating impasse which may call for third-party assistance:

> Positions tend towards rigidity because the protagonists are reluctant to budge lest any conciliatory gesture be misconstrued as a sign of weakness. Moreover, the parties may lack the imagination, creativity, and/or experience necessary to work their way out of the pit they have jointly engineered—not because they don't want to but because they don't know how. Thus, for a variety of reasons,

disputants are sometimes either unable or unwilling to move toward agreement of their own accord. Under the circumstances, third parties often become involved at the behest of one or more of the disputants, or on their own initiative.

They suggest and discuss a variety of ways in which a third party can help the parties break out of such an impasse. One way is by modifying the physical and social structure of the dispute. For example, the third party can structure communication between the principals; open and neutralize the site in which problem-solving takes place, impose time limits, and infuse resources. Another way is by modifying the issue structure. For example, the third party can assist the disputants to identify existing issues and alternatives; help them to package and sequence issues in ways that lead towards agreement; and introduce new issues and alternatives that did not occur to the disputants themselves. Finally, the third party can increase the disputant's motivation to reach agreement. For example, it can facilitate their making concessions without loss of face, engender mutual trust, encourage their venting and coming to grips with irrational feelings, and respect their desire for autonomy.

Another commentator, Jacob Bercovich, divides third party aims into process objectives and outcome objectives, each of which he in turn subdivides into two categories: (1) information search (*i.e.*, establishing communication, searching for common principles) and, (2) social influence (*i.e.*, persuading the parties to converge on an acceptable outcome). Bercovich sees third party behavior as implemented through certain tactics which he calls (1) reflective behavior (*i.e.*, receiving, transmitting and interpreting messages and signals reflecting and influencing how the parties perceive their situation); (2) non-directive behavior (*i.e.*, influencing the context and structure of the conflict by controlling publicity, controlling the environment, controlling resources, reducing pressure and recasting issues); and (3) directive behavior (*i.e.*, influencing the parties perceptions and motivation through making proposals, a judicious exercise of power and promises of resources).

Other commentators suggest other types of potential third-party contributions, or classify third-party objectives or functions in a somewhat different way. For example, Oran Young classifies third party objectives as: (1) informational (*i.e.*, offering information or increasing communication); (2) tactical (*i.e.*, offering services); (3) supervisory (*i.e.*, monitoring an agreement); and (4) conceptual (*i.e.*, offering new ideas for a settlement). Indeed, there is now a rich literature suggesting imaginative techniques through which third parties may help parties in an impasse "get unstuck"—for example, by creating a "hurting stalemate," providing "decommitting formulas" or "bypass solutions," "changing or reframing the game," using "single text procedures," and so forth. I have suggested elsewhere that a principal reason why disputing parties may not be able to reach a settlement agreement is that they distrust each other or are otherwise concerned with what they see as very serious risks potentially involved in such an agreement. In this case, third parties can play a crucial role in dispute settlement by helping the parties in a variety of ways to manage these risks—for example, by monitoring or verifying performance, serving as escrow agents, or providing guarantees. Third party risk management devices of this kind may be particularly useful, for example, in facilitating dispute-settlement arrangements in which distrust is a particularly serious obstacle, such as armistice or peace agreements or agreements seeking to resolve complex and emotional racial, ethnic or religious conflicts.

What about more directive techniques of third party intervention such as adjudication, in which third parties have authority themselves to determine how the dispute is to be settled?

* * *

First, adjudication can dispose of the matter. It is often more important to the parties that a dispute be settled than that it be settled in a particular way. Where negotiations are unsuccessful, adjudication or other third party disposition of the matter provides an alternative way in which the parties can put the dispute behind them and move on to other things.

Second, adjudication can permit concessions without "loss of face" or bureaucratic risk. Since adjudication involves an impersonal decision by a third party, neither of the governments of the parties (or the officials involved) can be held directly responsible for the outcome. There are probably a number of disputes where governments are relatively indifferent as to the outcome and would normally be willing to negotiate a compromise settlement, but where, for internal political or other reasons, they are unable to concede or even compromise the issue in negotiations. Third-party settlement is a politically useful way by which foreign offices can dispose of such problems without taking direct responsibility for concessions. In effect, they can "pass the buck" for not "winning" the dispute to the third-party tribunal—"Don't blame us, blame the judge!"

F. ASSESSMENT OF DISPUTE RESOLUTION PROCESSES: SUBSTANTIVE AND PROCEDURAL INQUIRIES

As you begin your study of public and private consensual processes for the resolution of disputes, you should consider both the procedural and substantive inquires that follow:

Procedural Inquiries

Who is the decision maker?

What is the decision making process?

What is the third party's role?

What are the guiding principles for decision making?

Are they legal or non-legal guidelines (such as industry standards)?

Formality? Privacy?

Consensual? Non-consensual?

What is the significance of the process' outcome? Is it binding? Is it appealable?

How does the cultural context shape answers to these questions?

Substantive Inquiries

What are society's and the parties' substantive goals in structuring the dispute resolution process?

What attributes are they trying to achieve and would be ideal in the process?

How do the parties prioritize these attributes?

In Western societies, these are attributes that are often valued:

   Efficiency

   Predictability

   Fairness/justice

   Effectiveness

How does the cultural context influence what are valued attributes of the process?

Notes and Questions

1. Given the vast reach of globalization, it may be that some of the consensual processes for dispute resolution will be more effective when combined with adjudicatory process. In the following excerpt, the author suggests combining conciliation with arbitration.

> The practical and cultural disadvantages of arbitration are fueling a growing interest in combining conciliation with arbitration, especially in Asia–Pacific commerce. "Conciliation"—often called "mediation" in the United States—is a process whereby the parties invite one or more third parties to help them negotiate a settlement. Asian parties may prefer conciliation for cultural reasons. Western parties may like conciliation for some of the same reasons that have led them from litigation to arbitration or for those that now sustain the alternative dispute resolution movement in the United States. Business persons generally may prefer to process disputes in a businesslike manner. In conciliation proceedings, the parties participate and retain control. They can resolve a dispute while preserving an ongoing relationship and enjoy flexibility without regard for formal procedures.

Conciliation, however, is not a completely satisfactory solution. Since its effectiveness in Asian domestic settings depends partly on social norms that support compromise, conciliation may fail in international transactions where similar norms are absent. Combining conciliation and arbitration may be a better solution. For Asian parties to international contracts, arbitration, and even litigation, are not unthinkable when all efforts at negotiation and conciliation have failed, the parties are no longer "friends," and a dispute continues to fester. At the same time, arbitration clauses are reassuring to Western parties who may want to hedge their bets on conciliation with a familiar and reliable backup. A practical advantage of combining arbitration and conciliation is that arbitration can impose a final and binding resolution to a dispute while conciliation alone might drag on indefinitely. Steven J. Burton, *Combining Conciliation With Arbitration of International Commercial Disputes*, 18 HASTINGS INT'L & COMP. L. REV. 637 (1995).

Do you agree with the author's suggestion? What are some benefits? Drawbacks?

2. Are there other consensual processes that you might combine for particular conflicts?

3. In addition to the barriers listed by Professor Mnookin, can you think of other barriers to the negotiated resolution of disputes?

4. What is the goal of the mediation process? One scholar has suggested that "the goals of the mediation process differ according to the culture of each participant. Therefore, a critical element of cross-cultural mediation is the mediator's ability to understand these different goals or 'conceptions' of the process, and to forge a process which satisfies the participants different conceptions." Cynthia A. Savage, *Culture and Mediation: A Red Herring*, 5 AM. U. J. GENDER & L. 269 (1996). Do you agree? Can you think of any examples of mediations in which the mediator possessed the ability described by Savage?

5. Can you develop a continuum of consensual processes based on the degree of directiveness of the third party? Do you think the same third party would be competent to perform all these third party roles? Or does each consensual process call for a different sort of third party? Some claim that in a med-arb process, the same neutral should not perform both functions of mediator and then arbitrator in order to maintain the integrity of each dispute resolution process. Do you think that the integrity of each consensual process depends upon avoiding the same neutral serving more than one process?

Chapter 3

THE ROLE OF CULTURE IN TRANSBORDER CONFLICT RESOLUTION

A. INTRODUCTION

International negotiators readily acknowledge the importance of culture in shaping solutions to conflict. Culture is the "perception-shaping lens" through which we both generate and experience conflict. There is, however, a big difference between acknowledging that culture is important and understanding why and how culture is so important.

This chapter begins with materials on why we should consider culture and the ways in which it is so pervasive in conflict. It explores myriad caveats to the consideration of culture. It then turns to specific tools for better understanding cultures: the ways in which cultures can differ and how these differences are illustrated in particular parts of the world and among certain groups.

The latter part of the chapter explores circumstances in which disputing parties have contrary cultural approaches and priorities. How do you resolve these differences? To what extent do we defer to any particular culture's values versus some more universally-recognized standard? What are ways in which the legal system and cultural norms relate and conflict in our attempts to resolve disputes?

We begin by considering two models, the cultural relativist model which defers to each culture and their particular cultural norms and the universalist model which advocates referring to a universally-recognized standard. We end with an example of a country where the legal system and the cultural norms have historically and currently conflict.

As you read this book, consider the issues and themes raised in this chapter. For instance, would parties from different cultures prefer mediation over litigation or arbitration? Why? Can you identify the cultural values embedded in the mediators' or arbitrators' reasoning? Isn't it natural for them to evaluate the parties' conduct in a way that is consistent with the standards of her or his culture? What cultural assumptions do they or a party from a socialist legal system or other legal system make? How do their assumptions affect their perception of the facts and their determination of who is "right" and who is "wrong"?

B. WHY CONSIDER CULTURE?

1. THE IMPORTANCE OF CULTURE

KEVIN AVRUCH & PETER W. BLACK, CONFLICT RESOLUTION IN INTERCULTURAL SETTINGS: PROBLEMS AND PROSPECTS

in CONFLICT RESOLUTION THEORY AND PRACTICE: INTEGRATION AND APPLICATION
131–40 (Dennis J. Sandole & Hugo van der Merwe eds., 1993).

To be fair, when one examines the concept of culture used by many theorists and practitioners in conflict resolution, one sees why it is so often relegated to a secondary place. In brief, "culture" in this view stands for rather superficial group differences. It is generally associated with descriptions of traditional, stereotypical modes of behavior, characteristic of some group of "others." Hence, such discussions of culture largely focus on questions of etiquette and tolerance. Culture is spoken of as though it were a thing, as if it were evenly distributed across members of the group of which it is an attribute, as though it were synonymous with "custom" and "tradition" and, finally, as if it were impervious to change through time. Such discussions also seem bedeviled by an intractable confusion between statements about cultural matters (those having to do, that is, with features of human consciousness) and statements about the actual behavior of individuals or groups of individuals. The point here is that culture is not reducible to behavior; to "know" a culture is not to be able to predict each and every act of each and every member of a group. In this vein, culture is sometimes treated merely as a label for group differences—as a way of naming the groups. This is especially true in intercultural conflict situations, where "culture" and "ethnicity" (or ethnic identity) are used synonymously. That these terms are unselfconsciously used this way by the parties to the conflict themselves—as well as by analysts or third-party interveners—is what makes the confusion intractable.

In contrast, our perspective on the role of culture in conflict arises from a conception of social life in which culture is seen to be a fundamental feature of human consciousness, the *sine qua non* of being human. It is held to be constitutive of human reality, including such behavioral manifestations of that reality as "conflict." Metaphorically speaking, culture is a perception-shaping lens or (still metaphorically) a grammar for the production and structuring of meaningful action. Therefore, an understanding of the behavior of parties to a conflict depends upon understanding the "grammar" they are using to render that behavior meaningful.

If one wishes to understand conflict behavior, it is particularly useful to attend to the indigenous understandings of being and action which people use in the production and interpretation of social action. These understandings, like all cultural knowledge acquired through social learning, are organized into sets of propositions and prescriptions of various levels of complexity and generality. The sets of understandings about conflict held *by the people involved* in a dispute are crucially important.

When the parties to a conflict come from different cultures—when the conflict is "intercultural"—one cannot presume that all crucial understandings are shared among them. Their respective ethnotheories, the notions of the root causes of conflict, and ethnopraxes, the local acceptable techniques for resolving conflicts, may differ one from another in significant ways. The first task of a third-party intervener in intercultural conflict situations is to pay serious analytical attention to these cultural dimensions. The third party must assay a *cultural analysis* of the situation.

2. CULTURAL ANALYSIS PROCESS

[*Author's Note*: What happens when individuals involved in a dispute come from different cultures? As the prior reading indicates, you cannot assume that everyone shares a common understanding about what caused the dispute or how to resolve the dispute. The cultural differences that precipitate different perceptions are the focus of the following reading. In it, Professors Avruch and Black introduce us to the process of "cultural analysis."]

Conflict resolution in intercultural settings requires, perhaps on the part of the parties to the conflict and most certainly on the part of the third-party intervener, an analysis of the conflict that is also a cultural analysis. This cultural analysis is preliminary to other aspects of third-party intervention, although it may well continue throughout the intervention. What does such an analysis consist of, and what are its entailments?

In the terms and analogies we have used, one's own culture provides the "lens" through which we view and bring into focus our world; the "logic" (known as common sense) by which we order it; the "grammar" by which it makes sense. Above all, our culture provides ways of seeing, thinking, and feeling about the world which in essence define normality for us—the ways things are and the way things ought to be. In intercultural encounters it is precisely one's sense of normality that may be put at risk. But in most people, a sense of normality is fairly well established and pretty well defended. So rather than question our own normality, we tend to assert the relative abnormality, the strangeness and bizarreness of the other: "the French are arrogant"; "the English are cold"; "Moroccans are untrustworthy." In most intercultural encounters, in fact, moments of noncomprehension and unintelligibility are deflected and dismissed by being glossed over by terms laden with value-judgments. Not only do the French think about this differently than we do, but they are "wrong" (arrogant, rude, etc.) to do so. Thus, intercultural encounters present us with situations (other peoples' behaviors and understandings) that appear strange and bizarre; our common sense labels them as such and our moral sense evaluates them as good or (more likely) bad. To revert to the lens metaphor, our own culture seems to us transparent, and the world seen through it seems to us veridical, simply the way things are. A glimpse of the world *through* another culture (one possible result of an intercultural encounter) presents us with areas of opacity, things we cannot see through clearly. We demarcate these; then we set about dismissing them.

A cultural analysis demands first that one *stops* at moments of noncomprehension and unintelligibility; that one resists deflecting them dismissively (and pleasurably) in moral terms; that one makes them— the seemingly opaque and unintelligible—the objects of scrutiny. In short, the analyst is well advised to remain reflexively attuned to the disconcerting moment. To turn to one's advantage the sensation of surprise is not an easy thing to do, however, because it demands that one resists such dismissive reflexes when being faced with the strange and bizarre. Second, a cultural analysis is a scrutiny with a peculiar sort of goal. "Cultural analysis," writes Raymonde Carroll, in a study of French–American cultural misunderstandings, is "a means of perceiving as "normal" things which initially seem "bizarre" or "strange" among people of a culture different from one's own." It is a way of making transparent that which first appeared as opaque. "To manage this," Carroll continues, "I must imagine a universe in which the 'shocking' act can take place and seem normal, can take on meaning without even being noticed."

The key word here is "meaning," of course. Since our culture provides us with systems of symbols by which meaning is asserted (or, as often as not, negotiated) and established in the world, a cultural analysis at root is the searching out of meaning in these systems of symbols. When directed towards a culture different from our own, such an analysis orients us to different meanings—other lenses, other logics, other grammars. Notice that in principle one can attempt a cultural analysis of one's own culture, and in practice as well, although many anthropologists deem this to be a much harder analysis—because one is usually not "stopped" by moments of noncomprehension and unintelligibility in dealings with one's own culture. This is exactly what one's own culture allows one to avoid. It takes a subtler mind and a more perverse sensibility (not to mention perhaps a case of chronic and clinical alienation), to allow oneself to be struck by, and stop at, the utterly familiar and veridical. And of course, conceptually, one result of a cultural analysis of one's own culture produces an effect opposite to that done on another culture. Aimed at one's own culture, such an analysis can have the eerie effect of rendering the previously "normal" both strange and bizarre. It can make opaque that which was transparent. It is almost always unsettling, very often critical, and so usually taken by others to be subversive—or surreal.

So much for what a cultural analysis is; how does one do it? Carroll uses the word "imagine" as a kind of shorthand answer to this question. Is this a methodology? Clearly any sort of analysis introduced with reference to subtle minds, perverse sensibilities, and clinical alienation—not to mention shameless recourse to metaphors like opacity and its opposite—is likely to seem problematic to social or behavioral scientists used to the comforting rigors of formal techniques for testing operationalized hypotheses. Nevertheless, there is a method for pursuing cultural analysis. Although it may take a certain sensibility to do it easily or well (and what methodology doesn't?), it certainly does not demand a mystical or occult one.

Here we follow (part of the way, at least) the now classic account found in Geertz, and its very lucid précis by Carroll. For Geertz, the essence of a cultural analysis is that it consists of "thick description," an ethnographic presentation of an event (a conversation, a person, a practice, a dispute, a belief . . . etc.) that stresses the placement of the event, for the social persons who enact it, within deeper and deeper, richer and richer, more and more layered contexts of meaning ("structures of signification," in Geertz's words). Carroll's interest lies in using cultural analysis to explore specific intercultural (French–American) misunderstandings; thus she emphasizes how one would go about describing something "thickly."

First, if one is trying to analyze the culture of another, be on the lookout for the bizarre: recognize the opacities. Be prepared to stop and avoid the social scientist's tendency to immediately explain (and explain *away*) the phenomenon by reference to causal theories—psychodynamic, materialist, ecological, or biological, to name a few. Because culture does not "cause" behavior—neither aggression, nor the business cycle, nor the grand flow of history—cultural analysis is not causal analysis. Precisely where causal analysis and cultural analysis come together, if they do, has been a matter of some considerable intramural debate between those committed to "interpretive" and "explanatory" anthropology. Simplifying the debate, one camp allows cultural analysis in as part of the ethnographic, descriptive stage—as a data-base-provider for the powerful Science (the theories of underlying causality) to come. The other camp asserts that cultural analysis *is* the science to come. When it comes to the understanding of human social action, these partisans maintain, the inscription and specification of meaning is the terminus (and an asymptotic one, at that) of our enquiry. For the first camp, ethnography serves Science; for the second, the science consists of Ethnography.

Our own position in this debate lies at neither extreme, but is rather more respectful of the search for causes (cybernetically construed, at any rate) than not. In fact, it is our respect for the power of causal theories—which tend to be indiscriminately omnivorous of databases in the hands of the naive or scientistic—that makes us place such a high premium on the avoidance of explaining away before one has the chance to explain. In this more limited sense, then, we agree with Geertz and Carroll that in cultural analysis one is not operating in the same conceptual domain as in causal analysis.

The second thing to be on the lookout for is the glossing of the strange with value-judgments ("the English are cold," "the French are rude," and so forth). These propositions are not so dissimilar in fact to the first set we advised avoiding: value-judgments are, after all, causal explanations put in the modality of a moral discourse; they are the "science" of our own culture's common sense. For most of us most of the time, the value-judgment, the moral accounting, is entirely sufficient as explanation. Too many social scientists, however, use value-judgments as a way-station to a fully causal explanation: "Why did your colleague say that to you at the departmental meeting? He is French, you know; they are rude … And why are they rude, you ask? Didn't you know they are all weaned with vinegar?" (Psychodynamic); "The red wine they drink to excess inhibits endorphin production" (biological); and so on.

Next, having been struck (stopped) by the opaque or the strange and having avoided moralizing, psychologizing, biologizing, ecologizing, or economicizing it away, one gets down to its proper, thick, description. This involves recording it ("inscribing" it, in the text-oriented work of these analysts) and, text now before you, contextualizing it. Simply put, this key procedure (or act of imagination in Carroll's term) requires that like "text" be put into different, deeper, and more widely ramifying frames of meaningful reference. As the frames of reference ramify, the initial strangeness should begin to ease; within the deepening and widening contexts of the cultural analysis, at least, the bizarre should begin to make sense, the opaque reveal the shadow of what lies behind it. One begins to translate. It is during this inscription/contextualization process that the true, the *interpretive*, nature of the enterprise emerges.

To call any analysis "interpretive" immediately raises questions of validity and verification. Such questions are justified. All interpretations—at least in our world—are not equal. An interpretation should be judged by how well it accounts for and explains—in the sense of "makes meaningful"—other aspects of the culture that appear bizarre, or the same aspect as it appears in the culture in other "texts." This is not, of course, "prediction" in the sense promised by covering-law, causal theories. It is closer to the "retrodiction" of a grammatical analysis: tell us the sentence just now uttered; we will tell you if it is grammatically appropriate in that language.

Finally, since one is always and necessarily doing this from the standpoint of one's own cultural presuppositions, the entire process is iterative. One is always in effect tacking back and forth in cultural analysis: between an interpretation that makes sense in the other

culture and a translation—for every translation is also an interpretation—that makes sense in your own. (This is a simple gloss on the
"hermeneutical circle" formed between interpreter and text.) In this
sense we would argue that a cultural analysis is in fact the paradigmatic
form of an enlightened intercultural encounter—one that is now ready
for problem-solving.

3. A HYPOTHETICAL INTERCULTURAL ENCOUNTER

[*Author's Note*: Professors Avruch and Black further illustrate with
an example of the cultural analysis process.]

Consider an American tourist in a foreign land. She does not speak
the language (needless to say). She asks an old man, a native of the
country, for directions to the train station. The old man does not speak
English. He looks at the tourist quizzically. The tourist repeats her
question, this time in a louder voice. From the old man another quizzical
look, perhaps a nod of the head or shrug of the shoulders. The tourist
speaks yet more loudly and, looking around, tries to imitate (pulling an
imaginary cord to train whistle: "choo, choo") the sound of a train. Now
the quizzical look becomes open amusement, but still without comprehension. The tourist looks around again and sees a young boy approaching them. "Do you speak English?" "A little." "Do you know where the
train station is?" "I do not, but I will ask this old man." And he does,
and the tourist will make her train.

What makes this little scenario the very model of an opaque intercultural encounter is, of course, the fact that neither party speaks the
language of the other. Our tourist tries to get around this first by raising
her voice (a reflexive, but not a bad, first option: in a monolingual
setting, it probably is the case that noncomprehension is linked to not
hearing the message, perhaps because of noise). Then she tries to bypass
speech and use an alternative channel of communication: gesture and
mimicry. The first option, raising the voice, consists of simply repeating
the original message in the original code and medium, but varying
physical parameter (amplitude). The second option is of a different order
entirely and consists of a transformation of the original message and
code. Here, the tourist is attempting a translation of her question into a
(gestural) code she believes is more universal than (even) English. Alas,
she is wrong, for in this native's land the gesture of pulling on a cord
signifies a bad attack of dysentery, while the sound "choo, choo"
conventionally signifies a male's appreciation of an attractive female.
Not surprisingly (but nevertheless fortunately), the old man is amused.
Luckily, a third party comes along—a native himself—who shares
enough of the tourist's linguistic code to be able to interpret and
translate the question.

A "cultural analysis" of this encounter could be rudimentary, indeed. The opacity, the noncomprehension, was simply the result of mutual nonsharing of linguistic codes, and the third party was an interpreter in the weakest sense of that term. Moreover, the problem that needed solution—directions to the train station—was simple enough and straightforward enough that the third party's admitted limitations as an interpreter (he spoke a "little" English) were not fatal. Moreover, in this scenario the older native was merely amused by the tourist's gestures—rather than offended, angered, insulted, and moved to retaliate in kind. If he had been, then we might imagine the third party as having a more substantial and difficult role to play. Correspondingly, our cultural analysis of the encounter (anger and passion have colored the opacity: why?) grows more complex. The tourist's recourse to a code—gesture and body language—that she thought was generic or universal turned out to be neither, although it was definitely full of meaning. The third party, *even if he understood what the tourist meant*, might find it harder to translate the gestures and placate his countryman. "Translation" implies that the third party attempts a cultural analysis of the tourist's gestures (what Americans *mean* by "choo, choo"), and "placation" implies that he communicates the results of his analysis to his countryman (and that such communication is feasible or likely: can a young boy mollify an old man, appropriately, in this culture? Maybe not, if the old man seems to get angrier and angrier). And now, the third party's limitations—intellectual, temperamental, or social—structural—as an interpreter (a cultural analyst) and problem-solver might well prove fatal.

This scenario—the revised one, in which the older native becomes angry—is a model intercultural encounter in another sense. For here we have an instance of a conflict that we can say with assurance is caused by "culture." To be more precise, the conflict is a result of cultural *differences* in the interpretation of meaning, by the parties, of the same events: the initial noncomprehension (what are you trying to say?) compounded subsequently by misapprehension (just who the hell are you accusing of diarrheal lechery?). Such intercultural conflicts "caused" by culture do occasionally occur, of course, and they are the ones most amenable to thin cultural analysis on the level of explaining to the parties involved the differential etiquettes at play. They are the ones where problem-solving can be reduced to simply correcting "a failure to communicate." But while such conflicts do occur, they should not be taken as representative of most conflictual intercultural encounters, and certainly not of conflicts of the deeply rooted sort.

This is so for two reasons. First, many intercultural encounters take place in shared linguistic settings, for instance nation-state diplomacy (where diplomats use English or French) or intranational interethnic disputes. In these cases, the shared language (the presumed mutual comprehension) can actually mask paralinguistic or other deeper cultural differences. Shared language can fool the parties into thinking much else, or all else, is shared as well. Second, and more profoundly, although it is only sometimes the case that cultural differences can themselves be said to account for *all* of the noncomprehension, and thus *all* of the reasons for the conflict, it is always the case that culture molds the ways in which the parties understand what the conflict is about, how to carry on through it, and what possible resolutions look like. In the rather homely and synthetic scenarios we have been spinning thus far, we can imagine the distinction in this way: If two parties, speaking different languages (cultures), think they are both vying for the same *pie*, but it turns out that one is really after the bottle of *lye*, then the dispute was about their noncomprehension, and a simple translation ought to solve the problem in a positive-sum (win-win) manner. But, if it turns out that both parties really do want the same pie (and each wants all of it), then translation serves only to clarify what the conflict is about (an important step, to be sure), but it does not represent its solution. The conflict is about control of valued resources; it is *about* the pie. Here we have encapsulated of the core of the "realist" position in international relations and much of the "materialist" position in the other social sciences. But the conflict also is very much about why certain resources—things like pies—are valued, about how one ought to fight over them (and how to fight to win), about how fights end, and about the costs, bearable and unbearable, involved. And these parts of the conflict, always present, are culturally constituted; they comprise ethnotheory.

4.　INTERACTIVE CULTURAL DYNAMICS AND INSTITUTIONAL CULTURES

While the foregoing readings introduced you to cultural analysis between two parties, a thorough and realistic assessment of the cultural context of disputes is more complicated. The interactive dynamics and varied roles of the participants trigger a whole array of inter-dependent cultural profiles.

PAT K. CHEW, THE PERVASIVENESS OF CULTURE

54 Journal of Legal Education 60, 66–69 (2004).

Consider a hypothetical alternative dispute resolution (ADR) process, as depicted in the Illustration. There are two parties, each party is represented by agents (presumably lawyers), and there is an arbitrator or mediator. What are each of their cultural profiles, and how do they conflict or complement each other?

Illustration of Interactive Dynamics of Cultural Profiles

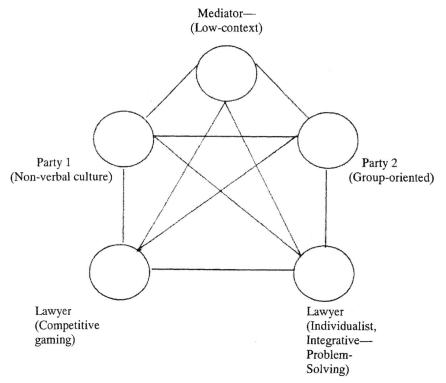

If a lawyer and her client have different profiles (for instance, what if the lawyer is more individualist-oriented but the client is more group-oriented), what agency-principal issues will arise? How will they prioritize objectives and strategies differently, given their varied values and conflict resolution styles? Given the critical role of the mediator, what if his or her cultural profile is distinctly different from one or both of the parties? For instance, if one party uses a mostly non-verbal style of communication, but the mediator is more direct and verbal and is generally not conscious of a non-verbal style, will that increase the probability that the mediator misconstrues the party's literal (and non-literal) communication and hence misunderstand the fundamental dispute or the party's underlying interests? As we consider other individual characteristics, such as age, race, class, occupation, or religion, how might that reconfigure each person's cultural profile? In what ways will each participant "frame" the dispute (defining the conflict, the interests of the disputing parties, and their own underlying interests) and then "game" the dispute (determining their strategy and how to implement that strategy)?

Once the framing and gaming strategies begin to emerge, how will the cultural profiles of the participants affect their interpretations and reactions to the amalgamation? How will each participant's perception (whether accurate or not) of every other participant cultural profile affect the dynamics? What are the interactive effects and how will they affect the options generated and any movement toward resolution?

Governing Institutions: What is the Broader Context?

In addition to the more apparent "people" components of the cultural context, we also should consider the institutional frameworks in which disputes occur. These frameworks provide the broader infrastructure—the rules, organizations, systems in which conflicts operate. These institutions may be formal with codified rules (such as legal statutes) and sanctioned interpretations and polices (such as those found in court opinions). In the alternative, these institutions may be creations of non-government private organizations—such as industries, neighborhoods, professional groups, religious groups, political groups—that have evolved over time to address business, moral, or social issues. These private institutions also have distinguishable values and rules of conduct, although they may not be directly articulated.

I posit that these "governing institutions" have cultural profiles of their own and may be critical in shaping the dispute resolution process. Two examples of types of governing institutions, the legal systems and industry groups, illustrate:

Legal System. Each legal system has its own distinctive attributes, embodied in both its procedural and substantive rules as well as the ways in which those rules are interpreted and enforced. Thus, the U.S. system with its particular historical basis and philosophy, is generally characterized by advocacy and adversarialness, adheres to the common law principle of precedents, and is theoretically predicated on notions of justice and individual rights. This cultural profile of the American legal system is apparent, for instance, in the resolution of legal disputes in the litigation process.

Particular subject areas of U.S. laws offer more specific cultural distinctions. In state corporate laws, for example, courts and statutes address disputes between shareholders and corporate management over whether executives have breached their fiduciary duties. What the courts value is apparent: managerial discretion, entrepreneurship, and risk-taking in the interest of the corporation's and shareholders' economic profits. Given this cultural profile, it is not surprising that the actual legal standard for directors' and officers' decision-making and fiduciary duties is low. Employment laws, although much more eclectic that state corporate laws, also generally prize managerial discretion but sometimes try to balance it against societal innovation and individual rights. Even ADR law is developing its own cultural profile, or perhaps more aptly labeled, its own "personality conflict." In its evolving jurisprudence, it struggles over ADR's original promise of efficiency and predictability versus its idealized aspiration to be a fairer and more humane forum than that offered by traditional litigation.

Industry. Industries and occupational areas often have their own distinct cultural profiles in resolving disputes. Within these industries and occupations, identifiable sub-cultures also emerge. For instance, the events surrounding the Enron debacle offered dramatic and timely examples of the cultural profile of the management of some large corporations. Sherron Watkins, former Enron vice-president, describes Enron's executives' culture of flamboyance, disregard for proprieties, and high-living. The cultural profiles of politicians, legislators, and the securities industry also are being revealed in their attempts to address the management and accounting problems that Enron revealed.

In an almost surrealistic way, the Iraqui War offered daily examples of the cultural profiles of two industries: the military (of both the U.S. and Iraq) and the media (of both the U.S. and other countries) covering the conflict. While utilizing advanced technology in its weaponry, the U.S. Coalition forces also adhered to strategies and priorities that are consistent with its culture and history. In prior American military campaigns, for example, the tactics of leapfrogging over enemy concentrations in route to an ultimate target and in focusing on the capital city as the ultimate target even while other major parts of the country are unconquered, have been time-tested although not always successful strategies.

The War also revealed aspects of the media's cultural profile. A newspaper analysis of **CNN** (a U.S. media station based in Atlanta) and **Al-Jazeera** (a Pan–Arab media station based in Doha, Qatar) revealed the priorities and official positions typical of media enterprises, no matter their nationalities. Both stations are "business operations competing for viewers and advertisers against increasingly aggressive rival and avidly seeking to please their target audiences." While they must make judgement calls, they both regard themselves as unbiased and politically independent. The comparative analysis, however, also revealed distinct traits of the cultural profiles of each station and their audiences. Offering numerous examples, it documented the "different lenses" through which the same conflict was seen. For instance:

> *Thursday, March 27: 6 a.m. EST, 2 p.m. in Baghdad.* On **CNN**, American paratroopers jump from a plane to open up the northern front in Iraq. On **Al-Jazeera**, a little Iraqui girl in a pink sweater stares out from her Baghdad hospital bed.

Questions

1. Think of a heated dispute where different parties experienced and described the conflict differently. Do a "cultural analysis" of the conflict. Also consider these issues: How did these differences come about? How did the individuals involved, the cultural norms, or the event itself contribute to these differences? If you were the mediator, how would these factors have influenced your way of handling the dispute or the eventual outcome?

2. Recall the excerpt on the Northern Ireland conflict in Chapter 1. How would you begin a cultural analysis of this conflict?

C. CAVEATS IN CONSIDERING CULTURE

Culture plays an integral role in international conflict resolution. At the same time, it is essential to keep in mind myriad caveats. This part of the chapter explores: the challenge of defining "culture," our inclination to stereotype, the temptation of being "the expert," and some hidden risks of the conflict resolution process. It then affirms that there are always varied versions of the same "story."

1. DEFINING CULTURE

The concept of "culture" has been the focus of much scholarly attention and debate, particularly in anthropology. An evolving definition is that "culture" is a common system of knowledge and experiences that result in a set of rules or standards; these rules and standards in turn result in behavior and beliefs that the group considers acceptable. Consistent with this broad definition, that individuals of different races, ethnic groups, religions, genders, and socioeconomic classes, for instance, have distinct cultures and cultural profiles. Furthermore, our culture shapes how we approach conflict and conflict resolution—including our values, norms, and conduct. It even influences how we define conflict itself and what we consider acceptable or desirable goals of problem-solving.

At the same time, a definition of culture recognizes the multiplicity, fluidity, and saliency of culture. Thus, it assumes that we are simultaneously a member of myriad cultural groups (multiplicity) and that our membership in a cultural group may change over time (fluidity). In addition, the extent to which we identify or are influenced by a particular cultural group may change depending on the situations in which we find ourselves (salience). This view of culture also is sensitive to the risk of overgeneralizing. Because you are a member of a particular culture does not necessarily mean that in any specific situation you would adhere to the rules or norms typically characteristic of that culture.

Michelle LeBaron and her colleagues have studied the evolving nature of culture and our understanding of it. They describe how the more recent literature reveals a "dramatic shift of focus." They note the trend toward "progressive questioning, deconstructing, and stripping away of what were once-assumed foundations," as illustrated by the themes of culture-bound perceptions and cultural construction of identity and knowledge.

> Although the terms perception and construction appear similar and often are used interchangeably, each term implies different assumptions about the nature of social reality. Perception suggests the presence of an objective social world which can be investigated and known. The hope is that an accurate knowledge of social reality may be accumulated that will help us to correct misperceptions and improve perception, enabling us all to "see" things in the same way.

The term construction suggests that there is no objective social reality "out there." Rather, we collectively construct or define what we believe to be the objective social world. In other words, through various processes (culture being one such process) we socially construct reality.

As LeBaron explains, the earlier research and literature on conflict resolution reflected a naive belief that culture is stable and assumptions of the transparency and accessibility by all of the "dominant" culture. In contrast, more recent research acknowledges culture as a "dynamic that both shapes and reflects experience" and that both dominant and multiple minority cultures may be more "opaque" and complex than assumed. In addition, scholars now are revisiting the varied meanings of fundamental terms and concepts:

> What do we mean by culture? What do we mean by competence? What do we mean by knowledge? What do we mean by fair practice? Through which cultural lens will we evaluate the boundaries of ethical behavior? These questions flow not only from an acknowledgment of the complexity of multiculturalism, but also from the decline of modernity and the questions inspired by postmodernism, feminist theory and social constructionism.... Words and terms must be chosen carefully and explained thoroughly, and none stand autonomous or free from critique.

ALISON DUNDES RENTELN, CROSS–CULTURAL DISPUTE RESOLUTION: THE CONSEQUENCES OF CONFLICTING INTERPRETATIONS OF NORMS

Willamette J. Int'l L. & Dispute Resolution 103, 113–15 (2002).

Some cases center on practices whose authenticity is in question. Then one must determine who is the legitimate representative of the group. Who can attest to the "centrality" of the custom with respect to the group's way of life? When an expert speaks on behalf of the ethnic minority group, this is offensive to members of the group who often are capable of explaining the practice themselves. Even if the group acknowledges the necessity of bringing in an "expert" with credentials to persuade a jury composed of non-members of the group, some may, nonetheless, resent the legal system for not taking their word for the existence of the tradition and for its central importance to their way of life.

Cases also arise in which conflict exists within the group as to the proper way to perform a ritual. For example, in Cha'are Shalom Ve Tsedek ("CSVT") a branch of the Orthodox Jewish community in France objected to the decision by the French government to have a central Rabbinical committee (ACIP, Association Consistoriale Israelite de Paris) maintain exclusive control over the ritual slaughter of animals. Unconvinced that the meat was sufficiently pure or "glatt," the organization filed a lawsuit. After CSVT lost in the French judicial system, it turned to the European human rights system.

After the European Commission on Human Rights concluded, by a vote of fourteen to three, that there has been a violation of Article 9 taken together with Article 14, France appealed to the European Court of Human Rights. Although the European Court of Human Rights thought ritual slaughter was protected under religious freedom, it accepted France's argument that there was a benefit in avoiding unregulated slaughter. In the end, the Court found no violation of religious freedom largely because it was not impossible for ultra-Orthodox Jews to find "glatt" meat; it was available in some places in France and in Belgium. The court also failed to see the significance of any difference in techniques used by the ACIP and the applicant: "[t]he only difference lies in the thoroughness of the examination of the slaughtered animals' lungs after death.

The Court explicitly said that the great majority of Jews accept the ACIP kosher certification system. The implication is that the dominant part of the minority should speak for the rest of the minority, i.e., religious pluralism includes pluralism within a single religious tradition. This controversy exemplifies well the concern of those who worry about oversimplifying religious practices. Obviously, divergent practices exist within the same group. Despite the variation with the group, however, one can say that ritual slaughter is part of Jewish customary law. Perhaps the real problem is that the dominant legal system decides which group to designate as the spokesperson for the minority group.

Although the group lost in the French courts as well as in the European Court of Human Rights, the case reveals conflict within the Orthodox Jewish community. The question of which individual or what group can speak on behalf of the entire minority group can be contentious.

---

2. RISKS OF OVER-ESSENTIALIZING

Generalizing about individuals from different cultures helps us to make some quick sense of a lot of complex information. The following reading, however, cautions us about some of the dangers of stereotyping.

JAMES K. SEBENIUS, CAVEATS FOR CROSS-BORDER NEGOTIATION

Negotiation Journal 121, 122–31 (Apr. 2002).

1. The John Wayne v. Charlie Chan Fallacy: Stereotyping National Cultures

Start with the obvious: All American negotiators are not like John Wayne and all Chinese negotiators are not like Charlie Chan. Or Bill

Gates and Mao Zedong. Or Michael Jordan and Zhu Chen, the phenomenal women's world chess champion who recently also defeated the world men's champion. We also know that some negotiators in southeastern France may bear more resemblance to northern Italian negotiators than to their Parisian compatriots. Likewise, the culture of western Chinese Uighers is far more akin to neighbors in Pakistan than comrades in Beijing. On another front, what is distinctively "Canadian" when its citizens vary from francophone Québecois to traditional anglophone Torontonians and to transplanted Hong Kong tycoons now living in Vancouver? In the face of such internal variation, we wisely caution ourselves against mindless stereotyping by nationality (as well as by gender, religion, race, profession, or age). Even so, in many situations it remains all-too-common to hear offhand remarks such as "all Chinese negotiators . . ." (as well as generalizations about "women . . ." or "engineers"). To combat this, a strong version of the anti-stereotyping prescription calls for ignoring nationality altogether in preparing for negotiation.

That advice by itself is too strong. Nationality often does have a great deal to do with cultural characteristics, particularly in relatively homogeneous countries like Japan. The careful work of many researchers confirms significant associations between nationality and a range of traits and outcomes. It would be foolish to throw away potentially valuable information. But what does information on a particular group's behavioral expectations or deeper cultural characteristics really convey? Typically, cultural descriptions are about *central tendencies* of populations that also exhibit considerable "within-group" variation. Suppose that a trait like "cooperativeness" (versus "competitiveness") is carefully measured by a psychological testing instrument for the citizens of Country X. The results will be a *distribution* with a few citizens rating highly cooperative, a few rating highly uncooperative, and the majority clustered around a more middle range.

* * *

In sum, remember that "national traits"—as well as traits supposedly associated with gender, ethnicity, etc.—are *distributions* of characteristics across populations, not blanket descriptions applicable to each individual. Be very cautious about making inferences about characteristics of specific individuals from different groups—even where the groups are, on average, sharply different. Avoid stereotyping and the "prototypicality" error of assuming an individual will exhibit the most likely group characteristic. Even if U.S. negotiators are on average more impatient, deal-focused, and individually oriented than their Chinese counterparts, be careful not to help amplify that stereotype in the mind of the other side. It is highly unlikely that many U.S.-Chinese negotiations will feature the equivalent of John Wayne pitted against Charlie Chan. Or Bill Gates against Mao Zedong. Or Michael Jordan against Zhu Chen.

2.   The Rosetta Stone Fallacy: Overattribution to National Culture

National culture clearly matters. But there is a tendency to see it as the Rosetta Stone, the indispensable key to describe, explain, and predict the behavior of the other side. Of course there are many possible "cultures" operating within a given individual. Beyond her French citizenship, an ABB executive may well be from Alsace, have a Danish parent, feel staunchly European, have studied electrical engineering, and have earned an MBA from the University of Chicago. National culture can be highly visible but, obviously, it is only one of many possible influences. For example, Jeswald Salacuse surveyed executives from a dozen countries to determine national tendencies on ten important bargaining characteristics, such as negotiating goal (contract v. relationship), orientation (win-win v. win-lose), formality level, communication style, risk-taking, etc. While his results showed significant national differences, he also analyzed the data according to profession and occupations of the respondents such as law, engineering, marketing, the military, diplomacy, accounting, etc. These categories, too, showed systematic association with different bargaining styles. Finally, Salacuse could also differentiate many of these style characteristics by gender. Other extensive studies extend and elaborate analogous findings: Nationality often matters when considering someone's bargaining characteristics but so too does gender, ethnicity, functional specialty, etc....

Attribution bias. Cultural differences, often evident in surface behavior, are easy to see; richer contextual factors frequently are not. In unfamiliar cross-border settings, factors like strategic incompatibility, politics, or even individual personality are less likely to be "blamed" for undesirable outcomes. The powerful but unconscious tendency to overattribute behavior to culture, all too often clouds negotiators' vision of the full range of factors that can affect a negotiation. Psychologists have extensively documented this dynamic, a systematic tendency to focus on supposed characteristics of the person on the other side of the table, rather than on the economic or other powerful contextual factors. The antidotes? First, remember that "culture" doesn't just mean nationality; instead there are many potentially influential "cultures" at work. Second, beyond "culture" are many other factors that have potential to affect negotiation behavior. Nationality can carry important information, but with many other cultures and many other factors at work, you should be careful not to treat your counterpart's passport as the Rosetta Stone.

3.   The "Visual Flying Rules" at Night Fallacy:
Falling Prey to Potent Psychological Biases

Just as trying to pilot by "visual flight rules" (VFR) at night or in a storm is hazardous, the psychology of cross-cultural perception can be treacherous. Beware the witches' brew of biases and psychological dynamics that can bubble up when one begins to label "other" groups, attribute characteristics to them, and act on these perceptions.

Self-serving perceptions of our own side. There is a powerful tendency, formally studied as "biased assimilation," for people to interpret information in negotiation self-servingly. For example, experimenters give a number of people identical information about a pending court case but randomly assign them to the role of plaintiff or defendant. When each person is asked for his or her private assessment of the probability that the plaintiff will win, those assigned the role of plaintiff on average give much higher odds than those (randomly) assigned to the role of defendant (but, again, on the basis of *identical* information). People tend to "believe their own lines" or self-servingly interpret information. Similar results have been found for corporate valuation results—done on the basis of the same data—by randomly assigned buyers and sellers. And this tendency runs deep: Back in the 1950s, researchers conducted an experiment at a boy's camp, sponsoring a jelly bean hunt among the campers. After the hunt, the boys were shown an identical picture of a jar of jelly beans. Each boy evaluated the total number of beans in the jar according to whether he was told the jar belonged to his own team or to the other side. The same photograph was estimated to contain many more beans when it was presented as "your team's" and far fewer when it was alleged to be the "other side's."

Partisan perceptions of the other side. If our capacity to process information critical of our own side is flawed, it is even more the case for our assessments of the other side in a conflict or negotiation. In part, this stems from the in-group/out-group phenomenon. Persons from different cultures, especially on the opposite side of the bargaining table, are more readily identified as belonging to an out-group, or the *Other*. Once that labeling is in place, powerful perceptual dynamics kick in (beyond the tendencies toward stereotyping and overattribution). Robert Robinson describes extensive research over the last 40 years, documenting an unconscious mechanism that enhances "one's own side, portraying it as more talented, honest, and morally upright" while simultaneous vilifying the *Other*. This leads to a systematic exaggeration of the other side's position and an overestimation of the extent of the actual conflict. As a result, negotiators are often unduly pessimistic about their ability to find common ground, and can be unwilling to pursue it.

Self-fulfilling prophesies. Such partisan perceptions hold the power to change reality by becoming self-fulfilling prophesies. The effects of labeling and stereotyping have been documented thoroughly to show that perceptions have the power to shape reality. Experiments testing the effects of teachers' expectations of students; diagnoses on mental patients; and platoon leaders' expectations of their trainees are only a few of many studies confirming that expectations prod behavior. At the negotiating table, the same principle holds true: clinging firmly to the idea that one's counterpart is stubborn, for example, is likely to yield intransigence on both sides, precluding the possibility of a compromise that might have occurred had the label of "obstinacy" not been so rigorously affixed.

In short, just as a pilot trying to navigate by visual flight rules at night or in a storm is prone to dangerous misjudgments, the psychology of perception in cross-cultural situations is rife with biases. Not only do we stereotype and overattribute to nationality, we are also poor at interpreting information on our own situation, vulnerable to partisan perceptions of the other side, and likely to act in ways that become dangerously self-fulfilling.

4.   St. Augustine's Fallacy: "When in Rome ..."

Assume that you have undertaken a full analysis of the culture of the person you will meet on the other side of the bargaining table. St. Augustine gave the classic cross-cultural advice: When in Rome, do as the Romans do. While this admonition certainly has merit, it is not always good advice. Steven Weiss has extensively developed the point that much better options may be available. For example, learning that the Chinese, on average, are more hesitant than North Americans to take risks is only a first step. Clearly, a responsive strategy would not mimic this hesitancy, but effectively anticipate it.

Rather than learning to behave as the Romans do (while in Rome or elsewhere), strategies should accommodate the degree of cross-table understanding each side has of the other. For example, consider the best approach for a U.S. manager on his first visit to Japan dealing with a Yale-educated Japanese executive who has worked extensively in Europe and North America. Here it would be sensible to let the Japanese take the lead. If a negotiator is far more familiar with a counterpart's culture than vice versa, the best strategy might be to embrace the counterpart's negotiating "script." If both sides are equally "literate," an improvisational and mutually-accommodating approach might be most appropriate. A lower degree of familiarity dictates bringing in locally familiar expertise, perhaps on your side and perhaps even as a mediator.

A great deal depends on how familiar you are with "Roman" culture and how familiar your "Roman" counterpart is with your culture. And of course you want to avoid the previous fallacies as well. The nationalities across the table from each other may be Chinese and U.S., but both players may be regulars on the international business circuit, which has its own, increasingly global negotiating culture. Again, assess—etiquette, deeper traits, negotiation-specific expectations, and caveats; do not assume and project your assumption onto your counterpart.

---

3.   FURTHER CAVEATS ABOUT PERCEPTIONS, CULTURE, AND THE DISPUTE RESOLUTION PROCESS

a.   John Paul Lederach, a Mennonite scholar and cross-cultural trainer of conflict resolution processes, invites us to contemplate other cultures through an "elicitive" approach, where we are engaged as active and nonjudgmental learners. More typically, he observes, our inclination is to be "prescriptive," coming as experts and considering our own culture as the standard by which other cultural approaches should be compared. By being more elicitive than ethnocentric, we stay open to the excitement of discovery and creation. JOHN PAUL LEDERACH, PREPARING FOR PEACE: CONFLICT TRANSFORMATION ACROSS CULTURES 3, 63–69, 89–92 (1995).

b.   In the classic narrative, "In a Grove," by Ryunosuke Akutagawa and the film *Rashomon* based on the Akutagawa narrative, we hear multiple and differing "stories" of the same tragic event in a Japanese bamboo grove, as told from the perspectives of different witnesses and participants among which are the following:

Masago tells the story of being raped by a robber in a bamboo grove. She is so shamed that she wants to kill herself and her husband, who has witnessed the crime and begs (with his eyes) to be killed. Fainting after killing her husband, she frees him from his shame but must go on living with hers.

The husband, *Kanazawa*, tells a different story of his scornful but beautiful wife. After being "violated," she betrays her husband, presumably as a way to protect herself. Left alone in utter despair and shame, he commits suicide.

The robber, *Tajomaru*, calmly describes how he lured the couple into the grove, intending to "satisfy my desire for her without taking her husband's life." After raping her, he is enraptured by her "burning eyes," and suddenly wants Masago to be his wife. He decides to "cross swords" with the husband as an honorable way to win her. He ultimately kills Kanazawa, but then discovers that Masago has escaped.

Each convincingly describes their perception of the causes of the conflict, the roles and motives of the participants, and the resolution of the dispute. We are left wondering: where is the truth? Does each person believe her or his own story and simply have a different perspective on what happened, or are they being intentionally deceptive? Is their reality shaped by a combination of their self-interest and their cultural upbringing? RYUNOSUKE AKUTAGAWA, RASHOMON AND OTHER STORIES (Takashi Kojima trans.) 19–33 (1952).

c.   As Sara Cobb and Janet Rifkin explain, not all narratives of an event receive the same respect. Using communication theory and focusing on the mediation context, they describe how parties to the mediation describe their versions of what happened. These narratives, depending on how the participants and mediators interpret them, become part of a "political" process in the sense that some become more dominant and some are suppressed or marginalized. Professors Cobb and Rifkin offer some interesting reasons why this may happen. First, they document that mediators intentionally or inadvertently value one narrative over another by the questions they ask and the summaries they offer. The mediators' intervention thus shapes the grounds on which agreement and disagreement can take place. Second, Cobb and Rifkin critique the mediation process itself as contributing to this marginalization of one disputant. They note a common pattern of the story told first by one of the parties (the initial narrative) becoming the dominant story and framing the issues, thus requiring the other party to respond to the pre-existing text. The mediation process also sets an "accusation/justification sequence in place that perpetuates adversarial interactions and reconstitutes one story as dominant." Are the mediators' and the parties' valuing of narratives shaped by their cultural upbringing? Sara Cobb & Janet Riskin, *Practice and Paradoxes: Deconstructing Neutrality in Mediation*, 16 LAW AND SOCIAL INQUIRY 53, 52–62 (1991).

d. Kay Schaffer and Sidonie Smith explore the previously untold narratives of victims of human rights violations from various time periods and cultures. They further describe how these stories have been used as part of a political process for eliminating human rights violations. As they describe it:

> Stolen Generation narratives [of the biracial children of indigenous people and White Australians] collectively reframe "well-intentioned" policies of assimilation as forms of cultural genocide. Testimonies and published life narratives by women in East and Southeast Asia, forced into sexual slavery by the Japanese Imperial Army during World War II, expose the institutionalized rape culture of forced prostitution during wartime as a violation of women's human rights. Narratives of political dissidents, like the letters from prison by China's champion of democracy Wei Jingsheng, often banned in their country of origin, find publishers elsewhere in nations receptive to their politics and only too ready to invoke the story told in order to exert pressure on non-compliant nations to address, justify, and modify their human rights record. Life narratives of displacement and cultural marginalization, such as those written by ethnic Turks in Germany, bring stories of second-class citizenship to the bar of public opinion around the world. Coming-out stories, such as Charlene Smith's narrative of rape and of her subsequent struggle to join other women to protest the inadequacy of HIV–AIDS counseling and treatment in South Africa, have focused national and international attention on the silenced stories of sexual assault and the scourge of AIDS in Africa. In the United States, Europe, and elsewhere, coming-out stories have played a critical role in the campaign to achieve human rights legislation for lesbians and gay men. KAY SCHAFFER & SIDONIE SMITH, HUMAN RIGHTS AND NARRATED LIVES 1–2 (2004).

Notes and Questions

1. There are many ways in which we acquire our own individual "culture," including the stories that we grew up with. Identify a favorite family story that deals with a conflict or dispute, either taken from a book or passed down orally. Reflect on how the story transmitted important values and approaches to resolving conflict.

2. Graphically depict your own "cultural map." You might begin by identifying key cultural groups to which you belong. For this exercise, you

can define "cultural group" broadly to include groups that have influenced how you perceive the world and what is important to you. These might include your family, ethnic, religious, school, or occupational group. Be creative in how you depict your map. It might be a circle with free-flowing lines to depict the relative importance of and interrelationships between each group.

3.   You have probably heard the stereotype of the "ugly American." What is meant by this expression? Consider how each of Professor Sebenius' caveats can be used to illustrate the danger of this stereotyping.

D.   UNDERSTANDING CULTURAL DIFFERENCES

1.   SOCIAL SCIENCE CONSTRUCTS

Social science research offers provocative insights into the way culture creates the backdrop for conflict. Social scientists have identified and studied constructs that can be used to describe approaches to conflict. These constructs are particularly useful in providing us with a conceptual basis to better understand and critique our own cultural profile and profiles of other cultures. They help us to answer the questions: *Who am I? Who are they?* These constructs identify patterns and attributes that distinguish one group of people from another— offering contrasts between the ways individuals approach conflict or conflict resolution.

The constructs of individualism/collectivism and high-context/low-context illustrate:

Individualist and Collectivist Cultures. One of the most widely researched of these social science constructs, the construct of individualism and collectivism has been used to analyze cultural differences in a range of contexts, both domestic and international. As Harry Triandis and others have explained, this construct focuses on what people value and how they orient their lives.

Individualist cultures are often more affluent, urban, and cultural complex. As the label suggests, individual and personal goals tend to have priority over group or societal goals. Individualists are emotionally detached from groups to which they belong. When solving problems, they are guided by a rationale cost-benefit analysis. When engaged in disputes, they are comfortable with being direct and confrontational. Individualist societies socialize their members to be self-reliant and independent. They become skillful at entering new groups. However, individuals tend to be lonely as well.

Collectivist cultures are often more agricultural and less developed. As the label suggests, group and collective needs and goals have priority over individual desires and rights. The self is defined in terms of the group to which the individual belongs. The ingroup often is hierarchical, group members tend to be homogeneous, and group norms are very influential. At the same time, strong distinctions are made between the ingroup and other groups (outgroups).

High-context and Low-context Cultures. Edward Hall and others have studied how groups and individuals think, act, feel, and interpret communication differently. In particular, they contrast the communication patterns and meanings of high-context cultures (associated with, for example, Chinese, Japanese, and Vietnamese) and low-context cultures (associated with, for example, North Americans, Germans, and Scandinavians).

In *high-context* cultures, the meaning of a message is embedded in the implicitly shared social and cultural knowledge of the group. Often what is not said and nonverbal communication are more revealing than the literal words. Individuals in high-context cultures are more likely to be non-confrontational and indirect in resolving conflict. They also tend to be more affective and intuitive, although they may not openly display these characteristics. Conflicts occur when the parties perceive that the norms of the group in a given situation are being violated.

In *low-context* cultures, communication and meaning are more literal and direct; what is said is the actual message. The parties do not customarily intend or seek interpretations beyond that. They also are more likely to be confrontational and direct in resolving conflicts. Low-context individuals tend to use factual, linear, and use inductive reasoning. Conflicts occur when an individual perceives that his or her own rights or values in a given situation are being violated.

Building on these premises, we can see that conflict also is manifested differently. Stella Ting–Toomey has written:

> In viewing the same conflict episode, for example, in an organizational setting concerning the rejection of a sales proposal by a North American supervisor in the [low-context culture] context, a North American subordinate will probably view the conflict episode very differently than a Japanese subordinate who has submitted the proposal. The North American subordinate will probably enter the conflict situation with heated discussion and issue-oriented arguments. He or she will probably produce facts, figures, and graphs to illustrate his or her case. In contrast, the Japanese subordinate [in a high-context culture] will probably be dumbfounded by the direct, outright rejection and will then proceed to analyze the conflict episode as a personal attack or a sign of mistrust. In fact, he or she will probably resign as soon as possible.

Low-context individuals are better able to disassociate the person involved in the dispute from the conflict issue. They "can fight and scream at one another over a task-oriented point and yet be able to remain friends afterwards." High-context individuals, however, bring to the table presumptions about appropriate roles and conduct for persons of a particular stature and background that are inseparable from the specific conflict. The often-heard principle "Separate the people from the problem" would be a cultural mismatch in a high-context culture.

In addition to individualism/collectivism and low-context/high-context, there are numerous other constructs. *Power distance* (indicating how disparities in power and equality are perceived), *masculinity/femininity* (indicating the extent to which people are expected to conform to designated social roles of men and women), and *uncertainty avoidance* (indicating how people react to the lack of structure and clarity) are examples of constructs that social scientists also are currently researching.

Research illustrates how these constructs can help us understand our own cultural profiles. One study by Alma Mintu–Wimsatt and Jule B. Gassenheimer, for example, compared the negotiation approaches of buyers and sellers in low-context and high-context cultures. People from the high-context culture (the Philippines) were less confrontational and emphasized interpersonal interactions more than those from the low-context culture (the United States). Consistent with their cultural profile, Filipino negotiators were inclined to consider the other party *(pakikisama,* or camaraderie) and to reciprocate behaviors demonstrated by the other party *(utang-na-loob)*—traits more consistent with a cooperative problem-solving approach. In contrast, the American negotiators were more competitive and self-serving.

2. CONSTRUCTS OF DIFFERENT CULTURES

Hazel Rose Marcus and Leah Lin further explore these constructs by describing the "conflictways" of Americans of various ethnic backgrounds. These individuals may maintain, merge, or ultimately abandon the cultural constructs of their family's countries of origin. Thus, Marcus' and Lin's discussion prompts us to reflect on the conflictways of those original countries, as well as increasingly multi-cultural American society. As you read their discussion of the conflictways of these groups, consider how their descriptions contrast with or complement the individualist/collectivist and low-context/high context constructs.

HAZEL ROSE MARKUS & LEAH R. LIN, CONFLICT-WAYS: CULTURAL DIVERSITY IN THE MEANINGS AND PRACTICES OF CONFLICT

in Cultural Divides 302, 313–27 (Deborah A.
Prentice & Dale T. Miller eds., 1999).
Conflictways in European American Contexts: Individual Rights and Autonomy

The meaning of conflict in many European American contexts, and particularly Anglo–American cultural contexts, reflects a view of the person as an autonomous entity who possesses individual rights and is motivated by a configuration of internal or personal values and goals. In European American cultural contexts, individuals are expected to express their *own* beliefs and pursue their *own* goals; it is their duty to do so because their ideas and attitudes literally define the self. Indeed, behavior is a reflection or expression of individual beliefs and goals. Within this cultural context, people defend conflict as perceived incompatibility in individuals' beliefs about an issue, or incompatibility in the accomplishment of their goals. These lay definitions are consistent with the mainstream social psychological view that conflict arises when incompatible activities occur, and that this incompatibility reflects differences in individuals' ideas, values, and goals.

European American conceptions of conflict are predicated on a notion of the person as an agentic performer of individual actions rather than a responsive being situated in and actively adjusting to a network of relationships. In contrast with the prevalent ideas and practices of Asian American, African American, and Mexican American contexts, conflict in European American contexts is not considered the product of the ongoing process of being in relationship with others. Conflict arises when the activities of two individuals interfere with one another. Thus, conflict emerges from incidental situations rather than as an inevitable consequence of relationality. For people with bounded, individualist selves, conflict with others can be self-defining or identity-promoting. It brings into sharp relief their own desires, preferences, and goals and provides the opportunity to verify or express them.

The paradigmatic expression of the European American perspective on conflict is articulated in Fisher, Ury, and Patton's best-selling handbook of negotiation strategy, *Getting to YES: Negotiating Agreement Without Giving In*. Even the title of this media sensation suggests that the goal of European Americans in conflict (consistent with the independent view of self) is to arrive at a solution without compromising personal integrity or making concessions. Careful observers of European American conflict, Fisher and his colleagues note that people in this cultural context tend to confront others directly while stridently promulgating a particular position that outlines the actions that they would be willing or unwilling to take. The authors of *Getting to YES* are critical of this positional bargaining strategy because it commits participants to unwise agreements, entails lengthy negotiations, and jeopardizes the long-term relationship between the parties. Nevertheless, the alternative strategy they offer also bears the unique stamp of the European American view of conflict: (1) separate the people from the problem; (2) focus on interests, not positions; (3) generate a variety of possibilities before deciding what to do; and (4) insist that the result be based on some objective standard.

First, by advising negotiators to distinguish the people from the problem, Fisher and his colleagues assume that the content of conflict may be extracted from the relationship between the participants (a peculiar idea in Chinese contexts). Moreover, they assume that this separation facilitates the reconciliation of problematic issues that are inherently extra-relational. They warn that in a positional bargaining situation, "the parties' relationship tends to become entangled with their discussions of substance." A common European American view is that the substance of a conflict lies in the different positions advocated by the participants. Instead, Fisher and his colleagues argue, in their discussion of their second tip, that the substance is the participants' individual interests. Although the authors try to revise the prevailing European American view of conflict, they view "interests" as a manifestation of a set of needs, desires, concerns, and fears that are internal to the person. Again, their suggested revision of European American conflictways is itself a reflection of that cultural view of the person.

In their resolution-oriented strategy, Fisher, Ury, and Patton also recommend that negotiators generate multiple solutions to the problem. They go so far as to suggest that these solutions be designed to maximize mutual gain. This advice appears to be at odds with the European American preference for single solutions and individual interests. However, ultimately the suggestion is directed toward a particularly European American goal: to identify and decide on a single, binding agreement. Although these authors advise negotiators to brainstorm many possible solutions, all but one of these are to be cast aside once a decision has been made. This decision is considered a primary and enduring outcome of the conflict rather than a transitory agreement that remains open to subsequent negotiation. Furthermore, they recommend that negotiators base their decision on "objective" criteria. "Logical" appeals to principles of fairness, efficiency, or scientific merit, they contend, eliminate competition between individual wills. This view presumes that the relational aspects of a conflict is inevitably a competition between independent agents, and that abstract principles can circumvent this supposedly counterproductive form of relationality to reveal an objectively correct solution.

Conflictways in Asian American Contexts: Giving Face and Avoiding Confrontation

Although Asian American construct ways of life and ethnic identities that distinguish them from Asians who live in Asia, some features of the cultural experience of this group overlap with that of Asians abroad, particularly since most immigration from Asia has occurred in the second half of the twentieth century. Oyserman and Sakamoto suggest that many contemporary Asian Americans are constructing complex identities that embrace some aspects of American traditions of individualism while still retaining many interdependent meanings and practices. Characterizations of conflict in Asian cultures can then be used to make some initial inferences about Asian American conceptions of conflict, although it is immediately evident that these practices may change in important ways as they come in contact with European American practices.

Analogous to the connection in a European American context between the meaning of conflict and an independent conception of self, the meaning of conflict of Asians reflects an interdependent view of the person. In Asian cultures, the self is defined in relationship to others and is viewed as part of a larger social unit. Conflict then is a disturbance or disharmony in the relationship between individuals. This disharmony may arise from disagreement about an issue, or even incompatible activities of the sort that are problematic in European American contexts. However, in Asian cultures, conflict is at heart relational rather than activity-oriented. . . .

Cultures that foster an interdependent view of self embed individuals in networks of relationships that are expected to endure across a lifetime. For conflict, the implications of this social system are threefold. First, the appropriate management of conflict is an important priority because the consequences of conflict are likely to persist over time. Second, the time available for reestablishing relational harmony is extensive because the relationship will continue to exist, even if in disharmony. Third, conflict is an inevitable part of relationships since they endure over such a long time. . . . From this perspective, once individuals have built a long-term relationship with one another, conflict is an irrepressible, nonpathological, perhaps necessary component of their relationship.

The enduring quality of many relationships in Asian cultures gives rise to the codification and institutionalization of procedures for managing conflicts. While people in European American contexts often seek conflict avoidance or resolution, Asian approaches aim for management or control of the conflict. These procedures recognize the differences between the participants and attempt to minimize the negative consequences of the differences prior to confrontation. As noted by Tu Mu, a Chinese poet of the T'ang dynasty, "He who excels at resolving difficulties does so before they arise."

In Japan conflict management is represented by the metaphor of nemawashi, or root binding. Binding the roots of a tree before transplanting it is thought to facilitate its growth following the transition. Analogously, in conflict situations, laying an interpersonal groundwork of discussion and consensus-building activities before taking action that addresses the conflict is thought to help reestablish harmony among the participants and prevent loss of face. Cohen suggests that informal contact in these contexts allows one to negotiate without negotiating.

Nemawashi is commonly accomplished by the use of three procedures. First, face-to-face talks among pairs of participants allow them to survey the conflict and persuade others that an appropriate action can be found. Second, in the ringi procedure, the participants circulate a written copy of a proposed action for endorsement. The circulation of the document serves to disseminate information about the action to those involved in the negotiation ahead of time and make participants aware of the emerging consensus. Third, neutral go-betweens may speak to individuals on both sides of a conflict to arrange its management.

* * *

All of the well-known strategies for conflict management in Japanese cultural contexts are readily comprehensible from a European American perspective; some, such as triadic management and displacement, are quite common. Yet the idea of managing conflict by trying to prevent it is much less well developed in mainstream settings. From a

European American point of view, conflict, although it can be negative in its consequences, is not altogether negative or undesirable. From the interdependent perspective, avoiding conflict, even if doing so entails acceptance or "giving in," is critical and identity-promoting. When selves are defined relationally or through interdependence, disturbing or destroying the relationship threatens self. In interdependent cultural contexts, it is critical to honor the opponent's face or to give face. "Face entails the presentation of a civilized front to another individual within the webs of interconnected relationships in a particular culture.... Face is a claimed sense of self-respect in an interactive situation." Once face has been taken away, it has to be given back by one's opponent; it cannot be restored in other ways. Ting–Toomey and Cole, in delineating problems of intercultural contact, note that while negotiators from interdependent contexts are often particularly concerned with honoring face, negotiators participating in independent worlds are often most adept at threatening face.

A variety of studies and anecdotal reports from European Americans doing business in China also suggest that people in Chinese cultural contexts are likely to be very attuned to the threat or presence of interpersonal conflict. Leung, in a comparison of conflict resolution styles in Hong Kong Chinese students and American students, reports that the modes of conflict resolution preferred by Chinese students were those assumed most likely to reduce animosity. Furthermore, informal procedures like mediation and bargaining were also preferred to explicitly confrontational procedures. In a similar study by Trubisky, Ting–Toomey, and Lin comparing Taiwanese and American students, the Taiwanese students favored the use of styles identified as "obliging" and "avoiding," "integrating," and "compromising." ... On the other hand, European Americans may understand indirectness as a lack of honesty or weakness in one's convictions rather than as a strategy for conflict management and consensus building.

Conflictways in Mexican American Contexts: Respect and Mutual Positive Feelings

Characterizing conflict from Mexican American perspectives is perhaps even more difficult than characterizing it from an Asian American perspective. Conflict in Mexican culture, and in Latin American cultural systems more broadly, has received only meager attention in the social sciences. The work that is available, however, suggests that a variety of values and practices remain important for people who have participated in Mexican cultural contexts even when they are quite fully engaged in American mainstream contexts. Most important, in contexts that are primarily Mexican and Mexican American the individual is viewed within a hierarchical system of relationships. One key quality for being a worthy or honorable person in this system is *simpatia*, or the ability to both respect and share others' feelings.

In many Hispanic and Latin American cultural contexts, a person who behaves properly, and thus is esteemed and fulfilled, is one who knows how to judge a social situation and engage in an appropriate level of relatedness, showing the proper courtesy and decorum depending on age, sex, and social status. The capacity to honor others, fulfill one's obligations, and give respect while maintaining respect, or the positive evaluation of others, is critical to a good standing in the community and to survival within the community. A resolution that ensures an individual's autonomy or guarantees individual rights is often less important in a conflict than resolution that is appropriate to the particular setting and maintains or restores an individual's pride and honor.

Compared to many European American contexts, in Mexican American contexts a great emphasis is placed on interpersonal reality and the maintenance of harmony in interpersonal relationships. A recent study compared the preferences of Mexican Americans and European Americans for different work situations. Given a choice, Mexican Americans preferred the work situation in which coworkers spend time getting to know each other and establishing relationships with one another before beginning to work. European Americans were more likely to choose the situation in which people cut to the chase and begin working almost immediately, believing that one should not waste time on social trivialities and that results are more important than relationships.

Conflictways in African American Contexts: Advocacy and Confrontation

Analyzing African American conflict meanings and practices is a particularly complex and potentially controversial endeavor. Conceptions of self in African American contexts reflect mainstream models of the autonomous agentic self, but they also reflect interdependent understandings of group identity and belongingness. African American contexts are often described as reflecting a communalism in which group concerns can transcend individual concerns more easily than is the case in primarily European American contexts. Moreover, in many African American settings a clear emphasis is placed on unity, cooperative effort, and collective responsibility. This type of interdependence may be a legacy of African notions of personhood and/or a continuing legacy of involuntary immigration, slavery, discrimination, poverty, and minority status, or some combination of all of these.

Somewhat in contrast to Asian American contexts, in African American contexts, people live within social contexts of friends and extended family but relate to these contexts in terms of separate individuals with unique thoughts and feelings. From this perspective, the self is publicly represented by the expression of these thoughts and feelings to others. The self is co-constructed by the individual and the social group as individuals direct their expressions toward relational others and the others respond to these expressions.

Kochman, in one of the few direct comparisons of some European American and African American behavioral styles, observes that in public debate or argument the "black mode," as he calls it, is often animated, interpersonal, emotional, and confrontational. In many African American cultural contexts, being animated or energetic is entirely appropriate in a dispute or conflict. In fact, discussions that are devoid of affect or dynamic opposition are unlikely to be taken seriously or regarded as significant. In an analysis of "black talk," Smitherman suggests that African American communication often requires a dialogue or a dynamic exchange between A and B, not A lecturing B. Moreover, because it is not universally held that emotion makes an argument less cogent, African Americans sometimes view efforts by European Americans to set aside feelings as unrealistic, illogical, or even politically devious. And indeed, in conflicts between blacks and whites, whites often observe that the level of black affect or anger was inappropriate and thus perceive the argument as illegitimate.

In African American cultural contexts, the meaning of conflict may be simultaneously individual and relational. Understood as a lack of agreement between individuals, African American notions of conflict sometimes imply that individuals have differing points of view but emphasize the discrepancy in participants' positions rather than focusing on the consequences of the discrepancy. In contrast, more European American definitions of conflict often focus largely on consequences, that is, the interference of incompatible beliefs or goals in individual activity.

Notes and Questions

1. Using the constructs described in the readings, describe yourself according to the individualism-collectivism constructs and the high-and low-context constructs. Also ask someone else who knows you well to describe you. To what extent are your self-perception and her or his perception different?

2. Referring to the "conflictways" that Marcus and Lin attribute to each racial and ethnic group, identify the conflictways with which you most identify and the conflictways with which you are the most uncomfortable. Are you typical or atypical of the ethnic group to which you belong?

3. Explore how these self-observations help explain your approach to conflict and conflict resolution. Is the United States characteristically individualist or collectivist, low-context or high-context?

4. Consider how you would approach resolving a dispute if the opposing party was collectivist while you were individualist, low-context while you were high-context, and had conflictways that are distinctly contrary to yours.

E. RECONCILING CULTURAL DIFFERENCES

1. CULTURAL RELATIVISM AND UNIVERSALISM

The materials in this chapter thus far have focused on how cultures differ in their approach to conflict resolution. What if cultural approaches conflict? How do you reconcile these differences?

Consider these dilemmas:

Dilemma One:

A delegation of American feminists attends a United Nations World Conference on Women in China, where delegations from countries all over the world meet. A critical issue arises: Given profound cultural differences among women from different countries, how can feminists maintain a global political movement while avoiding charges of cultural imperialism?

Dilemma Two:

You are a judge in a criminal case where the defendant is a recent immigrant to the United States. What if the defense presents cultural evidence as an excuse for her otherwise criminal conduct. Should the immigrant defendant be judged according to her own cultural standards rather than those of the relevant jurisdiction?

Dilemma Three:

A company is considering doing business in a foreign country where there are discriminatory employment practices and lax environmental protection laws. Should the company go along with the practices of the host country? Should the company reject the practices even though that decision would put them at a competitive disadvantage? Should the company simply refuse to do business in the country altogether?

Dilemma Four:

You are asked to resolve the case of an employee who has worked for your company for sixteen years. Though her work has been excellent for fifteen years, it has been unsatisfactory for the past year. If there is no reason to expect that performance will improve, should the employee be (a) dismissed on the grounds that job performance should remain the grounds for dismissal, regardless of the age of the person and his previous record; or (b) is it wrong to disregard the fifteen years the employee has been working for the company?

Two models, those of cultural relativism and of universalism, offer very useful conceptual tools for trying to reconcile these dilemmas. The *cultural relativist model* essentially advocates a deference to each culture and their cultural practices: "When in Beijing, do as the Chinese do!" The *universalist model*, in contrast, argues that there should be uniform global standards that all countries and peoples should adhere.

Each approach presents its own challenges. Under the cultural relativist model, the presumption is that cultural practices are clearly identifiable. As we've discussed earlier in this chapter, defining the "culture" and its attributes is seldom easy. Among other nuances, cultures are always changing, and there are often competing political, religious, or social authorities for defining cultural practices.

The universalist model also has definitional challenges. How and who decide what constitutes the universal norm? To what extent are these standards determined by global consensus versus the decision of a dominating and domineering group of countries, individuals, or interests?

Let's revisit the dilemmas posed above. Consider the varied perspective on how to reconcile these differences and on what roles the cultural relativisit and universalist models play.

Dilemma One:

> Feminist responses to this charge [of cultural imperialism] are complicated and sometimes conflicting. On the one hand, feminists note that culture and religion are often cited as justifications for denying women a range of basic rights, including the right to travel, rights in marriage and divorce, the right to own property, even the right to be protected by the criminal law on an equal basis with men. Women have much to lose, therefore, in any movement away from a universal standard of human rights in favor of deference to culture. On the other hand, feminists acknowledge that feminism itself is grounded in the importance of participation, of listening to and accounting for the particular experiences of women, especially those on the margins of power. Indeed, much feminist criticism of traditional human rights approaches has focused on the tendency of international policymakers to exclude women's experiences and women's voices. Thus, the claim that Western concepts of women's equality are exclusionary or imperialist strikes at the heart of one of feminism's central commitments—respect for difference.

> In short, both the move to expand universal human rights to include those rights central to women's condition and the move toward a relativist view of human rights are consistent with and informed by feminist theory. Indeed, the tension between them reflects a tension within feminism itself, between describing women's experience collectively as a basis for political action and respecting differences among women.

(From Tracy E. Higgins, *Anti-Essentialism, Relativism, and Human Rights*, 19 HARV. WOMEN'S L.J. 89–105, 111–15 [1996].)

Dilemma Two:

Allowing sensitivity to a defendant's culture to inform the application of laws to that individual is good multiculturalism. It also is good progressive criminal defense philosophy, which has as a central tenet the idea that the defendant should get as much individualized (subjective) justice as possible.

> For legal scholars and practitioners who believe in a progressive civil and human rights agenda, these illustrations also raise an important question: What happens to the victims—almost always minority women and children—when multiculturalism and individualized justice are advanced by dispositive cultural evidence? The answer, both in theory and in practice, is stark: They are denied the protection of the criminal laws because their assailants generally go

free, either immediately or within a relatively brief period of time. More importantly, victims and potential victims in such circumstances have no hope of relief in the future, either individually or as a group, because when cultural evidence is permitted to excuse otherwise criminal conduct, the system effectively is choosing to adopt a different, discriminatory standard of criminality for immigrant defendants, and hence, a different and discriminatory level of protection for victims who are members of the culture in question. This different standard may defeat the deterrent effect of the law, and it may become precedent, both for future cases with similar facts, and for the broader position that race-or national origin-based applications of the criminal law are appropriate. Thus, the use of cultural defenses is anathema to another fundamental goal of the progressive agenda, namely the expansion of legal protections for some of the least powerful members of American society: women and children.

(From Doriane Lambelet Coleman, *Individualizing Justice Through Multiculturalism*, 96 COLUM. L. REV. 1093, 1099, 1156–65 [1996].)

Dilemma Three:

There are some hard truths that might guide managers' actions, a set of what I call *core human values*, which define minimum ethical standards for all companies. The right to good health and the right to economic advancement and an improved standard of living are two core human values. Another is what Westerners call the Golden Rule, which is recognizable in every major religious and ethical tradition around the world. In Book 15 of his *Analects*, for instances, Confucius counsels people to maintain reciprocity, or not to do to others what they do not want done to themselves.

Although no single list would satisfy every scholar, I believe it is possible to articulate three core values that incorporate the work of scores of theologians and philosophers around the world. To be broadly relevant, these values must include elements found in both Western and non-Western cultural and religious traditions. . . .

In the spirit of what philosopher John Rawls calls *overlapping consensus*, one can see that the seemingly divergent values converge at key points. Despite important differences between Western and non-Western cultural and religious traditions, both express shared attitudes about what it means to be human. First, individuals must not treat others simply as tools; in other words, they must recognize a person's value as a human being. Next, individuals and communities must treat people in ways that respect people's basic rights. Finally, members of a community must work together to support and improve the institutions on which the community depends. I call those three values *respect for human dignity*, *respect for basic rights*, and *good citizenship*.

(From Thomas Donaldson, *Values in Tension: Ethics Away from Home*, HARV. BUS. REV. 3–12 [Sept.-Oct. 1996].)

Dilemma Four:

There is great potential for conflict when people from cultures having different orientations must deal with one another. This is particularly true when people who value universal rules deal with people who think each particular situation should be examined on its merits and that different rules might be appropriate for different people. Westerners prefer to live by abstract principles and like to believe these principles are applicable to everyone. To set aside universal rules in order to accommodate particular cases seems immoral to the Westerner. To insist on the same rules for every case can seem at best obtuse and rigid to the Easterner and at worst cruel.

[In a study by Hampden–Turner and Trompenaar on this case], more than 75 percent of Americans and Canadians felt the employee should be let go. About 20 percent of Koreans and Singaporeans agreed with that view. . . . As these results show, Westerners' commitment to universally applied rules influences their understanding of the nature of agreements between individuals and between corporations. By extension, in the Western view, once a contract has been agreed to, it is binding—regardless of circumstances that might make the arrangement much less attractive to one of the parties than it had been initially. But to people from interdependent, hight-context cultures, changing circumstances dictate alterations of the agreement.

(From RICHARD E. NISBETT, THE GEOGRAPHY OF THOUGHT: HOW ASIANS AND WESTERNERS THINK DIFFERENTLY . . . AND WHY 64–66 [2003].)

———————

In the following reading, Professor Abramson describes a practical multi-step approach to reconciling cultural differences. Of particular interest to our discussion is Step 5.

HAROLD ABRAMSON, INTERNATIONAL DISPUTE RESOLUTION: CROSS–CULTURAL DIMENSIONS AND STRUCTURING APPROPRIATE PROCESSES

in ALAN RAU, EDWARD SHERMAN & SCOTT PEPPET, PROCESSES OF DISPUTE RESOLUTION 918–21 (3th ed. 2002).

First, the attorney should learn a *conceptual framework* which can help her identify and understand cultural characteristics. The attorney must grasp the meaning of "cultural behavior" and how it is different from universal "human behavior."

Second, the attorney should fill-in this conceptual framework with a deep understanding of her *own culture or cultures*. An attorney is not always cognizant of the degree to which her own behavior is universal or culturally determined. Yet, it is though this personal lens that an attorney observes and assesses the negotiation behavior of others.

Third, the attorney should strengthen her conceptual framework with an understanding of the *culture or cultures of the other negotiator(s)*. Despite the difficulties in identifying cultural behavior, the attorney should try to identify and research the culture(s) of her client, the other attorney, and the other party.

Fourth, the attorney should learn to withhold judgments about the other side and instead view key negotiating behavior with an *open mind*.

* * *

Fifth and finally, the attorney should search for ways to *bridge* the resulting gap ... Gaps might be closed by the attorney negotiating a resolution or deferring to the other side's practice. The attorney could negotiate a solution through resort to an interest-based approach, where the interests behind the practices are respected. Parties also might negotiate a compromise. In the hypothetical, instead of viewing as bad faith the other side's claim that they cannot agree to anything without a consensus, the U.S. attorney might focus on how to respect their need for consensus while still meeting her needs for clients to be present with substantial settlement authority. The attorney, for example, could negotiate an arrangement in which the other side brings to the negotiation sessions all the people who must concur or at least be sure the absent people are available by telephone. Then, in the sessions, the consensus approach could be respected by giving members of the negotiating team ample time to meet privately.

As an alternative to negotiating over closure of the gap, one side may choose simply to defer to the other side's practice, especially when the other practice is not a deal-breaker or does not implicate core personal values. For instances, the U.S. attorney may defer to the other side's formal practices of carefully using titles and avoiding personal questions about family. The gap, however, can be difficult to bridge when the difference reflects engrained strategic practices, such as a conflict between a problem-solving style and haggling.

A hypothetical illustrates: A typical U.S. lawyer usually insists that signed business agreements cover many details and contingencies. The U.S. lawyer will likely interpret any reluctance by the other side to reduce details to writing as reluctance about the deal or a specific issue. In preparing for a cross-cultural negotiation with a Japanese lawyer, however, the U.S. lawyer should realize that his own preference for reducing everything to writing may be due to his own cultural upbringing and may not be a universal mode of behavior (step 2). The drafting of comprehensive contracts is taught in U.S. law school and reinforced in law practice. A Japanese lawyer may have been brought up differently (step 3). Instead of being concerned about the details of a written agreement, the Japanese lawyer may be more concerned about the business relationship, leaving for the written contract a general statement about the relationship and basic principles for governing the business deal.

In the negotiations, the U.S. lawyer should view the reluctance of the Japanese lawyer to put everything in writing as ambiguous behavior to be viewed with an open mind (step 4). This difference might be investigated through a conversation in which the U.S. attorney explains why he prefers detailed contracts and then inquires why the other attorney may not. If the U.S. attorney learns that the other side believes business deals are about relationships, not contracts, the U.S. attorney needs to find a way to bridge this resulting gap in practices. The attorney may close the gap by respecting the reasons for the different practices. He may negotiate a compromise in which both sides seek to cultivate a relationship of trust and then enter into a contract that may cover key obligations but not every conceivable contingency (step 5).

2. LAW IN ITS CULTURAL CONTEXT

Lawyers are experts in reading legal statutes and regulations literally and technically. When considering the laws of other countries, however, a mechanical reading of the laws is insufficient. Laws do not exist in isolation; they must be understood in the cultural context in which they operate. That is why legal conflicts and cultural conflicts are often so interdependent.

Thus, when considering how foreign laws are used and interpreted in international conflict resolution, it is important to identify which political or social factors most shape the laws. While these factors differ from country to country, these are examples of relevant inquiries:

- If this country was once a colony, what is the impact of that historical legacy? What are the politics of decolonization?
- What is the current political ideology and political agenda?
- What are the government's economic policies and priorities?
- What are the moral values and to what extent are they synonymous or in conflict with various religious values?
- Are there pressures for the country to be integrated into a regional or international legal or political framework?
- What is the country's attitude toward "the rule of law"?

The following reading further explores putting law in its cultural context, by considering China's attitude toward "the rule of law."

PAT K. CHEW, THE RULE OF LAW: CHINA'S SKEPTICISM AND THE RULE OF PEOPLE

20 Ohio State Journal on Dispute Resolution 43 (2005).

Laws cannot stand alone ... for when they are implemented by the right person they survive, but if neglected they disappear.... Law is essential for order, but the superior [person] is the source of law. So when there is a superior [person], even incomplete laws can extend everywhere. But when there is no superior [person], even comprehensive laws cannot apply to all situations or be flexible enough to respond to change.

Xunxi 210 B.C.[1]

When the West advises other countries on nation-building, it frequently signals the importance of the "rule of law" in the developing country's emerging political structure.... The West's implicit cultural assumption is that the rule of law is an inherently positive goal. This conclusion is based on an interrelated string of inferences. The rule of law is suppose to bring order and predictability to how a country functions. This order and predictability means that government and business operations are more transparent. This transparency promotes commerce in general, including foreign trade transactions and investment, which in the aggregate contributes to overall economic development. In addition, the West assumes that the rule of law is a predicate for the basic protection of human and civil rights. Given all of these positive associations, it is not surprising that the West sees the rule of law as "good" and a critical part of the infrastructure of emerging and transitioning countries.

By default, the West's implicit cultural assumption is that the absence of the rule of law is negative and inherently undesirable. This default situation is often considered synonymous with a society governed by the "rule of people" or sometimes more narrowly termed "the rule of man." In contrast to the situation described in the prior paragraph, a country without the rule of law is presumed to be uncertain and chaotic in its government and business functioning. Without formal legal rules, the West believes that how society operates is not transparent. This opaqueness in how things get done discourages trade including foreign investment, which in turn makes overall economic development more difficult. Instead of predictable legal rules, the fear is that the void will be filled with unpredictable and arbitrary human indiscretions. Furthermore, the West believes that the absence of the rule of law makes the basic protection of human and civil rights problematic.

The Western view of the rule of law, however, is not the only model. Alternative cultural assumptions about the rule of law exist. In contrast to the Western view, China historically and contemporaneously views the rule of law with skepticism. In fact, China has for many years analyzed the comparative merits of legal formalism (rule of law) and of cultural norms (rule of people). The Chinese have traditionally framed this issue as a debate between two schools of thought: the Legalists and the Confucians. China's own history and its observations of the West's experience with the rule of law further informs its perennial struggle

---

1. As adapted from Karen G. Turner, *Introduction: The Problem of Paradigms*, in THE LIMITS OF THE RULE OF LAW IN CHINA 3 (Karen G. Turner, James V. Feinerman & R. Kent Guy eds., 2000).

between these two approaches. Moreover, China's skepticism of the rule of law continues today.

A. *LEGALISTS V. CONFUCIANS*

This perennial issue has traditionally been framed as a long-standing debate between two fundamentally different approaches. The first is the Legalist approach traditionally termed "fazhi" or more recently termed "yifazhiquo"—what the West would label as the rule of law. The second is a Confucian approach-what the West has sometimes labeled as a rule of man but is more accurately translated as the rule of people from the Chinese word "renzhi."

The first recorded debate between the Legalists and Confucians is the story of Zi Chan, dating from 536 BC. Zi Chan, the prime minister of the state of Zheng, ordered that criminal laws be inscribed and prominently displayed. He intended this as "a dramatic gesture to demonstrate the permanence of the law and to assure the people that the law would be applied strictly according to its letter, free of government manipulation." This dramatic and public gesture, however, provoked social and political controversy over whether this Legalist approach to government was appropriate.

This debate, first occurring over 2000 years ago and repeated many times over in China, emphasizes the following arguments and counterarguments: The Legalists refer to the laws as "fa," defined as the positivist and formal statutes and codes of the government. Legalists argue that rulers should rely on these laws meticulously; rulers should not rely on their intellect, intuition, or arbitrary preferences. Just as craftspeople rely on their professional tools, such as their compass or their square, rulers should rely on the measurements and solutions dictated by the laws. By doing so, governing would be easier and the results would be predictable and uniform. Order is achieved by these predetermined rules and external systems.

The Confucians, on the other hand, argue that the rulers' paramount guides should be social and cultural norms. These rules of proper conduct, called "li," should be the basis for governing: "Li is the vehicle of government ... When li is dishonoured, government is lost." Thus, if there is a conflict, fa would have the lowest priority and li as the moral standard would have the highest priority. These cultural norms and moral imperatives have ancient roots and so would be the most widely accepted and authoritative. Furthermore, rulers exercising their discretion in the interests of the community is far more important than protecting the interests of any individual's needs. Rulers also can reinforce a long-standing system of hierarchical relationships between individuals, thus furthering the order and harmony achieved through a socially understood balance between internal forces and these relationships.

That the ruler order and the subject obey, the father be kind and the son dutiful, the elder brother loving and the younger respectful, the husband be harmonious and the wife gentle, the mother-in-law be kind and the daughter-in-law obedient; these are things in *Li*. That the ruler in ordering order nothing against the right, and the subject obey with[out] any duplicity; that the father be kind and at the same time be able to teach, and the son be filial and at the same time be able to learn; the elder brother, while loving, be friendly, and the young docile, while respectful; that the husband be righteous, while harmonious, and the wife correct, while gentle; that the mother-in-law be condescending, while kind, and the daughter-in-law be winning, while obedient; these are excellent things in *Li*.

Confucians further posit that fa is flawed in fundamental ways. Laws are inevitably incomplete and rigid. They must be constantly reviewed and analyzed. The uniformity that is valued by the Legalists is not important; in fact, uniformity can be viewed as unworthy since a particularistic approach that is tailored to unique circumstances better serves societal needs. A strict rule of law also is evidence that rulers cannot rule effectively by utilizing moral norms. Hence, laws are analogous to an external and physical force. Deference to the laws indicate that the rulers are weak in political power and the people are weak in character. As described by Confucius:

> If the people be led by laws, and uniformity sought to be given them by punishments, they will try to avoid the punishment, but have no sense of shame. If they be led by virtue, and uniformity sought to be given them by *Li*, they will have the sense of shame and moreover will become good.

Legalists counter these Confucian positions with a practical concern: How do you restrain the abuses of rulers whose main intent is maximizing their own political power? After all, Legalists note, rulers have "100 battles a day" in which decisions must be made and rulers' political indiscretion could lead to improprieties. Confucians recognize this paramount challenge, acknowledging that there is a risk of fallible humans wanting to gain unlimited power. Confucians, however, propose that moral education and indoctrination of rulers and people are the correct paths. Strengthening internal character is the answer; resorting to formal laws when faced with complex and important questions is inappropriate.

B. *Contemporary Application*

Chinese skepticism of the rule of law and China's struggle between the rule of law and the rule of people continues today.... As the Chinese have long recognized, the "rule of law" is only an abstraction that is not necessarily bad nor necessarily good; not necessarily immoral nor necessarily moral.... The effect of the rule of law also depends on its substantive terms and its policy objectives. While an ethnocentric West may assume that every rule of law necessarily provides for the same civil rights and economic ideologies that underlies the legal framework of Western countries, that assumption is myopic. There are instead innumerable forms of the rule of law—each of which reflects the politics, economy, religions, and cultures of the individuals and institutions that created and control the legal regime. In a country like China, where the legal infrastructure is still emerging, the rules of law may more accurately represent aspirational rather than currently viable legal principles. It also may represent a transitional set of statutes and rules, which will evolve as the country's economic, political, and societal systems mature.

As Margaret Woo explains, in the meantime, judges and politicians may interpret the rule of law in ways that facilitate the P.R.C.'s current political and economic agenda or their individual self-interests. In addition, China has consistently drafted and interpreted laws in ways that maximize the government's control and assure that it will have substantial flexibility in using the laws as tools to satisfy its needs.

As Randall Peerenboom suggests, China faces the threshold question of whether to have a rule of law and, presuming so, the critical challenge of selecting a model for its rule of law. He contrasts the Western conception of the rule of law with that envisioned by Chinese leader Jiang Zemin. The Western model is labeled the "liberal democratic version of the rule of law":

> [This model] incorporates free market capitalism (subject to qualifications that would allow various degrees of "legitimate" government regulation of the market), multiparty democracy in which citizens may choose their representatives at all levels of government, and a liberal interpretation of human rights that gives priority to civil and political rights over economic, social, cultural, and collective or group rights.

As Professor Peerenboom describes it, Jiang Zeming and other central leaders, on the other hand, propose a "state-centered socialist rule of law":

> [This model endorses] a State-centered socialist rule of law defined by, inter alia, a socialist form of economy (which in today's China means an increasingly market-based economy but one in which public ownership still plays a somewhat larger role than in other market economies); a non-democratic system in which the (Chinese Communist) Party plays a leading role; and an interpretation of rights that emphasizes stability, collective rights over individual rights, and subsistence as the basic right rather than civil and political rights.

While these two models offer the greatest contrast, hybrid models are also a possibility.

. . . Thus, as in other times in China's history, Chinese society is currently facing a period of economic, social, political, and legal evolution. It has historically debated and contemporaneously debates the primacy of a rule of law (that relies on a legalistic approach) versus a rule of people (that adheres to cultural norms and governmental discretion). It is not clear how China will resolve its current debate. There are various possibilities, as depicted in the matrix below. Introducing this matrix hopefully facilitates our thinking, while not presuming the outcome.

Matrix on Chinese Alternatives

A rule of people that . . .

		values a rule of law	rejects a rule of law
A rule of law that	. . . mirrors the rule of people	Alternative 4	Alternative 2
	. . . rejects a rule of people	Alternative 3	Alternative 1

Alternative 1 In Alternative 1, society rejects a legalistic approach. At the same time, the legal system rejects cultural norms. Under this alternative, the rule of law (advocating a legalistic approach) and the rule of people giving primacy to cultural norms, would predictably conflict. People would not recognize, follow, or consider credible the rule of law; and the law would discount societal values. In some ways, this describes the current situation where there is a disconnect between a rule of law and a rule of people.

In Alternative 2, society rejects a legalistic approach, even though the legal system mirrors cultural norms. This alternative may describe a transitional environment, when the legal system has incorporated societal values but society has not yet accepted a legalistic approach.

In Alternative 3, society values a legalistic approach, even though the legal system does not take into account or even rejects cultural norms. This is an unlikely alternative, given China's historical skepticism of the rule of law.

In Alternative 4, society values a legalistic approach. At the same time, the legal system mirrors cultural norms. This would appear to be the most optimal alternative for effective nation building. A rule of law and a rule of people would co exist but be in sync; both cultural norms and legal rules would facilitate societal functioning. This alternative, however, is not premised on any particular model of the rule of law or a rule of people. Thus, a Chinese rule of law may be based on liberal democratic principles or instead on more socialist ideology. Hence, as the West promotes the rule of law in China, China's affirmative response to its urging may be different than the West anticipates.

Notes and Questions

1. Assume you are an American lawyer representing the U.S. corporate partner in a proposed joint venture with a Chinese company. You are negotiating the joint venture agreement and anticipate discussing tomorrow the contract provision stipulating the dispute resolution process, including the choice of law, for any disputes between the joint venture partners. How and to what extent will you take into account China's approach toward the rule of law and the rule of people in your negotiations?

2. The film *The Story of Qiu Ju* (1993) depicts a dispute in a Chinese village involving a family who believes they were unfairly harmed by the chief of the village. The story describes the dispute resolution processes (both informal and formal) that ultimately prove inadequate for satisfying the parties' real needs.

After viewing the film, consider these questions:

- How would each party describe the dispute? What interests are at stake? Who or what would be affected by how the dispute was treated and resolved?

- In what ways did the cultural context shape the conflict and its resolution?

- In what way was the formal dispute resolution system and "the rule of law" effective or ineffective? What were the system's goals, and how did they complement or conflict with the parties' goals and the "rule of people?"

- What parallels and contrasts do you see between China's and the U.S.'s legal systems and cultural norms?

Part II

PRIVATE DISPUTES

Chapter 4

INTERNATIONAL NEGOTIATION AND MEDIATION IN THE PRIVATE SECTOR

Problem

You should acquaint yourself with this problem that will be used throughout this chapter.

MITSUBISHI MOTORS CORP. v. SOLER CHRYSLER–PLYMOUTH[1]

"Plaintiff Mitsubishi Motors Corporation (Mitsubishi) is a Japanese corporation which manufactures automobiles and has its principal place of business in Tokyo, Japan. Mitsubishi is the product of a joint venture between, on the one hand, Chrysler International, S.A. (CISA), a Swiss corporation registered in Geneva and wholly owned by Chrysler Corporation, and, on the other, Mitsubishi Heavy Industries, Inc., a Japanese corporation. The aim of the joint venture was the distribution through Chrysler dealers outside the continental United States of vehicles manufactured by Mitsubishi and bearing Chrysler and Mitsubishi trademarks. Defendant Soler Chrysler–Plymouth, Inc. (Soler), is a Puerto Rico corporation with its principal place of business in Pueblo Viejo, Guaynabo, Puerto Rico.

On October 31, 1979, Soler entered into a Distributor Agreement with CISA which provided for the sale by Soler of Mitsubishi-manufactured vehicles within a designated area, including metropolitan San Juan. On the same date, CISA, Soler, and Mitsubishi entered into a Sales Procedure Agreement (Sales Agreement) which, referring to the Distributor Agreement, provided for the direct sale of Mitsubishi products to Soler and governed the terms and conditions of such sales including providing for arbitration administered by the Japan Commercial Arbitration Association."

---

1. These facts are from a landmark U.S. Supreme Court case about whether statutory claims, in particular claims under U.S. antitrust laws, can be resolved in arbitration. For the full opinion, *see* 473 U.S. 614, 105 S.Ct. 3346, 87 L.Ed.2d 444 (1985).

Initially, Soler did a brisk business in Mitsubishi-manufactured vehicles. As a result of its strong performance, the minimum sales volume for its 1981 model year, as specified by Mitsubishi and CISA, and agreed to by Soler, was substantially increased. In early 1981, however, the new-car market slackened. Soler ran into serious difficulties in meeting the expected sales volume, and by the spring of 1981, it felt compelled to request that Mitsubishi delay or cancel shipment of several orders. About the same time, Soler attempted to arrange for the transshipment of a quantity of its vehicles for sale in the continental United States and Latin America. Mitsubishi and CISA, however, refused permission for any such diversion, citing a variety of reasons, and no vehicles were transshipped.

The reasons advanced included concerns that such a diversion would interfere with the Japanese trade policy of voluntarily limiting imports to the United States; that the Soler-ordered vehicles would be unsuitable for use in certain proposed destinations because of their manufacture, with use in Puerto Rico in mind, without heaters and defoggers; that the vehicles would be unsuitable for use in Latin America because of the unleaded, high-octane fuel they required was not available there; that adequate warranty service could not be ensured; and that diversion to the mainland would violate contractual obligations between CISA and Mitsubishi.

Attempts to work out these difficulties failed. Mitsubishi eventually withheld shipment of 966 vehicles, which apparently represented orders placed for production in May, June, and July 1981. In February 1982, Soler disclaimed responsibility for this shipment.

The following month, Mitsubishi brought an action against Soler in the United States District Court for the District of Puerto Rico under the Federal Arbitration Act and the New York Convention. Mitsubishi sought an order to compel arbitration in accordance with para. VI of the Sales Agreement. Shortly after filing the complaint, Mitsubishi filed a request for arbitration before the Japan Commercial Arbitration Association.

The complaint alleged that Soler had failed to pay for 966 ordered vehicles; that it had failed to pay contractual "distress unit penalties," intended to reimburse Mitsubishi for storage costs and interest charges incurred because of Soler's failure to take shipment of ordered vehicles; that Soler's failure to fulfill warranty obligations threatened Mitsubishi's reputation and goodwill; that Soler had failed to obtain required financing; and that the Distributor and Sales Agreements had expired by their terms or, alternatively, that Soler had surrendered its rights under the Sales Agreement.

Soler denied these allegations and counterclaimed against both Mitsubishi and CISA. It alleged numerous breaches by Mitsubishi of the Sales Agreement, raised a pair of defamation claims, and asserted causes of action under the Sherman Act, among other laws.

In the counterclaim premised on the Sherman Act, Soler alleged that Mitsubishi and CISA had conspired to divide markets in restraint of trade. To effectuate the plan, according to Soler, Mitsubishi had refused to permit Soler to resell to buyers in North, Central, or South America vehicles it had obligated itself to purchase from Mitsubishi; had refused to ship ordered vehicles or the parts, such as heaters and defoggers, that would be necessary to permit Soler to make its vehicles suitable for resale outside Puerto Rico; and had coercively attempted to replace Soler and its other Puerto Rico distributors with a wholly owned subsidiary that would serve as the exclusive Mitsubishi distributor in Puerto Rico.

The alleged contract breaches included wrongful refusal to ship ordered vehicles and necessary parts, failure to make payment for warranty work and authorized rebates, and bad faith in establishing minimum-sales volumes. The fourth counterclaim alleged that Mitsubishi had made statements that defamed Soler's good name and business reputation to a company with which Soler was then negotiating the sale of its plant and distributorship. The sixth counterclaim alleged that that Mitsubishi had wrongfully advised Soler's customers and the public in its market area that they should no longer do business with Soler.

Mitsubishi and Soler are looking for ways to settle the legal dispute.

A. INTRODUCTION

This chapter examines two primary consensual processes for resolving private disputes—negotiation and mediation. These processes are especially suitable for international commercial disputes:[2]

> The more complex the problem, the greater the need for a broader and flexible approach to solutions. In international disputes the problems are compounded by distance, different cultural understanding, political interference, changing commercial agendas and the many other potential hazards that can drive on this metaphoric bridge.

> Given the difficulties that are particularly present in international disputes, it is not surprising that to adopt a wholly legal approach to their resolution often brings enormous frustration and disappointment to all parties. . . .

> In its combination of flexibility alongside a degree of disciplined form, mediation is especially suited to the diversity—cultural, managerial, technical—of global business traffic. It renews time honoured ancient processes of community tribal adjustment at a 21st Century level.

This chapter begins with a definition of mediation in order to highlight the relationship between negotiation and mediation as well as to clarify the meaning of this widely and loosely used term.

2. *See* EILEEN CARROLL & KARL MACKIE, INTERNATIONAL MEDIATION—THE ART OF BUSINESS DIPLOMACY 2–3 (2000).

Mediation is simply a negotiation conducted with the assistance of a third party. Any process that can be legitimately classified as mediation should fit this generic definition. It should be noted, however, that there has been much debate over what processes can be rightfully called mediation, a term that has been liberally used by such diverse sources as judges, the United Nations, and the media. Even a television advertisement for an oven has presented its salesman as a "great mediator."[3] It just seems too late to justify a favored, circumscribed definition of mediation. It is more productive to focus on defining the adjective in front of mediation. Is the mediation problem-solving, transformative, evaluative, directive, or something else?

The second chapter on "International Conflict Resolution Processes" provided a valuable introduction to the basic processes of negotiation and mediation. Among other points, it noted the differing views of the appropriate role for the mediator. This chapter will examine various mediator roles that can be encountered in private international mediations.

Whenever you try to define mediation, you also inevitably encounter a favorite pastime riddle: What is the difference between mediation and conciliation? People discuss and debate it, speculate based on some particular experience, and usually end with the frustrating declaration that the terms can be used interchangeably, and if they should not be so used, will use them that way anyway. The riddle is compounded by the fact that some organizations use both words in their title without maintaining a distinction such as the U.S. Federal Mediation and Conciliation Service. Even the common suggestion that mediation is more of a Western term and conciliation is more of an Asian term is confounded by the fact that the UNCITRAL,[4] an arm of the United Nations that drafts model laws, called its 1980 Rules and its 2003 Model Law as ones on conciliation while defining the term in the Model Law to include mediation. Historically, conciliation abroad probably involved a more interventionist approach, a distinction still maintained in the recent definitions adopted by National Alternative Dispute Resolution Advisory Council (NADRAC) to the Australian Attorney–General:[5]

3. Maytag Corporation ran nationally a television advertisement that it called "The Great Mediator (pizza or casserole)." In the advertisement, the "Maytag Man" appears as "a great mediator" who has the answer to the question that has "aroused fierce passions for centuries: What's for dinner." The mediator presents a new range that can "cook two different foods, at two different temperatures, for one complete meal." The advertisement ran from August, 1999 to December, 1999. Interview with Nicole Kaczmarek, LB Works, Operations Manager, Advertising Agency for Maytag Corporation (July 2003).

4. "The United Nations Commission on International Trade Law (UNCITRAL) is the core legal body within the United Nations system in the field of international trade law. UNCITRAL was tasked by the General Assembly to further the progressive harmonization and unification of the law of international trade." See http://www.uncitral.org.

5. See National Alternative Dispute Resolution Advisory Council, Dispute Resolution Terms (last modified, Feb. 26, 2004), at www.nadrac.gov.au.

Conciliation-Mediation Distinction

In NADRAC's view, "mediation" is a purely facilitative process, whereas "conciliation" may comprise a mixture of different processes including facilitation and advice. NADRAC considers that the term 'mediation' should be used where the practitioner has no advisory role on the content of the dispute and the term "conciliation" where the practitioner does have such a role. NADRAC notes, however, that both "mediation" and "conciliation" are now used to refer to a wide range of processes and that an overlap in their usage is inevitable.

Mediation is a process in which the parties to a dispute, with the assistance of a dispute resolution practitioner (the mediator), identify the disputed issues, develop options, consider alternatives and endeavour to reach an agreement. The mediator has no advisory or determinative role in regard to the content of the dispute or the outcome of its resolution, but may advise on or determine the process of mediation whereby resolution is attempted. Mediation may be undertaken voluntarily, under a court order, or subject to an existing contractual agreement.

Conciliation is a process in which the parties to a dispute, with the assistance of a dispute resolution practitioner (the conciliator), identify the issues in dispute, develop options, consider alternatives and endeavour to reach an agreement. The conciliator may have an advisory role on the content of the dispute or the outcome of its resolution, but not a determinative role. The conciliator may advise on or determine the process of conciliation whereby resolution is attempted, and may make suggestions for terms of settlement, give expert advice on likely settlement terms, and may actively encourage the participants to reach an agreement.

Consider this answer to the riddle by Professors Rau and Sherman:

Conciliation appears to be a more familiar term in the international commercial context than mediation, although there can hardly be any substantive significance in the use of one term rather than the other. Attempts to distinguish between the two tend only to compound confusion. Donahey suggests that "practitioners from other countries" often make a distinction "based on the degree of involvement of the mediator or conciliator": While a mediator attempts to "bring the parties together to arrive at their own settlement of the dispute," a conciliator, on the other hand, will "evaluate the dispute and reach his or her own view as to a just resolution of the controversy," and then "propose terms of settlement based on that understanding." [M. Scott Donahey, *International Mediation and Conciliation*, *in* THE ALTERNATIVE DISPUTE RESOLUTION PRACTICE GUIDE § 33:1 (Bette J. Roth et at. eds., 1993)] * * * Yet other learned commentators will sometimes define these terms in precisely the opposite way. * * *

In any event such definitions appear pointless, what some academics might refer to as attempts to dichotomize a continuum. This is at best a difference of style or emphasis, and practitioners of mediation can be found who cover the entire spectrum between passivity and a high degree of "directiveness."[6]

This chapter initially considers what disputes are suitable for mediation as well as when they are ripe to go into mediation. Then, most of the chapter parses a mediation representation formula in which the distinctive aspects of international negotiations are first considered and then ways to negotiate in international mediations are examined.

B. DISPUTES SUITABLE AND RIPE FOR PRIVATE INTERNATIONAL MEDIATION

Before examining the distinctive issues in negotiations and mediations, this chapter considers when to turn to private mediation. When grappling with this threshold question, you should examine a number of factors. After summarizing the standard ones, ones that apply to both domestic and international disputes, this section discusses several distinctive factors relevant to assessing whether disputes that are international in character are suitable for mediation. It then considers factors to weigh when assessing whether cases suitable for mediation are ripe for mediation.

1. DISPUTES SUITABLE FOR MEDIATION

The suitability of a dispute for mediation does not depend on the dispute's substantive content; it depends on whether your client's process interests can be met in mediation. A client may prefer mediation because it might meet her interest in:

a.   Controlling the Outcome. She may want a process that gives her the power to retain control over the outcome of the dispute.

b.   Selecting a Forum That Addresses All Issues. She may want a process that can produce a global solution that goes beyond resolving the narrow legal issues that brought the parties to arbitration or court.

c.   Preserving or Improving a Continuing Relationship with the Other Party.

d.   Avoiding Establishing a Binding Precedent.

e.   Developing Creative Remedies. She may want to search for remedies that are not restricted to what an arbitrator or judge is likely to order.

f.   Forming an Enduring Settlement. She may desire a process that fosters implementation by involving parties in the nuanced shaping of the settlement terms.

---

6. *See* A. Rau & E. Sherman, *Tradition and Innovation in International Arbitration*   *Procedure*, 30 Texas Int'l L.J. 89, 105 n.89 (1995).

g. Maintaining Confidentiality. She may need an assurance of confidentiality before she will share critical information and settlement ideas with the other side.

h. Saving Time and Money.

I. "Cleaning-up" the Case. Even when she does not expect the case to settle fully in the mediation, she may want to gain a better understanding of her interests, clarify what issues need to be resolved, dispose of some issues, solidify a discovery schedule, and develop a plan for resolving any remaining issues.

j. Examining and Discussing Conflicting Views of the Facts or Law. This preview of the facts and law in mediation can provide a valuable reference point for parties who are trying to assess whether to accept a proposal on the table or to continue litigating.

k. Venting. A party may need a forum where she can feel that the other side has heard her or she can constructively discharge any built-up anger.

l. Overcoming Communication Problems Between Participants.

m. Dealing with an Unskilled Negotiator

n. Overcoming Conflicts Between Her and Her Attorney or Conflicts between the Opposing Attorney and His Client.

2. DISPUTES LESS SUITABLE FOR MEDIATION

Some party's process interests are less suitable for mediation. Even though these interests can occasionally be met in mediation, they usually are more meaningfully satisfied in other forums such as a court or possibly in arbitration. Interests that are less suitable for mediation include:

a. Establishing Precedent to Guide Future Conduct.

b. Deterring Future Litigation.

c. Securing Vindication.

d. Going for the Jackpot Before a Jury, Judge, or Arbitrator.

e. Overcoming Particular Impediments that are Especially Difficult to Overcome in Mediation such as:

i. Preserving a Principle. Your client may be unwilling to agree to any settlement in which he must compromise a personal principle or value.

ii. Other Party Is Inadequately Represented.

iii. Critical Party Is Not Participating.

iv. Other Party Is Engaging in Bad Faith Negotiations.

3. INTERNATIONAL DISPUTES SUITABLE FOR MEDIATION

Disputes that are international can present their own distinctive reasons for being suitable for mediation. In the following excerpt, consider the possible process interests of parties from different countries.

WALTER G. GANS, SAVING TIME AND MONEY IN CROSS–BORDER COMMERCIAL DISPUTES

Dispute Resolution Journal 52–54 (January 1997).

* * *

Neutral forum arbitration of those disputes has certainly become the method of choice insofar as binding adjudication is concerned. But it is often far more preferable to devise procedures to resolve these disputes informally—through structured negotiations, facilitation, through mediation or other non-binding modality, all with the assistance of a mutually respected neutral—before resorting to any binding process through a third-party decision maker. There are sound reasons for requiring disputants in most cross-border transactions to go through these informal procedures * * * before resorting to binding arbitration, or, in the rare case, litigation. What are some of these?

1. Cultural differences favor inclusion of informal processes. Most foreign companies (whether European, Latin American or Asian) do not favor, in the first instance, having their business disputes aired externally and decided for them by others. When it has become necessary to do so, it is often deemed a sign of failure on the part of the businessmen, who then tend to wash their hands of the matter, at which point it becomes strictly a legal matter to be handled by the lawyers.

Because it is so embedded in foreign culture, it is generally deemed not necessary—indeed, it often may be considered crass—to recite in a legal document informal and well-understood practices that business managers routinely use to resolve disputes. That's why ADR as we know it (apart from binding administered arbitration) was suspect in many quarters, at least in Europe and Japan. But with the sharp increase in all manner of transnational projects over the last several years, there is a greater understanding that the unwritten norms that pertain within a particular culture do not necessarily find acceptance in another. This is particularly the case insofar as that other culture is the United States. Accordingly, foreign-based companies are now much more prone to accept inclusion in the documents of even informal procedures that would be exhausted before resorting to the familiar binding adjudication.

* * *

2. Businessmen should control their disputes. There is now a view outside the U.S., which has been reinforced by the U.S. proponents of ADR, and that is finally taking hold in Europe and elsewhere, that dispute resolution should not be left exclusively to the lawyers. As mentioned, it is common practice abroad for foreign businessmen to resolve their disputes by themselves, informally, possibly with the assistance of a mutual friend or business acquaintance, but certainly not with the assistance of lawyers acting as such. If in the odd case that approach proved unsuccessful, then the matter migrated from a business disagreement to a legal dispute. At that stage, the business people bowed out and it became solely a legal matter leading to (hopefully) a so-called "correct" result: that is, one reached in a well-accepted court of law or arbitration. Expense at that point didn't really matter as long as the process was deemed to be fair or "correct."

We know that for the most part things have evolved differently in our culture. The trend here is for the business people to become active participants in dispute resolution, and for good reason. After all, such disputes typically arise out of a business transaction (legally formulated or not), or at least in a business setting. Why shouldn't those who are involved in the underlying business matter have an active stake in the resolution of the dispute emanating from it?

3. *Legal remedies are often too draconian to resolve business impasse.* Most disputes arising out of transnational transactions are business issues—what should be done if there's overcapacity? undercapacity? the need for new financing? Invocation of traditional legal remedies, as opposed to finding business solutions, is an admission that there's serious impasse and it cannot be resolved for whatever reason. Suing the other party for breach of contract or to compel dissolution or a buy-sell arrangement rarely serves the business goals as they were envisaged. Creative business solutions, on the other hand, will often resolve these problems, and the chances are better for achieving them if the respective managements recognize that dispute resolution is a management, not legal, responsibility. This can be facilitated by the lawyers who ideally would encourage management to adopt practical, cost-effective and timely solutions as opposed to proceeding immediately with costly and time-consuming adjudication. The legal advisers have the opportunity (even the duty) to counsel toward those ends, beginning at the transaction's negotiation stage, by incorporating in the contract dispute resolution processes and procedures that best facilitate a business solution. If that is not possible, then they should at least be knowledgeable and informed about modalities short of litigation that might be invoked and, finally, an arbitration procedure that makes best sense from the client's perspective.

4. *High incidence of disputes has led to greater scrutiny of costs.* Even in civil law countries which used to believe that the "correct" result was important regardless of expense, there is now a greater consciousness of the enormous costs attendant to adjudication in courts or even arbitration tribunals. Perhaps because of the higher incidence of international disputes, scrutiny of legal (along with other) expenses has become de regueur not only by U.S. but also by foreign companies operating in the global marketplace.

In addition to the process interests in this article, a party may have a particular process interest in:

a. Creating a Triggering Event to Convene a Settlement Discussion. Parties may need an excuse to meet, an excuse that provides them an opportunity to overcome such barriers to meeting as cultural obstacles to asking, geographic distances between parties, time zone inconveniences, and different languages. By turning to mediation, parties create an occasion in which these barriers that parties may not easily overcome on their own will be specifically addressed. When setting up a mediation, parties and the mediator will be compelled to discuss where and when to meet and whether an interpreter may be necessary to facilitate communications.

b. Avoiding International Arbitration or Litigation in the Domestic Courts of a Foreign Jurisdiction. Like parties in domestic mediations, parties from different countries may prefer a settlement process in order to avoid resorting to adjudication, their best alternative to a negotiated agreement (BATNA). However, in international legal disputes, the BATNA can be even more expensive and less certain than the BATNA in domestic disputes. In international disputes, a party may be compelled to participate in an international arbitration, posing the risks and expenses of a lengthy, formal arbitration process, or a party may be compelled to litigate in a domestic foreign court, posing all the risks and expenses of trans-border litigation. When compared to these alternatives, parties may prefer mediation because it can offer a significantly less expensive process that gives them significantly more control over the outcome.

c. Securing Help in Overcoming Cross–Cultural Obstacles. Parties from different countries might need a process that can help them recognize and overcome distinctive obstacles posed by their different cultural upbringings. They may need a mediation process with a skilled mediator who can help them bridge such cultural gaps as when an Asian or South American party, for instance, may be more interested in the relationship than the U.S. party who may be more interested in a detailed contract, or when the U.S. party wants extensive discovery while the civil law party sees no need for it.

4. DISPUTES RIPE FOR MEDIATION

When is the best point in the adjudicatory process to enter mediation? In other words, when is a case suitable for mediation ready for mediation? There are no hard-and-fast rules that would answer these questions. At an early stage, parties may be ready for a settlement process because they may not be too wedded to their positions and the litigation process may not have fractured their relationship. At a later stage, parties also may be ready to participate in a settlement process because discovery is mostly done, issues may have been narrowed through dismissal or summary judgment motions, and parties may feel more knowledgeable about the likely court outcome and litigation costs. Although minimum requirements can be articulated to help determine the best time to mediate (when parties know enough to adequately, although not necessarily thoroughly, evaluate the merits of their legal case and hence their best alternative to settlement), in practice pinpointing the best moment with precision is difficult.

The good news is that an imperfect timing decision will not normally damage your client's case. If you enter too early, you are just less likely to settle the entire case at that time. If you enter later than necessary, you may have only wasted money over-preparing the case. And, in both of these circumstances, you are still likely to benefit from the mediation. Even a case unsuitable for mediation will benefit from it at any point in the adjudicatory process. At a minimum, a competently conducted mediation will likely clean-up the case. As suggested earlier, parties will gain a better understanding of their interests, issues will be clarified, some issues might be settled, a discovery schedule may be developed, and what remains to be done to resolve the case will usually be illuminated, if not mapped out.

Notes and Questions

1. Which process interests for using international mediation do you find most persuasive? Can you think of other process interests that might be met in international mediations?

2. International mediations are not yet widely used for resolving international business disputes. This underutilization of mediation persists despite the impressive settlement record of domestic mediations[7] and despite the fact that most international organizations have promoted the use of mediations through exhortation and publication of rules.[8] Given the large number of process interests that can be met by mediation, why do you think mediation is underused for resolving private disputes?

3. Do you think the Mitsubishi–Soler Dispute is suitable for mediation? Do you think it is ripe for mediation?

C. DISTINCTIVE ISSUES IN INTERNATIONAL NEGOTIATIONS AND MEDIATIONS

The distinctive issues that arise in international negotiations and mediations can be illustrated when viewed through the lens of a formula

---

7. *See, e.g.,* Jeanne M. Brett, Zoe I. Barsness & Stephen B. Goldberg, *The Effectiveness of Mediation: An Independent Analysis of Cases Handled by Four Major Service Providers,* NEG. J. 259, 261 (July 1996) (The overall settlement rate was 78%.) and ROBERT C. MEADE & PHILIP FERRARA, PH.D., AN EVALUATION OF THE ALTERNATIVE DISPUTE RESOLUTION PROGRAM OF THE COMMERCIAL DIVISION: SURVEY RESULTS AND RECOMMENDATIONS 4–5 (July 1997) (The overall settlement rate was close to 70% for the Alternative Dispute Resolution Program of the Commercial Division of the Supreme Court, Civil Branch, New York County, New York State.).

8. ICC has offered conciliation services from its beginning in 1923, UNCITRAL in 1980, and ICSID in 1965. Interestingly, before WWII, the ICC handled more conciliations than arbitrations, but the number of conciliations dropped off after WWII while the number of arbitrations increased to the point that today most ICC cases are arbitrations with only a handful of conciliations. *See* W. LAURENCE CRAIG, WILLIAM W. PARK & JAN PAULSSON, INTERNATIONAL CHAMBER OF COMMERCE ARBITRATION 681–82 (2d ed. 1990).

for mediation representation.[9] This formula focuses on five central features of client representation. You *negotiate* in mediation to achieve the two goals of *meeting your client's interests* and *overcoming any impediments*. You negotiate in ways that take specific *advantage of the presence of a mediator* at each of the *key junctures* in the mediation process.

Compressed in this slender formula is an enormous amount of knowledge and skill that effective advocates should possess when representing clients domestically or internationally. The first three features consider how to be an effective negotiator. The next two features explore how to be an effective negotiator in mediations. This section unpacks the formula by examining each of the five italicized concepts as well as by highlighting cultural issues that may arise when resolving international disputes.

This section focuses on those issues that are distinctively international,[10] not on universal issues that are likely to arise in any negotiation or mediation. Universal negotiation and mediation issues are explored in depth in courses on alternative dispute resolution, negotiation, or mediation and therefore will be only mentioned. For example, because how to diagnose an impasse is covered in other courses, this section only explores obstacles that might arise due to the international character of the negotiation or mediation.

When this mediation representation formula is applied in the United States, it becomes imbued with unarticulated U.S. cultural values[11] that you should become conscious of when negotiating and mediating internationally. These usually unacknowledged cultural values are highlighted in italics in the following description of the U.S. version of the mediation representation formula. You negotiate using a *creative problem-solving approach* in mediation to achieve the two goals of meeting your *client's interests* and *overcoming any impediments* to settlement. Your negotiation strategy should take specific advantage of how a *U.S. trained mediator* can assist in resolving the dispute at each of the key junctures in a *problem-solving* mediation process. These cultural values will be explored and compared with values found in other countries.

1. APPROACH TO NEGOTIATIONS

You should know how to negotiate effectively with the other side and in mediations. Remember the connection between negotiation and

9. This formula forms the foundation of a book on how to effectively represent clients in a problem-solving mediation process. *See* Harold I. Abramson, Mediation Representation—Advocating in a Problem-Solving Process, Introduction (2004).

10. This discussion of distinctively international issues is based on materials published by Harold I. Abramson in *International Dispute Resolution: Cross–Cultural Dimensions and Structuring Appropriate*

Processes, in Alan S. Rau, Edward F. Sherman & Scott R. Peppet, Processes of Dispute Resolution: The Role of Lawyers ch. VI (3d ed. 2002).

11. This section refers to U.S. culture, not Western or North American cultures because these other common classifications are too broad for the materials used in this chapter.

mediation. Mediation is simply the continuation of the negotiations so you should know how to negotiate in a way that is suitable for gaining the optimal benefits from the mediation process.

Any negotiation has a structure in which well-recognized strategies and techniques are employed. This structure, along with its strategies and techniques, can be shaped by the negotiator's cultural upbringing. In the U.S., two archetypical negotiation approaches have been analyzed and critiqued in depth by numerous researchers and commentators; the two approaches have been labeled as adversarial or positional and problem-solving or interest-based.

In the more familiar adversarial approach to negotiations, each negotiator generally starts with firm, extreme and opposite positions and then makes calibrated concessions until the negotiators reach an impasse or are close enough to either split the difference or adopt one of the last offers on the table. Each party prepares for the negotiations by first establishing in his or her own mind the parameters of the negotiation dance which usually means forming a target goal, bottom line, and a specific opening offer strategy. Then, at the table, each party implements his or her opening offer strategy and engages in a negotiation dance of offers, counter-offers, compromises, and concessions. The dance consists of the carefully orchestrated movement of information, played to the battle music of partisan arguments, clever tactics, and sharp threats.

In contrast, a problem-solver that is creative does more than just try to settle the dispute. The problem-solver creatively searches for solutions that go beyond traditional ones based on rights, obligations, and precedent. Rather than settling for win-lose outcomes, the negotiator searches for solutions that can benefit both sides. To creatively problem-solve, the negotiator develops a collaborative relationship with the other side and negotiates in a way that is likely to result in solutions that are enduring as well as inventive. Such solutions are likely to be enduring because the negotiator works with the other side to fashion nuanced solutions that each side fully understands, can live with, and knows how to implement. They are likely to be inventive because the negotiator advocates for his or her client's interests instead of legal positions, uses suitable techniques for overcoming impediments, searches expansively for multiple options, and evaluates and package options imaginatively to meet the various interests of all parties.

The rational for adopting a problem-solving approach over the adversarial one in mediations is provided in the following excerpt.

HAROLD I. ABRAMSON, MEDIATION REPRESENTATION—ADVOCATING IN A PROBLEM–SOLVING PROCESS
1–6 (2004).

* * *

The mediation process is indisputably different from other dispute resolution processes. Therefore, the strategies and techniques that have proven so effective in settlement conferences, arbitrations, and judicial trials do not work optimally in mediation. You need a different representation approach, one tailored to realize the full benefits of this burgeoning and increasingly preferred forum for resolving disputes. Instead of advocating as a zealous adversary, you should advocate as a zealous problem-solver.

* * *

The familiar adversarial strategy of presenting the strongest partisan arguments and aggressively attacking the other side's case may be effective in court where each side is trying to convince a judge to make a favorable decision. But, in mediation, there is no third party decision-maker, only a third party facilitator. The third party is not even the primary audience. The primary audience is the other side, who is surely not neutral and can often be quite hostile. In this different representational setting, the adversarial approach is less effective if not self-defeating.

Many sophisticated and experienced litigators realize that mediation calls for a different approach, but they still muddle through the mediation sessions. They are learning on the job. Even though many attorneys prefer a problem-solving-type approach to negotiations, attorneys are still in the early stages of figuring out how to do it in mediations. Many attorneys went to law school before courses on dispute resolution were offered, and the dispute resolution courses that have shown up in law schools during the last twenty-five years have been largely limited to teaching students to be mediators, not advocates. Continuing legal education programs are only beginning to focus on teaching representation skills, with many programs limited to sharing anecdotal experiences and idiosyncratic advice. * * *

In this pitch for a problem-solving approach, I do not blindly claim that it is the only one that results in settlements. Attorneys frequently cite success stories when they use unvarnished adversarial tactics or a hybrid of adversarial and problem-solving strategies. The hybrid supporters claim that the best approach is a flexible one, a philosophy that surely is advisable in life generally as well as in legal negotiations. But, flexibility should not be confused with inconsistency. Shifting between adversarial and problem-solving tactics during the course of mediation can undercut the problem-solving approach. A consistent adherence to problem-solving will more likely produce the best results for clients.

* * *

Finally, for the skeptics who think that problem-solving does not work for most legal cases because they are primarily about money, I offer three responses.

First, the endless debate about whether or not legal disputes are primarily about money is distracting. Whether a dispute is largely about money varies from case to case. You have little chance of discovering whether your client's dispute is about more than money if you approach the dispute as if it is only about money. Such a preconceived view backed by a narrowly focused adversarial strategy will likely blind you to other parties' needs and inventive solutions. You are more likely to discover comprehensive and creative solutions if you approach the dispute with an open mind and a problem-solving orientation.

Second, if the dispute or any remaining issues at the end of the day turn out to be predominately about money, then at least you followed a representation approach that may have created a hospitable environment for dealing with the money issues. A hospitable environment can even be beneficial when there is no expectation of a continuing relationship between the disputing parties.

Third, the problem-solving approach provides a framework for resolving money issues. These types of disputes can sometimes be resolved by resorting to the usual problem-solving initiatives discussed throughout this book. If they fail, you then might turn to adversarial strategies, strategies that have been tempered and modified for a problem-solving process.

In short, the problem-solving approach provides a comprehensive and coherent approach to representation that can guide you throughout the mediation process. By sticking to this approach, you will be prepared to deal with the myriad of unanticipated challenges that inevitably arise as the mediation unfolds.

This problem-solving, interest-based approach may have been labeled, articulated, and studied in the United States, but it is not exclusively practiced in the United States. Consider this widely cited example of dispute resolution involving the Prophet Mohammed as mentioned in the Sunnah of Islam. The Prophet, serving in the role of a person who reconciles differences between people, illustrated how a distributive win-lose solution can be transformed into an integrative win-win one.[12]

> In the reconstruction of the ka'ba, a serious quarrel arose over the setting of the *Hajar al-Aswad*—the Black Stone. Each one of the four leaders of the Quraysh that was in dispute over this issue, was eager to have this honour and ensure he was not outdone by the others. There was an impasse. They could not agree. One of the leaders suggested that the first person to arrive at the *Haram* the next morning could be the one to place the *Hajar al-Aswad*. As it transpired, the Prophet (pbuh) was the first to arrive at the *Haram*. Not wishing to have the privilege all to himself, he

12. *See* Mohamed Keshavjee, *Alternative Dispute Resolution: Its Resonance in Muslim Thought and Future Directions*, SPEECH, Ismaili Centre, London 5–6 (The Institute of Ismaili Studies, Apr. 2, 2002).

asked each of the contesting tribes to select one leader. He then spread a sheet of cloth and put the *Hajar-at-Aswad* on it, asked the leaders to hold it at four ends and together raise it. Thus a serious conflict was averted by the Prophet's (pbuh) prudent action in giving all four leaders an equal honour of placing the stone.

This section assumes that the attorney plans to use a problem-solving approach in the negotiation and the mediation, a choice that is obviously culturally influenced. It is a negotiation approach that is especially suitable for mediation as a process that offers settlement opportunities that are different from those available in other dispute resolution processes such as judicial settlement conferences. A problem-solving negotiator in a cross-cultural settlement process comes prepared to deal with cultural differences throughout his or her negotiation and mediation representation including when: identifying the other side's interests (Subsection 2), diagnosing possible impediments (Subsection 3), enlisting assistance from a mediator brought up in another country (Subsection 4), and engaging in representation at key junctures in the mediation process (Subsection 5). The success of these initiatives does not depend on the other side negotiating as a problem-solver.

2. GOAL: ADVANCE INTERESTS

Your primary purpose in a problem-solving negotiation as well as in a problem-solving mediation, is to advance and meet your client's interests. Your client's particular interests can include ones that are distinctively a product of his or her cultural upbringing.

(a) Define Interests

What are interests? Some commentators have suggested that parties' interests are those shaped by Western cultural individualism, and that they fail to take into account other culturally-driven goals such as interdependence and relatedness. The critique sounds like this:[13]

> * * * interest-based * * * definitions typically narrow their focus on the parties directly engaged in the struggle or the conflict behavior. This combined with the cultural and social norms of individualism, individual autonomy, and independent existence of individuals, which are prevalent in the west, make such a definition appropriate in the western setting. Islamic settings, by contrast, both in theory and culturally, assume a great deal of social interdependence and community involvement even in interpersonal matters, which are more

13. *See* Amr Abdalla, *Principles of Islamic Interpersonal Conflict Intervention: A Search Within Islam and Western Literature*, 15 J.L. & RELIGION 151, 161–62, 165, 176 (2000–2001).

conducive to situational definitions that allow for a deeper and wider analysis of conflict situations.

* * *

The tendency in the American literature is to assume that a party in an inter-personal conflict will, and is encouraged to, define the issues based on an autonomous view of what his/her interests are. The literature describes a spectrum of defining issues that ranges from emphasizing one's own interest to considering other party's interests as well. * * *

Another element of defining issues in inter-personal conflicts is the consideration given to the relationship. The tendency in the American literature is to separate "relational goals" from "content goals," "substance" from "relationship," or "interests" from "relationships."

* * *

The discussion that will follow will suggest that Islamic theory and culture are based on interdependence and relatedness of community members. Relationship issues are in many instances as significant as issues of substance.

* * *

This strong sense of relatedness and community can be utilized to the benefit of conflict intervention in Islamic settings. A conflict intervener cannot assume that the community is made of independent autonomous individuals who expect that interpersonal conflict intervention will take place only between primary parties and the intervener. An Islamic setting is likely to engage and involve other entities (for example, extended family members) in any given conflict. This involvement of others can be a strength for conflict intervention, and would model Islamic norms and principles.

While this narrow view of interests can be encountered in the West, consider the broad definition of interests espoused by the leading U.S. proponents of interests-based negotiations, Roger Fisher and William Ury, as spelled out in their classic book, *Getting to Yes*.[14] They sharply

14. *See* ROGER FISHER & WILLIAM URY, GETTING TO YES 41, 48 (2d edition with Bruce Patton, 1991).

distinguish between the vital concept of interests and the commonly voiced positions of parties:

> * * * Interests motivate people; they are the silent movers behind the hubbub of positions. Your position is something you have decided upon. Your interests are what caused you to so decide.

> * * *

> **The most powerful interests are basic human needs.** In searching for the basic interests behind a declared position, look particularly for those bedrock concerns which motivate all people. * * * Basic human needs include:

> · security

> · economic well-being

> · a sense of belonging

> · recognition

> · control over one's life

Fisher and Ury do not ignore or subordinate concerns about a party's interest in relationships; they prominently recognized and examined this interest when they concluded that:[15]

> Every negotiator wants to reach an agreement that satisfies his substantive interests. That is why one negotiates. Beyond that, a negotiator also has an interest in his relationship with the other side.... Dealing with a substantive problem and maintaining a good working relationship need not be conflicting goals, if the parties are committed and psychologically prepared to treat each separately on its own legitimate merits. Base the relationship on accurate perceptions, clear communication, appropriate emotions, and a forward-looking, purposive outlook. Deal with people problems directly.

Len Riskin, in his classic article on the orientations of mediators, broadly defines interests to encompass "relatedness and community" when he suggests that third parties can approach parties' needs over a continuum of four levels from a narrow perspective of a legal dispute to the broad perspective of community interests:[16]

> 1.   Level I: Litigation Issues

> In very narrow mediations, the primary goal is to settle the matter in dispute though an agreement that ap-

---

15.   *See* FISHER & URY, *supra* note 14, at 19–21.

16.   *See* L. Riskin, *Understanding Mediators' Orientations, Strategies, and Tech-* *niques: A Grid for the Perplexed*, 1 HARV. NEG. L. REV. 7, 18–22 (1996).

proximates the result that would be produced by the likely alternative process, such as a trial, without the delay or expense of using that alternative process. The most important issue tends to be the likely outcome of litigation. "Level I" mediations, accordingly, focus on the strengths and weaknesses of each side's case....

2.   Level II: "Business" Interests

At this level, the mediation would attend to any of a number of issues that a court would probably not reach. The object would be to satisfy business interests....

Broadening the focus a bit, the mediation might consider more fundamental business interests, such as both firms' need to continue doing business, make profits, and develop and maintain a good reputation * * *

3.   Level III: Personal/Professional/Relational Issues

"Level III" mediations focus attention on more personal issues and interests.... Although Fisher, Ury and Patton tell us to "separate the people from the problem," sometimes the people are the problem. Thus, mediation participants often must address the relational and emotional aspects of their interactions in order to pave the way for settlement of the narrower economic issues. In addition, addressing these relational problems may help the parties work together more effectively in carrying out their mediated agreement.

Apart from these instrumental justifications, addressing these personal and relational problems can be valuable in its own right. Focusing on such issues may be important even if the mediation does not produce a solution to the narrower problems. In other words, a principal goal of mediation could be to give the participants an opportunity to learn or to change. This could take the form of moral growth or a "transformation," as understood by Bush and Folger to include "empowerment" (a sense of "their own capacity to handle life's problems") and "recognition" (acknowledging or empathizing with others' situations). In addition, the parties might repair their relationship by learning to forgive one another or by recognizing their connectedness. They might learn to understand themselves better, to give up their anger or desire for revenge, to work for inner peace, or to otherwise improve themselves. They also might learn to live in accord with the teachings or values of a community to which they belong.

4. Level IV: Community Interests

"Level IV" mediations consider an even broader array of interests, including those of communities or entities that are not parties to the immediate dispute. For example, perhaps the ambiguity in legal principles relevant to the Computec case has caused problems for other companies; the participants might consider ways to clarify the law, such as working with their trade associations to promote legislation or to produce a model contract provision. In other kinds of disputes, parties might focus on improving, or "transforming," communities.

Therefore, interests can be, and will be in this chapter, defined broadly to encompass most, if not all, needs of parties.

But, identifying these broad interests can be challenging when you consider that clients can more easily articulate their positions than they can their interests as a result of a lifetime of telling others what they want—whether they want to see a particular movie on Saturday night, have pizza for dinner, or be given money to compensate them for lost wages. Clients are rarely asked to voice what motivates them to want these things. They may want to see a particular movie because of their underlying interest in seeing an action movie or a romantic comedy. They may want pizza for dinner because they are looking for something quick and simple. They may want money because they habitually translate what they want into monetary equivalents when in fact they may really want something else like financial security.

You may find it difficult to identify your client's interests given this practice of taking positions compounded by your professional training and experiences that reinforce a positional, win-lose view of problems. Your legal education, the way the common law evolves, the pervasive and adversarial legal culture, the all too familiar routine of pursuing litigation, and traditional fee arrangements all shape and narrow a litigator's mindset. As a result, you may be professionally blinded to your client's interests. You may also be blinded to the other side's interests due to your own cultural upbringing, a point made in the next section on distinctively cultural interests.

In their book, Fisher and Ury explain that by simply asking "why?"(or variations of this question tailored for the cultural setting), you can overcome this blind spot and uncover your client and the other side's underlying interests. By bringing to the surface your client's underlying interests and surmising the interests of the other party, you can free both parties from the traditional contest over competing positions and identify what each side really needs from the negotiation and mediation.

(b) Distinctively Cultural Interests

In cross-cultural negotiations and mediations, you may discover less familiar interests that need to be met. You may think a dispute is primarily about money, for instance, when it is really mostly about protecting a principle, saving face, promoting particular community norms and collectivist interests, or preserving relationships. Although these interests are not unfamiliar to U.S. parties, these interests can be deeply compelling for parties from some non-U.S. cultures.

Cultural values may reveal the interests underlying negotiators' positions. Negotiators from cultures that value tradition over change, for example, may be less enthusiastic about economic development that threatens valued ways of life than negotiators from cultures that value change and development. This was the situation in which Disney found itself after purchasing a large tract of land south of Paris to construct Euro-Disney. Although EuroDisney promised jobs and economic development to an area that had high unemployment and few nonfarm jobs for youth, the local populace valued its traditional agricultural lifestyle. EuroDisney management, with its American values for economic development, had difficulty reconciling the local population's preferences for tradition over development.

The example also points out that the same values that generate cultural differences in preferences may also act as cultural blinders. Negotiators from one culture, expecting preferences to be compatible, cannot understand the rationality of negotiators from another culture whose views on the same issue are at odds with their own. It is generally unwise in negotiation to label the other party as irrational.[17]

In collectivist societies, such as in China and Japan, parties can have an interest in preserving face, a deeply ingrained personal value that involves being treated with respect and dignity, maintaining positive relationships, and preserving an honorable reputation and social standing in the community. "Face-saving" according to Fisher and Ury, however, "carries a derogatory flavor [in the English language]. People say, 'We are doing that just to let them save face,' implying that a little pretense has been created to allow someone to go along without feeling badly. The tone implies ridicule.... This is a grave misunderstanding of the role and importance of face-saving. Face-saving reflects a person's need to reconcile the stand he takes in a negotiation or an agreement with his principles and with his past words and deeds."[18]

17. *See* Jeanne M. Brett, Negotiating Globally—How to Negotiate Deals, Resolve Disputes, and Make Decisions Across Cultural Boundaries 8–9 (2001).

18. *See* Fisher & Ury, *supra* note 14, at 28.

Some parties also can have an interest in a solution appropriate for the community. In a study of mediation in an Islamic country, the author found:

> The settlement must be an appropriate outcome for the community as a whole as well as for the actual disputants. The group's interests guide the process. This is consistent with collectivist culture generally where communal and societal interests will preside over individual party interests. It enables this form of mediation to serve an educative role by articulating the social norms and providing acceptable behaviours and solutions for the disputants and for the community as a whole. In this way it differs from western mediations where confidentiality and privacy constraints, for the benefit of the individuals involved, limit a wider instructive role.[19]

Finally, consider these two international mediations where culturally shaped interests were not being met.[20] In one between two businessmen from Latin America and a U.S.-based multinational company, the lawyer from the U.S. Company could not fathom why the Latin American businessmen wanted an apology from the U.S. Company for its apparent negligence in losing a valuable commodity. It was not until the U.S. lawyers realized that the two businessmen had spent on legal fees and travel almost as much money as they were seeking in court that the U.S. lawyer understood that an interest other than money needed to be met. In another mediation, the defendant came to realize that a nonmonetary interest had to be met when the plaintiff from a West African country preferred litigating and losing (a significant risk according to the advice of his own attorney) than agreeing to compromise with a person whose business behavior offended the plaintiff's fundamental views of decency and personal ethics. These personal values had to be preserved in any mediated solution.

3. GOAL: OVERCOME IMPEDIMENTS

Disputing parties frequently encounter impediments in negotiations, and when they cannot overcome them on their own, they may turn to mediation. This section first suggests a methodology for classifying and overcoming impediments, and then it considers some of the distinctive obstacles that might arise in international negotiations and mediations.

(a) Classify Impediments

This excerpt explores one approach to identifying and overcoming impediments.[21]

---

19. *See* Ann Black, *Alternative Dispute Resolution in Brunei Darussalam: The Blending of Imported and Traditional Processes*, 13 BOND L. REV. 26 (Dec. 2001), *or* http://www.bond.edu.au/law/blr/vol13–2/black.doc.

20. Both disputes were mediated by co-author Harold Abramson.

21. The approach to conceptualizing impediments in this excerpt will be used throughout this chapter. However, Chapter 2 on International Conflict Resolution Pro-

HAROLD I. ABRAMSON, MEDIATION REPRESENTATION—ADVOCATING IN A PROBLEM–SOLVING PROCESS

104–08 (2004).

When you interview your client about the dispute and interests, you should inquire about any specific obstacles that might be impeding a negotiated resolution. This inquiry can be especially illuminating when you base your questions on an approach developed by one of a number of distinguished authors that have helped to demystify the murky world of impasse breaking.

My personal favorite, developed by Dr. Christopher Moore,[22] relies on taking three discrete steps that can produce a tailored-made strategy for overcoming impasses. His approach is built around his critical observation that impasses can be divided into five conflict categories that he labels as *relationship, data, value, interest, and structural.* Under his approach, you first inquire about the cause of the impasse; then you classify the cause in one of the five impasse categories; and finally you devise a suitable intervention for overcoming the impasse.

For instance, if parties are at an impasse because they have calculated different seller's lost profits that resulted from the buyer breaching a sales contract, you first would diagnose its cause, which may be different sales assumptions over the next twelve months. You would then classify the cause, which in this case, would be a data conflict. These first two steps enable you to get behind the impasse to the root of the conflict— conflicting views of a key assumption. This conclusion would give you the basis for devising a suitable intervention. In this case, you might simply focus your inquiry on the reasons for the different assumptions and ways to reconcile the differences.

This section explains Moore's five impasse categories as well as a few of his suggestions for how mediators might intervene * * *

Here are the five categories:

Relationship Conflicts can arise when parties are deeply upset with each other, cling to destructive misperceptions or stereotypes of each other, or suffer from poor communications.

The mediator can help parties identify the particular causes and help them classify the conflict as a relationship one. Then, the mediator can assist the parties in implementing a suitable intervention. The mediator might help the parties constructively explain to each other why they are upset, assist them in clarifying their perceptions of each other,

cesses offered another approach presented by Professor Robert Mnookin in which he classified impediments into strategic barriers, the principal/agent problem, cognitive barriers, and reactive devaluation.

22. *See* CHRISTOPHER MOORE, THE MEDIATION PROCESS 60–61 (1996) (Author presents Circle of Conflict in which five sources of conflicts are identified along with possible strategies for intervention).

focus on other ways to improve their communications, and cultivate their problem-solving attitudes. Relationship conflicts are common in disputes where parties distrust each other and are occupied with hurling threats.

Data Conflicts can be caused by inadequate, inaccurate, or untrustworthy information. Or, they can be caused by different views of what is relevant information or different interpretations of relevant data.

The mediator can help the parties identify the specific causes and to aid them in classifying the conflict as a data one. The mediator might intervene by helping the parties resolve what data are important, negotiate a process for collecting reliable data, or develop common criteria that can be used to assess the data. Data conflicts are common in court cases where parties may hold conflicting views of what happened, what might happen in court, or what is an appropriate interpretation of decisive data such as financial statements.

Interest Conflicts can arise when parties' substantive, procedural, or psychological/relationship wants conflict with each other.[23] Interest conflicts cover the classical positional conflict inherent in adversarial negotiations. They can be caused by parties wanting the same thing (such as property), wanting different amounts of the same thing (such as time), wanting different things that another is not prepared to give (such as one party wanting a precedent that the other party opposes), or even wanting something that another is not even aware of (such as an acknowledgment or an apology). Although many interest conflicts may be distributive, they can be integrative in nature, depending upon how the conflict is framed.

After clarifying the causes of the conflict and classifying it, the mediator can help parties pinpoint shared or non-conflicting wants, identify objective criteria for overcoming conflicting wants, and search for increase value and productive trades. Court cases typically present conflicting substantive wants because of the nature of the litigation process in which plaintiffs' attorneys draft complaints bursting with demands and defendants' attorneys draft answers that righteously reject almost everything.

Structural Conflicts often overlap with relationship conflicts and can be the murkiest to identify. The two most common as well as easiest structural obstacles to spot are impasses due to unequal bargaining power or impasses due to conflicting goals of attorneys and their clients, known as principal-agent conflicts. Other structural conflicts can be more subtle such as ones caused by no deadline, time constraints facing one side, missing key party, a party without sufficient settlement authority, geographical or technological limitations that impact disproportional-

23. In a problem-solving process in which the concept of "interests" performs such a vital and pervasive role, Moore's narrow and distinctive use of "interest" conflicts can be confusing. I prefer referring to wants or desire conflicts. Parties may reach an impasse because their substantive, procedural, or psychological wants or desires are in conflict with each other.

ly on one side, and unequal control of resources for resolving the conflict. Because structural conflicts frequently overlap with relationship conflicts, it can be difficult deciphering the nature of the conflict.

For example, an attorney-client conflict can be due to the structure of the relationship, a bad relationship between the attorney and client, or both. The mediator can help a side overcome an attorney-client conflict by exploring the details of the conflict. If it has arisen because the attorney thinks his client should settle while his client wants to pursue the litigation, for instance, the mediator can facilitate a discussion of the different views and ways for bridging possible differences. If the reason that the client wants to litigate is because she does not trust her attorney's advice, a reaction that suggests a relationship problem is impeding progress, the mediator might engage in initiatives to help mend the fractured attorney-client relationship.

A competent mediator will not do anything to neutralize a structural conflict due to a fair advantage of one party. When one side has greater bargaining power due to a stronger legal case, for instance, the mediator may help the disadvantaged party develop a realistic understanding of his legal options and then help the parties negotiate a resolution that recognizes the structural advantage of one side. When doing this, the mediator must be careful to avoid any appearance of siding with one party.

Value Conflicts can be the most intractable ones because they implicate a party's core personal or moral values. This narrow category can embrace matters of principle, ideology, or religion. A grassroots environmental group, for instance, may have difficulty settling with a housing developer because to do so might compromise the group's ideology to preserve all large tracks of open space.

The mediator may first help the parties clarify their core values because sometimes they might discover that their core values are not at stake or that both sides possess similar values and as a result, are not in conflict. Otherwise, the mediator may try to help parties work around their personal beliefs because compromise is usually unacceptable. The mediator can help parties search for an overarching shared goal, ways to avoid defining the problem in terms of a particular value, or solutions that do not compromise the value. Or, the mediator might assist parties in reaching an agreement to disagree. If the value conflict can be overcome by modifying the value, then, by definition, the conflict does not implicate a value. It is a conflict that fits within one of the other impasse categories.

Value conflicts can be difficult to recognize in court cases because values can be masked by all too familiar legal categories, arguments, and remedies. When a party wants to win in court, for example, the party may be motivated by the need for a clear victory to preserve a personal value—his personal integrity. A mediator might intervene by inquiring whether the party's personal integrity could be preserved in another process such as mediation.

(b) Overcoming Distinctively Cultural Impediments

In disputes between parties from different countries, impasses can arise due to conflicting predictions of what will happen in a foreign forum if the dispute is not settled (conflicting views of the BATNA). Under the section on international disputes suitable for mediations, we considered the challenges of predicting what would happen if the dispute were to be resolved in a foreign court or in international arbitration. This section considers another source of impasses, ones due to cultural differences—the subject of Chapter 3 on "The Role of Culture in Transborder Dispute Resolution." Any study of culture reveals numerous examples of behavior common in one culture that could be misinterpreted by someone brought up in another culture.

Miscommunication presents one area ripe for impasses in cross-cultural encounters, especially when parties are sharing information between low-context and high-context cultures. Of course, information sharing plays a central and decisive role in how a negotiation unfolds, regardless of the negotiation approach used. The cultural upbringing of each party can influence how information is conveyed by one party to another and how it is interpreted by the other party as well.

In a problem-solving approach, parties need to accurately share essential information in order to create value and locate creative, integrative solutions. In low-context cultures such as the United States, people share information overtly, with meanings conveyed in explicit and elaborate communication codes. The words spoken are what counts. In high-context cultures (such as Japan and China), words are only part of the broader shared social and cultural context for sharing information with others.[24] This next excerpt suggests how to convey information between high-and low-context cultures.

JEANNE M. BRETT, NEGOTIATING GLOBALLY— HOW TO NEGOTIATE DEALS, RESOLVE DISPUTES, AND MAKE DECISIONS ACROSS CULTURAL BOUNDARIES

14, 61–72 (2001).

Information is the currency of negotiation. Information about BATNAs, status, and other fair standards affects distributive agreements. Information about interests and priorities affects integrative agreements.

24. *See* Ting–Toomey, *Toward a Theory of Conflict and Culture, in* COMMUNICATION, CULTURE, AND ORGANIZATIONAL PROCESSES 71, 75–82 (W. Gudykuns, L.P. Stewart & S. Ting–Toomey eds., 1985).

When negotiators do not understand the information conveyed by the other party, integrative potential is almost always left on the table, and sometimes negotiations end in impasse.

* * *

Culture affects whether information is conveyed directly, with meaning on the surface of the communication, or indirectly, with meaning conveyed within the context of the message. Culture also affects whether information is conveyed at all.

* * *

Information

* * *

Cartoon negotiators [referring to a study] who reach integrative agreements have two characteristics in common. They are very interested in information in negotiation, and they have a strategy for getting it. There are three strategies for acquiring the necessary information to reach integrative agreements. All appear to be equally effective. [T]hey are not used with the same frequency in all cultures. Negotiators can share information directly with a series of questions and answers, comments on mutual interests and differences, and feedback. They can share information indirectly via a series of proposals, particularly multi-issue proposals. Negotiators can also agree to search for a second agreement after a first agreement has been reached. [The first two strategies are explained in this excerpt.]

Sharing Information Directly. Direct information sharing could be a series of questions and answers, comments on mutual interests and differences, or feedback about the correctness of a negotiator's inference. One party asks a question about the other party's preferences; the other party answers honestly and asks her own question in return. Negotiators might comment on what issues seem to be in their mutual interest and what issues are more important to one party than the other and correct erroneous conclusions * * *

Trust gets built in cultures where negotiators are comfortable with direct information exchange, when information is given by one negotiator and reciprocated by the other. Trust grows as each negotiator recognizes that the other negotiator is using the information provided to construct an agreement that takes into account both parties' interests. As trust grows, negotiators share more information and improve their joint agreement. Reciprocity is key to building trust. Just as trust blooms with reciprocal information sharing, trust fades when information is not reciprocated. Here is some advice for direct information sharing:

- Ask questions about interests or priorities. In general, ask questions about things that you would be willing to share information about in return. Asking questions has two purposes: getting information and building trust. Ask questions about reservation price or the absolute value or cost of an issue to the other party cautiously. If he answers such a question, he is likely to turn the question around and ask you to share your reservation price, which you may not want to do. When you fail to answer, trust is broken: you did not reciprocate.

- Give a little information about your own interests or priorities and then ask the question. This gives the other party something in advance of answering the question * * *

Negotiators from cultures where direct information sharing is not normative scoff at asking questions. Chinese managers in Beijing said to me, "Why should we bother asking the other party questions? We won't believe his answers, and he won't believe ours!" To be effective, direct information sharing requires truth telling, and truth telling requires trust. When there is no basis for trust, a different information-sharing strategy is needed. * * *

Sharing Information Indirectly. Indirect information sharing could be a series of proposals and counterproposals. Information gets shared in the following way. If you assume that the other will only make a proposal that is favorable to her interests, then you can infer the other party's priorities by noting how she changes your proposal in making a counterproposal. Consider a series of proposals that might be made in the Cartoon negotiation * * * The seller might propose $70,000 per episode, six runs, and up-front payment. The buyer might counteroffer $30,000 per episode, eight runs, and equal payments over the five-year contract. The first round of proposals does little more than provide a distributive picture for each party. The second round of proposals may be a bit more revealing. The seller might counter by saying, "If you want eight runs, I want payment up front." Multi-issue proposals force negotiators to link issues. When negotiators link issues, they build trade-offs into their deal. If the seller had linked price into a multi-issue proposal—"If you want eight runs, I want $60,000 per episode up front"—his proposal would have specified both the distributive outcome and the integrative agreement.

The Japanese negotiators in our study stand out in their use of proposals. [T]hey use proposals much more than expected. When you read through the transcripts of the Japanese negotiations and the U.S. negotiations, the difference in use of proposals is immediately noticeable. The Japanese negotiators might open the negotiation with a proposal. They are busy making proposals and counterproposals from the very beginning of the negotiation. The U.S. negotiators tend to begin by asking questions and wait to make proposals until after they have run out of questions.

* * *

When negotiators, like many of the Israelis in our study, are motivated to be self-interested (maximize their own outcome), the exchange of multi-issue proposals can result in an integrative agreement.

Self-interested negotiators can infer each other's priorities from the exchange of proposals. The proposal format keeps issues linked and forces concessions on low-priority issues in return for gains on high-priority issues.

When negotiators, like many of the Germans in our study, are motivated to be cooperative (maximize their own and the other's outcome), they do not need to link all issues into a proposal to reach an integrative agreement. They can reach agreements one issue at a time and reach an integrative agreement. They do so because they share information about priorities and engage in extended reciprocity. They concede on a low-priority issue because they expect a reciprocal concession from the other party on a subsequent issue that has high priority. . . .

Equivalent Proposals. Equivalent proposals are a particularly effective indirect information-sharing strategy when the other party is not forthcoming about preferences, refuses to make a counterproposal, or may be lying about her priorities and interests. Note the almost equivalent proposals in the context of the Cartoon negotiation. . . . Option A: price $46,000 per episode, six runs, and 25 percent up front and 25 percent in years 1–3 nets the buyer $1.5 million and the seller $0.9 million. If the seller turns down the offer, refusing to say more than ''not good enough,'' the buyer could put a second offer on the table, for example, . . . $55,000 per episode, eight runs, and 100 percent up front. The buyer then asks the seller whether he likes A or B better. If the answer is B. the buyer, knowing that the two proposals are almost equivalent from his own perspective, can then infer that the seller must be extremely sensitive to financing.

Dealing with Negotiators You Think Are Lying About Preferences.

Equivalent proposals are also an extremely useful way to manage a negotiator whom you think is lying about her preferences or a negotiator who puts a new issue on the table after you thought you had an agreement. In either case, make one proposal that you think should be acceptable and another that integrates the new issue or gives more on the issue you think has a false priority. Make sure the proposals are equivalent to you and anchored to give you as high a distributive outcome as you think is possible.

Alternatives J and K provide an example of using proposals to learn priorities when you think the other party is being less than forthright. Suppose the seller is suggesting that price is more important than receiving 100 percent of the money up front. The buyer could propose alternative J, which gives more on price and less on financing, and alternative K, which gives less on price and more on financing. The seller is now faced with deciding just how important price is in the context of financing. . . . Perhaps one reason why the Chinese managers with whom I worked in Beijing like using proposals is their concern with truth telling. Proposals, especially equivalent proposals, act like a truth serum.

———————

Consider these examples of how a party brought up in the U.S. could misinterpret a Chinese party's negotiation behavior or how a party with a Chinese cultural upbringing could misinterpret a U.S. party's behavior.[25]

Haggling and Compromise, Not Concession and Capitulation

"These moral values (adherence to hierarchical relationships to yield harmony and more concerned about finding the way than the truth) express themselves in the Chinese negotiating style. Chinese negotiators are more concerned with the means than the end, with the process more than the goal. The best compromises are derived only through the ritual back-and-forth of haggling. This process cannot be cut short. And a compromise allows the two sides to hold equally valid positions. While Americans tend to believe that the truth, as they see it, is worth arguing over and even getting angry about, the Chinese believe that the way is hard to find and so rely on haggling to settle differences."

No Without Saying No

"Rather than just saying no outright, Chinese businesspeople are more likely to change the subject, turn silent, ask another question, or respond by using ambiguous and vaguely positive expressions with subtle negative implications, such as *hai bu* cuo ("seems not wrong"), hai *hao* ("seems fairly all right"), *and hai xing or hai ke yi* ("appears fairly passable")."

These indirect means of rejecting proposals can result in a U.S. party, who is accustomed to confidently and unambiguously uttering "no" when called for and are accustomed to others doing the same, misinterpreting a Chinese "no" as close to agreement if not an agreement.

Harmonious Relationship More Important that the Contract

25. These quotes are selected from John L. Graham & N. Mark Lam, *The Chinese Negotiation*, Harv. Bus. Rev. 82, 84–90 (Oct. 2003) (Adapted and reprinted by permission of Harvard Business Review). The comments without quotations are not part of the article.

"In China, [i]n the final analysis, trust and harmony are more important to Chinese businesspeople than any piece of paper."

Such a disinterest by the Chinese party in reducing matters to writing might be misinterpreted by the U.S. party as avoiding particular commitments.

Nothing Settled Until Everything Settled

"Chinese negotiators tend to talk about those issues all at once, skipping among them, and from the Americans' point of view, seemingly never settling anything.... This difference in style can frustrate Westerners accustomed to measuring progress in a linear way.... [T]his difference in thinking style is the source of the greatest tension between negotiation teams. It also often causes Americans to make unnecessary concessions right before the Chinese announce their agreement.... Be prepared to discuss all issues simultaneously and in an apparently haphazard order. Nothing is settled until everything is."

Extreme Opening Offers

"Chinese negotiators will pad their offers with more room to maneuver than most Americans are used to, and they will make concessions on price with great reluctance and only after lengthy discussions. In fact, we have often seen Americans laugh at the Chinese base price or get angry at 'unreasonable' Chinese counteroffers.... In defending price positions, the Chinese use patience and silence as formidable weapons against American impatience and volubility. Westerners should not be put off by aggressive first offers by the Chinese; they expect both sides to make concessions eventually, particularly on prices."

Need to Save Face

"In Chinese business culture, a person's reputation and social standing rest on saving face. If Westerners cause the Chinese embarrassment or lost of composure, even unintentionally, it can be disastrous for business negotiations. The Chinese notion of saving face is closely associated with American concepts of dignity and prestige. *Mianzi* defines a person's place in his social network; it is the most important measure of social worth.... [W]hen those negotiating with the Chinese break promises or display anger, frustration, or aggression at the negotiation table, it results in a mutual lost of face. In the West, sometimes a mock tantrum is used as a negotiating tactic, but in China it invariably back-

> fires one way or another. Causing the Chinese business partner who brought you to the table to lost mianzi is no mere faux pas; it's a disaster.''

Cultural differences can be handled in the same way as you would deal with any impediment to settlement. Under the Moore approach, you would classify any difference and then develop a suitable intervention. Many cultural obstacles can be classified as interest conflicts that arise due to the parties' different cultural upbringings, upbringings that can foster conflicting wants and approaches to the negotiation. Such obstacles can arise in disputes between parties from different countries or between parties from within the same country when one party comes from a different region, a recently immigrated family, or a different religious, ethnic, or professional group. For bridging any cultural gaps, you might use the five-step approach examined in Chapter 3, Section E.

Notes and Questions

1. Do you think that the concept of interests is a universal or cultural one?

2. Does the definition of saving-face offered by Fisher and Ury comport with your personal view of the concept? Do you think their definition comports with the Asian view?

3. Are there any interests that you might identify for your client, the plaintiff, in the Mitsubishi–Soler Dispute that might be distinctively cultural? In order to avoid a miscommunication impasse, how might you convey information about your client's interests to the Japanese business parties who may process information indirectly?

4. An attorney could select a negotiation approach other than problem-solving. A different approach would impact on the choices made throughout the mediation process. If you were to use an adversarial, positional approach, what interests would you identify for the plaintiff in the Mitsubishi–Soler Dispute?

5. Consider the suggested list of possible cultural differences between a U.S. and Chinese negotiator that could become an obstacle to settlement. Select one for further analysis and recommend a negotiation strategy that would avoid the potential miscommunication and impasse, using the five-step approach for bridging cultural gaps suggested in Chapter 3, Section E.

6. Classify the likely cultural impediments in the Mitsubishi–Soler Dispute and suggest possible strategies for overcoming them.

4. USE PROACTIVELY THE PRESENCE OF THE MEDIATOR[26]

This section and the following one examine how to negotiate in mediations, first by identifying options for enlisting assistance from the

26. For a full discussion of ways that a problem-solving advocate might take advantage of the mediator's presence, *see* ABRAM- SON, *supra* note 9, at chs. 5.1, 4.2 (a) & (b), 3.2, 1.5, 1.6, and 2.4.

mediator and then by developing a representation plan for key junctures in the mediation process.

You will probably be in mediation for one of two reasons. You elected to use mediation because you and your client thought that a mediator might help the two sides resolve the dispute. Or, you were compelled to go into mediation. In both scenarios, you need to figure out how to benefit from this new person in the room. For you to take advantage of the mediator's presence, you ought to be familiar with how a mediator can contribute to resolving a dispute. What a mediator might do depends on her training, her practices, and what parties expect from her. Her various contributions can vary across cultures.

A mediator's role in managing the mediation process can be shaped by her cultural experiences. In an illuminating frame for examining mediator approaches, Dr. Christopher Moore suggests that to meet the needs of parties, "intermediaries also differ with respect to the degree of directiveness or control that they exercise over the dispute resolution process and the relative emphasis they place on the substantive, procedural, and psychological/relationship interests of the parties."[27]

> [I]ntermediaries vary along a continuum from highly directive to highly nondirective with respect to substantive issues, the problem-solving process, and the management of relationships between the parties. Kolb described the ideal types at the two ends of this spectrum: the 'orchestrators' and the 'dealmakers,' In brief, orchestrators generally focus on empowering parties to make their own decision: they provide mainly procedural assistance, and occasionally help in establishing or building relationships. They are less directive than are dealmakers and intervene primarily when it is clear that the parties are not capable of making progress toward a settlement on their own.

> In contrast, dealmakers are often highly directive in relation to both process and the substantive issues under discussion. Generally, they are very prescriptive and directive with respect to problem-solving steps, questions of who talks and to whom, types of forum (joint sessions or private meetings), and the types of interventions made. Dealmakers are also typically much more involved in substantive discussions and on occasion may provide substantive information to the parties, voice their opinion on issues under discussion, or actively work to put together a deal that will be mutually acceptable to the parties.

Over this continuum, mediators' roles can range from transformative to facilitative/problem-solving to evaluative to varying degrees of directiveness—including evaluative and wisely directive—to arbitral decision-making. Your ability to develop an effective representation plan depends on a clear understanding of the particular role(s) that will be

---

27. CHRISTOPHER MOORE, THE MEDIATION PROCESS—PRACTICAL STRATEGIES FOR RESOLVING CONFLICT 53–54 (2d ed. 1996).

performed by your mediator. Therefore, it is vital for you to clarify your mediator's role(s) before the first mediation session. The next four subsections consider the possible roles of mediators and the last subsection examines how each role can impact how you represent your client in the mediation.

(a) Examine the U.S. Problem–Solving Approach

In cross-cultural mediations, you should not mistakenly approach representation assuming that the mediator will perform as you are accustomed to mediators performing. U.S. practices reflect a culturally shaped view of mediation, a view that is vividly conveyed in the highly regarded Model Standards of Conduct for Mediators.[28] The definition of mediation in the Preface of Model Standards reveals much about how many people in the United States envision the mediator's role.

> Mediation is a process in which an impartial third party—a mediator—facilitates the resolution of a dispute by promoting voluntary agreement (or "self determination") by the parties to the dispute. A Mediator facilitates communications, promotes understanding, focuses the parties on their interests, and seeks creative problem solving to enable the parties to reach their own agreement. These standards give meaning to this definition of mediation.

This problem-solving/facilitative role for the mediator is implemented in three of the model standards. The first one on "Self–Determination" stresses that "the fundamental principle" of mediation provides that parties reach "a voluntary, *uncoerced* agreement" (emphasis added). The Comments further explain that: "The mediator may provide information about the process, raise issues, and help parties explore options. The primary role of the mediator is to facilitate a voluntary resolution of a dispute. Parties shall be given the opportunity to consider all proposed options. A mediator cannot personally ensure that each party has made a fully informed choice to reach a particular agreement, but it is a good practice for the mediator to make the parties aware of the importance of consulting other professionals, where appropriate, to help them make informed decisions."

The second and sixth standards reinforce party self-determination. The second standard on "Impartiality" views as "central to the mediation process" the obligation of the mediator to "remain impartial and evenhanded." The sixth standard on "Quality of the Process" directs the mediator to conduct the process in a "manner consistent with the principle of self determination by the parties." The Comments empha-

28. The Model Standards were prepared and approved by three leading organizations in the United States dispute resolution field: American Arbitration Association, the Litigation and Dispute Resolution Sections of the American Bar Association, and the Society of Professionals in Dispute Resolution (1992–1994). For a discussion of the Model Standards by the chair of the drafting committee, see John Feerick, *Toward Uniform Standards of Conduct for Mediators*, 38 S. Tex. L. Rev. 455 (1997).

size that the mediator should "refrain from giving professional advice. Where appropriate, a mediator should recommend that parties seek outside professional advice, or consider resolving their dispute through arbitration, counseling, neutral evaluation, or other processes."

In an in-depth analysis of the concept of party-self-determination, Professor Welsh suggests a more nuanced definition:

> In response to the concern that the original rich vision of self-determination is being lost, there may be a need to clarify the definition of self-determination in statutes, rules and ethical guidelines. It must be made clear that self-determination is different than parties' free will and requires more protection than parties' free will has received in traditional negotiation or in judicially-hosted settlement conferences. Specifically, statutes, rules, and ethical guidelines regarding self-determination could be rewritten to include: the parties' active and direct participation, communication, and negotiation; the parties' identification and selection of the interests and substantive norms which should guide the creation of settlement options; the parties' creation of potential settlement options; and the parties' control over the final outcome. In other words, the definitions should reference the indicia of party empowerment.[29]

Here is a fuller description of the role of the mediator in a facilitative problem-solving process. The specially trained neutral structures a process that provides disputing parties an opportunity to fashion enduring and inventive solutions that can go beyond what a court might be willing to do. In contrast with the more familiar settlement conference before a judge, the mediator has no decision-making power, maintains strict confidentiality, and involves clients deeply in the settlement process.

The mediator serves as the guide by managing a structured discussion that includes gathering specific information, identifying issues, interests, and impediments, and generating, assessing, and selecting options for settlement. The mediator employs a mix of techniques that are designed to encourage client involvement, explore clients' interests, and create a collaborative environment for settling the dispute. The mediator poses open-ended and focused questions, re-frames issues, conducts brainstorming session, and uses strategies for defusing tensions and overcoming impasses. The mediator may use private caucuses to gain confidential information and specialized methods for helping participants evaluate the strengths and weaknesses of their legal case. If the dispute does not settle, the mediator may help the participants design an alternative process for ultimately resolving the conflict.

During the mediation, you have a number of discrete opportunities for proactively enlisting assistance from the mediator.

---

29. *See* Nancy A. Welsh, *The Thinning Vision of Self-Determination in Court-Connected Mediation: The Inevitable Price of Institutionalization?*, 6 HARV. NEGOT. L. REV. 1, 80 (2001).

You might ask the mediator to:

- Facilitate the negotiation of a problem-solving process.

- Promote communications through the use of questioning and listening techniques.

- Manage the emotional dimensions of the conflict.

- Help generate options for settlement (e.g. brainstorming).

- Structure separately the inventing and deciding of settlement options.

- Help identify and overcome impediments to settlement, including the chronic impediment of clashing views of the court outcome (BATNA).

You also might solicit the mediator to use her control of the mediation stages to:

- Use the mediator's opening statement to set up a problem-solving process.

- Use the information gathering stage to secure venting and information for the specific purposes of understanding issues, interests, and impediments. [Opening Statements of Participants, First Joint Session, and First Caucus]

- Use the stage of identifying issues, interests, and impediments to ensure that this key information is clearly elucidated.

- Use the agenda formulation stage to ensure key issues and impediments are addressed.

- Use the overcoming impediments stage to overcome particular obstacles to settlement.

- Use the generating options stage to ensure creative ideas are developed. [inventing stage]

- Use the assessing and selecting options stage to ensure that your client's interests are met. [deciding stage]

- Use the concluding stage to ensure that any written settlement meets your client's interests or if no settlement, a suitable exit plan is formulated.

This classically U.S. problem-solving approach, adopted in the Model Standards and elaborated in the landmark negotiation book, *Getting to Yes*, has been explicitly incorporated in some mediation rules including international ones. For instance, it was copied almost verbatim in the rules negotiated between the Center for Public Resources (CPR), a U.S. based dispute resolution organization, and the China Council for the Promotion of International Trade (CCPIT), a Chinese based one when the two organizations formed the U.S. China Business Mediation Center. Consider Section 3 on Negotiations:[30]

---

30. *See* The CPR/CCPIT Mediation Procedure For Disputes Submitted to the U.S.- China Business Mediation Center, Section 3 (2004).

The mediator(s) may facilitate settlement in any manner the mediator(s) believe is appropriate. The mediator(s) shall help the parties focus on their underlying interests and concerns, explore resolution alternatives and develop settlement options.

The parties are expected to initiate and convey to the mediator(s) as many proposals for settlement as possible. Each party shall provide a rationale for any settlement terms proposed to the mediator(s).

Although the Model Standards' particular vision of the mediator's role reflects a widely practiced approach, and the dominate approach to training mediators in the United States , it is not the only one used. No culture can claim a single, monolithic mediation approach, and the United States is no exception. Two other substantially used approaches are evaluative and transformative mediation. A definition of evaluative mediation is provided in Subsection 4(b). Here is a definition of transformative mediation.

A transformative mediator engages in a mediation practice based on communication and relational theory. Instead of promoting the goal of settlement for the parties, the transformative mediator allows the parties to determine their own direction and supports the parties' own opportunities for perspective-taking, deliberation, and decision-making. The mediator focuses on the parties' interactions and supports their shifts from destructive and alienating interactions to more constructive and open interactions (referred to as empowerment and recognition shifts). In this model, parties are likely to be able to make positive changes in their interactions with each other and, consequently, find acceptable resolution for themselves, where such terms genuinely exist.[31]

The next section explores how a continuum of more directive approaches can be found in both the United States and around the globe.

Notes and Questions

What are the cultural as well as universal features of the U.S. version of problem-solving mediation?

(b) Search for Evaluation Power in Mediation Law, Rules, and Practice

Even when mediation law, rules, or practice contemplate a problem-solving process, they might confer on the mediator the power to evalu-

---

31. *See* ABRAMSON, *supra* note 9, at 71–72. *Also see* ROBERT A. BARUCH BUSH & JOSEPH P. FOLGER, THE PROMISE OF MEDIATION—RESPONDING TO CONFLICT THROUGH EMPOWERMENT AND RECOGNITION (1994). For an extensive resource list, see www.transformativemediation.org.

ate, usually in the form of the power to make recommendations. The recommendation power might include the power to evaluate the legal case, assess the reasonableness of settlement options, or offer settlement suggestions. As will be examined in Subsection 4(e), this short add-on power can change profoundly the character of the mediation process.

Examples of mediator recommendation power can be found domestically, in foreign domestic laws, and in the United Nation's model law. Mediator power to make recommendations was included in the recently adopted AAA International Dispute Resolution Procedures,[32] the Indian Arbitration and Conciliation Act of 1996,[33] and the new Model Law on International Commercial Conciliation of the United Nations Commission on International Trade Law.[34]

In the United States, even though the applicable law or rules might be silent on the subject, a widespread practice of mediators offering various types of evaluations can be found. The evaluative role of U.S. mediators can be described as follows:

> Evaluative: An evaluative mediator assists the participants in breaking impasses by contributing her views of the merits of the legal case, the consequences of failure to settle, and the benefits of particular settlement proposals. For instance, if each side has strongly conflicting views of the legal merits, the neutral might try to break the impasse by giving an evaluation of the merits of the dispute. By predicting the likely outcome in the adjudicatory forum, the neutral gives the participants a basis against which to assess the attractiveness of emerging options for settlement. If the case is not settling, the neutral might suggest how failure would impact on the interests of each party. If each side has strongly conflicting views of the benefits of a particular settlement proposal, the neutral might give an assessment of how the proposal benefits each side. The neutral might even present a proposal for adoption by the participants (sometimes known as the "mediator's proposal"). * * *[35]

Other unusual arrangements with the mediator having the power to recommend also can be encountered abroad. In one scheme not used

---

32. *See* Rule M–10 Authority of the Mediator, American Arbitration Association, International Dispute Resolution Procedures (Including Mediation and Arbitration Rules), Amended and Effective 1 July, 2003.

33. The Indian Arbitration and Conciliation Act of 1996, Article 67(4), adopted verbatim the Article 7(4) of the UNCITRAL 1980 Conciliation Rules.

34. United Nations General Assembly, Resolution 57/18 Model Law on Interna-

tional Commercial Conciliation of the United Nations Commission on International Trade Law, art. 6(4) (Jan. 24, 2003). The UNCITRAL Model Law incorporated the power to make proposals for settlement found in the UNCITRAL Conciliation Rules, art. 7(4) (Report of the UNCITRAL on the Work of it's Thirteenth Session, GAOR, Thirty-fifth Session, Supplement, No. 17, UN Document No. A/35/17 (1980)).

35. *See* ABRAMSON, *supra* note 9, at 71.

domestically in the United States, the mediator investigates the facts and law and issues a written report containing her recommendations. In another unfamiliar scheme, each party designates a mediator and then the mediators meet with each other to hammer out a resolution that is then presented to the parties for their confirmation.

(c) Search for Directive Behavior in Mediation Practice

Although laws and rules typically do not specifically authorize the mediator to be directive, they can indirectly restrict the degree of directiveness by requiring mediators to conduct the process in a way that ensures party-self determination and informed consent. Occasionally, they can preempt the directive power by mandating a facilitative approach. Regardless of the laws and rules, however, many mediators can be quite directive in practice by pressuring parties to agree to certain outcomes.

(1) Evaluatively Directive Mediators

Mediators who evaluate are not necessarily directive because mediators can offer evaluations without putting pressure on parties to adopt them.[36] In theory, evaluative power and directive power are different. In the U.S., however, mediators can implement their evaluative power by leaning toward directiveness. They can gently encourage or assertively press parties to move toward or adopt their evaluations.

In Continental Europe, the mediator's expected, if not preferred, role can be influenced by the mediator's civil law upbringing. In a study that compares mediation practices in Australia, a common law jurisdiction, with Germany, a civil law jurisdiction, Professor Nadja Alexander noted that in Germany: "Like the government legal centres offering conciliation services, most of the dispute resolution processes associated with these conciliation centres [chambers of commerce] do not follow an interest-based mediation model. Rather, the processes offered tend to be directive, interventionist and rights-based in nature." She then described similar practices by German judges who try to settle cases:

> German judges are required by law to attempt to settle a matter before hearing the case. This requirement has a long tradition in Germany and other civil law countries. * * * By comparison, no such legal requirement exists in Australia or

---

36. Professor Riskin, who recently modified his well known mediator classification system by replacing his facilitative-evaluative distinction with an elicitive-directive distinction, carefully distinguished the new label of directive from the old label of evaluative by pointing out that mediator evaluations can be either directive or non-directive. Directive mediators direct the parties toward a particular perspective or outcome while elicitive mediators elicits parties' perspectives and preferences. *See*

Leonard L. Riskin, *Decisionmaking in Mediation: The New Old Grid and the New New Grid System*, 79 NOTRE DAME L. REV. 1, 17–20, 30–33 (2003).

For an article that explores the boundaries of mediator evaluation as primarily a non-directive technique, *see* Donald Weckstein, *In Praise of Party Empowerment—and of Mediator Activism*, 33 WILLAMETTE L. REV. 501, 561–62 (1997).

other common law jurisdictions, although judicial attempts to get parties to settle may occur in some common law jurisdictions as a matter of practice rather than law.

Strictly speaking the civil law judicial 'settlement' function is not a form of court-related mediation, as it takes place within the courtroom and is conducted by the judge, who will directly hear the matter. In practice, judges' attempts to encourage parties to settle are very legalistic and interventionist. In fact, the majority of judges do not engage in a process that could be compared with facilitative mediation. Nevertheless this 'mediative' function of the judicial role has led to one of two views amongst the members of the German judiciary: (1) Mediation already occurs in the courtroom and therefore court-related programs are unnecessary; or (2) As mediation is, as a matter of law, part of the judicial role, judges are the natural and rightful mediators of disputes that would or could otherwise be determined by a court of law.

* * *

Finally, the settlement function of the German judge must be consistent with the overall objective of the judicial role, namely to find a legal solution for the disputants. According to Art 20 II of the German Basic Law the judicial role is bound by law and justice. Therefore, even while exercising their settlement function, German judges are required to lead parties towards a solution consistent with the relevant legal norms.[37]

A recent Italian legislative decree implementing a law regulating mediation of company disputes further reflected the evaluative directive attitude that can be found in civil law jurisdictions. In critiquing the decree, Italian Law Professor Giuseppe De Palo describes how it would operate:

The big problem with this legislative decree on mediation in corporate disputes comes from article 40 of Decree 5/2003, which mandates an "evaluative" mediation process. In fact, pursuant to article 40, if the parties are unable to agree, the mediator must make a final settlement proposal, which will be memorialized in a post-mediation report attesting the failure of mediation. Furthermore, article 40 continues, the parties must "take a definitive position" with respect of the mediator's final proposal, declaring what they would instead be willing to offer and accept. These party declarations, which are also mandated for inclusion in the post-mediation report, might then be used by the judge in any ensuring legal proceedings for fee-shifting.[38]

37. *See* N. Alexander, *What's Law Got to Do with It? Mapping Modern Mediation Movements in Civil and Common Law Jurisdictions*, 13 Bond L. Rev. 16, 23, 27–28 (Dec. 2001), *at* http://

www.bond.edu.au/law/blr/vol13–2/Alexander.doc.

38. *See* Giuseppe De Palo, *Crisis of Courts and the Italian Mediation Debate*,

Because many mediators within the U.S. and around the globe are known to exercise directively any evaluative power, you should take care to determine if your mediator might be directive in mediation.

(2) Wisely Directive Mediators

In some countries, disputing parties have experience with a "wise" third party who is a source of the "right" answers and is assertively directive. The wisely directive mediator investigates the dispute, evaluates it, and formulates and promotes solutions based on the wisdom for which he or she was selected. That wisdom could be informed by local cultural norms, religious values, and the mediator's leadership position, age, and legal knowledge. Parties expect to receive the evaluations and answers; parties also are expected to accept them. Therefore, while the role of the wise third party may be to "mediate," the third party effectively functions as a quasi-adjudicator imposing a resolution on the parties. Wisely directive mediators can be found in some Islamic countries and China, among other places.

Consider these mediation practices that are influenced by Islam and used in some Arab cultures. One observer, George Irani, noted that:

> In Lebanese culture, as in Arab culture in general, the mediator is perceived as someone having all the answers and solutions. He therefore has a great deal of power and responsibility. As one participant put it: 'If [the third party] does not provide the answers, he or she is not really respected or considered to be legitimate.[39]

Based on a study of three public disputes and his own experiences living and teaching in Cairo, John Murray observed the assertive role of third parties in Egypt.

> * * * [I]t is acceptable, indeed expected, that the third party will also apply pressure to help bring about agreement. This is why the resources and status of the third party are so valuable. Third-party pressure is welcomed even by those who feel its sting. * * *[40]

In a study of traditional rural mediation in Brunei Darussalam, a country with a strong Islamic influence, the author, Ann Black, documented these mediator behaviors:

> Equally important is for the mediator to have good knowledge of the rules to apply and to employ these to determine what is the right or fair outcome, and then to direct and guide the parties towards a similar solution. An ability to persuade,

INT'L J. OF DISP. RESOL. 17, 18 (Beilage–Germany, 2003).

39. *See* George Irani, *Islamic Mediation Techniques for Middle East Conflicts*, 3 MID. E. REV. OF INT'L AFF. 4 (June 1999).

40. *See* J.S. Murray, *The Cairo Stories: Some Reflections on Conflict Resolution in Egypt*, NEG. J. 39, 53–54 (Jan. 1997).

even to coerce parties by moral imperatives, to a settlement, is an attribute.[41]

In the chart below, Ms. Black highlighted differences between traditional mediation in a collectivist society of the sort she studied in Borneo and the Western form of mediation found in individualistic societies.[42]

**Table 1 Comparison of Features of Western
and Traditional Mediation**

Western /Independent Mediation [INDIVIDUALIST CULTURE]	Traditional/Iban Mediation [COLLECTIVIST CULTURE]
Goal of mediation is for parties to reach an agreement that ends the dispute to their mutual satisfaction.	Goal of mediation is to end the dispute between parties so that harmony can return to the longhouse community.
***	***
Mediators should not have social ties, or be related to, the disputants.	Mediators are connected to the disputants through social relationships or kinship ties.
Accreditation has objective basis—such as courses, professional qualifications, recognition by authoritative bodies.	Accreditation has subjective basis—trust and respect of that community. There is no training, other than community enculturation.
***	***
Mediations occur in private settings—an office/room neutral for the parties.	Mediations typically occur in a public setting—*raui* of the longhouse.
***	***
Mediators should be impartial, objective and even-handed.	Mediators should be fair, kind, loving and subjectively appraise options.
Criticism of disputants' behaviour or character is unacceptable.	Criticism is acceptable where this is relevant to the dispute.
Parties direct the outcome—mediator should not persuade or coerce.	Moral persuasion and coercion can be justified in the interests of the longhouse community.

---

41. *See* Black, *supra* note 19.

42. *See* Black, *supra* note 19, at 21, *or* http://www.bond.edu.au/law/blr/vol13–2/black.doc.

She also observed how the role of the traditional mediator, the wise third party who promotes particular outcomes, can diminish when people leave the intimacy of their villages that are bound by social and kinship ties for more anonymous living in urban areas.

Finally, focusing on private commercial disputes (intellectual property disputes) in a paper presented to an international conference on mediation, the Chairman of the Higher Board of Euro–Arab Arbitration System and a lawyer in Saudi Arabia, Salah Al–Hejailan, gave this wisely directive description of the mediator's role:

> The mediator is normally a person of a prestigious social standing who is known for his thorough knowledge, honesty and impartiality. Seniority and respect for elders are particularly resonant in the Arab World. Such a person enjoys the respect of the disputants who invariably feel satisfied with any award he may deem appropriate.[43]

China has its own long and rich history of mediation practice that has led to ten million mediators now serving on the People's Mediation Committees. These mediators, however, do not practice facilitative problem-solving mediation; their practice is fashioned by their own legacy.[44] Rather than maintaining impartiality and focusing primarily on ensuring party self-determination as prescribed in the Model Standards in the United States, these mediators come out of a tradition closer to the wisely directive approach. For over two thousand years, Chinese mediation practices have been shaped by traditional Confucian values of promoting self-criticism and compromising to preserve social harmony and personal relationships as well as centuries of imperial rule and control influenced by Confucian thought. During the twentieth century, mediation practices have been further influenced and reinforced by Maoist principles of promoting the Communist Party's values through self-criticism, education, and persuasion especially during the Cultural Revolution, post-Maoist Communist ideology tempered by a tenacious commitment to modernization, and recent Chinese government initiatives to modernize mediation practices.

Today, mediators serving on the People's Mediation Committees are known to stray from neutrality by taking sides and having some connection with the parties, and they can freely promote various social values, direct parties especially about what is right and wrong, and recommend solutions if not pressure parties to adopt them.[45] However, whether they

43. *See* Salah Al–Hejailan, *Mediation as a Means for Amicable Settlement of Disputes in Arab Countries* presented to WIPO Conference on Mediation, Geneva, Switzerland (Mar. 29, 1996), *at* http://arbiter.wipo.int/events/conferences/1996/hejailan.html.

44. *See* Eric Glassman, *The Function of Mediation in China: Examining the Impact of Regulations Governing the People's Mediation Committees*, 10 UCLA PACIFIC BASIN L.J. 460 (1992).

45. *See* Michael T. Colatrella, '*Court-Performed*' *Mediation in the People's Republic of China: A Proposed Model to Improve the United States Federal District Courts' Mediation Programs*, 15 OHIO ST. J. ON DISP. RESOL. 391, 404–408 (2000) ; Robert Perkovich, *A Comparative Analysis of Com-*

are mostly viewed as wise today is less clear. Many mediators are either political appointees or "elected" officials who may lack professional training and a respected status in their community. As suggested in the next several examples, wisely directive mediations may be moving toward an evaluatively directive form with the mediators acting aggressively directive.

The directive role of the mediators is vividly conveyed in this description of mediators handling an intense family dispute between a mother and daughter-in-law in Shanghai. "Mediators came in, spoke to the immediate family and their neighbors, then criticized each for not respecting the rights of the other. They articulated the rules and moral standards that, in the abstract, seemed to cover their situation, proposed a solution, and persuaded both parties to accept it."[46]

Recent Chinese initiatives, designed to modernize, professionalize and legalisticize the massive mediation program that operates through the seven million People's Mediation Committees, revealed much about aspiring mediation practices in China. The 1989 Regulations[47] reinforced and expanded upon by the 2002 Order of the Ministry of Justice[48] seek to clarify the role of mediators. According to these Regulations, mediators should educate people about the law and socialist morality, investigate facts and distinguish between right and wrong, and conduct "meticulous persuasion and so as to urge the parties concerned to understand each other, eliminate estrangement, and steer and help the parties concerned to come into mediation agreements."[49] While trying to implement these directives to educate, investigate, persuade, urge, and steer, mediators are obliged to ensure a voluntary process that abides by ethical policies promoting the mediators' professionalism, neutrality, fairness, and confidentiality. They must preserve for parties the right to decide whether to participate and whether to settle, "based on their own free will."

These competing obligations to be directive and ensure voluntary agreements do not apply only to the numerous mediations conducted by the People's Mediation Committees. Consider the mediator's role contemplated by the Conciliation Rules of the China Chamber of Commerce.[50] In the face of Article 4's emphasis that: "During conciliation

munity Mediation in the United States and the People's Republic of China, 10 TEMP. INT'L & COMP. L.J. 313 (1996).

46. *See* Kenneth Cloke, *Politics and Values in Mediation: The Chinese Experience*, 17 MED. Q. 69, 74 (Fall 1987).

47. Regulations Governing the Organization of People's Mediation Committees, Promulgated by the State Council on 17 June 1989.

48. Order of the Ministry of Justice of the People's Republic of China People's Mediation (No. 75), adopted at the working meeting of Ministers of the Ministry of Justice on Sept. 11, 2002 and promulgated to be effective as of Nov. 1, 2002. (The order

also provides for increase training of mediators, especially about legal knowledge, and establishes that the litigation rights of the parties cannot be barred on the grounds of a lack or failure of mediation.)

49. Order of the Ministry of Justice of the People's Republic of China People's Mediation (No. 75), adopted at the working meeting of Ministers of the Ministry of Justice on Sept. 11, 2002 and promulgated to be effective as of Nov. 1, 2002, Article 31.

50. *See* China Council for the Promotion of International Trade (CCPIT) and China Chamber of International Commerce (CCOIC), Conciliation Rules, arts. 4 and 5 (2000).

course, the principle of parties' free will must be observed," Article 5 describes a rather assertive process. "Conciliation shall be conducted on the *basis of ascertaining facts, distinguishing right from wrong and determining liabilities* while respecting the terms of the contract, abiding by the law, following international practice and adhering to the principle of being just, fair and reasonable in order to bring about mutual understanding and *mutual concession* between the parties. * * * (emphasis added)."

In a case study of arbitrators mediating a commercial dispute in China, the observer revealed rich details of how directive arbitrators-turned-mediators can be:[51]

- The arbitrator-mediator must be "amicable and patient—but this does not mean that any wrong attitude or unsuitable manner by a party is not criticized and corrected."

- One of the arbitrators-turned-mediator in the study "expressed his opinions, analyzing the cause of the dispute and each side's responsibility, asking both sides not be too emotional but to listen to reason, emphasizing that the dispute was of an economic nature, not political, hoping that P would not take too great account of their so-called losses of reputation and face. * * * "

- "D accepted the arbitrator's advice. * * * "

- "In mediation, arbitrators should first find out which party is likely to take the lead in making concessions, setting the ball rolling. Arbitrators should first try to persuade this party's chief representative or lawyer, who is comparatively not emotional but objective and who is willing to revise his viewpoints as the real facts to the disputes are gradually revealed after discussions with the other side, and will exchange ideas with the arbitrators."

The degree to which the history of mediation in China shapes the conduct of today's mediators is much studied and debated as the government and private sector try to modernize mediation practice by implementing more rigorous training and explicit professional conduct standards. In trying to transform mediation practice, China may be leaving behind the benefits of wise mediators that parties respectfully defer to and may be turning toward evaluative mediators that are aggressively directive.

(3) Distinguish Wisely Directive Mediation from Other Settlement Processes

The distinctive function of the wisely directive mediator should appear familiar to people in the United States knowledgeable about

51. *See* Huang Yanming, *Mediation in the Settlement of Business Disputes: Two Typical Examples of Cases Settled by Medi-* *ation at the CIETAC's Shenzhen Commission*, 8 J. INT'L ARB. 23 (1991).

evaluative mediation in which the mediator assesses the merits of the dispute or solutions, *judicial settlement conferences* in which a judge hints at what she might do in court or urges a particular settlement, and *nonbinding arbitration* where an arbitrator issues a decision on the merits. The function of the third party in these three familiar settlement processes and the wisely directive process are similar. The third party offers evaluations.

But parties' responses to third party evaluations in the U.S. are not similar to parties' responses to wisely directive evaluation in other countries. An evaluation from a U.S. mediator can provide valuable input but parties are relatively free to reject the recommendation as well as resist any pressure if the mediator is also directive. Parties can reject and resist with little consequence. An evaluation from a settlement judge can be riskier to repel especially if the parties want to avoid alienating the judge that might decide the case. Nevertheless, parties are not shy about resisting pressure when they must to protect their interests—a proud trait for those brought up in an individualistic society. And, a nonbinding decision by an arbitrator who will not be further involved in resolving the dispute can be freely rejected by the parties.

In contrast, an evaluation and pressure from a wise third party is received quite differently. Various case studies suggest that, based on history and experience in a collectivist society, disputing parties expect the wisely directive mediator to steer them toward the right solution, a solution that they are expected to accept. The third party may dress like a mediator but act more like an arbitrator.

Although wisely directive mediation may no longer be embraced intact by either mediators or parties in modern societies, its cultural influence can still be felt in the mediation practice of some regions around the globe.

(d) Search for Arbitrator Power in Mediation Practice

When formulating a plan to enlist mediator assistance, you will want to know whether the mediator might exercise the power to arbitrate. Although mediation and arbitration rules commonly bar third parties from switching roles from either arbitrating to mediating or mediating to arbitrating unless authorized by both parties, this switching option can be quite tempting in the heat of a mediation or arbitration, especially when fueled by a cultural practice.

Given the pressing goal to resolve the dispute, parties and neutrals can be less concerned about maintaining the integrity of each process and more concerned about doing everything possible to end the dispute. The temptation for a party to ask the mediator to arbitrate can be considerable when the parties have reached an impasse after spending an intensive day or more together mediating a dispute. The temptation to do the reverse and ask the arbitrator to mediate also can be considerable after parties have expended time and resources convening an arbitration with hand-picked neutrals and then see opportunities to avoid a lengthy arbitration by settling. Using the same neutral to both mediate and arbitrate saves the time and money of adjourning one process to select a new neutral who must then be educated about the dispute for the other process.

These savings can be magnified in international disputes where it can be especially difficult to select another neutral as well as to communicate and schedule sessions among neutrals, parties and attorneys who are from different countries. When everybody is already convened in one location for either the mediation or arbitration, parties can find the option of the neutral switching roles to be irresistible.

These benefits as well as the compromising risks posed by the neutral switching roles are widely known and still debated.[52] The primary risk is that one neutral may not be able to perform effectively the two distinctively different roles of arbitrator and mediator in the same case. In order to preserve the integrity of each process, the neutral must simultaneously maintain her *impartiality* as arbitrator and her *flexibility* as a mediator.[53]

The neutral as mediator must strive to preserve her impartiality when using various settlement techniques in order to avoid compromising her neutrality if she later arbitrates. As a mediator, she may solicit confidential information, hold ex parte meetings (caucuses), engage in "reality testing," and even assess merits of claims (evaluations). These initiatives may benefit the settlement process but can expose the arbitration process to legal attack. A party may challenge the arbitration award on the grounds that the mediator-turned-arbitrator was influenced by information learned during settlement efforts or had prejudged the case when she offered an evaluation of the merits of the case in the mediation. A party might even complain that the arbitrator retaliated against her in an arbitration proceeding for not heeding her advice during settlement discussions. Therefore, the mediator faces the daunting risk of engaging in settlement initiatives that may disqualify her as an arbitrator. In trying to reduce this risk, the mediator may avoid using some techniques that can be especially effective in mediations.

This switching option can be especially attractive when it comports with an ingrained cultural practice such as the one that can be found in many Asian countries[54] and in several Western European countries as well.

52. *See* Harold I. Abramson, *Protocols for International Arbitrators Who Dare to Settle Cases*, 10 AM. REV. INT'L ARB. 1, 3–4 (1999).

53. *See* CHRISTIAN BUHRING–UHLE, ARBITRATION AND MEDIATION IN INTERNATIONAL BUSINESS 203, 204 (1996). The author distinguishes *impartiality*, which "refers to the absence of pre-disposition with respect to the merits of the dispute" from *independence*, which

refers to being "capable of making their own judgment without being impaired by some type of dependence or obligation to a party."

54. *See* M. Scott Donahey, *Seeking Harmony: Is the Asian Concept of the Conciliator/Arbitrator Applicable to the West?*, 50 DISP. RESOL. J. 74 (Apr. 1995); Kenji Tashiro, *Conciliation or Mediation During the Arbitral Process—A Japanese View*, 12(2) J.

A favorable attitude toward mediators arbitrating can be found in some mediation rules. Consider the Conciliation Rules of the China Chamber of International Commerce, for instance. The specific wording of Rule 21 reveals a starkly positive attitude toward mediators arbitrating: "If conciliation fails, the conciliator(s) may be appointed by one of the parties as arbitrator(s) in the subsequent arbitration proceedings, *unless such appointment is opposed by the other party* (emphasis added)."

The rules of the Daini Tokyo Bar Association also reflect a positive attitude.[55] It states the general rule that if the parties in the mediation agree to go to arbitration, the "mediation procedure shall be converted to the arbitration procedures. In such case the Mediator(s) who has (have) undertaken the mediation procedure shall serve as the Arbitrator(s)." In the next subsection, however, it provides a way to opt out: " * * * should either or both of the parties wish to have different Arbitrator(s), such new Arbitrator(s) shall be selected. * * * "

The reverse procedure of arbitrators switching to mediate also can be found in rules and practice.

Consider the Introduction to the Chinese CIETAC (China International Economic and Trade Arbitration Commission) WebSite concerning its arbitration rules. It comments favorably on the practice of arbitrators mediating by pointing out that: "Many years of practice has indicated that the combination of arbitration with conciliation can make good use of the advantages of both arbitration and conciliation, so as to settle disputes more efficiently and turn hostility into friendship. It also may save parties expenses and help to maintain the friendly relations and cooperation between them. This practice in Chinese arbitration has received worldwide attention and approval."[56]

This supportive attitude toward a practice that is persistently condemned in the United States was unambiguously conveyed in a recent article co-authored by three Chinese lawyers. In analyzing the 1994 Chinese Arbitration Act, the authors criticized it for limiting mediation by the arbitrators to only when the litigants so agree: "It is China's unique innovation to combine arbitration with mediation, a method known as the 'med/arb.' This method should be recognized and supported in any future arbitration law. It should be further specified that a mediator may act as an arbitrator in the arbitral proceedings and the legitimacy of caucusing by arbitrators during the process of mediation should be accommodated, so to provide the basis for a combination between arbitration and mediation."[57]

INT'L ARB. 119 (1995); and Yanming, *supra* note 49.

55. *See* Daini Tokyo Bar Association's Rules of Procedure for Arbitration and Mediation, art. 24 (June 9, 2000).

56. *See* Introduction, Section XV. Combination of Arbitration and Conciliation, *at* www.cietac.org.

57. *See* Song Lianbin, Zhao Jian & Li Hong, *Approaches to the Revision of the 1994 Arbitration Act of the People's Republic of China*, 20 J. INT'L ARB. 169, 188 (2003).

The case study of arbitrators mediating in China, described in the section on wisely directive mediators, offered a window into the various ways that an arbitrator can deliberately and comfortably switch roles to settle disputes.

The Vice–Chairman of China International Economic and Trade Arbitration Commission (CIETAC) in Beijing, Tang Houzhi, when making the case for conciliation in arbitration, pointed out that China is not the only country that has found it advantageous for the same neutral to serve as both arbitrator and conciliator. He cited supportive policies in Hong Kong, India, Japan, Korea, Germany, Hungary, Croatia, Australia, and Canada.[58]

In a survey of U.S. and German practitioners,[59] German respondents reported that they "often" encountered arbitrators participating in settlement negotiations while U.S. participants reported that they "very rarely" saw arbitrators do this. When asked about the propriety of arbitrators participating in negotiations, 92% of German respondents thought it was appropriate, while 71% of U.S. respondents rejected this role for arbitrators.[60]

These practices of neutrals switching roles in some parts of the world can impact on your plan for involving the mediator in settling the dispute as well as how you and your client might participate throughout the mediation. Therefore, you should clarify whether the mediator will have the power to arbitrate before you develop a mediation representation plan.

(e) Impact of Different Roles on Mediation Representation

Your entire approach to interacting with and enlisting assistance from the mediator can be shaped by how transformative, facilitative, evaluative, or directive the mediator might be or whether the mediator might arbitrate the dispute.

The materials on various mediator roles suggest a continuum of cultural influences and practices around the globe. Although it is always risky to generalize, because no country has a monolithic approach, generalizations based on likely cultural propensities can at least sensitize attorneys to look for a range of possible mediator roles. A tentative continuum might be constructed with China and Islamic countries being the most directive, civil law countries next, followed by the U.S. and

58. *See* Tang Houzhi, *The Use of Conciliation in Arbitration*, presented to WIPO Conference on Mediation, Geneva, Switzerland (Mar. 29, 1996), *at* http://arbiter.wipo.int/events/conferences/1996/tang.html.

59. See BUHRING-UHLE, *supra* note 51, at 188–96.

60. These different attitudes may be converging as parties are exposed to different cultural practices, leading to U.S. lawyers becoming more acquainted with Asian practices of conciliation and Asian lawyers becoming familiar with the more adversarial U.S. model of arbitration. *See, e.g.*, Rau & Sherman, *supra* note 6, at 89, 105–09. In a survey, attorneys appeared more receptive to settlement initiatives by arbitrators than the actual practice of international arbitrators.

Australia, with English practices and transformative mediation in the U.S. being the most facilitative. Whether this continuum withstands the still ongoing study of global mediation practices or is replaced by a reformulated, more nuanced one remains to be seen. Any continuum of mediator roles should not be blindly followed. Its value is in offering a framework for discerning, testing, and verifying mediators' roles when formulating a plan for intelligently interacting with the mediator. Any of these mediator roles can singularly shape your entire representation strategy, as suggested in the following excerpt.

HAROLD ABRAMSON, PROBLEM–SOLVING ADVOCACY IN MEDIATIONS: A MODEL OF CLIENT REPRESENTATION

10 Harvard Negotiation Law Review (2005).

* * *

For example, realizing that the mediator will stay in a problem-solving mode gives an attorney the freedom and security to share information including interests, brainstorm options, recognize weaknesses in his or her client's legal case, and be open to creative solutions other than the ones in the legal papers. The attorney can feel comfortable asking the mediator for help, whether in sorting out interests, facilitating an evaluation of the legal case, or developing multiple options. The attorney also has much freedom and security with a transformative mediator who is trained to support whatever sort of process is structured and implemented by the attorney, client, and the other side, although the attorney cannot rely on the mediator's expertise or initiatives to create or direct a process, as the transformative mediator is committed to being non-directive.

In contrast, consider the impact of mediator evaluation on advocacy. Whenever an attorney comes near me and this topic, I ask the same simple question: Does knowing that the mediator might offer an evaluation influence how you would represent your client in mediation? The answer has been yes every time.

Mediation evaluations can take a variety of forms. For instance, mediators may assess the reasonableness of settlement options, assess consequences of not settling, or recommend settlement proposals either as the mediation unfolds or as a "mediator's proposal."

Knowing that the mediator may formulate one or more of these types of evaluations can induce the attorney to approach the mediation more like an adjudicatory process than a negotiation. This mediator role can change the nature of the mediation process. Instead of viewing the mediator as a facilitator with whom the attorney can have candid conversations, the attorney is likely to view the mediator as a decision-maker who must be persuaded. Instead of formulating a negotiation strategy based on meeting parties' interests, the attorney is likely to formulate a strategy designed to convince the mediator to recommend a favorable evaluation.

Consider in what specific ways an attorney would circumscribe his or her representation if the attorney thought the mediator might evaluate. Would the attorney and his or her client talk less candidly if the attorney were to take into account the possibility of the mediator performing any of these other roles? Would the attorney avoid recognizing any weaknesses in his or her legal position, other than the safely obvious ones, to the mediator or the other side? Would the attorney eschew compromises, especially ones that deviate from the remedies sought in the legal case? Would the attorney hide and disguise information in order to avoid coloring unfavorably the mediator's view of the dispute? Would the attorney be likely to advance partisan legal arguments at the expense of interest-based creative option building?

Affirmative answers to these questions prompt many attorneys to return to the traditional adversarial approach so familiar in the courtroom in which the attorney withholds unfavorable information, hides any flexibility to avoid implying a lack of confidence in the legal case, and presents carefully crafted partisan arguments and positions that are designed to persuade a decision-maker to act favorably.

Alternatively, an attorney might problem-solve but in a selective way that reduces the risk of an unfavorable assessment by the mediator. In such a constricted problem-solving approach, an attorney could still share and advocate his or her client's interests and engage in such problem-solving moves as brainstorming options and designing creative solutions, but only up to a point. The attorney will avoid sharing information or showing flexibility that may risk a less favorable evaluation from the mediator.

This strategic behavior can dilute the potential of a problem-solving process by limiting the ability of parties to uncover optimal solutions. Withholding information may hide important matters relevant to devising solutions. Hiding flexibility may cramp the search for imaginative solutions.

I have seen first-hand how attorneys and clients withhold unfavorable information and flexibility. In one instance after three days of arbitration hearings, the parties agreed to convert the proceeding into a final-offer arbitration process in which each side would submit a final offer, and I would select one. The final offers barely resembled what each side advocated during the hearings. While this anecdote is surely not surprising because an advocate would never be expected to reveal acceptable settlement terms during an adversarial hearing, it illustrates the point that should be as obvious as what happened in the anecdote. There is a tendency to hide flexibility in an evaluative/adjudicatory process. This point was further illustrated in a recent case where I was operating as a mediator who might evaluate. After four hours of mediating and reaching an impasse, both sides selected the mediator's proposal scheme where I would formulate a proposal that each side would either accept or reject without advising the other side unless both sides accepted. The party that took the most inflexible position in the mediation and tenaciously hid any hint of legal vulnerability accepted a mediator's proposal that was one-third of its uncompromising position in the mediation.

* * *

In view of this strategic need to hide information and flexibility, an attorney may be induced to fashion this constricted form of problem-solving advocacy, one that is based on a narrowly focused adversarial plan and presentation. Such an approach would require a sophisticated and nuanced form of advocacy in order to minimize stifling the creative problem-solving potential of the mediation process. The advocacy would consist of a blended problem-solving-adversarial strategy that could not be implemented casually because of the need to carefully identify and segregate risky from safe information and then to artfully and persuasively disclose only the safe information. It is a strategy that would need to be actuated proficiently in the heat of the mediation, realizing that too much candor might result in a less favorable mediator assessment and too little candor might result in a less optimal negotiated result.

An attorney might be more confident pursuing a constricted problem-solving approach if the type of carefully designed safeguard in the Center for Effective Dispute Resolution (CEDR) Mediation Rules was adopted. The rules ensure that all participants approve an evaluation role at the optimum moment in the process as well as limit the type of evaluation. The rules give the mediator *conditional* recommendation authority: "If the Parties are unable to reach a settlement in the negotiations at the Mediation, and only if all the Parties so request *and the Mediator agrees*, the Mediator will produce for the Parties a *nonbinding recommendation on terms of settlement*. This will not attempt to anticipate what a court might order but will set out what the Mediator suggests are appropriate settlement terms in all of the circumstances." (emphasis added)[61] CEDR's Guidance Notes state that "The intention of paragraph 12 is that the Mediator will cease to play an entirely facilitative role only if the negotiations in the Mediation are deadlocked. Giving a settlement recommendation may be perceived by a Party as undermining the Mediator's neutrality and for this reason the Mediator may not agree to this course of action."

---

61. *See* CEDR Model Mediation Procedure and Agreement, para. 12 (Oct. 2002). For a somewhat less strict approach, *see* The CPR/CCPIT Mediation Procedure For Disputes Submitted to the U.S.-China Business Mediation Center § 7 (2004) and Daini Tokyo Bar Association's Rules of Procedure for Arbitration and Mediation, art. 25 (Advisory Opinion) (June 9, 2000).

Notes and Questions

1.   The Italian legislative decree, referred in the section on Evaluatively Directive Mediators, envisioned the mediator providing an evaluation in the form of a final settlement proposal. Why did the excerpt discussing the decree suggest that the decree contemplated that the mediator might perform a directive role?

2.   What are the practical differences, if any, between a wisely directive mediator and an evaluatively directive mediator? Would you represent a client differently depending on which role you anticipated your mediator performing?

3.   For what types of disputes would you prefer a: (a) problem-solving mediator, (b) an evaluatively directive mediator, (c) a wisely directive mediator, or (d) a nonbinding arbitrator?

4.   Is there a tension between a mediator engaging in a directive mediation and a mediator ensuring that any resulting agreement is voluntary and respectful of party-self-determination? If you were a directive mediator, how would you ensure a voluntary agreement that respects each party's right to self-determination? If you were an attorney before a highly directive mediator, what would you do to ensure a voluntary result for your client?

5.   What would you do before and during the mediation session to guard against a mediator whose cultural upbringing may encourage him to slide into the role of arbitrator? If you prefer the practice of the mediator switching roles to arbitrate, what safeguards would you want to adopt to preserve the effectiveness and integrity of both the mediation and arbitration processes? If you thought the mediator might switch to arbitrate, would you further modify the constricted problem-solving representation approach described in the excerpt on *Problem-Solving Advocacy in Mediations*? If so, in what specific ways might you modify the approach?

6.   For the Mitsubishi–Soler Dispute, assuming that you are representing the defendant Soler, what flexibility would you hide and what information would you withhold because the mediator will be evaluatively directive?

7.   The *Problem-Solving Advocacy in Mediations* excerpt suggests that an attorney might be more confident pursuing a constricted problem-solving approach if the safeguards in the Center for Effective Dispute Resolution (CEDR) Mediation Rules were adopted. Re-read the rule in the excerpt and describe what protections it would give you and then indicate what risks, if any, must still be anticipated.

8.   Consider these suggestions for blending a U.S. facilitative-problem-solving approach with a traditional Malay–Islamic approach that slants toward wisely directive. Extract the distinct stages of mediation based on the U.S. model of opening statements by mediators and parties, identifying interests, generating options, assessing options, and formulating agreement. Are there any other ways that you might modify these stages to move closer to a problem-solving approach while still respecting Malay–Islamic traditions and values?

Working with Malay Clients[62]

Difficult mediations should be scheduled after the Friday afternoon prayers at the mosque. Perhaps the parties and the mediator can have a simple meal together just before the mediation. Community elders, the religious teacher, and key members of the family should be present. At the opening of the mediation, the religious teacher asks all parties if they would like to join in a prayer for peaceful resolution of the dispute. Prayers are offered and parables from the Koran are shared to set the tone for the mediation and to remind parties of their common religious and community values. Parables can be used to reframe disputants' mind-set toward a more generous and forgiving state.

Disputants may be given the option of representing themselves or being represented by a family elder. Other than these parties who participate directly in the inner circle, all other family members sit in the "outer circle" as observers. In facilitating and controlling verbal behaviors and reframing ideas, the mediator can use key phrases, proverbs, and parables from the Koran or from Malay literature. Ground rules can be reinforced by referencing passages on acceptable behavior from the Koran or well-known Malay parables. During the option generation stage, the mediator can test options by asking parties if their solutions are congruent with community standards of fairness and good conduct. In the event of a deadlock, the mediator can suggest that the parties examine certain sections of the Islamic and Malay literature for guidance. The mediator can grant private time for each of the two families to meet, discuss, and generate options. The mediator and other influential resource persons such as community elders and religious leaders can also help guide parties toward acceptable options. When the final agreement is reached, parties can offer a prayer of thanks together before departing.

5. DEVELOP REPRESENTATION PLAN FOR KEY JUNCTURES IN THE MEDIATION

Opportunities to advance interests and overcome impediments are presented at key junctures in the mediation process. You should be familiar with the key junctures in your process so that you know at what points in the mediation you might engage the other side and enlist assistance from the mediator. The term "junctures" is used to identify the points in the mediation for which you should develop a tailored negotiation plan. Junctures are not the same as stages in that stages identify the sequential steps in the mediation process. Junctures and stages, however, can overlap.

---

62. *See* Ho–Beng Chia, Joo Eng Lee–Partridge & Chee–Leong Chong, *Traditional Mediation Practices: Are We Throwing the Baby out with the Bath Water*, 21 CONFLICT RESOL. Q. 451, 460 (Summer 2004) (In Singapore, the authors compare a Western version of institutional mediation with traditional Chinese mediation and traditional Malay (Islamic) mediation).

In a U.S. mediation process, there are a number of junctures that offer opportunities for advancing interests and overcoming impediments.[63] In this section, you will consider four junctures in which distinctively international issues might arise. These issues can arise when: (1) selecting the sort of mediator that would be suitable for the mediation, (2) engaging in pre-mediation contacts with the mediator, (3) participating in joint sessions and caucuses, and (4) dealing with any post-session issues.

(a) Juncture: Selecting a Mediator

You need to select a mediator who will perform the roles contemplated by both sides and will be qualified to handle a dispute between parties from different countries.

(1) Selecting Approaches

There is no more important decision in mediation representation than choosing the roles that you want your mediator to perform. You want to be sure that you select a mediator who will employ the mix of approaches and techniques that you think are warranted. Do not rely blindly on the flexible authority typically found in mediation rules. Hidden in apparently harmless language can be found unstated as well as unexpected cultural practices that impact on what assistance the mediator may provide as well as the way you ought to represent your client. At this early juncture, both sides should agree on the roles they want performed by the mediator, an undertaking that is ripe for differing cultural preferences that require attention and skillful negotiation.

Several recent rule innovations have not left to chance this vital discussion of mediator roles.[64] The Oslo Chamber of Commerce Rules, for instance, provides specifically that "The Mediator, in cooperation with

---

63. In addition to the junctures considered in this text, there are a number of other junctures that offer opportunities for advancing interests and overcoming impediments. They include when (1) initially interviewing your client, (2) approaching the other attorney about the use of mediation, (3) preparing your case for mediation, (4) preparing your client, (5) participating in joint sessions and caucuses, (6) drafting a settlement agreement or developing an exit plan from an unsuccessful mediation, and (7) completing any post-session tasks.

64. See, e.g., A voluntary European Code of Conduct for Mediators, adopted on July 2, 2004 in Brussels, also expects the mediator to ensure that the parties resolve what role they would like the mediator to perform.

3.1 The mediator shall satisfy himself/herself that the parties to the mediation understand the characteristics of the mediation process and the role of the mediator and the parties in it.

The mediator shall in particular ensure that prior to commencement of the mediation the parties have understood and expressly agreed the terms and conditions of the mediation agreement including in particular any applicable provisions relating to obligations of confidentiality on the mediator and on the parties.

Instead of the Code suggesting appropriate mediation practices, however, it simply states that the mediator should be competent and knowledgeable of the mediation process. See 1.1, 1.2, and 1.3.

the parties, shall see to it that an Agreement is made"[65] that covers what the parties want to empower the mediator to do. The rules recently negotiated between CPR Institute for Dispute Resolution (CPR), a U.S. based organization, and the China Council for the Promotion of International Trade (CCPIT) also requires mediators to be proactive:[66]

> Mediators shall ensure that prior to commencement of the mediation the parties have understood and expressly agreed:
>
> the purpose and general procedure of the mediation
>
> the role of mediators and of the parties
>
> the obligation of confidentiality on the mediators and on the parties mediators' fee arrangement.

The ICC adopted what might be a unique approach.[67] Instead of labelling the third party as a conciliator, the Rules refer to a Neutral who will first "seek to reach agreement upon the settlement technique." The *Guide to ICC ADR* defines several ADR settlement techniques and, in doing so, distinguishes carefully between Mediation as a facilitative process where the Neutral is "not requested to provide any opinion...." and Neutral Evaluation where the Neutral provides "a non-binding opinion or evaluation." If the parties do not reach an agreement, the default technique is Mediation.

These prophylactic measures are particularly appealing because they ensure that parties face essential design questions and formulate a suitable process before the first mediation session. The more typical rules, however, do not impose a specific obligation on the mediator. Instead, the rules give parties the option of negotiating the details of the particular roles. And, if they do nothing, the default process in the rules control. The default rules usually give the mediator broad authority to do what is "appropriate" along with occasionally predictable as well as unexpected powers such as caucusing and recommending solutions. When left unregulated by a specific negotiated agreement or by specific rules, the mediator will conduct the mediation based on his or her cultural upbringing and training, and not all mediators follow familiar U.S. practices.

You should consider what suitable mix of mediator's approaches you prefer and should negotiate for these. Here is a brief description of four basic inquiries: How do you want the mediator to manage the mediation process? How do you want the mediator to view the dispute? How do you

65. Oslo Chamber of Commerce, Rules of the Arbitration and Dispute Resolution Institute of the Oslo Chamber of Commerce, art. 34 (2003).

66. The CPR/CCPIT Mediation Procedure For Disputes Submitted to the U.S.-China Business Mediation Center, App. D–Professional Ethics, § 3 (2004).

67. *See* ICC ADR Rules, Art. 5 (July 1, 2001) and Guide to ICC ADR 11–15 (June 2001), *at* http://www.iccwbo.org/index_adr.asp#model_clause. The ICC transformed its 1988 Rules of Conciliation into these new ADR Rules.

want the mediator to involve the clients? And, how do you want the mediator to use uses caucuses, if at all?

How do you want the mediator to manage the process?

The range of options was discussed extensively in Section C.4 on "Use Proactively the Presence of the Mediator." Mediators can perform as transformative, facilitative, evaluative, and variously directive mediators; they also can perform as arbitrators. You will want to clarify which role or roles you prefer the mediator to perform.

One particular culture practice requires special attention: the selected mediator might pressure parties to settle. This directive practice was examined in Section C.4(c). One check against mediator pressure can be found in the right of party self-determination. Professor Jackie Nolan–Haley points out that the informed consent requirement strives to limit the "mediator power to control only the process in which parties' decisionmaking occurs, while the parties retain the power to decide and control the outcome."[68]

Unfortunately, studies in the U.S. have shown that courts tolerate considerable mediator pressure to settle. It is the remarkable exception when a court will find pressure to be so overbearing as to constitute unambiguous coercion and as a result void an agreement as not "voluntary" or one not based on "free will"[69] And, if the self-determination value is so weakly implemented in its place of origin, you have plenty of reason to be concerned about how much it will be respected in countries where mediation has not been built on this fundamental principle. The wording of many rules outside the United States does not offer much hope. The rules either omit anything on self-determination or only give it lip service by parroting the language without supplying any meaningful standards that would give enforcement a chance.

Even the new voluntary European Code of Conduct for Mediators,[70] that signals a serious concern about informed consent, lacks a standard that could facilitate enforcement.

> 3.3   The mediator shall take all appropriate measures to ensure that any understanding is reached by all parties through knowing and informed consent, and that all parties understand the terms of the agreement.

An unusual exception can be found in the European Commission (EC)'s Green Paper on Alternative Dispute Resolution in Civil and Commercial Law (Presented by the Commission of the European Communities, April 19, 2002) (Com 2002). The EC Green Paper confronted

---

68. *See* Jacqueline M. Nolan–Haley, *Informed Consent in Mediation: A Guiding Principle for Truly Educated Decisionmaking*, 74 Notre Dame L. Rev. 775, 791 (1999).

69. *See* Welsh, *supra* note 27, at 1, 59–79. *Also see* Nolan–Haley, *supra* note 66, at 775, 793–812.

70. This voluntary code of conduct was issued by a group of dispute resolution leaders on July 2, 2004 in Brussels. It is hoped that the code will be adopted by a number of European dispute resolution organizations.

forthrightly the need to promote genuine consent. It forcefully made the case for aggressive action to ensure real consent and recommended several strong protective measures including giving parties a period of time to reflect before signing or a period of time to retract after signing.[71]

3.2.2.2 The validity of consent

83. The parties' agreement is the essential and, from a certain standpoint, the most sensitive stage of the procedure. Indeed, care must be taken to ensure that the agreement concluded is genuinely an agreement. If the final agreement does not reflect the real wishes of the parties, that is, the actual compromise which the parties are willing to accept, with all that this implies in terms of waiver of their original wishes, ADR mechanism has not achieved its primary objectives, i.e. the genuine resolution of the dispute and the social pacification that ensues. Further problems can therefore be anticipated. For example, the validity of the agreement may be disputed, the responsibility of the third parties may be set at issue on the grounds that he "extracted" an unfair agreement from one of the parties, etc. In particular, in the event of an economic imbalance between the parties, the notion of a certain protective formalism is required when it comes to concluding and signing the agreement. All steps must be taken to guarantee the validity of the consent expressed. It would therefore appear that there is a need for a period of reflection before the signing or a period of retraction after the signing of the agreement. There is also the need to analyze the possibility of providing for a confirmation stage at which the validity of the agreement is verified prior to becoming an enforceable decision. A judge or notary would be in charge of this proceeding, though specialised bodies such as Chambers of Commerce might take their place in specific subject areas.

If you want to guard against aggressive mediators, you should consider adopting a protective measure when negotiating the mediation rules and roles. You might draft a provision that provides a meaningful opportunity to enforce a right to party-self determination while tailoring the provision to avoid becoming a source of wasteful collateral litigation over whether it has been violated. This drafting task can be a challenging one.

How narrowly or broadly do you prefer the mediator to define the presenting problem(s) in the dispute?

Whether you want to select a mediator who approaches the dispute narrowly or broadly depends on the needs of your client.

---

71. *Also see* Welsh, *supra* note 27, at 1, 86–92 (Author suggests imposing cooling-off periods before agreements become effective in order to preserve party self-determination.).

A mediator may approach a dispute at one or more of four "levels" of problem definition according to Professor Leonard Riskin, as described in the Section C.2 on defining interests. At Level I—Litigation Issues, the neutral focuses narrowly on the legal case, its strengths and weaknesses, and what would likely happen in the adjudicatory forum. At Level II—"Business" Interests, the neutral broadens the focus to consider interests that an adjudicatory resolution could not satisfy but are important to the participants. A resolution that involves re-structuring a business relationship is the classic example. At Level III—Personal/Professional/Relational Issues, the neutral invites parties to consider more personal issues and interests. As Professor Riskin pointed out, "mediation participants often must address the relational and emotional aspects of their interactions in order to pave the way for settlement of the narrower economic issues." At Level IV—Community Interests, the neutral reaches for a broad "array of interests, including those of communities or entities that are not parties to the immediate dispute."

How deeply do you or your client want to participate in the mediation session?

Mediators have different practices regarding how to involve you as the representative and your client.[72] Some third parties prefer to involve only your client, leaving you on the sideline; other third parties prefer involving you, putting your client on the sideline; and still others prefer involving both you and your client actively. You may want to clarify with the other side and the mediator the degree that you and your client would like to participate in the mediation session. For instance, if you prefer a problem-solving process, you usually will want your client to be present and to participate actively. You will want to select a mediator who knows how to constructively and actively involve your client and the other client in the mediation session while respecting your attorney-client relationship. If you are convinced that your client should not participate or should participate only restrictively, then you should select a neutral who knows how to conduct mediations primarily through attorneys.

How do you prefer that the mediator use caucuses?

Rather than leaving to chance the use of caucuses, you ought to clarify with the other side and the mediator how caucusing, if any, will be used. For instance, if you prefer a problem-solving process that is designed to promote collaboration, out-of-the-box legal thinking, and creative solutions, you may want to ask the mediator to keep the parties together interacting and to either avoid caucusing or only use them selectively, especially to help bridge cultural gaps. Caucusing options and when to use them will be considered in Section C.5(c)(2) on "Using Caucuses."

---

72. *See* ABRAMSON, *supra* note 9, at 191–92.

(2) Considering Training and Impartiality

The mediator should have training and experience that goes beyond the basics. The mediator should be an expert in dealing with a range of cross-cultural differences, including likely cultural obstacles, and have experience working with an interpreter if parties do not have equal competence in a common language.

You also may want a mediator who is impartial, a common expectation in the United States, although agreeing on who is impartial can be more difficult in disputes between parties from different countries. In this next excerpt, three options for solving the impartiality challenge are suggested.

HAROLD ABRAMSON, MINING MEDIATION RULES FOR REPRESENTATION OPPORTUNITIES AND OBSTACLES

1 Journal of International Dispute Resolution 40 (European Law Publishers and Verlag Recht und Wirtschaft Heidelberg, Germany, January 2004) and 15 American Review of International Arbitration (2005).

How do you select a mediator in a cross-border dispute that both sides view as neutral? Parties must be confident in the mediator's neutrality so that they will trust disclosing information and trust the mediator's initiatives. Even though professional mediators know to scrupulously maintain their neutrality, parties may still be skeptical of any mediator from the country of another party.

Mediation rules occasionally include a default mediator selection process designed for parties from different countries.

The *mediator from a third country* approach is used in the UNCITRAL Model Law. It suggests that the person recommending a mediator "shall take into account the advisability of appointing a conciliator of a nationality other than the nationalities of the parties."[73] The *one from each country* approach is taken in a Chinese rule where each party appoints a mediator and the two mediators jointly conciliate the case.[74]

If you elect the co-mediation solution, rules can provide different approaches to selecting the mediators. The Chinese and a German rule adopt the international arbitration model of party-appointed third parties; each party appoints a conciliator.[75] But, the UNCITRAL Model Law, while preferring this approach in earlier drafts and characterizing it as the "prevailing view," ultimately rejected this approach in favor of

73. *See* United Nations Commission on International Trade Law, Draft Guide to Enactment and Use of the UNCITRAL Model Law on International Commercial Conciliation, art. 5(4) (May 27, 2002).

74. *See* China Council for the Promotion of International Trade (CCPIT) and China Chamber of International Commerce (CCOIC), Conciliation Rules, arts. 9(3), 12 (2000).

75. *See* German Institution of Arbitration, DIS Mediation/Conciliation Rules, § 7(2) (Jan. 1, 2002).

requiring parties to "endeavour (sic) to reach agreement on . . . concilia-tors" unless they agreed on a different procedure.[76]

A third approach, implicit in rules that are silent on selecting international mediators, is to select a *qualified mediator in the location of the mediation*. Realizing that the mediator has no decision making power, a party may not be too concerned about the country of the mediator as long as the mediator has excellent credentials and experi-ence.

Ultimately, you will have to come to terms with what selection process will give you confidence in the mediator. Fortunately, these concerns are not as weighty in mediations as in arbitrations. In media-tions, you have the safeguard of simply walking away from the mediation if you lose trust in the mediator while in arbitrations, you must demon-strate prejudice as a basis for disqualifying the neutral.

This standard U.S. requirement for impartiality may not be as important to parties from some other countries. John Murray, in report-ing on his study of three public disputes and his own experience during his extended stay in Egypt, for instance, observed less of a need for impartial third parties in Egypt.

> * * * Parties in the West also assume that a third party should be impartial, preferably someone as independent and new to the dispute as an American judge is to the case he/she hears at trial. Westerners have difficulty accepting the idea that a mediator could be one of the participants, or someone who holds power over the parties.

> * * *

> * * * Egyptians find it hard to visualize a detached or neutral intervener. What could someone like that have to con-tribute to settling the dispute? To intervene, someone must be part of the community, have something at stake.[77]

(b) Juncture: Pre–Mediation Contacts with the Mediator

You should consider whether you can, want, or are expected to have any contact with the mediator before the mediation session. There are two basic types of pre-mediation contacts: meetings with the mediator and the submission of written materials.

Practices regarding pre-mediation contacts can vary among coun-tries as well as within each country. Consider the variety of practices

---

76. *See* United Nations General Assem-bly, Resolution 57/18 Model Law on Inter-national Commercial Conciliation of the United Nations Commission on Internation-al Trade Law, art. 5(2) (Jan. 24, 2003).

77. *See* Murray, *supra* note 38.

among U.S. trained mediators. Regarding pre-mediation meetings, some hold them with both attorneys, others hold ex parte meetings with each attorney, and some have no pre-mediation contact. Regarding pre-mediation submissions, some mediators invite each side to submit any materials that they choose; others limit the length; some specify what materials to submit; and still others prefer to receive nothing. Regardless of local practices and preferences, the need for pre-mediation contact with the mediator is even greater in disputes between parties from different countries than in domestic disputes because international mediations are inherently fraught with opportunities for misunderstandings and conflicting expectations. Pre-mediation contacts can be desirable for clarifying the role of the mediator and the structure of the process as well as for preparing the mediator for the session.

There are a number of issues that should be resolved with the mediator before the first session. Several of them can present distinctively international dimensions. Here are four to consider.

(1) Convening a Mediation Session

In international mediations, the optimal arrangement—where parties, attorneys, and the mediator meet to mediate—can be cumbersome to schedule and costly to convene. Some of these challenges can be eased through the use of technologies, as suggested here and further examined in Chapter 6 on Resolving Disputes Online:

* * * International disputes involve parties from different countries who are usually spread out geographically and over different time zones. The participants may have no language in common, may have to communicate with each other through interpreters, and may face other cross-cultural obstacles when trying to understand each other.

In an effort to reduce these practical obstacles to convening everyone at a single location, mediators are starting to experiment with the use of new technologies for convening sessions. These new technologies, when intelligently used with face-to-face sessions, can create a cost-effective, hospitable environment for international mediations.

* * *

These technologies can be used in combination with face-to-face sessions, giving the participants a number of ways to meet during the course of a mediation. One scenario could be as follows: In the first session, everyone meets together in one location during which time the participants develop a working relationship with each other and the mediator. The participants become educated about the mediation process, parties present each of their "stories," parties' interests are explicated and understood, and issues are defined. Before adjourning, the participants develop an agenda and assignments for the next session. If they have developed a sufficient working relationship, participants may not need to meet in one location for the next session. Instead, they may be able to meet technologically. For the second session, they may meet through *teleconferencing* at which time each of the parties may report any information collected and further refine the issues. Then, they may agree to meet a third time through *videoconferencing*. By now, the parties may be ready to resolve some of the most contentious issues and even come to an agreement in principle. Next, a fourth session may be held in a *chat room* or on a *whiteboard* where the parties can exchange specific drafts in an effort to resolve some of the details, especially about some of the noncontroversial aspects of the settlement. Then, they may follow a *store and forward* approach in which detailed drafts are prepared and forwarded for comments, giving each party time to reflect and return comments. Finally, they may all convene again in one location to work out the final details and sign the settlement agreement.[78]

(2) Using Interpreters

You may need to retain an interpreter to ensure that language differences in the mediation session do not become a barrier to settlement. Misunderstandings can defeat one of the primary advantages of mediation: opening up productive communications. Therefore, you should not casually select an interpreter; you should select a professional who is qualified to interpret the substantive exchanges that are likely to take place in the mediation. You also need to know how to work effectively and efficiently with an interpreter.

It is good advice to meet with the interpreter before the mediation session to discuss the substantive nature of the dispute and what the participants expect from the interpreter during the session. This meeting offers a valuable opportunity to acknowledge the vital and demanding work of the interpreter and to begin developing a smooth working relationship. The interpreter should be briefed about the dispute and the technical vocabulary that might be used during the session. The interpreter should be advised to interpret every word that is spoken and to specifically not summarize what is said in order to avoid the risk of failing to convey critical details. You may want to invite the interpreter to offer cultural advice before and during the session. A qualified interpreter should understand the culture in which the language is spoken and therefore might be able to recognize cultural differences that arise and to suggest possible ways to overcome them.

(3) Ensuring Adequate Confidentiality

Confidentiality in the mediation, considered by many in the West as one of the great benefits of mediation, can be less secure internationally

---

78. *See* Abramson, *supra* note 10, at 932–34.

than you might be accustomed to at home due to less developed and untested laws in many other countries. Even though virtually every set of mediation rules provides some confidentiality, in that what happens in the mediation cannot be used in a related legal proceeding, the precise scope of protections can vary. There is still intense debate in the U.S. about how much protection is necessary and the appropriate wording to achieve it, a debate connected with a U.S. and international initiative to promote uniformity in mediation rules and protections.[79] Therefore, you should carefully assess whether the rules you are considering will provide sufficient protection as well as will be enforced in relevant jurisdictions.

(4) Involving Parties with Knowledge and Settlement Authority

As in any mediation, you want to be sure that people with knowledge and settlement authority will be attending, a well-recognized requirement in the West, and one that can be difficult to satisfy when one of the parties is a government agency or a corporation. Within a hierarchical governmental or corporate structure, it can be a formidable undertaking to determine who has sufficient settlement authority and knowledge of the dispute to participate meaningfully.

Selecting the right parties poses additional challenges in societies that follow a decision-making process that is different than practiced at home. Instead of vesting decision-making in an identifiable authoritative leader, as commonly found in the United States, decision-making may be vested in a negotiating team that decides by a cumbersome consensus-making process, for instance, as practiced in such places as China and Japan.[80] In societies with extended closely knit families such as in the Middle East, the leader of the party's family—whose presence may be more important than the presence of the party involved in the dispute—may be the decision-maker as suggested by this observer:[81]

> Family in the Middle East is dominated by the powerful role patriarchy plays in decision-making. The father's authority in his family is an integral part of the more general authority system. Patriarchal authority maintains not only the genealogical cohesiveness of the family but also the cohesiveness of social life. This patriarchal pattern of power is made concrete and takes shape in the primacy of the zaim (leader) of the family. The zaim controls and defends the cohesiveness

79. The Model Law on International Commercial Conciliation, adopted by UNCITRAL and recommended by the United Nations General Assembly in 2002, is designed to promote uniformity in mediation law among nations. The Uniform Mediation Act, approved by the National Conference of Commissioners on Uniform State Laws in August, 2001 and amended in August, 2003 to coordinate with the UNCITRAL Model Law, is being considered for adoption by a number of states in the United States.

80. *See, e.g.*, JESWALD W. SALACUSE, MAKING GLOBAL DEALS 68–69 (1991).

81. *See* Irani, *supra* note 37, at 6.

of the family inside the group as well as in the relationships between the family and other families. The zaim
acts as the family referee and sanctions conflicts that
erupt within the family, while controlling the solidarity
and support within and between family members. He
acts as the family's ambassador towards outsiders.

Questions and Notes

1.   Here are two examples of how an attorney might prepare a plan in
mediation to bridge cultural gaps.[82]

> *Example 1*: In a successful mediation, you, as a typical
> U.S. lawyer, might insist on a signed agreement that
> covers many details and contingencies. However, the
> other side, a Japanese party and lawyer, may resist
> elaborating such details, creating an obstacle to draft-
> ing the settlement agreement. You, as a culturally
> sensitive lawyer, might view this difference as one that
> could be due to conflicting cultural interests. In investi-
> gating the impasse, you might realize that your own
> preference for reducing everything to writing may be
> due to your own cultural upbringing. The drafting of
> comprehensive contracts is taught in U.S. law schools
> and reinforced in law practice. A Japanese lawyer may
> have been brought up differently. Instead of being
> concerned about the details of the written agreement,
> the Japanese lawyer may be concerned about the busi-
> ness relationship, leaving for the written agreement a
> general statement about the relationship.
>
> When developing a strategy for overcoming this im-
> passe in the mediation, you should avoid the instinctive
> reaction that the other side is trying to evade resolving
> key issues. Instead, you should view the other side's
> behavior with an open mind. From a Japanese cultural
> perspective, they may not be hesitating; they just may
> not be interested in the details of the written agree-
> ment.
>
> This interest conflict might be investigated in a joint
> session by each party explaining why the party prefers
> or is disinclined to put details in writing. You might be
> able to overcome this obstacle by discussing and re-
> specting the reasons for the different practices and
> then negotiating a compromise. The clients might seek
> to cultivate a relationship of trust and enter into a
> written settlement that covers key obligations but not
> every conceivable contingency.

82.   ABRAMSON, *supra* note 9, at 180–81.

Example 2: Your mediation representation plan would be shaped by your analysis of any potential cultural obstacles* * * For example, when preparing for the mediation, you may have learned that in addition to valuing personal relationships over contract details, the other side recognizes and respects hierarchy and rank and communicates subtlety and indirectly instead of forthrightly and unambiguously.

* * *this information would influence what you and your client do throughout the mediation process. First, you would want to select a mediator who is sensitive to and capable of mediating disputes between parties with different cultural upbringings. Assuming you decided to bridge any cultural gaps by respecting the differences, you and your client would behave culturally sensitively in each contact with the other side: when participating in the pre-mediation conference, when presenting opening statements, and when participating in joint sessions. For instance, you and your client would communicate graciously and not brutally bluntly, would be respectful of the ranks and formalities to which the other side is accustomed, and would support cultivating a genuine working relationship. You and your client would interpret the other side's communications though their cultural lens of subtle and indirect methods of communicating. Instead of expecting the other side to flatly say "no" to a proposal, for example, you would look for other clues such as the way the other side delays giving an answer. In a caucus with the mediator, you may enlist his advice and assistance in presenting proposals to the other side in a way that is less likely to be misinterpreted due to their different cultural filter.

2. If you are representing a U.S. client in a dispute with a business in India, which option would you choose for selecting a mediator that would meet your needs for impartiality? Why would this selection procedure be acceptable to the other side?

3. What additional credentials and experiences would you look for when selecting an experienced domestic mediator for a private international dispute?

4. Draft a clause that provides for meaningful enforcement of a right to party self-determination. Be sure the provision includes a clear standard for compliance that minimizes the risk of collateral litigation over its interpretation.

5. Here is an agenda for a pre-mediation conference in a domestic mediation. For an international mediation involving the Mitsubishi–Soler dispute, assuming that you are representing the defendant Soler,

identify and discuss what, if any, distinctively international matters you would explore under each item.

Pre-Mediation Conference—Agenda[83]

___a. Verify mediator's mix of approaches to the mediation

___b. Verify other side's approaches to the mediation.

___c. Verify attendance by best client representatives with sufficient and flexible settlement authority.

___d. Verify time, date, place, and length of session.

___e. Resolve what information you need from the other side before or by the session.

___f. Resolve whether the mediator plans to have any ex parte conversations with each side before the session.

___g. Consider signaling the likely interests of your client.

___h. Consider broaching a discussion of possible impediments.

___i. Ask about the pre-mediation submission, if questions still unresolved.

___ Determine whether the mediator wants you to submit any pre-mediation materials.

___ Determine what the mediator wants included in the pre-mediation submission.

___ Determine whether the mediator will share any information in the submission with the other side.

___ Determine that if the mediator plans to share any information, whether the mediator wants you to send the entire submission or a portion to the other side.

___j. Identify any other issues that need to be resolve in the pre-mediation conference.

(c) Juncture: Mediation Session

In the mediation session, a number of distinctively international representation issues can arise. Under Sections C.1–4, several issues were examined including how to identify cultural interests and cultural impediments as well as ways to enlist the assistance of different types of mediators. In this section, we consider the challenges faced when preparing opening statements, using caucuses, fashioning suitable solutions, and resolving distributive conflicts.

(1) Presenting Opening Statements

Presenting your side of the dispute, commonly called opening statements in the U.S., poses a daunting challenge because the audience can

---

83. ABRAMSON, *supra* note 9, at 225–26.

be so unreceptive. The audience is not a neutral third party trained in and dedicated to listening; it is the suspicious, if not distrustful and hostile other side. Attorneys and clients typically struggle and strive to present their issues, interests, and possible solutions in ways that will be heard by the other side who probably thinks they have already heard it all and expects only self-serving statements. In international mediations, you confront the additional challenge of reaching parties from a different cultural upbringing. They will hear your opening statements and any remarks during the session through their cultural filter that might distort what you intend to communicate. You need to identify the other side's likely cultural filters and then present in a way that accounts and corrects for possible distortions.

For example, if you want a yes or no answer from a party who needs to preserve face and who communicates indirectly, you ought to carefully avoid putting the other side in an awkward or embarrassing light and be tuned into indirect ways in which the other side might say no. If the other side is from a formal and hierarchical culture where rank is important, then you should select a client to present your side's opening statement who is of equal rank with the other party so that the other side will feel respected and therefore receptive to listening.

(2) Using Caucuses

You should determine whether you think it might be advantageous to meet separately with the mediator during the mediation session. Most rules authorize mediators to meet separately with each side, an approach commonly labeled as caucusing in the United States. But, giving the mediator caucusing authority does not necessarily mean it will be used or used optimally. As has been observed in the United States, caucusing practices among mediators can vary from primarily caucusing, to selective caucusing, to no caucusing:[84]

> (1) Some mediators and advocates prefer a *no caucus approach* because they believe the mediator should work with the parties in joint sessions in which the parties share information directly with each other. They mistrust caucuses because of how private meetings with the mediator can taint the neutrality of the mediator. Caucusing also can undermine the opportunity for parties to work together to resolve their own problems because caucusing cuts-off vital direct communications and creates undue reliance on the mediator, who is the only person with a full view, for transmitting reactions and information between sides and for fashioning a solution.

> (2) At the other extreme, some mediators as well as advocates prefer a *mostly caucus approach* in which the sides meet jointly only at the beginning of the mediation and then again at the end when signing the settlement agreement. You and your

---

84. *Id.* at 205–10 (2004).

client have little opportunity to interact directly with the other side. By primarily using caucuses, the mediator insulates hostile parties from each other and as a result limits the opportunity for the dispute to escalate. The mediator carefully screens and tightly manages the flow of information and the way proposals are framed and presented.

(3) Other mediators and advocates prefer a *selective caucus approach* in which most meetings are held in joint sessions in order to promote communications between the parties and preserve the mediator's neutrality. These mediators and advocates limit caucusing to narrow and laser-sharp purposes that they believe can be accomplished only in private meetings. Under this approach, you and your client are able to communicate directly with the other side as well as to meet in caucus with the mediator to share sensitive information, test risky proposals, or guard against reactive devaluation,[85] among other purposes.

In a problem-solving process in which you want to promote communications and sharing of information, you would normally restrict caucusing to selective purposes. In international mediations, another selective purpose should be considered. Private meetings with the mediator could be used to reduce cultural distortions and bridge cultural gaps.

By meeting with each side separately, the mediator, a trusted intermediary, might be able to accomplish things that cannot be achieved when both sides are in the same room. For instance, the mediator might be able to facilitate building a consensus among the members of a side that does not decide by a leader. The mediator may be able to communicate more effectively with one side because the mediator's style of communication may be more compatible with that side's than the other side's communication style. Or, the mediator, as a non-party, may be a person that can help parties save or preserve face, as suggested in this excerpt:[86]

Direct Versus Indirect Confrontation and Culture

Confrontation becomes less direct when it is no longer face to face, as when negotiations are carried out * * * by agents, such as lawyers or intermediaries, or through mediators.

* * *

Direct confrontation is consistent with the action-oriented and solution-minded communication that is characteristic of low-context cultures. It typically challenges the status quo—an act that is discouraged in hierarchical cultures and a right that is protected in egalitarian cultures. Direct confrontation also disrupts harmony, a value in collectivist cultures.

---

85. Reactive devaluation describes the tendency of parties to devalue any proposal presented by any other party.

86. *See* BRETT, *supra* note 17, at 104–07.

Underlying the preference for indirect confrontation is a particular concern for face. Face refers to the self-image one projects to others. Respect is the currency by which face is maintained. Disrespect affronts face; respect confirms it. Although face is not unimportant to people from individualist and egalitarian societies, it seems to be more important to people from collectivist and hierarchical cultures. Maintaining face both confirms the person's acceptance in a society (collectivism) and that person's status within the society (hierarchy). It is easier to maintain face using an indirect approach than negotiating directly, where negotiations could escalate with either or both parties becoming emotional and showing disrespect. When disputing is carried out indirectly through third parties, the disputants are buffered from each other. Third parties may also remind disputants, either directly or indirectly through their presence, of the importance of relationships and social harmony, factors that may be forgotten in the midst of emotional face-to-face negotiations.

The mediator can be a person that parties may be more frank with than they can with each other. For this reason, there is a tradition of using intermediaries (zhongjian ren) to settle disputes in China. The Chinese mode of indirect communications, desire to save face, and related reluctance to say no can make intermediaries valuable, as suggested in this excerpt on the use of intermediaries in China:[87]

Only a native Chinese speaker can read and explain the moods, intonations, facial expressions, and body language Chinese negotiators exhibit during a formal negotiation session. Frequently, only the zhongjian ren [intermediary] can determine what's going on. When an impatient Westerner asks what the Chinese think of a proposal, the respondents will invariably offer to kan kan or yanjiu yanjiu, which means, "Let us take a look," or "Let us study it"—even if they think the proposal stinks. This is where the zhongjian ren can step in because he is an interpreter not so much of words as of cultures. Often, the two parties can say frankly to the intermediary what they cannot say to each other. In China, the intermediary—not the negotiator—first brings up the business issue to be discussed. And the intermediary often settles differences.

Caucusing with the mediator also can be advantageous in collectivist societies where the third party's suggestions can give face-saving cover for a party reluctant to make concessions. It was this insight that explained why a study in Turkey, an Islamic dominated country, showed that Turkish subjects, when compared to U.S. subjects, registered "a higher preference for third party help and a lower preference for direct contact with the other party in a conflict situation."[88]

---

87. *See* Graham & Lam, *supra* note 23, at 82, 87.

88. *See* M. Kamil Kozan & Canan Ergin, *Preference for Third Party Help in Con-*

(3) Generating and Assessing Options (The Apology)

When developing and assessing options for settlement, you should be vigilant for solutions that seem unusual but yet essential for the other side. These unexpected viable options might be responsive to the cultural interests of the other side. You will recall the earlier discussion of interests that can be deeply cultural; they can include interests in protecting a principle, saving face, meeting collectivist needs, and preserving relationships. These culturally shaped interests may call for culturally shaped solutions.

Consider this commentator's view of suitable remedies in mediation involving a Chinese party:

> One must not make the mistake of assuming that the Chinese dismiss monetary compensation completely. On the contrary, disputes involving money must be resolved by the use of money. What needs noting is the fact that monetary compensation does not come across as the *only solution* in a mediated award. Often, the wronged party expects, or in cultural parlance, *demands*, more than that. A monetary award may suffice to repair the wrong done at the inter-personal level or at the level of transactions. However, it may do little to restore what the wronged party perceives to be a loss of face, reputation or good standing in the eyes of the community. * * * [I]n addition to a monetary award, [ancillary remedies] may take the form of the offering of mediating tea which serves to demonstrate respect and restore face. Feasting is another common remedy, acting as a public acknowledgment of the conclusion of a dispute.

> * * *

> The offer of a public apology represents a most common and usual form of remedy in conflict resolution with the Chinese. * * *

> What is worth noting again is the public, not private, nature of remedies in Chinese dispute settlement. The remedy is consistent with the characteristic Chinese cultural inclinations towards homocentricity, the subjugation of personal rights, and the Confucian value of group harmony. The offer of an apology serves to vindicate the injured party's private rights by using the public medium. It is, therefore, seen as a powerful means of regaining one's face, reputation and standing.[89]

flict Management in the United States and Turkey—An Experimental Study, 29 J. Cross-Cult. Psych. 525, 528–30, 534 (1998). *Also see* Chia, Lee–Partridge & Chong, *supra* note 60, at 451, 453–54 (Traditional Chinese mediators use caucuses to help "the parties 'save face' and prevent 'inappropriate' actions that may jeopardize the 'staging' of appropriate conduct by either or both parties.").

89. *See* Bee Chen Goh, *Remedies in Chinese Dispute Resolution*, 13 Bond L. Rev.

This deeply ingrained need to restore face in particular cultures by giving and receiving apologies was vividly demonstrated recently when five Japanese citizens were taken hostage in Iraq. According to a report in the New York Times,[90] the hostages experienced returning home to the public embarrassment of having been taken hostage as more stressful than the terror of being held hostage and facing a gruesome execution. Each hostage went to Iraq for different reasons: to start a nonprofit organization to help Iraqi street children, as a freelance photographer, as a freelance writer, and as a member of an anti-war group. The official reaction from the United States government was praise. "Well, everybody should understand the risk they are taking by going into dangerous areas," said Secretary of State Colin L. Powell. "But if nobody was willing to take a risk, then we would never move forward. We would never move our world forward. And so I'm pleased that these Japanese citizens were willing to put themselves at risk for a greater good, for a better purpose. And the Japanese people should be very proud that they have citizens like this willing to do that." In stark contrast, these citizen initiatives were considered unforgivable in Japan because they were pursuing individual goals in defiance of the government and causing difficulties for Japan. The need to apologize extended to the hostages' family members who felt compelled to participate in a very public process. They held a press conference to bow deeply before the nation to apologize for the trouble that their family members caused Japan.

Public apologies also can be necessary in commercial matters. After failing to comply with Japanese legal requirements, Citigroup officials publicly apologized; they bowed deeply before reporters and television cameras. "Such formal public apologies are expected in Japan from companies accused of wrongdoing and are seen as a necessary first step in repairing relationships with regulators and corporate clients."[91]

Consider this excerpt on the power of apology and how it impacts on the giver and the receiver.

DONNA L. PAVLICK, APOLOGY AND MEDIATION: THE HORSE AND THE CARRIAGE OF THE TWENTY–FIRST CENTURY

18 Ohio State Journal on Dispute Resolution 829, 843–47 (2003).

1.　Apology's Impact on the Giver and the Receiver

* * *

"[T]he restoration of a harmonious relationship is attained by the denial of one's self-serving and self-preserving tendencies." Thus, to correct the power imbalance, the giver must begin by acknowledging and

4–6 (Dec. 2001) *at* http:// www.bond.edu.au/law/blr/vol13–2/Goh.doc.

90. *See* Norimitsu Onishi, *Freed From Captivity in Iraq, Japanese Return to More Pain*, N.Y. TIMES, Apr. 23, 2004, at A1.

91. *See* Todd Zaun, *Citigroup Tries to Repair Its Image in Japan*, N.Y. TIMES, Oct. 26, 2004, at W1.

painfully embracing his or her deeds and admitting wrongdoing. By admitting wrongdoing, the giver of the apology begins to take responsibility for the results of his or her actions. As the giver's responsibility increases, shame increases, and the giver begins to experience some of the loss of self-esteem that the victim has experienced. Conversely, the victim's burden of responsibility decreases, and his or her self-esteem and identity begin to rebound. The balance of power slowly starts to shift. "Apology is a form of non-coercive power-balancing enacted by parties in which the powerful offer their vulnerability and through recognition, the injured/humiliated are empowered."

After accepting responsibility, the giver then must express sorrow or regret. The expression of sorrow for the violation is central to apology; it is apology's energizing force. The element of sorrow, often expressed as empathy for the victim, causes the giver to feel anxiety about the damaged relationship, guilt for having hurt the victim, shame for violating a moral rule, and loss of self-respect. Sorrow for having caused the victim to suffer helps to diminish or end the victim's pain; this occurs through the exchange of shame between the giver and the victim. This transfer of shame from the victim to the giver lies at the heart of forgiveness.

Through forgiveness, victims are able to release their feelings of corrosive anger toward givers. Forgiveness also allows victims to let go of their resentment that a moral harm has been done, or to at least contain it. Consuming resentment can cloud the victim's moral reasoning, effect behavior, and stifle personal growth. Forgiveness frees victims from the control and events of the past and allows them to move forward with life. Expressions of sorrow and forgiveness relieve givers of feelings of guilt and shame that they have harbored. When anger, guilt, and shame no longer act as a divide between the victim and offender, forgiveness can facilitate reconciliation.

Finally, apologies can help heal. Acknowledgment of the violation, coupled with an expression of regret or contrition, can have a profound effect on the victim. "If such expressions [in the form of apologies], are accompanied by a request for forgiveness, the healing process will be underway * * * " "When we apologize * * * we stand naked. No excuses, appeals to circumstance, etc., can elicit that which alone can release, eradicate, and renew: forgiveness and, hence, redemption."

2. Apology's Impact on the Relationship

Apology sends a message of caring. It demonstrates caring for the victim simply by acknowledging that the violation has occurred. It removes the perception that the giver feels superior or is indifferent. Apology dispels the perception that the victim is being ignored. Thus, apology validates the victim. This causes the victim to have a more favorable impression of the giver and decreases negative feelings and feelings of anger or aggression toward him or her. "Apology mediates between frustration and aggression and can ameliorate an injured person's hostility toward the wrongdoer." A decrease in the victim's anger and hostility can prevent further deterioration of the relationship and escalation of the conflict. It also minimizes the desire for retaliation.

An authentic apology, coupled with the desire to make amends, "serves the crucial function of repairing relationships after injury" by restoring trust. Trust is essential for any continued or future relationship. Without an apology and an expressed desire to make amends, why should the victim believe that the offender will not repeat the offensive behavior? Apology cements the relationship by reinforcing or repairing the damaged trust that is integral to interpersonal connections. Thus, repairing the frayed or severed relationship restores the balance of power between giver and receiver by helping the victim and the offender regain their internal needs for esteem and belonging (i.e., affiliation in the moral community). They are then capable of moving forward.

Consider this comparison of the role of apology in Japan with its role in the United States:

HIROSHI WAGATSUMA AND ARTHUR ROSETT, THE IMPLICATIONS OF APOLOGY: LAW AND CULTURE IN JAPAN AND THE UNITED STATES

20 Law and Society Review 461–62, 466–69,
471–74, 475–76, 478–79, 492–93 (1986).

* * *

Americans are said to be less likely than Japanese to apologize formally to those they have injured. When faced with a charge that they have seriously wronged another person, Americans typically will deny or challenge the claim or may try to explain and justify their actions. Unlike their Japanese counterparts, neither civil nor criminal defendants in the United States are called upon to express personal apology to those they have injured or to the society whose rules they have violated. An American who is found to have wronged another is likely to consider that paying the damages or accepting punishment ends further responsibility and that there is no need for personal contrition or apology to the injured individual. In fact, were any legal authority—perhaps a judge or the police—to seek an apology from an American as part of the settlement of a serious dispute, such an apology would probably be perceived as either insincere, personally degrading, or obsequious. In contrast, a basic assumption in Japanese society seems to be that apology is an integral part of every resolution of conflict. Offenders too willing to submit to damage payments or other punishment without expressing apology are suspect. Indeed, an offer to pay the damages or accept other punishment without offering apology is considered insincere (not sei-i) in the Japanese context.

* * *

A. A Fable of Apology and Mutual Dependence

A fable may clarify our point [about different attitudes toward apology.] In Aesop's Fables, as told in the West, a mouse boasts to his friends that he is not afraid of a lion, who is sleeping peacefully nearby. To prove his courage, the mouse jumps on the head of the sleeping lion, who awakes and captures the insolent mouse. Desperate but undaunted, the mouse tries to negotiate his way out of this perilous situation. "Free me and someday I will save your life," he brashly promises. The lion thinks this self-aggrandizing mouse is ridiculous, but, because it happens that he is not hungry, he lets the mouse go. Time passes and one day the lion is trapped by a hunter's net. The mouse comes by and chews the net, releasing the lion and thereby keeping his promise. The lion thus learns the lesson that even a blowhard little mouse can rescue him and is not too small to be his friend.

The version of the same tale that is told to Japanese children is somewhat different in that the mouse does not boast to his fellow mice (they do not appear in the story). Instead, the absent-minded mouse climbs onto the head of the sleeping lion by mistake. The lion awakes and captures the mouse. The mouse apologizes profusely in tears for his terrible mistake and unforgivably impolite behavior. The lion feels pity for the mouse and lets him go. The reader is never told whether the lion is hungry, for that is irrelevant to this version of the tale. The Japanese mouse is deeply grateful to the lion for his generosity and kindness. Later, when the lion is trapped, the mouse comes by and "pays back the indebtedness" (on gaeshi). Now the obligation has shifted, and the lion, grateful to the mouse, expresses regret that he had previously behaved arrogantly toward the mouse. The lion then apologizes to the mouse, and they become faithful friends.

* * *

II. THE ELEMENTS OF APOLOGY

Apology becomes important when it provides significant evidence of the state of mind of the apologizer. From a Westerner's perspective the ambiguities of apology are therefore intimately tied to the uncertainties of human intention and their potential for manipulation. Apology relies too heavily on inferring from an external act the presence of a state of mind—remorse or nonhostility—and therefore seems to be too subject to manipulation by deceitful people who say they are sorry but do not mean it. Even when there is no conscious intention to deceive, the formal aspect of the act of apology inevitably tends to convert it into a conventional or stereotyped ceremony. Some of the more flowery forms of apology in English, for example "I beg your pardon," or "Oh, I'm terribly sorry," are used most commonly in precisely those minor social situations in which the literal meaning of the words are very unlikely to express the actual state of mind of the person saying them. Conventionality can erode the content of the concept and obscure its meaning. From a Western point of view, these features make apology a dangerous foundation upon which to build an important legal structure.

One way to retrieve the essential connotations of the concept is to ask what constitutes a meaningful apology. For instance, one may ask whether a person can meaningfully apologize without acknowledging that

1.   the hurtful act happened, caused injury, and was wrongful;

2.   the apologizer was at fault and regrets participating in the act;

3.   the apologizer will compensate the injured party;

4.   the act will not happen again; and

5.   the apologizer intends to work for good relations in the future.

* * *

IV.   APOLOGY AS AN ADMISSION OF THE WRONGFULNESS OF THE ACT

* * *

Many Japanese seem to think it is better to apologize even when the other party is at fault, while Americans may blame others even when they know they are at least partially at fault. Americans, as a group, seem more ready to deny wrongdoing, to demand proof of their delict, to challenge the officials' right to intervene, and to ask to speak to a lawyer * * *

An apology in the Japanese cultural context thus is an indication of an individual's wish to maintain or restore a positive relationship with another person who has been harmed by the individual's acts. When compensation or damages are to be paid to the victim, it is extremely important that the person responsible expresses to the victim his feeling of deep regret and apologizes, in addition to paying an appropriate sum. * * * In dealing with those who have offended them, the cultural assumption of social harmony would lead the Japanese to accept the external act of apology at face value and not to disturb the superficial concord by challenging the sincerity of the person apologizing. The act of apologizing can be significant for its own sake as an acknowledgment of the authority of the hierarchical structure upon which social harmony is based. At a deeper psychological level, the restoration of a harmonious relationship is attained by the denial of one's self-serving and self-preserving tendencies. In this context, the external act of apology becomes significant as an act of self-denigration and submission, which of itself is the important message. Then the internal state of mind of the person who tenders the apology is of less concern. Conversely, if an offender is too willing to offer reparation without indicating his repentance and expressing apology, the response of other Japanese is likely to be unaccepting.

* * * Thus it appears that the Japanese view an apology without an acceptance of fault as being insincere, while an American is more likely to treat an exculpatory explanation as the equivalent of an apology at least to the extent that it is accompanied by a declaration of nonhostile intent in the future.

* * *

V. APOLOGY AND DISASSOCIATION

* * * [A]n apologizing individual splits herself into two parts, the part that is guilty of an offense and the part that disassociates itself from the delict and affirms a belief in the offended rule. In this way apology is likely to involve a disassociation from that part of the self that committed the unacceptable act.

This disassociation can be accomplished in a variety of familiar ways: The bad behavior might be attributed to some external agency; it may be said to have been unintentional, unwitting, or otherwise not the work of the conscious self; or the individual might claim to be a new and different person who is no longer chargeable with the delicts of his old self. "Oh, I'm sorry, I didn't mean it!" is a typical American apology.

* * *

VI. LEGAL ASPECTS OF APOLOGY

Despite the obvious social and moral significance of apology, its legal implications are somewhat uncertain both in Japan and the United States. These uncertainties arise at several levels. At a formal level, the norms of substantive rights and liabilities announced in the codes and court decisions rarely treat apology as a significant factor. In American civil law, for example, we found no clear instance in which apology serves as a defense to a cause of action. A person is not relieved of liability for causing harm because he or she has apologized for the injury. The closest instance to the use of apology as a defense is the doctrine, now largely embodied in statute, that a retraction or apology mitigates damages in a defamation suit. If the retraction or apology is effective, the plaintiff is permitted to recover only actual damages, which in the vast majority of cases leaves the plaintiff with a moral victory but no substantial monetary recovery. Thus in states with such a statute or common law rule, an apology is a practical bar to a libel action, although the law does not quite say that. A somewhat similar situation exists in criminal law. Apology is not a defense to a criminal charge, but in both Japan and the United States the codes and rules permit apologetic behavior to be considered in mitigation of punishment. * * *

Uncertainty regarding the legal consequences of apology arises at two other levels as well. The procedural and evidentiary legal structures of Japanese and American law treat apology quite differently, although an apology is likely to have an impact on the outcome of a case in both systems. In American law, a statement that meets the standards of a sincere apology discussed above might also be characterized as an admission of liability admissible against the utterer. As we shall suggest, the law of evidence in America is torn between the pull to encourage compromise settlement of disputes by a process that is likely to include an apology and the countervailing attraction to a common lawyer of an admission, that "queen of proof," which can be used to prove the claim despite the hearsay rule and other artificial strictures that make proof at common law so complex. Such rules of evidence do not play a role in the judge-centered Japanese trial. As in the United States, few Japanese lawsuits are resolved by judgment after a full judicial trial. * * * What is notably different in Japan is the extent to which the court process includes and may actually require that the parties undertake to resolve the dispute by "conciliation" (chotei) and "compromise" (wakai). In such a process, the tender of an apology is a crucial step toward resolution and has important practical consequences, even if the provisions of the civil code that define the legal obligations of the parties say nothing about apology.

* * *

VIII. CONCLUSION

We said earlier that there are real differences in apologetic behavior in Japan and the United States. We are even more confident that there are differences in the significance that is attached to such behavior or to the failure to apologize in each nation. Americans attach greater significance and legal consequence to the perceptions of autonomy and internal coherence, thus making apology important as an expression of self. This leads apologetic behavior to be accompanied by a justification or an emphasis on the acceptance of liability along with responsibility. The act of apology must accordingly spring from internal motivations, not from the request of external authority, and must not be weakened by mixed motives. In Western eyes, ambiguity and ambivalence detract heavily from the worth of an apology. Sincerity in an apology means internal coherence and wholeheartedness.

* * *

Apology may be given a lower legal priority in the United States because American society does not place as high a value on group membership, conformity, and harmonious relationships among people as Japanese society does. In a social context that highly values group hierarchy and harmony, the appearance of conflict is likely to trigger a search for accommodation and compromise that will restore the sense of group coherence. An emphasis on individual autonomy, in contrast, is likely to lead to the vigorous assertion of narrowly defined personal interests that will appear in polar conflict with the rights of others. Compensation for the economic damage done may thus become more important to the hurt party than the restoration of the relationship that has been threatened. The admission of fault is dominant, and one may refrain from making an apology in order to protect oneself from demand for undue compensation. * * *

Although apologizing in the United States may be rare for the various cultural and legal reasons highlighted in the Wagatsuma and Rosett article, a recent surge of articles have been assessing and promoting apologies in the United States.[92] Professor Jonathan Cohen, in his article on "Advising Clients to Apologize,"[93] suggested how an apology can add value to a legal settlement by subtracting insult from an injury, preventing escalation of a dispute and future antagonistic behavior, and repairing a damaged relationship. An apology also can ease the way to serious settlement negotiations and mitigate the corrosive effects of feeling guilty and regret.

Based on several experimental studies, Professor Jennifer Robbennolt presented findings on how apologies can impact on efforts to settle legal disputes.

JENNIFER K. ROBBENNOLT, APOLOGIES AND LEGAL SETTLEMENT: AN EMPIRICAL EXAMINATION

102 Michigan Law Review 460, 506–07 (2003).

* * *

As a general matter, the results of the present study provide evidence that a full apology that both expresses sympathy for the victim's injuries and accepts responsibility for those injuries influences a variety of perceptions and attributions about the situation and the other party that might lead to a settlement or allow the parties to begin discussions. Full apologies were seen as more sufficient apologies, as evidencing more regret and a greater likelihood of care in the future, and as offered by people of higher moral character. Full apologies favorably altered assessments of the conduct leading to the injuries and changed the emotions of the injured party so as to reduce anger and increase

92. *See, e.g.,* Jennifer G. Brown, *The Role of Apology in Negotiation,* 87 Mar-quette L. Rev. 665 (2004); William K. Bartels, *The Stormy Seas of Apologies: California Evidence Code Section 1160 Provides a Safe Harbor for Apologies Made After Accidents,* 28 W. St. U. L. Rev. 141 (2000–01); Max Bolstad, *Learning From Japan: The Case for Increased Use of Apology in Mediation,* 48 Clev. St. L. Rev. 545 (2000); William Bradford, *'With a Very Great Blame on Our Hearts': Reparations, Reconciliation, and an American Indian Plea for Peace with Justice,* 27 Am. Indian L. Rev. 1 (2002–03); Charles R. Calleros, *Conflict, Apology, and Reconciliation at Arizona State University: A Second Case Study in Hateful Speech,* 27 Cumb. L. Rev. 91 (1996–97); Jonathan R. Cohen, *Advising Clients to Apologize,* 72 S. Cal. L. Rev. 1009 (1999); Jonathan R. Cohen, *Legislating Apology: The Pros and Cons,* 70 U. Cin. L. Rev. 819 (2002); Taryn Fuchs–Burnett, *Mass Public Corporate Apology,* Disp. Resol. J., July 2002, at 27; Elizabeth Latif, *Apologetic Justice: Evaluating Apologies Tailored Toward Legal Solutions,* 81 B.U. L. Rev. 289 (2001); Erin Ann O'Hara & Douglas Yarn, *On Apology and Consilience,* 77 Wash. L. Rev. 1121 (2002); Aviva Orenstein, *Apology Excepted: Incorporating a Feminist Analysis into Evidence Policy Where You Would Least Expect It,* 28 Sw. U. L. Rev. 221 (1999); Donna L. Pavlick, *Apology and Mediation: The Horse and Carriage of the Twenty–First Century,* 18 Ohio St. J. Disp. Resol. 829 (2003); Lee Taft, *Apology Subverted: The Commodification of Apology,* 109 Yale L.J. 1135 (2000), and Deborah L. Levi, *The Role of Apology in Mediation,* 72 N.Y.U. L. Rev. 1165 (1997). *Also see* Ken Blanchard & Margaret McBride, The One Minute Apology (2003).

93. Cohen, *supra* note 93, at 1009, 1015–23, 1023–27, 1027–42.

sympathy for the offender. Full apologies were seen as mitigating potential damage to the relationship, were more likely to lead to forgiveness, and inclined injured parties to look more favorably on the settlement offer. In addition, the results of the first study demonstrated that full apologies, through these effects on perceptions and attributions, increased the likelihood that the settlement offer would be accepted.

Accordingly, full apologies that include accepting responsibility for the incident may facilitate the settling of lawsuits. These "responsibility-accepting" apologies, however, are precisely the type of apologies that most clearly raise concerns about the effects of apologizing on liability decisionmaking and are not likely to be protected by evidentiary rules protecting apologies. Making a statement that admits fault and that might be admissible at trial, while improving the prospects for settling the case, is thought to increase the risk that the offender will be found liable.

For this reason, there is growing interest in ways in which offenders can apologize without exposing themselves to the same risks attendant to a full, responsibility-accepting apology. [This sort of partial apology can consist of sincere expressions of sympathy that fall short of admitting liability.] The present research suggests that the effects of such partial apologies are complex and identifies several aspects of the case that defendants ought to take into account when considering a partial apology. First, the effects of partial apologies on settlement decisionmaking appear to be much more complicated than the effects of full apologies. On the whole, partial apologies did not appear to facilitate settlement in the ways hoped by proponents. The most consistent finding was that partial apologies tended to be no better (or worse) than not offering an apology. Across both studies, regardless of the level of responsibility and the level of injury, there were no differences between those receiving partial apologies and no apology in their evaluations of the offender's conduct, the offender's regret, the offender's belief that he or she was responsible, damage to the relationship, anger, the degree to which the offer would make up for the injuries, or forgiveness.

More troubling for the efficacy of partial apologies, however, were some indications that a partial apology has the potential to influence attributions in ways that are unlikely to facilitate negotiation, particularly when the offender's responsibility for the incident was more clear or when the resulting injury was more severe. Where the offender's responsibility was more clear, participants reported less sympathy toward the offender and predicted that the offender was less likely to be careful in the future when a partial apology was offered. Where the resulting injury was more severe, offering a partial apology increased attributions of responsibility to the offender and resulted in the offer being perceived as less likely to make up for the injuries received. Moreover, the results of the first study demonstrated that partial apologies may increase injured parties' uncertainty about whether or not they are inclined to accept or reject a particular settlement offer. These results suggest that not only do partial apologies not facilitate settlement in the ways that full apologies do, but that offering a partial apology may change perceptions in ways that could impede the discussion.

On the other hand, there were some indications that, under the right circumstances, even a partial apology might be somewhat beneficial. Both when the responsibility for the incident was more ambiguous and when the injury was less severe, a partial apology was viewed as more sufficient than no apology. In addition, when the responsibility for the incident was more ambiguous, the offender's conduct was rated more favorably when a partial apology was offered than when the offender failed to offer an apology. Particularly where the offender's responsibility was less clear, participants were somewhat more open to apologies that did not accept responsibility. This suggests that there may be circumstances under which a partial apology is beneficial and (at least somewhat) better than failing to offer any expression of sympathy at all.

Professor Robbennolt's studies have also suggested that protected apologies are not less effective or less valued than unprotected ones. She found that an evidentiary rule that protected the apologizer from liability did not undermine the value of the apology to the recipient.

Professor Cohen, in his article on counseling clients to apologize, also considered how parties can give "safe" apologies (what Professor Robbennolt called protected apologies) in the United States, realizing that the one of largest barriers to apology lies in the fear of it establishing liability.[94] He suggested several ways that parties may more safely apologize, although he recognized that none of the options ensured absolute safety. The best known option relies on the rules of evidence that exclude settlement discussions from trial, but as anyone who has examined Federal Rule of Evidence 408 knows, these sorts of rules offer traps for the unsophisticated. Parties can remove some of the Rule 408–type traps by drafting a confidentiality contract but a judge may not feel bound by a private agreement, even a carefully crafted one, if the excluded evidence would contravene a greater public policy in hearing the evidence. A better option would be to secure a judicial order, thus overcoming the risk that an unsympathetic judge might not enforce a private agreement, although persuading a judge to issue an order can be difficult. Even if successful, the judge or an appellate court might later find a reason to modify the order. Finally, court rules and state statutes designed to preserve confidentiality in mediations offer a promising option because their legal protections are tailored to serve the needs of this particularly suitable setting for weighing whether to apologize and for framing apologies. The scope and limitations of these mediation

---

94. Professor Cohen also suggested several other barriers to apology. He indicated that clients may be concerned that an apology can justify extracting an additional monetary payment, be demeaning, show a weakness that can invite the wrath of others, or risk voiding insurance coverage.

specific protections, however, are still unfolding in rules, legislatures, and court decisions.[95]

Notes and Questions

1.   Outline several key points that you think Soler and its attorney in the Mitsubishi–Soler dispute should cover in their opening statements. Next, consider how you would present these points in a way that would likely be heard by Japanese parties on the other side?

2.   The readings suggest examples when private meetings with a mediator might help avoid a cross-cultural impasse. Can you think of any other cultural situations where caucusing might be effective?

3.   What are some of the cultural factors that discourage offering apology in the United States? What considerations would you advise your client to weigh when deciding whether to offer an apology? To seek an apology? If your client needs an apology, would you ask your client to consider taking less money than he or she could probably secure in the settlement in return for receiving an apology?

4.   How would you test whether an apology might be an option important to the other side? Given what you read about apology in Japan, how would you approach a Japanese party about your client offering an apology? In the Mitsubishi–Soler dispute, do you think the Japanese plaintiff might find an apology desirable? Would a partial apology by defendant Soler facilitate or hinder efforts to settle the dispute? Consider Professor Robbennolt's discussion of how partial apologies can impact on settlement efforts.

5.   Were you surprised by Professor Robbennolt's suggestion that protected apologies may not be less effective or less valued than unprotected ones? Why do you think that a recipient might value an apology that did not expose the apologizer to legal liability?

6.   Some litigators are thrilled with the option of their clients offering apologies as long as the apologies cannot be construed as conceding legal responsibility. They figure this could be a great deal for their clients. By simply offering words of apology, their clients would not have to pay as much money or, better yet, may pay nothing. Seems like a no-brainer, they have concluded. The readings consider the risk of strategic and insincere apologies, however. Draft an apology for Soler in the Mitsubishi–Soler dispute that meets the five criteria found in the Wagatsuma and Rosett article. Would you want to modify the apology in any way to account for the risks of offering it? If you did, would that safe apology still be a full one?

7.   In recognizing that apologies can contribute to preventing and settling lawsuits, a number of state legislatures in the United States have begun considering and in some cases have adopted laws designed to make the legal environment more hospitable for offering either apologetic expressions of sympathy or fault-admitting apologies. For a status report of what is

95. In the United States, the National Conference of Commissioners on Uniform State Laws conducted an extensive study and debate of the scope of necessary protections in mediations and drafted the 2001 Uniform Mediation Act. The draft was approved by the American Bar Association and is now being considered for adoption in a number of states.

happening in the United States that also examines the arguments for and against various approaches, see Cohen, *Legislating Apology: The Pros and Cons*, 70 U. CIN. L. REV. 819 (2002).

(4) Resolving Distributive Issues

As the session moves rapidly toward closure, a difficult distributive issue can crystallize and block the way home. This last issue may be resolved in only one way, in a way that benefits one party at the expense of the other. It is usually about how much money one party will pay the other.

To resolve a distributive dispute, negotiators traditionally turn to a dance of offers and counteroffers. The dance can range from simple to complex and from combative to collaborative.[96] The dance begins with opening offers and can follow a carefully calibrated pattern of concessions that are played to an orchestra of arguments, warnings, affirmative promises, emotional appeals, humor, silence, and other moves designed to advance one party's position at the expense of the other. An adversarial negotiator can dance very competitively using aggressively a full range of gentle and harsh steps; a problem-solving one can modulate these steps to produce a collaborative dance. But, other versions of the dance can be performed. One particularly distinctive one has been labeled the haggle. It is best known as the method of choice in the Middle Eastern bazaar although variations are practiced throughout the world. Its particular steps are shaped by the culture of the practicing parties. In this next excerpt the author, an experienced haggler, translated his experiences and strategies into the following pithy advice and rules for success.

MAX EDISON, HOW TO HAGGLE—PROFESSIONAL TRICKS FOR SAVING MONEY ON JUST ABOUT ANYTHING

11–13, 29–39 (2001).

CHAPTER III: TESTING

Well as a pawnbroker, I get maybe 20 different people trying to sell me stuff every day, and if I guess wrong too often I'm out of business. * * * So to preserve tranquility, I've gotta be right at least 95 percent of the time. I boost the odds in four ways [three are included].

1. I collect newspaper advertising inserts from the local chain stores. Every time I see something on sale at Wal–Mart or Home Depot, I know it'll be coming through the pawnshop at one point or another. Even if my customer, the seller, paid full price, I'm only going to give him a fraction of the sale price. * * *

---

96. *See* ABRAMSON, *supra* note 9, at 47–51, 263–64. For a more thorough treatment of approaches to distributive issues, see CHARLES B. CRAVER, EFFECTIVE LEGAL NEGOTIA- TION AND SETTLEMENT ch. 7 (4th ed. 2001) and MELISSA L. NELKEN, UNDERSTANDING NEGOTIA- TION ch. 2 (2001).

2. I have a big stack of catalogs that tell me the wholesale and/or retail prices on everything from guns to diamonds to CD players.

3. Now that our shop has full-time Internet access, I check online auctions and classified listings to see what other people are trying to get for the same equipment in similar condition. One of the neat things is that stuff sells so darn cheap on the net.

Chapter IV—Psyching Em Out

Haggling is a psychological warfare, no doubt about it. Make a slip and you pay too much, or receive too little, for the stuff you're dickering over. Well, there are some unwritten rules to haggling, which a lot of people know, and then there are dirty tricks, which are known only to few.

UNWRITTEN RULES

* * * Most everybody who's any good at haggling knows these rules, and if you break one they get annoyed.

1. Play "hard to get." If a seller can tell that you are in love with an item, he knows he can get his top price. Instead, pretend to be mildly, but not formally, interested in the piece you're looking at. Don't fall in love, and try not to come back three or four times in the course of the day to look at it. While this shows the seller that you're serious about the item, it also shows him that he can take you for pretty close to sticker price.

2. If you make an offer, that offer stands unless a counteroffer is made. One of the biggest complaints I have about some of my Hispanic, Somali, and other African customers is that I'll have a TV priced at, say, $75. They'll offer $60, and I'll accept, because I can knock 20 percent off the top of anything. Then they'll offer $50, which really cheeses me off and makes me challenge them to put up or shut up.

Then again, haggling in Mexico is different. Merchants put wildly inflated price tags on their stuff (at least the stuff they want to sell to tourists), then accept, eventually, a price that is 10 percent of that.

4. Buyers, if you and the seller can't quite come together on the price of an item, ask him if he's got anything to throw in on the deal. * * * If it's a VCR, he might throw in a couple of free movies. Whatever makes you feel better about paying his final price. * * *

5. Never show your whole hand at once. If you're willing to pay $80 for an item, for example, offer $60 (or even $40). You never know—the other guy might take it. Even if he passes or counteroffers, he'll feel like some progress is being made. Sellers, never give your lowest price right off the bat (unless you're desperate to get rid of a piece). * * *

6. Along the same lines, sellers should never let the buyer know how much they paid for an item. * * *

7. It's important to nail down beforehand whether sales tax is included or not. Once buyer and seller agree on a price, that price should be solid.

DIRTY TRICKS

There are certain things you can do that boost your profits or drop your buying price by taking advantage of the other person's weaknesses. Whether these strategies are moral or not is none of my concern. They happen, and you ignore them at your peril. These include:

1. Try to determine how desperate the other party is. One of the first things you should be asking is, "Why are you selling?" If the answer is, "I need the money," you have a sucker on your line. He's just admitted to you that he's desperate to sell. When someone admits that he's desperate, he's also admitted that he'll take a much lower price for what he's got for sale. * * *

2. Try to knock the crap out of whatever he's got for sale. Let me put that another way. Nobody likes to be abused or have their stuff abused. Be polite, but point out flaws in the merchandise. * * * The fact is, few people really know what they've got or what it's worth. * * *

5. Totally * * * lie. The chances are good that the seller really doesn't know how much his stuff is worth, much less what anyone is willing to pay for it. You can tell him that the particular model he's got isn't selling very well, or it has some weird hidden defect, or that Wal–Mart is selling it new for half what he paid (which is not altogether impossible). Whatever story you choose, stick with it and try to get your story straight before he starts questioning you.

6. [I]t's always good to have excuses for not paying top dollar, too. One of my favorites is, "Gee, I'd really like to sell it to you at that price, but I've gotta be able to look my business partner in the face." You could substitute the phrase, "but I've gotta look out for my bottom line, or else I'm out of business," or "I've got dollars invested, but I'm not willing to take a loss on this," or "These really don't sell well around here."

8. Whether you're a buyer or a seller, don't trust anyone. One of the key sayings around our pawnshop is one we stole from a car dealer: "Question: How do you know when a customer is lying? Answer: When his lips are moving." That about sums it up. As a pawnbroker, I get lied to at least half a dozen times a day. I don't take personal offense at it, but I recognize that it happens and I know who's doing it.

    Anyway, your buddy Harvey may swear up and down that his VCR works perfectly, but you'll save harsh feelings later by testing his stuff now. * * *

STUPID MOVES

There are some things that you may have been taught to do which are of no use whatsoever in haggling. It's best to break yourself of these habits before you do any more damage.

The first one is saying, "I've got other people looking at it." Every second-rate haggler seems to think this is a good device to motivate a buyer, and maybe it is—at least a buyer who doesn't know anything about haggling. To a seasoned wheeler-dealer, though, this a cheap, transparent dodge to try to get someone to buy something he otherwise wouldn't.

Notes and Questions

1. Examine the excerpt by Max Edison in which he offered detailed advice and rules for effective haggling. Try to extract and label any generic negotiation strategies by using negotiation nomenclature. And, then, critique these generic strategies.

2. Based on your analysis of the excerpt, construct a model of haggling for resolving distributive conflicts in an international negotiation or mediation. Would you describe the model as problem-solving? If not, can you construct a haggling model that could be fairly described as problem-solving?

3. Are there norms of proper behavior in the haggling process that if violated will derail or destroy the process? What norms are suggested in the excerpt? Are there other norms that might apply in other cultures? As a buyer, have you ever engaged in a haggle in which the seller cut off the negotiations because you did something other than bid too low for the item? Do you think that the seller cut off the negotiations because you violated some unstated rule of ethical haggling?

4. Before class, you should go to a local market where haggling is done to bargain for the lowest price you can get for an item. Then, parse your haggling experience by identifying the stages, strategies, and what you would do differently the next time.

(d) Juncture: Post–Session: Enforcing Settlement Agreements

Enforcing an agreement to settle a dispute resolved in an international mediation poses fresh challenges with an elegant solution, as this excerpt suggests:[97]

> In cross-border disputes, attorneys should give special attention to how any resulting settlement agreement will be enforced. In domestic disputes, attorneys know that they can always fall back on the local U.S. court in the jurisdiction in which the agreement was signed to remedy any breaches. In

97. See Abramson, supra note 10, at 936–37.

cross-border enforcement actions, the local court option in a foreign country can be less reliable and take more time and expense. Attorneys need to retain local counsel in the breaching party's country and commence a lawsuit in a foreign jurisdiction with all the risks and uncertainties of transnational litigation. These burdens of cross-border enforcement can be less onerous, however, in a foreign country with a mature legal system where the client does regular business and already has local counsel.

In cross-border disputes, parties can more easily enforce a settlement agreement when it is the by-product of an arbitration proceeding. Rather then assuming the risks of enforcing a settlement agreement in a transnational lawsuit, parties can request an arbitral tribunal to incorporate the settlement agreement into an arbitration award. This option is explicitly authorized by both domestic and international arbitration rules. The resulting "consent" award may be enforceable in foreign jurisdictions under the relatively reliable procedures of the New York Convention on Recognition and Enforcement of Foreign Arbitral Awards.

This method of enforcement works relatively smoothly for parties who sign a settlement agreement after the arbitration proceeding has been initiated and the arbitral tribunal formed. If no tribunal has yet been constituted, however, parties have several other options for facilitating enforcement. First, parties could add to a settlement agreement a personal jurisdiction clause. Under the clause, parties would agree to submit to the personal jurisdiction of a domestic court for the purpose of enforcing a settlement agreement. Second, parties could simply include in a settlement agreement a clause that provides that any breaches would be resolved in arbitration. This is an obvious precaution that can be too easily forgotten. The arbitration clause would give an aggrieved party access to an arbitration process that would produce an award enforceable under the New York Convention. Third, parties could initiate an arbitration proceeding for the purpose of securing a consent award. This strategy would increase the expense and time in connection with settling a dispute but may be worthwhile in order to give parties the added security offered by a consent arbitration award * * *

The Stockholm Chamber of Commerce Rules contain a rare provision that explicitly provides a procedure for enforcing settlement agreements through an arbitration award. Parties can agree to appoint the mediator as an arbitrator and "request him to confirm the settlement agreement in an arbitral award."[98] The resulting "consent" award can then be enforced under the New York Convention.

The European Commission of the European Union is considering a proposed directive to convert settlement agreements into enforceable instruments. It would provide that:

> Member States shall ensure that, upon request of the parties, a settlement agreement reached as a result of a mediation can be confirmed in a judgment, decision, authentic instrument or any other form that renders the agreement enforceable under national law, provided that the agreement is considered as binding contract in accordance with the applicable law to the agreement.[99]

Notes and Questions

Assume that you are representing the defendant U.S. party High–Tech in a dispute with the plaintiff, an Italian–Chinese joint venture, Prosando. Both sides have agreed to mediate the dispute in Beijing. An associate in your law firm has put together a Case File that includes a description of the dispute, background on the Chinese mediator, proposed mediation rules, and other materials that might help you understand the cultural setting of the mediation. You will need to read the Case File to answer these questions.

1. Based on reading Files 3–5 that contain laws regulating the People's Mediation Committees, information on the practice of the same neutral mediating and arbitrating, and two articles on the history of mediation in China, do you think the Government is trying to move the role of mediators away from a wisely directive approach and toward an evaluatively directive one, as suggested in Section C.4(c)(2)? In answering this question, cite specific language in the Regulations and Order as well as sections of other materials in the three files.

2. After reading File 1—Description of Dispute, identify both parties' interests and any potential impediments.

3. After reading File 2—Mediator's Resume and Interview Notes, classify the approach to the mediation that you think Mr. Lu will actually use. Explain the basis for your prediction.

4. After reading Files 1–5, which rules in File 6—Proposed Mediation Rules would you want to modify and why? Describe the specific changes that you would want to make. Are there any specific rules that you would want to add?

5. What would you and your client want to emphasize in the opening statements if you were planning a problem-solving approach before a problem-solving mediator? Outline the key points. In what particular ways would you modify the opening statements knowing the mediator might be of the

---

98. Stockholm Chamber of Commerce, Rules of the Mediation Institute, art. 12 (Apr. 1, 1999).

99. *See* Article 5(1) of Preliminary Draft Proposal for a Directive on Certain Aspects of Mediation in Civil and Commercial Matters (no date on draft).

sort you identified in Question 3? Intent on pursuing a constricted problem-solving approach (as described in the excerpt in Section C.4(e) on "Impact of Different Roles on Mediation Representation"), how would you further modify your side's opening statements if you thought the other side viewed the mediator as wisely directive even though you might see the mediator as directively evaluative?

6. Consistent with advancing High Tech's interests and avoiding the potential impediments, suggest a productive response to each of these statements by the Chinese side, the plaintiff.

(a) Plaintiff says: "I have been embarrassed by the sudden termination of the distribution agreement in China. We were actively negotiating with a number of potential distributors in Central and Southern China at the time we received the notice. And we are still disturbed that your company resisted giving us the most recent technology to distribute as if we were from a third-world country."

(b) Plaintiff's Attorney says: "My client wants damages in the amount of $39 million." You are outraged by such a high demand, convinced that under their most optimistic scenario, they would not be able to prove damages of more than $5 million.

Case File

List of Contents

File 1: Case Facts

The Dispute

Prosando v. High–Tech[100]

Prosando, an Italian–Chinese joint venture based in Beijing, is a distributor of office and business equipment.

In January 1990 Prosando entered into an exclusive five-year distribution contract with High–Tech, a California computer manufacturer. Prosando agreed to establish a distribution network for High–Tech's

---

100. ©1994. The CPR Institute for Dispute Resolution (formerly known as the Center for Public Resources/CPR Legal Program), 366 Madison Avenue, New York, NY 10017, www.cpradr.org. (Permission granted to change Prosando party to an Italian–Chinese joint venture.). Reprinted with permission. All rights reserved.

Future A and B minicomputers throughout China and to use High–Tech's trademark in doing so.

The English-language contract, negotiated by persons who spoke English as a second language, raised questions regarding termination rights. One provision gave High–Tech a limited right to terminate the sole distribution aspect of the contract if Prosando failed to develop a distribution network by June 1991, one-and-one-half years into the contract. Another alleged termination provision appeared at Clause C but contained blanks as follows:

> *Buyer must place a noncancellable blanket order for 100 of the products totaling one million U.S. dollars upon execution of this agreement for delivery on or after _____. (Left blank in the contract.)*

> *On each calendar year commencing in _____ (left blank in the contract) the parties will agree on the minimum quantity requirements for the subsequent twelve-month period. If agreement is not achieved, either party may terminate this Agreement upon prior 90 days written notice.*

Loss of profits or prospective profits arising from termination were addressed as follows:

> *Upon termination of this Agreement becoming effective: (a)Neither party shall be liable to the other for loss of profits or prospective profits of any kind or nature sustained or arising out of or alleged to have arisen out of such termination.*

After the contract was signed, High–Tech withheld shipment of equipment pending legal department review of the contract. Six months later, despite Prosando's reluctance, the parties agreed to allow High–Tech to retain distribution rights for itself in exchange for a 10% commission on such sales to Prosando.

After the renegotiation, Prosando's first order for 50 units (not the allegedly required 100) was shipped. In October 1990 Prosando placed another order for 20 units which it cancelled in January 1991. Throughout the second half of 1991, Prosando sought changes and delays in the payment terms.

In January 1991 High–Tech discontinued the Future A system and introduced the Century series but refused to negotiate its distribution with Prosando. High–Tech claimed the contract expressly contemplated that new computer lines need not be offered to Prosando. After another six months (one-and-one-half years into the contract), High–Tech finally agreed to allow Prosando to distribute Century.

During the first two years of the contract, Prosando's sales and establishment of a distribution network were so slow that by June 1992 only four Beijing distributors were in place. None were in place outside of Beijing.

In June 1992, two and a half years into the Agreement, without prior warning, High–Tech notified Prosando that the contract would be terminated within 30 days for clear and unequivocal breach of the Agreement by Prosando's:

1. Failure to use its best efforts to resell the products within the assigned territory to the total dissatisfaction of the Seller, since Prosando has placed orders for only 88 units of products.

2. Failure to establish the "distributor" network on or before June 30, 1991.

3. Failure to submit or negotiate any subsequent annual purchase commitments.

Upon receiving this notice, Prosando continued to sell its remaining High–Tech equipment. Prosando initiated an arbitration proceeding in Beijing claiming $10 million in damages for breach of contract and fraud; $20 million for loss of business reputation; $6 million for lost profits for 5 years; and, actual reliance damages of $3 million expended on the contract (including capitalized loans, leasing of premises, personnel, promoting and advertising the product, travel, etc.) They seek compensatory damages for High–Tech's fraud in entering into a contract to provide equipment that was soon to be cancelled.

High–Tech denied all allegations and counterclaimed for $126,000 for equipment shipped.

In late 2000, the parties agreed to try mediation to be administered by the Beijing Conciliation Centre.

File 2: Mediator's Resume and Notes from Interview

Resume

John Lu

Attorney at Law

Beijing, China

Jlee@ATTS.com

Education

Beijing University, Law 1982

Columbia University Law School, LL.M. 1988

Mediation Training and Experience

Mediator, People's Mediation Committee, Beijing, 1979–1981

Mediation Training–Beijing Conciliation Centre, January 1997 (5 days)

Advanced Mediation Training–Harvard Law School, June 2000 (5 days)

Conciliator, The Beijing Conciliation Centre of CCPIT/CCOIC, 1997–present

Employment Experience

Attorney, China Energy Corporation, Shanghai 1982–1987

Attorney, Dell Computers, Round Rock, Texas 1989–1995

Attorney, Private Practice (domestic and international business transactions) 1995–present

Personal Information

Born in Nanjing, China

Speaks Mandarin

Fluent in German and English

Enjoys Chinese and Italian Opera

Notes from Telephone Interview of Mediator—October 2, 2000

1. Mr. Lu identified himself as a facilitative, problem-solving mediator who uses the approaches learned at the Harvard advanced mediation training program. He also frequently uses caucuses. He feels he has the expertise to offer credible recommendations and evaluations, but will do so only if solicited by one of the parties.

2. He has mediated about 100 cases of which about ten involved disputes between distributors and their foreign distributees.

3. Mr. Lu has negotiated numerous distribution agreements while working at Dell and in private practice. He also has litigated a dozen disputes that have arisen under distribution agreements.

4. He has published a widely read and highly regarded article in China on how to avoid destroying business opportunities under distribution agreements. The article contains his personal advice on how to maintain healthy business relationships. The article has not been translated into English.

File 3: Law Regulating People's Mediation Committees

CONSTITUTION OF THE PEOPLE'S REPUBLIC OF CHINA
(Adopted on December 4, 1982)

Article 111. The residents' committees and villagers' committees established among urban and rural residents on the basis of their place of residence are mass organizations of self-management at the grassroots level. The chairman, vice-chairmen and members of each residents' or villagers' committee are elected by the residents.... The residents' and villagers' committees establish committees for people's mediation, public security, public health and other matters in order to manage public affairs and social services in their areas, mediate civil disputes, help maintain public order and convey residents' opinions and demands and make suggestions to the people's government.

REGULATIONS GOVERNING THE ORGANIZATION OF PEOPLE'S MEDIATION COMMITTEES PROMULGATED BY THE STATE COUNCIL ON 17 JUNE, 1989[101]

Article 1 The present Regulations are formulated with a view to strengthening the establishment of people's mediation committees, settling promptly any civil disputes, promoting solidarity among the people, safeguarding social security and facilitating socialist modernization and construction.

Article 4 Adult citizens who are upright, able to strengthen solidarity among people, enthusiastic about people's mediation, equipped with a certain amount of legal knowhow and adept in policy interpretation shall be elected as committee members of people's mediation committees.

Article 5 The task of a people's mediation committee is to undertake mediation in civil disputes, disseminate through mediation such legal information as the law, statutes, rules, regulations and policies of the state, and to educate people on the observation of law and order and the respect of social morality.

Article 6 Mediation work undertaken by people's mediation committees shall follow closely these principles:

(1) mediation shall be undertaking in conformity with the law, statutes, rules, regulations and policies of the state or, where no relevant stipulations exist, in accordance with social ethics;

(2) voluntary mediation on the basis of mutual equality shall be undertaken; and

(3) the rights to litigation of the parties concerned shall be respected; a people's mediation committee shall not employ lack of mediation and failure of mediation as reasons to stop the parties concerned from bringing a lawsuit to the people's court.

Article 8 When mediating in a dispute, a people's mediation committee shall place emphasis on investigation and facts. A clear distinction shall be made between right from wrong. A people's mediation committee shall also be reasonable and patient in the course of mediation to facilitate conciliation between the parties concerned.

Article 10 People's governments at grassroots level shall give support to agreements reached through mediation by people's mediation committees which are in conformity with the law, statutes, rules, regulations and policies of the state, and correct those agreements in discordance with the law, statutes, rules, regulations and policies of the state.

Article 12 Committee members of people's mediation committees shall keep the following disciplines:

101. In comparing the original 1954 regulations with the new 1989 regulations, the author suggests that major themes of the new regulations include the "preeminence of law and the resulting need for accountability to the law" and an effort to increase the professionalism of the mediators. Whether these goals have been achieved has not yet been determined. *See* Glassman, *supra* note 44.

(1) practice of favouritism and fraudulence is forbidden;

(2) harassing, attacking and taking revenge on the parties concerned are forbidden;

(3) insulting and penalizing the parties concerned are forbidden;

(4) disclosure of the secrets of the parties concerned is forbidden; and

(5) acceptance of invitations to dinners and gifts is forbidden.

ORDER OF THE MINISTRY OF JUSTICE OF THE PEOPLE'S REPUBLIC OF CHINA PEOPLE'S MEDIATION

(No. 75)

Some Provisions Concerning the Work of People's Mediation which was adopted at the working meeting of Ministers of the Ministry of Justice on September 11, 2002 is hereby promulgated to be effective as of November 1, 2002.

Article 4. The people's mediation committee shall observe the following principles in the mediation of private disputes:

a. Conducting mediations on the basis of laws, regulations, administrative rules and policies. Where there are no explicit provisions in laws, regulations, administrative rules and policies, they shall conduct mediations on the basis of socialist morality;

b. Conducting mediations on the basis of the free will and equality of both parties concerned;

c. Respecting the litigation rights of the parties concerned, and may not prevent them from lodging lawsuits with the people's court on the ground of not conducting mediations or failing to settle the disputes through mediations.

Article 6. In the people's mediation activities, the parties to disputes shall enjoy the following rights:

a. Deciding at their own free will to accept, refuse to accept or to terminate mediation;

b. Requesting relevant mediators to withdraw;

c. Refraining from suppression and constraint, expressing their true will and making reasonable claims;

d. Coming into mediation agreements at their own free will.

Chapter II People's Mediation Committees and People's Mediators

Article 17. The people's mediators shall observe the following disciplines in the mediation of disputes:

a. They may not seek private gains by unlawful means;

b. They may not suppress or revenge against the parties concerned;

c. They may not insult or punish any of the parties to the disputes;

d. They may not disclose any of the privacies of the parties concerned;

e. They may not accept any treat of gift of other people.

Article 18.

* * * To perform his duties, a people's mediator shall stick to the principles, love his work and provide services warmly. They shall be honest and keep his promise, behave decently, show self-discipline, be uncorrupted, pay attention to study, and incessantly improve their accomplishment of law and ethics as well as mediation skills.

Chapter III Acceptance of Private Disputes

Article 23. The people's mediation committees shall accept disputes for mediation upon the request of the parties concerned. Where none of the parties requests, they may volunteer for mediation, unless the parties show objection to mediation. . . .

Chapter IV Mediation of Private Disputes

Article 25. To mediate a dispute, the people's mediation committee concerned shall appoint a people's mediator as the chairman, and may, where necessary, appoint a number of people's mediators to participate in the mediation.

Article 26. When mediating a dispute, the people's mediation committee shall inquire the parties concerned about the facts and plots of the dispute, know the claims and grounds of both parties, and where necessary, make investigations for verification purposes, and make good preparations for the mediation.

Article 29. The mediation of disputes by the people's mediation committee may be conducted in public where it is necessary, and the relatives, neighbors of the parties concerned and the people of the local place (or the entity concerned) to be audiences in the mediation, unless the privacy or business secret of the parties concerned is involved or any of the parties concerned shows objection.

Article 31. The people's mediation committee shall, on the basis of finding out the facts, discriminating the liabilities of each party, and according to the characteristics of the parties concerned, the nature of the dispute, difficulty, situation of development, etc., take various flexible ways to conduct patient and meticulous persuasion and so as to urge the parties concerned to understand each other, eliminate estrangement, and steer and help the parties concerned to come into mediation agreements.

Chapter V People's Mediation Agreement and the Performance Thereof

Article 36. The parties concerned shall voluntarily perform the mediation agreement. The people's mediation committee shall pay return visits to the performance of the mediation agreement and put the situation of performance to record.

Article 37. Where the parties concerned refuses to perform the mediation agreement or become regretted after coming into an agreement, the people's mediation committee shall deal with the different situations according to the following rules:

> a. Where the parties refuse to perform the agreement without good reasons, it shall persuade and urge them to perform the agreement;
>
> b. If the parties concerned argue that the agreement has not been properly made or the people's mediation committee finds that the agreement is not properly made, it shall, upon the consent of the parties concerned, alter the agreement by a second mediation, or cancel the original agreement and come into a new one;
>
> c. If any of the parties still refuses to perform the people's mediation agreement after being urged, it shall inform the parties concerned that they may request the basic-level people's government to deal with the dispute or file a lawsuit with the people's court on the ground of performing, altering or canceling the mediation agreement.

Chapter VI Guidance to the People's Mediation Work

Article 40. The judicial administrative organs at all levels shall pay attention to the training of the people's mediators by various means so as to constantly improve the quality of the people's mediators.

File 4: Practice of Same Neutral Mediating and Arbitrating

See Section C.4(d) in this chapter on "Search for Arbitrator Power in Mediation Practice"

Arbitration Law of the People's Republic of China

(Adopted at the Ninth Standing Committee Session of the

Eighth National People's Congress on August 31, 1994)

Article 51. The arbitration tribunal may carry out mediation prior to making a ruling. The arbitration tribunal shall mediate when the litigants agree to mediation. If the mediation fails, a ruling should be made promptly.

If an agreement has been reached through mediation, the arbitration tribunal shall draw up a written mediation, which has the same legal effect as a ruling letter.

File 5: Articles on Mediation in China

MICHAEL T. COLATRELLA, JR., COURT–PERFORMED MEDIATION IN THE PEOPLE'S REPUBLIC OF CHINA: A PROPOSED MODEL TO IMPROVE THE UNITED STATES FEDERAL DISTRICT COURTS' MEDIATION PROGRAMS

15 Ohio State Journal on Dispute Resolution 391, 395–400, 404–06 (2000).

II.   MEDIATION IN CHINA

For more than two thousand years, mediation, or tiaojie, has been the primary means of resolving disputes in China. The popularity of mediation as a method of dispute resolution in China is a product of primarily three related but distinct sociopolitical forces—Confucian philosophy, an inadequate and underdeveloped legal system, and Maoist principles. Each of these factors, which are grounded in both the cultural values and the historical development of China, discouraged the use of formal litigation and fostered the resolution of disputes through private settlement, often with the assistance of a third party.

1.   Confucian Philosophy

Confucian philosophy, which dominated Chinese culture for more than two thousand years and is still a significant force in modern Chinese society, traditionally encouraged individuals to settle their disputes privately and, if necessary, involve the community, extended family, clans, and guilds for dispute resolution assistance. Confucius taught that the primary goal of all human endeavors, including government, is to promote and preserve the natural harmony that existed among men and between man and nature. It was a person's duty, according to Confucius, to preserve harmony through one's behavior, guided by the rules of polite conduct (li). Litigation, a form of conflict, disrupted the natural harmony and amounted to "a public admission of some personal failing . * * * " The Chinese therefore came to embrace compromise or yielding (jang) as the socially acceptable way to resolve disputes, which "requires one to yield on some points in order to gain some advantage on others." Another Confucian principle which influences conflict resolution is the "spirit of self-criticism." One who assumes a spirit of self-criticism examines his conduct to determine whether it is the cause of the conflict. This humbling act, in turn, invokes a positive response from the other party and hopefully leads to harmony. Thus, mediation always has been consistent with Confucian values.

2. An Inadequate and Under–Developed Court System

The popularity of mediation in imperial China was in large measure also attributable to an inaccessible and inadequate court system. Many localities had no court, and litigants often were forced to travel great distances to lodge formal civil claims. If litigants could overcome the obstacle of distance or were fortunate enough to live close to courts, their case was handled by magistrates or magistrate assistants that had no legal training and who often were corrupt. The magistrates or their assistants were known to accept bribes and extort "customary fees" from litigants, which led to a general distrust of the courts and which gave rise to the expression "win your lawsuit and lose your money." Magistrates also were frequently "harsh and degrading" to litigants. It was not unusual for the court to use torture to obtain evidence from a litigant or to incarcerate him pending trial and during a prolonged appeal process.

Despite the advent of the rule of law (fa) during the third century B.C., which slowly wove its way into Confucian principles, imperial China retained its strong bias against lawsuits embodied in Confucian principles. Imperial rulers were unconcerned with the inadequacies and corruption that plagued the court system. Imperial philosophy toward litigation and the frequent abuses of the courts are captured in a statement made by the K'anghsi Emperor (1662–1722): "[L]awsuits would tend to increase to a frightful amount, if people were not afraid of the tribunals, and if they felt confident of always finding in them ready and perfect justice . * * * I desire, therefore, that those who have recourse to the tribunals should be treated without pity, and in such a manner that they shall be disgusted with [the] law, and tremble to appear before a magistrate." Such sentiments paint a grim picture of the plight of litigants in imperial China and, not surprisingly, encouraged mediation's widespread use and popularity.

3. Maoist Thought

With the onset of communism in China in the twentieth century, the popularity and acceptance of mediation continued as it was, viewed as furthering the notions of social harmony which characterize communist thought. After the overthrow of the Ch'ing Dynasty in 1911, China was embattled in a tumultuous and bloody political struggle over the country's leadership, from which the Communists ultimately emerged victorious. As a result, the People's Republic of China was established in 1949 under the leadership of Mao Zedong (Mao), and the process of creating a new legal system modeled after the former Union of Soviet Socialist Republics began.

Mao immediately recognized how the deeply rooted Confucian concepts of compromise and self-criticism mirrored and served communist ideals and goals. Analogous to Confucian thought, Mao believed that in a communist society, individual interests should be de-emphasized in favor of promoting social harmony and the common good on behalf of society as a unit. Therefore, disputes between individuals in a communist society should be "resolved not through defeat of one party over the other, but by the movement of both to a new plane of unity higher than the one out of which the [dispute] originally developed.'' Thus, the Communist party adopted mediation as a means to promote social harmony and control, conducting mediation with the assistance of ''party cadres'' or People's Mediation Committees (Committees). In addition to resolving disputes and avoiding the cost, delay, and ''undesirable dissonance'' of litigation, mediation by party members or organizations also served as a means of ''educating'' the people and implementing party policy.

B. Mediation in Modern China

Mediation continues to be China's most popular method for resolving disputes and is an integral part of civil procedure in its court system. Unlike the United States, the Chinese judiciary is not a separate, coequal branch of government within the Chinese legal system, but rather one of many ''arms'' of the central government, lacking the independence, power, and prestige often associated with our court system. Litigation in this environment often is perceived as lacking the impartiality and fairness that Americans typically enjoy and contributes to the preference of the Chinese for mediation. Although China is seeking to create a more modern legal system committed to the rule of law in order to engender greater confidence in its ability to adjudicate cases fairly, for the benefit of its own citizens as well as to compete in the international economic market, it is still deeply committed to the concept of institutionalized mediation.

* * *

2. Civil Procedure and Mediation

Given the historical unreliability of the litigation process in China, it is not surprising that mediation plays a central role in China's ordinary procedure for resolving civil disputes. China's present Code of Civil Procedure was adopted officially in 1991 after functioning almost ten years on a provisional basis, and an entire section of the Code is dedicated to describing mediation's proper use, evidencing its prominence in China's ordinary civil procedure. Participation in mediation is voluntary, but judges occasionally employ subtle, and sometimes more forceful, pressures to encourage parties to mediate disputes. Participation in mediation is commonly expected of and anticipated by parties and is viewed by the courts to be an efficient way to resolve disputes and promote social stability.

The mediation process itself, which typically is conducted by a single judge even if a collegiate panel of judges ultimately will hear the matter in the event that a resolution cannot be reached, is informal and bears close resemblance to an American settlement conference. While there is no parallel provision in the United States Federal Rules of Civil Procedure requiring a judge to apply a particular set of values or even the law to facilitate a settlement, in practice a Chinese mediation proceeds very much like a settlement conference in America. The most similar feature between the two processes is that neither employs a uniform method or system by which the mediation or settlement is conducted. In both systems, it is left to the judge's discretion as to when, how long, and in what manner to conduct mediation or a settlement conference. This obviously leads, in both systems, to great disparity in how each process is conducted even within each system. Nevertheless, the Chinese judge uses many settlement techniques that would be very familiar to his American counterpart. Chinese judges often will meet separately with parties, something referred to in American mediation terminology as "caucusing." The judge sometimes will suggest a settlement proposal he or she believes would be fair or point out to the parties the particular weaknesses of their claim or defense, giving them cause to re-evaluate the strength of their position. Finally, a judge might simply, as is done so often in the United States, emphasize the potential economic benefits of a particular settlement whereby a litigant can avoid the additional legal expense and uncertainty of court adjudication.

Chinese mediation differs from the American settlement conference in a few ways. Article 85 of the Code of Civil Procedure of the People's Republic of China provides that "[w]hen hearing a civil case, a people's court shall * * * conduct mediation on the basis of clear facts and distinguishing from right and wrong." Thus, within the theoretical framework of the mediation process is an evaluative element in which the judge applies a set of normative values to help facilitate settlement—values that are rooted in both the judge's cultural and legal experience * * *

ROBERT PERKOVICH, A COMPARATIVE ANALYSIS OF COMMUNITY MEDIATION IN THE UNITED STATES AND THE PEOPLE'S REPUBLIC OF CHINA

10 Temple International and Comparative Law Journal 313–27 (1996).

B.　Community Mediation in the PRC

The Peoples' Mediation Committees are the most widely known institutions for dispute resolution in the PRC. There are approximately 10 million mediators who comprise approximately 7 million committees. For every civil dispute that goes to court, probably five or ten are resolved by the committees. The 1982 Constitution of the PRC ordained that each residents' and villagers' committee was to organize a Peoples' Mediation Committee. These committees have a statutory basis in the 1954 Provisional Organizational Principles for the Peoples' Mediation Committees. The Principles set forth, inter alia, the responsibility of the committees to mediate, under the supervision of the Peoples' Courts, ordinary civil disputes, community and family disputes that might not rise to the level of a violation of law, as well as minor criminal cases. The decision to mediate is to be voluntary and mediated settlements must conform to the law. * * *

The Ministry of Justice assisted in the establishment and operation of the committees, including the necessary training and monitoring of the work of the members of the committees. Under the regulations, mediation committees are to be organized within each neighborhood, village, and/or workplace. The individual mediators are chosen by the members of the neighborhood. No formal training is required, but in most instances those chosen are elders who enjoy the respect of the community and are trusted to be fair.

Chinese mediators, like mediators from the United States, utilize a continuum of skills and strategies ranging from establishing and enhancing communication to engaging in problem solving. Moreover, they also follow [similar] procedural steps * * * However, they may also decide questions of fact, make recommendations for possible solutions, and give advisory opinions. This has led one commentator to point out that Chinese mediators mobilize such strong political, economic, social and moral pressure upon one or both parties that there may be some doubt as to the voluntariness of the process.

1.   Xiliani Huitong Committee

While in the PRC our delegation met with four neighborhood committees to discuss their experiences using mediation. The first, in Beijing * * * consisted of seven individuals who were chosen from among the retired workers in the neighborhood because those individuals were regarded as experienced, wise, and mature. * * * While mediating, the committee would investigate the facts comprising the complaint and then 'persuade and educate' the disputants. Although the committee does not adjudicate the dispute, it must ensure that any settlement conforms to the law.

* * *

3.   Chang Zing Committee

* * * This committee also consists of neighborhood residents who are retired workers and chosen because they are enthusiastic, healthy, educated, have some knowledge of dispute resolution, and are "on good terms" with the other residents of the neighborhood. They are trained for three to five days and one additional day each month regarding the substantive law and negotiating skills. * * * Once involved, the mediation committee will attempt to resolve the dispute, but if a mediated settlement cannot be achieved the mediator may issue a "mediator's verdict."

The committee described its efforts in three disputes. The first involved a dispute between two families which led to a report to the committee that a fight was to take place. The committee, acting on its own initiative, intervened and investigated the facts, determining which party initiated the dispute. The mediators then impressed upon the party that initiated the dispute that if he did not pay monetary damages, as requested by the other disputants, there was the likelihood of continued conflict and then he would bear even more responsibility than he did at that point * * *

4. Suzhou Committee

* * * [T]heir purpose, in the words of Section Chief Jin Zhao Wen, is to 'make people happy' and to see that people "live in harmony." The committees make findings of liability and culpability after investigating the dispute in question and do so, not only to resolve the dispute, but also to lead to self-criticism.

* * * In one, a son objected when his widowed mother found a boyfriend after the son married and moved away. In reaching a mediated settlement the committee reminded the son that now that he had married he was happy, but that his mother was alone. In turn, the committee also urged the mother to wait six months before marrying her boyfriend so that her son would calm down. The second case involved a dispute between two merchants which led to one threatening the other. The committee called in the parents of the party who had made the threat and asked that they 'educate' him which led to a settlement.

III. CONCLUSION

Based on this brief survey of the experiences of local Chinese mediation committees, similarities and differences between community mediation in the PRC and the United States are evident. In both countries, the mediators follow similar mediation steps and procedures. In both countries initial statements are taken from the parties, there is restatement of the facts by the mediator, and the use of caucus is present in mediation. The efforts of the Chan Zing mediators to encourage families to realize that they only faced further fighting and conflict without an agreement was a classic form of BATNA. The efforts of the Chan Zing mediator to ask one party in an assault case to regard her conduct in light of the other disputant's demand to inflict injury on her as she did, is what United States mediators would regard as the 'flipside' technique. Finally, when the Chang Zing mediators asked the angry grandson to consider his conduct in light of his grandmother's age and short remaining life, they moved him to test his position in light of reality.

Despite these similarities, differences between community mediation in the United States and the PRC are readily apparent. Moreover, I believe that some of these differences are not only profound, but may be attributed to, inter alia, the fundamental religious, political, social, and cultural differences between our two countries. The impact of Chinese religious and political philosophies are first and foremost evident in the fact that disputants, as part of a mediated settlement, engage in self-criticism. This appears to be a reflection of the Confucian li and jang and the establishment of harmony as the perfect ideal. In addition, the fact that Chinese mediators often act on their own initiative and make findings of liability and culpability, often leading to imposed solutions, is consistent with the slant put on li by modern concepts of Maoism. The Maoist influence is also felt by the practice of Chinese mediators to 'persuade and educate' disputants and the mediation committees' responsibility for the implementation of Party policies, such as family planning policies.

———————

File 6: Proposed Mediation Rules

China Council for the Promotion of International Trade(CCPIT)
China Chamber of International Commerce(CCOIC)
CONCILIATION RULES
(Selected Rules)
2000

Article 1. These Rules are formulated with a view to settling by means of conciliation (mediation) disputes arising from the fields of economy, trade, maritime business, etc. so as to promote the development of international and domestic economic exchanges.

* * *

Article 4. During conciliation course, the principle of parties' free will must be observed.

Article 5. Conciliation shall be conducted on the basis of ascertaining facts, distinguishing right from wrong and determining liabilities while respecting the terms of the contract, abiding by the law, following international practice and adhering to the principle of being just, fair and reasonable in order to bring about mutual understanding and mutual concession between the parties and help the parties to reach an amicable settlement agreement thereof.

* * *

Article 7. Each of the Conciliation Centres maintains a Panel of Conciliators. The conciliators are selected and appointed respectively by CCPIT/CCOIC and its Sub-councils from among impartial and upright personages with special knowledge and/or practical experience in economy, trade, finance, security, investment, intellectual property, technology transfer, real estate, construction contract, transportation, insurance and other fields of commerce, maritime business and/or law.

* * *

Article 9. When applying for conciliation, the applying party must satisfy the following requirements:

(4) Appoint or authorize the Conciliation Centre to appoint one conciliator from the Centre's Panel of Conciliators;

* * *

Article 12. The two appointed conciliators shall jointly conciliate the case. The parties may also agree to have a sole conciliator to conciliate the case alone. If the parties have had such agreement but cannot agree on the appointment of the sole conciliator, the appointment shall be made by the Conciliation Centre.

* * *

Article 14. The conciliator(s) may conduct conciliation in the manner he or they deem(s) appropriate.

Article 15. Experts of relevant professions may be invited to participate and assist in the conciliation work if the conciliator(s) consider(s) it necessary and the parties agree. The expenses required shall be borne by the parties.

* * *

Article 17. Conciliation proceedings shall terminate on the day on which one of the following circumstances emerges:

(1) the Conciliation Statement is made in case of successful conciliation ;

(2) the conciliator(s) think(s) that success of conciliation is impossible and declare(s) in writing a termination of the conciliation proceedings; or

(3) the parties or one party declares in writing to the conciliator(s) to the effect that the conciliation proceedings be terminated.

Article 18. The conciliator(s) may meet or communicate with the parties in the manner he or they think(s) appropriate.

Article 19. When the conciliator(s) receives(s) information from one party, the conciliator(s) may disclose or not disclose it to the other party; however, if one party gives information to the conciliator(s) and requests that the information be kept confidential, the conciliator(s) shall respect the party's request.

Article 20. The parties shall cooperate in good faith with the conciliator(s) to submit materials and produce evidence and come to conciliation meetings on time, etc. in compliance with the requests of the conciliator(s).

Article 21. If conciliation fails, the conciliator(s) may be appointed by one of the parties as arbitrator(s) in the subsequent arbitration proceedings, unless such appointment is opposed by the other party.

Article 22. If conciliation fails, the parties shall not invoke any statements, views, opinions or proposals that have been put forward, proposed, admitted or indicated to be acceptable by the parties or the conciliator(s) in the course of conciliation as grounds for claim or defence in the subsequent arbitration proceedings or litigation proceedings.

Chapter 5

DRAFTING DISPUTE RESOLUTION CLAUSES[1]

A. INTRODUCTION

Private parties in international disputes can face a tumultuous and uncertain dispute resolution route, a route that can be improved by parties drafting their own dispute resolution clauses.

If private parties rely on the default process for resolving disputes, they cannot count on access to a compulsory, binding international court system. There is none. Their default process is to resort to the national court system of one of the parties, but cross-border litigation presents a host of risks that can make the litigation process enormously expensive and unpredictable.[2]

More than one domestic court may have jurisdiction, making it easy to forum-shop and posing the risk of concurrent lawsuits in two or more countries.[3] The pendency of a lawsuit in one country is not usually grounds to stop a lawsuit in another country, leaving it to the discretion of local judges to decline jurisdiction under the unpredictable doctrine of "forum non conveniens."[4]

Uncertainty over which substantive law a domestic court will apply interjects another risk into cross-border litigation. This uncertainty

1. This chapter is an expanded adaptation of the chapter by Harold Abramson, *International Dispute Resolution: Cross–Cultural Dimensions and Structuring Appropriate Processes, in* RAU, SHERMAN & PEPPET, PROCESSES OF DISPUTE RESOLUTION 938–58 (3d ed. 2004).

2. See C. BUHRING–UHLE, ARBITRATION AND MEDIATION IN INTERNATIONAL BUSINESS 17–37 (1996); JACK J. COLE, JR., INTERNATIONAL COMMERCIAL ARBITRATION: AMERICAN PRINCIPLES AND PRACTICE IN A GLOBAL CONTEXT ch. 1, §§ 1.8.1–1.8.2 (1997); and Lawrence Perlman & Steven C. Nelson, *New Approaches to the Resolution of International Commercial Disputes*, 17 INT'L LAW. 215, 218–25(1983).

3. An unambiguous choice of forum clause can help reduce the risk of parallel lawsuits.

4. Under the 1968 European Convention on the Jurisdiction of the Courts and the Enforcement of Judgments in Civil and Commercial Matters (Brussels Convention), almost twenty European countries agreed to rules that eliminate the risk of parallel litigation.

There is even the opposite risk that courts in both jurisdictions may decline jurisdiction, leaving the parties without access to any court system.

exists because of the international nature of the transaction, which connects it with two or more legal systems,[5] and is exacerbated by the difficulty in predicting how a local court will interpret the selected law.

Moreover, a local court judgment may not be recognized or enforced in a foreign jurisdiction. There is no widely adopted multilateral treaty to support res judicata that would bar re-litigation of the same claim in a foreign court or to ensure enforcement of a domestic court judgment in a foreign country.[6]

Finally, parties can find litigating in foreign courts inhospitable. Foreign judges may favor parties from their own country due to personal sympathies or worst yet, corruption. The judges may lack experience in business affairs and may apply local laws that are inadequate for dealing with international business disputes. Trials may have to be conducted in a foreign language under less familiar rules or what might be viewed as less desirable civil law inquisitorial procedures. And, additional costs may have to be incurred for retaining a second attorney, one knowledgeable of procedure and law of the foreign jurisdiction.

Although some of these transnational litigation risks can be reduced by parties agreeing to which national court system will be used (choice of forum provision) and which law will be applied (choice of law provision), these provisions still leave parties with a dispute resolution process with other significant risks and expenses. And the process also is limited to declaring who is right and wrong and producing solutions that are narrowly legalistic. Many of these risks, expenses, and limitations, however, can be minimized if not avoided by parties designing their own flexible private dispute resolution system, known as an ADR clause (alternative dispute resolution clause).

When drafting an ADR clause, three distinct issues require attention.

> 1) What should be the content of the clause? Clauses are usually short and to the point, and each word counts. You need to choose the words knowingly and with care.

> 2) What set of dispute resolution rules should be incorporated in the clause and should any of the specific rules be modified or supplemented? Virtually all dispute resolution institutions offer their own procedural rules to govern mediations and arbitrations. These various rules can either be adopted intact or modified to meet special needs of the parties. Of course, parties can create their own rules from scratch, but this

---

5. A clear choice of law provision will reduce this uncertainty.

6. The Doctrine of Comity can be asserted to gain recognition of a foreign judgment but its application is fraught with uncertainty. Also see Brussels Convention mentioned in footnote 4. An effort is now underway by the Hague Conference on Private International Law to draft and push for adoption of a Hague Convention on Judgments. See Lawrence W. Newman & Michael Burrows, *Proposed Hague Convention on Judgments*, 220 N.Y. L.J. 3 & 29 (Dec. 30, 1998).

option would be an expensive route to essentially re-inventing much of what has already been devised and tested by others.

3) Should the dispute resolution process be administered ad hoc or by an independent professional organization? Neither mediation nor arbitration is a self-executing process. Both processes require administrative attention to run smoothly and effectively.

B. DRAFTING MEDIATION CLAUSES

The previous chapter considered the suitability of using mediation for resolving international disputes. This section considers what key provisions to include in an agreement to mediate. You should avoid blindly adopting wholesale a boilerplate clause that incorporates by reference a set of mediation rules. The clause and incorporated rules may need to be modified to cover any distinctive needs of the parties from different countries.

As should have been evident from the Chinese dispute exercise in Chapter 4: International Negotiation and Mediation in the Private Sector, a good starting point is to examine studiously a pre-existing, tested, and recognized set of mediation rules. You can choose among numerous off-the-shelf rules that are offered by a multitude of national and international organizations.

Each set of rules is usually limited in number and is quite compact. The various sets of rules typically cover many of the same issues, offer remarkably similar approaches, and rarely contain any uniquely international provisions. They cover procedures for initiating and terminating a mediation and for appointing a mediator. They address the role of the mediator, conduct of the mediation, confidentiality of the process, and matters related to payment for mediation services. Differences, however, can be found that might present unexpected opportunities and obstacles when developing a mediation representation plan. These occasional differences can relate to the procedure for mediator selection and the roles vested in the mediator, as should have been evident in the Chinese exercise. Moreover, the more deeply you examine the rules, as also should have been evident in the exercise, the more likely you are to discover that a difference may be culturally-based.

Here are three examples of suggested mediation clauses:

1) The London Court of International Arbitration recommends: In the event of a dispute arising out of or relating to this contract, including any question regarding its existence, validity or termination, the parties shall seek settlement of that dispute by mediation in accordance with the LCIA Mediation Procedure, which Procedure is deemed to be incorporated by reference into this clause. LCIA Mediation: Procedure and Costs (June 24, 2002).

2) The American Arbitration Association (AAA) suggests: If a dispute arises out of or relates to this contract, or the breach thereof, and if the dispute cannot be settled through negotiation, the parties agree first to try in good faith to settle the dispute by mediation in accordance with the International Mediation Rules of the International Centre for Dispute Resolution before resorting to arbitration, litigation or some other dispute resolution procedure." AAA International Dispute Resolution Procedures (July 1, 2003).

3) The ICC (International Chamber of Commerce) suggests this mediation-type clause: Obligation to submit dispute to ADR with an automatic expiration mechanism. In the event of any dispute arising out of or in connection with the present contract, the parties agree to submit the matter to settlement proceedings under the ICC ADR Rules. If the dispute has not been settled pursuant to the said Rules within 45 days following the filing of a Request for ADR or within such other period as the parties may agree in writing, the parties shall have no further obligations under this paragraph. ICC ADR Dispute Resolutions Services at www.iccwbo.org/index_adr.asp.

Notes and Questions

1. Compare the mediation clauses suggested by the London Court of Arbitration, AAA, and ICC. Which key words or phrases would you want further clarified and which clause would you prefer and why?

2. Develop a checklist of issues to consider when negotiating over a set of proposed rules and a mediation clause for future international disputes. You should draw upon the discussion of distinctive issues in international mediation that were considered in the previous chapter.

3. Find on the Internet a set of mediation rules. In view of the issues identified in Question 2, examine the rules to determine whether they are satisfactory, whether you would like to learn more about how any of the rules are likely to be interpreted, and whether you would want to modify any of the rules.

4. Which of the issues identified in Questions 2 and 3 do you think are likely to be controversial when negotiating a clause and rules with an attorney from either Continental Europe or China? What cultural factors, if any, might explain any differences?

C. DRAFTING ARBITRATION CLAUSES

Although the focus of this text is on consensual processes, you should have some basic understanding of adjudicatory processes that give protection to parties in the event that mediation fails. The two primary adjudicatory options for backing up mediations are transnational litigation and arbitration. Both options have in common the designation of a neutral third party who will hear the case and issue a decision that will bind the parties and bring the conflict to closure. For international business disputes, the more widely used of these two options is arbitration because it ameliorates a number of the risks and concerns that complicate transnational litigation.[7] Instead of parties contending with the gaps in transnational litigation law and any troublesome features of different national court systems, parties frequently prefer designing a private, supranational dispute resolution process that operates separately from disparate national court systems. But, the private process does not operate independently; national court systems still perform an essential gap filling and enforcement function in case a party needs to enforce an agreement to arbitrate or an arbitration award.

1. ARBITRATION AS AN INTERNATIONAL ADJUDICATORY PROCESS

In comparing transnational litigation with international arbitration, it has been suggested that international arbitration is not really an alternative to litigation but is simply a better way to litigate international business conflicts.

CHRISTIAN BUHRING–UHLE, ARBITRATION AND MEDIATION IN INTERNATIONAL BUSINESS

141–43 (1996).

* * *

[I]t appears that the reasons why international commercial arbitration has become the principal means of dispute resolution in international business have more to do with the specific problems of litigating international disputes in national courts than with the desire to create a type of procedure that is fundamentally different from litigation.

The two considerations that stand out as the most significant advantages of international commercial arbitration, the *neutrality* of the forum and the *international enforceability* of the results clearly address two fundamental problems of transnational litigation: whether justified or not, players in international commerce do not seem to have confidence in the complete neutrality of national courts towards foreign litigants and therefore have a strong desire to avoid having to stand trial in the other side's "home court." This consideration is particularly important if one of the parties is a government or a state-owned entity because on the one hand governments are reluctant—and sometimes prevented by constitutional constraints—to submit to the jurisdiction of an another government and on the other hand private entities tend to abhor the prospect of confronting a sovereign in its own courts.

---

7. *See* GARY B. BORN, INTERNATIONAL COMMERCIAL ARBITRATION IN THE UNITED STATES 5–9 (1994) and RICHARD H. KREINDLER, ARBITRATION OR LITIGATION? ADR ISSUES IN TRANSNATIONAL DISPUTES, 79 DISP. RESOL. J. 79 (1997) (Both authors point out how the advantages of arbitration cannot be guaranteed. For example, Born notes that countries hostile toward arbitrations have enacted laws that pose obstacles to the enforcement of arbitral awards.).

The participants in international commerce seem to be painfully aware of the deficiencies of the legal framework of transnational litigation and particularly the problems of enforcing judgments in a foreign jurisdiction:

> If for judgments there existed a convention similar to the New York convention, 50% of the big international commercial arbitrations would be court litigation.

A consideration that was regarded as less relevant but that is clearly connected to the enforceability aspect is the degree of *voluntary compliance* with arbitral awards which, according to the ICC is very high. Although there are no data available on *why* parties comply voluntarily, it is plausible to assume that an effective enforcement mechanism operates as a strong motivation.

The next group of advantages of international arbitration that were considered significant are, again, unrelated to any search for "alternative" methods of dispute resolution. *Confidentiality* simply means that the public—and the competitors—are excluded from the proceedings but it has no bearing on what type of procedure it is that is being conducted behind closed doors. And the objective of having the dispute decided by a "judge" with *expertise* in the subject matter and of curtailing the excesses of protracted *discovery* and lengthy *appeals* have to be understood as the desire to improve the quality and effectiveness of litigation rather than to create a different type of procedure.

Finally, the objectives which are at the heart of the quest for more informal, "alternative" methods of dispute resolution, the desire to achieve a process that is *faster, less expensive* and *more amicable*, seem to have only marginal relevance for the choice of arbitration in international commerce. This may be due either to the perception that, in international arbitration, these advantages do not materialize, or that these qualities are not among the real priorities of the participants. Both reasons seem to be—at least in part—true: more than one half of the respondents denied that arbitration is less expensive and more than one third disputed the notion that it was faster or more amicable. And only about one tenth of the respondents affirmed that speed, cost savings and amicability were "highly relevant" factors for the choice of arbitration as a method of dispute resolution. As one practitioner explained:

> * * * parties are often not that concerned with costs because their main preoccupation is with the outcome of the procedure; the advantage of arbitration is not to cut costs, it is a tailor-made procedure that emphasizes quality.

In sum, what international arbitration offers and what the participants expect is not an "alternative" to litigation but *a system of litigation that works in an international context* and avoids the pitfalls of transnational litigation in national courts.

Notes and Questions

Do you find convincing the contention of Christian Buhring–Uhle that international arbitration is "not an alternative to litigation" but is "*a system of litigation that works in an international context* and avoids the pitfalls of transnational litigation in national courts"? Can this same point be made about the use of domestic arbitration? If so, then what does it mean to describe a process as an alternative dispute resolution method?

2. CONTENT OF ARBITRATION CLAUSES

The same general inquiry that applies to drafting a mediation clause applies to drafting an arbitration clause: What key provisions should you include? Just as when drafting a mediation clause, you should avoid blindly adopting wholesale a boilerplate clause that incorporates by reference a set of arbitration rules. You may need to modify the clause as well as the rules to better serve the needs of parties from different countries.

This negotiation takes place in a historical context[8] in which procedural practices in international arbitrations have been changing, especially so during the 1970s and 80s, toward a more trial-like process. International arbitrations developed initially as an informal process cultivated in Continental Europe, primarily in Paris under the auspices of the ICC. In the civil law tradition, international arbitrators gave considerable attention to the law while giving little attention to developing and considering the facts. The arbitrations were dominated by Continental academics and an exclusive "club" of people engaged in business affairs.

During the 1970s and 80s, the pressures exerted by the increased participation of Anglo–American law firms in international business deals transformed international arbitrations. When the major U.S. law firms went international, they exported what they knew best: how to aggressively represent their clients in adversarial proceedings. U.S. lawyers were determined to employ a U.S. style litigation strategy in arbitrations. These pressures led to what became known as the increasing "judicialization" of international commercial arbitrations. It is in this cultural context that arbitration rules are evolving and differences can arise when negotiating over arbitration rules and clauses between U.S. common law lawyers and civil law lawyers from other counties.

UNCITRAL and every significant dispute resolution institution offer comprehensive arbitration rules. Unfortunately, however, it is not unusual for parties to adopt a set of rules without examining them. Parties can incorporate them unthinkingly into a dispute resolution clause. They then hope that, if the arbitration rules must be activated, any surprises

---

8. *See* YVES DEZALAY & BRYANT G. GARTH, DEALING IN VIRTUE—INTERNATIONAL COMMERCIAL ARBITRATION AND THE CONSTRUCTION OF A TRANSNATIONAL LEGAL ORDER chs. 3,4,5 (1996). *See* *also* Rau & Sherman, *Tradition and Innovation in International Arbitration Procedure,* 30 TEX. INT'L L.J. 89 (1995).

in the pre-packaged rules will be small ones. In international deals, the risks of bigger surprises are bigger, increasing the importance of addressing critical design issues before a conflict arises.

Again, a good starting point is to examine studiously a draft clause and a proposed set of pre-existing, tested, and recognized set of arbitration rules. Parties should give special attention to a number of issues that can impact the quality and substantive outcome of the arbitration process. Consider the issues posed in this excerpt and the following Notes and Questions.

LUCY F. REED, DRAFTING ARBITRATION CLAUSES

International Business Litigation & Arbitration 2000.
624 PLI/Lit 563, 565–577 (Practicing Law Institute, February 2000,
PLI Order No. H0–005R) (2000 Practising Law Institute)

Introduction

The arbitration clause may be the last thing on the minds of everyone involved in negotiating a contract. Should a dispute arise, however, it may ultimately prove to be the most important clause of all. Substantive rights and obligations so carefully negotiated under a contract will only be as good as the award issued by the tribunal eventually responsible for giving effect to them.

* * * The following may serve as a rough guide to the essential issues which must be addressed by parties and their advisers when negotiating and drafting the arbitration clause in an international contract * * *

Sample multi purpose clause

In all but exceptional cases, advisers should avoid ad hoc arbitrations and adopt intact one of the model clauses provided by the specialist arbitral institutions. Alternatively, the following is a sample multi purpose clause containing the key elements required in a good arbitration clause, which can be used in conjunction with any institutional rules. The components of this clause are explained in detail below:

> Any dispute, controversy or claim arising out of or in connection with this contract, including any question regarding its existence, validity or termination shall be finally resolved by arbitration under the Rules of [name of institution] in force at [the date hereof/the date of the request for arbitration], which Rules are deemed to be incorporated by reference into this clause.
>
> The tribunal shall consist of [a sole/three] arbitrator[s].
>
> The place of the arbitration shall be [city].
>
> The language of the arbitration shall be [language].

* * *

1.4.5 Applicable substantive law

The applicable substantive law (or lex causae) is the law governing the merits of the dispute (i.e. the parties' substantive rights and obligations under the contract) and should always be specifically chosen and clearly stated in the contract. The law governing the arbitration agreement (and its interpretation) will generally be that of the contract of which it is a part. This should not be confused with the law governing the arbitration itself (the lex arbitri, or lex fori i.e. the procedural law governing the conduct of the arbitration proceedings), which will be the national law of the country in which the arbitration takes place (the seat—see section 2 below for further details). Although it is vital to specify the applicable substantive law, it is common and in fact preferable to have a "governing law clause" separate from the arbitration clause in a contract to avoid confusion. However, it is perfectly acceptable to specify the applicable substantive law as part of the arbitration clause, so long as it is clear that the provision is independent from the other elements of the arbitration clause and relates to the contract as a whole.

2. Seat of the arbitration

2.1 Importance of seat of arbitration

The seat of the arbitration is the place (city and country) in which the arbitration legally takes place (as compared to where the tribunal may meet physically). It is one of the essential elements should be agreed by the parties and clearly specified in the arbitration clause. decision has far reaching implications as the choice of seat determines, inter alia, the procedural laws which will govern the arbitration proceedings and the national courts to which the parties must resort to supplement the proceedings and enforce those rights and obligations not within the jurisdiction of the arbitration. There are also important practical reasons for choosing a particular country to host the proceedings. Although the administering institution, if one is appointed, or the arbitrator(s) generally can select the seat if none is specified, the result may be unexpected, and differ substantially from that which the parties would have chosen freely.

2.2 Favorable legal environment for proceedings

The most important factor to consider is the legal environment of a particular country; that is its laws and courts. Advisers should carefully review the legislation and jurisprudence of the desired seat to ensure that their choice is "arbitration friendly." Issues to consider in any review include the following:

2.2.1 Enforceability of agreement to arbitrate

First and foremost, it is vital that local laws will allow local courts to enforce the parties' agreement to arbitrate and not instead assume jurisdiction over the dispute. To be sure of this, the seat country should be a signatory to the 1958 New York Convention on the Recognition and Enforcement of Foreign Arbitral Awards (the New York Convention) which obliges signatories to stay (suspend) any court proceedings brought in breach of an arbitration agreement and refer the parties to arbitration.

* * *

2.2.5 UNCITRAL Model Law

Some countries should be avoided their legislation applicable to international arbitration is outdated, unclear, conflicting and difficult to navigate. One shorthand way of ascertaining whether an unfamiliar country has a legislative framework suitable for international arbitration is to check whether that country has adopted the UNCITRAL Model Law on International Arbitration. The Model Law is intended to be an internationally acceptable law based upon the principle that the local courts in the place of arbitration should support but not interfere with the arbitral proceedings. Countries can enact the Model Code fully or partially taking into account crucial local legal requirements or idiosyncrasies. Advisers should be sure to check that any local amendments made to the Model Law do not substantially detract from its acceptability * * *

2.3 Enforceability of the award

2.3.1 New York Convention country

Inability to enforce the final award makes a nonsense of the entire arbitration procedure, hence the question of enforceability of award is one to be carefully considered at the outset when choosing the seat. Choosing a country which is a signatory to the New York Convention is vital not only to ensure the enforceability of the arbitration agreement, but also the enforceability of the eventual award. The country is the seat of arbitration will determine the "nationality" of the award. As the New York Convention contains a well-subscribed reciprocity reservation, when the victorious party comes to request the courts of the country where the assets of the losing party are located enforce the award, the courts of a signatory country need not automatically enforce an award granted in a non signatory country. Although there exist other conventions dealing with the enforcement of awards, the New York Convention is the most important and widely accepted.

* * *

3. Choosing the arbitrators

* * *

3.2 Method of selection

The method of selection depends on the number of arbitrators. Where there is one arbitrator the clause should specify that appointment be by designation of the appointing authority, if one exists or by agreement of the parties, which can be difficult. Where three arbitrators are to be appointed, the usual course is for each party to nominate one (where there are only two parties) and for the third to be agreed either by the parties or the two nominated arbitrators or designated by the appointing authority. Alternatively, the appointing authority may designate all of the arbitrators. In multi party arbitration proceedings, the appointing authority often designates all three arbitrators.

———————

Access to the New York Convention, formally known as the Convention on Recognition and Enforcement of Foreign Arbitral Awards[9] and referred to in the Reed article, has been a vital factor in making international arbitrations so attractive and so widely used. In what is probably the most important treaty in the field of international dispute resolution, the signatory countries gave up some of their sacred sovereignty by agreeing to enforce in their local courts arbitration awards issued by foreign arbitration tribunals. Over one hundred and thirty nations have ratified the New York Convention.

The key features of the New York Convention can be found in its first five articles. Article I establishes the general obligation of a state to recognize and enforce foreign arbitral awards. The Article also gives each state the option to limit this obligation to awards made in the territory of another contracting state (reciprocity reservation) and to disputes that are commercial under its own national law (commercial reservation). The United States has adopted both of these reservations. Article II limits enforcement of *agreements to arbitrate* to agreements that are (1) in writing and (2) that a local court does not find to be "null and void, inoperative or incapable of being performed." When these two conditions are met, the local court will refer the parties to arbitration. Article III imposes a national treatment-type obligation; a contracting state will not impose "substantially more onerous conditions" on enforcement of foreign awards than enforcement of domestic awards. Article IV establishes the only conditions that must be satisfied by a party who seeks *enforcement of an arbitration award*. The conditions deal with authentication and certification of the award. Article V(1) sets forth grounds for refusing recognition and enforcement of a foreign award, grounds that can be asserted by a party against whom enforcement is sought. In addition to grounds familiar in domestic arbitration laws (e.g. procedural defects and lack of arbitrability), a court can refuse recognition when the foreign award had been set aside in the foreign country. Article V(2) sets forth grounds for a local court to act on its own motion to refuse recognition and enforcement. The two grounds are when the subject matter is "not capable of settlement by arbitration under the law" of the local country and when recognition and enforcement "would be contrary to the public policy" of the local country.

At the celebration of the fortieth anniversary of the New York Convention in 1998, scholars and practitioners from around the world

———————

9. 1958 Convention on Recognition and Enforcement of Foreign Arbitral Awards 21U.S.T.2517, 330 U.N.T.S.38, T.I.A.S. No. 6997 (1959) (known as the New York Convention). See Appendix G.

convened for the day at the United Nations to consider what the treaty had accomplished and what should be done to improve it.[10] Everyone seemed to agree that the New York Convention had been a great success. Participants nevertheless suggested several areas for improvement. Procedures for local enforcement should be more uniform among different states.[11] Article II(2)'s provision on only enforcing arbitration agreements in writing should recognize the validity of agreements created by modern means of contract formation.[12] A supplementary convention should be adopted to provide for foreign enforcement of provisional and conservatory relief.[13] Finally, a local court should not be barred from enforcing a foreign award because a foreign court nullified the award, especially when the reasons may be considered internationally intolerable.[14] Participants thought that these improvements could be implemented through adoption of a supplementary treaty or more likely through enlightened domestic law or judicial interpretations.

Notes and Questions

1. When drafting an arbitration clause and selecting rules, you should give special attention to a few additional issues.

a. Party–Appointed Arbitrators

In international arbitrations, parties ardently favor tripartite tribunals in which each party appoints an arbitrator and then either the party-appointed arbitrators or an appointing institution selects the chair of the tribunal. This is the usual selection procedure according to Lucy Reed in her article.

This appointment scheme raises the elemental issue whether an arbitrator appointed by a party must be independent and neutral. In domestic arbitrations, party-appointed arbitrators are sometimes described as non-neutral or partisan arbitrators who are not held to the same standards of neutrality and independence that applies to other arbitrators. This policy is reflected in the recently adopted *Code of Ethics for Arbitrators in Commercial Disputes*. It permits parties to appoint arbitrators that may be "predisposed toward deciding in favor of the party who appointed" the arbitrator,

---

10. New York Convention Day—June 10, 1998 A/CN.9/1998/INF.1 (U.N., 20 May 1998).

11. *See* Robert Briner, *Philosophy and Objectives of the Convention, in* New York Convention Day—June 10, 1998 A/CN.9/1998/INF.1, at 2–3 (U.N., 20 May 1998).

12. *See* Neil Kaplan, *New Developments on Written Form, in* New York Convention Day—June 10, 1998 A/CN.9/1998/INF.1, at 5–6 (U.N., 20 May 1998).

13. *See* V.V. Veeder, *Provisional and Conservatory Measures, in* New York Convention Day—June 10, 1998 A/CN.9/1998/INF.1, at 8 (U.N., 20 May 1998).

14. *See* Jan Paulsson, *Awards Set Aside at Place of Arbitration in* New York Convention Day—June 10, 1998 A/CN.9/1998/INF.1, at 10 (U.N., 20 May 1998). For a contrary view, see William W. Park, *Duty and Discretion in International Arbitration*, 93 Am. J. Int'l L. 805, 814 (1999):

Deference to good faith annulments often furthers the very same interests as enforcement of the arbitration agreement and award, holding the parties to their bargain. Just as an agreement to arbitrate in London means driving to hearings on the left side of the road, so it means that proceedings are subject to the English Arbitration Act.

and then provides for a number of exemptions from traditional restrictions on arbitrators including allowing the arbitrators to communicate with the appointing parties during the arbitration proceeding until the arbitrators start to deliberate.[15]

Party-appointed arbitrators in international arbitrations, however, strive for greater neutrality and independence than in domestic arbitrations. The degree of neutrality and independence guides how attorneys interact with their party-appointed arbitrators before and during the arbitration proceeding. Consider how much neutrality and independence are expected in the relatively new AAA International Arbitration Rules. Article 7(2) states: "[n]o party or anyone acting on its behalf shall have any ex parte communication relating to the case with any arbitrator, or with any candidate for appointment as party-appointed arbitrator except to advise the candidate of the general nature of the controversy and of the anticipated proceedings and to discuss the candidate's qualifications, availability or independence in relation to the parties, or to discuss the suitability of candidates for selection as a third arbitrator where the parties or party-designated arbitrators are to participate in that selection. No party or anyone acting on its behalf shall have any ex parte communication relating to the case with any candidate for presiding arbitrator."[16] This preference for party-appointed arbitrators is surprising because it appears to violate the principles of neutrality and independence that form the foundation of judicial justice.[17] Yet, parties commonly select this procedure for various reasons:

> In arbitration, parties accept virtually non-appealable finality of the arbitrators' decision largely in exchange for the ability to participate in the selection of their tribunal rather than accept an anonymous, governmentally chosen decision maker—a judge—whose rulings may be less predictable but generally are subject to appellate review.... Party-appointed arbitrators also may be expected to play a role in selecting the third arbitrator, bringing their judgment and experience to bear on this important task. James H. Carter, *Living with the Party–Appointed Arbitrator: Judicial Confusion, Ethical Codes and Practical Advice*, 3 AM. REV. 153(1992).

> At least one of the persons who will decide the case will listen carefully—even sympathetically—to the presentation, and if the arbitrator is well chosen, will study the documents with care. That fact alone is likely to spur the other arbitrators to study the documents as

---

15. *See* Code of Ethics of Arbitrators in Commercial Disputes Cannon X.C & E (Joint Committee of ABA and AAA, effective Mar 1, 2004) (revision of 1977 code).

16. *See* AAA International Arbitration Rules, arts. 7(2) (July 1, 2003).

17. Alan Scott Rau, *Integrity in Private Judging*, 38 S. TEX. L. REV. 485, 497–514 (1997).

well, whether or not they would have done so in any case. Thus the presence of a well chosen party-appointed arbitrator goes a long way toward promising (if not assuring) a fair hearing and a considered decision.

* * *

[I]n an international case a party-appointed arbitrator serves as a translator. I do not mean just of language. . . . I mean rather the translation of legal culture, and not infrequently of the law itself, when matters that are self-evident to lawyers from one country are puzzling to lawyers from another. Andreas F. Lowenfeld, *The Party–Appointed Arbitrator in International Controversies: Some Reflections*, 30 TEX. INT'L L.J. 59, 65 (1995).

Given these justifications for a party-appointed selection process and the AAA international rules where limited interviews of candidates are permissible, what can an attorney ask a candidate? During the arbitration proceeding, what ex parte contacts, if any, can an attorney have with his or her party-appointed arbitrator? Consider how specific you can be during an interview or a proceeding without violating the AAA Rules. If the arbitration rules are silent on ex parte contacts, can you interview a candidate alone and can you have any ex parte contacts during the proceeding? If the answer is yes to either question, what do you think you can discuss during these ex parte encounters?

b. Interim Relief

Whether interim relief by a court in aid of arbitration—in the form, for example, of an attachment or a temporary injunction—is available can often be unclear. It is important, therefore, for parties to investigate relevant arbitration rules and national laws to determine whether they can secure interim relief in court or from the arbitration panel pending the issuance of the arbitration award.

c. Language

The arbitration clause should specify the language of the arbitration proceeding because the parties may not speak a common language in an international arbitration. Parties usually assume that the language of the arbitration will be the language of the contract containing the arbitration clause, but do not leave this assumption unverified. Furthermore, it may not always be the sensible choice depending on the background of the parties and circumstances of the case.

d. Currency of Awards

Parties may want to resolve the currency in which any awards or settlement will be paid. If the choice is among currencies that are freely convertible in international markets, parties should resolve which party will assume the foreign exchange risk. Foreign parties also should determine whether the local law where the arbitration is taking place requires the foreign party to accept payments in the local currency because this could be a problem if the local currency is not freely convertible. The party then must determine whether the local government permits foreigners to exchange local currency for hard currency.

e. Waiver of Sovereign Immunity.

If one of the parties is a governmental entity such as a state-owned automobile manufacturer, the other party should determine whether the governmental entity has waived its immunity from lawsuits. Many countries have adopted laws that waive sovereign immunity for "commercial acts." To be safe, the non-governmental party should negotiate a waiver of sovereign immunity that would be included in the dispute resolution clause of the business contract.

2. When drafting an arbitration clause, an attorney's position on a provision may be shaped as much by her cultural upbringing as by her strategic view of what best serves the interests of his or her client. Three examples of culturally shaped positions that can be masked as strategic ones are summarized here. For the first example on discovery, draft a provision that accommodates the different views of civil and common law lawyers.

a. Discovery

Different philosophies about discovery can shape each party's views of the appropriate level of discovery in arbitrations. U.S. lawyers are taught in law school and in practice to engage in thorough pre-hearing discovery. Many civil law lawyers view the U.S. style of discovery as excessive and oppressive, especially the broad and liberal view of what is discoverable and the wide use of depositions. Civil lawyers are brought up to rely on restricted discovery, limited to the production of relevant, critical documents. It is in this environment of competing upbringings that parties negotiate discovery provisions that both sides can live with. In practice, discovery in arbitrations reflects a philosophy closer to civil law than common law norms.[18]

b. Punitive Damages

Parties from different parts of the United States and around the globe follow different views on whether arbitrators should have the power to award punitive damages. Even if parties agree to vest the tribunal with the authority, a local court that views the payment of punitive damages as a violation of local public policy may still not enforce the award.

c. Awarding Costs of Arbitration

Parties may enter negotiations with a cultural preference for either the English or American Rule for determining who will pay attorney fees and the other costs of arbitration. The American rule of each party

---

18. Jack J. Coe, Jr., International Commercial Arbitration: American Principles and Practice in a Global Context 242–44 (1997).

paying her own costs regardless of outcome is not the practice every-where.[19] Many civil law jurisdictions follow the English rule of the loser paying.

3. In her sample multi-purpose clause, Lucy Reed begins with this language: "Any dispute, controversy or claim arising out of or in connection with this contract, including any question regarding its existence, validity or termination shall be finally resolved by arbitration...."

Recalling that every word counts when drafting clauses, identify each key issue that the clause addresses as well as each solution adopted in the clause.

D. DRAFTING MULTI–STEP CLAUSES

Designing a comprehensive private dispute resolution system is more essential for parties from different countries than for parties within the same country. At least when you fail to plan for domestic disputes in the U.S., you can call the other side to try to settle the dispute, and if that fails, turn to a familiar and stable public court system. For international disputes, however, you should consider whether you want to avoid the uncertainty of an ad hoc settlement process as well as the default process of transnational litigation with its additional risks and unfamiliarity.

You should not wait until an international dispute arises to design a private dispute resolution system. By waiting, you may face the unwieldy obstacles of again convening attorneys and possibly clients when relationships are strained and participants are separated by large distances, time zones, culture and language. Ideally, international parties should design their private process at the time the business relationship is being formed.

The dispute resolution design that is becoming standard incorporates a simple and discrete two-step process of first trying mediation and then, if it is not completely successful, going to arbitration for a final resolution. Known as med-arb clauses, the process is structured like this one recommended by the ICC.[20]

> In the event of any dispute arising out of or in connection with the present contract, the parties agree to submit the matter to settlement proceedings under the ICC ADR Rules. If the dispute has not been settled pursuant to the said Rules within 45 days following the filing of a Request for ADR or within such other period as the parties may agree in writing, such dispute shall

19. See DAN B. DOBBS, DOBBS LAW OF REMEDIES, § 3.10 (vol. 1, 2d ed. 1993) (description of American rule including comparison with English rule).

20. See http://www.iccwbo.org/index_adr.asp#model_clause. The clause re-fers to ADR rules that specify that unless parties agree to another settlement technique, mediation will be used (Article 5(1) & (2)). Also see James T. Peter, Med-Arb in International Arbitration, 8 AM. REV. INT'L ARB. 83 (1997).

be finally settled under the Rules of Arbitration of the International Chamber of Commerce by one or more arbitrators appointed in accordance with the said Rules of Arbitration.

This basic two-step design can be supplemented by more elaborate sequencing and mixing of dispute resolution options. Which design is optimal for a party depends on the circumstances at the moment the parties are designing the clause. In this section, three different configurations are examined. Each option encompasses a process sequence that combines arbitration with settlement processes. The first option, Neg–Med–Arb, and the second one, Dynamic Med–Arb, may be suitable at the time parties are negotiating a business deal or when a dispute first arises. The third option, Arb–Med–Arb, can be appealing when a dispute is already in arbitration.

1. NEG–MED–ARB

KATHLEEN M. SCANLON, MULTI–STEP DISPUTE RESOLUTION CLAUSES IN BUSINESS– BUSINESS AGREEMENTS

SJO34 ALI–ABA, 6–15 (Mediation And Other ADR–Dispute Resolution For The 21st Century, American Law Institute–American Bar Association Continuing Legal Education September 18–19, 2003) (Copyright 2003 Kathleen M. Scanlon, Special Counsel, Heller Ehrman White & McAuliffe. All Rights Reserved).

* * *

For many decades, stand-alone, standardized arbitration clauses had been the extent of ADR clause drafting in many business-to-business agreements. If litigation, rather than arbitration, was contemplated, provisions relating to forum selection, choice-of-law and a few other select items may have been addressed in the contract. Presently, much more sophisticated drafting is required, including issues relating to multi-step clause drafting.

A multi-step dispute resolution clause provides for sequential stages of dispute resolution. Multi-step clauses typically provide for a period when the parties engage in a consensual process—such as negotiation or mediation—before resorting to an adjudicatory process such as arbitration or litigation. The rationale underlying such an approach is that the negotiation or mediation stage affords the parties an opportunity to develop creative, business-oriented solutions before investing time and money in an adversarial process such as arbitration or litigation.

* * *

II. Multi–Step Clause Overview

More and more leading companies across a cross-section of industries are using some form of multi-step dispute resolution clauses in their agreements when appropriate. Negotiation and/or mediation are commonly used prior to the parties resorting to arbitration or litigation.

A. Sample CPR Multi–Step Clause (Negotiation–Mediation–Arbitration)

CPR provides numerous model multi-step dispute resolution clauses to assist counsel in their drafting tasks. All of the CPR model clauses are intended to be customized by counsel for the particular transaction at hand and should not be included in a contract on a pro forma basis. The Model Multi–Step Clause provided below contains three steps—Negotiation–Mediation–Arbitration.

CPR Model Clause

"(A) The parties shall attempt in good faith to resolve any dispute arising out of or relating to this [Agreement] [Contract] promptly by negotiation between executives who have authority to settle the controversy and who are at a higher level of management than the persons with direct responsibility for administration of this contract. Any person may give the other party written notice of any dispute not resolved in the normal course of business. Within [15] days after delivery of the notice, the receiving party shall submit to the other a written response. The notice and response shall include (a) a statement of that party's position and a summary of arguments supporting that position, and (b) the name and title of the executive who will represent that party and of any other person who will accompany the executive. Within [30] days after delivery of the initial notice, the executives of both parties shall meet at a mutually acceptable time and place, and thereafter as often as they reasonably deem necessary, to attempt to resolve the dispute. All reasonable requests for information made by one party to the other will be honored.

All negotiations pursuant to this clause are confidential and shall be treated as compromise and settlement negotiations for purposes of applicable rules of evidence.

(B) If the dispute has not been resolved by negotiation as provided herein within [45] days after delivery of the initial notice of negotiation, [or if the parties failed to meet within [30] days after such delivery,] the parties shall endeavor to settle the dispute by mediation under the CPR Mediation Procedure [then currently in effect OR in effect on the date of this Agreement], [provided, however, that if one party fails to participate in the negotiation as provided herein, the other party can initiate mediation prior to the expiration of the [45] days]. Unless otherwise agreed, the parties will select a mediator from the CPR Panels of Distinguished Neutrals.

(C) Any dispute arising out of or relating to this [Agreement] [Contract], including the breach, termination or validity thereof, which has not been resolved by mediation as provided herein [within [45] days after initiation of the mediation procedure] [within [30] days after the appointment of a mediator], shall be finally resolved by arbitration in accordance with the CPR Rules for Non–Administered Arbitration [then currently in effect OR in effect on the date of this Agreement], by [a sole arbitrator] [three independent and impartial arbitrators, of whom each party shall designate one] [three arbitrators of whom each party shall appoint one in accordance with the 'screened' appointment procedure provided in Rule 5.4] [three independent and impartial arbitrators, none of whom shall be appointed by either party]; [provided, however, that if one party fails to participate in either the negotiation or mediation as agreed herein, the other party can commence arbitration prior to the expiration of the time periods set forth above.] The arbitration shall be governed by the Federal Arbitration Act, 9 U.S.C. §§ 1–16, and judgment upon the award rendered by the arbitrator(s) may be entered by any court having jurisdiction thereof. The place of arbitration shall be (city, state)."

*　*　*

III.　Special Drafting Issues Checklist for Multi–Step Clauses

*　*　*

C.　Condition Precedent and Enforcement Issues

*　*　*

2) Multi–Step Language Addressing Enforcement–Related Remedies

Within the multi-step clause itself, some parties also address remedies for failure to satisfy the multi-step ADR conditions. For example, in a real estate transactional document, the contract provided that failure to mediate prior to litigation or arbitration resulted in a forfeiture of any entitlement to attorney fees:

> Buyer [and] Seller ... agree to and shall mediate any dispute or claim between them arising out of this contract.... The mediation shall be held prior to any court action or arbitration.... Should the prevailing party attempt an arbitration or a court action before attempting [to] mediate, THE PREVAILING PARTY SHALL NOT BE ENTITLED TO ATTORNEY FEES THAT MIGHT OTHERWISE BE AVAILABLE TO THEM IN A COURT ACTION OR ARBITRATION
> *　*　*　*

*　*　*

3) Jurisdictional Issues in Multi–Step Arbitration Clauses

　　a.　Who Decides Whether Nonbinding Process Has Been Satisfied—Court, Arbitrator, Mediator?

When a dispute arises over whether the parties have satisfied the nonbinding ADR process stage in the context of a multi-step clause that provides for arbitration as the final step, who decides the compliance issue—the court, arbitrator, mediator (if mediation is part of the clause)?

Although tangential litigation over such an issue is counterproductive to the intent and spirit of contractual multi-step ADR clauses, such litigation (unfortunately) exists.

During the past U.S. Supreme Court Term (2002–03), the Court stated that "gateway procedural disputes" are to [be] resolved by the arbitrator, and are not questions of arbitrability for the court [See *Howsam v. Dean Witter Reynolds, Inc.*, 537 U.S. 79, 123 S. Ct. 588 (2002)]. Similarly, the vast majority of state courts and the law that has developed under the Federal Arbitration Act (FAA), 9 U.S.C. §§ 1–16, hold that, in the absence of an agreement to the contrary, issues of substantive arbitrability—i.e., whether a dispute is encompassed by an agreement to arbitrate—are for a court to decide, and issues of procedural arbitrability—i.e., whether prerequisites such as time limits, notice, laches, estoppel, and other conditions precedent to an obligation to arbitrate have been met—are for the arbitrators to decide. Moreover, Section 6 of the recently revised Uniform Arbitration Act, the Revised Uniform Arbitration Act (2000) ("RUAA"), provides that:

> (c) An arbitrator shall decide whether a condition precedent to arbitrability has been fulfilled and whether a contract containing a valid agreement to arbitrate is enforceable.

Are questions concerning enforcement and satisfactory compliance with nonbinding ADR processes included in a multi-step arbitration clause "gateway procedural disputes" for the arbitrator or questions of arbitrability for the court? Many courts faced with this precise issue refer the matter to the arbitrator, either explicitly or implicitly as a condition precedent issue for the arbitrators. However, some courts have decided the compliance issue themselves, instead of deferring to the arbitrator. In some of these latter cases, a thoughtful discussion, if any, of the jurisdictional issue is lacking. In these instances, courts presumably operate under enforcement provisions of arbitration statutes as a basis for addressing these procedural issues. In a sparse number of other cases, courts have viewed the condition precedent requirement as limiting the arbitrator's authority to hear the dispute—i.e., arbitrator only empowered to hear disputes that have been mediated. Thus, it is a question of arbitrability and not procedure under this framework. Query the soundness of the latter analysis, particularly in light of the most recent wave of U.S. Supreme Court decisions showing a reluctance by the Court to construe arbitration agreements.

And last, in at least one instance, the court referred the compliance issue to mediation. Specifically, when the contract provided that "all claims, disputes and other matters in question arising out of or related to this Contract or breach thereof shall be submitted to non-binding mediation which shall be a condition precedent to any party initiating litigation ... [and only if mediation does not settle the dispute] "either party may submit the dispute to mandatory, binding arbitration ... ," the court reasoned that "[s]ince the question of whether the proper procedural steps have been followed is a dispute arising out of the Contract, the Contract requires the mediator to attempt resolution prior to arbitration.''

From a practical standpoint, to avoid any tangential litigation over satisfactory compliance and its related jurisdictional issue, counsel may consider including in their multi-step clauses explicit authorization for the arbitrator, and not the court, to decide these condition precedents issues.

Notes and Questions

1. What are the advantages of a three-step Neg–Med–Arb clause for resolving a dispute that is international? Of course, the three-step clause is not a panacea for all risks that can arise when facing an international dispute. What are the drawbacks of such a private process? Under what circumstances might you counsel against incorporating such a dispute resolution clause into a business contract?

2. Under the Sample CPR Multi–Step Clause, what are the consequences for a prevailing party who circumvents the mediation stage and goes to arbitration or court? What other incentives might you design and incorporate into the clause to motivate good-faith participation?

3. Who would you rather handle any disputes regarding whether a party has satisfied the nonbinding ADR process before going to arbitration—the judge, arbitrator, or mediator? What are the advantages and drawbacks of each third party?

2.   DYNAMIC MED–ARB

In the following excerpt, Christian Buhring–Uhle transforms the basic two-step Med–Arb option into a more dynamic process in which parties shift back and forth between consensus-based and adjudicatory processes until the dispute is resolved.

CHRISTIAN BUHRING–UHLE, ARBITRATION AND MEDIATION IN INTERNATIONAL BUSINESS

371, 389–91 (1996).

* * *

How Mediation Windows Work

... [S]ettlement facilitation during an on-going arbitration in the form of low-intensity mediation efforts by the tribunal itself are a common feature of the practice of international arbitration. By contrast, a full-scale mediation as a separate procedure in the "shadow" of an on-going arbitration, and with the participation of high-level executives from the parties, is less usual though not entirely uncommon. It can be conducted by the tribunal or by a separate mediator. Such a "mediation window" does not necessarily disrupt the arbitration since there are long periods during any arbitration where no hearings are conducted and the participants simply prepare for the next step in the proceedings. Setting aside a few days for a mediation attempt—the maximum duration will be of one or two weeks—is therefore possible without causing a noticeable disruption.

* * *

[T]he guiding principle for dispute resolution process design should be to maximize the consensual element in any solution and to have third-party decisionmaking available but to limit it to the indispensable minimum.

3. BASIC ELEMENTS OF THE SYSTEM

[T]he two main elements of the proposed system for dispute resolution process design are *interest-based negotiations* and a *rights-based adjudication* procedure as a *back-up* in case no agreement is reached.

The best way to achieve consensus is through negotiation. Since interests are the yardstick for commercial dispute resolution the *negotiations* should be primarily *interest-based*. There are a number of ADR techniques, most notably mediation, that can improve the effectiveness of negotiation. They should therefore be considered when structuring the negotiation element of the system.

Previous chapters have shown that arbitration is the most effective *back-up* available in international commercial disputes. Litigation, however, is also a rights-based adjudication procedure and has to be considered as an option in specific contexts where arbitration is not available or where international agreements such as the Brussels Convention have improved the legal framework for transnational litigation.

There are two intermediate steps between these two principal elements: *rights-based negotiation* as a filter to adjudication and *loop-backs* as a way to revert to interest-based negotiation.

Rights-based negotiations are an important *filter* to adjudication. Rather than incurring the costs of going through an adjudication procedure the parties try to anticipate its result in negotiations. These negotiations typically take the form of an exchange of legal arguments and a confrontation of conflicting predictions about the outcome of the back-up procedure. This form of "bargaining in the shadow of the law" characterizes conventional settlement negotiations. It can be enhanced through certain forms of predictive ADR, most notably mini-trials and related mediation structures. In practice, interest-based and rights-based negotiation are blended into one procedure which in the shadow of an impending adjudication is dominated by rights-based negotiation. However, it is important to make this distinction, mentally and through the structure of the process, in order not to loose sight of the ultimate goal of dispute resolution process design—a consensual solution that reconciles the interests of the parties on the highest possible level. Both interest-based and rights-based negotiations can be brought to their maximum effectiveness through the assistance of a mediator but in mediation, too, it is important to distinguish problem-solving and predictive techniques in order to accomplish the two objectives of realizing the interests of the parties and having their rights respected.

A *loop back is* a structure that permits the participants of a rights-based adjudication procedure to revert to interest-based negotiation, always in line with the guiding principle to maximize consensus and to minimize third-party decisionmaking. Examples for loop backs are mediation windows in arbitration and post-award-settlements which through negotiation try to improve the result of adjudication.

Notes and Questions

Map out conceptually Buhring–Uhle's Dynamic Med–Arb Process. Under his approach, what is the difference between interest-based and rights-based negotiations? As a participant in such a process, how would you shift from the first to the second and why would you want to? What is the difference between the use of "mediation windows" in an international arbitration and the use of mediation in a domestic court proceeding? Draft a dispute resolution clause that implements the Dynamic Med–Arb Process.

3. ARB–MED–ARB

This section considers the opportunities for a third party to assist in settling a dispute after the parties have activated the international arbitration clause and selected the arbitrators. This process sequence can be called Arb–Med–Arb.

This process sequence is already familiar to litigators. A court case can be funneled into a separate mediation process either as a result of an agreement or a court order. If the case fails to settle in mediation, the case returns to court for final resolution. This process sequence also can be used in international arbitrations; parties can elect to channel the arbitration case into a separate mediation process and, if unsuccessful, to return the case to arbitration.

As an alternative to referring the case to a separate mediator, the arbitrators could try to settle the dispute. This option can be a practical one that takes advantage of the rare occasion when all the international participants are together for the arbitration, and it avoids delays due to the time it would take to select a mediator and reconvene again for the mediation. This is a controversial process design, however, because of the inherent difficulties posed by one neutral trying to serve two starkly different processes. Much has been written about the risks to the integrity of each process.[21] As a result, international arbitrators seldom assist in settlement efforts.[22]

21. *See* Chapter 4 C.4(d) on "Search for Arbitrator Power in Mediation Practice."

22. *See* Christian Buhring–Uhle, Arbitration and Mediation in International Business

International arbitrators have been known, however, to occasionally resort to settlement techniques that range from mild to intensive interventions.[23] Arbitrators may (1) suggest that parties try to negotiate a settlement of the case, (2) actively participate in settlement negotiations (at parties' request), (3) propose a settlement formula (at parties' request), (4) meet with parties separately to discuss settlement options (with parties' consent), (5) hint at possible outcome of the arbitration, and (6) render a "case evaluation" (at parties' request). The more intensively arbitrators intervene, the more controversial the intervention.

In this next article, Professor Mnookin described how an arbitration panel that he served on performed not only the roles of arbitrator and mediator but also the role of a process designer.

ROBERT H. MNOOKIN, CREATING VALUE THROUGH PROCESS DESIGN

11 Journal of International Arbitration 125, 126–30 (1994).[24]

* * *

A. *Bitter Conflict*

In September 1985, I was appointed a member of a three-person panel to arbitrate a dispute between IBM, the largest computer company in the world, and Fujitsu, the largest computer company in Japan and now second in the world only to IBM. The arbitration involved a fundamental conflict over intellectual property rights to operating system software—the large and complex computer programs that manage the internal functions of a computer and facilitate the use of application software.

In the early 1970's, Fujitsu decided to develop and market IBM-compatible operating system software for mainframe computers. When Fujitsu released its first such system in 1976, IBM did not claim copyright protection for its operating system software, and there was some question whether copyright law applied to computer software at all. Two years later, IBM registered a copyright for new releases of its compatible software. By 1983—seven years after Fujitsu first issued its IBM-compatible software—it had become clear that such software was indeed protected by U.S. copyright law. IBM confronted Fujitsu with allegations that Fujitsu's operating system programs violated IBM's intellectual property rights.

188–92, 193–96, 211 (1996) (Attorneys appear more receptive to settlement initiatives by arbitrators than the actual practice of international arbitrators!).

23. *See* CHRISTIAN BUHRING-UHLE, ARBITRATION AND MEDIATION IN INTERNATIONAL BUSINESS 188–92 (1996).

24. Fujitsu selected Robert H. Mnookin, a Stanford University professor of law, ADR expert, and founder of the Stanford Center for Conflict and Negotiation. Professor Mnookin is now at Harvard Law School. IBM appointed John L. Jones, an American computer industry executive. The two party-appointed arbitrators selected a chairman who retired before the first award was rendered.

After several months of negotiations, the two companies attempted to resolve their disputes by executing two agreements. The 1983 Settlement Agreement granted Fujitsu immunity and waiver of IBM claims with respect to past and future distribution of Fujitsu's programs in exchange for payments from Fujitsu to IBM. The 1983 Externals Agreement required each party to provide the other with information relevant to compatibility, so-called "external information."

These agreements quickly broke down because they failed to define clearly what information Fujitsu could use in future software development, how it could use it, and at what price. Indeed, the appendix in which the parties were to set the price for external information was left blank. The two parties also failed to agree on the extent to which Fujitsu could use its original IBM-compatible programs as a software development base.

In 1985, IBM filed a demand for arbitration pursuant to the 1983 Settlement Agreement, accusing Fujitsu of copying its software in violation of copyright law and IBM's rights under the 1983 agreements. Fujitsu denied violating IBM's rights and accused IBM of failing to live up to its obligations to provide Fujitsu with interface information under the 1983 agreements.

For IBM, at stake was the protection of billions of dollars of investment in the development of its operating software program. For Fujitsu, at stake was its ability to remain in the IBM-compatible operating systems software business. At stake, too, were the enormous sums of monies invested by Fujitsu's customers to develop applications programs to operate in IBM's or Fujitsu's IBM-compatible operating system environment. Angry and embittered by the collapse of the 1983 agreements, each party was prepared to spend enormous sums of money fighting it out.

From the outset of this arbitration in 1985, the panel sought to help the parties create value that would resolve the conflict in a manner that would further each party's legitimate interest and create value for both. In taking on this task, we were immediately faced with two barriers presented by traditional assumptions about arbitration itself.

The first barrier is inherent in the structure of tripartite arbitration which tends to push the process toward position-taking within the panel itself. While this may lead to eventual compromise, it usually fails to provide room for problem-solving and exploring options for creating value for expanding the pie.

The second barrier is procedural. The exclusive reliance on traditional arbitration proceedings may inhibit the parties and the panel from developing value-creating opportunities.

Here's how we dealt with each of these barriers:

Rejecting the "Partisan" Model

The adversarial positions of the parties often are mirrored in the decision-making process of the three-arbitrator panel, where the two party-appointed arbitrators often battle for the heart and mind of the neutral chair. I'll call this the "partisan" model of tripartite arbitration. In this model, each party-appointed arbitrator continues to meet privately with his or her respective party and counsel, to pursue their adversarial strategies. As a result, the panel's deliberations often mirror the parties' arguments. This process might eventually lead to a coalition between the Chair and one of the party arbitrators, or, alternatively, the Chair may end up mediating a compromise solution between the two arbitrator/advocates. Either way, there is little room for mutual problem-solving or a value-creating approach.

We rejected this partisan model from the outset of the IBM–Fujitsu arbitration. We made it clear to IBM and Fujitsu that the two arbitrators originally appointed by the respective parties would not play partisan roles. Indeed, at its first meeting, the panel ordered that there be no *ex parte* contact or communications.

Most importantly, the panel committed itself to furthering the fundamental interests of both parties in the arbitration process. We recognized that by becoming independent of the parties, and by adopting a problem-solving approach to the panel's own discussions, the panel could exercise its authority and freedom to effectively address the parties' interests and maximize joint gains.

In fact, our arbitration took a further unusual turn. In 1987, panel Chairman Donald McDonald resigned. Rather than appoint a new Chair, the parties empowered my colleague, Jack Jones, and me to retain jurisdiction over the arbitration as a two-person panel until the year 2002. How do we break a tie? We are authorized to hire a third arbitrator if we need one, even for a specific issue. But we haven't needed one, and I don't believe we ever will, because Jack and I have been committed to a problem-solving approach throughout our tenure. There has never been a split vote, because there is never a vote at all. Instead, we have worked together in a collaborative way to further the interests of the parties in the arbitration process.

We were still faced, however, with a second procedural barrier—the limitations of an exclusive reliance on traditional forms of arbitration. Throughout the proceedings in addition to immersing ourselves in the substance of the various claims and counterclaims, we gave a great deal of thought to the dispute resolution process. We asked ourselves whether following traditional methods of adjudication would always be the best way to resolve the dispute in this case, and we concluded that this traditional approach had serious deficiencies.

This conclusion required us, with the consent of the parties, to take responsibility for the process design. Our task was to fashion a flexible dispute resolution process responsible to the particular and changing circumstances and capable of achieving a successful resolution of the many disputes brought before us.

In filing for arbitration, IBM initially brought claims against Fujitsu with respect to a number of specific Fujitsu operating system programs.

The programs at issue involved hundreds of thousands (and in some cases millions) of lines of codes, representing an investment of hundreds of millions of dollars of research, development and programming time.

The parties were locked into extreme positions, positions that were hardened by the uncertainties each party faced. Their claims and counter-claims were framed entirely in terms of the past: interpretation of the agreements, legal rights under ambiguous law, what did or did not happen. IBM claimed that broad copyright protection and restrictions in earlier agreements protected its programs from use by Fujitsu in its software development. Fujitsu, or the other hand, argued that the scope of copyright protection was narrow, and that its entitlement under the earlier agreements was very broad.

A program-by-program adjudication of the parties' disputes would have been bitter, protracted and costly, taking years of discovery and formal arbitration hearings. But worse yet, with a case-by-case common-law approach, the panel might never catch up, particularly given the rate of technological change and the fact that Fujitsu would be continuing to develop and release new IBM-compatible programs during the proceedings.

Dispute Resolution Strategy

The panel concluded that the most effective way to help the parties create value was to adopt a radically different, forward-looking approach.

* * *

One of the advantages of arbitration is that with the consent of both parties, a wide variety of dispute resolution techniques, including mediation, may be employed. With the consent of the parties Jack Jones and I acted as mediators to probe the interests underlying each party's positions and to encourage problem-solving.

It became clear that Fujitsu's paramount interest was to develop IBM-compatible software through its independent development efforts. Fujitsu suggested that it did not require internal design information from IBM programs, but, instead, only external interface information—information specifying what the IBM programs did, not information about how IBM did it. Another interest of Fujitsu was to obtain security against future claims by establishing *ex ante* immunity procedures.

IBM's main interest was to protect its valuable intellectual property. To the extent that Fujitsu had any access to IBM programs, IBM's interests also include ensuring that Fujitsu did not copy internal design information contained in IBM programs, and that IBM received full and adequate compensation for external interface information contained in IBM programs extracted by Fujitsu.

Our exploration suggested to us that the parties had a common interest in reducing uncertainty regarding exactly what IBM information Fujitsu would be permitted to use in an independent software development process. Moreover, differences in the parties' interests made it possible for the panel to create value even under the complex circumstances involved in the IBM–Fujitsu arbitration. Through the process of mediation, the panel saw the possibility of separating the peel from the pulp if certainty could be established concerning the scope of external interface information and that external information could be separated from internal design information.

As a result of our mediation efforts, the parties set aside the 1983 agreements and executed a new 1987 agreement that provided a framework for the resolution of all issues in dispute. It provided that the panel would create a Secured Facility regime that would regulate Fujitsu's access to and use of IBM programming material for a transition period lasting approximately ten years. With respect to Fujitsu's old programs, the parties agreed that, at a price to be established by the panel, Fujitsu would purchase a paid-up license in exchange for immunity, waiver of claims, and an express right to use these programs as part of Fujitsu's software development base.

To pursue the parties shared interest in certainty about applicable legal requirements, the parties authorized the panel to create the rules that would govern each party's use of the other's mainframe programming materials for the transition period. The rules to be established in this arbitration would bind both parties, irrespective of copyright law.

* * *

This stage involved creating the instructions to define external interface information and rules to implement the new regime. Technical teams from each party, including software developers and counsel with expertise in software development, played central and constructive roles. Negotiations between these teams—encouraged, guided and focused by the panel—were more productive than had previously been possible between the parties and their counsel. This process resulted in an extensive set of rules and procedures that currently govern the Secured Facility Regime in its day-to-day operation.

* * *

We did not frame our strategy in terms of penalties or exoneration for past conduct. Rather, as a result of mediation, the parties agreed that Fujitsu would purchase a paid-up license—at a price determined by the panel—that would allow Fujitsu to use, with immunity, in future software development, all of its old IBM-compatible programs. By relying largely on written submissions, we held expedited hearings that lasted less than ten days to determine the fair price. We required Fujitsu to pay IBM U.S. $396 million for this paid-up license.

* * *

[T]he panel assured the parties that it would conduct independent compliance monitoring. We hired independent experts to serve as Facility Administrators and staff to ensure that the applicable facilities of each party are operated in accordance with the strict and elaborate safeguards.* * * The panel also hired an independent technical consultant to assist with inspections at the facilities of each company where programming materials of the other are surveyed or reviewed.

Notes and Questions

1.   In the IBM–Fujitsu arbitration, identify each of the dispute resolution processes that were designed by the arbitrators.

2.   In view of the reservations about the same person serving as mediator and arbitrator in the same case, why do you think the IBM–Fujitsu arbitration was successful? Review the benefits and risks that were considered in Chapter 4—International Negotiation and Mediation in the Private Sector, Section C.4(d) on "Search for Arbitrator Power in Mediation Practice."

3.   Can you extract from the IBM–Fujitsu experience any principles that could guide future arbitrators who are considering taking on the additional roles of mediating and assisting parties in designing and implementing other methods of dispute resolution?

4.   Draft a dispute resolution clause that would provide neutrals the authority to function the way they did in the IBM–Fujitsu arbitration.

This next article suggests how international arbitrators may safely settle cases by following safeguards that are designed to preserve the impartiality of the neutrals while giving them some flexibility to facilitate settlement.

HAROLD ABRAMSON, PROTOCOLS FOR INTERNATIONAL ARBITRATORS WHO DARE TO SETTLE CASES

10 American Review of International Arbitration 1–2, 7–15 (1999).

* * *

[The author emphasized that the protocols are designed to create a small opening through which arbitrators can try to settle cases. This excerpt lists the twelve protocols and includes explanations for three of them.]

Ideally, I think international arbitrators should stay out of the direct settlement business. I favor the optimal arrangement in which the neutral who tries settling a case is different from the neutral who decides the case. This arrangement preserves the impartiality of the neutral as decisionmaker while giving the neutral as settler the maximum flexibility to do her job well.

But as a pragmatist, I worry about lost opportunities for settlement in international arbitrations. It is extremely cumbersome to convene all the parties and attorneys. The first opportunity to meet face-to-face may be the first day of the arbitration hearings (or the night before in a foreign city while recovering from jet-lag). This may be their first real opportunity to discuss settling the case. In this paper, I consider whether these settlement discussions can be facilitated by the arbitrators.

* * *

In this section, I suggest a series of protocols that parties and their neutral(s) should follow. These protocols may work best when settlement initiatives are restricted to quasi-mediations. In some limited situations, adopting these protocols may make it feasible for arbitrators to engage in real mediations.

(1) Neutral is Trained in Both Processes * * *

(2) Neutral Consents to Serve Both Roles * * *

(3) Neutral as Settler Will Respect Principle of Party Self–Determination
* * *

(4) Clients with Settlement Authority Should Be Present * * *

(5) Documents and Statements in Settlement Process are Confidential
* * *

(6) Neutral as Settler Will Not Evaluate Merits, Evidence or Reasonableness of Positions

Any evaluation by the neutral as settler poses a significant risk of compromising the neutral's impartiality if she resumes the role of arbitrator. The arbitrator who offers an evaluation during the settlement process may appear to have prejudged the case when the arbitration proceeding resumes. When the neutral returns to arbitrating, the neutral also may discover that the evaluation done in the settlement process may contaminate her view of the record in the arbitration proceeding. This protocol barring evaluations directs the neutral as settler to resist slipping prematurely into an adjudicatory mindset....

This restriction should not be interpreted to bar a mediator or quasi-mediator from helping the parties evaluate the case. The settler can still ask even-handed questions about the quality of evidence, credibility of witnesses, clarity of law, and likelihood of success in the arbitration proceeding. The settler can introduce to the parties the use of decision tree analysis to help the parties assess alternatives to settlement. * * *

(7) Neutral Will Not Caucus, Unless Parties Agree to Exception

Arbitrators turned settlers increase the risk of compromising their appearance of impartiality when they hold private meetings. The excluded party may become concerned that the neutral played one party against the other during settlement efforts. The excluded party also may become suspicious that the other party corrupted the neutral's view of the case under circumstances where the excluded party could not challenge the information. Presumably for these reasons, international practitioners have judged caucuses as the least appropriate technique for arbitrator-turned-mediator.

Barring caucuses means barring the use of a tool that many quasi-mediators and mediators consider vital for settlement efforts to be successful. Many settlers believe that private meetings create a unique and safe opportunity for neutrals to help parties vent and release anger, clarify positions and interests, and assess the acceptability of alternative settlement options. * * *

(8) Parties Agree to Reconfigure Arbitration Panel to Suit Settlement Process

Arbitrators can take many different pathways toward helping parties settle a case. Each pathway offers different ways for preserving the impartiality of the neutral as arbitrator while opening opportunities for settlement. Many of these pathways are built around the flexibility offered by the usual international tribunal of three arbitrators. Five configurations are considered here although other permutations can be imagined. [This excerpt describes one option.]

[W]hen a typical panel of a neutral chair with two party-appointed arbitrators is constituted, the two party-appointed arbitrators could work together as a settlement team without the participation of the chair. This arrangement would preserve the neutrality of the chair who would not be tarnished by settlement efforts.

The settlement team could serve as quasi-mediators or even full-fledged mediators. They might function like a panel in a minitrial, hearing the parties' claims and helping them settle the dispute. The settlement team of party-appointed arbitrators may even be permitted by the parties to use caucuses because the third arbitrator, the chair, remains in reserve, insulated from the settlement process (Protocol 7). The settlement team should caucus only as a team which means each party-appointed arbitrator should avoid any *ex parte* contacts with the appointing party.

If settlement efforts are unsuccessful, the chair could serve as a sole arbitrator. This option, however, may be resisted by many international attorneys who prefer their party-appointed arbitrators to participate in the deliberations. In the alternative, all three arbitrators could hear the case. The impartiality of the panel may survive because any partiality by the party-appointed arbitrators would off-set each other, leaving the chair with the neutral and decisive role in the deliberations.

(9) Arbitrator Will Not Be Influenced by Information Revealed in Settlement Process * * *

(10) Parties Agree Not to Challenge Arbitrator or Award Based on Combined Roles * * *

(11) Settlement Initiatives Should Not Unduly Delay the Arbitration Proceeding * * *

(12) Parties Consent to Combined Processes * * *

Notes and Questions

1.   Do the protocols establish sufficient safeguards to protect the impartiality of arbitrators who try to settle cases? Which protocols are central to preserving arbitration's neutrality? Do the protocols disable arbitrators from engaging in meaningful efforts to settle? Are there other configurations of tripartite tribunals that can serve the twin goals of maintaining the impartiality of the arbitrators and giving them sufficient flexibility to engage in effective settlement efforts? Did the parties or arbitrators in the IBM–Fujitsu case violate any of the protocols? If so, why did the settlement efforts still succeed?

2.   Who is in a less risky position to help parties design dispute resolution processes—mediators or arbitrators?

3.   Why is it generally acceptable for judges, but not arbitrators, to try settling their own cases? Is it easier to justify the same person serving as mediator and arbitrator in international arbitrations than domestic ones?

E.   SELECTING INSTITUTIONAL OR AD HOC ADMINISTRATION OF PROCESSES

Should you retain a professional organization to administer the dispute resolution process, or should you self-administer the process, known as ad hoc administration? This section considers some of the factors to weigh when deciding whether to out-source or self-administer a process.

Administration by one of the reputable international organizations in the business of administering dispute resolution processes can be helpful and convenient. These professional organizations have their own trained staff, facilities, and procedural rules to govern dispute resolution processes. They are primarily in the arbitration business although they also serve mediations. The organizations can be sorted into two groups: ones that handle virtually any business dispute[25] and ones that specialize in handling only certain types.[26]

These professional organizations become more attractive to use the more complex the conflict is because of the more administrative tasks that someone must handle. To set up an arbitration, someone must prepare and send notices to parties, administer the procedures for selecting arbitrators, arrange the scheduling of hearings (time, date, and place), and deal with any post-award enforcement issues. A reputable neutral institution has the know-how to handle these administrative

25.   Examples include the International Chamber of Commerce (ICC), American Arbitration Association (AAA), London Court of International Arbitration (LCIA), The Arbitration Institute of the Stockholm Chamber of Commerce, and the CPR Institute for Dispute Resolution.

26.   Examples include the International Center for the Settlement of Investment Disputes (ICSID), China International Economic and Trade Arbitration Commission (CIETAC), Commercial Arbitration and Mediation for the Americas (CAMCA), and World Intellectual Property Organization Arbitration Center (WIPO).

details, offers its time-tested rules, provides a list of qualified neutrals, and most importantly, insulates arbitrators from the parties. Moreover, an experienced institution can offer its expertise in determining whether an award meets legal requirements for enforcement in multiple jurisdictions. An arbitration process administered by a highly respected institution also gives its award additional credibility when a party seeks voluntary or legal enforcement.

Professional organizations can be especially valuable for administering an international arbitration because an international arbitration can be more complicated than a domestic one. Straightforward tasks of communications and scheduling become more complicated when parties and neutrals reside in different countries, speaking different languages. There also is a greater likelihood that parties will need professional translators, bilingual stenographic transcripts, and an understanding of different foreign legal requirements for enforcing agreements to mediate or arbitrate, settlement agreements, and arbitral awards.

Comparatively, mediations are generally less complicated to administer than arbitrations. Nevertheless, independent administration can be convenient, especially for inexperienced parties who do not have access to a list of mediators and are unsure what it takes to set up a mediation. They also may lack knowledge of the legal requirements for enforcing settlement agreements abroad and lack easy access to professional translators and suitable meeting space abroad.

But this expertise and convenience can be costly; these institutions charge substantial administrative fees (much less for mediations than arbitrations) and can take time to provide their services.

As an alternative, parties can self-administer the process, although neutrals and parties can find it cumbersome and at times awkward to both self-administer a process and participate in it. This option, however, is still worth considering because it can be more flexible and cost-effective as well as quicker, if certain critical conditions are met: if parties are cooperating, if they can efficiency negotiate the administrative details to be done, and if the neutrals and parties can proficiently handle the administrative responsibilities without compromising the neutrality of the neutrals.[27] However, even with ad hoc administration, parties usually find it helpful to select an "appointing authority"[28] to handle the vital stage of selecting the arbitrators or mediators and to be available to handle any challenges.[29] For parties preferring ad hoc

---

27. The United Nations Commission on International Trade Law (UNCITRAL), which does not serve as an administering institution, has published helpful instructions on how to organize arbitral proceedings. UNCITRAL Notes on Organizing Arbitral Proceedings, U.N. Doc. V.96–84935.

28. A number of established institutions are willing to serve as an "appointing authority" including the ICC, AAA, CPR and Stockholm Chamber of Commerce.

29. In CPR's Commentary for its Non–Administered International Arbitration Rules & Commentary, CPR suggests that "[t]he assistance of a neutral organization to serve as appointing authority may nevertheless be valuable in selecting the Tribunal or deciding a conflict of interest challenge to an arbitrator. Under CPR's International Rules, a Neutral Organization on which the parties agree will perform these limited functions. (*See* Rules 5, 6 and 7)."

administration, they can choose rules designed for self-administration[30] such as the ones formulated by the United Nations Commission on International Trade Law (UNCITRAL.)[31]

The need for professional administration can be less for mediations. They can be simpler to administer once the mediator is selected because the process can require less paper work, fewer participants, and less need to insulate neutrals from the parties, making it easier for mediators to handle scheduling times and places of sessions as well as exchanging any documents or briefing papers.

Notes and Questions

This section considered various factors to weigh when deciding whether to contract-out or self-administer a single process. Obviously, self-administering a multi-step process would be more complicated. Would you ever choose to self-administer a Neg–Med–Arb process? If so, under what circumstances would you do so?

30. CPR also has designed rules specifically for ad hoc administration. See CRP's Non–Administered International Arbitration Rules & Commentary (1995).

31. UNCITRAL's arbitration rules, adopted by the General Assembly of the United Nations, are designed to be broadly acceptable in countries with different legal and economic systems, whether common law or civil law jurisdictions or capital-exporting or capital-importing nations.

UNCITRAL is not a dispute resolution institution. UNCITRAL was established by the General Assembly of the United Nations in 1966 to promote "the progressive harmonization and unification of the law of international trade" (G.A. Res. 2205, 21 U.N. GAOR, Annex 3, U.N. Doc. A/6396 and (Add. 1 & 2) (1966), *reprinted in* 1 Y.B. COMM'N INT'L. TRADE L. 65 (1968–70), U.N. Doc. A/CN.9/SER.A/1970).

Membership in UNCITRAL is limited to nation-states. Among its many significant contributions, it adopted Arbitration Rules in 1976 (U.N. Doc. Sales No. E.7 v. 6 (1977)), Conciliation Rules in 1980 (U.N. Doc. A/35/17 (1980)), Model Law on International Commercial Arbitration in 1985 (U.N. Doc. A/35/17 (1980)), and updated its Notes on Organizing Arbitral Proceedings in 1996 (U.N. Doc. V.96–84935).

Chapter 6

RESOLVING DISPUTES ONLINE

A. INTRODUCTION

Q: Why is Cybersettle[1] better than arbitration, mediation or other ADR?

Traditional ADR is more expensive, time consuming and often results in unpredictable settlement outcomes. With Cybersettle, the amount of the settlement is always under your control and your bargaining position is never compromised.[2]

This claim by Cybersettle that its online dispute resolution service provides an alternative to alternative dispute resolution forms the central inquiry of this chapter. Do the remarkable and still emerging innovations in online dispute resolution (ODR) offer viable alternatives, dare we say, to *traditional* forms of alternative dispute resolution such as mediation and arbitration?

ODR has been labeled as the fourth party at the dispute resolution table:[3]

* * * Three is also a familiar number in traditional dispute resolution, where there are usually considered to be three parties to the process: the two disputants and the third party neutral. Even when there is a multiparty dispute with many disputants, ADR is still commonly thought to be three-sided, with all of the disputants grouped together as the two disputants and the mediator or arbitrator as the third party.

* * * [W]e propose that you think of ODR as shaped somewhat differently, as having not three parties but four, as being a square or rectangle instead of a trian-

---

1. Cybersettle is a private company that designed a double-blind bid system for resolving money disputes. Its automated negotiation system is described in the next section on "Online Facilities and Processes."

2. *See* Cybersettle webpage on attorney questions: http://www.cybersettle.com/faqs/attyfaq.asp#.

3. *See* Ethan Katsh & Janet Rifkin, Online Dispute Resolution 93–94 (2001).

gle. The "fourth party," the new presence "at the table," is the technology that works with the mediator or arbitrator. Just as the role of a third party can vary in different contexts, so can the role of the fourth party. It can, in different circumstances, be more or less relied upon and be more or less influential, but the role, nature, and value of this fourth party needs to be understood and recognized.

The fourth party does not, except in a few well-defined instances * * *, *replace* the third party. But, it can be considered to *displace* the third party in the sense that new skills, knowledge, and strategies may be needed by the third party. It may not be coequal in influence to the third party neutral, but it can be an ally, collaborator, and partner. It can assume responsibilities for various communications with the parties, and the manner in which the third and fourth parties interact with each other will affect many parts of the dispute resolution process.

Interest in this fourth party has been fueled by the emerging cyber marketplace, a marketplace of transactions taking place over the Internet, known as e-commerce. These buyers and sellers need access to cost-effective and efficient means to resolving disputes that arise from these online transactions. These buyers and sellers need a dispute resolution process that is inexpensive—one in which the costs are much lower than the purchase price of the commodity. Going to court or convening a mediation are not viable resolution methods for these modest transactions.

Although you are unlikely to represent clients in these modest disputes, you ought to be knowledgeable about online dispute resolution options in order to serve other clients' needs. You may be asked to counsel a client who is trying to resolve his own dispute in an online process. He may want to know whether he should participate in an automated "blind bidding" negotiation, for instance, a method described in the next section, and, if so, what strategies to employ. A business client may ask you to evaluate an existing ODR process or design one for an online dispute resolution clause that she wants to include in either her customer (B2C) contracts or business (B2B) ones.[4] A client may need you to represent him in an online mechanism for a dispute arising out of a substantial online or offline transaction, especially an international one. You might even choose to build a practice to provide client services in online processes.

---

4. B2C refers to contracts between businesses and their retail consumers. B2B refers to contracts between businesses.

Online dispute resolution processes present a number of advantages.[5]

1.   For e-commerce transactions and modest offline transactions, online processes may offer the only financially feasible option for resolving these low dollar value disputes.

2.   For substantial offline transactions, especially international ones, online facilities can offer ways to reduce the expense, enhance the efficiency, and improve the effectiveness of dispute resolution processes.

3.   An asynchronous ODR process can operate twenty-four hours a day, seven days a week, at the parties' and mediator's convenience. Such a mechanism is particularly useful when parties are located in different time zones. Also, participants can access all the documents and discussions at any time and from anywhere they have Internet access.

4.   Interactions can be rational and considered in an asynchronous process. Participants and mediators have the time to reflect, consult others, and craft thoughtful communications, an opportunity that reduces the risk of making damaging and impetuous remarks, an especially significant risk when parties are intensely hostile.

5.   There is no travel inconvenience for the parties, their attorneys, and the mediator.

6.   No expenses are incurred to provide a neutral facility at which to conduct the mediation.

7.   Because the proceedings can take place with everyone at their usual place of business, documents and research materials can be readily accessible.

8.   Everyone's time is used productively. There is no dead time between sessions or while waiting at the session for the next stage in the mediation process.

9.   The mediator may caucus with one side without artificially interfering with the flow of the mediation.

10.   In cross-border transactions, ODR reduces the risk of being dragged into a foreign court system.

The obvious drawback of ODR is the loss of face-to-face, spontaneous, and sustained interactions between the parties, attorneys, and the mediator. This drawback will be examined in detail throughout this chapter.

Section B introduces you to the online world by describing several online facilities and dispute resolution processes. Section C suggests how these online facilities can be used to supplement or replace offline negotiations, mediations, and arbitrations. Section D considers how to determine whether ODR might be acceptable to participants. Section E, the central segment of this chapter, assesses some of the criticism leveled

---

5. *See, e.g.*, JOHN COOLEY, MEDIATION ADVOCACY 256–58 (2002) and Gibbons, Kennedy & Gibbs, *Cyber-Mediation: Computer-* *Mediated Communications Medium Massaging the Message*, 32 N.M. L. REV. 27, 42–43 (2002).

against the use of ODR and possible responses. Finally, Section F raises several legal issues posed by using ODR.

Notes and Questions

As you proceed through this chapter, continue to consider whether ODR can be fairly described as an alternative to *traditional* alternative dispute resolution processes. Also, continue to consider whether you can identify other advantages of using online dispute resolution processes.

B. ONLINE FACILITIES AND PROCESSES

This section introduces you to the online world—background that is essential for this chapter. It defines key terminology, explains several of the technological facilities available online, and describes a range of online processes.

The three basic and most widely used online facilities are email, instant messaging, and videoconferencing. These facilities operate in cyberspace, the virtual world that can be accessed by anyone who has access to the Internet. Through these facilities for communicating and interacting, whether simultaneously or asynchronously, people can meet without meeting face-to-face.

Email

Electronic mail is now the most commonly used means for communicating online. Emails may consist of text and include attachments that contain text, photos, motion pictures, music, and exact replicas of original documents. Exchanging emails do not require real time interaction, thus permitting participants to ponder and respond with care. And the messages can be sustained as a thread as well as stored and categorized for later use.

Instant Messaging

Instant messaging provides a private chat room where participants can exchange text messages in real time. It functions like a meeting on the Internet with participants communicating with each other through the interactive exchange of text messages, thereby creating an online conversation without interruptions. The exchanges can be stored for later references.

Videoconferencing

Videoconferencing permits participants from different locations to hear each other, see each other, exchange documents, and collaborate in editing drafts. And they can do all this in real time. However, it is not a perfect substitute for a face-to-face meeting. Unless parties have access to the latest technology, the video can be choppy and the screen small. Nonverbal communications, so vital to in-person communications, can be distorted because facial expressions can be unclear and eye contact difficult to make due to the angle of the camera. Also, participants unfamiliar with the technology or unaccustomed to appearing in front of a camera may not interact naturally. These difficulties can be compounded by cultural differences and the lack of generally accepted code of etiquette for behaving during a videoconference. Nevertheless, videoconferencing in which participants use the latest technologies and prepare carefully can be an effective option for meeting when parties cannot convene in the same room.

Videoconferencing is also is the most expensive technological option due to the combination of three significant costs. Participants must incur the cost of buying desktop conferencing software and hardware (video camera and speakers), establishing a large screen videoconferencing facility, or renting a videoconferencing facility. Participants must pay the cost of a high-speed, long-distance transmission connection among the participants in the videoconference. And, in less advanced countries, it may take some effort and extra expense to secure access to videoconferencing technology.

This next excerpt describes briefly a number of online dispute resolution processes.

MELISSA CONLEY TYLER & DI BRETHERTON, SEVENTY–SIX AND COUNTING: AN ANALYSIS OF ODR SITES, A REPORT OF RESEARCH CONDUCTED FOR THE DEPARTMENT OF JUSTICE, VICTORIA, AUSTRALIA

Proceedings of the UNECE Forum on ODR 2003 http://www.odr.info/unece2003.

* * *

3.2.1 Types of Online ADR Offered

Online ADR has adapted a range of traditional ADR processes for use online, including complaint handling, arbitration, mediation, facilitated negotiation and case appraisal. * * *

In addition, a number of online-specific techniques have been developed to take advantage of the new technology; these include automated negotiation and negotiation support. Mediation and arbitration have been the most prevalent forms of online ADR.

Key Terms

Facilitated negotiation is the simplest form of online ADR in which an online space is provided where parties can negotiate directly. Since the space is designed and run by rules set by the provider, the dialogue is in fact a facilitated one. * * *

Online mediation can be via email or, on more modern systems, through a secure website. * * *

Online arbitration can be through submission of documents only or via videoconferencing. * * *

Case appraisal is where a neutral party considers a dispute and provides advice as to the facts, law and possible outcomes. Mock trials provided by iCourthouse ask a virtual "jury" to make a non-binding determination of issues through a web platform. Alternatively, a neutral evaluation ("advice" or "recommendation") can be requested from an expert or expert panel through providers of neutral evaluation. * * *

Automated negotiation is an innovative form of online ADR that does not have an exact offline analogue. The key difference between this and other online ADR is that it is fully automated and software driven. No human intervention is involved. Automated negotiation includes processes such as "blind bidding" where parties submit confidential settlement offers for a number of rounds. A computer program automatically notifies them of a settlement at the arithmetic mean once the amounts are sufficiently close. * * *

Negotiation support systems have also been designed to take advantage of the online medium. They are expert systems that allow manipulation of negotiation variables by one or both parties to help them plan and conduct negotiations. * * *

Complaint Handling is a process where a party can make a complaint to a third party who will communicate a demand for redress to the respondent. Complaints can then be handled by processes such as facilitated negotiation, mediation, case appraisal or arbitration. Complaint handling is often used to resolve consumer disputes. * * *

––––––––––

Two of these online options, "automated negotiations" and a "negotiation support system," should be further explained because they are less familiar processes that also uniquely harness the opportunities offered by an online environment.

An *automated negotiations* scheme has been designed by Cybersettle. Its electronically orchestrated negotiation process works this way:[6]

> 1. Offers. The claims professional submits basic information and three confidential offers of settlement into the Cybersettle system. These Maximum Offers represent the most a claim can settle for during any respective attorney "round."

> 2. Other Attorney. Once the claim is submitted, the other representative is instantly notified and a username and password is provided. After logging in and reviewing the claim information he/she may enter up to three Minimum Demands, round-by-round. The attorney Round 1 Minimum Demand is compared to the claim professional's 1st Maximum Offer and so forth.

6. *See* www.cybersettle.com.

* * * The Minimum Demand represents the least the claim can settle for during the respective round.

3. Settlement Formula. For each attorney Minimum Demand, Cybersettle adds 20%, thus creating a "range" of settlement between the Minimum Demand and the calculated Maximum Settlement Amount. If, in any given round, the Maximum Offer is greater than or equal to the Minimum Demand., the claim will settle for the average of the two amounts up to the Maximum Settlement Amount.

4. Settlement Example

Maximum Offer	Minimum Demand	Maximum Settlement	Result
$16,000	$32,000	$38,400	No Settlement
$20,000	$26,000	$31,200	No Settlement
$24,000	$22,000	$26,400	SETTLEMENT

Claim Settles in Round 3 for $23,000 (Average of $22,000 and $24,000).

A highly structured *negotiation support system* was designed by SmartSettle.[7] A hand-picked facilitator, using a specially designed textual and graphical online screen, assists the parties in identifying key issues and characterizing each side's interests. Then in an online caucus, each party quantifies each interest with both a worst and best expectation and also assigns a value to the relative importance of each interest on the basis of a scale from 0 to 100. These values are converted onto a graph that is privately available to each party on an interactive screen. The graph quantifies the worst and best scenarios with a relative value. Each party's screen shows his or her private information as well as any shared information.

Based on each party's private graph of proposals and preferences, each party begins submitting offers and counteroffers. If an agreement is not reached, parties can request that SmartSettle generate suggestions within the bargaining range that has been narrowed by the concession process. If the parties reach an impasse, the parties can request Smart-Settle to generate an "equivalent" proposal. SmartSettle then generates a reformulated proposal, already acceptable to one party that might be acceptable to the other one. If the parties so choose, SmartSettle can

---

7. *See* http://www.smartsettle.com.

continue to generate equivalent proposals until they find a mutually acceptable solution.

C.   HYBRID AND EXCLUSIVELY ONLINE PROCESSES

This section examines various ways in which online facilities can be used to supplement or replace offline negotiations, mediations and arbitrations

1.   NEGOTIATION AND MEDIATION

This excerpt considers the vital role of the mediator in selecting online facilities to improve communications as well as various options for incorporating online facilities.

LLEWELLYN J. GIBBONS, ROBIN M. KENNEDY & JON M. GIBBS, CYBER–MEDIATION: COMPUTER– MEDIATED COMMUNICATIONS MEDIUM MASSAGING THE MESSAGE

32 New Mexico Law Review 27, 35–37, 62–68 (2002).

* * *

e.   Choosing a means of communication [by the mediator]

* * * As the mediator moves beyond establishing the basic ability to communicate at a distance, the mediator must also plan to achieve higher order needs of the mediation, i.e., how the particular technology will affect the mediation process. The mediator must consider whether technology should be used to distance the parties psychologically, to bring the parties together, to speed the process up, or slow the process down. Technology is a variable that may manipulate the mediation. Using technology, the mediator may selectively filter out cues that detract from the mediation or add cues incrementally as needed to facilitate mediation. The mediator may also slow down communications by using asynchronous technology (e.g., email) or speed up response using synchronous technology (e.g., instant messaging).

The purpose of mediation, whether physical or virtual, is to "facilitate communications, promote [] understanding, [and] focus [] the parties on their interests and creative problem solving to enable parties to reach their own agreement." For effective mediation, the mediator must gain the trust and respect of the parties through impartiality and effective use of mediation skills. The mediator adds to the process by enriching the context in which the parties communicate. The mediator is also a sounding board to facilitate communication between the parties. The mediator may do this by active listening; that is, "hearing" and restating the parties' unspoken communication. Active listening acquires not just verbal cues; a good active listener notices the incongruity between the verbal message and a party's body language. In online mediation, the mediator must pay attention to the use of emotions, emoting, delay or lag time in communication not attributable to technology, and the creative use of grammar, text, or graphic symbols. Active listening is the explicit importation of the parties' kinesic and paralinguistic communications into the mediation process. In either physical presence mediation or virtual mediation, the mediator accomplishes empathic communication by "attending, paraphrasing, reflecting feelings, and summarizing." Alternatively, the communication may be a neutral perspective on one party's likelihood of success in future actions. This clearly communicates how the other party views the dispute. In any formalistic category of successful mediation, the sine qua non of mediation is the mediator as communication-facilitator. This enriching context facilitates or improves the possibilities for the parties to communicate their interests and needs and to reach a resolution.

While some mediations absolutely require the physical presence of the parties involved, others may be resolved more effectively online. Determining which is which will require a knowledgeable mediator. Skillful selection and use of technology may overcome lack of physical presence and, in some cases, the lack of physical presence may be an asset. For example, one study demonstrated that when negotiators are motivated to maximize joint outcomes, the use of rich media to communicate will result in a greater total sum of party satisfactions than those negotiations using leaner media. But, when negotiators are motivated to maximize their own outcomes, the rich media quickly revealed the conflict. Therefore, "[c]omputer conferencing technology may be superior for competitive bargaining tasks because the absence of visual communication prevents the negative socioemotional angst from adversely impacting task performance." Consequently, parties should include CMC options in an analysis of factors related to choice of negotiation strategy.

* * *

III. PRACTICE OF ONLINE MEDIATION

In selecting tools for online mediation, the mediator should be aware of the cultural impact of the chosen technology. Frequently the participants will be from different real-world and technological cultures and may react to mediation technology differently. For example, if face saving is an instrumental skill in a party's culture, technology should be chosen to allow the possibility of face saving. When mediating between two individuals of different status in a culture where status is instrumental, the mediator may wish to level the playing field by using technology that eliminates status cues, thus empowering the lower status individual or technology to re-create those cues.

A. Online Programs

There are many ODR programs. These programs fall into three primary classifications: (1) programs that use computer-mediated communication merely to facilitate the administration of physical-presence mediation; (2) hybrid-mediation programs, those in which the mediator may use virtual-presence, physical-presence, or some mixture of the two during the course of the mediation; and (3) virtual-mediation programs, which exist entirely online and rely solely on virtual presence during the course of the mediation. Of the virtual-presence mediation programs, there are two main categories: those that use technology as an aid to a human mediator and those that rely on the software-as-mediator to bring resolution to the dispute. Both uses of technology in mediation present interesting possibilities, opportunities, and challenges.

1. Physical–Presence and Virtual Administration

Existing mediation providers are increasingly moving onto the Internet to advertise their mediation services. Many online mediation services do not actually mediate online but rather provide information online or allow parties to complete forms or complete other administrative tasks online. The actual mediation takes place in the physical presence of the mediator and the parties. The use of technology to reduce expenses and to facilitate the routine administration and tasks associated with scheduling mediation does not implicate the concerns raised in this article.

2. Hybrid Mediation

Hybrid-mediation projects use both face-to-face (physical presence) and online (virtual presence) mediation techniques. The mediator may start the mediation in person, allowing the parties to develop an impression of each other. The mediator may then proceed online to work through the issues, but at any point in the mediation process where a face-to-face meeting would be helpful, the mediator may bring the parties together. This eclectic approach to mediation permits the mediator to fashion a suitable mediation process to meet the social, emotional, and financial needs of the parties under almost all circumstances.

* * *

3. Virtual–Presence Mediation

The virtual-mediation projects may easily be classified into two groups: those projects that use technology to assist the human mediator and those projects that rely solely on technology to mediate the dispute.

a. Technology in Aiding Human Mediator

In the human adjunct programs, the technology is merely one more tool for the mediator, but the mediator does not meet with the parties face-to-face. The mediator selects from a palette of options depending on the nature of the dispute, the technology available to the parties, and the relationship between the parties. This type of mediation permits the mediator to take advantage of any opportunities presented by the parties to assist them in reaching a settlement. Since this is the most flexible form of mediation, it should be the preferred option in the vast majority of online mediations when the dispute presents complex issues and interests that are not readily quantifiable.

The University of Massachusetts Online Ombudsman Office is considered the premiere online mediation program. This online dispute resolution program focuses on disputes rising out of online activity. The dispute resolution utilized in this program is predominantly mediation. The program selectively incorporates technology in the mediation process and uses technology to enhance the capabilities of the mediator. Upon receiving a complaint, the mediator contacts the other party via email, informs the party about the program, and asks whether the party is willing to mediate. Each party then has the opportunity to present its wants, needs, desires, and claims. The mediator then attempts to distill the fundamental issues and relevant facts. This agenda-setting phase may require several attempts before the mediator expresses the dispute in a manner acceptable to the parties. This process of schema and correction is repeated, with the parties growing closer until they agree. "The mediator facilitated the information exchanges by providing a buffer, soliciting discussion and responses, and reformulating not only the dispute but also the claims of each party in search of that ground where a deal might be constructed. At the decision point, if there was not the necessary movement for determinative resolution, the disputes were considered at impasse and largely left dormant (or to the devices of the parties themselves)."

b. Technology as Mediator

For some mediation projects, the role of the mediator in setting the agenda and facilitating the process is vested entirely in the code of the software used by the project. These programs work well when the economic value of the dispute is easily quantifiable, the parties do not seek personal reconciliation, and there are opportunities for mutually beneficial exchange. In contrast, they do not work well when the issues are not readily reducible, or where repeat players require an adjustment to their relationship.

An example of a code-based mediation program is Cybersettle, a patented double-blind bidding process [described earlier in this chapter].
* * *

c. Software Assistance

Any analysis of online mediation would be incomplete without including at least an introduction to some of the various types of software that may facilitate the mediation process. Through the use of such software, parties may be able literally to visualize their positions or gain a better understanding of the adverse party's position. * * *

---

2. ARBITRATION

Arbitration is an easier process to move online than mediation:

> * * * It is possible to move arbitration online without departing in major ways from the offline model because arbitration is a simpler communication process than mediation. Roles are clearer and exchanges may be

fewer. This does not mean that there are not some challenges, but only that overall, it will be easier to develop online arbitration models, and there will be less variation among online arbitration Web sites.[8]

At this early stage of development, exclusively online arbitrations have been primarily built around the exchange of emails with attachments. Based on these submissions, the arbitrator renders an award, as exemplified in the *American Arbitration Association Supplementary Procedures for Online Arbitration.* The AAA procedures, however, also authorize parties and the arbitrator to create a more elaborate online process including a hearing, which is defined as "meetings of the parties before the Arbitrator, whether conducted in-person or by telephone, video-conference, or other means."[9]

The potential of online adjudication is suggested by the Michigan experiment to create the first Cyber Court. Consider the possibilities envisioned by these draft rules that are designed to create a wholly virtual court.

LUCILLE M. PONTE, THE MICHIGAN CYBER COURT: A BOLD EXPERIMENT IN THE DEVELOPMENT OF THE FIRST PUBLIC VIRTUAL COURTHOUSE

4 North Carolina Journal of Law & Technology 51, 55–56, 62–65 (2002).

* * *

Recently, Michigan passed legislation that would establish the nation's first public and fully virtual court. * * * Under its proposed program, Michigan's Cyber Court will not be limited to one specific physical location, but will operate primarily in cyberspace using e-mail, electronic filing systems, videoconferencing, and Web broadcasts. Judges, lawyers, parties, witnesses, and the public will participate in a bold experiment that will test the limits of these technological innovations beyond the physical limitations of current high tech courtrooms. * * *

* * *

II.   Draft Rules and Procedures for Michigan Cyber Court

With the passage of H.B. 4140, the State Bar of Michigan, through its Cyber Court Rules Workgroup, moved quickly to draft Special Rules for Electronic Practice in Cyber Court. * * * In creating the special practice rules, the Workgroup sought to balance the need for adequate specificity in the rules to guide Cyber Court parties, attorneys and the courts, with the desire to retain a certain degree of flexibility to respond to future technological developments.

---

8. *See* ETHAN KATSH & JANET RIFKIN, ON-LINE DISPUTE RESOLUTION 138 (2001).

9. *See* American Arbitration Association Supplementary Procedures for Online Arbi-

tration, Definition d and Procedure 9 (Jan. 1, 2001).

A party's ability to operate within the virtual court hinges primarily upon being classified as an "authorized electronic filer." As defined under the draft rules, an authorized electronic filer must sign an agreement with the Cyber Court in which that party agrees to comply with court mandated electronic security procedures. These procedures include the use of digital signatures, identification of a current e-mail address for receiving electronically transmitted materials, payment of the applicable service fee, and full compliance with the authorization agreement establishing one's electronic filing status. * * *

While some state and federal courts allow for limited electronic filing of court documents, the proposed Cyber Court rules vastly expand the materials that can be transmitted electronically. Once a party is registered, they may make service of process through e-mail or by facsimile without prior party consent, provided that the other party is also an authorized electronic filer. If the parties agree to use the Cyber Court, they may electronically transmit pleadings and other court papers to one another and the clerk of the Cyber Court. The draft rules also allow for electronic motion practice with parties filing motions and responses thereto along with briefs and affidavits electronically. In addition, registered filers may submit scanned copies of certified documents and notarized sworn statements. Depositions that are recorded electronically may also be filed electronically with court approval. A document is "filed" when the document accesses the information processing system of the Cyber Court and when applicable fees are paid * * *. The Cyber Court is open twenty-four hours a day for the purpose of electronically filing documents and to provide for flexible scheduling of court proceedings in different time zones.

* * *

Pre-trial conferences, hearings and other court proceedings can be carried out through audio, video or Internet conferencing. The Cyber Court judge is not limited to one location, but may sit in any technologically appropriate space with distant parties, attorneys, and witnesses allowed to appear electronically from satellite locations. Hearings open to the public may be accessed through physical attendance or live closed circuit television broadcasts at the primary or satellite locations as well as through live Web casts. * * *

Notes and Questions

Begin to consider the different ways that you might design hybrid or exclusively online dispute resolution processes. Later in this chapter, you will be asked to design online dispute processes for a hypothetical dispute.

D. CRITERIA FOR ACCEPTABLE ODR

Online processes are bound to be unwelcomed by parties unfamiliar with them, unsure of their viability, or unhappy with their experiences online. This next excerpt considers what criteria must be met before ODR might be acceptable to a user.

ETHAN KATSH & JANET RIFKIN, ONLINE DISPUTE RESOLUTION

73–90 (2001).

* * *

The Fundamentals of ODR

This chapter focuses on what we believe must be the three fundamental features or building blocks of any ODR system. These are the following:

- Convenience

- Trust

- Expertise

Very simply, no ODR system will be used or be successful unless it is convenient to use, provides a sense of trust and confidence in its use, and also delivers expertise. Described a little differently, such systems needs to facilitate access and participation, have legitimacy, and provide value.

The challenge of ODR is not simply to provide some level of convenience, trust, and expertise, but to provide the right mix of convenience, trust, and expertise for users to particular contexts. Different people may have different needs or expectations for one or more of these factors. For example, what is sufficient trust for one will be insufficient for another. Whether trust is more important than the other factors and whether a high level of one factor can compensate for a low level of another will also be different for different people. Three things, however, are clear.

> 1. Everyone faced with a choice of whether to use an ODR system or process will make a calculation or assessment involving these three factors. It is this assessment that will determine whether one system will be used over another and whether online systems can compete effectively with offline systems.

> 2. Some measure of each of the factors must always be present. Every system must contain all the factors at some threshold or minimum level. Except for situations where one is compelled to participate and given no options at all, such as when one receives a summons

from a court, it will be rare that a high level of one factor can compensate for complete absence of another.

3. Threshold levels of all three factors must be met for all the parties. To do this may lead to providing less than desired levels for one or both parties.

The relationship between the three factors of convenience, trust, and expertise can be compared to the relationship between three sides of a triangle. In the convenience, trust, and expertise triangle, the length of each side represents how high a level of the factor is present. As with all triangles, our triangle of convenience, trust, and expertise can come in many different shapes because the length of each side can vary greatly as the level of one of these factors increases or decreases. What is necessary for the triangle to remain a triangle, or for the ODR system to be a legitimate ODR system, is for all these factors to be present in some measure.

The Convenience, Trust, and Expertise Triangle

* * *

The weights given to the three factors of convenience, trust, and expertise will vary among people and will also vary depending on context. If, for example, a problem is important to you and other options are not present, you might participate in a process even if it is not very convenient. On the other hand, if the problem is not very important or is not very complex, you might be willing to work with a third party with less expertise than would be acceptable in a more complicated or important matter.

* * *

There is no objective way to measure the three factors to ascertain whether, in any particular ODR process, there is a sufficient amount of each. In any initial design of online dispute resolution processes, the challenge should be to do as much as possible to further the three goals of access and participation, legitimacy, and value, and, at a minimum, provide enough of each to meet some threshold value. We can expect that early versions of a system will bring relatively low levels of each factor. If the system is used and is even moderately successful, one can assume that threshold levels have been met. In subsequent versions, attention should be paid to trying to raise the levels of each.

* * *

One very simple but useful way to visualize where the strengths and weaknesses of an ODR system are is to draw a triangle that you believe represents the ODR system. * * *

* * *

Convenience

In the category of convenience we include any logistical and financial factors that positively or negatively affect access to and participation in the process. What forces are present that affect the disputant's assessment of whether to begin or participate in the process? In the IRS example, a threshold level of convenience, trust, and expertise was probably met by both mail and phone. For us, talking on the phone would probably be more convenient than writing a letter, but for others the opposite might be true. Interestingly, the IRS did not suggest going to the local IRS office, something we might agree is less convenient than phone or mail. Yet, for some individuals, other factors, for example, in the context of a letter from the IRS, might be more important than convenience, and going down to an IRS office might be the option selected. [H]owever, the goal of an ODR system will often be not to provide the highest possible level of convenience. Here, the IRS probably does not want people appearing at its offices when other choices better meet the agency's own personnel and budgetary needs.

Would an online option have been more convenient or less convenient than those offered? Many might prefer an online option and find it highly convenient, but, of course, for those without Internet access at all, it would not meet any threshold convenience level. For those with a very slow Internet connection the measure of convenience would be lower than for those with a high-speed Internet connection.

* * *

We generally support the use of communication forums that allow one to respond at one's convenience. We thus prefer asynchronous communication options, such as email and Web based conferencing, to chat rooms where everyone must participate at the same time. However, there should not be rigid rules about this but rather a policy that allows the third party to select among appropriate options. Some media may provide more opportunities to equalize power among the parties than other media and what is convenient will vary in different contexts and for different disputes.

While it may seem to many readers that the phone is quick and the most universally accessible medium, that may not be a correct assumption. From March to December 2000, SquareTrade handled over 30,000 disputes for a variety of online marketplaces. Disputants from over eighty countries were involved. They were in different time zones and often with different language capabilities. When the Web, in some way, breaks down language barriers and time zone differences, it becomes a decidedly more convenient forum.

* * *

We shall return to the issue of convenience when we discuss options for working with the parties, but it is clear that as more people become comfortable online, as speeds of transmission increase, and as software becomes easier to use, the convenience bar for the least capable of the disputants will rise. It is also clear, however, that convenience will always be one of the three factors since as levels of comfort with participating online increase, expectations of what disputants should be capable of doing may also increase, and software that allows more complex interactions among the participants is continually developed. As long as one party finds the ODR context less convenient or accessible than the other, the issue of convenience will need to be considered in developing ODR systems.

Trust

The great benefit of the online environment is commonly understood to lie in the area of convenience. We can send email to anyone on the planet, and we can do it from wherever we might be, whether we are on the ground or, if we have the right equipment, in the air flying somewhere. In general, whatever it is that we find to be miraculous about the online world more often than not will fall into the category we have loosely called convenience.

* * *

Trust is in a very different realm from convenience. We believe, frankly, that trust is as important for the success of any Web based enterprise as convenience, but we also recognize that it is easily ignored and neglected. While lack of convenience creates a feeling of frustration, lack of trust results in a feeling of risk. With convenience, the question is whether it is easy enough to do something. With trust, one can do something but one may not want to do it because of concern that what one wants is not what one will get.

Trust is something that may be irrelevant if a user finds it difficult to negotiate a site. But trust becomes highly relevant when there is convenience and a user feels able to conduct a transaction on the site. At this point, a whole set of questions will surface, all of which contribute to how much risk a user feels in using the site.

* * *

Consider ClicknSettle, CyberSettle, or some other blind bidding venture. These processes are only usable when there is a single issue over which the parties disagree and that issue is quantifiable, such as money. Advocates of such process argue that when money is the issue there is nothing to lose, because if there is no agreement, no party will be any worse off than if the process had not been used. In spite of this, "engagement rates," the rates at which second parties agree to participate, tend to be less than 50 percent. Why aren't they higher?

Blind bidding companies do understand that parties must have trust that confidential information will not be revealed to the other side. Therefore, they have all put measures in place to make their sites highly secure. But that does not seem to be enough. Nor is it enough that these sites are easy to use and certainly meet all measures of convenience. What is instructive here is that there is simply risk in doing something new. It may be that authorization from the company is needed to depart from traditional practice. There may be a need to file some forms to explain to the company that one is doing something differently from colleagues who are handling claims in the traditional manner. Whether or not the cause of the engagement rate is one of these factors or something else, any company offering a new service needs to anticipate that there will be some risk to whoever is willing to try something new.

* * *

Building trust online involves providing information to customers that tells them something about the party they are dealing with. The value of a seal or trustmark, such as those offered by SquareTrade.com, the Better Business Bureau, or WebAssured, is that a third party is providing information about the Web site owner. The Web site owner is not simply saying that he will participate in ODR if a problem arises but that he has a formal agreement with a third party to do so. Trust comes, therefore, from information on the third party's site and the reputation of the third party.

* * *

In traditional mediation and arbitration, taking some action to build trust is usually at the top of the mediator's or arbitrator's agenda when the parties first meet. Traditional ADR recognizes that parties have not necessarily completely committed themselves to either the mediation process or the particular mediator, and a goal of a first meeting is both to present information about the process and also to create an environment that will support a decision to continue.

Building trust in an ODR process should be a key concern in the design of the Web site. Potential users of ODR will begin making judgments about the value of the service the first time they see the opening screen of the ODR site. There is a challenge, therefore, that is not present in face-to-face dispute resolution, since more effort needs to go into anticipating questions and concerns that users might have. . . .

We often see attempts to build trust by presenting information about how much benefit can be gained from using the site, how the site has been successfully used in the past, and how successful the founders or managers of the site are. Such information is really data about expertise, which is something we shall discuss in the next section. This is useful information to give to users, but it confuses trust with expertise. Expertise concerns whether the site has the resources and skills to successfully resolve the problem. Trust is about whether what is being promised will be delivered and about whether or not what the site is saying about itself and its expertise can be delivered.

Expertise

The Net is an ever-growing, indeed infinitely expandable, information and knowledge space. It is increasingly easy to deliver information to anyone and to any place from anyone in any other place. Delivering useful, valuable, and expert information, however it not the same as delivering expertise. Sometimes, we recognize, information alone may be sufficient to fulfill what a user needs, and easy, cheap access to information is what the Net excels at. Often, however, something more than information is required. In this sense, expertise requires an interactive informational process, one where the Web site receives information from a user, processes it in some way, provides some analysis and results to the user, and perhaps then begins the process again.

* * *

The principle challenge of expertise, however, goes beyond providing useful information. Expertise is delivered as part of a process, which can be a one-on-one process like an interview, or a more complex process like mediation. In an online mediation, information would certainly be provided to the parties as part of the process, but the parties will find value in the process only if the mediator does something more. The mediator needs to respond appropriately to communications, to keep the parties "talking," and to move them somehow toward a mutually acceptable solution.

Notes and Questions

1. Various national and international organizations have recommended ways to promote trust in ODR. Some organizations have promoted disclosure of critical information without indicating what substantive policies ought to be adopted. Other organizations have identified substantive policies that should be adopted.

2. The American Bar Association's Task Force on Electronic Commerce and Alternative Dispute Resolution took primarily a disclosure approach. The task force formulated a detailed set of best disclosure practices:[10]

[Selected] RECOMMENDED BEST PRACTICES BY ONLINE DISPUTE RESOLUTION SERVICE PROVIDERS

III. MINIMUM BASIC DISCLOSURES

ODR providers should disclose the following minimum level of information:

B. Terms and conditions and disclaimers;

C. Explanation of services/ADR processes provided;

D. Affirmation that the ODR proceeding will meet basic standards of due process, including (1) adequate notice to the parties; (2) an opportunity for the parties to be heard; (3) the right to be represented or to consult legal counsel at

---

10. *See Addressing Disputes in electronic Commerce: Final Recommendations and*   *Report,* 58 Bus. Law. 415, 458–68 (Nov. 2002).

any stage of the proceeding; and (4) in an arbitration, an objective decision based on the information of record.

V. COSTS AND FUNDING

VI. IMPARTIALITY

ODR providers must disclose all matters that might raise a reasonable question about the impartiality of the ODR provider or its neutral(s). * * * Specifically ODR providers should disclose the following:

A. Relationship to Others Concerning Providing ODR Services. * * *

B. Selection Process of Neutrals. * * *

C. Ethical Standards for Neutrals. * * *

VII. CONFIDENTIALITY, PRIVACY, AND INFORMATION SECURITY

ODR providers should be prohibited from disclosing any personally identifiable information without the party's affirmative consent. ODR providers should disclose [confidentiality policies]:

VIII. QUALIFICATIONS AND RESPONSIBILITIES OF NEUTRALS

IX. ACCOUNTABILITY FOR ODR PROVIDERS AND NEUTRALS

X. ENFORCEMENT

ODR providers should disclose:

A. If they provide any assistance in enforcing any agreement, award or decision reached or rendered through an ODR process.

B. Whether they cooperate with law enforcement officials so instances of fraud can be detected and prosecuted.

XI. JURISDICTION AND CHOICE OF LAW

3. Global Business Dialogue on Electronic Commerce (GBDe), a worldwide CEO-led business initiative to assist in creating a policy framework for developing a global online economy, formulated a number of substantive recommendations. In its 2003 New York Recommendations for dealing with business-to-consumer (B2C) disputes in electronic commerce, GBDe recommended the following substantive policies for regulating the use of arbitration:[11]

Binding Arbitration

Merchants should generally avoid using arbitration that is binding on consumers because it may impair consumer confidence in electronic commerce.

11. *See New York Recommendations, Summit* 2003, 57, 59 (Global Business Dialogue on Electronic Commerce, 2003, www.gbde.org).

Arbitration that is binding on merchants as an obligation of membership in a trustmark program, on the other hand, serves to promote consumer confidence in electronic commerce. Arbitration that is binding on consumers should only be used in limited circumstances, and where it clearly meets the criteria of impartiality, transparency and public accountability. Consumer decisions to engage in binding arbitration must be fully informed, voluntary, and made only after the dispute has arisen.

* * *

Consumer Awareness

* * *

* * * Equally, the merchant shall not seek a commitment from the consumer to use binding arbitration prior to the materialization of the dispute, where such commitment would have the effect of depriving the consumer of the right to bring an action before the courts.

4. The Transatlantic Consumer Dialogue also proffered substantive recommendations. The Dialogue is a forum of U.S. and European Union (EU) consumer organizations which develops joint consumer policy recommendations to the U.S. government and the EU to promote the consumer interest in policy making. In its 2000 Recommendations on alternative dispute resolution, it urged adoption of a number of substantive policies including:[12]

ADR systems to resolve consumer complaints in the context of e-commerce should be based on the following principles.

* * *

4. ADR systems should be designed and presented as a voluntary option for consumers, not as a legal or contractual requirement.

* * *

6. ADR systems should be independent. They should be operated by reputable third parties, which could include government, nonprofit organizations, for-profit entities that are not directly involved in the disputes, or any combination thereof. If ADR systems are offered

---

12. *See Alternative Dispute Resolution in the Context of Electronic Commerce,* Doc. No. Ecom 12–00 (Feb. 2000, www.tacd.org).

by trade associations or other industry groups, they should be separate and independent, and operate in consultation with consumer organizations. * * *

* * *

10. Decisions on behalf of consumers should be binding on the other party, except that appeals could be made on grounds of mathematical mistake or other technical problems. Meaningful enforcement of decisions rendered through ADR is essential. If ADR systems are operated by trade associations or other industry groups to which companies belong, compliance with ADR decisions should be a requirement for maintaining membership. Failure to comply with ADR decisions should also be a basis for those who facilitate the vendor's sales, such as online auction sites, operators of billing systems, etc. to deny future services to the seller. * * *

11. Consumers who submit disputes to ADR systems should not be asked to waive their legal rights, nor should they be restricted or blocked from resorting to other avenues of recourse that would normally be available if they are not satisfied with the outcome. * * *

5. These disclosure and substantive policies are recommended to promote trust in the use of ODR. Which approach do you think is most likely to build trust: the disclosure or the substantive approach? What minimum substantive features would you need before trusting an online mediation or arbitration process? Are these needs any different than what you would require before trusting an offline process?

6. You will have an opportunity to apply these three criteria of convenience, trust, and expertise to a number of processes in the next section.

E. CRITIQUE OF ODR

How much trust and expertise can be offered by ODR? Are the suggested responses adequate to gain your trust or to persuade you that ODR offers value-added expertise?

This first excerpt addresses two major objections to online mediation—the lack of a face-to-face meeting and the lack of a paradigm to guide mediators. It then considers what is loss in "computer mediated communications" as well as what can be restored through a more sophisticated use of online tools.

LLEWELLYN J. GIBBONS, ROBIN M. KENNEDY & JON M. GIBBS, CYBER–MEDIATION: COMPUTER–MEDIATED COMMUNICATIONS MEDIUM MASSAGING THE MESSAGE

32 New Mexico Law Review 27, 43–54 (2002).

* * *

D.   Misconceptions and Problems

The major challenge to online mediation is to overcome resistance based on inexperience. This section will discuss two of the major objections to online mediation. First, there is an unexamined assumption that physical presence, face-to-face dispute resolution is superior to dispute resolution mediated by other communication channels. Secondly, there is a perception that there is no paradigm to guide mediators in the uncharted realm of cyberspace. Neither perception is necessarily true.

1.   There Is No There, There: Physical Presence versus Virtual Presence

As one commentator observed, "the great paradox of online mediation is that it imposes an electronic distance on the parties, while mediation is usually an oral form of dispute resolution designed to involve participants in direct interpersonal contact." This so called paradox is really not a paradox at all. While it is true that mediation is usually conducted in a face-to-face setting, the distance is not imposed on the parties as a result of being on the Internet. Rather, the distance is imposed by the parties' physical locations. In this sense, online mediation imposes or offers an electronic nearness for the parties. It is this proximity that is the starting point for facilitating communication online.

Traditional mediation allows the parties to observe one another as they react to the mediation process. Depending on the technology used, online mediation may limit opportunities to observe the opposing party's spontaneous body language or verbal responses throughout the mediation process. Even if spontaneous body language or verbal responses are perceptible, the communicative media alters how they are understood. Under some circumstances, the lack of body language may be an advantage. Due to the lag time in online mediation, the parties will have more opportunity to think about their disputes and to respond in a manner that will promote resolution to the dispute or to dwell on perceived slights and become agitated.

Another misconception is that email will be the main (sole) technology used in online mediation. Although email is the predominant form of communication on the Internet, it is not the sole form of communication. There are many other technologies that can be used for online mediation. As online mediation evolves, mediator training should evolve to cover the technologies available for mediation. While the actual forum (virtual versus physical) is different, the basic principles of mediation still apply and may be enhanced as new technologies become available.

Based on their experiences with unmoderated lists, some mediators worry that the virtual presence mediation will degenerate into an online flame war absent the social sanctions that moderate human behavior in the physical presence of other individuals. This is potentially a positive characteristic of Computer–Mediated Communication (CMC); CMC promotes equality in the communicative marketplace. "The lack of nonverbal cues about physical appearance, authority, status, and turn-taking allows users to participate more equally and with more extreme affect on CMC systems than in many face-to-face interactions." This concern of runaway socioemotive content is based on unmoderated list serves. The mediator is the moderator for virtual or physical presence mediation and is responsible for the decorum and tranquility of the mediation.

Finally, there is a misconception that physical presence mediation is neutral while virtual mediation favors those with computer skills. Face-to-face mediation tends to advantage individuals who are physically attractive, articulate, well-educated, or members of a dominate ethnic, racial or gender group. Both forms of mediation advantage those with different skill sets. The reality is that "embedded in every tool is an ideological bias, a predisposition to construct the world as one thing rather than another, to value one thing over another, to amplify one sense or skill or attitude more loudly than another." As one commentator observed,

> The routine use of a medium by someone who knows how to use it typically passes unquestioned as unproblematic and "neutral"[;] this is hardly surprising since media evolve as a means of accomplishing purposes in which they are usually intended to be incidental. And the more frequently and fluently a medium is used, the more "transparent" or "invisible" to its users it tends to become. For most routine purposes, awareness of a medium may hamper its effectiveness as a means to an end. Indeed, it is typically when the medium acquires transparency that its potential to fulfill its primary function is greatest.

Mediators assume that because they use the medium of physical presence mediation often and the vast majority of their life experience is based on physical presence communication, it is neutral and transparent. Rather, it too advantages some participants and subordinates others. Mediators must realize that

> [a]ny medium facilitates, emphasizes, intensifies, amplifies, enhances or extends certain kinds of use or experience whilst inhibiting, restricting or reducing other kinds. Of course, [the] use of any medium for a particular task may have advantages over "the alterna-

tives" (such as "saving" time or labour), but use always involves a "cost." There are losses as well as gains. A medium closes some doors as well as opening others, excludes as well as includes, distorts as well as clarifies, conceals as well as reveals, denies as well as affirms, destroys as well as creates. The selectivity of media tends to suggest that some aspects of experience are important or relevant and that others are unimportant or irrelevant. Particular realities are thus made more or less accessible—more or less "real"—by different processes of [communication].

A mediator's purpose is to serve as a neutral third party who facilitates communication between the disputants. Whether the medium is physical presence mediation or virtual mediation, it is incumbent upon the mediator to ensure a level playing field if the mediation is to be successful. In the online context, this will require the mediator to actively consider the role of communications in the mediation process.

2. Cross–Cultural Paradigm of Online Mediation

Mediators looking for an analogous communications model to guide online mediation may usefully consider cross-cultural mediation. Online mediation differs from physical-presence mediation in that it is, in essence, almost always a form of cross-cultural mediation. Culture may embrace disparate and wide-ranging elements or culture may be defined solely as language or by a method of communication. "Language is culture. Language structures meaning, determines perception, and transmits culture. It communicates thought and subjective cultural experiences at deep and subtle levels." "[E]ach new technology not only extend[s] the reach of human communication, it also alter[s] the ways in which humans relate[] to information and to each other." The existence of an Internet culture may be found in its sui generis method of communication that has fashioned a new worldview. Correspondingly, in the course of online mediation, the mediator may become a cultural interpreter to bridge the communications "gap" in online communications. On the Internet, the mediator may no longer retire solely to the default rules that social conventions and verbal-language supply. In particular, those conventional usages of body language, verbal-language, and shared assumptions based on physical impressions may be lacking in some forms of online mediation.

As an online cultural interpreter, the mediator must first teach the technology to the parties. This is analogous to finding a common language in a cross-cultural negotiation. Once the parties, with the help of the mediator, have selected the technology for the mediation, the mediator must spend time helping the parties to develop paralinguistic cues to replace those that are lacking in virtual, as opposed to face-to-face, communication. This is really no different from mediating face to face between individuals from different cultures. The mediator in either context educates both parties in the expected social and communicative norms. In cross-cultural mediation, parties may misinterpret. To avoid misinterpretation, parties must learn to understand the sender's intended signs. The sender can learn, for example, that a common greeting is considered an insult in another culture and can refrain from using it. The receiver may also learn that the "deadly insult" was intended as a polite gesture. In physical presence mediation, the mediator educates the parties concerning cultural differences in order to eliminate "noise." In online mediation, the mediator tries to minimize "noise" caused by the technology or the parties.

Another problematic "cultural area" in online mediation is how the parties and the mediator process time. "[T]here appears to be a continuum of time orientation, with monochronic time on one end and polychronic time on the other." Monochronic individuals or cultures tend to prefer to do one thing at a time and have a high need to complete a task before moving to another task or topic. They tend to think in a linear manner and process information in a sequential orderly manner. Polychronic individuals or cultures tend to attempt to accomplish several things simultaneously. Monochronic or polychronic individuals do well in their respective cultures but may experience difficulties in communicating with individuals of the other orientation. Online mediation permits the mediator to create an environment that mediates between these two orientations. For example, email allows for multiple topics to be discussed simultaneously; yet, threading the topics focuses each thread on only one issue.

Another assumption concerns the extent to which cultures expect individuals to know about situations. "A culture in which information about a procedure is rarely communicated is a high context culture. Members are expected to know how to perform in various situations, but the rules of the cultural performance remain implicit. The context is supposed to be the cue for behavior." "In a low context culture, on the other hand, information is abundant, procedures are explicitly explained, and expectations are discussed frequently." Communication often breaks down when an individual from a high context culture attempts to communicate with an individual from a low context culture. Communications break down because the underlying assumptions or the "context" of the communication are rarely understood by both parties, much less discussed or explicitly stated. The high context individual assumes that the low context individual understands and would, in fact, perhaps be insulted if she filled in the contextual gaps, while the low context individual waits in frustration for the additional information necessary to understand the task. Because the ODR takes place in a uniquely communicative medium, the mediator may use technology to insure that the parties are sharing common assumptions and bridge the high/low context cultural issues without unnecessarily offending either party.

Computer-mediated communication is best characterized as a specific form of cross-cultural communication, even for individuals sharing a common culture. The role of the mediator remains the same but the selection of techniques may change. Because mediators have engaged in cross-cultural mediation since the earliest days of mediation, mediators already have at least rudimentary skills to apply to online mediation. Mediators must apply this knowledge to the technological tools provided by the Internet.

II. COMMUNICATION AND MEDIATION

Ideally, the choice between dispute resolution alternatives should be informed. Disputants and their lawyers should possess sufficient information to examine critically the relationship between the processes that exist in face-to-face mediation and those processes that exist in online mediation. This section will discuss the basic communication paradigm, the theoretical perspectives on Computer–Mediated Communication (CMC), the theoretical perspectives on legal mediation, and whether a better understanding of CMC theory would assist legal mediators.

A. Communication Defined

"Computer-mediated communication is simply the application of computing machinery to the process of communication." In order to resolve (mediate) disputes in either physical presence or virtual presence, communication must take place. Of the essential elements of communication, the most significant difference between virtual and physical presence dispute resolution options is the channel. To determine the viability of online mediation, one must consider the medium used to transmit the message, i.e. the channel of communication.

B. Computer–Mediated Communication

While social science commentators agree that the singular difference between computer-mediated communication and face-to-face communication is that non-verbal cues are reduced or eliminated in CMC, there is no agreement on the effect that this has on the communicative process. Two major theoretical explorations of cue loss in CMC have focused on the social information processing approach and the "cues-filtered-out" approach, and on how individuals process CMC information (social information process). Social influence theory posits that social influences affect individual perception of media richness. In contrast, media richness theory posits that "media richness" is an immutable characteristic of each form of communication media. Traditional legal scholarship of online mediation tends to focus doctrinally on the lack of nonverbal cues to the detriment of alternative theoretical perspectives. This emphasis discourages legal commentators from identifying tools that can reintegrate cues into the online mediation process and discourages commentators from attempting to change social attitudes toward CMC. This section presents the theoretical perspectives that inform current understanding of CMC as a prelude to the authors' identification of tools for reintegration of cues in CMC and presentation of reasons for use of CMC.

1. Cues–Filtered–Out Theory

Early CMC research utilized Social Presence Theory and the Media Richness Theory to develop the cues-filtered-out approach." Media Richness Theory posits that communicative technologies possess unique capabilities for transmission of the complete context of the communicative act. Under this theory, technologies import various levels of ambiguity. "Ambiguity is a function of a medium's richness, that is the capability of (a) facilitating feedback, (b) communicating multiple cues, (c) presenting individually tailored messages, (d) and using natural language to convey subtleties." Many forms of CMC are extremely limited in their ability to transmit cues. "The rank order of media in terms of richness is face-to-face, telephone, electronic mail, personal written text (letters, memos), formal written text (documents, bulletins), and formal numeric text (computer output)." The richer the media, the greater the capability to reduce ambiguity. This characterization of communication media would seem to argue for employment of the most cue-rich medium. However, richer media and the increase in completeness may cost more than less rich media. Thus, if the task involves higher levels of ambiguity, leaner media will accomplish the same task more efficiently.

Social Presence Theory hypothesizes that the psychological state of being "present" is a function of the quantity and quality of the cues one receives with the communication. The social information processing theorists note that many of the prior studies supporting the cues-filtered-out theories were one-shot studies of extremely short duration in which the parties had neither the time nor motivation to create a positive impression.

2. Social Information Processing Theory

The social information processing theorists contend that the distinguishing characteristic between physical presence and virtual presence communication is the rate of impression formation, rather than question whether impression formation is possible. Further research and field experiments led some researchers to question the cues-filtered-out approach (media richness theory). Subsequent research suggested "that bandwidth was an insufficient predictor of CMC effects on the nature of social interaction." Consequently, given sufficient time, frequency of communication, and motivation, individuals engaged in virtual presence communication will develop impressions that are of equal accuracy as those engaged in physical presence communication. "The more often an individual spends time communicating with others on-line, the more easily s/he can adapt to the lack of nonverbal and contextual cues and the more satisfied s/he becomes with the relationship."

3. Social Influence and Communication Media Theory

The Social Influence model posits that an individual's media perception and use are influenced by others and the objective features of the communication's technology. Individuals view different objective features of a given medium of communication differently. Selecting media for a specific mediation task is not an objective choice as pure Media Richness theories suggest; the sender must consider the receiver and his or her social context. Accordingly, the Social Influence Model proposes that media selection and use is subject to social influence, subjectively rational, not motivated by efficiency concerns, and "designed to preserve or create ambiguity to achieve strategic goals."

4.   CMC and Online Mediation

CMC is merely the channel through which communication takes place. The seminal question in online mediation is whether CMC as a channel is capable of carrying the data without unduly interfering with the receiver's ability to convert the data to understanding and knowledge so as to permit mediation. A related question is the effect of CMC on the sender's and receiver's respective physical and social filters that organize how the individual selects and uses data.

The most restrictive of the theories of CMC are the cues-filtered-out approaches. If online mediation is feasible using the most restrictive CMC paradigm, then online mediation is also possible under the less restrictive paradigms. Under the cues-filtered-out approach, the mediator must consider the amount of ambiguity inherent in the medium supporting the mediation, and as the level of ambiguity becomes more crucial, the mediator should evaluate the costs of richer media with the benefits of reducing ambiguity. The social information processing theory teaches that online mediation may under some circumstances take longer so that the parties can form impressions of their counterparts. "Most studies of interpersonal relationships within computer-mediated environments have [noted that problems] with the lack of nonverbal and contextual cues can be apparently overcome as participants in on-line relationships increase the time they spend using the medium and the more familiar they become with it." These approaches do not preclude virtual presence mediation. Rather, these approaches teach that e-mediators will have to work harder to reintegrate cues into the online mediation and to reduce unnecessary ambiguity.

The social influence theory teaches that the mediator will have to work to select media on an ad hoc basis that is acceptable to the parties and work to help the parties accept the technology. But over time, as individuals become more CMC savvy, this will be less of an issue until the communications technology becomes transparent through its ubiquitous nature. Although each of these theories envisions a slightly different role for the mediator, all of these theories support CMC as a possible tool for mediation.

C. *Mediation*

Legal literature reflects a recognition of communicative value of nonverbal signals in lawyer-client interviewing and counseling, negotiation, mediation and trial practice. Eye contact, facial expressions, or trunk lean may provide significant information regarding a mediating party's preferences. This section explores the effect on CMC of the availability of nonverbal cues or their substitutes.

1. Spatial Dynamics

Spatial dynamics concerns the effects of environmental conditions surrounding each party during the mediation. These environmental conditions include the party proximity to other parties and the mediator, party physical reactions (body language) toward other parties and the mediator, and the party reactions to the time or duration of the mediation. Proxemics, kinesics, and chronomics profoundly affect attitudes of the parties and can affect the ultimate outcome of the mediation.

a. Proxemics

Proxemics refers to the parties' physical orientation to one another throughout the mediation process. This physical orientation is one factor that may affect the attitudes of the parties throughout the mediation. For example, parties sitting across a table from one another may unconsciously promote adversarialness. Separating the disputants on opposite sides of the table may create a psychological barrier to communication, recognition, or agreement. Whereas seating parties next to one another on the same side of the table creates a less oppositional tone. Elimination of the physical barrier may enhance the impression of a shared common place and psychologically, a shared common predicament.

* * *

Conceptually, proxemics does not appear relevant to text-based communication. It does, however, relate to videoconferencing and graphical avatar conferencing. In one study involving highly collaborative tasks using videoconferencing, subjects did not prefer the "collaborative" side-to-side position; rather they preferred the more "competitive" face-to-face position when videoconferencing. While subjects preferred to be in person, face-to-face, for collaborative tasks, subjects were generally satisfied with videoconferencing. This study provides support for the media richness theory and for those attorney-mediators who contend that online mediation is only realistic when videoconferencing becomes viable.

When individuals were graphically represented in cyberspace by an avatar, proxemics was important. An avatar is a graphical representation of the user that interacts with other graphical representations, including those of other users. One study found that even graphical representations have "personal distance" space among other avatars. The further avatars were apart, measured in pixels, the more likely an individual would perceive the conversation as appropriate. The closer avatars appeared on screen, the greater the social attraction between the parties. In sum, whether measured in feet or pixels, distance matters. Research suggests that designers of online mediation software products, or mediators who use off-the-shelf products to create a graphical virtual environment for the mediation, need to consider proxemics in their design.

b. Kinesics

"Kinesics" concerns the communicative aspects of physical reactions of parties toward one another. Body language is absent in the text-based online mediation process and will probably be difficult to re-create. It is present in videoconferencing, but not to the same extent as in physical presence mediation. Without a face-to-face interaction between the parties, parties are more likely to express any response to comments made textually, whereas if the parties were in the same room together, the reaction would be more likely to involve body language rather than verbal expression. Textual expression may be more accurate and authentic than a "read" of ambiguous and culturally determined body language.

c. Chronomics

Time is an important consideration in physical presence mediation. The time each party has to speak and the duration of the mediation may have a profound impact on the attitudes of the parties. If both parties do not receive equal time to state their position, the one receiving less time may feel slighted or even feel that the mediator is biased. This in turn can lead to increased hostility and lowered cooperation. Since text-based online communication permits the parties to participate to the extent they desire, greater or lesser participation should raise fewer inherent equity and bias issues. In addition, online mediating parties may avoid the time pressures to concede experienced by negotiators in face-to-face negotiations with pre-set itineraries for returning home.

2. Paralinguistics

Paralinguistics is the study of the influence of verbal pitch, rate, volume, and mediating tone of the parties. While the Internet is largely text based, the sender has several text options for sending paralinguistic cues. The best-known paralinguistic devices on the web are emoticons. Emoticons are ASCII text characters used to express emotion, such as :-) for a smile or :-(for a frown. Some programs allow for graphic representations of emotion, for example for a smile or for a frown. For example, Cindy saying, "Robin, you're awful." is ambiguous and is quite different from Cindy saying, "Robin, you're awful (smiley face image)." Since individuals cannot modulate the volume of their voice in text based discussions, ALL CAPS is known as shouting. Another option is "emoting." Emoting represents an action and is usually expressed in the third person, for example, messages sent by Cindy such as "Cindy crying, 'Robin, you're awful'" or "Cindy saying flirtatiously, 'Robin, you're awful.'" These cues may be used either in synchronous or asynchronous communication. Modern email programs give individuals the option of using different fonts, font sizes, and colors. All of which may be used to communicate paralinguistically and to enrich lean text-based communication.

––––––––

This next excerpt further considers what is loss without face-to-face encounters and then suggests what can be gained by effectively using the computer screen to improve communications online.

ETHAN KATSH & JANET RIFKIN, ONLINE DISPUTE RESOLUTION

9–10, 136–37, 140–41 (2001).

* * *

The Nature of ODR

[T]he single question we are asked most often about ODR concerns how dispute resolution can possibly succeed without face-to-face encounters. The easiest response to this is that there are many disputes where face-to-face meetings are not feasible, and in these cases, without ODR there would be no dispute resolution process at all. ODR, we indicate, is not meant to replace or be a substitute for face-to-face settings when they can be part of the process. For online disputes, therefore, where parties may be located at great distances from each other, it is not hard to persuade even skeptics that ODR is useful and appropriate.

Although the argument that ODR can be employed when face-to-face meetings are not possible is accepted without much resistance, it may, we confess, turn out to be a bit too facile an answer. We do not think that ODR can or should replace face-to-face meetings, but as ODR grows, we do believe that it will affect the overall process of which face-to-face meetings are a part. But ODR may not *replace* face-to-face meetings but it may *displace* them in the sense that the perceived need for them may change, the frequency with which they are held may change, and how they are conducted may change.

ODR, when used in offline disputes, may not yet appear to be a competitor or substitute for the face-to-face encounter. We are, quite clearly, far from being able to provide as flexible and interactive a communications process online as a meeting in a physical place. We are also not at a point where we can anticipate how videoconferencing might be employed and when it will be widely and reliably available. Where the value of ODR is likely to be recognized first in offline contexts, is at points in the process of negotiation, mediation, or arbitration that occur before or after a face-to-face meeting. While we recognize that face-to-face encounters are information-rich experiences, we also believe that what happens in between such meetings is, in terms of communication, impoverished and information poor. What we do not see noticed by the very same people who point out to us to the great value of face-to-face encounters, is that the communications environment in which ADR is pursued *between* face-to-face meetings is often not even considered to be a period of time in which progress toward resolution is anticipated. Online tools can change this.

* * *

The task of the online mediator, like the task of the offline mediator, must be to employ the most appropriate and powerful verbal and nonverbal tools available. Many of the verbal tools that we have, such as email and Web-based conferencing, are already in common use. For verbal communication, we shall explore ... some of the challenges in how to use written language to respond to various kinds of situations that often arise during an online mediation process. Again, the level of interactivity online may not be able to match the level of interactivity in a face-to-face encounter, but the online environment also has some novel resources for enabling the participants to express themselves efficiently and appropriately.

Resources for online nonverbal communication are less familiar than textual tools. While offline nonverbal communication is largely identified with the cues, signals, and other "between the lines" communication, the key to nonverbal online communication and interaction lies in how we employ the screen and what we can learn from the screen. It is intriguing that design of the screen is normally referred to as the inter*face*. This term means that there is influential information on the screen that has nothing to do with the words we see on the screen. This inter*face*, like a person's face, can be employed to communicate meaning and can shape how the verbal content is received.

Just as the meaning of words communicated face to face is influenced by how the words are communicated, words communicated electronically are influenced by how they are displayed.... The screen, by its appearance and design, is itself an image that functions to structure communication. The screen is the context in which interaction occurs, and it does have an effect on the message. In many ways it is quite analogous to tone of voice and demeanor in that the screen provides a shape and mood to whatever is being communicated. Most importantly, just as voice and demeanor are almost bonded to the actual words being used, the screen is "a part of the conversation rather than an adjunct to it."

One reason we are optimistic about ODR is because there is not simply content, words, and images, but a frame, the screen, around all communication. An important facet of the "fourth party" that we spoke of earlier is the screen, which can add authority, quality, and trust to the online mediation process. Products that use the screen well will enhance the chances for success and add value to the expertise of the mediator. Products that do not recognize the power of the screen will miss out on the numerous ways in which the interface itself can enhance convenience, build trust, and raise expectations that the process will provide value.

* * *

Online Mediation

* * *

When we hear reservations expressed about what we are calling screen to screen, it is often about the limits of text and verbal communication on the screen. After all, face-to-face communication allows one to discern from something other than what is being said whether or not someone is to be trusted or believed. It may reveal how passionately a disputant feels about something. It may even communicate something about whether there is some willingness to compromise. Compared with this rich level of communication, the screen seems to be a negative— something that hides rather than reveals emotion, and that provides no assistance in evaluating sincerity.

What we are calling "screen to screen" cannot and should not be expected to provide the same kind of communication that occurs face to face. It should, however, enable us to take advantage of opportunities that the screen provides to display information, update information, and acquire intelligence based on experience. We generally do not favor the use of real time or "chat" sessions to resolve disputes because these are largely textual exercises that add little that might compensate for the lack of face-to-face contact. When we have experimented with such sessions, the mediators have found that they are rushed, pressured to respond quickly, and less able to control the flow of information among the disputants. They may, in such sessions, be able to exert pressure on the participants to reach settlement, but they have generally felt that such sessions are poor copies of traditional face-to-face meetings.

In such real time sessions, the role of the screen fades away. We may, at some point, find that real-time videoconferencing can indeed duplicate the face-to-face session. What we are most interested in at the moment, however, is in taking advantage of the richness of the display and the powerful technology that connects it to others.

———

This excerpt raises concerns about the independence of some online processes including how the provider or neutral working for the provider might face conflicts of interest.

BENJAMIN G. DAVIS, DISCIPLINING ODR PROTOTYPES: TRUE TRUST THROUGH TRUE INDEPENDENCE

Proceedings of the UNECE Forum on ODR 2003 http://www.odr.info/unece2003.

* * *

II.　Structural independence tensions: triangular conflicts.

* * * Analysis of these models [of dispute resolution for business-to-business electronic commerce] focuses on independence of the dispute resolution procedure. The analysis highlights the problem of what might be termed triangular conflicts of interest. * * *

* * *

B.　Model 2: Structural independence tensions in Business to business marketplaces—the owner/member tension

In business to business marketplaces, there are contracts between the market place owner and each member ("owner/member contract") and contracts that arise from the contracting between members of the marketplace ("member1/member 2 contract"). The degree of control by the owner may vary but the expectation is that the owner may insist on a standard dispute resolution method for all owner/member contracts. The owner may have substantial authority with the members of the marketplace due to it being a dominant enterprise or a coalition of dominant enterprises in a given industry or function. On the other hand, consistent with party autonomy, the parties to the member1/member2 contract may settle on the same or different means of dispute resolution.

In the cases where the dispute resolution service provider for the owner/member contract is the same institution as that foreseen in the member1/member2 contract, careful attention would appear warranted as to neutral selection. Because the owner may have substantial business interests with regard to any given member, it would appear prudent to avoid actual bias or the appearance of bias. To assure this, the neutral selected by the dispute resolution service provider should have no connection to the owner or make full disclosure to the parties to the member1/member2 contract of any links to the owner. The same would appear true in the case of disputes under the owner/member contract where member1/member2 contracts are present. It would appear prudent that a neutral with ties to member2 for example who may have substantial business interests with member1 would disclose such interests to the owner and member1 in an owner/member1 dispute—again—to preserve the integrity of the process.

Example: Construction Company A owns a construction marketplace website. Subcontractor 1 and subcontractor 2 are members of that site having each signed an owner/member agreement with Construction Company A. Subcontractor1 and subcontractor 2 sign a contract unrelated to Construction Company A. Construction Company A contracts with Subcontractor2 in an unrelated contract. A dispute arises between Subcontractor1 and Subcontractor2 under the agreement they signed within the marketplace. All contracts foresee the same dispute resolution service provider. Care should be taken in the appointment of any neutral to avoid bias or the appearance of bias which might occur if the neutral has ties to Construction Company A.

I am unaware of any sites that address this tension in neutral selection.

C. Model 3: Structural independence tensions in Business to business services in trust services

In Business to Business services in trust services, the tension is one that arises from being at the border between business to business electronic commerce and business to consumer electronic commerce. One example is in the area of privacy policies. To the extent a company purchases consumer privacy dispute resolution services from a trustmark or seal, both parties are engaged in Business to Business electronic commerce (the company and the trustmark/seal organization). The trustmark or seal may undertake examination itself or appoint a third party neutral to examine any complaints filed by the consumer. To the extent the trustmark has on its Board of Directors representatives of the company about which the consumer files a complaint, it would appear prudent that recusal mechanisms be in place and disclosed as part of the operation of the trustmark or seal to avoid the actual bias or appearance of bias as regards dispute resolution of consumer complaints concerning that board member. In addition, tensions may arise in situations where significant clients of the board member are the subject of consumer complaints under the mechanism. * * *

Example1: French consumer has a privacy complaint against Microsoft Corporation and its controlled U.S. subsidiaries ("Microsoft"). Microsoft provides in its declaration as part of the EU–US Safe Harbor Program that privacy policy dispute resolution is to be provided by www.truste.org. A representative of Microsoft sits on the Board of Directors of www.truste.org.

Example2: A user of Verisign trust services has a dispute with Verisign with regard to its privacy policies. Verisign provides that its privacy policies are reviewed by www.truste.org. A representative of Verisign sits on the board of www.truste.org.

I am unaware of any clear rules that address these concerns at the site.

III. Further structural independence tensions: Embedded and non-embedded dispute resolution service providers and panels vs. inhouse dispute resolution service providers

Where the dispute resolution service provider is embedded (i.e. owned by the owner of the marketplace or has a significant component of its caseload and revenue being generated by this specific activity) tensions as to structural independence increase. While any dispute resolution service provider wants to please the party(ies) that determine whether it will be allowed to continue to have the cases it is handling, the embedded provider is in a more precarious position as its life is dependent on this one stream of cases. . . . Where the control interest of the key entity are not consistent with independence of the dispute resolution service provider, pressure to conform to the key entity's wishes comes to bear on the dispute resolution service provider. Where the dispute resolution service provider is not so embedded (i.e. has multiple streams of cases) pressure on integrity will be less as there is no particular interest in having results that favor one key entity over another (this could be viewed as a diversification effect or a volume effect).

This tension between embedded and non-embedded is heightened in the situation where a dispute resolution service provider is providing the neutral role inhouse. In that setting, the survival interest of the dispute resolution service provider will influence the inhouse "neutral" who will be tempted/pressured to make decisions that favor the interests of the key entity that is the client of the provider.

Notes and Questions

1. Katsh and Rifkin concluded that, "We generally do not favor the use of real time or 'chat' sessions to resolve disputes because these are largely textual exercises that add little that might compensate for the lack of face-to-face contact." Why do you think they drew such a negative conclusion about the use of "chat" sessions like instant messaging? Do you agree with their conclusion? Can you envision occasions during an online mediation where a chat session may be useful?

2. The cyber-mediation excerpt by Gibbons, Kennedy, and Gibbs examined the non-verbal cues and other forms of communication that are reduced or eliminated when moving from offline, face-to-face encounters to online ones. It also examined some of the tools for enriching online communications. What do the authors believe is lost when communicating online, and what can mediators do to help parties reintegrate some of what is lost? Do you think adopting their recommendations could result in reconfiguring online communications to approximate offline communications? What if anything cannot be restored online?

3. In cross-cultural mediations, in what ways might the use of online communications reduce the risks of cultural obstacles? In what ways might the use of online communications contribute to cultural obstacles? If you were the mediator in a dispute between parties from New York and Tokyo and wanted to reduce the risks of a cultural obstacle preventing resolution, what key points would you want to make in an emailed opening statement to the disputing parties and their attorneys? In answering these questions, consider not only the materials covered in this chapter but also materials covered in the chapter on "The Role of Culture in Transborder Dispute Resolution" and the materials on cultural impediments in the chapter on International Negotiation and Mediation in the Private Sector."

4. What is the added value (expertise) of using automated negotiations or a negotiation support system? In other words, what does each of these dispute resolution processes offer that you would not be able to accomplish on your own by just calling the other side to negotiate a settlement? What opportunities might be lost by using each of these options?

5. Is the pressure (identified in the Davis article) favoring the interests of the embedded service provider reduced when the provider uses a large panel of independent neutrals?

6. If you were asked to design an online mediation process for a trade association and its members, what would you do to ensure the structural independence of the process? Assume the trade association is a state bar association that wants to establish an online mediation process for handling fee disputes between attorney members and clients.

7.   a. If you were asked by a business client whether it should incorporate into a customer contract the use of a particular online mediation service, how would you assess the structural independence of the service? Assuming your client plans to sell photography equipment online to retail consumers, assess the independence of Square Trade's mediation service based only on the information available on its website. *See* www.square-trade.com. Further assess Square Trade's mediation service based on the criteria suggested by Katsh and Rifkin for convenience, trustworthiness, and added value (expertise)?

7.   b. Assess the arbitration process offered by Online Resolution based on the criteria suggested by Katsh and Rifkin for convenience, trustworthiness, and expertise. *See* www.onlineresolution.com.

8.   Assuming that you are mediating online using a facilitative-problem-solving approach, critique the following hypothetical mediation conducted through emails. Identify specifically which of the mediator's emails you think were effective and why, as well as which ones you would rewrite and why. How would you change the content of the emails if you were an evaluative mediator?

JAMES C. MELAMED, MEDIATING ON THE INTERNET TODAY AND TOMORROW

1 Pepperdine Dispute Resolution Law Journal 11, 20–24 (2000).

* * *

Framing Discussions with Email

As examples of how a mediator may frame mediation discussion with email, consider the following samples. Note that these are sample emails that are to be modified by the mediator, in his or her professional discretion. While imperfect, these mediator communications demonstrate the type of structuring and framing of discussions that is available through email.

Subject: Online Mediation; Getting Started

Hello party 1 and party 2:

Thank you for using Online Mediation. I am the mediator assigned to your case. My profile is available at . * * * I am currently reviewing the case and will be composing some questions to begin the process. I will be sending that message to everyone involved within the next couple of days.

If you have questions about the process or would like to send me additional information, you may reply to this message. Remember "Reply" will send the message to me alone. "Reply All" will send the information to me and the other party.

Again, thank you for participating. I will be back to you soon.

Your Online Mediator

Subject: Time to Get Started

Hello. This is your friendly online mediator again.

Unless I hear otherwise, I will assume that you are satisfied with my selection as your mediator. I will do my best to assist you.

I want to confirm that you understand the voluntary nature of this process and also that you have complete decision-making power. I also want to confirm that our discussions are confidential. No communication will be held against anyone in any possible future contested action.

Please let me know of any questions that you have as we begin our discussions. Perhaps the best place to begin is to ask for each of you to summarize:

1. The Issues that you believe need resolution.

2. Your Interests (what you would like taken care of)

3. The Options (different ways we could solve the issues).

Thanks for working with me to resolve this matter. I will be back in touch as soon as I have heard from each of you. I encourage you to do a "reply all" on this message so that we can share this information. If you want to communicate with me individually, you should use a "reply" message or a separate message.

Your Online Mediator

Subject: Perhaps Some Discussion Between You Would be Helpful

Greetings,

I want to confirm for each of you that I have read your responses on the Online Mediators intake form and your respective descriptions of the situation.

I am thinking, to the extent that you desire, that it might be good for each of you to more fully share with one another (not just me) your concerns and your suggestions for improving the situation.

Also, do you have any questions for one another?

Your Online Mediator

Subject: How Can We Make This Work for Everyone?

Hi Folks,

Understanding that we may not settle this matter in a way that will be ideal for either of you, we can only settle this matter if we have some flexibility from each of you.

What degree of flexibility would you be willing to demonstrate if the other was also so forthcoming?

Can you think of any exchanges of arrangements that might be acceptable to you both?

Can you think of any package deals that would work?

Are there any other ways that you could benefit one another?

Your Online Mediator

Subject: How Important Is It For You To Settle This Matter?

Hi,

I sense your frustration.

I would like to hear from each of you as to the relative importance of solving this matter and being done with it.

How could we do that in a way that you could both support?

Your Online Mediator

Subject: Time to Make Some Progress

Hi,

Thanks for working with me and the process thus far.

My understanding is that the fundamental question is how can we best solve these issues:

(List Issues as "How can we best . . ." or "What is the best way for us to . . .")

Let me now ask, what specific proposals for resolution would you like to make to the other that you believe they may accept?

Your Online Mediator

Subject: Let's Think About This Creatively

Hi,

Can you think of two different sets of arrangements, either of which would be acceptable to you?

What would you need to receive to agree to the other's proposal?

What would you be willing to give, that you understand they desire, if they were willing to go with your suggestions?

Thanks for your consideration.

Your Online Mediator

Subject: A Set of Arrangements for Your Consideration

Greetings,

As we have not been able to easily resolve this matter through direct exchange between you nor through my shuttle efforts to date, I am thinking that this might be a good time for me to describe a possible set of arrangements that I believe may work for both (all) of you.

In offering this possible "reference point," I want to emphasize that this is not necessarily the resolution that I recommend. I have not even processed the information in that way. Rather, this is the resolution that, if you were to ask me, I would think that you would both (all) most likely be able to support.

I ask that you give this "reference point" your fullest consideration and please let me know whether it might possibly be acceptable, if acceptable to the other(s), or of any fine tuning that would be necessary for these arrangements to become acceptable.

Thanks for your consideration and efforts!

Here is the reference point set of arrangements that I ask you to consider:

Your Online Mediator

Subject: Confirming Your Agreement

Greetings,

The purpose of this message is to confirm what I understand you agree to as a means of resolving this matter.

It is my understanding that you agree as follows:

Terms of Agreement

1.

2.

3.

Please let me know if I have misstated this agreement or if I am missing any important pieces.

Your Online Mediator

---

9. Let's try to use ODR for resolving a conventional international legal dispute, a trademark dispute.[13] These questions provide you the opportunity to incorporate the use of one or more of the three basic online facilities into an online process.

Trademark Dispute

Deodorant Soap[14]

Super Manufacturing, an American company, entered into a licensing contract with ExtraClean, a British company, to manufacture deodo-

---

13. For a discussion of the role of the attorney in online mediation and arbitration, see JOHN COOLEY, MEDIATION ADVOCACY ch. 8 (2d ed. 2002) and JOHN COOLEY &

STEVEN LUBET, ARBITRATION ADVOCACY ch. 8 (2d ed. 2003).

14. The facts of this dispute are loosely based on *Lever Bros. Co. v. United States*,

rant soap under its "Powerful Protections" trademark for sale in Great Britain.

The British version of the soap had to be re-formulated to suit local tastes and circumstances. The British version lathers less and smells different. It also is designed for "hard water" common in Britain while the American version work bests in the "soft water" available in most American cities.

The packaging of the U.S. and U.K. products is also somewhat different. The British "Powerful Protections" logo is written in script form and is packaged in foil wrapping and contains a wave motif, while the American "Powerful Protections" logo is written in block form, does not come in foil wrapping and contains a grid pattern. There is small print on the packages indicating where they were manufactured. The trademarks are registered in both the United States and Great Britain.

Three years after ExtraClean began manufacturing and selling Powerful Protections in Great Britain, a British third party distributor called Personal Products started selling the soap in parts of the United States despite the objections of Super Manufacturing. After negotiations failed, Super Manufacturing sued Personal Products for trademark infringement, unfair competition, and damages in the amount of one million dollars for lost sales. It seeks to enjoin Personal Products from further selling the deodorant soap in the United States because the British version has created substantial consumer confusion and deception in the United States about the nature and origin of this merchandise; it has received numerous consumer complaints from American consumers who unknowingly bought the British version and were disappointed. Personal Products has responded that sales are going well in the United States, that there is no consumer confusion in the marketplace (the central factual issue in a trademark case), and that Super Manufacturing is trying to eliminate competition.

The parties have agreed first to try mediating the dispute and then if unsuccessful, to resort to binding arbitration. They also have agreed that the mediation will take place in New York City and the arbitration will take place in London.

When answering these questions, consider whether and when you would use email, instant messaging/chat rooms, and videoconferencing.

a. Mediation

When planning the use of ODR, you should consider how mediation can follow a number of stages. They can include: An Opening Statement of the Mediator; Gathering Information (Opening Statements of Parties and Attorneys, Discussions in Joint Sessions and Caucuses); Identifying Issues, Interests, and Impediments; Overcoming Impediments; Generating Options; Assessing and Selecting Options; and Concluding (Agreement or Impasse).

299 U.S. App. D.C. 128, 981 F.2d 1330 (1993).

i. In what ways might you use one or more online facilities in the Trademark Dispute to supplement a traditional face-to-face mediation at particular stages of the mediation process?

ii. For the Trademark Dispute, design an exclusively online mediation process that meets the criteria of Katsh and Rifkin for convenience, trust, and expertise. Construct a process that covers all the stages of mediation. Indicate what might be lost in this exclusively online process.

b. Arbitration.

When planning the use of ODR, you should consider how arbitration can follow a number of stages. They can include: Opening Statement of Arbitrator(s); Opening Statement of Each Attorney; Presentation and Cross–Examination of Each Side's Case; Rebuttal; Closing Statements; Submission of Briefs; Deliberation by Arbitrators; and Issuance of Award.

i. In what ways might you use one or more online options in the Trademark Dispute to supplement a traditional face-to-face arbitration at particular stages of the arbitration process?

ii. For the Trademark Dispute, design an exclusively online arbitration process that meets the criteria of Katsh and Rifkin for convenience, trust, and expertise. Construct a process that covers all the stages of arbitration. Indicate what might be lost in an exclusively online process.

F. LEGAL ISSUES

ODR presents a number of legal issues due to the easy access it offers to a dispute resolution process from anywhere around the globe. These cross-border encounters can involve parties across state borders within the United States or across international borders. Several of the legal issues posed by these online encounters are considered in the next two articles.

LLEWELLYN J. GIBBONS, ROBIN M. KENNEDY & JON M. GIBBS, CYBER–MEDIATION: COMPUTER– MEDIATED COMMUNICATIONS MEDIUM MASSAGING THE MESSAGE

32 New Mexico Law Review 27, 37–39 (2002).

* * *

2. Legal Context for Online Mediation

The purpose of this section is not to resolve any of the many complex legal issues related to mediation in the online context, but rather to identify a few of the legal issues that will influence online mediation. The "location" of the virtual mediation is legally significant. In the physical world, the place of the mediation is readily identifiable.

Parties who negotiate and mediate in Florida can reasonably assume that Florida law governs. The parties may vary some of the default rules and assumptions by contract. But, what if the mediator is physically in California, one party is in New York, and the other is in Florida and they are communicating using the Internet in an attempt to mediate an ecommerce dispute? Which jurisdiction's laws will govern the mediation? The laws governing the mediation are important. For example, some jurisdictions have professional licensure standards to qualify as a mediator; some jurisdictions provide for mediator immunity so that the mediator has no or limited liability, and the ethical obligations of the mediator may vary by jurisdiction. Whether a given act within the mediation process may rise to the unauthorized practice of law is a question of state law. In some jurisdictions, the mediator's assistance to the parties in reducing the resolution to writing or the mediator's candid evaluation of a party's chance of success should the case proceed to litigation may result in a charge of unauthorized practice of law either against the attorney-mediator who may not be admitted in a jurisdiction that may assert some interest in the mediation or against a lay-mediator who is not an attorney in any jurisdiction. The legal and evidentiary effects of statements made during the mediation vary by jurisdiction. Many jurisdictions provide confidentiality concerning the use of statements made during mediation. For example, statements made during the course of mediation may not be used as evidence in later judicial proceedings. Statements made to or by the mediator are privileged and confidential. Clearly, the mediation laws of a jurisdiction may affect how the parties and the mediator proceed in a highly charged dispute.

Unlike arbitration, the literature discussing the role of the law governing the mediation is scarce, but one may look to arbitration by analogy and synthesize some possible ground rules. The law governing the arbitral proceedings is, in almost all cases, the law of the arbitral situs. The arbitral situs is the place where the parties agreed that the arbitration would take place. This is often a legal fiction because, frequently for the convenience of the parties, the actual physical proceedings may occur in a different jurisdiction or multiple jurisdictions. There is no reason why the mediator and parties could not select in the agreement to mediate in a jurisdiction whose laws support the mediation process. By analogy, courts should give the agreement to mediate the same deference they give an agreement to arbitrate and apply the law of the chosen jurisdiction. These issues are unresolved and may present complex choice of law questions in the ecommerce and online mediation context. Until these issues are resolved, and depending on the nature of the dispute, prudent lawyers must consider the legal advantages of knowing which laws govern the mediation process. This lack of legal certainty may, in a few instances, hinder the growth of online mediation.

KAREN STEWART & JOSEPH MATTHEWS, ONLINE ARBITRATION OF CROSS–BORDER, BUSINESS TO CONSUMER DISPUTES

56 University of Miami Law Review 1111, 1130–36 (2002).[15]

* * *

III.   Enforcement Problems as an Impediment to Online arbitration

Although online arbitration has the potential to provide the essential legal framework needed for the continued development of cross-border B2C commerce, it is unlikely that Internet stakeholders will be willing to invest the time and capital in developing practical online arbitration systems unless they can be sure that awards will be enforced. Despite the conclusions of many international meetings that online arbitration should be a primary means of resolving cross-border disputes, besides the ICANN process there are no other successful international ventures at online arbitration. The main reason for this is the lack of a reliable means for enforcing online arbitration awards.

A.   United Nations Convention on the Enforcement of Arbitral Awards

The most widely used means of enforcing international arbitral awards is the United Nations Convention on the Enforcement of Arbitral Awards (the "New York Convention"). The New York Convention, however, was drafted in 1958 and obviously could not have contemplated arbitration in cyberspace. It is therefore doubtful that the New York Convention can provide the predictable means of award enforcement required for the development of cross-border online arbitration.

* * * The New York Convention was an attempt to limit the involvement of national courts in the arbitral process, to restrict the number of options that a losing party could utilize to avoid the enforcement of awards, and to ensure the enforcement of foreign arbitral awards. * * * The New York Convention only governs foreign arbitral awards and is typically implicated when the seat of the arbitration occurs in Country One but enforcement of the award is sought in Country Two. Because the seat of the arbitration is generally chosen by agreement of the parties for reasons of convenience and access to evidence, the seat of the arbitration often differs from the place of enforcement. As a practical matter, the place of enforcement, however, is generally the country in which process over the losing party's assets can be obtained with the help of national courts.

There are, nevertheless, some very important caveats to the general principle that foreign arbitral awards will be enforced under the New York Convention. Article V of that convention provides that an award may be set aside by the domestic courts where the arbitration occurs.

---

15. For other legal issues posed by on-line arbitration, see Hornle, *Online Dispute Resolution—More Than The Emperor's* *New Clothes*, Proceedings of the UNECE Forum on ODR 2003 http://www.odr.info/unece2003.

Moreover, the award may not be enforced by the courts of the country where enforcement is sought if the award violates the public policy of any involved country. Article V, therefore, is a limit to the general goal of the New York Convention, namely enforcement of foreign arbitral awards, because it gives power back to the national courts to decide whether they should be set aside. Once in a national court, the losing party may bring up defenses to the enforcement of awards that are available under national law.

Although Article V impedes the enforcement of arbitration awards rendered both online and offline, it has an even greater potential to prevent the enforcement of online arbitral awards. This is true for two reasons. First, the New York Convention requires all contracts for arbitration to be in writing and signed by the parties. This presents an Article V problem because many countries have not yet come to agree that electronic contracts satisfy this requirement. Second, the New York Convention provides for a commercial reservation that allows signatories to refuse to enforce arbitral awards that are not considered "commercial." This reservation has been adopted by fifty-one of the contracting and extension states. Although generally given broad interpretation, it has received the narrowest and strictest international interpretation in support of the general international antipathy towards the arbitration of B2C disputes. The consensus has been that these disputes are not commercial. Thus, either the court at the seat of the arbitration may set aside the award, and/or the courts at the place of enforcement may refuse to enforce it. When an arbitration award is rendered online, aside from other defenses generally available to delay or avoid compliance with foreign arbitral awards, the losing party has two additional defenses: (1) failure to meet the writing requirement; and most importantly (2) that the award falls under the commercial reservation.

    1.   writing requirement

* * *

The text of the Convention does not make clear whether the law at the seat of the arbitration or at the place of enforcement should determine if the writing requirement is met. However, because Article V of the Convention allows either the national courts at the seat of the arbitration to set aside the award, or the courts at the place of enforcement to refuse to enforce an award, a problematic situation arises whenever a contract for arbitration does not meet the writing requirement for either of the two countries.

While the United States has enacted legislation explicitly giving effect to electronic agreements, other contracting and extension countries have refused to follow suit. When parties from countries with conflicting legislation become embroiled in a dispute, a party disfavoring online arbitration may use the law of either country as a defense on the grounds that an agreement for arbitration never existed.

2. commercial reservation

The commercial reservation presents the biggest hurdle to the use of online arbitration in cross-border B2C disputes. The New York Convention was drafted for the purpose of enforcing arbitration agreements in commercial disputes, generally defined as disputes between two businesses. One of the goals of the New York Convention was to ensure that contractual clauses, in particular a contractual provision for arbitration, would be enforced. Because the New York Convention's aim is to uphold the contractual agreements of businesses, a valid argument could be made that when two businesses are engaged in an online transaction in which the record between them evidences an intent to resolve all disputes by means of online arbitration, then in keeping with the spirit of the New York Convention, the agreement should be enforced. The New York Convention, however, offers no such underlying policy favoring the enforcement of agreements for arbitration where one of the parties is a consumer. To the contrary, one of the central purposes of the commercial reservation was to prevent the mandatory enforcement of pre-dispute arbitration clauses when one of the parties is a consumer. Thus, whereas business parties about to enter into a contract containing an arbitration clause could stipulate that an electronic agreement is a writing and further agree on the seat of the arbitration, the commercial reservation, in an attempt to protect consumers, removes consumers' power to bind themselves, at least prior to the dispute, to resolve it by any means of arbitration.

Notes and Questions

1. In view of the various issues that you might have to resolve under the law of the site of the mediation, what can you do to ensure that your preferred law will be applied in an international online mediation?

2. How important is it for parties to have access to the New York Arbitration Convention to enforce an award from an online international arbitration involving an online B2C transaction or a modest online B2B transaction? What are some of the practical obstacles to relying on the Convention for enforcing an award? What alternative approaches might you devise to provide parties an efficient means of enforcement?

Part III

PUBLIC DISPUTES

Chapter 7

INTERNATIONAL NEGOTIATION AND MEDIATION IN THE PUBLIC SECTOR

A. INTRODUCTION

The field of modern conflict resolution is predominantly a study of negotiation and mediation under a wide variety of contexts and practices. This chapter begins with an overview of international negotiation and then offers an understanding of negotiation as preventive diplomacy. The materials consider structural, fairness and justice issues in international negotiation as well as some of the barriers to successful negotiation. Despite the appeal of negotiation as a form of preventive diplomacy, we challenge you to think about the conditions under which it is appropriate to refuse to engage in the negotiation process.

The second part of the chapter explores the mediation process as it is practiced in the public international arena. The materials focus on concepts of mediator leverage and neutrality and the timing of mediator interventions. Finally, the materials in the latter part of the chapter present some models of international mediation practice. Through the lens of case studies, we examine mediation practice in situations of intractable and deadly conflict.

As you read the materials in this chapter you should keep in mind the issues discussed in earlier chapters dealing with negotiation and mediation in the private sector and think about the following questions. What are the differences between public, private and domestic negotiation and mediation practice? What are the similarities? How relevant is the American model of mediation in international practice?

B. INTERNATIONAL NEGOTIATION

Negotiation commands a central position in international conflict resolution as an alternative to the use of force in resolving conflicts and disputes between nations and ethnic groups. In fact, Article 33 of the United Nations Charter lists negotiation as the first method of settling inter-State disputes. Often, negotiations are conducted in the shadow of the actual or threatened use of force. Negotiators, therefore, must be skilled at managing conflict in the midst of power struggles. In both bilateral and multilateral negotiations, negotiators must understand: a) the role of power and the effect of asymmetrical relationships in ethnic conflicts, b) the role of agents who negotiate for others, and c) the importance of cultural factors in these conflicts.

How negotiators can achieve such an understanding has been the subject of considerable study by scholars. Watkins and Rosegrant have proposed "breakthrough" principles for international negotiators that include: continual shaping of the negotiation structure, paying careful attention to process design, and employing force when necessary.[1] Rubin and Zartman have identified several personality traits of effective negotiators. These traits include: flexibility, interpersonal sensitivity, inventiveness, patience, tenacity, and trust.[2] Perhaps the most valuable skill is the ability to change the perception of what is at stake in any given conflict. By recognizing that conflict emerges from the parties' perceptions of reality, negotiators can have an enormous impact on the resolution of the dispute.

1. NEGOTIATION AS PREVENTIVE DIPLOMACY

A form of preventive diplomacy has emerged from the need to develop conflict prevention.[3] The term "preventive diplomacy" was first used in 1960 by former UN Secretary–General Dag Hammarskjold in an attempt to avoid having local struggles become superpower conflicts.[4] Thirty years later, another UN Secretary–General, Boutros–Ghali, adopted a similar approach in response to the development of ethnic and regional conflicts during the Cold War. In *Agenda for Peace,* Boutros–Ghali defined preventive diplomacy as "... action to prevent disputes from arising between parties, to prevent disputes from escalating into violent conflicts and to limit the spread of the latter when they occur."[5]

Preventive diplomacy, therefore, means that proactive, conscious efforts should be made to prevent conflicts from escalating. David Hamburg provides the following distinction between preventive and ordinary diplomacy:

> In operational terms, it resembles conventional diplomatic practice and uses a similar repertoire of policy tools, including information gathering, official and

1. MICHAEL WATKINS & SUSAN ROSEGRANT, BREAKTHROUGH INTERNATIONAL NEGOTIATION: HOW GREAT NEGOTIATORS TRANSFORMED THE WORLD'S TOUGHEST POST-COLD WAR CONFLICTS (2001).

2. Jeffrey Z. Rubin, *The Actors in Negotiation, in* INTERNATIONAL NEGOTIATION: ANALYSIS, APPROACHES, ISSUES 104–09 (Victor A. Kremenyuk ed., 2002) [hereinafter KREMENYUK, INTERNATIONAL NEGOTIATION].

3. I. WILLIAM ZARTMAN ed., PREVENTIVE NEGOTIATION: AVOIDING CONFLICT ESCALATION (Carnegie Commission on Preventing Deadly Conflict, 2001) [hereinafter ZARTMAN, PREVENTIVE NEGOTIATION].

4. DAVID A. HAMBURG, NO MORE KILLING FIELDS: PREVENTING DEADLY CONFLICT 117 (2002).

5. BOUTROS BOUTROS-GHALI, AN AGENDA FOR PEACE (1992) (rev. ed. 1995).

track-two negotiations, mediation and confidence building measures. However, preventive diplomacy is distinguished by its forward-looking character, its emphasis
on systematic early warning and early response. Traditional diplomacy, by contrast, has typically been ad hoc
and reactive, more geared to limited crisis management
than to a principled program of fundamental violence
prevention.[6]

Negotiation is the most basic form of preventive diplomacy. At a fundamental level, it requires a change of attitude between adversaries.
Zartman suggests that it is necessary for negotiators to direct attention
to the task of changing stakes.[7] This involves refocusing the parties'
perceptions of what is at stake in the conflict. By reframing issues and
helping parties consider possible trade-offs, it may be possible to achieve
this end.

2. THE DECISION TO REFRAIN FROM NEGOTIATING

Notwithstanding the central importance of negotiation in the international conflict resolution regime, the recent surge of terrorist activity
suggests that there may be situations in which refusal to negotiate is a
justifiable position. Of course, much depends upon how the term negotiation is defined. In the following excerpt Professor Robert Mnookin offers
a framework for decisionmaking when parties are considering whether
or not to participate in negotiation.

ROBERT H. MNOOKIN, WHEN NOT TO NEGOTI-
ATE: A NEGOTIATION IMPERIALIST RE-
FLECTS ON APPROPRIATE LIMITS

74 University of Colorado Law Review 1077 (2003).

* * *

The term "negotiation" is hardly self-defining. The U.S., for example, has a stated policy of not negotiating with terrorist groups that have
kidnapped American citizens. But in a number of instances, this policy is
not seen as inconsistent with "dialogue" or "talks" or "contacts" with
the hostage-holders. In the words of L. Paul Bremer, former Chief of the
State Department's counter-terrorism program: "We will always talk to
anybody about the welfare of American hostages, but we will not
negotiate because that implies making concessions." In contrast, Spain's
former interior minister suggested that "dialogue" of any sort with
Basque rebels would be inconsistent with Spain's no-negotiation policy.
Indeed, by manipulating the meaning of "negotiation" these examples
suggest parties will often seek to loosen or tighten self-imposed limits.

Negotiation scholars have defined "negotiation" in a variety of
ways. When the definition is very broad, it may include nearly any type

---

6. *See* HAMBURG, *supra* note 4.

7. ZARTMAN, PREVENTIVE NEGOTIATION *su-*
pra note 3, at 314–16.

of interaction in which a party in a conflict is trying to influence someone else, even if there is no direct communication. Through moves away from the negotiation table, a disputant is often trying to shape the other side's perception of possible outcomes; thus, negotiation can be defined in a way that is so broad that any move by a disputant can be seen as part of a negotiation. Note that if tacit communication is included within the definition's scope, then tactical actions in a war or procedural moves in a lawsuit can be seen as part of a negotiation process.

On the other hand, it can be defined so narrowly as to exclude dialogue about a problem when one party takes a firm position and is unwilling to compromise.

For purposes of this paper, I define negotiation as a joint decision making process involving interactive communication in which parties that lack identical interests attempt to reach agreement. This definition requires active communication, as well as a mixed-motive game, in which not all interests are aligned.

* * *

. . . refusals to negotiate can often simply be a tactic that is used as part of the negotiation process. A negotiator might proclaim a refusal to negotiate, or threaten to end negotiation, simply as a "hard-bargaining" tactic. In such a case, the proclaimed refusal to negotiate is intended only to extract additional concessions from the rival in exchange for agreeing to negotiate. When the decision not to negotiate is strategic, on the other hand, it should not be seen as a negotiation tactic; rather, it is a preference for an alternative course of action: either abstaining from any interaction ("walking away") or resorting to coercive measures (the court or the sword).

In the present discussion, I narrow my interest to the strategic decision of not entering into the negotiation. The implicit assumption of many negotiation imperialists—that everything is or should be negotiable—certainly doesn't describe the world. In the family, at the workplace, and in the market, many matters are said to be "non-negotiable." A department store won't haggle over the price of its ties and a restaurant won't negotiate the price of an entrée. A political leader may refuse to negotiate with a terrorist kidnapper. Sometimes the refusal to negotiate may be unwise. But sometimes it is better not to negotiate. What considerations are and should be taken into account in deciding whether to negotiate at all? In various contexts, where a party refuses to negotiate, what reasons are typically used to justify that decision? How should a party think about and decide whether to enter into or begin a negotiation at all?

II. A Framework for Decision Making

* * *

My framework poses six questions that should be addressed, four of which draw from negotiation analysis. Negotiation imperialists—myself included—suggest that in preparing for a negotiation a party should identify its own interests and those of the other parties; think about each side's BATNA; try to imagine options that might better serve the negotiators' interests than their BATNAs; and ensure that commitments made in any negotiated deal have a reasonable prospect of actually being implemented. These same considerations are equally valid in informing an individual's decision whether one should enter into a negotiation. In addition, one must also consider the expected costs—both direct and indirect—of engaging in the negotiation process, as well as issues of legitimacy and morality.

A. Interests

What are my interests? What are my counterpart's interests? The analysis begins by identifying one's own interests: long-and short-term, intangible and tangible, indirect and direct. One should then proceed to consider, given the available information, the interests of the other parties. Negotiation theory teaches, among other things, that it is necessary to probe beneath stated demands and positions and ask, what is important to the other side? What do they value? It is in light of these interests that an analyst can assess the benefits and costs of alternative courses of action.

B. BATNAs

What is my best alternative to negotiation? What is my counterpart's? The second set of questions concerns alternatives to negotiation, or BATNAs. In deciding whether to negotiate, it makes sense to consider one's legitimate alternatives to negotiation. Indeed, each party to a conflict must assess its possible alternatives and how those alternatives serve its interests.

One alternative might be to do nothing, or ignore the conflict. Another alternative might be to engage in self-help or unilateral action. In many contexts, the existence of an institutional structure or hierarchy may make negotiation unnecessary because one party can impose its will very effectively by fiat or command. In an army (and some organizations) a superior can order a subordinate to undertake some task and reasonably expect his command to be followed. Parents are often advised not to negotiate bedtime with their young children. And a teacher in school would most often impose on the students the date and time of the final exam. In some contexts, a party can initiate an institutional process that can coercively impose an outcome. For example, when a party has a legal claim, an alternative might be to bring a lawsuit, which if successful, will require the other party to do certain things. Where effective self-help is readily available, it may also serve as an alternative to negotiation. This is understood by every bigger child who snatches a toy from a smaller one. At the same time, it also suggests the need to consider the legitimacy of a self-help alternative, especially when it involves the use of force.

C.   Potential Negotiated Outcomes

Are there potential negotiated outcomes that can satisfy my interests and those of the other party better than our respective BATNAs? The third question requires an assessment of possible negotiated agreements. If a party has an alternative that is clearly superior to any possible negotiated agreement, why negotiate? Because negotiations are not devoid of costs, negotiating only makes sense if there are reasonable prospects for a negotiated agreement, superior to each party's BATNA. Even if there are potential negotiated agreements that better serve the interests of each party, this is not the end of the analysis for three more questions must be addressed.

D.   Reliable Counterpart

Is there a reliable negotiation partner? Is there a negotiation counterpart with whom I can negotiate a sufficiently enforceable deal? Even when one can imagine a negotiated deal that better serves each party than its best alternative, it may nonetheless make no sense to initiate negotiations if one believes the other party would never uphold its end of the bargain and there is no effective mechanism for enforcing the negotiated deal. In some instances, it may simply be a matter of trust. In other contexts, there may be no representative who has the capacity to bind a set of stakeholders.

Consider the plight of a real estate developer who owns a large parcel of land in a residential neighborhood that she wishes to use to build a small shopping center. Various neighbors object and threaten to bring suit (and thus delay the development for a matter of years) if the city's zoning commission grants a variance. The developer may be willing to negotiate a deal that might benefit all concerned, but there may be no organization or representative that has the power to bind all the neighbors. If there is no reliable counterpart, entering into a negotiation would be a futile—and potentially costly—exercise.

E.   Costs

What are the expected costs, direct and indirect, of negotiation? A rational decision obviously requires a consideration of costs. There are costs associated with the process of negotiation, regardless of whether a deal is made.

1.   Direct Transaction Costs

Whether one is making a deal or resolving a conflict, the process of negotiation imposes transaction costs on the parties, who must invest time, money, manpower, and other resources. Negotiation can absorb the attention and energy of persons whose time is valuable. It can cost money because a party may need to hire professionals or experts to assist. The amount of costs depends, naturally, on the type of negotiation involved, its prospective duration, the necessary logistics for the process, etc. Entering into a used-car dealership does not entail the same transaction costs as negotiating an arms-control agreement with a rival country.

* * *

Beyond the immediate transaction costs, direct costs also involve the disclosure of information, which may be exploited by the counterpart in future actions, regardless of whether an agreement is achieved in that instance. Exposing intelligence-gathering capabilities, a company's vulnerabilities, or even personal desires may prove detrimental in future interactions with the same party.

2.   Indirect or Spillover Costs

Apart from the direct transaction costs, there may be a variety of indirect or spillover costs. Entering into a negotiation may affect a party's reputation: People's instincts may tell them that if someone is willing to settle, there must be something to the claims against them. The mere willingness on the part of a defendant to negotiate a plea bargain with the district attorney might be perceived as an admission of guilt. Reputation costs increase where a negotiating party has previously stated a policy of not negotiating in similar instances, as where a company has declared in the past that it would refuse to negotiate frivolous lawsuits and see them through in court, but is willing to negotiate with a current plaintiff.

Reputation is somewhat related to another type of spillover costs. A demonstrated willingness to negotiate here may serve as an adverse precedent, creating an incentive for other potential claimants later. Even if negotiating a resolution of this single dispute may make sense in light of the immediate cost savings, the precedent of a negotiated settlement here may bring a flood of similar claims later. An employer may refuse to negotiate with unlawfully striking workers if the employer believes that negotiation may only encourage future employees to go on strike. For example, in 1981 when 11,400 air traffic controllers went on strike for higher wages and better working conditions, President Ronald Reagan and the Federal Aviation Administration (FAA) refused to negotiate, fired the striking controllers, hired replacements, and barred the strikers from ever being re-employed by the FAA.

In a similar vein, numerous countries around the globe, such as the U.S., Britain, France, Italy, Germany, Israel, the Philippines, Guatemala, Peru, and Russia have a declared policy of refusing to negotiate with terrorists. This refusal, as I shall show later, is no doubt driven by additional considerations, but it is also intended to avoid providing incentives for further extortions by future terrorists.

Beyond the costs associated with the parties "at the table," there are also spillover costs "behind the table" relating to one's constituencies or coalitions. The decision to enter into negotiations may have an adverse effect on those whom you will need to rally to your cause in the event negotiations fail. Apart from your own constituents, there can also be effects on coalitions—those whom you may need as allies if negotiations fail.

A dramatic example with respect to constituents relates to Winston Churchill's refusal to accept an invitation to begin negotiations directly with Mussolini—and indirectly with Hitler—in May of 1940. Churchill had just become Prime Minister, France had very nearly been overrun, and tens of thousands of British troops appeared to be trapped around Dunkirk. The Battle of Britain had just begun, and German bombers had launched their attack. While Churchill's refusal to negotiate reflected a number of considerations, one of which was his skepticism that Hitler would abide by any deal that might be at all acceptable to his government, a primary reason for Churchill's refusal related to his concern that the act of negotiating with the Axis would have a devastating impact on the morale of his constituents and their ability to make the sacrifices necessary if negotiations failed.

A decision by one member to negotiate separately may have a devastating effect on the viability of a previously effective coalition. Liggett's decision to negotiate with a plaintiff in a tobacco suit generated a flood of lawsuits and settlements across the country because of its devastating impact on the previously effective coalition among all the major tobacco companies, which for years had insisted on litigating to the end all tort claims.

C. Legitimacy and Morality

What considerations of legitimacy and morality should be taken into account? In considering the benefits and costs of the decision whether to negotiate, there is no avoiding questions of legitimacy and morality. One aspect was mentioned earlier: when thinking about alternatives to negotiation, one must consider the legitimacy of those alternatives. A bigger child may have the power to grab the toy of a younger and smaller sibling, but most parents would prefer that the child not exercise that alternative but instead ask to use the toy. A self-help alternative to negotiation may not be considered legitimate, at least without some institutional approval. Few doubted the capacity of the U.S. to bring about a regime change in Iraq, but many have questioned the legitimacy of the American resort to force in the absence of U.N. Security Council authorization.

The mere process of negotiation with a counterpart is perceived as conferring some recognition and legitimacy on them. Providing a counterpart with "a place at the table" acknowledges their existence, actions, (and to some degree) the validity of their interests. To avoid validation of interests or claims, countries have often refused to negotiate with rebels or insurgent groups, denying them any recognition or legitimacy. Thus, for decades, Israel refused to negotiate with the Palestinian Liberation Organization, Britain denied any status from the Irish Revolutionary Army, the Spanish would not negotiate with the Basque separatist rebels, Peru would not engage in a dialogue with the Tupac Amaru, and Russia announced an absolute policy of not negotiating with the Chechen rebels. In addition, the interest of denying recognition and legitimacy has also largely determined the relationships between Israel and some Arab countries and between China and Taiwan.

The policy of refusing to negotiate with terrorists derives not only from the fear of conferring legitimacy or recognition, but also from aversion to rewarding past bad behavior. When previous interactions have failed to satisfy the claims of a party, satisfying its claims under the pressure of violence implies that violence was indeed worthwhile. This consideration, of course, is problematic. Although most of the national liberation movements around the world have employed violence in their struggle to gain independence or self-determination (among very few Gandhi-like exceptions), once violence is employed it usually entrenches political rivals, at least in the short term following violence.

Perhaps the most renowned example of a refusal to negotiate for moral considerations is Sir Winston Churchill's refusal to negotiate directly or indirectly with Adolph Hitler in May of 1940. For Churchill, the refusal derived not only from the questionable effectiveness of such negotiations, given the dismal history of Hitler's negotiations with Chamberlain, or the potential effects of failed negotiations on his fellow citizens, but also from a strong moral aversion to "doing business with the devil." Churchill truly believed that Britain had a deep moral obligation, on behalf of itself as well as the rest of the world, to fight Nazi Germany. In relation to British advocates of appeasement, he said: "An appeaser is one who feeds a crocodile—hoping it will eat him last."

3. STRUCTURAL ISSUES IN INTERNATIONAL NEGOTIA-TION

The process of international negotiations has three significant stages. The first—the planning stage—involves determining that all relevant parties are represented at the bargaining table. Even though it may be more difficult to reach an agreement with multiple parties and issues,[8] in terms of the long-term durability of an agreement, inclusion prevents disgruntled parties from disrupting or sabotaging the agreement.

The second significant stage of international negotiation involves the process of issue identification. Theorists have identified three categories of issues: conflicts over interests, conflicts over values, and mixed interests and values.[9] Under the first category, parties may have different views about the distribution of specific resources. Under the second category, conflicts in values exist where the parties have different, and possibly incompatible, ideological values, principles, and belief systems. Research has demonstrated that negotiations over conflicts in values present the most difficult challenges and often require the assistance of a mediator to reach agreement.[10] Of course, any negotiation can involve disagreement about both matters.

---

8. *See* Rubin, *supra* note 2, at 100, 102.

9. CHRISTOPHER DUPONT & GUY-OLIVIER FAURE, *The Negotiation Process, in* KREMEN-YUK, INTERNATIONAL NEGOTIATION 51, *supra* note 2, at 51.

10. *Id., citing* H. TOUZARD, LA MEDIATION ET LA RESOLUTION DES CONFLITS [Mediation and the Resolution of Conflicts] (Paris: PUF 1977).

Finally, the third stage of international negotiation involves information exchange and bargaining. During this stage, two predominant bargaining models are evident: positional bargaining and problem-solving. Positional bargaining tends to be adversarial in nature and directed towards what theorists have labeled as "value claiming" behaviors. Problem-solving bargaining, on the other hand, focuses on both parties' underlying needs and interests and is directed toward "value creating" behaviors.[11]

As a practical matter, actual negotiations do not follow a clear-cut positional or problem-solving model. Value claiming and value creating behaviors are inherent in every negotiation and the challenge for negotiators is to manage the tension between both strategic approaches in the same negotiation. Pruitt suggests four techniques that can assist negotiators in avoiding the tensions between value claiming and value creating behaviors, or what he labels the dilemma between contending and problem-solving: (1) sequencing in time, *e.g.,* going from contending to problem-solving; (2) taking a contentious public stance coupled with covert (secret) problem-solving; (3) firm flexibility; and (4) developing a working relationship with the other party.[12]

Given the realities of contemporary global politics, the traditional approach to negotiation, positional-based bargaining, which is largely influenced by power differentials, is giving way to joint problem-solving approaches.[13] In the following excerpt, the authors describe how one political party in Northern Ireland employed a problem-solving approach in the negotiations leading up to the Good Friday/Belfast Agreement in 1998.

JACQUELINE NOLAN–HALEY & BRONAGH HINDS, PROBLEM–SOLVING NEGOTIATION: NORTHERN IRELAND'S EXPERIENCE WITH THE WOMEN'S COALITION

Journal of Dispute Resolution 387, 394–97 (2003).

* * *

Strategies for Developing a Sustainable Agreement

Throughout the negotiations, the Women's Coalition remained focused on its twin goals of including women on an equal footing with men and achieving accommodations upon which a stable and peaceful future could be built. The new, creative approach of the Coalition prevented the formation of rigid bargaining positions. In this way, its internal practices modeled behavior for the multi-party negotiations.

---

11. David A. Lax & James K. Sebenius, The Manager As Negotiator 29–34 (1986).

12. Dean G. Pruitt, *Strategy in Negotiation, in* Kremenyuk, International Negotiation, *supra* note 2, at 86–88.

13. Kremenyuk, International Negotiation, *supra* note 2, at 28–31 (2002).

The Coalition entered the negotiations with a specific frame of mind—to reach a settlement that could move Northern Ireland beyond the regular cycles of conflict in every generation. Specifically, the Coalition sought a durable settlement that could win the consent, allegiance, and active support of all. For the Coalition this mean engaging in a comprehensive set of problem-solving strategies:

—Structuring an inclusive negotiation process involving all those who had been successfully elected to participate in the negotiations, as well as consultation with other interest groups that were not directly represented;

—Generating a comprehensive and complex discussion agenda that would address the needs and interests of all the participants;

—Building relationships and helping others to transform relationships;

—Contributing positively with ideas and solutions rather than with negatives;

—Listening and demonstrating genuine comprehension of others' ideas and paying attention to body language and dynamics;

—"Interpreting" between other parties to ensure that differences in positions were clear and could be addressed without conflict being exacerbated by confusion over communication or language; and

—Building cross-party collaboration and consensus.

Inclusion and Democracy

The Coalition's vision of inclusion extended even to paramilitaries. For example, before and during the two years of negotiations, the Coalition consistently promoted full participation of all elected parties, even when some parties with paramilitary links were excluded from time to time over the failure to honor cease-fires. This approach differed from that of many other political parties who argued vociferously for the exclusion of certain parties from the talks and refused to dialogue with them when they were present.

The Coalition took a significant step to make inclusion meaningful by convincing the parties to change the governing Rules of Procedure for negotiations so that all parties shared in the decision-making power. Its understanding of inclusion went beyond the involvement of all political actors to achieve engagement, whenever possible, with civic leaders from across the spectrum of society. Consistent dialogue between Coalition negotiators and a broader constituent base, through monthly open meetings and larger consultative conferences, enable the Coalition to keep those outside the talks abreast of developments at the negotiating table. It also helped to keep negotiators in touch with the views and feelings on the ground. This in turn formed part of the feedback the

Coalition could share within the talks and, specifically, bring to the attention of the Independent Chairs. The dialogue with the public helped to prepare them for compromises that would be required in the long term, allaying fears about an agreement that was too extreme.

Publishing its inclusive and problem-solving platform in the *Irish News*, the Coalition argued that it was necessary to address the fears and concerns of all other participants, engage in discussion with all, value and build on others' ideas whenever possible and frame and reframe contributions in a manner that would lead to solutions. It described itself as "solution-focused," and argued "that all parties and interests have to be heard if realistic political options are to emerge." This approach was in marked contrast to the negotiating behavior of some of the traditional political parties who would defend their own position at all costs, support it with intemperate language and wild assertions in the media to keep supporters in line, herd supporters in a particular direction, and threaten the entire process while doing so.

Establishing New Standards of Negotiating Behavior

The Women's Coalition was determined to play its part in creating a different expression of democracy that would allow negotiation to flourish. An abnormal and deviant political culture that indulged in antagonistic, bullying, sectarian, and sexist behavior had thrived during years of conflict and had become embedded as normal in the minds of politicians, the media, and those working in the political arena. Demonizing people and parties was standard practice, while open and democratic debate based on well-presented arguments, especially on contentious issues, was rare. . . .

Northern Ireland had been damaged by decades of adversarial and violent politics. It was clear that such behavior was a barrier to dialogue and serious engagement. Abuse was used as a tool to thwart substantive negotiation and political progress. Fundamental change was required if more women were to be encouraged to participate in politics. The Coalition decided that this negative language and behavior had to be interrupted and that it would challenge old attitudes and set new standards for respect and competence. It refused to accept abuse as normal political banter and constantly confronted disrespectful attitudes and actions with a view to fostering inclusion, respect, and political progress. It worked to free to concept of compromise from negative connotation of the word "traitor." These efforts played a more important role in the negotiation process than has often been credited by observers.

Dialogue and Consensus

A key reason women wanted to be involved in the negotiations was to argue for and demonstrate a different way of doing things—concentrating on solutions to shared problems rather than on mutually exclusive aspirations, and driving negotiation by values and visions for the future rather than protecting historical certainties. . . .

Throughout the negotiations, Coalition representatives continued collaborative practices of checking the views of others and seeking to reach accommodation across a wide variety of differing interests. Such practices, combined with their prior experience in cooperative efforts, helped the women approach the peace talks confident that their strategies were in the best interests of promoting dialogue and consensus. Every effort to describe the Coalition as 'unionist' or 'nationalist,' for example, or to drive a wedge between women from different religious or political traditions by insisting that the Coalition take a position on the constitutional status of Northern Ireland, met with failure.

4. IMPEDIMENTS TO NEGOTIATION

Negotiation can succeed or fail. In fact, many international negotiations result in failure. Understanding how and why negotiations fail requires an understanding of cultural differences and how they can establish barriers to successful negotiations. Negotiations can be impeded by strategies, cognitive problems, insufficient coordination, lack of reciprocity, failures in trust-building, and linked negotiations. In the following excerpt, the author considers multiple impediments to successful negotiation of Sri Lankan ethnic conflict.

DAVID M. ROTHENBERG, NEGOTIATION AND DISPUTE RESOLUTION IN THE SRI LANKAN CONTEXT: LESSONS FROM THE 1994–1995 PEACE TALKS

22 Fordham International Law Journal 505, 506–07, 510, 525–66 (1998).

INTRODUCTION

On October 13, 1994, four negotiators from the government of Sri Lanka arrived in the rebel-held territory of the Liberation Tigers of Tamil Eelam ("LTTE") to begin face-to-face peace talks with the LTTE. After eleven years of civil war that left over 34,000 dead, both sides realized that a window of opportunity for negotiating a peaceful solution to the intractable military conflict had emerged. The mood throughout the island of Sri Lanka was euphoric. Thousands of ordinary Tamil civilians, who gathered to witness the arrival of the opposing-government delegation, streamed through LTTE barricades in an outpouring of support for the peace process, throwing flower petals and kissing the hands of the government officials. The opportunity for a peaceful resolution of the violent civil war was historic.

Six months later, the LTTE abrogated a cessation of hostilities agreement by attacking a Sri Lankan Navy ship. The government of Sri Lanka responded by mounting a major offensive to recapture all LTTE-held territory. The years since the breakdown of the peace talks have been characterized by intense military conflict.* * *

How did this happen? How did the Sri Lankan government and the LTTE move so quickly from embracing a historic opportunity for peace to all-out war? Careful analysis of the 1994–95 Sri Lankan peace talks reveals that a major obstacle in the negotiations was a poorly designed process. Despite the momentous nature of the talks, and despite the captivation of the country that the talks inspired, the government and the LTTE failed to consider systematically-important process issues of the negotiations.

* * *

I. The Historical Background

To understand the 1994–95 peace talks, it is necessary to examine briefly the historical roots of the conflict. Such an overview will not only identify the major issues, positions, and parties involved, but also offer insights into the undercurrents influencing past peace efforts that continue to hinder the modern peace process. Three such undercurrents are: 1) the legacy of deep mistrust between the parties, even when settlements are reached, 2) the omnipresence of intra-party rivalries leading to the encouragement of chauvinist sentiments, and 3) the tendency to dismiss issues of process in efforts to ease ethnic tensions.

* * *

K. Historical Trends: Process–Oriented Obstacles to Peace

To understand the process-oriented obstacles of the 1994–95 talks, it is helpful to further explicate their historical roots. Even this brief survey of the Sri Lankan ethnic conflict highlights important historical trends that inform our understanding of the talks. The legacy of deep mistrust between Tamil parties and the government, for instance, grew out of failures within the peace process and has become a fundamental barrier to negotiations. The government's inability to implement the BC Pact and the Senanayake–Chelvanayakam Pact ("SC Pact") produced acute suspicion within the Tamil leadership of the government's commitment to honoring its obligations on the ethnic question. This tension between "agreement in principle" and "agreement in practice" resurfaces distinctly in the 1994–95 talks. Deep mistrust developed through more subtle means as well. Military actions and the government's inclination to offer what it knew would be unacceptable to Tamil parties, as the Thimpu Talks suggest, led Tamil leaders to interpret the government's actions as a calculated decision to negotiate in bad faith. Indeed, Tamil groups consider the government's efforts to ease the ethnic tensions, such as the BC Pact or the 1978 constitutional reforms, as little more than token attempts to provide a temporary reprieve in ethnic polarization. The rhetoric and the concern over bad faith and tokenism remain central to the 1994–95 peace talks. Finally, the government's approach to the armed conflict, in which bombing campaigns and an economic embargo create extreme hardships on the Tamil non-combatants, served to raise the level of mistrust and antipathy between Tamil and Sinhalese leaders. Efforts to build trust, therefore, are first tied to stopping violent confrontation. As the 1994–95 talks indicate, however, initially limiting peace talks to cease-fire issues creates distinct obstacles to long-term peace.

The Sri Lankan government has developed an equally strong mistrust of the LTTE. After all, the LTTE is the party that abrogated the recent cease-fires. The LTTE broke the cease-fire following Thimpu, pulled out of the Indo–Sri Lankan Accords, and ended the talks with Premadasa. The result of such abrogation was suspicion and a seriously harmed dialogue between the parties. In fact, following the LTTE's abrogation of the talks with Premadasa, virtually no communication existed between the government and the LTTE until the beginning of the 1994–95 talks. Moreover, the LTTE's approach to armed confrontation has been perceived by the Sinhalese public and leadership as extraordinarily brutal, and, in turn, generates increased apprehension. The LTTE has shown not only a willingness to silence Tamil moderates and to assassinate government officials, but also to engage in suicide bombings that injure innocent civilians. Any efforts at peace that do not seek to systematically improve the level of trust between the government and the LTTE have little chance of long-term success, to which the 1994–95 talks unfortunately attest.

A second historical trend in the process-oriented failures to ease ethnic tensions in Sri Lanka is the pervasive existence of intra-party rivalries which breed chauvinistic and nationalistic sentiments. The story of Sri Lanka's modern ethnic conflict is largely the story of competition between the UNP and the SLFP to capture the nationalist vote. This competition is not hidden. Agreements with the Tamil leaders, such as the BC Pact and the SC Pact were breached by the Sri Lankan government precisely to maintain the support of chauvinist back-benchers. More subtly, the rivalry between the UNP and SLFP led the Sinhalese parties to distance themselves from proposed legislation, such as the 1980 District Development Council Act, which sought to devolve power to Tamil parties. The competition between Sinhalese parties, combined with the lack of protection of minority rights in Sri Lanka's constitution, heightened ethnic tensions and impeded efforts to resolve the conflict peacefully.

On the Tamil side, intra-party rivalries served to silence moderate voices. The LTTE has been ruthless in its efforts to elevate itself as the only voice for the Tamil people. The LTTE's campaign of terror against Tamil militant groups that abided by the Indo–Sri Lankan Accord is a case in point. Although the LTTE remains the dominant voice of the Tamil movement and diaspora today, the remnants of its historical competition with other Tamil parties remain significant. That is, the LTTE may feel the need to attain a settlement that is better than a settlement that non-violent Tamil parties might be able to attain, such as the current Devolution package, in order to justify the armed resistance, the sufferings of the Tamil people, and the LTTE's extreme leadership. Intra–Tamil rivalries not only suppressed moderate Tamil voices, but also may have raised the bar in the 1994–95 talks.

. . . . peace and reconciliation efforts largely ignored issues of process. Attempts to amend the constitution in 1978, for example, were conducted without preparatory discussions on how to include Tamil leadership in the reform process. Instead, the constitution was amended without Tamil input. Similarly, the Thimpu talks lacked a systematic preparatory process, leading each party to advocate positions that were unsuitable to the other. The Indo–Sri Lankan Accord explicitly excluded Tamils from the process of peace. Although all Tamil parties accepted the Accord, the LTTE's stake in the agreement was seriously undermined by the design of the negotiation process in which it was prohibited from participating. Finally, the Premadasa talks, which were conducted directly with the LTTE, represented an ad hoc methodology in which agreements were left unwritten and the process was never formalized. Without serious consideration of how to structure peace negotiations, the government and the LTTE were unable to generate serious commitments to peace.

* * *

III.   THE LESSONS OF THE 1994–1995 PEACE TALKS

* * *

A.   Lack of an Operating Framework

Perhaps the most glaring weakness in the 1994–95 peace talks was the absence of an operating framework within which the peace negotiations would take place. A set of general objectives was never agreed upon in advance of the first round of negotiations, and the 1994–95 talks therefore began with both sides very unclear about what issues would be addressed and how the negotiations would be structured. In fact, the government negotiators were given "no mandate," according to one government negotiator, other than to build a good rapport with the LTTE and to begin understanding their positions. Rajan Asirwatham, another government negotiator, echoed the same sentiment, explaining that the government was seeking only to understand the problems and expectations of the LTTE in the first round of negotiations. The 1994–95 peace talks thus began in a very unconstrained environment in which both sides could begin to share their interests and positions.

It is not surprising then that the first round was characterized by open and informational exchanges. Since the end of the Premadasa–LTTE talks, the Sri Lankan government and the LTTE had not been in direct communication with each other. Certainly the new PA had no special knowledge of the latest LTTE positions for arriving at a negotiated settlement. When Kumaratunga became Prime Minister, advocating a peace platform, neither the government nor the LTTE knew exactly what peace talks would mean. Also, at the time of the first round of peace talks, Kumaratunga was the Prime Minister under a UNP President and was awaiting November's presidential election. Shared leadership helps explain why the government moved slowly and carefully at the first round. The idea to begin the talks in a free and open manner in order to build trust and to establish common ground seemed a reasonable approach to both the government and the LTTE at the time.

Without a clear understanding of what would be discussed or how the negotiations would be structured, the first round therefore began in an ad hoc manner. For example, the LTTE's first move was to suggest an effort to curtail the massive Tamil suffering in the north, followed by a cease-fire. At the time of the first round of talks, much of the LTTE-held area was without electricity and phone service, was subjected to indiscriminate bombing, and was facing serious shortages of medicine, food, petrol, and most commercial goods. The LTTE asserted that undertaking a rehabilitation effort in the Northern and Eastern Provinces would help to create the conditions for peace and a sense of partnership in the peace effort. The government, eager to rebuild the Northern and Eastern Provinces and to win the support of those populations, agreed that economic development would be the initial topic of the negotiation and expressed the hope that political issues would be discussed simultaneously. A mutual understanding, however, of how the rehabilitation issues related to the political issues was never attained.

The LTTE thought of rehabilitation issues as a dire necessity that was the "basic right" of Sri Lankan citizens in the Northern and Eastern Provinces. The government, on the other hand, viewed rehabilitation issues, at least in part, as a bargaining chip. That is, the government expected that as it showed a willingness to help rebuild the North and the East, the LTTE would simultaneously begin discussions on a political solution. Without a clear understanding of the general approach of the talks, it is easy to see, in hindsight, how such misunderstandings helped lead to a breakdown in the talks. The government became increasingly suspicious of the LTTE when political issues were not discussed, and the LTTE became increasingly skeptical of the government's delivery on rehabilitation issues. Pressure for political dialogue only exacerbated Tamil resentment. The government envisioned a political solution at the heart of the talks, whereas the LTTE seemed to believe that economic issues and normalization of life in the North and the East were the primary aims. This incongruence of understandings was never resolved.

Neither the LTTE nor the government spent much time simply talking about the peace process. Just as critical, the government and the LTTE failed to talk about talking about the peace talks. The two sides simply arrived in Jaffna hoping that some discussion and good faith effort would lead to peace. In fact, a central criticism levied against the government is that it structured and conducted the talks with "arrogance and naiveté." One political commentator argues that the "cardinal assumption" of the government's approach was that overwhelming pressure on the LTTE and some flexibility by the government would result in a peace settlement. Malinda Maragoda, a UNP adviser, blames the breakdown on "sheer inexperience and incompetence in management." It seems, however, that both sides are guilty of failing to develop a mutually understood framework to the negotiations. The LTTE, which hosted the talks and set the agenda, bears responsibility for not allotting enough time to discussing and to detailing the general objectives of the peace talks and the actual process that the talks would employ. Usually, such issues are worked out in advance of peace talks. For instance, in the successful negotiations between Peru and Ecuador over disputed territory, the U.S. mediator credits the detailed mandate, painstakingly formulated before the peace talks, as the basis of the success of the talks. Similarly, negotiators of the 1991 Treaty on Conventional Forces in Europe credit the success of the twenty-one-month-long negotiations on the mandate agreed upon before the negotiations took place. In the Sri Lankan context, the development of a general framework was noticeably, and disastrously, absent.

* * *

Another element missing from the framework of the negotiations was an agenda. According to government negotiator Dr. Uyangoda, there was no fixed agenda of the 1994–95 talks. Neither side undertook an analysis of potential peaceful arrangements and neither side approached the negotiations with a detailed plan. The date and subjects of each round of negotiations were typically decided in letters rather than in face-to-face meetings. It was unclear, for instance, when political issues would be the focus of a round of negotiations. Kumaratunga's letters to Prabhakaran indicate that the government thought that discussion of political issues would occur at the beginning of the peace talks, by the second round, and blame the LTTE for stalling and being insincere by not setting a date for political discussions. The LTTE may have been purposefully stalling, but it also may have had a different understanding of the timetable of the negotiations. Without an agenda, and without efforts during negotiations to arrive at a coherent agenda, the two sides were free to conceive competing understandings of when important issues, such as future political arrangements, would be discussed.

Finally, the absence of an operating framework for the peace talks reflects a fundamental lack of preparation. The hazy manner in which the negotiations were conceived and structured implies that adequate preparation was not undertaken. It was more than that, however. There seemed to be a conscious effort not to prepare in-depth for these historic negotiations. Government negotiators, for instance, did not study past negotiations and were instructed not to speak with former negotiators in an effort to protect them from skepticism and prejudice. Such purposeful lack of preparation, according to former U.S. Ambassador to Sri Lanka, Teresita Schaffer, prevented the government negotiators from realizing the importance of contentious issues, such as the problem of the Pooneryn camp, that arose as sticking points in previous negotiations.* * *

B.   Agent Issues: Perception and Status of the Government Delegation

Another major process-oriented obstacle was the perception by the LTTE that the government had sent a low-ranking delegation to the talks. While the LTTE sent a delegation comprised of its deputy political leader, the head of Jaffna political section, the head of its economic division, and the head of its administration, the LTTE believed the government had sent mere messengers.* * * This perspective created two problems. First, at a time when each side was gauging the other's commitment to peace, the LTTE began to form an impression that the government was not serious about ending the ethnic conflict. Second, the LTTE felt rebuffed, believing that there was a purposeful rejection of parity between itself and the government in the negotiations.* * * The status of the delegation became a serious psychological obstacle to the peace process.

* * *

Beyond the psychological obstacles, the status of the delegation affected the actual process of the talks. The government delegation was not empowered to make important substantive decisions, but was instructed to return to Colombo after each round to allow the President and her Security Council to make final decisions. This approach, combined with a lack of planning on both sides, led Kumaratunga and Prabhakaran to exchange letters focusing on the most controversial issues. For instance, discussions of a political arrangement to end the civil war were never discussed during the peace talks. According to an insider who has read all of the non-public letters exchanged, however, political issues were the subject of several letters. The status of the government delegation, therefore, may have inadvertently helped create a two-tier negotiating system in which peace talks were held for economic and rehabilitation issues and letters were exchanged to deal with more controversial issues. A lack of coherence between these two dimensions of the peace process and a marginalization of face-to-face dialogue for the most controversial issues were two serious process-oriented impediments that seem to have resulted from the status, or perceived status, of the government's delegation. Although it is not wholly unusual for leadership to engage each other on the most sensitive aspects outside of the official negotiation, the apparent disunity between the talks and the letters may have limited the ability of the negotiators to arrive at a settlement.

Finally, the status of the delegation may have had an effect on the implementation of agreements reached in the negotiations. The government did not send top-ranking defense department officials, but rather only two officers representing the Army and Navy* * * to advise the government negotiators on the modalities of a cease-fire agreement.* * *

C. The Use of Letters

In the 1994–95 peace talks, Kumaratunga and Prabhakaran exchanged approximately forty letters. Their correspondence was meant to jump start stalled talks, to appeal to the opposing leadership for appropriate action, to make demands, to express the importance of issues, and to discuss the most controversial subjects. The use of letters, however, is a difficult way to express ideas and to explain positions. Developing a common understanding of approaches and solutions to any ethnic conflict is an enormous task. Hours and days of direct negotiations often fail to produce common understanding. At the very least, however, parties to a long negotiation can explain, refine, and revise the technique of communication, including listening, so that they feel reasonably comfortable that what they say is understood in the way that it was intended. Writing, on the other hand, forces the author to choose permanently certain words and styles, leaving greater opportunity for the recipient to attach a different or competing meaning to those words. When the objective is explaining one's interests, options, and alternatives, the use of the written word in place of direct communication is a more difficult and risky technique. The fact that the letters exchanged in the Sri Lankan context were typically short in length further highlights the dangers of communicating complex ideas through writing.

* * *

D.   Inside the Talks: The Procedures

* * *

A second error in the negotiation process was a distinct lack of an informal dimension to the negotiations. Building trust and arriving at meaningful exchanges is a difficult task in negotiations, particularly for warring parties. Mediators of ethnic conflicts have suggested that informal activities are often essential to getting negotiators to trust each other and to begin meaningful exchanges.

* * *

The tenor of the talks did not just exclude informal processes, but was decidedly too formal. There was a level of protocol in the talks that had negative repercussions. For example, each negotiating team had its national flag on its side of the table. When pictures of the LTTE delegation negotiating under its own flag, a symbol of independence to many, hit the Sri Lankan newspapers, there was an uproar among Sinhalese nationalists. The government and the LTTE had to react to the backlash that arose out of this unnecessary formality. Although the use of flags may have great symbolic value, the practicalities of arriving at a negotiated settlement necessitated restricting protocol and formalities that were likely to cause controversy. This lack of forethought further shows how the structure and process of the talks were more accidental than the product of a calculated approach.

Thirdly, both sides failed to engage in brainstorming sessions during the peace talks. The technique of brainstorming in its most simple form includes exchanges between parties about possible options and potential arrangements for improving a current conflict. In an open and non-binding format brainstorming helps parties identify options that can facilitate efficient trades and create value for both sides.* * *

E.   The Structure of Implementation

One of the critical issues in the breakdown of the 1994–95 talks was the implementation of agreements reached in negotiations. Quite simply, the instruments, institutions, and process necessary to oversee the implementation of agreements were not effectively created during those meetings.* * *

Not only were instruments of implementation lacking, but also there was a noticeable absence of monitoring institutions.* * *

A final flaw in the structure of implementation was a lack of adequate trust-building steps. Trust-building steps are easily implementable agreements that are designed to demonstrate commitment to the process and to help develop a common stake in the negotiations. At the start of the talks, the government and the LTTE released political prisoners to show their good faith in the negotiating process. Aside from these initial actions, however, there were surprisingly few steps taken to build trust. The LTTE did release two captured policemen that had been engaged in a hunger strike, but only after significant urging from a non-governmental envoy that met with LTTE leaders in March 1995. The creation of confidence building exchanges simply was not systematically pursued in the Sri Lankan peace talks.

Moreover, the negotiation's approach of beginning economic reconstruction before discussing a political arrangement, left the LTTE with few responsibilities in which it could show its commitment to the peace process. Other than maintaining the cease-fire agreement, the LTTE could not demonstrate to the public any ostensible responsibilities that it could prove it was fulfilling. The LTTE's complaints regarding the government's performance were viewed by many as strategic rather than sincere, precisely because the LTTE had so few pro-active commitments that it needed to perform.

* * *

IV. Recommendations

The lessons extracted from the process of the 1994–95 peace talks imply needed reforms for productive dialogue in the future. In this section, six recommendations are presented for revising the process of the talks. The suggestions are directed toward practitioners of peace in Sri Lanka.

A. Employ Third–Party Mediation

Even in this brief presentation of obstacles in the process of the 1994–95 Sri Lankan peace talks, the deep mistrust and miscommunication between the government and the LTTE is apparent. Both sides have a history of such increasing polarization that even attempts to build rapport were misconstrued or understood in vastly different contexts. The status of the government's delegation is a prime example. As described earlier, the government's decision to name a pro-Tamil delegation was interpreted by the LTTE as a purposeful affront and rejection of parity because none of the negotiators had high official standing in the new government. After years of bitter conflict and rare and brief dialogue, the parties were unfamiliar and inexperienced in the process of communication in such a setting.

Mediators facilitate communication by assisting each side in framing and presenting their interests and positions, as well as receiving and interpreting messages. Successful negotiated settlements in ethno-political conflicts have been influenced decidedly by employing professional mediators. In the Sri Lankan context, a mediator could have impacted two features of the negotiation.

First, a mediator could have helped prevent harmful unilateral action. In the Sri Lankan peace talks, both sides took unilateral steps rather than joint action to advance the dialogue. In virtually every instance, however, such action, even if employed in good faith, had damaging ramifications. For instance, the government's action to announce a large scale reconstruction program for the Northern and Eastern Provinces was not warmly received by the LTTE, as the government expected. Rather, the LTTE viewed this unilateral action as a strategic move by the government to marginalize the LTTE from the popular investment program. The LTTE demanded that a joint commission be created so that policies and credit could be shared. The result was a delayed and ineffective reconstruction program that failed to please both sides. Although a mediator might not solve underlying tensions between, for example, the level of capital invested and the amount of credit received, a mediator can help the parties recognize conflicts that are not readily apparent to the parties because they are separated by such psychological, historical, and even geographical distance.

Similarly, a mediator can help the parties recognize zones of agreement. Perhaps the greatest concession by the LTTE in the 1994–95 peace talks was its change in position from a total commitment to the creation of an independent Tamil Eelam to the acceptance of a potential federal arrangement. This concession was major. Rarely do separatist guerrilla organizations accept possibilities less than full independence. This refusal partially explains why twentieth-century civil wars tend to last for many years, or even decades. Yet the significance of such a concession was not fully understood by the government and Sri Lankan people. The reflections of negotiators, journalists, and academics do not seem to appreciate the magnitude of this development. A mediator, by aiding the parties in communicating the difficulties and importance of such a concession, can help both sides identify and appreciate joint gains and common interests more effectively.

After the third round, both the government and the LTTE recognized that the progress of the talks was adversely affected by internal miscommunications. The government, in fact, suggested that a mediator be brought into the peace process. Ironically, the process of this suggestion underlines the fundamental difficulties that the parties experienced in the absence of a mediator. That is, the government, in a letter to Prabhakaran, and through public statements, suggested the use of an intermediary and, after private discussions with the French government, advocated that former French Ambassador to Haiti, Francois Michel, be named as mediator. The LTTE rejected the intermediary as a friend of the government, and perhaps more importantly, voiced opposition to a negotiation process where the consideration of a mediator was conducted unilaterally. The negotiations were so disconnected that even the consideration of a mediator was itself subject to harmful unilateral action.

As previously noted, the LTTE is also guilty of unilaterally injurious action. One example is its ultimatum demanding certain action on penalty of a resumption of hostilities. While a mediator may not be able to insist that parties continue to negotiate, a mediator can help the parties better understand the consequences and the gravity of their actions. By encouraging cooperation and by assisting the parties in shaping their positions as warnings rather than as threats, a mediator can help prevent the parties from inadvertently locking themselves into untenable positions.

A second important role for a mediator in the Sri Lankan context would be in assisting the implementation of agreements. A mediator can impact three dimensions of implementation. First, a mediator can draft the actual agreements that the parties reached during the negotiations. As stated earlier, one of the barriers to implementation in the 1995–95 peace talks was the absence of written, measurable guidelines, especially in regard to the lifting of the embargo. A mediator can not only help the parties realize the importance of such guidelines, but also would be uniquely positioned to do the drafting. Such assistance could provide greater objective criteria for judging and critiquing the behavior and commitments of the parties.

A mediator could also be instrumental in developing and overseeing monitoring institutions. Efforts to establish monitoring committees in the 1994–95 talks were hampered by an unclear process and poor coordination. These committees, in the end, could not function effectively, leaving each side to wage public relations campaigns against the other for violating the peace process. One of the principal advantages of employing a mediator is to include an objective party to monitor the actions of the parties and to speak out against violations. A mediator can help to develop an expansive framework for ensuring the parties' commitments. For instance, despite the attempt to create monitoring committees for the cease-fire, there was little effort to develop independent monitoring of the embargo. Undertaking such an enterprise might not be exceedingly difficult. A few observers at relevant checkpoints could have helped the parties to identify problems and to discourage violations. Moreover, the use of an objective and independent party to discover and to relay such information can mitigate the bitterness and suspicion that accompanies complaints in the absence of a mediator. As developers of monitoring institutions, mediators bring legitimacy and independent pressure on the implementation of the agreements reached.

Finally, mediators can help the parties design internal dispute resolution techniques for overcoming impasses in the peace process. In the 1994–95 talks, stumbling blocks were typically dealt with through increasingly threatening letters and ultimatums. No discussions took place, before or during the negotiations, to consider how the parties should approach impasses. A professional mediator at the very least can help the parties consider different options for moving the dialogue forward. Such options include a secret summit between more senior representatives, direct contact between the leadership, or a delay in the negotiations in which the parties are instructed to refine positions and to suggest alternatives. There are numerous approaches to handling impasses and a professional mediator can guide the parties to explore options. Again, such a role by no means ensures more productivity. It does, however, create a more carefully and deliberately constructed process which in turn makes it more difficult for the parties to resort to violence once again.

B. Develop an Operating Framework

For peace talks to succeed, it is essential that they are structured around a mandate of common objectives. The attempt to develop such a mandate will inform the parties early on if there is enough general agreement to expect tenable peace negotiations. Should such efforts fail to identify zones of agreement, then full peace talks are not likely to be worthwhile and may in fact be counter-productive. Because such face-to-face peace talks are rare and require the initiation of extraordinary developments, a missed opportunity could result in a degeneration of communication and a further distancing between the parties. This occurrence, unfortunately, has been the Sri Lankan experience. Exploratory talks and open exchanges are needed prior to the official talks and ensuing public scrutiny to enable the parties to reach broad zones of agreement before full peace negotiations can take place.

* * *

C. Communicate Through Non–Written Means and Establish a Hotline Option

* * *

In addition to in-person, senior level negotiation, the government and the LTTE need to create regular, open lines of communication to provide an alternative process for continuing the peace dialogue. A hotline, for instance, between the leadership of the LTTE and the government can serve the same intended purpose of letters—to jump-start stalled talks, to express the importance of issues, and to appeal for appropriate action. Although negotiations remain the more effective method of communication and ought to be the focus of any peace process, a hot-line can provide a second avenue for exchange and explanation between the parties in urgent situations.* * *

D. Use Non–Public Dialogue

The type of exploratory talks that this Article advocates as a precursor to actual peace talks may not be politically feasible or desirable if held publicly. The political maneuvering between the government and the LTTE, and the pressures on each to claim victory for its respective constituency and to present favorable national and international images seriously undermines the open, honest, and creative exchanges necessary for a successful negotiation. In Sri Lanka, holding such public exploratory talks could irresponsibly generate deep expectations, which, in turn, would make exploratory talks even more difficult and guarded. To minimize such outside pressures and to avoid creating unrealistic expectations, exploratory talks may be more effective if held secretly.

---

5. ISSUES OF JUSTICE AND FAIRNESS IN INTERNATIONAL NEGOTIATIONS

There is a great deal of debate about the extent to which justice and fairness norms should influence international negotiations.[14] The traditional view based on the realist tradition of international law rejects the relevance of these norms on the ground that there is no universal criterion of justice through which outcomes should be judged. Realists argue that power relationships are relevant when considering outcome.[15] Recent scholarship, particularly in the area of international trade, suggests, however, that justice norms, including notions of procedural justice, do influence international negotiations both in the initial agenda-setting stage, the actual bargaining phases, and throughout the implementation stage.[16]

Notes and Questions

1. The Women's Coalition was formed in April 1996 in Northern Ireland by a group of women from all walks of life, with different political orientations, and who participated in different religious traditions. In order to run for election as a Coalition member, there were two essential qualifications: (1) candidates had to have views on the issues and problems facing them and their community and (2) they had to be willing to seek a political accommodation that was inclusive of all interests. Unlike most of the other political parties that participated in the Peace Negotiations, the Women's Coalition did not represent a particular sectional interest. Under joint, rather than single leadership, it concentrated on three basic issues: inclusion and accommodation, equality, and human rights. All actions were informed by these principles, and every woman participating in the election for the Coalition signed a pledge to uphold them.

How would the problem-solving principles of accommodation, inclusion, and relationship-building employed by the Women's Coalition during the

---

14. *See* ZARTMAN, PREVENTIVE NEGOTIATION, *supra* note 3, at 100.

15. CECILIA ALBIN, JUSTICE AND FAIRNESS IN INTERNATIONAL NEGOTIATION 4 (2001).

16. *Id.* at 100–40.

peace negotiations in Northern Ireland be transferable to other negotiations involving religious and ethnic conflicts in deeply divided societies? Would these principles have relevance for the 1994–95 negotiations in Sri Lanka?

2. Under what circumstances would the techniques used by the Women's Coalition Party during the peace negotiations in Northern Ireland not be helpful in a conflict situation?

3. As discussed earlier, conflict often does not lie in objective reality but in the parties' perceptions of what is at stake. What role did perceptions play in the Sri Lankan conflict and to what extent did they act as barriers to the negotiated resolution of the conflict?

4. Identify some of the psychological barriers to the Sri Lankan peace negotiations. How might they have been overcome?

5. The author emphasizes the *ad hoc* manner in which the Sri Lankan peace negotiations were conducted and criticizes the negotiators' use of letters. What advice would you have given on the structure the negotiations if you had been consulted as a process expert? Would e-mail have been an appropriate vehicle of communication?

6. Negotiators often engage in informal activities to humanize the negotiation process. Why is the humanizing process important in negotiations? Would sharing meals have made a difference in the Sri Lankan peace negotiations of 1994–95? Can you think of other informal activities that could humanize the negotiation process?

7. Both the Northern Ireland peace negotiations and Sri Lankan 1994–95 peace negotiations were affected by positional and hard-bargaining strategies. To what extent are hard-bargaining tactics and strategies influenced by culture?

8. There has been a great deal of discussion about the role of justice in the peace-building process in conflict-ridden societies. Much less consideration has been given to the role of justice norms during actual negotiations. A recent study of the Rambouillet/Paris negotiations begins to fill the empirical void. Germany, France, United States, United Kingdom, Russia and Italy recommended these negotiations in 1999 to resolve the Kosovo conflict. NATO supported the negotiations and agreed to stop its use of force while they were being conducted. The final peace terms were integrated into UN Security Council Resolution No. 1244. In discussing the role that justice played in these failed negotiations, one author has stated that the failure to incorporate the norms of justice into the negotiation process made it difficult to achieve a lasting peace. Paul R. Williams, *The Role of Justice in Peace Negotiations, in* POST-CONFLICT JUSTICE 115 (M. Cherif Bassiouni ed., 2002). What justice norms might have made a difference in the failed Sri Lankan peace negotiations of 1994–95?

9. To what extent do the barriers to negotiation described by Professor Mnoonkin in Chapter 2, have relevance in the Sri Lankan negotiations of 1994–95?

C. INTERNATIONAL MEDIATION

1. MEDIATION IN PUBLIC DISPUTES

Like negotiation, mediation has an important place in the conduct of international conflict resolution. It is a form of assisted negotiation and functions as a catalyst to achieving negotiated settlements—parties who are incapable of resolving their conflicts seek third-party assistance in their negotiations. Although mediation is listed in Article 33 of the United Nations Charter as a procedure used by *States* to manage disputes, *ethnic groups* within States increasingly resort to mediation as a means of conflict resolution. The complexity and violence of ethnic conflict pose a significant challenge to practitioners of mediation methodologies.

The practice of public international mediation is far-reaching in scope and also in the number of actors it affects. It ranges from various forms of informal assistance, such as problem-solving workshops, to formal interventions by States, international, regional, and transnational organizations, and individuals. While efforts to reach consensus on a universal definition of mediation have been as unsuccessful in the international arena as they have been in domestic settings, it is possible to identify some common characteristics of mediation and mediator activities in the international context. In the following excerpt, Jacob Bercovitch proposes a set of uniform characteristics.

JACOB BERCOVITCH, ED., INTRODUCTION: PUTTING MEDIATION IN CONTEXT

Studies in International Mediation 5 (2002).

* * *

1. Mediation is an extension and continuation of the parties' own conflict management efforts.

2. Mediation involves the intervention of an individual, group or organization into a dispute between two or more actors.

3. Mediation is a non-coercive, non-violent and ultimately non-binding form of intervention.

4. Mediation turns a dyadic relationship into a triadic interaction of some kind. By increasing the number of actors from two to three, mediation effects considerable structural changes and creates new focal points for an agreement.

5. A mediator enters a dispute in order to affect, change, resolve, modify or influence it in some way.

6. Mediators bring with them, consciously or otherwise, ideas, knowledge, resources and interests of their own, or of the group they represent. Mediators are often important actors with their own assumptions and agendas about the dispute in question. Mediators can often be both interested and concerned parties.

7. Mediation is a voluntary form of intervention. This means the parties retain their control over the outcome (if not always the process) of their dispute, as well as their freedom to accept or reject mediation or mediator's proposals.

8. Mediation operates on an *ad hoc* basis only.

---

2. MEDIATION PRINCIPLES AND CONCEPTS

In considering the general characteristics of effectiveness in mediation, it is important to remember that, depending upon the length and intensity of a conflict, parties value different attributes in a mediator. For example, in studies of the use of mediation in cases of deadly conflict, researchers found that the value added by mediators was procedural, rather than substantive and that impartiality was the attribute most valued by the parties to the conflict.[17] In other contexts, such as the Vatican's mediation of the century-long conflict between Chile and Argentina over the Beagle Channel, the mediator's patience was considered the most desirable virtue.

The term "multi-party" mediation refers to the involvement of several third-parties in the resolution of a conflict. Multiple interventions can take place either simultaneously or throughout the life of a conflict.[18] The post-Cold War era has witnessed significant growth in the practice of multi-party mediation as regional coalitions, international organizations, and transnational organizations have become increasingly committed to containing violent conflict. However beneficial such efforts may be, the combination of diverse groups and conflicting agendas pose serious coordination problems. International scholars have observed that the challenge to leadership is a daunting one:

> Experience in such varied places as the former Yugoslavia, Somalia, Cyprus, Mozambique, Central American, and Central Africa points to the growing need for comprehensive thinking and coherence of unity of action. While it may be gratifying to professionals and specialists in various types of third party intervention to imagine that each can operate unburdened by the other's baggage and free from heavy-handed coordination mechanisms, the reality is that chaotic interventions will produce at best random results.[19]

---

17. Melanie C. Greenberg et al., Words Over War: Mediation and Arbitration to Prevent Deadly Conflict 344 (Carnegie Commission 2000).

18. *See* Chester A. Crocker et al., Herding Cats: Multi-Party Mediation in a Complex World 10 (1999) [hereinafter Chester A. Crocker et al, Herding Cats].

19. Chester A. Crocker, Fen Osler Hampson & Pamela R. Aall, *Two's Company But Is Three a Crowd? Some Hypotheses about Multiparty Mediation, in* Studies in International Mediation 228, 251 (Jacob Bercovitch ed., 2002) [hereinafter Bercovitch, International Mediation].

Leverage refers to a mediator's power to exert pressure on the parties to persuade them to accept a particular proposal.[20] The tactics of exerting power and leverage differ with different mediators and what constraints are imposed upon them. States, super-powers, regional, transnational, and international organizations have different types of resources that can increase leverage. Scholars have identified several types of resources that mediators can bring to the table including the powers related to reward, coercion, expertise, legitimacy and information.[21] In order to be successful, mediators must have leverage. Whether leverage is of the "carrot" or "stick" variety depends largely upon the mediator's motivation and external political influence.

The use of mediator leverage is invariably linked with mediator neutrality and impartiality. One of the longstanding characteristics of Western mediation practice is adherence to the value of mediator impartiality. The *Standards of Conduct for Mediators* identify impartiality as a central principle of mediation practice.[22] Frequently, scholars use the term impartiality interchangeably with neutrality, and this confluence has caused considerable confusion in practice. Impartiality implies an absence of bias or favoritism. Strictly speaking, a neutral mediator has no power over the parties and no personal stake in the outcome.

Whether mediator neutrality is possible in the circumstances of public international mediation is doubtful. As Jacob Bercovitch has observed: "Any intervention that turns a dyad into a triad simply cannot be neutral."[23] In the context of multi-party mediation,[24] some scholars believe that mediators should impose a settlement where they have the power to do so or where the parties share a consensus for settlement.[25] In cases of armed conflict, scholars have further observed that neutrality may be unworkable or that mediators may be only partially effective:

> ... armed conflicts are cross-cultural, typically involving estranged communities with a lack of understanding for the competing goals and interests of the other parties involved. Consequently, an independent third party without a vested interest in the outcome, utilizing a structure not in tune with the context of the mediation, will reach a partial settlement at best.[26]

20. Marieke Kleiboer, *Great Power Mediation: Using Leverage to Make Peace, in id.* at 127.

21. *See* BERCOVITCH, INTERNATIONAL MEDIATION, *supra* note 19, at 240.

22. STANDARD II, JOINT CODE, STANDARDS OF CONDUCT FOR MEDIATORS, ADOPTED BY THE AMERICAN BAR ASSOCIATION, AMERICAN ARBITRATION ASSOCIATION, AND THE SOCIETY OF PROFESSIONALS IN DISPUTE RESOLUTION (1994). The proposed 2005 revision of the Standards by the American Arbitration Association, American Bar Association and Association for Conflict Resolution, the successor organization to the Society of Professionals in Dispute Resolution, retains the emphasis on impartiality.

23. JACOB BERCOVITCH, THE STRUCTURE AND DIVERSITY OF MEDIATION 6 in INTERNATIONAL RELATIONS: MULTIPLE APPROACHES TO CONFLICT MANAGEMENT (Jacob Bercovitch and Jeffrey Rubin eds., 1992).

24. CHESTER A. CROCKER ET AL., HERDING CATS, *supra* note 18, at 3–14.

25. CHESTER A. CROCKER ET AL., HERDING CATS, *supra* note 18, at 52.

26. John D. Feerick, *The Peace–Making Role of a Mediator*, 19 OHIO ST. J. DISP. RES. 229, 241 (2003).

Finally, empirical studies suggest that mediator bias can allow the mediator to influence the parties to arrive at a positive outcome.[27]

3. MODELS OF INTERNATIONAL MEDIATION PRACTICE

There is no clear consensus on appropriate or uniform models of mediation practice. Domestic ADR literature is replete with debates about evaluative and facilitative, directive and non-directive forms of mediation. The evaluative or directive mediator engages in a wide set of activities ranging from offering minimal suggestions to outright manipulation, while the facilitative, non-directive mediator focuses more upon helping the parties to communicate with each other.

Similar models and debates exist in international mediation practice. For example, under a structuralist model of mediation—a form of mediation that is like evaluative mediation—mediators operate with multiple sources of leverage in addition to their traditional powers of persuasion. Zartman and Touval describe such leverage as including: extraction, the power to produce an attractive position from each party; termination, the ability to withdraw from the mediation; deprivation, the ability to withhold resources from one side or to shift them to the other; and gratification, the ability to add resources to the outcome.[28] This social-psychological model, which is similar to the facilitative or non-directive mediation model, emphasizes some tenets of problem-solving negotiation by focusing upon the underlying needs of the parties and creating opportunities for enhanced communication, changed attitudes, and creative decision-making.[29]

In the following excerpt, the author discusses a predominant American mediation model, what she labels, "Neutral, Low–Power Mediation," and illustrates its weakness when utilized in situations of violence, power asymmetry, and military crisis.

MELANIE GREENBERG, MEDIATING MASSACRES: WHEN "NEUTRAL, LOW–POWER" MODELS OF MEDIATION CANNOT AND SHOULD NOT WORK

19 Ohio State Journal on Dispute Resolution 185 (2003).

* * *

Mediation is such a universal dispute resolution process, used in so many formal and informal settings around the world, that it is impossible to make a claim for American dominance of the field or American hegemony over any particular type of mediation. American diplomats use

---

27. Peter J. Carnevale & Sharon Arad, *Bias and Impartiality in International Mediation*, in RESOLVING INTERNATIONAL CONFLICTS: THE THEORY AND PRACTICE OF MEDIATION 39–51 (Jacob Bercovitch ed., 1996).

28. I. William Zartman & Saadia Touval, *International Mediation in the Post–Cold War Era*, in MANAGING GLOBAL CHAOS: SOURCES OF AND RESPONSES TO INTERNATIONAL CONFLICT 455 (Chester A. Crocker *et al.* eds., 1996).

29. Crocker et al., *Two's Company But Is Three a Crowd?*, BERCOVITCH, INTERNATIONAL MEDIATION, *supra* note 19.

such a wide range of mediation styles in their mediation of international armed conflict (from Richard Holbrooke at one extreme, using NATO force as a backdrop to his muscular persuasion of the parties at Dayton, to George Mitchell in Northern Ireland, using only the force of his will and perseverance to influence the parties to reach the Good Friday Agreement), that there is no way to single out a typically American style.

However, there is one form of mediation that dominates the domestic landscape of American mediation, which mediators have used with wildly mixed results to resolve international armed conflict. This form of mediation, which I call "Neutral–Low Power Mediation" [hereinafter NLP mediation], would be instantly recognizable to anyone involved in a law school mediation seminar, a victim-offender mediation program, a community mediation program, a divorce mediation, a labor mediation, or a peer mediation program in an elementary school. While NLP mediation is neither a strictly American invention, nor exclusive to American conflicts, its pre-eminent role in the landscape of mediation in this country is extraordinary. . . .

II.   Characteristics of NLP Mediation

The hallmark of NLP mediation is a mediator whose primary role is to help the parties in their own communication and negotiation. This form of mediation is typically an extension of the parties' own bilateral or multilateral negotiations, rather than a forum in which the mediator tries to browbeat the parties into agreement, or to push through solomonic judgments.

Within an NLP mediation, the roles of the mediator and parties are fairly circumscribed. The mediator can show a strong hand in shaping the process of the mediation, but not in influencing a particular outcome. Specifically:

- The mediator is expected to be neutral, with no bias toward any of the parties.
- The mediator typically brings no resources of his or her own and does not have power beyond moral persuasion to coerce a party into action.
- The mediator has full control of the mediation process, though parties usually have the power to accept or reject ground rules at the start of the mediation.
- The mediator keeps confidences and does not have the discretion to impart confidential information, even when it might benefit the parties.
- The mediator can ensure fair process but is not expected to impose a solution on the parties (though the mediator might suggest potential solutions, based on the parties' description of their own interests and potential areas of agreement).
- The mediator can help balance power dynamics within the mediation (for example, ensuring that each party gets equal

time to talk, making sure each party has the resources to attend particular meetings, etc.) but cannot unilaterally take measures to render a party more or less powerful in an absolute sense.

The parties, too, have obligations and powers within the NLP mediation:

- Parties are expected not to "forum shop" during the course of the mediation (though they may have recourse to the courts if mediation breaks down).

- Parties either help set the ground rules or agree to the mediator's ground rules.

- Parties are expected to participate in good faith, not using the mediation as a delaying tactic, venue for stonewalling, or means solely for extracting confidential information from another party.

- Parties agree to keep information revealed in the mediation confidential (unless there are agreements otherwise).

- Mediation may or may not be binding, depending on the context, the rules governing the mediation, and the desires of the parties.

- The solution "belongs" to the parties, and not to the mediator.

There are great advantages to NLP mediation. The process is transparent, nimble, and procedurally fair. It allows for creativity and catharsis. The outlook of NLP mediation is egalitarian and optimistic, with an emphasis on developing a roadmap for future action. These characteristics, especially when combined with the ability of participants to pursue more binding, judicial processes if the mediation breaks down, make NLP mediation a powerful and attractive tool for resolving a wide range of disputes.

However, there are disadvantages to NLP mediation, as well. NLP mediation is difficult to enforce, and does not work well to rein in spoilers. Procedural justice does not always lead to normative justice, and the lack of procedural safeguards can leave less powerful parties with no recourse. NLP mediation is not geared toward deep-seated societal conflict, which tends to require iterative, multi-level intervention, combining elements of muscular diplomacy, mediation, and grass roots initiatives.

The weaknesses of NLP mediation are amplified in contexts of violence, power asymmetry, and military crisis. In these situations, NLP mediation has the potential to be not only ineffective, but also morally suspect and dangerous. In the United States, NLP mediation is not used in cases of violent crime (victim-offender mediation does not encompass crimes such as assault, rape or murder), and tends not to be used in contexts where the power imbalances between parties are so blatant and inexorable that any mediated resolution would be tainted (for example, sexual harassment suits). Beyond the boundaries of the United States, the use of NLP mediation in situations of armed conflict has led, in at least two very high profile cases, to great human suffering on the ground and shame for the international community.

While NLP mediation is usually taught as a neutral, transparent process, it is actually quite value-laden. Mediation often has a strong forward-looking component, rather than exclusive focus on adjudicating past wrongs. The mediator presumes good faith on the part of the parties. Issues of culture and power tend to be subjugated to a more neutral definition of interests and joint goals, even in more transformative settings.

These values and presumptions, which make the mediation process nimble and forward-looking in many contexts, can be disastrous in situations of deep-rooted, intractable conflict, in which leaders manipulate international intervention to suit their own strategic aims. Parties, even when they profess to be in good faith, often continue to shift the balance of the power on the ground, through violence, as the mediation is taking place. With the lack of an international police force, no entity can prosecute this extra-mediation violence, and the mediator must come to terms with the new power realities as the mediation unfolds. Power differentials between (and even among) the parties can hinder negotiation and can lead to coerced, ineffectual, or unjust agreements. The implementation of mediated peace agreements can be derailed by resentful, less powerful parties, or "spoilers" who never took part in the negotiations.

---

4.   TIMING OF MEDIATION INTERVENTIONS

In general, disputing parties are not ready for mediation until they have an incentive to accept the mediator's assistance.[30] Under what conditions will disputing parties accept mediation and be willing to move forward to agreement once they are involved in the mediation process? This question implicates theories of mediation readiness and ripeness. Zartman describes ripeness as a "mutually hurting stalemate" where both parties have sufficient strength to cause some damage to the other but neither has the capability of achieving an unequivocal victory. The stalemate may not be a fixed time but occur through a series of opportunities. A somewhat broader "readiness theory" offered by Pruitt suggests that motivation and optimism are the key factors in determining when mediators should enter a conflict. According to Pruitt, this moment exists "when the parties are maximally motivated to settle but are having difficulty meeting or going forward—when they are fed up with the conflict but are unable to escape it."[31]

---

30. I. WILLIAM ZARTMAN, RIPE FOR RESOLUTION: CONFLICT AND INTERVENTION IN AFRICA (1989).

31. Dean Pruitt, *Mediator Behavior and Success in Mediation, in* Bercovitch, STUDIES IN INTERNATIONAL MEDIATION, *supra* note 19, at 50.

Linked to the issues of readiness and ripeness are questions of "missed opportunities" discussed in the following excerpt:

I. WILLIAM ZARTMAN, COWARDLY LIONS: MISSED OPPORTUNITIES FOR DISPUTE SETTLEMENT

18 Ohio State Journal on Dispute Resolution 1, 2–8, 10–15, 19 (2002).

* * *

II. Opportunities

Opportunities are favorable moments for achieving a purpose—a suitable combination of conditions for accomplishing a goal. The opportune moment to do something is not just "whenever," but is contextually determined in relation to the conflict. Interventions require an "entry point" or occasion that invites foreign action. Need alone does not justify action; there must be some definable opening for external parties to enter, and if there is not, it must be created. Opportunities or entry points can be defined by events or by context.

Events that require or justify a mediatory reaction can be either scheduled or unscheduled. In a few instances, a scheduled event such as an election requires a response that could make a major difference in the subsequent course of actions. Examples include the fraudulent count announced after the 1985 elections in Liberia, where American rejection would have triggered both internal and external reactions; or the cancellation of the November 1987 elections in Haiti, which occasioned a cut in aid but little more; or the restoration of Aristide in 1994, which was not followed by measures to restore the state as well; or the 1996 elections in Yugoslavia, where the opposition received polite notice from Washington but no help.

More frequently, unscheduled events or crises invite an external response. The 1995 shelling of Sarajevo galvanized the NATO allies into intervention in Bosnia, and the 1991 advances of the Eritrean and Tigrean rebels on Addis Ababa brought in United States mediation. But neither the 1988 massacre of dispossessed Somali tribesmen in Hargeisa, the 1991 and 1993 military and civilian riots in Kinshasa and other Zairean cities, the 1995 and 1996 pogroms of targeted ethnic groups in the Kivus of eastern Zaire, the 1991 military coup against the elected Haitian government in Port au Prince, nor the 1994 unconstitutional installation of a new president in Haiti brought any effective response. In an event-defined opportunity, scheduled or unscheduled, the response must be immediate; otherwise, the opening closes and the justification appears lame.

When there is no event, scheduled or unexpected, to require a response, the opportunity is to be found more broadly in the context of the conflict. Significantly, this is the more frequent case. The established model indicates that a ripe moment for initiating mediation is composed of a mutually hurting stalemate, out of which parties seek or are responsive to help in extricating themselves. Such a stalemate was seized on ... by the All–African Council of Churches in 1972, when the southern and northern Sudanese armies bogged down in civil war; by the United States in 1987, when the UNITA–South African and Cuban–Angolan armies checked each other at Cuito Carnevale; by Portugal in 1990, when the opposing forces in Angola fought to an impasse at Mavinga; by Sant' Egidio and supporters in 1990, when drought and destruction brought the Mozambican civil war to a deadlock.

Parties to conflicts have repeatedly allowed ripe moments to slip away as evidenced by the following: in Lebanon in March 1978, July 1982 and March 1984, factions engaged in a civil war were deadlocked and hurting but not helped out of their impasse; in Liberia in June 1990, in April 1992 or July 1993, parties were brought to a ceasefire but no effective measures for ending the conflict. Other instances when ripe moments for conflict resolution were missed existed in June 1990 when the Yugoslav republics were deadlocked over the future of the federation, in October 1998 when the Serbian government and the Kosovars were at an impasse over the Kosovo issue, and in Somalia in March–June 1991 just after Siad Barre's fall. A mutually hurting stalemate may motivate conflicting parties themselves to negotiation but it is often the vehicle for third party intervention if the parties are not motivated to seize the moment on their own.

But in some instances, there was only a soft stalemate with a painful but bearable effect, and the interveners were required to create an event or an opportunity to justify their action. Intervention therefore had to be sold to the conflicting parties themselves (as well as to the interveners' public); it was a lifebuoy thrown to a swimmer rather enjoying the excitement of the surf and oblivious to the approaching tidal wave that was visible to the thrower. The image shows that a soft stalemate requires third party intervention, even more than does a hard or hurting stalemate. In these instances, the opportunity is artificial, to be constructed out of the unstable conflict or impending collapse before it really blows up at a less convenient time for both conflicting parties and vulnerable bystanders. "You're going to be involved willy-nilly," noted Joseph Alpher of the Mideast conflict in 2001, "and so it is better to take the initiative than be dragged in by some dramatic event, which ... is almost certainly going to be a negative one."

Finally, there are moments of opportunity when the conflict undergoes a momentary calm, opening the possibility of creating a longer lasting, more stable outcome. It is generally evident that measures are needed to make the pause in the conflict permanent by addressing the causes of the conflict and establishing mechanisms to prevent its reoccurrence. The opportunity may come from an informal lull in the conflict, from a more explicit ceasefire, or even from a meeting of the parties. The point is that it offers an opening for specific measures for it is not self-perpetuating and will fall apart at the next incident if not seized and solidified. In half the instances, third parties took advantage of a momentary lull to summon the conflicting parties to a conference to fill the political vacuum and reinstitute the state, but then failed in reality because they did not invest commensurate energy in follow-through.

* * *

Missed opportunities are not merely missed moments; they tend to be failures to gain entry into a whole phase of a conflict, after which entry is no longer or much more rarely possible, and the phase changes into something less penetrable. Opportunities are not revolving doors, where entry appears at regular intervals. They constitute a period of time in the life of the conflict when preventive diplomacy is possible and after which entry becomes much more difficult. Not only opportunities, but whole periods of opportunity were missed in Yugoslavia, Liberia, Haiti, Somalia, and Zaire–Congo. Consequently, these countries and their citizens, the regions, and the external powers have had to live with the consequences.

III. Interest

Need is not opportunity, but opportunity is not interest. For an opportunity to be seized or missed, a third party must have an interest in involvement. The enormous losses that missed opportunities entail, and their effect on regional or global relations, provide a humanitarian interest in intervention. Realists, to the contrary, would argue that humanitarian interest is not a negligible concern for the United States. Whether in the Cold War or in regional conflicts, states act to protect and advance their values, not just their structural position. The importance of human life to the American system of values gives humanitarian interest a special salience. As American inaction on the Rwandan genocide in 1994 and official attempts to avoid the "G-word" demonstrate, humanitarian interest and the value of human life anywhere is not absolute, but it is strong. Joseph Nye has indicated that "[a] democratic definition of the national interest does not accept the distinction between a morality-based and an interest-based foreign policy. Moral values are simply intangible interests," and British Foreign Secretary Robin Cook has denied the distinction between "promoting our values [and] pursuing our interests."

Incredibly, the fate of Lebanon, Somalia, Zaire, Yugoslavia, Liberia and Haiti have, on crucial occasions, not been considered of interest to the United States, Europe, or their own regions, nor has the importance of their announced collapse to the fate of their region in general been deemed worthy of motivating U.S., European or neighbors' involvement. If the loss of 500,000 Yugoslav lives, 500,000 Somalis, 150,000 Liberians, 120,000 Lebanese, 100,000 Zaireans, and 5,000 Haitians as a result of direct killings at the hands of their own countrymen does not provide a compelling humanitarian interest, it is not because these losses were not foreseeable and foretold. If humanitarian interest was not enough motivation, the importance of each case in regard to American and other Western foreign policy values such as good governance, democracy, regional stability, economic accountability and access, and external responsibility should have been.

But even for those who hold to the distinction between values and interests, there is a national or strategic interest in managing deadly conflict and state collapse. Collapsed states tend to be vacuums, drawing in outside forces to fill the empty political space. That space is then occupied by regional conflict, perpetuating the state collapse, exacerbating the domestic conflict, extending the regional conflict, and forcing extra-regional powers to take sides against their interests. If the struggle to occupy the vacuum engages neighbors in pursuit of their interests, it is broadly in the interest of outside powers to see the collapsed state recover and take care of its own affairs.

* * *

IV. Early Awareness and Early Action

The strongest reason for early action, when options are still available, is that later action is more expensive, forced and constrained; inaction is costly in its consequences. In all of the cases, the US—to focus on the leading country—was obliged to enter the conflict late, after having avoided chances to take lesser action earlier. When it finally adopted a policy, substantial damage had already been done. Many of the deaths and displacements were accompanied by frightful human abuses—rapes, massacres, destruction of homes and places of worship, and other brutalities. These are some of the costs that need to be calculated in making the decision not to act.

These losses had even greater secondary effects. Socially and psychologically, they left deeply scarred and wounded people.* * *

Society was also shattered by the conflict. Population displacement destroyed the social tissue, traditional norms of respect and authority were trashed, and social institutions such as church and school were left in ruins. Social geography, patterns, and structures were seriously altered in generally unproductive and antagonistic ways; societies generally underwent leveling and proletarianizing, with massive influxes into the cities. The new leadership tended to appeal to, be representative of, and derive its support from this new social sector. The youth suffered tremendously in all of the countries, with heavy implications for the future. Education was interrupted, unemployment became endemic, drugs took hold, and child soldiers were scarred in their formative years.* * *

Furthermore, the conflicts destroyed national as well as personal economies. It was not simply that some buildings were destroyed and needed rebuilding, or that some people lost their jobs or even savings. The entire national economic systems of the six countries were demolished.* * *

Normally the list of costs stops here, or earlier, but the collapse of a third sector—the political sector-also bears heavy consequences. When the state is privatized, as in Zaire/Congo and Liberia, or pulverized, as in Somalia, or drawn and quartered, as in Yugoslavia, or contested, as in Lebanon, or hijacked, as in Haiti, it loses its legitimacy as well as its ability to function. Collapsed states are not simply rebuilt like a fallen statehouse portico; they need reconstruction from the foundations. Not only is it a long and complex job, but it is also a void that foreign forces and international institutions cannot adequately fill. . . .

V. Excuses

In all thirty instances of missed opportunities in the six collapsing states, early warnings were more than adequate, proposed measures would likely have been successful, and the cost of collapse in terms of lives and money may have been much less than the final actual costs. In half the instances, the policy proposals involve merely strengthening initiatives that have already been taken. So why were the opportunities missed?

The most specific reason is that the measures were contrary to the policy supporting the status quo, even as the status quo was falling apart. The United States long held to the policy of "Mobutu or Chaos" and the whole Troika worked hard to make that mantra come true. Like Mobutu, Doe was long viewed as a bulwark against communism, and his regime's assistance in giving the United States a toehold in West Africa was viewed with gratitude. In Haiti, U.S. policy and opinion was sharply divided between supporters of Haitian business and advocates of Haitian populist democracy; this dulled the thrust of any effort to secure a rapid return of President Aristide. Thus, in many cases, the safe status quo was preferred to risky change and as a consequence, these states continued to slide down the slippery slope toward collapse. A well-crafted alternative that reduces risk and follows through with supports and controls is needed to counter the costly policy favoring the status quo.

Another reason opportunities were missed was a fear of casualties. The official fear of military deaths was encouraged by the Bush administration as early as 1991 by the manner the Gulf War was touted; the fear was then played to the hilt by the Clinton administration. Instead of developing such themes as leadership, post-Cold War order, U.N. usefulness to American objectives, regional security regimes, protection of human rights, and values as interest, the United States, joined by other Western countries, hid behind its own rhetoric about casualties even when the danger of deaths was minimal. As a result, it allowed forces of disorder and spirals of violence to prove its point. A little exemplary firmness in Liberia, Somalia, and Yugoslavia in 1990 or in Liberia, Somalia, Zaire, Yugoslavia, and Haiti in 1991 would have involved few or no troops and would have forestalled much larger troop use and danger later. The absence of such a response showed the forces of disorder in these countries that their actions were unchecked. Thus, a firm response not only inhibits specific disorder in the short run, but it also inhibits its escalation in the long run.

A third reason for the missed opportunities was a lack of mediation skills. Frequently, as in Lebanon, Liberia, and Somalia, mediation was attempted but failed because it was not well conducted. There were no skilled authoritative mediators, often because of a shortage of experience and training in the tough business of preventive diplomacy (especially in West Africa and the Middle East). Keeping the parties engaged, devising trade-offs, thinking through consequences and follow-through, working out details, installing dispute-resolution mechanisms, developing ties and relationships, were skills, which were absent in crucial conferences of the parties. Provision of a skilled mediator was required to complement the demarche.

Inhibitions also derived from Cold War considerations in the late 1980s and Gulf War concerns in the early 1990s. But usually Cold War inhibitions on the U.S. side were the result of a bogus calculation. Support and participation in the Damascus and Lausanne negotiations would have left the United States in a stronger position in the Middle East, particularly with Syria, which was claimed as an ally by the Soviet Union, but also with Saudi Arabia, Muslims, and Christians in Lebanon. The idea that Doe and Barre were bulwarks against communism in Africa, which was invoked to inhibit preventive diplomacy in 1985 and 1988, respectively, is farfetched especially in light of the fact that neither of their oppositions were communist.

The Gulf War blocked U.S. and U.N. attention to a number of promising demarches in two major directions. It monopolized official attentions, leaving no space for dealing with other issues, and it dominated the possibilities of building alliances and coalitions in 1991, since the United States was already too deeply in political debt to its allies on the Gulf front to be able to contract additional debts on other issues. Yet, the judgment that the United States can only handle one crisis at a time is simply not true in the absolute, since the United States has frequently been called on to deal with "two front" diplomacy. Yet, these very considerations should have worked in the other direction. Given that the proposed preventive diplomacy demarches were not of crisis magnitude, authority to deal with them should have been delegated and they should have been handled, with support from the Assistant Secretary and Regional Bureau level, before they became crises.

* * *

VI. Foreign Policy and International Relations

In the last analysis, the major reasons for missed opportunities lie at the feet of some of the leading tenets of conflict management in the post-Cold War era. These reasons include a paralyzing worry over mission creep, a fixation on exit strategy, a fear of military engagement and casualties, an aversion to "nation-building," and most broadly, an unwillingness to bear the responsibilities of international leadership in the post-Cold War era. These policies and attitudes have hampered effective action and allowed opportunities to slip away in blood, only to reappear as impositions at times when it is most difficult to adhere to them.

* * *

The major reasons for missed opportunities also lie at the feet of some of the leading tenets in the study of international relations, which in turn influence policymakers' thinking on what is possible and desirable. International relations theory is torn between the realist notions of state supremacy and the liberal and constructivist assumptions that the state is increasingly bypassed by a multitude of other actors. To the first, perhaps paradoxically, what is not a state does not matter, and to some, what is not a great power does not matter at all. The need to construct and support legitimate authority in the softer areas of the globe where it does not exist is not considered important to the interest of the major states. The liberals and constructivists do not do much better.

Notes and Questions

1. What is the mediator's role in neutral, low-power (NLP) mediation? Given the advantages and disadvantages of this mediation model, can you identify current conflicts where it would be helpful?

2. John Paul Lederach, a Mennonite scholar, offers a different view of the importance of timing in helping parties to resolve conflict. Instead of Zartman's focus on concepts of ripeness and seizing opportunities, Lederach looks toward the concept of cultivating relationships:

> The cultivation metaphor suggests that a deep respect for, and connection to, the context is critical for sustaining a change process that is moving from deadly expressions of conflict to increased justice and peace in relationships. The context of protracted deadly conflict, like soil, is the people, commonly shared geographies but often sharply differing views of history, rights and responsibilities, and the formation of perception and understandings based on cultural meaning structures. Cultivation is recognizing that ultimately the change process must be taken up, embraced, and sustained by people in these contests.

[Jean Paul Lederach, *Cultivating Peace: A Practitioner's View of Deadly Conflict and Negotiation*, in CONTEMPORARY PEACEMAKING: CONFLICT, VIOLENCE, AND PEACE PROCESSES 35 (John Darby & Roger MacGinty eds., 2003).]

What is your view on the relative importance of timing in resolving conflict? Of cultivating relationships? Are both views compatible?

3. Professor Melanie Greenberg has written that in Bosnia it was outside mediators who determined when the situation was ripe for resolution. Melanie C. Greenberg & Margaret E. McGuinness, *From Lisbon to Dayton: International Mediation and the Bosnia Crisis*, in WORDS OVER WAR: MEDIATION AND ARBITRATION TO PREVENT DEADLY CONFLICT 71 (Carnegie Commis-

sion 2000). To what extent does this assertion challenge Zartman's theory of ripeness?

4. Identify a conflict that resulted in human rights abuses. How might these abuses have been prevented or minimized with earlier intervention in accordance with Zartman's theory in *Cowardly Lions: Missed Opportunities for Dispute Settlement*?

5. After evaluating the outline of the thirty instances of missed opportunities identified in *Cowardly Lions: Missed Opportunities for Dispute Settlement*, identify some situations in the world today in which a conflict is ripe for resolution, specifically a situation that is ready and does not need to be artificially created. Is it easier to recognize these situations after they have been resolved?

6. Given the costs of later intervention, Zartman advocates early awareness and action. What prevents the United States from earlier engagement in conflict?

7. To what extent are economic considerations, which Zartman mentions only in passing, a determinant in the decision of a third-party nation to involve itself in international conflicts?

5. CASE STUDIES IN INTERNATIONAL MEDIATION

As you read the case studies of international mediation in the next section, consider the following questions: (1) To what extent are economic considerations a determinant in the decision of a third-party nation to involve itself in international conflicts? (2) Article 2 (Section 7) of the UN Charter honors the international law principle of sovereignty and territorial integrity that prevents international and regional organizations from becoming involved in the resolution of interstate conflicts such as the Eritrean War. At what point should the world community disregard the norms of sovereignty in favor of intervention to resolve conflict? How does Professor Zartman respond to claims of the sovereignty norm?

(a) Peacemaking Role of the Mediator

The fluidity of mediation practice in the international context gives mediators broad latitude in structuring and conducting the process. The following reading discusses Senator George Mitchell's role in mediating the peace talks that led to the Good Friday/Belfast Agreement in 1998 in Northern Ireland and his adaptation of American labor relations practices to the situation in Ireland.

JOHN D. FEERICK, THE PEACE–MAKING ROLE OF A MEDIATOR

19 Ohio State Journal on Dispute Resolution 229 (2003).

* * *

A. An Intractable Conflict

The conflict is often expressed in religious terms as a clash between Catholics and Protestants. To be sure, religion plays some part, as do lack of employment and other socio-economic factors. At the center of the conflict, however, is the issue of national identity. A great many Protestants want to keep Northern Ireland in union with the United Kingdom and, consequently, they are called Unionists. A great many Catholics favor Northern Ireland becoming part of the Republic of Ireland and thus are labeled Nationalists. Not every Protestant or Catholic in Northern Ireland, however, can be identified with these points of view. Nevertheless, these competing identities lead to divisions on political, social, and cultural levels. Intractable and incessant division is further perpetuated by a perceived threat each community has regarding the other.

Beginning in the 1980s and continuing through the mid–1990s, a number of important milestones occurred as a result of negotiations that took place between the British and Irish governments. These British–Irish agreements included: an Anglo–Irish Agreement in 1985, expressing a commitment that only the people of Northern Ireland could change its constitutional status; a Downing Street Declaration in 1993, setting out a general formula for participation in the peace talks by political parties associated with paramilitary organizations; and a Frameworks Document of 1995, creating the International Body on Decommissioning and setting a course for all-party negotiations. Also during this period the Irish and British governments had separate discussions with the political parties that had allegiances to them. Among these were discussions between the Irish government and the major Nationalist parties in the North, namely, the Social Democratic Labor Party and Sinn Fein (the political wing of the Irish Republican Army (IRA)). All of these discussions led to cease-fires in 1994 by the IRA and the Combined Loyalist Military Council. The British and Irish governments served a critical mediation function in laying the groundwork for the peace negotiations that began in June 1996.

Senator Mitchell's appointment in 1996 to chair the all-party talks was foreshadowed by his assignments in Northern Ireland in 1995, after leaving the United States Senate. First he was appointed by President Clinton to organize a trade and investment conference. Then he was chosen as one of three members of the International Body on Decommissioning established by the Frameworks Document of 1995. In the process he became familiar with Northern Ireland, its people, leaders, and history. Many in Northern Ireland also came to know him. Looking more closely at the peace talks as a possible case study of mediation at its best, one finds the most careful of attention given by Senator Mitchell to every aspect of the process.

In a word, Senator Mitchell's style was one of extreme sensitivity to the process, the rules adopted, the views and positions of the parties, and to the independence of his office. Although the selection by the British and Irish governments to chair the talks was objected to by some of the political parties, he was given many opportunities to demonstrate his independence and he did so. At the very outset, he agreed, in the face of strong Unionist objections, to change the rules that had been agreed to by the British and Irish governments for the talks. The Senator said, "I felt throughout the discussions that ultimately my ability to be effective would depend more upon my gaining the participants' trust and confidence than on the formal description of my authority."

The multi-party talks began with the development of a set of rules of procedure, which took almost two months to put in place. By July 1996 there was agreement on the rules of procedure, which included provisions dealing with non-compliance by a party with respect to the conditions for entering into the talks, the formula for voting on proposals, and the confidentiality of the talks. A period of several months then followed to develop a very brief and general agenda for the opening plenary session, and on October 15, agreement was reached. Once a general agenda had been established, substantive negotiations could begin, taking place along three tracks or strands. However the issue of decommissioning—Unionists wanted paramilitary arms to be given up before negotiations could begin—arose postponing substantive negotiations for some months.

During discussions on decommissioning and subsequent negotiations, Senator Mitchell and his colleagues conducted many meetings with the parties through the use of strands to deal with global kinds of issues, subcommittees, smaller group meetings, and informal and individual meetings. They constantly put questions to the parties, asking for their responses and positions, both orally and in writing. They sought to understand each party's needs and fears and then to communicate them to the other parties as well as allowing the parties to directly communicate with each other through various formats. They created options for the parties to consider, drew them into every aspect of the process, and used caucuses, shuttle diplomacy, and smaller group discussions to find areas of agreement. Plenary sessions were convened judiciously to receive reports, to have exchanges at times, and to deal with important issues affecting the talks that had arisen. By November 10, 1997, opening discussions were complete and the parties were ready to get into active negotiations. To jump-start the negotiations, Senator Mitchell created a document identifying the key issues for resolution to generate some give and take. As he noted, "only when all the issues were seen together could all the parties get a sense of where the necessary trade-offs and compromises might be made."

Throughout the negotiations, Senator Mitchell and his colleagues paid a great deal of attention to the importance of symbols, appearances, and ways to facilitate communications. For example, while most of the negotiations took place at Stormont, a suburb of Belfast, they were commenced in an undistinguished government office building rather than the building from which a Protestant-dominated Parliament once governed the North. Similarly, when some of the negotiations left Belfast, they were held in both London and Dublin so that both communities would not see a tilt in favor of the other. Care was also given to limiting the number of people who would be present at key meetings in order to encourage dialogue, and also to whether the presence of a stenographer or note taker might chill discussion. As the negotiations entered 1998, the agenda became more specific and the meetings more frequent with a deadline imposed to build a momentum toward an agreement. Senator Mitchell expressed the importance of a steadfast deadline in reaching an agreement.

I began to think about a deadline, earlier than the one at the end of May that Blair had already set . . . without a hard deadline these people just would not decide anything: the decisions are so fraught with danger for them that they would just keep talking and talking and talking. Eventually, this process would just peter out or, more likely, some dramatic outside event—some new atrocity—would just blow it up. Either way, it would fail. It had to be brought to an end; that was the only possible way to get an agreement. A deadline would not guarantee success, but the absence of a deadline would guarantee failure.

Eventually Easter weekend of 1998 was set as the deadline and the parties unanimously agreed. On April 10, 1998, after nearly two years of talks and negotiations, an agreement was reached.

The process reflected a number of approaches and mechanisms used in the field of American labor relations, such as committees and subcommittees, smaller group discussions, and the creation of committees in the final agreement for issues that were not capable of resolution at the point of the final agreement. Far more than format, location, and the like was the constant sensitivity of the Senator to each of the parties engaged in the process. He met with them frequently and separately over every aspect of the talks, made sure their views were understood and advanced, sought their suggestions for solutions, and circulated to them for comment drafts of documents containing questions, issues, and options. The respect he gave to each made it their process and inspired confidence in him and his colleagues.

The manner in which Senator Mitchell conducted himself throughout the talks made its success possible. For example, despite the confidentiality of the talks, leaks were commonplace, and yet, the parties came to understand that the Senator (and his colleagues) would make no exception for themselves regarding the confidential nature of the talks. This proved providential because when the first draft of the final agreement was circulated in April 1998, confidentiality was of critical importance and when Senator Mitchell demanded it at that point, the parties complied. Also interesting to note, in terms of the personal role of a mediator, is the tone struck by Senator Mitchell in his public statements. When he spoke to the press at different junctures, his accounts of the negotiations were terse, but he always expressed hope that an agreement could be found. Nothing was conveyed that could be misinterpreted or that exalted the role or importance of the mediator. Throughout, Senator Mitchell helped build toward an agreement by reminding the parties that the people wanted peace and that the alternative to an agreement was not acceptable.

Senator Mitchell's service as chair of the peace talks was, I believe, a testament to the viability of American mediation in international dispute resolution. He brought to his assignment extraordinary personal qualities (most importantly listening, patience, and perseverance) and superlative experience at the center of American politics. The discipline that he brought to his office and the respect he gave to each party engaged in the process are a model for anyone asked to mediate a dispute, whether or not in a context of armed conflict.

(b) Mediation of Armed Conflict

The following excerpt describes the Track II diplomacy efforts of the Carter Center's International Negotiation Network [INN] to mediate one of the longest civil wars in African history between the government of the People's Democratic Republic of Ethiopia (PDRE) and the Eritrean People's Liberation Front (EPLF) in 1989. A Peace Agreement signed in Algiers in 2000 finally resolved this seemingly intractable conflict. The mediation model employed was the use of an eminent person as the convenor.

DALE E. SPENCER & HONGGANG YANG, LESSONS FROM THE FIELD OF INTRA–NATIONAL CONFLICT RESOLUTION

67 Notre Dame Law Review 1495 (1992).

* * *

"The Forgotten War" is a label that has been applied to the conflict between the PDRE and the EPLF. It was one of the longest running civil wars in African history, raging for thirty years, and yet remained relatively unknown except to scholars and relief workers. In 1989, the INN spear-headed negotiations between the PDRE and the EPLF, seeking a peaceful resolution to the conflict. From the mediation process, the INN gained valuable experience applicable to both the theory and the practice of conflict resolution.

III.   THE PDRE/EPLF NEGOTIATIONS

A.   Historical Background

Ethiopia is one of Africa's oldest civilizations and the seat of Africa's symbol of the pacific resolution of conflicts—the Organization of African Unity ("OAU"). Over the last hundred years this loosely knit state has brought different nationalities (*e.g.*, Eritreans, Somalis, Oromos, Tigreans) under the imperial rule of an essentially feudalist Amharic ruling class.

Ethnic conflicts have been recurrent in Ethiopia where Eritrea, facing the political and cultural predominance of the Amharans, has had the strongest claim to self-determination. In recent history, both the Amharans and the Eritreans were victims of colonialism. Ethiopia was colonized for five years by the Italians, and Eritrea was under the colonial rule of Italy from the late 1880s until 1941. The 1889 treaty of Wuchale between Italy and Ethiopia established Eritrea's borders as they exist today. The Eritrean territory was a concession to the Italians in exchange for their agreement not to colonize other parts of Ethiopia.

For the last three decades, the Eritreans have waged a guerrilla campaign against the armies of Ethiopia. The resistance movement evolved into the EPLF. When asked for the three most important issues that must be resolved to attain peace, the EPLF answered "self-determination, self-determination, and self-determination." Conversely, when questioned about the principle behind its fight against the EPLF, the PDRE response was "national unity and sovereignty."

After years of perpetual civil war, Ethiopia is now among the poorest countries in the world, spending seventy percent of its Gross National Product for military needs while maintaining the largest standing army in sub-Saharan Africa. The losses for both Ethiopia and Eritrea have been staggering. Eritrean children go to school in caves underground, when possible. For three generations the Eritreans have experienced only a steady onslaught of bombing raids, death, and destruction. While the world watched in horror between 1984 and 1985, a deadly famine struck Ethiopia. Recurrent drought and famine continue to strike the region which lacks the necessary infrastructure development to adequately feed and care for its people.

B.   The Peace Talks

The INN began its concentration on the PDRE and the EPLF conflict almost a full year before initially convening the parties. Following a working session with a group of scholars, the INN Secretariat began an analysis of the historical, political, economic, and cultural aspects of the conflict. We tried to overcome the biases found in the written analyses and conducted a number of preliminary interviews with scholars, policy analysts, and relief agencies to gain knowledge and insight into the sociocultural differences of the parties. Later, we convened several highly targeted briefing sessions to discuss approaches and frameworks for a mediation initiative. One of the prerequisites for INN involvement is being invited in by all major parties. To meet directly with the leadership of both sides and explore opportunities for a peaceful solution, we made a field trip to the Horn of Africa in the spring of 1989.

As a result of our trip, both the PDRE and EPLF leadership extended invitations to begin a mediation process. We learned that both sides wished the international community to be informed of their negotiations. One of the initial conclusions was that the conflict was virtually intractable. At one level, our strategy was to devise and implement steps to transform the members of the negotiation team from warriors into problem solvers. At another level, we realized that because the parties were so entrenched in their adversarial roles, our best approach might be to create a process that would be used by the parties for their own purposes but which would result in a temporary cessation of the fighting, saving lives in the short term. We hoped that changing circumstances would lead to long-term options for peace.

The principal INN objectives in this effort were fourfold: to act as a catalyst, to create conditions for progress, to reach an agreement for an extended cease-fire, and to act where governments and regional organizations had been unable to act. We devised the multipath, multiphased approach discussed previously in order to meet these objectives.

In September, 1989, under INN auspices, representatives of the EPLF and the PDRE attempted to negotiate a peaceful settlement to their conflict. The parties placed only three requirements on the peace process: first, that it be conducted by a neutral third party; second, that the talks be made public; third, that no preconditions be set by either side. In compliance with their ground rules, each negotiating session began and ended with a highly publicized, and often highly divisive, press conference. The parties would frequently use the media opportunity to castigate each other.

Representatives from each side spent two weeks together at the Carter Center of Emory University in Atlanta. Convened by former President Carter, the parties worked on preliminary agreements that would provide the framework for later substantive talks. In November and December of 1989, the parties met for a second round of preliminary negotiations in Nairobi, Kenya. Again under the leadership of President Carter, they worked for over a week on the remaining preliminary issues. At the end of the Nairobi peace talks, both sides signed an agreement on fourteen procedural matters including language, venue, agenda, record keeping, and publicity.

Following the two rounds of procedural negotiations, the remaining unresolved issues were fairly straightforward—would the U.N. accept an invitation to serve as an observer if it were invited by only one party, the EPLF, and would observers merely be witnesses or would they also serve as mediators. Initially, the U.N. would not accept unless invited by both sides, relying on the prohibition in the U.N. Charter. This presented the negotiation team with a procedural Catch–22. The only way to reach an agreement on the observer question was through a mathematical formulation that allowed each side a limited number of unrestricted choices, combined with certain jointly chosen observers. The PDRE had maintained that the conflict was an internal affair of a sovereign nation and not within the purview of either regional or international organizations. The EPLF exercised its unilateral choices to name the U.N. and OAU as observers. However, the EPLF radio also broadcast the mathematical formulation for the selection. Knowing that it was not invited by the government of Ethiopia, the U.N. declined to accept the invitation because Ethiopia is a member-nation. The EPLF used the U.N. refusal to attend the substantive peace talks as a partial justification for the resumption of its military offensive. Only when the PDRE government was substantially weakened by the combined EPLF/TPLF (the Tigrean People's Liberation Front) military assaults did it capitulate on the observer question and authorize President Carter to invite the U.N. on behalf of both the PDRE and the EPLF.

* * *

IV. LESSONS

Peace talks seem to be most fruitful without the spotlight effect and constant posturing caused by the presence of mass media, although in this case the parties were unwilling to engage in the negotiations without such exposure. The interest of the press in the peace talks served ultimately as a strong incentive for both parties to show good faith in staying in the peace process. At the same time, each round of negotiations required damage control after the press conference, due to the parties' use of the media for blaming, labeling, and other divisive tactics. If an early agreement can be reached to have a totally private negotiation, or at a minimum, an agreement not to make a public statement during the sessions, progress can be achieved more readily.

Direct participation and joint actions of all of the major parties should be encouraged. The negotiating parties in this case might have included players such as the TPLF, who were then involved in parallel negotiations with the PDRE mediated by the Italian government. There was communication between the two ongoing negotiations, but the outcome might have been different had all of the parties been brought together in light of the similar military stand taken by the EPLF and the TPLF. The continued TPLF gains on the battlefield became one of the determinants for the peace process at the negotiations between the EPLF and the PDRE.

The creation of gains for both sides will greatly assist the parties in dealing with public opinion back home. Gains need to be seen by the parties as being greater than the cost of staying engaged in the conflict. It is important that both sides leave the negotiations feeling like winners. Our efforts to develop such joint gains for the PDRE and the EPLF never reached complete fruition since the process was interrupted before they were fully developed.

The third party should realize that the negotiating parties may have hidden agendas that can impact the process. In the case of Ethiopia/Eritrea, thirty years of bitter fighting left the groups extremely reluctant to be at the negotiating table together. Each was using the media attention generated by the talks to advance their cause. Either could have used the lull in fighting occasioned by the negotiations to strengthen their military position to prepare for a massive strike if the talks broke down. It is not uncommon in such protracted conflicts for the parties to leverage the process to secure gains on the battlefield and in the battle for public opinion. The EPLF may have been "playing the talks" as merely a part of a larger, master strategy to at last have their case heard by the United Nations, the court of last resort. This would certainly explain their choice of the U.N. as an observer and their insistence that all observers not only witness, but also mediate.

The importance of sociocultural differences cannot be overlooked. Third parties are rarely able to create a solution that will be as acceptable as one coming from the participants. Those who "own" the conflict will know the best approaches to ending it. Moreover, there will be less resistance to solutions that come from the parties than from those that are seen as being imposed on them. The direct participation in designing their own solutions is correlated with the empowerment of the parties to solve their own problems. As a corollary, the third party must be careful to give both sides credit when progress is made during the negotiations so that one side or another is not seen as taking all the credit when the continued progress depends on both.

We attempted to work with the World Bank and the International Monetary Fund to provide a major development package that could be introduced when a peaceful solution materialized, in essence, a carrot to offer as a negotiation incentive. These kinds of incentives can be tied to the negotiations so that the parties will see a direct benefit attributable to a specific agreement. They could even be developed in a sliding scale way so as to give greater incentives for major progress.

The role of a third party acceptable to all is correlated with its perceived neutrality and fairness. It is imperative that there be a clear understanding of the role of any third party, whether it be as a mediator, as an observer, or some other capacity; and that there be close communication with all sides in the dispute. We realize that the role of any individual is limited by his or her personal, social or political background, mortality, and acceptability to the parties in particular contexts. Therefore, the INN has expanded its original concept of using a single eminent person to convene a series of mediations, to developing a cadre of such eminent persons who might conduct more negotiations or use their combined influence to transform political thinking on regional and global levels.

(c) Mediation of Deadly Conflict

When do traditional principles of mediation exacerbate rather than resolve conflict? In an earlier section, Melanie Greenberg describes a predominant American model of mediation identified by such characteristics as confidential sessions and a neutral mediator with no powers beyond that of persuasion. In the following excerpt discussing Rwanda and Bosnia, she describes how disastrous that model can be in the case of deadly conflict.

MELANIE GREENBERG, MEDIATING MASSACRES: WHEN "NEUTRAL, LOW–POWER" MODELS OF MEDIATION CANNOT AND SHOULD NOT WORK

19 Ohio State Journal on Dispute Resolution 185 (2003).

* * *

In Bosnia and Rwanda, NLP mediation was an insufficient tool to stop the bloodshed or prevent genocide. In both cases, all the danger signs pointed to failure: the mediated agreements failed to satisfy powerful spoilers; the mediations took place on a highly visible stage, with top government leaders, during a time of crisis and tension; problem-solving trumped relationship building; and numerous red flags pointed to a lack of commitment by important parties.

The use of NLP mediation in Bosnia and Rwanda, rather than alleviating the conflict in those desperate countries, allowed intransigent and irredentist leaders breathing room to organize and conduct ethnic cleansing, and to pursue their military aims under cover of mediation. In Bosnia, the mediation was little more than a fig leaf for the assertive military intervention that the United States and the European Union were unwilling to employ in the conflict. In Rwanda, the mediation effort was sincere and well executed, but the lack of cohesion between the Hutu representatives, and the exclusion of powerful spoilers from the talks, led to a failure of implementation, and to the ensuing genocide. In each of these cases, all six of Kressel's red flags for mediation failure waved horribly from the start. These cases illustrate the danger of trying to use mediation to create a safe space, while ignoring practical realities on the ground, power dynamics between the parties, and structural difficulties in the societies that make reconciliation extremely difficult.

A.　Bosnia

Bosnia was the first test of Europe's ability to manage deadly conflict within its borders after the fall of the Soviet Union. Even as diplomats proclaimed the dawning of a new day in Europe, power-hungry and intransigent leaders were preparing to carve up Yugoslavia, with dire consequences for many of its citizens.* * *

The United States, about to enter into a presidential election campaign, was noncommittal. The United Nations authorized a peacekeeping force for the sole purpose of guaranteeing the delivery of humanitarian aid. NATO was unwilling to use military force to stop the ethnic cleansing, and individual European States also refused to send troops. Instead, the United Nations and the European Community suggested a joint mediation effort, to try to resolve the Bosnian conflict. Cyrus Vance agreed to mediate on behalf of the United Nations, and the respected British diplomat Lord David Owen, agreed to represent the European Community. Vance and Owen acted under the auspices of the International Conference on the Former Yugoslavia (ICFY), a loose forum of

European nations established in September 1992 to monitor and resolve the unraveling situation in Yugoslavia.

The mediation took the form of a classic NLP mediation. The mediators held very little leverage over the parties, and were unable to rally international military support to enforce any agreement. As Lord Owen reflected in his memoirs, "The daunting challenge for the ICFY in November 1992 was whether, armed only with moral authority and weak economic sanctions, and with no credible threat of selective counterforce, we could roll back the Serb confrontation lines and create a new map." The central goals of the mediation were to stop the fighting, to roll back some of the 70% of Bosnia that the Bosnian Serbs had commandeered through ethnic cleansing, and to keep Bosnia a multi-ethnic state. The parties to the mediation were Milan Panic, a Serb who had moved to the United States and led a multinational drug company; Dobrica Cosic, a Serb intellectual whom Milosevic had appointed to be president of the rump Yugoslavia; Mate Boban, the Bosnian Croat leader (communicating closely with Franjo Tudjman in neighboring Croatia proper); Alija Izetbecovic, the president of the Bosnia and leader of the Bosnian Muslims; and later Slobodan Milosevic himself.

Vance and Owen, after discussions with the parties, developed a plan that would divide Bosnia into ten cantons, three with a Serb majority, two with a Croat majority, three with a Muslim majority, and one with a mixed Croat–Serb majority. Sarajevo, the tenth canton, would be ruled by a loose coalition of three groups. On the positive side, the Vance–Owen Plan kept Bosnia intact as a multi-ethnic, non-partitioned state, did not change international borders, and did not give the Bosnian Serbs territory contiguous to Serbia proper. On the negative side, the plan rewarded the Bosnian Serbs for their ethnic cleansing by granting them more land than they had before the war; the governmental structure was too weak to rule the fragmented country; and the land swaps would be impossible without military enforcement.

The Vance–Owen Plan failed quickly, for reasons predictable when NLP mediation is used in situations involving deep-rooted violent conflict. The mediation was highly visible, and focused on a specific outcome, rather than on a change of relationship between the parties. Even more important, the mediators lacked any leverage or enforcement power, and the conflict was utterly "unripe" for resolution. In order for the Vance–Owen Plan to succeed, military intervention and peacekeeping forces were necessary for overseeing land swaps, and the threat of military force was needed to soften Serb intransigence in accepting the Plan. This military muscle was not forthcoming in any way from the International Community. Peacekeepers were allowed only to assure humanitarian aid, with tragic results in Srebrenica and other Muslim enclaves. NATO was unwilling to commit to air strikes, and, most important, the new President Clinton was unwilling to back the Vance–Owen Plan with force. He proposed, instead, a policy of "[L]ift [the arms embargo] and strike [the Serbs]," which Secretary of State Warren Christopher seemed to know would be a non-starter for European countries fearful of having their peacekeeping forces come under American or NATO fire. With no enforcement policy, the mediators and the parties knew that the process was ineffectual. They counted on using a plan with contradictory interpretations that the parties could all sign, in the hope that these contradictions could be negotiated once peacekeepers were in place and the violence had died down.

* * *

B. Rwanda

While the fighting continued in Bosnia, a genocidal wave of ethnic cleansing erupted in Rwanda in 1994. The Rwandan genocide of 1994 followed a NLP mediation effort that produced the Arusha Accords (a power sharing agreement between Tutsi exiles, the Rwandan Patriotic Front, and a coalition of Rwandan government parties). The failure of the Arusha Accords resulted neither from a bad-faith mediation effort, nor an unskilled one. The Arusha Accords were a classic "facilitative dialogue" type of NLP mediation that produced an elegant and substantively rich agreement for power sharing. However, the lack of cohesion among the Rwandan delegation, and the exclusion of key spoilers from real power in the Accords, set the stage for genocide in the implementation period following the Accords. A mediator with the power to offer incentives to the spoilers, and to ensure adequate peacekeeping troops following the Accords—the kinds of powers not generally available to NLP mediators—might have been able to avert the grisly deaths of between 500,000 and one million people. This was a clear situation in which a facilitative style of mediation produced results, yet was not a powerful enough tool to firmly resolve a fraught situation of potential violence.

* * *

While Tanzanian president Yoweri Musevina convened the talks, the key mediator of the Accords was Ami Mpungwe, a distinguished Tanzanian diplomat. Before beginning the Accords, Mpungwe met frequently with top US and French diplomats, and exhaustively studied recent peace agreements in Cambodia, Liberia, Namibia, and South Africa to see if lessons could be applied in Rwanda. He also studied the academic literature of peacemaking, looking for sustainable solutions for Rwanda.

Mpungwe fashioned the mediation process as a combination of settlement talks over specific political issues and facilitative dialogue, to resolve the underlying causes of tension between Hutus and Tutsis. He tailored the process to combine elements of problem-solving and transformative elements, but the process kept a profile very close to pure track-one diplomacy, as each of the representatives was in constant contact with top leadership. As Mpungwe saw it, the mediation had several goals, and his job was largely facilitative:

First, the structure of the process should be designed to facilitate communication between the two parties. Second, the process should last for a long time to allow for changing perceptions as well as negotiation of a detailed text. Third, his own role, and that of his negotiation team, was not to hammer out a deal between the two but to facilitate dialogue and communication, channel input from the "observers," and create an environment in which the parties to the process could reach a mutually acceptable agreement. Moreover, Mpungwe's desired outcome was clear: not just a settlement that would freeze the conflict for a brief period, but a political resolution to the conflict and its (perceived) underlying causes, one that would be durable and even a model for African internal conflict.

This is a classic NLP mediation, with elements of a facilitated public peace process—but with none of the deniability and secrecy that allow risk taking in non-diplomatic settings. The red flags that Kressel raises to predict mediation failure flew briskly in the Arusha Accords. There were certainly high levels of conflict between Hutus and Tutsis, with additional political complexity between the neighboring countries harboring Tutsi refugees and the Rwandan government led by President Juvenal Habyarimana. There was low motivation to reach agreement, and low commitment to mediate on the part of at least one of the key parties. While the RPF stood to gain a great deal from the talks (inclusion back into Rwandan government), and sent a high-level delegation to make sure their aims would be accomplished, the Rwandan delegation had much to fear from the Accords and had far less incentive to mediate. They were stuck between a rock and a hard place. On one hand, they needed an agreement that would wrest the country away from civil war and from international pressure to mend the Hutu–Tutsi rift. On the other hand, the potential loss of power of many of the President's cronies and other hard-line groups made compromise nearly impossible. A mutually hurting stalemate did not exist strongly enough to counter the hard-liners' fear of losing power, and so the conflict was not truly ripe for balanced, low-power mediation.

* * *

What are the lessons to be learned from the Arusha Accords? The genocide was not pre-ordained. A strong, coordinated peacemaking effort that was able to force the government of Rwanda to share power (using military "sticks" and economic "carrots" in the process) might have been successful. But the area was not seen as strategic for the United States (especially in light of the recent debacle in Somalia), and no African body was strong enough to impose a strong Dayton-like arrangement on Rwanda. Once the genocide began, the United States refused to acknowledge the severity of the violence, and was not willing to take the political risk of sending troops (the State Department studiously avoided any mention of the "g" word—genocide—that would have required action). The United Nations did not feel compelled to act on General Dallaire's desperate requests, without strong Security Council support. In this situation, perhaps no mediation effort could alone have resolved the deep problems underlying the Rwandan political situation. A coordinated spectrum of grass-roots dialogue, "public peace processes" that would have allowed for political movement in a confidential setting, and strong-armed, public mediation with a strong coordinator, might have been able to prevent a slide into bloodshed. Certainly, NLP mediation by itself, even if brilliantly and sensitively conceived and competently executed, only set the stage for future disaster.

Notes and Questions

1.   One of the "lessons learned" offered by the author of the excerpt on the Sri Lankan conflict was that a mediator would have been helpful to prevent harmful unilateral action and to assist in implementation of the agreement. Do you agree?

2.   In reviewing the stages of mediation, the implementation stage will be most challenging in the case of intractable conflict; in post-conflict societies, the real work of mediation begins after the peace agreement is signed. Social and economic infrastructures must be rebuilt, alienated communities must learn to live together, and mechanisms for the protection of human rights must be established.[32] To what extent did Senator George Mitchell's mediation strategy contribute to the successful implementation of the Belfast/Good Friday Agreement? Where would you locate his mediation approach—in the structuralist or social psychological models of international mediation?

3.   What are some pragmatic reasons for the UN's refusal to engage in the conflict between the PDRE and the EPLF without the Ethiopian government's consent?

4.   Identify the "lessons learned" from the interrupted negotiations in the Ethiopian conflict. Do any of these lessons have a bearing upon the Sri Lankan conflict? To what extent did cultural differences influence either of these negotiations? How would you distinguish the negotiating contexts in Ethiopia, Sri Lanka and Northern Ireland?

5.   What were the sources of the mediator's leverage in the Ethiopian negotiations? What impact did their leverage have upon the mediator's neutrality and impartiality?

6.   Can you think of some situations when governments or individuals negotiated with terrorists or violent groups where the results have been positive?

7.   Through Norway's intervention, a ceasefire ended the fight between the Tamil Tiger rebels and the Sri Lankan government in February 2002. Peace talks broke down in April 2003 over Tamil Tiger demands for greater autonomy. As of August 2004, Norway has been attempting to revive peace negotiations in order to prevent a return to civil war. In the excerpt that you read, the author discusses the benefits of third-party mediation in the Sri Lankan conflict with the Tamil Tigers. What geopolitical characteristics should a third-party mediator in this conflict have? Do the Norwegian interveners meet these requirements?

---

32.   Jan Egeland, *The Oslo Accord: Multiparty Facilitation through the Norwegian* Channel, *in* CHESTER A. CROCKER ET AL., HERDING CATS, *supra* note 18, at 544.

8.   Do you agree with the assertion that "neutral low-power" models of mediation should not be employed in cases of deadly conflict? Are there any circumstances involving deadly conflict in which such mediation models might be helpful?

9.   As discussed earlier in Chapter 2, in domestic mediation practice, informed consent is considered by many scholars and practitioners as the foundational value of mediation. Do you think that the principle of informed consent has relevance in the practice of public international mediation? How relevant was this principle in the Northern Ireland peace talks? The Ethiopia/Eritrea conflict? Rwanda? Bosnia?

Chapter 8

PROCESSES FOR MANAGING ETHNIC CONFLICT

A. INTRODUCTION

The persistence and complexity of ethnic conflict in the post Cold–War era argues for giving greater attention to processes that address the needs of multi-ethnic States. These States face the challenge of developing structures that will prevent ethnic conflicts from erupting into wars that will threaten the foundations of civil society. The potential for violence and destruction poses a particular threat to emerging democratic States where there are conflicts over scarce resources.

The materials in this chapter describe processes and philosophies that may have the potential to resolve or at least manage ethnic conflict and establish the foundations of peacebuilding. The chapter begins with a discussion of pre-negotiation activities: problem-solving workshops, the public peace process and sustained dialogue. The materials then consider the relevance of legal processes, fact-finding, reconciliation, and co-existence work. The end of the chapter examines the use of arbitration in managing ethnic conflict. Although the concern of this textbook is with consensual processes, we offer a discussion of arbitration because in some cases, it has significant value in resolving territorial disputes between ethnic groups. The materials in Chapter 9 explore some of these processes more fully in the context of organizational structures such as Truth Commissions and tribunals.

As you read these materials, you should consider the role of culture in the use of these processes. Are some ethnic groups more inclined to favor a particular form of conflict resolution? Are there processes for managing ethnic conflict that might be rejected by specific ethnic groups? Does your understanding of cultural differences through social science constructs (e.g., individualist and collectivist cultures; high-context and low context cultures) assist you in responding to these questions?

B. PRE–NEGOTIATION PROCESSES

1. PROBLEM–SOLVING WORKSHOPS

Problem-solving workshops, a form of Track II diplomacy, bring together members of conflicted societies in a private, academic setting to listen to each other's views of the conflict. Developed by Professor Herbert Kelman and his colleagues who worked with Israeli and Palestinians citizens, the workshops seek to establish a climate in which trust can develop and communication take place. In this sense, they may be considered a significant part of the pre-negotiation process. Problem-solving workshops may also be helpful in overcoming obstacles during the actual negotiations and in implementing agreements reached in negotiation.[1]

2. PUBLIC PEACE PROCESSES

Some conflicts are so intractably locked in their early stages that conventional mediation or negotiation are of no avail. In such cases, pre-negotiation or pre-mediation activities are needed to change relationships and pave the way for formal peacemaking. Harold Saunders, the originator of the public peace process, defines this method as "sustained action by citizens outside government to change the fundamental relationship between citizen groups in conflict."[2] The process involves bringing together non-official representatives of various groups to a conflict to begin a discussion about the problem. Such meetings between individual citizens have the benefit of defusing tensions and promoting group understanding. They can also establish the foundation for future negotiations. The public peace process intervention model has been utilized successfully in a number of world situations, including South Africa,[3] U.S. and Soviet Union conflicts, Palestinian and Israeli conflicts, and conflicts between Armenian–Azerbaijanis and Armenians.[4]

A variation of the public peace process is the process of "sustained dialogue." In the following excerpt Harold Saunders offers a five stage framework for dialogue among parties in deep-rooted conflict. His reflections are based on prior experiences in the Arab–Israeli Palestinian peace process, as founding U.S. co-chair of the Dartmouth Conference Regional Conflicts Task Force, and his work with parties from the former Soviet republic of Tajikistan after civil war broke out in the early 1990s.

---

1. Herbert C. Kelman, *Interactive Problem–Solving: Informal Mediation by the Scholar–Practitioner, in* STUDIES IN INTERNATIONAL MEDIATION 167–68 (Jacob Bercovitch ed., 2002).

2. Gennady I. Chufrin & Harold M. Saunders, *A Public Peace Process,* 9 NEGOTIATION J. 155–156 (April 1993).

3. Peter N. Bouckaert, *The Negotiated Revolution: South Africa's Transition to a* Multiracial Democracy, 33 STAN. J. INT'L L. 375, 382 (1997).

4. *See* Herbert C. Kelman, *Informal Mediation by the Scholar/Practitioner, in* MEDIATION IN INTERNATIONAL RELATIONS: MULTIPLE APPROACHES TO CONFLICT MANAGEMENT 64 (Jacob Bercovitch & Jeffrey Z. Rubin eds., 1992).

HAROLD H. SAUNDERS, SUSTAINED DIALOGUE IN MANAGING INTRACTABLE CONFLICT

Negotiation Journal 85–91 (January 2003).

* * *

A Five–Stage Dialogue Process

We have conceptualized the experience in the Regional Conflicts Task Force in the 1980s and through countless hours in nonofficial Israeli–Palestinian dialogue as a five-stage process. This is not an artificial construct but rather the conceptualization of that experience, describing how interactions among the same participants in repeated dialogue sessions seem to unfold over time. In the early 1980s, Evgeny Primakov said, "We will begin the next meeting where the last meeting ended." This made possible developing a cumulative agenda with questions sharpened and carried from one meeting to the next; building a common body of knowledge that participants could test between meetings; and learning to talk and work analytically together. By 1989, we were developing scenarios together to analyze how regional conflicts might evolve and how the superpowers might respond to avoid direct confrontation.

The five-stage framework is not intended as a rigid template but rather as an analytical and working framework to permit moderators and participants alike to understand the progression of relationships in their work together: Those stages are:

- *Stage One:* Either people on different sides of a conflict decide to reach out to each other, or a third party creates a space for dialogue and invites conflicting parties to come together there. People in conflict decide to engage in dialogue—often with great difficulty—because they feel a compelling need to build or change a relationship to resolve problems that hurt or could hurt their interests intolerably: These participants are themselves a microcosm of their communities.

- *Stage Two:* They come together to talk—to map and name the elements of those problems and the relationships responsible for creating and dealing with them. In early meetings, they vent their grievances and anger with each other in a scattershot way. This venting provides both the ingredients for an ultimate agenda and an opportunity for moderators to analyze and "map" the interactions—to understand the dynamics of the relationships. This stage ends—at least for a time—when someone says: "What we really need to focus on is...."

- *Stage Three:* In much more disciplined exchanges, participants probe the specific problem they have identified with these aims: (1) to name the most pressing problem to reflect the concerns of those affected by it; (2) to probe the dynamics of the relationships underlying that problem; (3) to lay out broadly possible ways into those relationships to change them; (4) to weigh those choices and to come to a sense of direction to guide next steps; (5) to weigh the consequences of moving in that direction against the consequences of doing nothing; and (6) to decide whether to try designing such change.

• *Stage Four:* Together, they design a scenario of interacting steps to be taken in the political arena to change troublesome relationships and to precipitate practical steps. They ask four questions: What are the obstacles to moving in the direction we have chosen? What steps could overcome those obstacles? Who could take those steps? How could we sequence those steps so that they interact—one building on another—to generate momentum behind the plan for acting?

• *Stage Five:* They devise ways to put that scenario into the hands of those who can act on it.

The focus is on *transforming relationships* throughout the five stages. In this process of sustained dialogue, there is always a dual focus: Participants, of course, focus on concrete grievances and issues, but always the moderators and participants are searching for the dynamics of the relationships that cause the problems and must be changed before the problems can be resolved.

In this process, the concept of relationship is essential. It is defined rigorously in terms of five components—five arenas of interaction in constantly changing combinations within and between the parties interacting: (1) *identity,* defined in human as well as in physical characteristics—the life experience that has brought a person or group to the present; (2) *interests,* both concrete and psychological—what people care about—that bring people into the same space and into a sense of their dependence on one another—interdependence—to achieve their goals; (3) *power,* defined not only as control over superior resources and the actions of others but as the capacity of citizens acting together to influence the course of events without great material resources; (4) *perceptions, misperceptions, and stereotypes*; and (5) the *patterns of interaction*—distant and close—among those involved, including respect for certain *limits* on behavior in dealing with others.

The story of the Inter–Tajik Dialogue "within the Framework of the Dartmouth Conference," as participants came to call it, can be told as unfolding in four chapters:

• From March 1993 through March 1994, the group met six times, during which participants moved from being barely able to look at each other to playing a significant role together in paving the way for government and opposition decisions in early 1994 to engage in formal peace negotiations under a U.N. mediator. In March 1994, just before negotiations began, they produced their first joint memorandum, "Memorandum on the Negotiating Process of Tajikistan."

- From April 1994 through June 1997, three Dialogue participants served as members of the two negotiating teams in the U.N.-mediated Inter–Tajik Negotiations. One of them served throughout that period and is now the Deputy Foreign Minister of Tajikistan. Another is Minister of Industry. The third was a vice-chair of the Uzbek Association in Tajikistan, who served on the government team. This period ended with the signing of a peace agreement.

- From July 1997 through February 2000, five participants in the Dialogue served in the Commission on National Reconciliation, which was established in the peace agreement of June 1997 to oversee implementation of the provisions of that agreement. Other Commission members joined the Dialogue when the Commission's work ended.

- From April 2000 to the present, members of the Dialogue and other Tajikistani citizens formally registered their own nongovernmental organization, the Public Committee for Promoting Democratic Processes in Tajikistan. Their strategy is one of peace-building. They are working on four tracks: (1) creating a complex of dialogue groups in six regions of the country, which began by discussing how to integrate the only legal Islamic party in Central Asia into a "secular, democratic" polity; (2) holding public forums on major national issues such as drugs, education, and poverty in major regions of the country; (3) experimenting with three Economic Development Committees in towns particularly torn apart during the civil strife, where deliberative practices are being used to address economic problems in those communities—their own elaboration of building "social capital"; and (4) workshops over two and a half years in collaboration with the Ministry of Education and three professors from each of eight universities, to develop curricula, a text, teaching materials, and courses in resolving conflict and peace-building.

Early in each of these four phases, participants in the Dialogue stated and then restated their objectives, thereby establishing goals against which to judge their progress. In August 1993, they said, "What we need to work on is starting a negotiation between the government and the opposition on creating conditions so refugees can go home." After negotiations began in April 1994, they asked themselves whether they should continue the Dialogue. Their answer was emphatic: "Yes. We helped to get negotiations started. Now we have to assure that they succeed. Our objective now is to design a political process of national reconciliation in Tajikistan." At this point, participants assured the government of Tajikistan that the Dialogue would not interfere with the work of the negotiators but would rather think beyond the negotiations and concentrate on ways of preparing the citizens of Tajikistan to implement whatever agreements came from the negotiations. After the peace agreement was signed in June 1997, they stated their purpose as establishing the elements of democracy in a "united, democratic, secular, peaceful Tajikistan." In February 2000, after the end of the formal transition period defined by the peace agreement, their further defined objective is captured in the four-track program of the Public Committee described earlier.

One additional framework has been useful for analyzing this work. Participants in the Inter–Tajik Dialogue in October 1996 coined the phrase "multilevel peace process." In their joint memorandum following their seventeenth meeting they wrote: "It is necessary to broaden public participation in the efforts to achieve peace by developing a multilevel peace process in order to assure the widest possible involvement in achieving the implementing a peace agreement." They recognized the importance of the official peace process—the formal negotiations at the top of the political pyramid. They were deeply engrossed in their own "public peace process" involving members of the policy-influencing community, mostly outside government, at the upper-middle level of the body politic. But they also recognized the work in civil society where much of the fighting in the civil war took place. The key for them was the interaction among all those levels.

The formulation, "multilevel peace process," emerged from an exchange in the Dialogue in which one participant recounted the following experience: He had served with a joint opposition-government commission to negotiate a cease-fire in a region where fighting had cut a critical east-west road. When he had finished his account of negotiations involving field commanders, municipal officials, local elders, and other community interests, another Dialogue participant said: "The reason our cease-fires rarely hold is that they have been negotiated between the president and the leader of the opposition without any reference to the people on the ground with interests at stake and with guns. What we need is a multilevel peace process that connects the local people with the top-level negotiators through working groups."

Judging "Success": An Ongoing Self–Evaluation

Within these frameworks—the five-stage process of sustained dialogue, the concept of relationship, and the multilevel peace process—a process of evaluation takes place. In any complex political process, the cause-and-effect relationship between one actor and any outcome in the larger political process may be unknowable with any precision. My bottom line is that building a habit of ongoing self-evaluation into the process of dialogue is far superior to the necessarily unrooted comments of an outside evaluator. There is no judgment more authentic than that of the people whose lives are at stake. Two examples underscore this point:

First, in August 1993, participants in the Dialogue's third meeting decided to focus on how to start a negotiation between the government and the opposition. In the fourth meeting, they discussed in detail how that might be done. They identified as a major obstacle the fact that the opposition was physically fragmented, ideologically diffuse, and geographically dispersed. Pro-government participants asked: "Who from the opposition would join a negotiation? How would we find you to invite you?" Within a month, opposition factions met in Tehran, Iran, wrote a joint platform, and created an opposition coordinating center in Moscow. Two participants in the Dialogue signed that platform, and brought it back to the fifth meeting of the Dialogue. They submitted to two days of questioning by pro-government participants; their answers were written down. The pro-government participants left the meeting saying: "We believe the foundations for negotiation now exist. We will report to our government." A month later, the government accepted the invitation from a U.N. emissary to join U.N.-mediated peace talks.

Did the Dialogue play a role in paving the way for negotiation? Yes, certainly. At the very least, as a senior government official later made the point, it was impossible any longer to argue that talks between the government and the opposition were impossible. Can the Dialogue claim exclusive credit for starting negotiations? No, of course not. Individuals in government and in opposition circles were already struggling with the question of how to end the violence, and the U.N. emissary was pressing on behalf of the U.N. Security Council to begin negotiation. The work of the Dialogue was one factor in contributing to conditions in which a decision to negotiate was made.

Second, in June 1995, the peace negotiations were stymied over the question of how to create an institution to oversee national reconciliation. The opposition for some time had proposed a Commission on National Reconciliation to be created as a supra-governmental organization in lieu of a coalition government, which the government had rejected. The dialogue produced a joint memorandum containing three options. In one, they suggested positioning a National Reconciliation Commission *under* the authority of the negotiations to oversee the implementation of the peace accord through four sub-commissions. Their very first joint memorandum, that the negotiating teams establish four sub-commissions to deal with such issues as returning refugees, demilitarizing armed elements, economic rehabilitation, and constitutional reform. The purpose was for the negotiators in dealing with these specific problems to begin actual work involving elements of the bureaucracy and the society. That was the pattern which the National Reconciliation Commission ultimately adopted. Can the Dialogue claim credit for designing the Commission on National Reconciliation as ultimately established by the peace agreement? No, the idea had been in the air for some time, although participants in the Dialogue feel that the idea of positioning the Commission under the authority of the negotiating teams originated in the Dialogue itself.

Finally, evaluation depends heavily on what questions are asked. For instance, a normal evaluator's question might be: Can you demonstrate what impact your intervention had on producing a peace treaty? Our answer is that the Dialogue played a significant role but others probably played a more significant role. It is certainly possible, as one of the long-time participants has done, to document the interplay of ideas between the Dialogue and negotiators or members of the Commission on National Reconciliation, but exactly who gets how much credit for what is unknowable. (I was at Camp David with Presidents Carter and Sadat and Prime Minister Begin in 1978; one of my roles was to produce each of 23 successive drafts of the Camp David Accords. I could not know—exactly who was responsible for each formulation and reformulation in that intense mediating process in which conversations took place around the tennis courts, over meals, and during walks in the woods, as well as around various working tables.)

Another way of posing a question can be found in the first grant proposal the U.S. team wrote to a U.S. foundation at the beginning of the Inter–Tajik Dialogue: "We want to *see whether* a group can form from within a conflict to design a peace process for its own country." Implicit in this approach has been the notion of continuous self-evaluation—evaluation as part of an unfolding open-ended political process. Neither participants nor the moderators have waited for outside evaluation to determine how they were progressing. At each stage, participants in the Dialogue have reviewed their progress and stated a new objective for themselves. They have moved from being barely able to look at each other in the first meeting to producing 21 joint memoranda in 32 meetings. Then together without any initiative from the Russian–U.S. team, they have formed their own Public Committee for Promoting Democratic Processes in Tajikistan. They have developed their own strategy for peace-building.

There is no doubt in my mind that this group is pursuing the most coherent strategy for peace-building in the country, and is taking solid and even measurable steps it has designed for itself. The more important point is that this has been an open-ended political process with new steps being defined that could not in any way have been envisioned at the beginning of the process. Posing an objective—possibly with too narrow a definition—for evaluators' judgment could have closed the door on the opportunity for participants to make continuous mid-course corrections and move beyond premature definitions of success.

Another framework for judging the success of the Dialogue itself lies in the five-stage process laid out by the management team. In the first six meetings, the Dialogue participants clearly moved through all five stages of the dialogue as they learned to think and talk together and then actually to produce a joint memorandum together which laid out a design for the negotiations they had helped begin. After that, we learned that a well-established dialogue group will in each meeting work its way through at least the last two or three stages of a dialogue as the participants come together, talk about the situation in their country since the last meeting, probe one or two of the most important issues in depth, and produce a joint memorandum about it. This provides the opportunity for judging success at each meeting.

Notes and Questions

1. Do you think that the story of the Inter–Tajik Dialogue can be repeated for other deep-rooted conflicts?

2. To what extent do cultural considerations play out in public peace processes or the concept of sustained dialogue? Can you think of some ethnic groups who would not favor such processes?

3. If you were conducting an evaluation of the sustained dialogue process based on Saunders' account, what would you conclude?

4. In thinking about processes that are helpful in resolving ethnic conflict, how important is it to consider conflict *within* ethnic groups? Consider the following reflections in formulating your response.

> There are many aspects to intractability, but I would like to surface one aspect that I believe has not received adequate attention. We usually focus our attention on differences between identity groups. For instance, for twenty years, we concentrated on dialogues between Israelis and Palestinians. I have often reflected, however, that we really should have been spending our efforts on dialogues *within* identity groups—that is, among Israelis on how they would define their state and among Palestinians on how they would define theirs.

> Today, there are hundreds—probably thousands—of Israeli and Palestinian veterans of dialogue-type interactions, many of those veterans in high places. They have now produced technically viable solutions to most of the important issues in negotiation—a statement that could not have been made a decade ago. *But*, they have been overwhelmed—silenced—by a minority committed to derail the peace process because they have a vision of an outcome that may well be different from the majority within their own groups. The present violent minority might well have been marginalized or contained had they been dealt with in dialogue over the past decade.

> This point is dramatically visible in the Israel–Palestine case. It is less visible beneath the surface, but no less important in the latent tensions between ethnic, racial, religious, and culturally defined groups in the cities of the world.

[Harold H. Saunders, *Sustained Dialogue in Managing Intractable Conflict*, Negotiation J. 85, 92 (January 2003).]

C. LEGAL PROCESSES

In the struggle to develop political solutions to ameliorate ethnic conflict, many multi-ethnic States have chosen to disregard legal norms as a viable tool of conflict resolution. In the following article, the author argues that, in the life of an ethnic conflict, there is an intermediate moment at which a conflict has arisen but has not reached the crisis point. The intervention of legal processes to formulate and implement legal norms at this juncture may have a transformative effect. The following "thick description" case study of the Ethiopian system examines the advantages of using legal processes to resolve and manage ethnic conflicts. As you read this material, think about what constitutes an ethnic group. Are there any characteristics that are shared by the three ethnic groups described in this reading?

ELENA A. BAYLIS, BEYOND RIGHTS: LEGAL PROCESS AND ETHNIC CONFLICTS

25 Michigan Journal of International Law 529, 556–601 (2004).

* * *

II. Legal Process Models at Work in Ethnic Conflict Resolution

* * *

The Ethiopian system has three distinctive qualities: it establishes a permanent, ethnic focused institution that grants some measure of standing to all ethnic groups; it is structured to employ complementary consensual and adjudicative processes; and it relies on constitutional interpretation to resolve national disputes. * * * Each. * * * raises a fundamental question about the appropriate role of legal process in ethnic conflicts that deserves further consideration: Should states ever recognize ethnic groups? Which aspects of legal process might be effective in resolving ethnic conflicts? And what kinds of constitutional principles and standing will be appropriate for the ethnic conflict context?

* * *

A. *The Ethiopian System*

1. Structure

* * *

The extremity of Ethiopia's circumstances has fostered a willingness to adopt extreme political strategies. Foremost among these is its policy toward its ethnic groups. When it established its new government in 1994, Ethiopia adopted a political structure that it calls "ethnic federalism." It organized the regional states of its federation as nearly as possible along ethnic lines. All ethnic groups, not just minority or indigenous groups, have the constitutional right of self-determination. That right is nearly absolute, including not only cultural rights, but self-government, statehood, and even secession.

In the broadest sense, this is a classic political structural solution to ethnicity: Ethiopia has designed the framework of its political institutions with the express purpose of defusing ethnic tensions and preventing ethnic conflicts. But unlike most such solutions, it incorporates and emphasizes ethnicity rather than attempting to counterbalance or ignore it. Other countries have structured at least some regional states along ethnic lines, but only rarely is this the exclusive method of drawing borders. And the universal and virtually unqualified right of secession held by Ethiopia's Nationalities is, to my knowledge, unprecedented.

Ethnic federalism is controversial. Critics charge that using ethnicity as a building block for the government feeds nationalist fervor and sets the stage for inter-ethnic violence. Some argue that the right of secession in particular is a catalyst for conflict, and that its guarantees of self-government are hopelessly divisive and complex. Others claim that ethnic federalism is a mere sham to disguise the hegemony of a single ethnic group.

Notes and Questions

1. Do you agree with the critique of ethnic federalism that it creates an environment for inter-ethnic conflict?

2. Can you think of other countries afflicted by ethnic conflict where it might be helpful to use ethnicity as a building block for the government?

ELENA A. BAYLIS, BEYOND RIGHTS: LEGAL PROCESS AND ETHNIC CONFLICTS

25 Michigan Journal of International Law 529, 556–601 (2004).

* * *

Ethiopia's conflict resolution system is centered in the institution of the House of the Federation, the upper house of Parliament. While the lower house has legislative powers and its members are elected from districts within each regional state, the House of the Federation has a different composition and role. It is composed of representatives from each of the Nationalities. It does not have traditional legislative powers but rather is charged by the constitution with maintaining the country's ethnic, regional and federal relationships. This includes the roles of dispute resolution and constitutional interpretation.

Under the auspices of this constitutional authority, the House of the Federation effectively has jurisdiction over all ethnic disputes, whether formal or informal, legal or political, big or small. Because the regional states are defined by their ethnic composition, the House of the Federation's powers with respect to the regional states are interrelated with its powers with respect to Nationalities, and inter-state disputes are often ethnic disputes as well. Similarly, because the constitution establishes Nationalities rather than individuals as the fundamental constituents of the Ethiopian federation, many aspects of the constitution and constitutional interpretation will have at least some ethnic aspect, well beyond the express Nationality rights themselves.

Apart from the constitutionally prescribed procedures for handling Nationalities' petitions for statehood or secession, the House has discretion under the constitution to create whatever procedures it sees fit for adjudicating these disputes. When the Berta and Silte cases were first taken under consideration, the House was still developing its procedures and no law had yet been passed governing its activities. Under a more recent law consolidating the House's authority, the House maintains considerable flexibility. The procedures set forth in this law to some extent represent the prior practice of the House. Certain elements, however, are aspirational, such as specific deadlines for issuing decisions, and stricter exhaustion, standing and other admissibility requirements.

Most cases are intended to move through a multi-stage process. Upon receiving a petition, the House initially encourages direct negotiation between the parties. If this fails, the case progresses to mediation by House representatives, and then to adjudication by the House as a final measure. The exceptions to this pattern are cases that call for constitutional interpretation, claims by Nationalities for enforcement of constitutional rights, and border disputes: in these cases the House's role is adjudicative.

Ethiopia's conflict resolution system is thus a blend of the legal and the political on several levels. At the institutional level, the House of the Federation is a quintessentially political body, but one that has been designated for adjudicative purposes. At the process level, the act of constitutional interpretation is a trademark legal process, but one that is fraught with political concerns, while processes of mediation and adjudication are used in both legal and political settings. Finally, ethnic conflicts are themselves often an unstable combination of the legal and the political. The procedures set forth in the constitution and the relevant law are described in extremely broad terms, and could be carried out in ways that pushed the House's adjudicative style either more toward the political or toward the legal aspects of its role. Accordingly, it is through the practices that the House is developing to carry out its hybrid role that the balance between the legal and the political will be drawn.

Implementation of this program has not been a panacea for Ethiopia's ethnic conflict. Indeed, it is too early to assess the system's ultimate success. Ten years into the existence of the new constitution and its conflict resolution system, implementation is just beginning. But the preliminary successes and failures in the Berta, Silte, and Ormeo cases offer insight into the potential of processes focused specifically on ethnic conflict, point to concerns that should be addressed in determining whether and how to offer such processes, and suggest factors that may weigh on their ultimate effectiveness.

2. The Berta: Mediation

When the Berta Nationality walked out of the Benshangul–Gumuz regional parliament over the issue of proportionate representation, they brought it to a halt. The Benshangul–Gumuz government asked the Prime Minister's Office to intervene, but the Berta reportedly rejected the proffered negotiators as likely to favor the regional government. The Benshangul–Gumuz government and the Berta then jointly appealed to the House of the Federation to consider the case under the auspices of its constitutional authority over inter-ethnic and regional conflicts.

The House of the Federation has established a Committee for States' Affairs to mediate conflicts between Nationalities and between regional states, and to address ethnic and regional concerns. This committee will accept a case upon the request of both parties, or upon the request of one party if they have failed to resolve the problem between themselves after two years. As both the Berta and the regional government had requested its participation, the committee delegated mediators from among its members to meet with them.

The mediators' preliminary goal was to negotiate a framework for resolving the representation issue. The first step was to persuade Berta representatives to return to the regional parliament. To change the Berta's representation—even if an agreement were reached—the regional state would have to amend its constitution. This would not happen overnight. In the meantime, what would keep this conflict from becoming a crisis would be to enable the regional parliament to begin governing again. The mediators achieved this goal: the parties agreed to a temporary compromise provisionally allocating additional representatives to the Berta in return for their agreement to return to the legislature. The second step was to develop a procedure for moving forward. To this end, the mediators created an independent commission to study the parliamentary representation in the region and provide a recommendation that would be binding on both parties.

With this framework in place, the Berta returned to participate in the regional government and the immediate crisis, together with its immediate and escalating costs, was resolved. But the basic conflict carried on.

The commission's study of regional representation unearthed more complexities. While the Berta might have been underrepresented in the regional government, the Nationalities that were not indigenous to that region—comprising 47 percent of the population—were not entitled to any political representation at all. In addition, the question of political representation overlapped with issues of resource allocation by the regional government, of the proportionality of representation in the federal government, and of the use of regional languages. These factors, as well as mundane procedural delays, led to an extension of the study period from 45 days to over two years. The mediators referred the legal questions to the House's Legal Committee. Debate on the study's purportedly binding recommendations continues to date, and at the time this was written, no solution had yet been implemented.

3.   The Silte: Constitutional Interpretation

The Silte community's appeal for recognition as a Nationality, independent of the larger Gurage Nationality, raised basic questions about ethnicity. What defines a cognizable ethnic group? Should ethnicity be determined by self-definition or are there objective factors that should be considered? Who should decide: the group seeking independence, the larger ethnic group, or some third party? These were vital questions not only for the Silte and the Gurage, but also for the many other ethnic communities that were part of larger, recognized Nationalities, and therefore for the country as a whole.

The Ethiopian constitution provides a substantive definition of a Nationality and sets forth Nationality rights, but does not delegate authority or create a process for recognizing Nationalities. Until the Silte's petition, the government had relied on long established ethnic categories used under previous governments in carrying out the census to define its Nationalities. When the Silte formally petitioned for new recognition as Nationality, they forced the government to confront these jurisdictional and procedural questions.

As required by the constitution, the House had established an advisory body, the Council of Constitutional Inquiry ("the Council"), to carry out the actual work of interpreting the constitution. The Council is composed of legal experts, including the President and Vice President of the Federal Supreme Court, and also includes three members of the House who are not required to have any legal expertise. The House and the Council have the authority to accept petitions for interpretation directly from a wide range of parties. Upon accepting a petition for constitutional interpretation, the Council performs the legal analysis and presents a recommendation to the House, and the House considers the recommendation and issues a final decision.

The process of constitutional interpretation is accessible enough on paper, but in reality it required some tenacity for the Silte's claim to be heard. Although at the time there were no formal legal barriers to submitting a petition, the House's decision to exercise its jurisdiction is discretionary. The Southern Nations' government did not want to take any action in the Silte case until it had obtained an authoritative judgment on its jurisdiction and the procedure it should follow. The House, however, refused to consider the petition until the Southern Nations government had issued its own final decision in the matter. Between the Southern Nations' repeated attempts to persuade the House to accept the petition, and the regional process of reaching a decision after it abandoned these efforts, several years elapsed.

When the Council at last turned to the Silte case, it focused its opinion on the jurisdictional and procedural questions, affirming the substantive constitutional definition of a Nationality with little comment. In the absence of direct constitutional guidance, the Council turned to latent constitutional principles for guidance. From the central place the ethnic rights of self-determination occupy in the Ethiopian constitution, the Council discerned a constitutional intent to give unrecognized ethnic communities control of the process of determining their status. Accordingly, the Council granted the primary authority for determining identity to the petitioning community, and created a four step process. First, community representatives must present a petition for recognition as a Nationality to the regional state government. In response, the regional state must conduct a study of whether the community has met the constitutional definition of a Nationality and present the study to the petitioning community. That community must then vote on the issue through a popular referendum. If the results of the referendum and the study are in agreement, then the decision is final. But if either party is aggrieved, it can petition the House for review. However, the House's review will be limited to determining whether the *process* followed was constitutional, and it apparently will not review the merits. Notably absent in this structure is any role for the larger concerned community, in this case the Gurage Nationality from whom the Silte were seeking to separate.

This process was immediately put into use. The House of the Federation adopted and promulgated the Council's recommendation. The Silte council petitioned for recognition, the regional state conducted its study, and the Silte people voted for independent Nationality status. None of the parties appealed to the House of the Federation for reconsideration of the result, so the matter was at last at a close. The Silte were recognized as a Nationality, received the related political benefits, and set up their own independent self-administration. The immediate dispute between the Silte, the Gurage and the regional government was resolved. Since then, other communities seeking recognition have done the same.

4.   The Oromo: The Limits of the System

The Oromo ruled Ethiopia and its many peoples for several centuries, until they were superceded by the Amhara Nationality. Since then, the Oromo have been dominated by smaller ethnic groups, first the Amhara, and now the Tigreans. The Oromo Liberation Front ("OLF") was a secondary player in the war against the communist Derg regime in the 1970s and 1980s, which was eventually won by a collation of ethnically defined militia dominated by the Tigrean military forces. In the post-war political process of developing the current government, the OLF felt itself shut out by the Tigrean political party. The OLF walked out of the constitution drafting process and has since refused to participate in elections.

The Oromo are now represented in the regional and federal governments by a new political party, which critics allege is a mere sham propped up by the Tigreans so as to be able to claim participation by all ethnic groups. The OLF is active as an opposition group operating in the sphere of protest and sometimes violence. It complains of political oppression and politically motivated arrests of Oromo, as well as pervasive social bias against them. The situation is volatile: there were demonstrations, property destruction, and mass arrests of Oromo students at Addis Ababa University in January 2004 when the university refused permission for an on-campus Oromo cultural event.

Although the Ethiopian constitution provides for all recognized Nationalities like the Oromo to have the right to secede, the OLF has not instigated the political process for secession. Although the constitution also guarantees rights of equal treatment and self-government, the OLF also has not brought its claims to the House of the Federation either for mediation or as constitutional claims. Rather, they have continued to protest outside the established ethnic conflict resolution process.

5.   Key Factors in the Berta, Silte and Oromo Cases

Underlying the differences between the Berta, Silte, and the Oromo's experiences with the Ethiopian conflict resolution system are certain key factors that seem to have played a role in shaping those experiences. In each case, both the nature of the dispute and the identity of the group affected the group's perception of and reaction to the available dispute resolution mechanisms. And in each case, that reaction created dynamic relationships with broader effects beyond the resolution of the immediate dispute.

There are two distinctive aspects to the nature of the disputes themselves. First, each dispute is embedded in complex, ongoing interrelationship, both amongst the ethnic groups themselves, and between those groups and the political and legal systems. Even when the dispute seemed initially to present a simple either/or question, the process of dispute resolution peeled away that superficial dichotomy and exposed layers of legal and political concerns. In the Berta case, the initial question about proportional representation revealed underlying inequities and questions about rights to representation for non-indigenous groups. In the Silte case, their demand to the regional state government for recognition revealed ambiguities in the substantive definition of a Nationality and the need for a process and criteria for addressing their demand. This revelatory effect complicates the task of bringing the immediate dispute to a conclusion, but raises the possibility that the process could have a fundamental effect on the relationship between the parties by providing a forum for addressing those underlying tensions.

Second, while none of these disputes presents itself as a candidate for a simple solution, some are a better fit with the remedies available under this system than others. The Berta and Silte's claims are for allocation of rights and benefits that are defined by the Ethiopian federal system and could be provided within it. In contrast, the OLF is challenging the underlying legitimacy of the system, including the House's authority over dispute resolution.

These differences in the fit between the system and the claims affected the groups' participation in the conflict resolution system in several ways: by influencing their interest in participating in the system, by shaping how they expressed their claims, and by affecting the ability of the system to respond to those claims. The Berta and Silte, whose interests corresponded to those recognized by the system, naturally had a greater interest in participating than the Oromo, whose interests fell outside the system. This in turn gave the Berta and the Silte an incentive to express their interests in the terms understood by the system. There were likely some underlying concerns that drove the Berta and Silte to seek greater political power, whether economic, reputational, cultural, or something else entirely. Enticed by the rewards for participation gin the system, those various underlying concerns were transformed into claims for the legal rights recognized in the system: proportionate representation and formal recognition. The Berta and Silte then found the system generally, if imperfectly, responsive to their concerns: both groups' claims were accepted into the system and considered by it.

Next, not only the character of the disputes, but also the identity of the groups themselves affected their participation in the conflict resolution process. The first important characteristic is the group's internal organization. Attempts to define group rights and pursue group claims are often plagued by problems of defining group membership and agency. The Berta and Silte are cohesive social groups with pre-established members and leadership, minimizing these problems. The Oromo, in contrast, are a diffuse group without reliable internal leadership structure or group consensus on the OLF's cause. It would be difficult for the OLF to claim to represent the entire Oromo Nationality or to identify its actual members.

Of course, it is not by chance that the Berta and Silte do not suffer from the agency and membership problems that are common to group claims. Rather just as the system's recognition of certain rights has encouraged ethnic groups to shape their claims to match those rights, so the availability of opportunities for Nationalities to claim those rights has encouraged ethnic groups to establish internal leadership structures and processes that will permit them to do so. As small ethnic groups that gain disproportionately greater rewards by participating in the system, the Berta and Silte have greater incentives than the OLF to position themselves to do so.

A second influential characteristic is each group's level of involvement in the political system as a whole. The conflict resolution system is, after all, not the only way that ethnic groups claim their rights. Rather, they claim them first and foremost through participation in government. And the success of political and structural incentives for participation in the government seems to reinforce participation in conflict resolution processes as well. Because the House is composed of representatives of the Nationalities, disputing Nationalities like the Berta and the Gumuz are already invested in the House as an institution, and it has responsibilities to them as its constituencies. The Silte, although not yet involved in the House, were seeking to be a part of it. In contrast, the OLF has refused to take part in the current government on principle and so not only has no pre-existing relationship with the House but is formally opposed to it. This sense of constituency is a central theme in the structure of the Ethiopian system.

Finally, the expressive function of bringing a claim to the House favors the participation of groups like the Berta and Silte rather than the Oromo. Parties may be looking not just for process or for resolution, but for the imprimatur of an outside authority or for a means of expressing the seriousness of their dispute. For small groups like the Berta and Silte to submit their local conflicts to the House symbolizes the dispute's importance and seeks the acknowledgment of a higher authority. These are satisfactions that the Oromo, a large group with a national conflict, cannot expect. Since the federal government is the other party to their dispute, mere consideration of their claims by the House would serve as an expression of federal power rather than federal respect.

Taken as a whole, these factors suggest that there is a dynamic relationship between the ethnic groups, the political system as a whole, and the conflict resolution system. There are certain qualities inherent in these conflicts and groups that make them more amenable to participation in and resolution by the conflict resolution system: a cohesive group position on an issue, for example, or a claim that fits neatly into the political structure as it exists. But the ethnic groups also engage in an active process of reshaping their identities and claims, when they see it to their advantage to so in order to participate in the system.

This also indicates that a conflict resolution system could be a tool for recasting ethnic interrelationships and roles in society, for the better or the worse. Whereas ethnic conflict may seem inchoate when it is undirected and takes place solely in social and political realms, the existence of a mechanism for resolving those conflicts to their advantage may encourage ethnic groups to narrow and hone their claims to specific concerns with specific remedies and to develop decision-making structures that will enable them to pursue those claims. That possibility raises important questions. Common wisdom has it that granting rights to ethnic groups may stir up more disputes or intensify old ones. Whether this is right or wrong, does granting access to process raise similar concerns?

On a more hopeful note, if we assume that ethnic groups will continue to play social roles in ethnic-identified societies and that access to process might encourage them to play a productive rather than a destructive role, what kinds of roles would the state encourage them to take on? What sort of incentives will encourage them to accept those roles? And in the context of dispute resolution, what kinds of processes and institutions will promote these goals?

* * *

The Ethiopian system provides one set of answers to these questions. It has three distinctive qualities: 1) it establishes a permanent conflict resolution institution that is composed of ethnic representatives and grants a measure of standing to all ethnic groups; 2) it uses complementary consensual and adjudicative processes; and 3) it treats ethnic relationship as a primary subject of constitutional interpretation.

Other states make use of some of these mechanisms and permit ethnic groups to participate in their court systems or other legal processes in limited ways. Some states have established permanent ombudsmen or commissions to address minority and indigenous concerns. Some permit members of minority and indigenous groups to seek interpretation and enforcement of constitutional rights. The Ethiopian system, however, appears to be singular in combining all three qualities.

However, the Ethiopian approach is distinctive in a more consequential sense than merely as a happenstance aggregation of these particular constituent parts. Other states may permit ethnic groups to make use of their legal processes when those groups can accommodate their identities and claims to those processes, by meeting the ordinary judicial system's requirements for standing and jurisdiction. But ordinary judicial procedures are designed primarily for individuals and for the state, not for groups, particularly in civil law systems. The Ethiopian system aims to design processes that accommodate the identities and claims of its ethnic groups, by granting some standing to all groups and authorizing some jurisdiction over all disputes.

In so doing, the Ethiopian system challenges the usual assumptions and questions about the relationship of ethnic groups and legal process. Rather than asking whether ethnic groups can be rights holders or have the capacity to participate in legal process, it asks how legal process can be accommodated to the needs and conflicts of ethnic groups. Which qualities of legal process lend themselves to ethnic conflict resolution, and how can legal process be put to service of the goal of maintaining an ethnic-identified multi-ethnic society?

1. Three Institutional Qualities: A Permanent, Ethnic–Composed Institution with Standing for Ethnic Groups

The House of the Federation is a permanent institution that is composed of ethnic representatives and grants standing to ethnic groups. These characteristics reflect and respond to the realities of ethnic conflict discussed in Part II, above. Accepting the inevitability of conflicts between ethnic groups, the Ethiopian government created a permanent conflict resolution system rather than relying on ad hoc interventions. Recognizing that the formally ethnic-blind ordinary courts in Ethiopia lack both the institutional capacity to handle any kind of group claims and the credibility to handle ethnic claims in particular, the House is focused specifically on resolving ethnic disputes and made up of ethnic representatives. By granting standing to all ethnic groups, the Ethiopian system makes legal processes available for all inter-ethnic disputes. In so doing, the Ethiopian system both acknowledges the complexity of Ethiopian inter-ethnic relationships and the need for processes that can address all ethnic groups' claims, whether they are a local majority or minority.

a. Permanence Offers Practical Advantages

A permanent specialized system presents certain typical advantages, and the Ethiopian system makes use of these advantages to address the realities of ethnic group conflicts. The House has the opportunity to develop expertise and good practices over time, which is a benefit in the context of complex, interwoven ethnic relationships and disputes. A permanent institution is positioned to address recurrent, pervasive social concerns over the long-term, by mandating and supervising the implementation of new processes or institutional reforms, for example. If controversies should arise in the future about the study and referendum process that the Council of Constitutional Inquiry established in the Silte case, the Council will be available to respond to those new issues.

In addition, the House is already constituted and organized, so that it should be readily available as disputes arise. Initiating a dispute resolution process requires some measure of political will and is sometimes seen as a loss of face or a signal of a weak relative bargaining position. Indeed, one aspect of training for mediators is the art of bringing reluctant parties to the negotiating table. Triggering a pre-existing mechanism with an established institution is less controversial, requires less imagination and effort, and is therefore more likely to occur than calling for new ad hoc processes. The availability of a dispute resolution process can also provide an additional incentive to negotiate reasonably and peaceably outside that system, by posing the threat that the third party institution may bring the matter to a less advantageous solution that can be reached directly.

Furthermore, the existence of a permanent institution promotes not just participation, but early participation. Even after the parties do begin an ad hoc process, delays in beginning the process can be socially and politically costly and tend to make resolving the dispute more difficult. Easy cases now may well be hard cases later, after they have become contentious. And while lingering conflicts between private parties might not concern the state much, multi-ethnic states know that unaddressed inter-ethnic discord all too often festers into unrest.

In this regard, early entry into the process also serves a diversionary purpose: by removing the dispute from its social and political context, its social and political costs may be contained. Once a process for addressing their concerns had been initiated, both the Silte and the Berta permitted the involved local political institutions to carry on with their ordinary business instead of holding those institutions hostage to their dispute. The Oromo conflict, in contrast, is being played out in the socio-political arena, with disruptive and sometimes violent results.

b. Ethnic Composition Builds Ethnic Constituency

It is common wisdom in Ethiopia, right or wrong, that the credibility of government institutions depends on having proportionate ethnic representation within them. A demand for proportionate representation in every institution presents a heavy and at times unbearable burden that can undercut other institutional mandates. However, in institutions that address ethnic interests, proportionate representation may foster a vital sense of constituency among ethnic groups. The nurture of and reliance on a sense of ethnic constituency is one of the central themes of the Ethiopian system.

In particular, ethnic representation in the House seems to promote both a general sense of constituency and also a practice of participating in the House as an institution. Because the Nationalities have representatives in the House and take part in its activities over the long-term outside the context of any particular dispute, they have continuous access to, investment in and oversight of it. As discussed above, there is a dynamic relationship between the Nationalities and the political system: when given access to the system, Nationalities tend to shape their identities, internal organization, and claims to make use of that access to their advantage. Although it is impossible to pinpoint the motivation of the involved groups, in the Berta, Silte, and Oromo cases, political participation, or an interest in it, correlated with participation in conflict resolution, and vice versa.

If successful, the development of a sense of constituency in the House could have profound ramifications for the dispute resolution process. In any given dispute, it should encourage the involved Nationalities to bring their claims there. Over time, repeated individual acts of participation may establish a practice of resort to the House to resolve conflicts, and therefore a practice of using legal processes to resolve ethnic disputes. As discussed below, such practices may take on a life of their own, creating not just possibilities, but expectations of participation.

In this sense, the creation of a permanent institution specifically intended for ethnic conflicts could gradually reshape the social perception of ethnic conflict. If ethnic disputes are treated and resolved as ordinary disputes subject to rational procedures, they will eventually be regarded as such. The very existence of a permanent institution like the House of the Federation thus could undermine the social expectation that inter-ethnic disputes will constitute pure exercises of power.

But while the permanence and ethnic composition of the House present a transformative possibility, these qualities also run the risk of entrenching existing oppositions and hostilities. Particularly because constituency rather than independence is the basis of the institution's credibility, it risks accreting institutional biases or becoming a pawn to powerful players and coalitions. The problems of reliance on constituency rather than independence are at their peak in the context of constitutional interpretation.

The use of the House of the Federation, an ethnically representative body, to carry out the typically judicial role of constitutional interpretation underlines the high Ethiopian valuation of ethnic concerns in constitutional interpretation. It also relies again on a sense of constituency rather than an independent adjudicator to establish the process's legitimacy among ethnic groups. However, in so doing, this choice blends legal and political roles in ways that threaten to undermine other fundamental goals of constitutional interpretation, such as maintaining separation of powers.

As an initial matter, it is important to understand the place of the Ethiopian system in the range of methods of constitutional interpretation. Although Americans understand the essence of judicial review to be the power of the ordinary courts to interpret the constitution and to nullify laws as unconstitutional, this is not the shape of judicial review in many states. Ethiopia is unusual but by no means unique in giving the power of constitutional interpretation to the upper house of its Parliament.

Indeed, many states have a considerably more limited vision of the role of judicial review than does the United States. These states permit review only of certain kinds of constitutional claims under limited circumstances, relying to a large degree on political mechanisms to hold government power in check and enforce civil liberties. In general, states have authorized a wide range of institutions to interpret their constitutions, and the scope of that authority varies significantly in terms of jurisdiction, power to nullify a law, binding effect of the judgment, and enforcement. For example, most states do provide for some form of judicial review, putting the power to interpret the constitution and nullify some contradictory government actions in the hands of some independent judicial or quasi-judicial body. But only about one-third of those states follow the United States in decentralizing this authority to the ordinary courts as a whole. The others vest the interpretative power in a special constitutional court or council, vest it solely in the highest ordinary court of the land, or use some mixture of these systems. Only a few states do not provide for authoritative constitutional interpretation at all.

But even when considered within the context of this variety of roles and institutional mechanisms for constitutional interpretation, the Ethiopian choice of the House as its constitutional interpreter raises a red flag about political control of the process. At times, assigning this authority to a non-judicial branch has been a signal of a repressive government disinterested in active review. While there are a number of democratic, stable, and rights-respectful nations that operate under a system of parliamentary interpretation of the constitution, those nations tend to have other internal incentives for voluntary adherence to the constitution that Ethiopia lacks.

In the Ethiopian case, this decision prioritizes the credibility created by a sense of ethnic constituency over the legitimacy and check on the political branches made possible by having an independent, nonpolitical body interpret the constitution. For reasons of sheer numbers if nothing else, it would not be possible to have representatives of all ethnic groups among the members of a constitutional court, whereas the House is composed of representatives of all the Nationalities. If it is true that Ethiopia's ethnic groups would not accept constitutional determinations that came from a non-representative body, then the credibility of those determinations among ethnic groups is better guaranteed by ensuring constituency than independence. The costs of this trade-off are more acute, of course, in cases that do not affect ethnic interests, and so this trade-off also represents a judgment that ethnic issues will be a primary concern of constitutional interpretation.

There is no doubt, however, that the decision to vest the power of constitutional interpretation in a political body does not sit easily with respect for the values promoted by separation of powers and systems of strong judicial review. Ethnic issues are only a few of those that must be addressed by constitutional interpretation, and active, independent constitutional courts have played a vital role in building respect for constitutional values in new democracies as well as old. In light of these concerns, ethnic constituency building ought not take precedence over independent adjudication where constitutional interpretation is concerned. Furthermore, as discussed below, processes for ethnic conflict resolution may be more effective generally if they are based in multiple institutions, rather than in a single, ethnic-focused system.

c. Risks and Rewards of Standing for Ethnic Groups

While the House grants standing to its Nationalities to bring quite a number of claims, its recognition of ethnic groups is not unqualified. Although Nationalities can be parties to virtually any claim, it is far easier for government entities to initiate a claim quickly than for a Nationality to do so. Under the new law organizing the House's procedures, regional state councils are automatically accepted as proper representatives of the state's interests, but Nationalities must prove agency and also must demonstrate that they have exhausted state remedies for their claims. While this is likely a wise safeguard against some forms of chicanery, it does place an additional burden on Nationalities and complicate the process of bringing claims for them. In addition, Nationalities can bring only those constitutional claims that relate to their constitutional rights, while states can petition for hearing of any constitutional claim. Since regional state councils tend to be dominated by the majority ethnic group in the region, these rules in fact give systematic advantages to regional majorities (acting as regional states), over regional minorities (who participate as Nationalities). Finally, while the House has heard claims affecting communities that have not been recognized as

Nationalities, as it did in the Silte case, its new procedural law does not provide a specific mechanism for such communities to bring claims.

Thus, while the kind of institution embodied by the House in theory could serve as a venue of first resort for ethnic groups in conflict, in fact the House's rules of admissibility, standing, and exhaustion mean that it serves as a venue of last resort, after other mechanisms have been tried and have failed. These limits on ethnic standing undercut the benefits promoted by the House's permanence and ethnic composition to some extent. The House presents a venue for most ethnic claims eventually, after exhaustion requirements are satisfied and so long as a regional state will bring those claims that a Nationality or smaller community is not specifically authorized to bring. However, it does not offer automatic, immediate access to legal process for all claims. Accordingly, it is less likely that ethnic groups will develop a practice or expectation of making use of the House's processes to resolve their conflicts, and less likely that the House will be able to intervene early in a conflict and prevent if from escalating.

These questions of the appropriate standards for ethnic group standing and admissibility of ethnic claims, however, beg a more fundamental question: whether it is ever wise to give official recognition to ethnic groups or to design legal processes specifically for resolving ethnic disputes. This question is particularly acute in the constitutional setting, as discussed in the next Section, but it presents concerns even in consensual and ordinary adjudicative proceedings.

It is worth noting again at this juncture that many multi-ethnic states will not find it in their interests to make use of legal processes for resolving ethnic disputes. Rather, there are a subset of multi-ethnic states that have an obvious need for some form of ethnic conflict resolution: that is, multi-ethnic states where ethnic identity is primary, ethnic division is deep, and recurrent debilitating ethnic disputes pose the primary threat to the existence of the state.

In considering whether it is appropriate to grant some form of standing to ethnic groups, it is also important to consider that state recognition of ethnicity poses a risk for ethnic groups as well as for the state. In the past, such recognition has been limited and often negative. To be sure, some constitutions contain protections for ethnic minority or indigenous groups, either in the form of group rights, protections against discrimination on the basis of ethnicity, or political structures such as autonomous regions or set aside parliamentary seats. But other constitutions have enshrined limits on citizenship that have been either obliquely or overtly based on ethnicity, and many have not addressed ethnicity at all. Political policies targeted at ethnic groups are far more common, sometimes protecting minority and indigenous peoples, but sometimes targeting particular groups for sanction or oppression. There is no doubt that state recognition of ethnicity has often been to the detriment of ethnic groups in the past, and that, whatever its ostensible purpose, such recognition creates risk of misuse.

Acknowledging the legitimacy of these concerns, two observations suggest that some multi-ethnic states should nonetheless run the risks associated with legitimizing ethnic identifications in order to gain the benefit of legal process for ethnic conflict resolution. First, if an ethnic conflict exists, whether sham or genuine, the multi-ethnic state's fears have already been realized: ethnicity has become a source of conflict. While there is a risk that recognition of ethnic groups may catalyze an escalation in ethno-political rhetoric, it is certain that the state must find some way of dealing with ethnic conflict in order to survive. In this context, recognizing ethnic groups as parties for the purpose of adopting conflict resolution processes may present a measured risk that is worth taking.

Furthermore, it appears that it is not so much ethnic identification itself as unresolved and festering ethnic disputes that pose an imminent threat to the multi-ethnic state. One reason that ethnic identification is persistence is that ethnicity often serves a positive purpose by constructing vibrant, valued communities. Beyond their cultural and social value, these communities may play a positive political role, governing themselves successfully and authentically representing the interests of their members. Indeed, they may be more popular, credible, and effective than non-ethnic political institutions. Nor is it even the development of disputes between ethnic groups that makes ethnic conflict destructive. After all, disagreements readily and ordinarily arise and are resolved just as readily and ordinarily between and within all communities, however defined.

Rather, the primary threats that ethnic conflict poses to the state seems to be twofold: the use of ethnicity by political or community leaders to stir up conflict as a means to power, and the failure to resolve inter-ethnic conflicts, whether genuine or political shams, in an orderly and peaceful way. The first threat is one that legal process can address only indirectly, by undermining political rhetoric asserting that there is no effective remedy for ethnic conflict, and by actually resolving claims.

The second threat presented by ethnic conflict, that of unrest spurred by lingering unresolved conflict, is one that can and ought to be addressed directly by law and legal process. Where ethnic conflict is already occurring, early diversion of the disagreement into a conflict resolution process before it becomes intractable offers some hope of preventing the dispute from escalating. Granting standing to ethnic actors and recognizing their claims is necessary to this process.

Mere acknowledgment of ethnic identifications in the conflict resolution context, without more (such as creation of new political rights or mandatory identification of all citizens with a particular ethnic group, for example), ought to pose a relatively small risk of catalyzing ethnic conflict, as compared to acknowledgment of ethnic identifications in other contexts. However, there is a specific risk to legitimizing legal institutions as an appropriate venue, and legal processes as an appropriate mechanism, for ethnic dispute resolution. Just as democratic processes have been co-opted by political and community ethnic leaders and used as tools of nationalism and ethnic warfare, so too could legal processes.

This raise several questions: Does ethnicity pose a risk that is greater or different in kind than other political interests that have been known to hijack legal processes? What safeguards might be established against misuse of the legal system for this purpose, as structural guarantees of judicial independence protect against misuse of the courts by the political branches of government?

* * *

b. Generating Legal Norms and Practices

If the ability to bring disputes to some sort of conclusion provides the measure of success, using multiple and complementary processes seems to provide an advantage. In light of the serious social and political ramifications of unresolved ethnic disputes, this is no small matter. But there are other considerations: equality, efficiency, fairness, enforceability and credibility among them.

Precisely because ethnic groups do play such a significant role in ethnic-identified societies, the social effects of these processes are a vital concern for the state. As discussed below, the Ethiopian system on its face promotes a particular social goal: self-determination for its ethnic groups. Certainly the results of the constitutional interpretation in the Silte case seem to advance this purpose. However, as discussed below, other multi-ethnic states will likely have other predominant concerns, such as security and equality among their ethnic groups, and so their practices will need to be guided by ad judged against different norms.

There is a lively debate about the essential social purpose and functioning of legal processes, spurred not only by the infiltration of ADR into legal systems, but also by the social effects of public interest litigation and by the critical legal studies movement. Division on these questions is particularly acute when it comes to questions like the one before us: the appropriate processes and institutions for deciding group disputes of public significance. The discussion began with opposing principles. Owen Fiss and other advocates of litigation before a judge promoted authoritative adjudication based on external, neutral legal principles as a potent agent of institutional and social change, and emphasized the importance of formal procedures as a protection for weaker parties. Advocates of consensual systems, in contrast, contended that the parties themselves can better create durable solutions that promote their primary, often underlying goals, and that their direct, active participation in self-defined processes is crucial to this end. Critical legal scholars, meanwhile, saw in both systems flawed assumptions of neutrality and equality that merely mask the use of law as a vehicle for power.

As this debate has progressed, new approaches and theories have emerged. A middle ground has developed, based on the proposition that different processes will have roles to play in serving different sorts of disputes, and that relevant factors can be identified to provide models for choosing between processes in the context of any given dispute. In the private sector, some businesses and industries have developed complex hybrid, multi-stage models, beginning with defined and directed negotiation, and progressing into increasingly adjudicative and coercive mechanisms in later stages if consensual processes fail. The goals envisioned for legal processes in public disputes have also evolved: Nathalie des Rosiers, for example, argues for a therapeutic approach, calling upon courts to play an expressive role rather than an adjudicative one.

It is worth noting that each of these positions, new and old, presupposes the existence of effective, competent courts that are ready and able to consider claims if called upon to do so. For ethnic conflicts, this is often untrue. Indeed, in the ethnic conflict context, there may well be no legal processes of any kind to address the dispute at hand. Therefore, the challenge that we face in considering processes for ethnic conflict is not to determine an ideal among the available legal processes, but rather to develop any effective legal process at all.

In this light, while this debate raises many interesting legal process issues, I would like to on only two: the capacity of legally processes to create law, and the risk that legal processes will be used in bad faith or to destructive ends.

If there is both substantive law and formal legal processes to enforce that law, then adjudicative and consensual models' processes may offer distinctly different advantages: binding versus nonbinding judgments, and an obligation to uphold legally prescribed norms versus an ability to expressly compromise those norms, for example. But when there is little or no substantive law, and particularly in contexts in which enforcement mechanisms are meager, these distinctions begin to collapse.

In this context, consensual processes as well as adjudicative ones may generate law by establishing practices of participating in those processes and adhering to the substantive norms that result. In the Ethiopian context, the Berta's established practice of participating in the House of the Federation facilitated their consent to the House's jurisdiction over their dispute. If this new practice endures and is repeated, the jurisdiction of the House over such disputes may eventually become obligatory, in that the expectation of participation in the House's mediation process may become as absolute as if that jurisdiction were formally mandatory, and the social and political costs of refusing to participate may play an enforcement role as effectively as formal sanctions. If the Berta case were to reach a substantive result reallocating representatives among locally non-indigenous as well as indigenous groups, this result itself could also become an institutional norm within the House's mediation process. Thus, because it is a permanent institution with institutional memory, the mediation system may in time develop its own customary or common law.

This capacity of various kinds of processes to generate law suggests that the most important goal of ethnic-identified states should be to draw ethnic groups into ongoing participation in legal processes. Legal processes will not only become a habit of dispute resolution but also may over time themselves generate the law necessary to resolve those disputes. Much as states participate in international law, gradually developing and complying with common norms through iterative processes of interpretation, implementation and repudiation that extend far beyond traditional legal contexts, so might ethnic groups be drawn into participation in and creation of domestic legal norms for their behavior by participation in legal processes of all sorts.

If this is so, then the potential effect of legal processes in controlling ethnic conflict transcends the resolution or containment of any particular disputes. But if so, then its potential to cause destructive results through generation of destructive norms also transcends the risks associated with bad faith participation in any given dispute.

In each model of legal process, the safeguards against destructive use of the process can be readily subverted by a bad faith actor. In the adjudicative model, formal processes and a neutral judge are intended to winnow out false claims and evidence, if not false motives, and to mitigate power differentials between the parties. But if the judge herself is biased, this safeguard fails. Consensual models protect against destructive results by their reliance on the agreement of the parties, and on the active participation of a third party neutral to address differences in power. But if all of the parties are acting in bad faith, they can nonetheless hijack the process. Finally, if there is not just individual but institutional bias, the risk of generating destructive law is acute. If the mediation institution develops its own common law by means of the practices of the parties, that common law could perpetuate and enforce the biases inherent in those collective practices.

In this respect, having multiple, complementary legal processes is not just a matter of maximizing the chance of successful resolution of an immediate dispute or providing multiple contexts for participation in legal processes and generation of legal norms and compliance. Rather, the use of multiple processes centered in multiple institutions helps to mitigate this risk of bad faith, and enforcement of constitutional principles in particular must serve as a vital safeguard against destructive norms. Bad faith on one level may be counterbalanced by good faith on another; biased norms or practices in one institution ought to be corrected by the norms and practices of another. This possibility creates complexities, of course—what if the norms and practices between levels and institutions are truly different? What if, for example, ethnic communities consistently vote for recognition as independent Nationalities, and regional states consistently determine that they are ineligible according to the constitutional standard? If there are such divergences, the development of productive constitutional principles and useful constitutional interpretation will be vital to controlling and limiting them.

———————

Notes and Questions

1. What does the author mean by "legal" processes?

2. What are the key characteristics of the Ethiopian ethnic conflicts? What threat do such conflicts pose to the state?

3. What are the risks and rewards of granting standing to ethnic groups?

4. Discuss the practical advantages of having a permanent, ethnic-composed institution with standing for ethnic groups. What are the disadvantages of such an institution?

5. In what ways does the Ethiopian system fail to address ethnic concerns in an effective manner?

6. What are the fundamental concerns that the Ethiopian system raises for the use of legal process in addressing ethnic conflict?

7. Having read the detailed description of the Ethiopian system, how would you respond to the question raised by the author, namely whether it is ever wise to give official recognition to ethnic groups or to design legal processes specifically for resolving ethnic conflicts?

D. FACT–FINDING

The bilateral fact-finding process in which one or more persons conducts an independent investigation of disputed facts may be a useful form of resolving ethnic conflicts, particularly where the disputing parties give the fact-finder the power to make recommendations. The following case study is a thick description of the use of fact-finding in the Israeli–Palestinian Peace Process.

ARTHUR LENK, FACT–FINDING AS PEACE NEGOTIATION TOOL—THE MITCHELL REPORT AND THE ISRAELI–PALESTINIAN PEACE PROCESS

24 Loyola of Los Angeles International & Comparative Law Review 289 (2002).

I. Introduction

The peace process between the Israelis and the Palestinians requires creative concepts for conflict resolution. The "Oslo" process, which began as a series of discussions in Norway among academia, created a full range of legal and social relations between the Israelis and the Palestinians. It used a range of differing methods and creativity to deal with seemingly irreconcilable issues between the parties. The basic concept of the process was to begin with the "easier" issues and then gradually build a trusting relationship to tackle the most difficult points of conflict. The series of agreements, signed by Israel and the Palestine Liberation Organization between 1993–1999, were not merely written agreements. Rather, the agreements were steps in a process of reconciliation and confidence building that would lead towards addressing the most contentious issues. Despite the first genuine attempt to deal with these permanent status issues at Camp David in July 2000, violence erupted between the Israelis and the Palestinians in September 2000.

In the days following these confrontations, the Israelis and the Palestinians, together with the active involvement of the United States and others (Egypt, Jordan, United Nations and the European Union), began to consider additional methods of conflict resolution to cease violence and return to a more constructive path. The parties involved decided to form a fact-finding body to examine the facts and causes of the violent outbreaks, and to propose ideas to prevent their recurrence. The idea to form such a body was first proposed at a summit in Paris on October 4, 2000. The Israelis and the Palestinians reached an agreement on the proposal at a second summit that took place in Sharm el-Sheikh, Egypt on October 16–17, 2000. Former U.S. Senator George J. Mitchell chaired the Sharm el-Sheikh Fact–Finding Committee (the Mitchell Committee). In April 2001, the Committee published the Mitchell Report, which summarized its findings and recommendations.

* * *

III. Background to the Conflict

Israel and the Palestinians had a history of negotiating and reaching agreements even before the memorable handshake between Yitzhak Rabin and Yasser Arafat on the U.S. White House lawn on September 13, 1993. That handshake signaled a mutual recognition and a shared goal to gradually end enmity in the region. A series of agreements were signed, yet a number of setbacks challenged the attempt to foster a relationship. Ehud Barak was elected Prime Minister of Israel in May 1999 on the platform that he would expedite the negotiation process between the parties. In September 1999, the parties committed to a fifteen-month timeline for implementing agreements and working together to resolve remaining issues.

In Spring 2000, Barak reached the conclusion that a summit meeting between the leaders was a necessary catalyst to reach a historic agreement. At the invitation of the United States, the parties met at Camp David, near Washington D.C. with U.S. representatives led by then-President William J. Clinton. From July 11–25, 2000, for the first time, the parties openly discussed the most difficult "permanent status" issues of the Israeli–Palestinian conflict. These issues included Jerusalem, the refugees, settlements and recognition of an independent Palestinian state. Despite the marathon meetings and twelve days of seclusion, the parties did not reach an agreement.

Tensions subsequently increased between Israel and the Palestinians. The United States blamed the Palestinians for the failure to reach a successful resolution at Camp David. In response to the conclusion of the summit, President Clinton said:

> [T]he Palestinians changed their position; [they] moved forward. The Israelis moved more from the position they had ... I was not condemning Arafat, I was praising Barak. But I would be making a mistake not to praise Barak because I think he took a big risk. And I think it sparked, already, in Israel a real debate, which is moving Israeli public opinion toward the conditions that will make peace. So I thought that was important, and I think it deserves to be acknowledged. Prime Minister Barak announced that the proposals made at Camp David were void, and stated the Palestinians were responsible for their rejection of the Israeli offers. In Israel, Barak was criticized for making such far-reaching offers without success. Arafat embarked on a month-long international tour to discuss with world leaders the possibility of a unilateral Palestinian declaration of independence. At the end of his tour, Arafat realized the international community would not support a unilateral action by the Palestinians on the diplomatic front. Simultaneously, rhetoric regarding the threat of violence in the region increased as a result of the deadlock in the peace process. Nevertheless, secret negotiations continued in the region and in Europe.

On September 27, 2000, violence erupted in the region when a roadside bomb exploded, wounding two Israeli soldiers at the Netzarim Junction in the Gaza Strip. The next day, opposition leader Ariel Sharon visited the Temple Mount in Jerusalem. Generally, in Israel, this action was considered to be a domestic challenge to Prime Minister Barak. On September 29, protests in the Temple Mount area occurred during and after Friday Muslim prayers. That afternoon, four Palestinians were killed and fourteen Israeli policemen were wounded. Violence reached the West Bank and Gaza.

Diplomatic efforts began in an attempt to quell the violence. On October 4, Prime Minister Barak and Chairman Arafat met in Paris with French President, Jacques Chirac, and U.S. Secretary of State, Madeline Albright. The parties agreed upon some "Points of Understanding," which included a commitment by both sides "to reduce and eliminate friction and confrontation." Additionally, the parties preliminarily agreed that the United States would develop with the Israelis and the Palestinians, as well as in consultation with the United Nations Secretary General, a committee of fact-finding on the events of the past several days.

Notwithstanding the promising nature of the agreement, Arafat refused to sign at the last moment.

IV.   Formation of the Mitchell Committee

On October 16 and 17, the Israeli and Palestinian leaders met again at a summit in Sharm el-Sheikh, Egypt. Other summit participants included President Hosni Mubarak of Egypt, U.S. President Clinton, King Abdullah from Jordan, U.N. Secretary General Kofi Annan and Javier Solana, European Union High Representative for Common Foreign and Security Policy. The summit concluded with the parties agreeing to the establishment of a fact-finding committee. The parties additionally agreed to issue public statements calling to end violence, renew security cooperation and work towards further negotiations.

Regarding the fact-finding committee, President Clinton said:

[T]he United States will develop with the Israelis and Palestinians, as well as in consultation with the United Nations Secretary–General, a committee of fact finding on the events of the past several weeks and how to prevent their recurrence. The committee's report will be shared by the U.S. President with the U.N. Secretary–General and the parties prior to publication. A final report shall be submitted under the auspices of the U.S. President for publication.

The parties later agreed the committee would be chaired by former U.S. Senator George J. Mitchell, and would include four additional members: former Turkish President Suleyman Demirel, Norwegian Foreign Minister Thorbjorn Jagland, former U.S. Senator Warren Rudman and Mr. Solana.

The Israelis and Palestinians manifested a willingness to play a role in determining the mandate for the Mitchell Committee. The Committee, however, feared that such a focus would be counterproductive and impractical in light of the already tense atmosphere. Further, the terms sought by the parties might encumber the Committee's flexibility and independence. The Committee instead focused its mandate on two letters sent by President Clinton to Senator Mitchell, which outlined goals and working procedures for the Committee. In the second letter, dated December 6, 2000, President Clinton wrote:

First, the Committee should ensure that it is, and is perceived to be, fair and impartial. Specifically, the Committee should operate in a transparent manner, allowing the parties to view material offered by the other party and to comment on one another's presentations. Also, as was agreed at Sharm, both sides should have an opportunity to review the report and give comments to the Committee before it becomes final.

Second, the Committee should seek to avoid any action that could further inflame the already very tense situation.... (T)he Committee should conduct its work in confidence rather than through hearings.... Finally, if the Committee chooses to retain professionals for assistance, they should conduct their work quietly outside the glare of publicity and should share the results only with the Committee. If these experts conduct individual interviews or gather materials in the region relevant to the Committee's mission, they should do so privately and inform the Committee of their work, which the Committee would bring to the attention of the parties for further comment.

Third, the Committee should strive to steer clear of any step that will intensify mutual blame and finger-pointing between the two parties. As I noted in my previous letter, 'the Committee should not become a divisive force or a focal point for blame and recrimination but rather should serve to forestall violence and confrontation and provide lessons for the future.' This should not be a tribunal whose purpose is to determine the guilt or innocence of individuals or of the parties; rather, it should be a fact-finding committee whose purpose is to determine what happened and how to avoid it recurring in the future...."

V.   Fact–Finding Activities

In late November 2000, the parties assigned points of contact to work with the Mitchell Committee. Representatives of each side were invited to meet with the Committee members in New York for initial consultations. At that meeting, the participants were asked to submit a written presentation to the Committee by the end of December. Additionally, the parties were informed that Committee members would visit the region for introductory meetings on December 11 and 12. Further, the Committee would consider additional visits as deemed necessary. Both parties were expected to respond to the initial written presentations at a later date.

Despite the agreement reached at Sharm el-Sheikh, none of the terms written by President Clinton on October 17, 2000 were effective except for the development of the Mitchell Committee. At the conclusion of the summit, Prime Minister Barak publicly called for implementation of the terms of the agreement, including cessation of violence. Chairman Arafat, however, did not make a similar declaration, although a statement was made on Palestinian television noting that "the Palestinian leadership" instructed the Palestinian forces to follow up on the activities agreed to at Sharm el-Sheikh. Unfortunately, no security cooperation was initiated and the violence continued.

An additional diplomatic attempt to end the violence took place in Gaza at a meeting between Chairman Arafat and then Israeli Minister for Regional Cooperation, Shimon Peres. The parties agreed to issue a "Joint Statement on the Cessation of Violence" on November 2, 2000. Before the statement was issued, however, a car bomb exploded in a Jerusalem market, killing two Israelis.

A.   Written Submissions

Each party submitted two rounds of documents to the Committee. These documents offered subjective narratives of the prior events and the deteriorating relationship between the parties. The documents were similar to legal brief arguments on substantive and procedural issues. The parties presented their views by way of videos, maps and aerial photos. Both sides also submitted views on how they saw the completion of work by the Committee including its recommendations as well as quickly publicizing their submissions through media sources including the Internet. They attempted to use the submissions to gain advantages in the diplomatic circles and the public opinion. Many meetings took place with both the Committee members and the technical staff including officials, victims of violence, NGO's and academia. The benefits of this process included providing a forum for venting their concerns and frustrations, as well as introducing the Committee and its staff to the nuances of the conflict. The presentations additionally enabled the Committee to direct its efforts towards pragmatic recommendations.

B. Palestinian Initial Submissions

In December 2000, the Palestinians presented two submissions to the Mitchell Committee. On December 11, 2000, the Palestinians presented their Preliminary Submission of the Palestine Liberation Organization to the International Commission of Inquiry to the Committee members during their visit to the region. This submission primarily addressed procedural issues, but it also presented Palestinian claims regarding the conflict. Then on December 30, the Palestinians presented A Crisis of Faith: Second Submission of the Palestine Liberation Organization, which was their primary written presentation of facts. Together, these two presentations emphasized the central positions of the Palestinians in the Israel–Palestinian conflict far beyond the issues of violence during the previous three months, including the major historical issues between the sides.

The Palestinian submissions offered a historical overview of the region. The papers detailed issues ranging from the U.N.'s partition plan of 1947 to the "dashed expectations" of the Palestinians as a result of the peace process. Although not expressly stated, the papers conveyed a message that the events were not a reaction to one specific event, but instead a combination of disappointments culminating over an extended period. As a result, the Palestinians saw no other option but to resort to violence in order to end the regional stalemate. In other words, the Palestinians saw themselves as merely reacting to the Israeli violence— actual physical violence as well as political and economic threats. The authors noted that more than seven years after signing the Declaration of Principles, most Palestinians had come to the conclusion that this faith was misplaced. The Palestinians viewed Israel's attitude towards the implementation of the signed agreement is perhaps best captured in late Prime Minister Rabin's assertion that 'no dates are sacred.'

The Palestinians' primary problems with the peace process included the continual building of settlements, and Israel's non-compliance with obligations taken as part of the various agreements already signed by Israel and the Palestinians. As for the settlement issue, the authors presented the Israelis' continued policy of a "military-enforced dual system, and the persistent infringement upon Palestinian civil, political and economic rights by Israeli occupation forces" as the basis of the intifada of 1987–1993.

Further, the bulk of the Palestinian presentation blamed Israel for the events of the three months following the eruption of violence. The central issues detailed by the presentation were violence against civilians ("a one-sided war"), including a range of statistics regarding the number of dead and wounded, international principles regarding the illegal use of force by Israel and a detail of different methods allegedly used "to kill and injure Palestinians." The submission also described the Palestinians' economic losses as a result of the violence.

The Palestinians emphasized the role of the international community, as envisaged by the Palestinians. They saw the Mitchell Committee as an opportunity to internationalize the conflict. Disappointed with the results of the direct negotiations with the Israelis, the Palestinians presented the view that a greater involvement from the international community would be helpful. The Palestinians hoped that the Mitchell Committee, like other international fora such as the U.N. General Assembly and the Commission on Human Rights would be of use in promoting their position in the conflict. The Committee mandate itself was presented as resulting not only from the agreement reached between the parties at Sharm el-Sheikh, but also from the Fourth Geneva Convention and U.N. Security Council Resolution 1322 (2000). From the Palestinian perspective, Israel's violation of international laws and norms in recent violent attacks, in addition to the thirty-three years of occupation of the West Bank and Gaza, was the central reason for encouraging the involvement and shared responsibility of the international community.

The Palestinians concluded their presentation with eight recommendations to the Mitchell Committee. A majority of the recommendations emphasized the "root causes" of their conflict with the Israelis rather than the specific events. The recommendations included: (1) a demand for compliance with the Fourth Geneva Convention, (2) an end to violence against the Palestinian civilian population, (3) a lift on restrictions on freedom of movement of persons, vehicles and goods, (4) a freeze on settlement construction and expansion, (5) a gun control imposed on Israeli settlers, (6) a call for Israeli compliance with the past agreements, (7) a deployment of an international monitoring and implementation mission and (8) an end to further attacks in the Palestinian controlled areas.

C. Israel's Initial Submission

Israel submitted the First Statement of the Government of Israel on December 29, 2000. The presentation emphasized that the Palestinian leadership strategically encouraged violence after being perceived by the international community as the cause of the Camp David Summit failure. The Israelis claimed that the Palestinians blatantly violated their commitment to a peaceful dispute resolution by choosing violent confrontation instead of continued diplomatic dialogue. The goal was to provide the Palestinians with an opportunity to reestablish their historical position as the underdogs in the conflict. The presentation detailed the history of agreements reached between the Israelis and the Palestinians. It stressed the repeated and comprehensive obligations that were ignored by the Palestinian Authority to work towards preventing incitement, violence and continually fighting terror. There is a detailed attempt to respond to a claim raised against Israel relating to the disproportionate use of force.

The summary of Israel's position regarding the violence was stated as:

> Israel did not seek the present confrontation. It was, and continues to be, imposed upon Israel by the Palestinian side. Within the severe constraints of the events of recent weeks, Israel's actions have been directed towards containing the confrontation, protecting persons not directly involved in the conflict and their property, and avoiding casualties to its military and police personnel in the performance of their task. Israel has also been concerned to minimize serious injury to those actively engaged on the Palestinian side.

> While it has not always been possible, in the extreme circumstances of the on-going violence, to meet all of these objectives, Israel firmly maintains that it has acted in a measured and responsible fashion in the circumstances.

Israel detailed its concerns regarding the practice and policies of the Palestinians including the exploitation of children by sending them to participate in violent protests, promoting acts of violence and terror directed at the Israeli civilians, specific acts of barbarism, official and religious incitements, the release of terrorist detainees from prisons, and the failure of the Palestinian Authority to confiscate illegal weapons. In a significant number of incidents, the Palestinian snipers hid in crowds of civilians and opened fire. Additionally, the torture and lynching of two Israeli reservist soldiers in Ramallah, and the destruction of the Jewish holy site of Joseph's Tomb, were cited as examples of the nature of the threat towards any Israeli national who fell into the hands of the Palestinians.

The authors of the report compared the Palestinian riots to "armed conflict short of war," thus mandating the application of the rules of engagement of the Israeli military within the context of these events. The nature and methods employed by the Israeli military were described in detail to refute any claim of excessive use of force. The paper detailed the various types of non-lethal weapons available to Israel, but claimed that since the violence initiated by the Palestinians involved live-fire, non-lethal weapons were often not a viable option.

The submission included a long series of quotes taken from articles by the international media citing public statements made by the Palestinian leaders addressing these points. A series of aerial photos, maps and even a collection of video clips were included with the Israeli document.

The Israelis recommended that the Palestinians stop the violence and return to the terms of the previous agreements reached between the parties in an effort to ensure security for the citizens of the region. The Israelis further proposed concrete measures, such as ending Palestinian incitement, returning terrorists to prison and renewing security cooperation. Israel also proffered a number of confidence building measures it would be disposed to undertake in an effort to "build the feeling of security and progress on all sides."

D.   Activities of Technical Staff

After the parties submitted their presentations to the Committee at the end of December 2000, the Mitchell Committee sent a delegation of approximately twelve aides, described as a technical staff, to gather evidence and meet with the parties to assist the five principal members of the Committee in their fact-finding task. This diverse group included nationals from various countries appointed by the Committee.

The Palestinians welcomed the technical staff and organized a wide series of meetings and presentations. They also submitted two additional documents on specific issues of interest regarding the conflict, in addition to a relatively large number of documents prepared by a variety of Palestinian and international organizations.

The Israelis, on the other hand, already frustrated by the shortcomings of the Sharm el-Sheikh Summit's failure to end violence, were preparing for elections in early February 2001. They deemed activities of the technical staff as extensions of the ambiguous mandate promulgated by the Mitchell Committee, and continued to be concerned by a lack of agreement on the terms of reference for the Mitchell Committee. After the technical staff visited the Temple Mount on January 13, 2001, without coordinating the visit with the Israeli officials, Israel decided to temporarily suspend its cooperation with the Mitchell Committee.

Newly elected Prime Minister Ariel Sharon renewed ties with the Committee. He noted that while he believed "the setting up of the Committee was a mistake of the previous government . . . Israel would cooperate with the Committee and extend it any necessary assistance to find out the truth [as] Israel does not fear an examination of the facts." One reason for this decision was the active involvement of Shimon Peres, the Minister of Foreign Affairs in Sharon's government. This surprising new partnership was a key component in Sharon's formation of a unified national government. Peres argued that for a new government to build international credibility, it would be counterproductive to be perceived as being responsible for the dissolution of the Mitchell Committee.

Prime Minister Sharon welcomed a second visit of the Committee members on March 21, 2001. During the four-day visit to Israel and the Palestinian areas, the Committee members held discussions with Sharon, Peres, Arafat and other political and military leaders, as well as meeting with victims of violence from both sides. Following this second visit, members of the technical staff remained in the region for four more days for further meetings with the Israeli officials to complete the fact-finding efforts of the Committee.

E.   Written Responses of the Sides

Both parties responded to the other party's submissions. Israel and the Palestinians submitted their responses around the time the Committee members made their second visit to the region.

1.   Palestinian Response

In the Third Submission of the Palestinian Liberation Organization to the Sharm el-Sheikh Fact-finding Committee, the Palestinians responded to the Israeli claims regarding the root of the violence, the Israeli characterization of the situation in the region as an "armed conflict" and other specific points raised in the Israeli submission.

Regarding the root causes of the violence, the Palestinians reemphasized their dashed expectations from the peace process. According to the Palestinians, the interim period had to be viewed comprehensively, not only the short period since Camp David. The Palestinians noted that despite the Israeli assertions to the contrary in their presentation, the Palestinian efforts to promote peace and security during the interim period were significant. The authors noted that the Israeli "allegation is belied by the Palestinian Authority's significant accomplishments in preventing violence during the Interim Period and overlooks the legal constraints imposed on its law enforcement efforts."

The document detailed Palestinian efforts to prevent violence, including actions against illegal possession of weapons. The document also presented the efforts of the Palestinian Authority to educate people in order to fight incitement. At the same time, it was argued that the acts of Israeli provocation, such as settlement activities, broken deadlines and economic and personal restrictions on Palestinians, were part of the frustration and disappointment felt by the Palestinians throughout the peace process. Counterclaims about the Israeli statements and actions in connection with incitement, such as claims of hate speech by Israeli politicians and religious leaders, were presented to rebut Israeli claims regarding the Palestinian incitement created by textbooks. Finally, the Palestinians characterized the Israeli proposals at Camp David as a dramatic departure from the principles agreed to between the parties as modalities for making peace, and thus falling short of the Palestinians' requirements regarding a peace agreement. According to the Palestinians, Barak's offer did not meet the Palestinians' need regarding Palestinian refugees, the final status of Jerusalem and other central issues.

As for the Israeli use of force, the Palestinians noted a distinction in international law between an uprising and an armed conflict. Furthermore, the Israelis' obligations and legal standards, as an occupying force, within internationally recognized frameworks, remain unchanged. Thus, the Palestinians claimed that if the occupation ended, so would the uprising. The Palestinians emphasized:

> [t]he elements necessary for establishing an "armed conflict" as a matter of international law are not present; that demonstrations are resistance to occupation; and that Israel, as an occupying power has a duty to ensure that the Palestinian people are protected. Rather, Israel's classification of the current uprising as an "armed conflict" is predicated simply on the presence of firearms at some, and not all, demonstrations. And, it is a means by which Israel attempts to derogate from its obligations as set out in international law.

In concluding the legal aspects of the conflict, the authors of the Palestinian presentation stated that the key to understanding the events was not as claimed by the Israelis:

> The link between settlements and the present intifada is clear: many of the acts of violence carried out by Israeli soldiers and settlers, that have resulted in Palestinian deaths and injuries, have taken place on the heavily defended roads leading to the settlements or in the proximity of the settlements. Israel is not under threat—the Palestinians are. And they will continue to be unless and until the international community puts an end to Israel's goal of separating the Palestinian people from its land—and controlling the former while annexing the latter.

2. Israeli Response

In its response, Israel reiterated its overall view of the continuing conflict and addressed specific allegations raised by the Palestinians. The Israelis discussed what they considered to be a series of factual and legal misrepresentations in the Palestinian submissions, particularly regarding claims of the use of excessive force and alleged assassinations by the Israel Defense Forces.

At the beginning of the statement, the Israeli authors commented on the nature of the Palestinian presentations:

> The Palestinian submissions are notable for what they leave out. Nothing is said—not a single word—of Palestinian policies and practices over the past five-and-a-half months. Nothing is said about attacks on Israeli civilians, about the ongoing incitement to hatred and violence, about the release of terrorist detainees, about the calculated exploitation of children, about the use of illegal weapons, about the destruction of Jewish Holy Sites ... Above all, nothing is said about ending the violence. It is quite extraordinary that in four Palestinian submissions to the Committee there is not a single word about the ending of the bloodshed; about stopping the attacks. The omission is telling. The message is clear. It has even been expressed by senior Palestinian officials. Palestinian attacks

against Israelis will not end until Israel accepts Palestinian demands.

As for Israel's use of force, the authors reemphasized their position that Israel acted in a measured and proportional manner in response to the Palestinian violence. Additionally, they noted that the Israeli civilians and armed forces have come under violent attacks by persons who do not wear uniforms, often in crowded civilian areas. The Israelis argued that these individuals cannot claim to be civilians or receive the protection afforded to civilians. Thus, those who took part in the attacks cannot claim immunity, and therefore it is permissible, in accordance with international law, to target those who directly take part in hostilities.

As to the issue of economic damages, Israel posited that despite shared Israeli and Palestinian interests in economic cooperation, the Palestinians have no inherent right to work in Israel or to receive automatic economic benefits. In the Israelis' opinion, economic cooperation and commercial interaction must be viewed as byproducts of peaceful interaction between people. Israel enacted restrictive measures for security reasons. Similarly, allegations of environmental damage and collective punishment were rejected. In conclusion, Israel emphasized its interest in ending violence and ensuring security for its citizens.

VI.   Conclusions of the Committee—The Mitchell Report

Prior to publication, during the first week of May 2001, the Sharm el-Sheikh Fact–Finding Committee Report was presented to U.S. President George W. Bush, to Israel and the Palestinians, and to the Secretary General of the United Nations. Upon presentation, the sides were asked to offer comments to be appended to the final published report. While official publication waited for the parties' comments, the media immediately and widely documented the details of the report. On May 21, 2001, the full report, including the comments, was publicly released.

A.   Details of Report

Despite the Mitchell Committee's mandate "to determine what happened and how to avoid it recurring in the future," the Report predominantly emphasized the future. In fact, the Report purposely did not answer many central fact-finding questions within the mandate. The Report's authors appeared to believe that any detailed fact-finding into such a tense atmosphere would not only challenge the Report's credibility and its chance for acceptance, but might even exacerbate the problems in the region.

Instead, the Report included proposals to assist the parties in stopping the violence, rebuilding confidence and returning to the negotiating process. The Committee noted that its mandate was not a solution to the conflict or a determination of the scope of the negotiations, but rather a strategy to address the previous eight months of crisis. The Report set forth a modest goal. It recommended a path for stopping the violence and returning the parties to the negotiating table. In that context, the Report was a valuable success.

The Report offered some analysis of the events, primarily by presenting each party's positions, in many cases without comment or resolution. In presenting the facts and making the recommendations, the Report scrupulously attempted to avoid placing blame on either party. This political balancing act sometimes went too far, blurring one side's unique responsibility within a specific issue. For example, the uniquely Palestinian responsibility to prevent the use of illegal weapons was presented in the Report's Recommendations by stating, "the parties should abide by the provisions of the Wye River Agreement prohibiting illegal weapons." Similarly, incitement was noted with equal measure.

The bulk of the Report, however, discussed the proposal's prospective impact. The Report's conciliatory tone offered a path towards a return to the peace process. The recommendations emphasized three distinct stages: (1) an end to the violence; (2) the rebuilding of confidence; and (3) resuming negotiations. The "principal recommendation" urged each side to recommit themselves to the spirit of Sharm el-Sheikh and to implement the decisions made there in 1999 and 2000. This quasi-philosophical observation expressed a need for the two sides to return to bilateral cooperation.

In its opening words, the Report emphasized that the sides "must act swiftly and decisively to halt the violence." Also, the sides must rebuild trust, which can be accomplished by implementing a series of proposed confidence-building measures. The proposals covered a range of subjects such as halting incitement, the issue of Israeli settlements, rejecting and combating terror, a renewal of economic cooperation, protection of holy sites, as well as responsibilities and procedures of security forces by both parties. These actions were important to resume "full and meaningful negotiations" based upon "mutual agreements and understandings" reached between the parties. This method was wise, as it offered small, incremental steps away from violence, while moving towards building faith and achieving the ultimate interest of all concerned—peace negotiations. It also offered political benefits to both sides, which could assist in domestic marketing for the adherence to the plan terms.

While the recommendations addressed most of the major issues regarding current violence, some key issues were apparently intentionally omitted from the operative portion of the Report. Key examples include: (1) the conclusion that an international presence would not be appropriate without the agreement of the two sides; (2) lack of determination regarding the Palestinian allegation of "assassinations;" (3) the Israeli claim as to the Palestinian Authority's role in the planning and coordination of the start of violence; (4) the extent to which Ariel Sharon's visit was responsible for the outbreak of violence; and (5) any determination about the legality of positions or accountability of either party in international law. The decision to omit these issues further underscored the Report's emphasis on conciliation as opposed to traditional fact-finding. The Committee's goal to present a politically acceptable report to both parties prevented conclusions on any of these central fact-finding issues.

B. The Parties' Responses—Differing Interpretations

Both parties quickly announced a general acceptance of the Mitchell Committee findings. In the introduction letter to the parties' responses, the Committee noted: "We are grateful for the generally positive tone of all of the comments, and we are struck by the convergence of the parties' views on our report." In fact, in the weeks following its publication, the acceptance of the Mitchell Report had become a central aspect of the parties' diplomatic posture. Nevertheless, in their official responses, the two parties offered widely differing interpretations of the Report and some criticism to many of its findings. Senator Mitchell anticipated such a reaction when he commented, before the submission of the responses, "[l]ook, it's human nature. They're going to say they like the parts that agree with their positions and they dislike the parts that don't agree with their positions. That's what I fully expect will occur."

1. Israeli Response

A key aspect of the Israelis' response to the Mitchell Report was the understanding of the Report's recommendations as four distinct stages. The Israelis regard the fulfillment of each stage as a necessary precursor to proceed with the process. Thus, the first stage of ending the violence needs to be achieved before enacting the other steps and recommendations. A "cooling-off" period would follow, which would allow for the enactment of confidence building measures so that negotiations could finally resume. In its written response, Israel noted its dispute with the findings regarding the settlement issue, as well as the Report's criticism of actions taken by Israeli Defense Forces.

2. Palestinian Response

Conversely, the Palestinians determined that the Mitchell Report's findings and recommendations should be accepted and implemented concurrently. Without Israel directing an immobilization of settlement activity, as the Report recommended, there would neither be an end to violence nor acceptance of any other terms of the proposal. To deal with the implementation issues, the Palestinians urged the involvement of the international participants from the Sharm el-Sheikh Conference of October 2000. The Palestinians expressed disappointment with the non-legal nature of the findings, as well as the Report's failure to accept the Palestinian demand regarding an international presence in the region.

C. Diplomatic Efforts

In May 2001, despite the release of the Mitchell Report, violence continued in the region. The killing continued during the days following the release of the Report.

One hour after the release of the Report, Secretary of State Colin Powell expressed the United States' support for the Report, tendering an interpretation that could be seen as consistent with both the Israeli and the Palestinian interests. Powell, however, noted that the Report should be interpreted within a framework of a timeline leading to direct negotiations. He additionally emphasized the importance of various confidence-building measures, including the need to halt settlement activity. Finally, Powell announced plans for increased U.S. diplomatic involvement in the region.

The international community overwhelmingly approved and supported the findings of the Report. Many regarded the stature of the Committee members coupled with the pragmatic nature of the document as a positive instrument for the region. Active participation from European Mitchell Committee members Javier Solana and Thorbjorn Jagland were incentives for support from other European nations. Any achieved success would strengthen Europe's desire to be a "player" and not merely a "payer" in Middle East diplomacy. The Bush Administration, wary of its increased involvement in the Israeli–Palestinian conflict, viewed the Report as a "lifeline" for both parties, and a way to bolster America's regional presence.

Around the time of publication of the Mitchell Report, Israel implemented a unilateral cease-fire, overcoming the first obstacle proffered by the recommendations. Nevertheless, Palestinian violence ensued with the murder of twenty-one Israeli youths by a terrorist suicide bomber outside a discothèque in Tel Aviv on June 1, 2001. In the face of these deaths, Yasser Arafat was under extreme diplomatic pressure to move towards a fragile ceasefire agreement. On June 13, 2001, George Tenet, Director of the Central Intelligence Agency, brokered a ceasefire agreement based on the central points of the Mitchell Report. Despite these attempts to quell the violence, tensions have escalated in the months that followed. Nevertheless, both sides continued to publicly emphasize their continued commitment to the Mitchell Report and to the Tenet workplan. For months after their publication, these two documents were the only peacekeeping guidelines accepted by the parties and the international community.

VII. Relevance for the Peace Process and Conflict Resolution

In most ways, the experience and results in forming a fact-finding committee regarding the violence in the Middle East were far from successful. As detailed above, the primary goal of the October 2000 Sharm el-Sheikh Summit was to implement a cease-fire, however, violence continued and evolved for months. The Committee also failed in nearly all of the other terms of cooperation set forth in the agreed Presidential Statement. In fact, the only term that took force was the formation of the Mitchell Committee. The Committee's original goals were an introspective attempt to analyze the recent violence and to find a solution to prevent its recurrence. When it became readily apparent that the violence would continue, the Committee and the parties involved realized that an immediate end to the violence was now their paramount objective.

From a purely legal standpoint, in terms of fact-finding, this material change in circumstances might have warranted a stop to the work of the Committee in that the terms and agenda set out and agreed upon between the parties had markedly changed. It is doubtful whether Israel would have agreed to such a mandate at the outset. At the same time, Israel made a conscious decision to continue its involvement with the Committee, perhaps to avoid being perceived in the international community as the party that rejected a potential solution to the conflict.

From the Palestinian perspective, the goal of internationalizing the conflict and the search for negotiating forums outside the "Oslo agreements" were equally attainable by conciliation as by fact-finding. The Palestinians had not achieved any tangible diplomatic gain from the months of violence and held out hope that the Mitchell Committee would offer it some sort of diplomatic victory. Therefore, despite the material changes, the parties continued their cooperation. This tacit agreement officially changed the essence of the mission from one of fact-finding to one of conciliation.

In its desire to reach a politically viable solution, the Committee avoided certain facts and determinations. The Committee instead emphasized solutions that would allow both sides to either willingly or reluctantly accept its terms. While the Committee achieved that goal, it alone did not create the necessary leverage to induce the sides into carrying out the recommendations of the Report.

While the Report received much respect and was widely lauded both regionally and internationally, it failed to induce the parties to end the violence. Despite being widely supported and the fact that no other viable proposal exists, its long-term effect is unclear. Despite the fact that both sides continue to profess their "acceptance" of the terms of the Mitchell Report, it is questionable that there is either the political will or the proper environment conducive to implementing the terms of the Report. In fact, the violence continued for months after the publication of the Report. As with any other fact-finding committee, the acceptance of its findings ultimately depends on the interests of the sides. While those interests may come in time, and the method may in fact be laid out in the Mitchell Report, it was certainly not the strength or influence of the legal mechanism of fact-finding or conciliation that will influence the parties.

It is unclear that either "fact-finding" or conciliation is the focus of the parties today. Even the terms of the Mitchell Report may not have true support from the parties. The Palestinians, interested at the beginning of the process, and certainly continue to have a strategic interest in increased international involvement, it is not clear that they have an interest in paying a price, such as returning to negotiations under the original conditions of the Oslo peace process that may be required by truly adapting the findings of the Mitchell Committee. Perhaps the continuing discussions regarding the use of international observers to enforce the Report, despite the express findings of the Committee, are an effort to disregard the findings, freeing the Palestinians to continue to search for a more favorable forum. Israel, though uninterested in the mission at its inception, now has a stake in requiring an implementation of the cease-fire. Some in Israel, however, may also be less interested in the price it may have to pay, domestically, for a settlement freeze. This point is yet to be tested, and it remains dependent upon a true cessation of violence by the Palestinian side.

Most states are unwilling to adopt fact-finding measures for comparatively mundane issues. In fact, there is no successful precedent in recent history for a use of fact-finding or a conciliation commission in a case of such existential importance as the Israeli–Palestinian conflict. It is possible that the Mitchell Committee may contribute to the negotiation process that would ultimately end violence between the parties. This will happen when both sides are ready to not only hear proposals, but also to make difficult compromises. The fact-finding element of the Mitchell Committee, however, did not achieve this result. Rather, local concerns and decision making prodded by international pressure, could one day reach this goal without a fancy "blue ribbon panel."

Thus, while the Report was an earnest effort by the individuals who seemed interested in bringing this chapter of violence between the Israelis and the Palestinians to an end, it is doubtful that the Report served as a turning point in the conflict. It was unlikely that it had the possibility of doing so in the first place. Other attempts to inject an international presence, such as observers or monitors, will have a similar fate. Ultimately, for a breakthrough to occur, the political and popular leadership within the Israeli and the Palestinian communities must demonstrate a desire to support a non-violent breakthrough that will demand an openness to co-exist. External intervention efforts, such as the Mitchell Committee, cannot serve as a replacement for local decisions and actions of dialogue and peacemaking between the sides.

Notes and Questions

1. Given the background of the conflict described in this case study, how realistic was the idea of fact-finding as a process of conflict resolution?

2. If you had been a member of the Mitchell Committee, what do you think your response would have been to the Palestinian and Israeli initial written submissions in December 2000?

3. To what extent might your initial response change after reading each group's response to the other party's submissions?

4. What were some of the strengths and weaknesses of the Mitchell Committee's report?

5.   In Chapter 1 we discussed the role of perceptions in contributing to conflict. To what extent did the parties' perceptions explain their differing responses to the Mitchell Committee report?

6.   How significant is the international community's approval and support of the Mitchell Committee report?

7.   Based on the developments in this case study, do you think that fact-finding can ever be used successfully for "intractable" conflicts?

8.   Given the benefit of hindsight, would it have made sense for the Mitchell Committee to have stopped at some point and re-negotiated their mandate?

9.   Based on the materials in Chapter 3, construct a "cultural analysis" of the conflict described in this case study?

10.   After reading the parties' submissions and responses, are you able to determine whether each group is part of a high-context or low-context culture?

E.   RECONCILIATION

The increase in inter-ethnic conflict has brought with it an increased interest in the role of religion and faith-based diplomacy in the management and resolution of conflict. A growing literature supports recognition of peacemaking efforts informed by religious values.[5] For example, against the background of the South African experience, Archbishop Desmund Tutu has been a strong proponent of forgiveness and reconciliation:

> I really want just to say to you that I have gone through the crucible of the Truth and Reconciliation Commission and have been devastated by the extent of the evil revealed in that process.... I have looked into the abyss of human evil and seen the depth to which we can in fact plumb. But paradoxically one comes away from it exhilarated by the revelation of the goodness of people. You encounter people who, having suffered grievously, should by right have been riddled with bitterness and a lust for revenge and retribution. But they are different.[6]

Reconciliation is connected with notions of restorative justice, a concept that seeks to rehabilitate the social relationships affected by a conflict rather than to simply punish parties for crimes committed.[7] Does

---

5.   *See, e.g.,* Douglas Johnston, ed., Faith-Based Diplomacy: Trumping Realpolitik (2003).

6.   Archbishop Desmond M. Tuto, *Foreward, in* Foregiveness and Reconciliation: Religion, Public Policy, and Conflict Transformation x, xi (Raymond G. Helmick, S.J. & Rodney L. Petersen eds., 2001).

7.   Mica Estrada–Hollenbeck, *The Attainment of Justice through Restoration, Not Litigation: The Subjective Road to Reconciliation, in* Reconciliation, Justice, and Coexistence: Theory and Practice 65, 74 (Mohammed Abu–Nimer ed., 2001) [hereinafter Reconciliation, Justice and Coexistence].

reconciliation have any place in the constellation of processes for the management and resolution of ethnic conflict? Scholars have suggested that restorative justice approaches to conflict resolution such as problem-solving workshops, mediation, and interest-based negotiation are more likely to promote reconciliation than the legalistic justice devices of the criminal court system.[8]

In Chapter 9 we will discuss the concept of reconciliation within the context of Truth and Reconciliation Commissions. The following excerpt presents the case for a reconciliation policy for Nigeria in the wake of that country's violent troubles.

PHILIP C. AKA, NIGERIA: THE NEED FOR AN EFFECTIVE POLICY OF ETHNIC RECON-CILIATION IN THE NEW CENTURY

14 Temple International & Comparative Law Journal 327 (2000).

I. INTRODUCTION

Nigeria needs an effective policy of ethnic reconciliation as part of a broad-based strategy for conflict management in the new century. The issue is fair and equal treatment for all 248 or so ethnic groups that make up modern-day Nigeria. Should the country seek to achieve such equitable treatment through a specific policy of reconciliation for past inequities against aggrieved ethnic groups within its polity? Or should it seek to do so via the installation of broad general constitutional-institutional reforms? In the past, Nigeria tended to adopt one or the other of these two strategies rather than utilize both simultaneously. Following the civil war, under the Gowon regime, the country adopted a reconciliation policy, which was later abandoned for a strategy emphasizing constitutional-institutional innovations following General Yakubu Gowon's overthrow in July of 1975.

Our argument is that Nigeria needs a well-tailored policy of reconciliation, in addition to any other strategy or strategies the country chooses to adopt for promoting ethnic harmony and reducing conflict. A reconciliation policy of this kind should redress inequities to marginalized groups like, the Igbos, and oil-producing minorities in the Niger Delta, like the Etches, Ibibios, Ijaws, Ikwerres, and Ogonis. One other conflict such a policy could address is the Yoruba grievance arising from the nullification of the 1993 presidential election presumed to have been won by the late Chief Moshood Abiola, a Yoruba. However, the election of Gen. Olusegun Obasanjo, also a Yoruba, is believed to have rectified the injustice. Gen. Obasanjo's nomination and election as President was supported and backed by the same northern establishment of Hausa-Fulani military leaders who cancelled the Abiola election. The marginalization of the Igbos followed from the civil war, while that of oil-producing communities in the Niger Delta region arose from the environmental despoilation from oil exploration in these communities. Since

8. *Id.* at 77–82.

coming into office on May 29, 1999, the new civilian government of Gen. Obasanjo has pursued policies of "inclusiveness and equity rather than patronage." The orientation is as it should be and a refreshing step in the right direction after many wrong-headed policy steps under a succession of military dictators. However, to be truly effective, as well as to promote ethnic harmony and to reduce conflicts, any inclusive policies the government pursues must also integrate a well-tailored program of reconciliation for past inequities to aggrieved ethnic groups that have left them marginalized in the body-politic.

II. DEFINING RECONCILIATION

Reconciliation is the successful restoration or reestablishment of harmony following a conflict and entails "bringing [conflicting] parties together to overcome their own differences." It is what happens after every violent conflict, without which any supposed "settlement 'merely set[s] the stage for the next war.'" Although an established strategy for conflict resolution, reconciliation recently is coming into vogue as a secular concept in the aftermath of the work of the Truth and Reconciliation Commission in South Africa. Whether in South Africa or Latin America (Chile and Argentina), where reconciliation was actually pioneered in the resolution of human rights problems, the underlying notion is the same: truth-telling concerning past misdeeds or voluntary confession of those misdeeds is a precondition for national healing and "is crucial for sustainable peace." Lasting reconciliation is built on "[mutual] forgiveness" and it must give former enemies "faith again in civil institutions, in justice, and in the rule of law."

Conceptualized as a policy, reconciliation goes beyond reactive fire fighting and embraces institutionalization of a framework for fairness. The main idea is to build "institutions and conventions that ensure justice" for aggrieved ethnic groups, majority and minority alike. It entails the establishment of "deliberate institutional frameworks" like a peace and reconciliation commission that would recommend interventions for redress of longstanding grievances. . . .

We stated earlier that Nigeria alternates reconciliation with the strategy of institutional reforms. A more correct statement of the situation, however, is that the only time the country had a reconciliation policy was under the Gowon government in the aftermath of the Biafran war. Gowon's reconciliation was a one-case, one-beneficiary policy applied mainly to the Igbos. A civil war is always a traumatic and devastating experience for any country that has the misfortune to go through it and a policy such as Gowon's, designed to minimize or remove the pains from such an experience, is justified. Similar single-issue-oriented agencies or commissions or both have been set up in the past to look into various demands of ethnic minorities in the country generally, and those of oil-producing minorities in particular. It is not this case-by-case approach that we have in mind here. Rather, our advocacy is for the development of one reconciliation policy that will apply in all cases of marginalization. A reconciliation program of this kind is remedial—the idea being to (a) leave in place a framework for the institutionalization of fairness to aggrieved ethnic groups, whether majority or minority; and (b) deal with problems before they fester and become intractable.

III.   NATURE OF ETHNICITY AND ETHNIC POLITICS IN NIGERIA

Nigeria originated as a creation of British colonialism. The country comprises over 200 ethnic groups: many of them tiny and not politically influential; three of which collectively make up about two-thirds of the population. These "ethnic triumvirate," as one analyst dubbed them, are the Hausa–Fulanis (two groups so closely integrated culturally and politically that they are often counted as one), the Igbos, and the Yorubas. These majority ethnic groups have long dominated the politics of the country. In the First Republic (1960–1966), the country operated a federal system of government that was so lopsided in its structure that these ethnic triumvirate were "in effect, governmental as well as ethnic categories." Following the creation of more states, beginning in 1967, a decline has occurred in the share of national power these majority groups collectively wield. They still, however, control over 50 percent of the states in the country.

Each of the three majority ethnic groups form the dominant group within its geographic domain: Hausa–Fulanis in the North; Igbos in the southeast; and Yorubas in the Southwest. But it is a dominance that smaller ethnic groups within each affected geographic region, aiming also to integrate their own influence upon regional and national life, have been known to challenge. Thus, in the colonial and post-colonial years up to the period before the creation of more states in 1967, minorities within each of the then regions feared and resented the domination of the "big tribe" within their geographical area. A recent minority challenge that departs significantly from this "regional" pattern is the Ogoni uprising or campaign, which arguably was directed against all three majority groups or to the Nigerian state as a whole. Unlike all previous domination challenges, the campaign also attracted international attention largely, due to the high-profile leadership of Ken Saro–Wiwa.

Like most parts of Africa, ethnicity in Nigeria is a "factor of exclusiveness" that dominates political and economic life. "Acceptance and rejection" on ethnic grounds "characterize social relations" in the country. Ethnic cleavage or division in Nigeria is "expressed inevitably through inter-ethnic discrimination in jobs, housing, admissions into educational institutions, marriages, business transactions, or the distribution of social welfare services." It is also more often than not "accompanied by nepotism and corruption."

For all the constitutional and institutional reforms designed to reduce its impact on political life, to date, ethnicity forms "the basis on which political values are defined, articulated, contested, or challenged" in Nigeria. Ethnicity evolved as a cleavage in Nigeria with colonialism and achieved its fullest development and manifestation following independence. In the country, like much of the rest of Africa, "the ethnic group continues to act as a significant pole around which people mobilize to make claims upon the state."

* * *

In responding to the oil-producing communities demands for more equitable treatment, the Nigerian government has used both institutional and non-institutional devices or strategies. The institutional means included the creation of new states and the application of the federal character principle. These devices did not help the oil-producing communities much. The first, state creation, was initially invented with minorities in mind. But after the first exercise in 1967, more majority-dominated states than minority ones were created. After 1967, new states became a majority group game and no longer favored minorities. The federal character principle and the other institutional means the government used, have not been helpful. This is mainly because, as Osaghae and others have pointed out, the principle has been inconsistently applied by various Nigerian governments. If the principle is upheld, "the days when major groups only were relevant competitors for power" in Nigeria would, as Osaghae asserted, be "past and gone."

In addition to constitutional-institutional means, the Nigerian government also used non-institutional concessions "made up of a mixture of carrot and stick" to respond to the demands and the anti-oil protests of oil-producing minorities. Unfortunately, as we shall show, these concessions entailed more stick than carrot. For the carrot, the government unveiled development programs designed to promote the welfare of oil-producing communities. In 1961, it established the Niger Delta Development Board (NDDB). NDDB was charged with responsibility for agricultural development projects in the Niger Delta, but was ineffective and "was regarded as little more than a public relations exercise." The Oil Mineral Producing Areas Commission (OMPADEC), formed in 1992, and charged with responsibility for coordinating "development projects in oil-producing communities," was meant to be a more substantive concession. However, the Commission is badly run, inefficient, its allocations are mismanaged, and its operations are seriously plagued by official corruption. As Jedrzej G. Frynas, who has carefully studied this topic, noted, "[t]he failure of the OMPADEC to channel resources to the oil producing areas illustrates the use of public oil revenues for the private benefit of specific individuals at the expense of village communities affected by oil operations on the ground." To make matters worse, "a significant proportion of" what little monies oil companies set aside for their oil-producing communities are "misappropriated by oil company staff, local contractors or chiefs."

As opposed to concessions involving development projects, the government, together with the oil companies, unfortunately has been noted better for the stick of repressive security measures it uses in response to anti-oil protests. The violence involved in the hanging deaths of the Ogoni Nine is too well-known. But these security measures aimed against anti-oil protesters have also included extra-judicial killings, rapes, arbitrary arrests, beating and floggings, harassment, and intimidation. Frynas, in his work, well described the machinery the government designed to dispense these security measures:

> In dealing with anti-oil protests, the authorities used regular units of the police and the army as well as the navy. The Nigerian authorities also created special units of the security forces, consisting of the police and the military, to deal with anti-oil protests such as the Rivers State Internal Security Task Force in 1994.... In addition to assistance by state security services, oil companies maintain their own security forces. These security forces are drawn from the Nigerian police and perform duties at oil installations. Paid by the oil companies, they are known as Shell Police or Mobil Police.

The dispensing of these measures sometimes has been deadly for affected communities. For instance, in reaction to an alleged impending attack on oil facilities at Umuechem in 1990, the Mobile Police (a branch of the Nigerian Police noted for its brutality) moved in with teargas and gunfire, killing about 80 people and destroying about 500 homes. The demonstrators, many of them youths, were neither violent nor armed. What is so disconcerting about the massacre in Umuechem is that force did not have to be used. Shell had been operating in the area going back to the "late 1950s, resulting in the pollution of a stream, destruction of farm crops, and other losses to property. The community had received little or no compensation, while villagers called for social amenities such as the provision of electricity." Rather than respond peacefully to the legitimate claims of dissatisfied community members, Shell chose force with these deadly outcomes.

After 1975, the government abolished the principle of revenue allocation to states based on derivation (locally collected revenue or share of contribution to government revenue) and replaced it with a special account for the oil-producing areas. Abolition of the derivation principle meant that "a higher share of the oil revenues generated in their local areas was allocated to states that were non-oil producing." Oil-producing minorities believed the abolition to be to their detriment, and their most widespread demand was a reversion to the status quo ante that prevailed before 1975. Conflicts between these oil-producing minorities with the government on the one hand and between these minorities and oil companies on the other escalated following the abolition of the derivation formula....

Nigeria needs an effective policy of reconciliation, additional to any general strategies it adopts. Nigeria also needs to promote ethnic harmony and reduce conflicts within its society. Problems of ethnic reconciliation "are not those which will disappear with time if left unattended to." If the diverse marginalization experiences of Igbos and oil-producing minorities teach anything, it is that ethnic grievances do not go away until a government acts affirmatively, for example, through an effective reconciliation policy, to remove those grievances. A reconciliation policy of the kind we envisage here should address the grievances of the Igbos arising from the distortion in their political and economic position in Nigeria due to the civil war. And it should tackle the age-long marginalization of the oil-producing communities in the country's River Niger Delta.

The challenge Nigeria confronts and must meet head-on in the 21st century is to find an "effective formula" "to bring ethnic competition, class conflict, social diversity, and the like into a . . . productive synthesis." One way to achieve that synthesis is the timely redress, via a reconciliation policy, of injustices to aggrieved ethnic groups within the country. Although a reconciliation policy is, by its nature, remedial, a policy of the kind we have in mind here, to be effective, must integrate a measure of pro-activeness. The idea being to catch problems and address them before they fester in the way the disparate grievances examined here did. In addition to supplementing and reinforcing other strategies for conflict management, a reconciliation policy is also good for democracy.

* * *

Given its origins as an arbitrary collection of disparate ethnic groups, as opposed to aggregation of peoples with common history or shared collective experiences of nationhood, Nigeria has been, understandably, more than a trifle concerned about national unity. * * *

The challenge relatively new states like Nigeria face "is to imbue [their] unity with purposes which . . . truly reflect the needs and aspirations of [their] people." Nigeria's unity is enhanced only when oppression of any ethnic group ceases and the political system "is adjusted to accommodate the legitimate aspirations of every group . . . and the . . . members of every constituent group feel equal and secure in [the country]." "To keep Nigeria one," as Wole Soyinka once quipped, "justice must be done." Nigerians must aim in the new century to make their country "a nationally-owned instrument for the enforcement of equity."

In the post-Cold War era, cleavages like ethnicity and religion are superseding ideological and geopolitical forces as "the new global schisms." The practical implication for an ethnically complex society, like Nigeria, is that close attention needs to be paid to ethnic conflicts. Such increased attention should include proper reconciliation, through appropriate policy, of past violent disputes, like the Biafran war, whose settlement left so much to be desired. Progressive countries take ethnic reconciliation seriously.

F. COEXISTENCE

Compared to reconciliation efforts, coexistence is a more modest effort to begin the rehabilitation process in the aftermath of inter-ethnic violence and conflict. Co-existence is distinguishable from the notions of forgiveness and personal peace involved with reconciliation. As Michael Ignatieff has observed, "It is a colder word and more rational too."[9] Some scholars, however, view the goal of achieving durable and fair co-existence as an aspect of the reconciliation process. Viewed from this perspective, co-existence is a foundational aspect of peacebuilding, reconciliation, and attaining sustainable justice.[10]

Coexistence is as much a philosophy as a process of restoring equanimity in post-conflict societies. In the following excerpt, the author discusses the philosophy and nature of coexistence work.

EUGENE WEINER, COEXISTENCE WORK: A NEW PROFESSION

in Eugene Weiner, ed., The Handbook of Interethnic Coexistence 13–17, 19–21 (1998).

* * *

Coexistence work consists of getting people to participate in an intimate encounter with their ethnic enemies. Like the meeting between the two great enemies of the Cold War that took place in that helicopter, it is the absurdity that unfolds before their eyes that enhances conditions for ethnic peace. Although, as we shall see, the concept of coexistence had a controversial inception, it is a doctrine that enabled President Bush and Prime Minister Gorbachev to sit together in that helicopter. The commitment to coexistence at that moment may have saved the world from destruction in the twentieth century, and, if given a chance, it may succeed in doing so again in the twenty-first century as we deal with the horrors of ethnic conflict.

* * *

Coexistence implies not only that differences exist between individuals, groups, nation-states, and civilizations but that they are fundamental. Coexistence means "to exist together, in conjunction with, at the same time, in the same place with another." According to the *Oxford English Dictionary*, the term was negatively expanded and applied during the course of the twentieth century to an essential *lack* of coexistence between the Soviet and capitalist ideological systems. The term "competitive coexistence" was sometimes used in the framework,

---

9. Michael Ignatieff, *Afterward: Reflections on Coexistence*, in Antonia Chayes & Martha Minow, eds., Imagine Coexistence: Restoring Humanity After Violent Ethnic Conflict 326 (2003).

10. Louis Kriesberg, *Changing Forms of Coexistence*, in Reconciliation, Justice, and Coexistence, *supra* note 7, at 47–63.

but it was the term "peaceful coexistence" that was understood to be different in quality from "peace." Although "peaceful coexistence" began initially under Lenin's influence as an ideological cover for covert and overt aggression and deception, it has undergone development and finally transformation in the course of the past six decades. In its latest transformation, the concept has become a welcomed clarion call for a more enlightened and less antagonistic relationship between the Soviet Union and the West. In 1989, the Soviet policy of peaceful coexistence was redefined to include such principles as non aggression, respect for sovereignty, national independence, and noninterference in internal affairs.

During the period of its most controversial usage, coexistence was deemed to be compatible with propaganda against, and isolation from, divergent groups as well as the encouragement of uprisings. There are, therefore, those who would say "good riddance" to a term so tainted by ambiguous usage. However, in our view such a move would be a serious mistake. * * *

First, the idea of coexistence has functioned as an important restraint on the self-fulfilling logic of many ideological movements. Ideologies with totalistic eschatological visions—and there have been many in the twentieth century—are dedicated to the destruction of their enemies. They require convincing reasons to justify anything less than a totally dedicated effort at such destruction. These totalistic, combative, confrontational visions—such as fascism, communism, and some nationalistic, ethnic doctrines—sometimes need to be saved from themselves. This has been true as well for some missionary, zealous versions of the free-market economy. The concept of coexistence with the alien Other most fundamentally grants that alien Other the *right to exist*. It functions as a check and restraint on totalistic visions that seek the annihilation of an enemy viewed as the incarnation of evil. Once people are willing to agree to coexist, they begin to embrace a less toxic vision, one that may settle for something other than a complete victory over the enemy.

Second, the idea of coexistence also creates a useful and needed interregnum. Without the concept of coexistence there are only two orders of time for totalistic visions: the time of the totally dedicated struggle and the time of victory or defeat. The idea of peaceful coexistence creates a third order, an "in-between" time. It is a hiatus when one concedes that one will have to learn to live with the enemy "temporarily." In reality, it may turn into a hiatus without end: and that is precisely its social usefulness. The concept of coexistence provides a period during which other things can happen apart from the awful struggle itself. For example, when periods of peaceful coexistence begin, there are opportunities for noncombative personalities to emerge as leaders within the antagonistic groups. The onset of a coexistence era allows common interests (such as economic ones) to emerge among the antagonists, giving both parties a strong stake in making the temporary stage a permanent one.

It is this ongoing dynamic that, we believe, makes the concept of coexistence a particularly useful one in the resolution of intractable ethnic conflicts. Coexistence appeals to self-interest while affirming the right of the Other to life. The self-interested realization that one's own existence is dependent on the existence of the Other is an important stage in the humanization of conflict. It can be a prelude to a durable peace. We do not reject the ultimate desirability of such goals as reconciliation, amity, true peace, and cooperation. They are certainly desirable. However, it seems likely that the best means towards the achievement of these aims is to create a situation of minimalist coexistence, where antagonists "simply" allow others ... to live. Although aiming low and succeeding may have the disadvantage of not resolving conflicts definitively, aiming high and failing can (and frequently does) lead to disenchantment, discouragement, cynicism, and helplessness, which can then contribute to the re-escalation of conflict.

Coexistence is at once a philosophical orientation toward reality, a goal to be achieved, and a method for achieving that goal. As a philosophical orientation, it is based on a tragic, pessimistic view of the human condition. The assumption is that many intended improvements are futile and achieve nothing, and some attempts to improve the human condition actually makes things worse. This is what Hirschhorn calls the "perversity of human interventions" and Merton calls the "unintended negative consequences of planned social action." "Improvements" frequently jeopardize achievements that are already in place.

Coexistence work thus tends to concentrate neither on the deep psychological level nor on the macro-societal, political, and economic levels. It does not pretend to resolve either deep-seated, long-lasting hatreds or fundamental, structural injustice. Coexistence work goes on where ethnic enemies actually interact: in the street, in neighborhoods, in institutions of higher learning, in hospitals, in sports clubs, in business enterprises, in community groups, in religious organizations. Its "live and let live" philosophy informs its work mainly within the institutions of civil society. Thus coexistence work, while taking a dim view of human nature, is nonetheless activist, pragmatic, incremental—and hopeful.

* * *

The Nature of Coexistence Work

How could the creation of a new profession—the coexistence worker—contribute to the lessening of ethnic conflict, and what would the sphere of work specific to such a profession look like? As has been noted, the most ferocious conflicts in the world have tended to be between ethnic groups within the nation-state rather than between them. These have been some of the most devastating civil wars of the second half of the twentieth century—e.g., Sudan (the forty-year intermittent civil war between north and south), Nigeria (the Biafran Civil war, 1967–70),

Pakistan (the 1971 secession of Bangladesh), and Lebanon (from 1975 through 1990).

Coexistence work between ethnic groups within a single nation-state encourages antagonistic groups to exist together in civil society by avoiding confrontation. It encourages measures of compromise that enable these groups to live together despite conflicting interests. It seeks to do this, no matter how hate-filled the environment has become, by persevering in its work of enabling groups to discover their common humanity. Coexistence work continuously attempts to blunt differences by making ad hoc arrangements to overcome crises and providing opportunities for face-to-face dialogue. It is based on the conviction that the cumulative effects stemming from a mindful awareness of common existence are far-reaching in their influence. Through the recognition of a common humanity and making compromise into a habit, a climate of hopefulness is created. In such a climate social and political arrangements can be designed to address long-standing grievances and to redistribute privileges equitably, which have been selfishly monopolized.

Coexistence work is predicated on the belief that all its efforts *will* eventually pave the way toward greater consensus, cooperation, reconciliation, and a generosity of spirit, and that if this is not achieved, at least excessive violent conflict will have been prevented. Coexistence work is a way to get through the day—alive. Coexistence practitioners work in the most difficult of times when coexistence is the only alternative to continuing all-out conflict. It is the last gasp of civilized hopefulness, the hope that human beings can be brought to their senses by not indulging in their fantasies of domination and the destruction of enemies, real and imagined.

Coexistence work attempts to call forth habits, skills, and qualities of character that form effective democratic citizens. It helps create civic virtues such as the capacity to listen and hear alternative views and interests, to attend to the common good, and to create a greater sense of belonging. It is the work of creating moral anchors that hold the overall societal framework intact and expose the absurdity of attempting to deny the human face of one's antagonist when it is actually seen.

Coexistence work can occur on many levels, but fundamentally it adopts a bottom-up-perspective, in which one pays less attention to national politics (who is in power, how they use it, and how likely they are to keep it), or to the issues of war, peace, or territorial integrity. It is therefore frequently damned with faint praise, and is regarded as noncontroversial and somewhat innocuous. The really high-impact work of social amelioration is viewed as taking place on the level of legal rights, human rights, economic readjustment, etc. Increasing the civility in a society is seen as beneficial, but it is often viewed as a palliative to paper over deeper cleavages and inequalities. The truth is that there are, indeed, times of acute crisis, when this view is basically right. However, in the scheme of everyday life, coexistence work does make a difference. It matters more than a little whether one's ethnic food differences are taken into account when sick in a hospital, or if, because of ethnic origins, one is discriminated against in getting a job, an apartment, entering a university, getting a governmental entitlement, or simply being related to politely. These events are not the stuff of history but they are the stuff of everyday life for most people, most of their lives. Consequently, our answer to those who would neglect the less glamorous aspects of creating a civil society for the more dramatic, fundamental structural changes, is that the work of coexistence must continue until those more basic changes are in place. Indeed the work of coexistence must go forward or those structural changes may never happen. It is the example of coexistence work that may cause the structural changes to occur, precisely because people have not lost hope, and because they have seen that coexistence is possible.

For almost a century now in many parts of the world, this bottom-up perspective has been systematically undermined. Most notably in Eastern Europe and mainland China, a major ingredient of democratic society has been missing. Among the first acts of totalitarian, ideologically based regimes has been the destruction of free, voluntary citizen associations. In those countries where civil society was destroyed, the state assumed complete responsibility for looking after the interests of the people. Voluntary associations of citizens in the pursuit of their economic, cultural, or religious interests were regarded as subversive competition to the state. It was the state's ideological agenda that determined what was good and bad, and therefore the state did not need to be prompted by the interests of citizens as they themselves defined these issues or sought to pursue them.

In the West, on the other hand, there has been a consistent appreciation of these voluntary associations. John Locke, the intellectual father of the American Revolution, saw government as the trustee of civil society (interests as defined and pursued by ordinary citizens). Insofar as it helped the ordinary people in the realization of their pursuit of life, liberty, and wealth, the government gained legitimacy or lost it. This is precisely the opposite perspective from the ideological world of totalitarianism. Under democracy, the government must prove that it is a faithful executor of the public will. Under totalitarianism, on the contrary, the people must demonstrate their embodiment of state aims or they are at the mercy of its coercive authority. However, while the democratic form of government has indeed given rise to a plethora of associations of like-minded citizens who pursue their interests, these associations have tended to be overshadowed by the sheer power and capacity of the state to achieve its goals. It is the President of the United States that we all know, rather than the president of the local neighborhood association, banking company, or tenant association. In comparison to the ultimate authority of the state, all these other forms of association may have seemed inconsequential.

This was true until 1989. It was in that year that some institutions of civil society succeeded in making the kind of major changes that everyone assumed no small association could accomplish. It was the Civic

Forum in Czechoslovakia and the Solidarity movement in Poland organized years before that succeeded in creating a bloodless revolution that brought down one of the most despotic and coercive regimes in history. It was not the government bureaucracy, nor the military, nor political leaders that did this job. It was ordinary people who banded together to address the central questions in their lives. The movement had a moral force that was unstoppable. It was a revolution from the bottom rather than the top.

People in pursuit of their interests can, on occasion, achieve miracles. The voluntary organizations through which coexistence can be pursued are capable of doing things that central governments cannot easily do, and thus add further legitimacy to the coexistence project.

Notes and Questions

1. How would you compare the Baylis approach to resolving ethnic conflict in Ethiopia with Akra's approach in Nigeria? Are there any commonalities?

2. Evaluate how each of the following hinder unity in Nigeria: a) ethnicity, b) religion, c) class, d) northern and southern geography, e) urban and rural differences.

3. What incentives exist for the current Nigerian leadership to create a policy of reconciliation such as the one suggested by the author? How do the incentives and lack of incentives affect the chances that a policy of reconciliation will be enacted?

4. Does Akra minimize the role that tribal hostilities continue to play in the allocation of political and economic power in Nigeria?

5. How would you describe the reconciliation policy envisioned by Akra? Is such a reconciliation policy to create unity in Nigeria a realistic possibility or simply an idealistic dream?

6. Reflecting on the role of religion and faith-based diplomacy, consider the factors that may drive a group's decision to seek assistance from religious leaders and institutions rather than secular ones.

> Put another way, at what point do religious values become secular ones, and what difference does that make for the long-term durability of agreements? A recent example from Northern Ireland illustrates the interpretive problem. When the IRA offered an apology in July 2002 for the murders it had committed thirty years earlier, during the time of the infamous "Troubles," can it be said that was an act motivated by religious concerns? Alternatively, was it, as the skeptics argued, a purely political gesture? Or, is this a more complex inquiry that defies either/or categorization?

[Jacqueline Nolan–Haley, *The Intersection of Religion, Race, Class, and Ethnicity in Community Conflict*, NEGOTIATION J. 351, 352 (Oct. 2002).]

7. Did you find the case for coexistence strategy persuasive?

8. John Paul Lederach suggests that the concept of conflict transformation is more helpful in describing the project of peacebuilding and peacemaking than terms such as "resolution" or "management."

> Over the past years the idea of conflict transformation has emerged in the search for an adequate language to describe the peacemaking venture* * * Transformation provides a more holistic understanding which can be fleshed out at several levels. Unlike resolution and management, the idea of transformation does not suggest we simply eliminate or control conflict, but rather points descriptively towards its inherent dialectic nature. Social conflict is a phenomenon of human creation, lodged naturally in relationships. It is a phenomenon that transforms events, the relationships in which conflict occurs, and indeed its very creators.

[JOHN PAUL LEDERACH, PREPARING FOR PEACE: CONFLICT TRANSFORMATION ACROSS CULTURES 17 ((1995).]

Do you think that peacebuilding is connected to coexistence work? Is Lederach's view of conflict transformation helpful for advancing coexistence?

9. In your view, how realistic is the bottom-up perspective of coexistence work?

10. When do you think that a coexistence strategy might be viable? Can you think of any particular countries where this philosophy would be effective in making structural changes?

11. What are the long-term implications of coexistence?

G. ARBITRATION

While the focus of this text is on consensual processes for resolving conflicts and disputes, international arbitration has such a longstanding role in the resolution of political disputes between States that it should be considered as a viable process for resolving ethnic territorial disputes. Among the major benefits of this process are the parties' power to select the arbitrators, the forum, and the procedural rules that will be used. Hearings are generally conducted with regard to the specific dispute, and the parties can request that the proceedings be private.

In the wake of increased ethnic conflict, arbitration has become a valuable mechanism for resolving issues between parties with a history of ethnic and religious conflict. The following excerpt discusses the successful use of arbitration to resolve territorial disputes between India and Pakistan and Egypt and Israel.

CARLA S. COPELAND, THE USE OF ARBITRATION TO SETTLE TERRITORIAL DISPUTES
67 Fordham Law Review 3073 (1999).

* * *

Ever since Great Britain and a recently independent United States agreed to submit a border dispute to arbitration in 1794, in accordance with the Jay Treaty, international arbitration has proved a useful method of settling limited territorial disputes between nations. One of the most attractive features of arbitration is that the proceedings are generally conducted in ad hoc courts of arbitration specifically designed to deal with a particular dispute. The parties can participate in defining the issue to be adjudicated, and they have the power to select the arbitrators, the forum, and the rules of procedure that will be used to settle the dispute. Arbitration also provides the parties with the option of holding hearings in secret. Thus, arbitration provides an appealing forum for nations that have decided to resolve their differences through peaceful means because it is much more flexible than a permanent court and allows the parties to maintain more control over the proceedings.

Arbitration has been used in the past, with much success, to settle limited issues of territorial sovereignty. The question remains, however, as to whether it is an appropriate dispute resolution mechanism to settle ethnic-based claims to land. The proliferation of ethnic-based violence in the context of the secession and breakup of states currently poses one of the greatest threats to public order and human rights. But these conflicts are not only about ethnic groups seeking self-determination through political independence and statehood; they are fundamentally issues about control over land. Thus, constructing effective means to peacefully resolve territorial disputes is a matter of profound importance.

* * *

A. The Rann of Kutch Arbitration

The dispute between India and Pakistan over the Rann of Kutch ("The Rann") has been heralded as "one of the major instances of international arbitration in the post-war period." The object of the arbitral tribunal was to determine a sector of the boundary between the territory that, in British times, was known as Sind (now part of the Islamic Republic of Pakistan) and the State of Kutch and other Native Indian States (now part of the Province of Gujarat in the Republic of India). The Rann (or marsh) of Kutch spans approximately 200 miles across the southern portion of the Indo–West Pakistan border. It has been described as a "desolate wasteland" because it is practically uninhabited and has little economic or strategic value.

1. Background

The territorial dispute had century-old origins, but it became acute shortly after India and Pakistan emerged as independent states in 1947. India claimed the Rann as part of its territory, while Pakistan insisted that the boundary ran through the "middle of the Rann or approximately along the 24th parallel." Early in 1965, India, claiming that Pakistan illegally patrolled the Rann north of the 24th parallel, posted border guards along the line. Pakistani troops fired upon and cleared India's outposts in April. Hostilities increased and during the next several weeks Pakistani and Indian forces engaged in battles involving several thousand troops. Shortly after the fighting began, Britain began negotiations, and soon afterwards, in an agreement dated June 30, 1965, both parties agreed to a cease fire and to submit the dispute to settlement by arbitration.

In accordance with the agreement, Pakistan and India each nominated a non-national as member of the tribunal, and the Secretary General of the United Nations appointed the Tribunal's Chairman. Prior to the commencement of oral hearings, and in accordance with the rules of the Tribunal pertaining to discovery, a delegation from Pakistan visited New Delhi to inspect and obtain copies of maps and documents in Indian Government archives. A delegation from India visited Islamabad for the same purpose. The terms of the cease-fire agreement provided that the parties would undertake "to implement the findings of the Tribunal in full as quickly as possible," and the parties agreed that the Tribunal should remain intact until its findings had been implemented.

2. Issues and Arguments

The first issue to be decided by the Tribunal was "whether the boundary in dispute [was] a historically recognized and well-established boundary." The Tribunal examined voluminous documentary evidence, including British maps and surveys dating largely from the period between 1870 and 1947. The Tribunal concluded that "there did not exist ... a historically recognised and well-established boundary in the disputed region."

The second main issue was whether Great Britain should be held, by its conduct, to have recognized, accepted, or acquiesced in the claim of the former State of Kutch (now part of India) that the Rann was Kutch territory. Such a determination would preclude Pakistan, as successor of Sind and thus of the territorial sovereign rights of Great Britain in the region, from successfully claiming any part of the disputed territory. The Tribunal relied primarily on maps published by the British Government in India of a conterminous boundary roughly coinciding with India's claim. This boundary had become a constant feature on all maps produced as surveys of India after 1907. India also offered into evidence the fact that assertions of the Rao (Ruler) of Kutch that the Rann was his territory had not been contradicted by the British authorities for approximately seventy-five years prior to independence. Further, India presented reports in which both the Rao and the British had stated that the Rann was Kutch territory. The Tribunal concluded that these three grounds of India's case were all acts of relinquishment by the British, and that they had the effect of leaving "the disputed territory, or the greater part thereof, in the hands of the sovereign or sovereigns who by reason of geographical proximity were there to receive it."

* * *

The Tribunal noted that evidence relating to acts of sovereign rights over the territory must be evaluated with the nature of the territory in mind. Two facts were crucial in the understanding of what would constitute sovereign functions in this situation: (1) much of the territory in dispute was uninhabitable; and (2) the two entities were agricultural societies at the time relevant to the proceedings. Thus, the activities and functions of government were limited to the imposition of customs duties and taxes on land, livestock and agricultural produce, and to the maintenance of peace and order. The Tribunal found that the activities of neither Kutch nor Sind authorities within the majority of the Rann were sufficient to constitute continuous and effective exercise of sovereign authority. The Tribunal concluded, however, that Sind did exercise sovereign control over certain portions of the territory known as Dhara Banni and Chhad Bet, areas that are raised above the level of the Rann and were used by Sind inhabitants as grazing pastures.

Based on Sind's acts of sovereignty over Dhara Banni and Chhad Bet, the Tribunal awarded these areas to Sind's successor, Pakistan. The Tribunal also awarded a peninsula of land, known as Nagar Parkar, to Pakistan, even though Pakistan had not established legal title to it. The Tribunal based this decision on the fact that the area was wholly surrounded by Pakistani territory. Thus, the Tribunal reasoned that awarding the area to India would inevitably lead to friction and conflict. With regard to the remainder of the territory, the Tribunal concluded that the evidence of Sind sovereignty over the majority of the Rann was insufficient to establish sovereignty. The Tribunal thus relied primarily on the evidence produced by India of British relinquishment of rights over the Rann, and awarded the remainder of the territory, approximately ninety percent of the Rann, to India.

3.   Preliminary Analysis

The Rann of Kutch Arbitration was extremely successful in resolving a territorial dispute between two nations with a history of conflict. Throughout the proceedings, the parties cooperated with each other and with the Tribunal. Neither side questioned the authority of the Tribunal, and both sides worked together to implement the decision. This success can be attributed to several factors. First, the issues before the Tribunal were well-defined. Additionally, the parties had previously agreed that the boundary was conterminous between the two nations and that, therefore, the territory in dispute had to belong to one or the other, which further limited the scope of Tribunal's authority. Second, as the Tribunal noted, the dispute was essentially factual in nature. The parties did not focus their arguments on complex legal issues, but relied instead on testimony and documentary evidence. The Tribunal, in turn, relied on the weight of this evidence and the relative strength of the parties' arguments in rendering its decision. Other than incidentally, the Tribunal did not have to enunciate or expound potentially contentious principles of international law.

More important to the success of the arbitration was that the dispute over the Rann did not represent a major political dispute between the two countries. The Rann had little economic or strategic value and was sparsely populated. Thus, although large-scale fighting preceded the arbitration proceedings, the dispute was more symbolic than substantive. Furthermore, shortly after the cease fire, both nations had shifted their attention to disputes over Kashmir and Punjab, areas more vital to the interests of both countries.

B. The Taba Area Arbitration

The successful arbitration of the dispute over the Taba area between Egypt and Israel "represent[ed] a significant milestone in the development of relations between the two formerly warring nations." The objective of the arbitral tribunal was restricted to deciding the location of fourteen boundary pillars of "the recognized international boundary between Egypt and the former mandated territory of Palestine," thus deciding the status of the Taba area, a strip of land in the Sinai on the shore of the Gulf of Aqaba.

1. Background

The origins of the dispute can be traced to 1906, when Turkish forces occupied the coastal settlement of Taba but were forced to withdraw under British pressure. After negotiations between Anglo–Egyptian and Turkish representatives, a territorial agreement was reached ("the 1906 Agreement") and the border between Egypt and the Ottoman Empire was fixed as running through Taba. In 1915, however, a British military survey produced a map that showed the border as running along a line approximately three-quarters of a mile to the north-east of the 1906 line. The 1915 line became the boundary with Egypt under the British Palestine Mandate and remained as such when Israel proclaimed itself an independent state in May 1948. In the June 1967 war between Israel and Egypt, Israel captured the Sinai peninsula from Egypt, bringing the Taba area under Israeli control.

In the March 1979 Treaty of Peace between Israel and Egypt, Israel agreed to withdraw its troops from the Sinai and to recognize "the full exercise of Egyptian sovereignty up to the internationally recognized border between Egypt and mandated Palestine." Pursuant to the Treaty of Peace, a joint commission was formed to demarcate the boundary. When survey teams reached the Taba area, the parties could only agree on the placement of three boundary pillars. Despite negotiations, the parties failed to agree on the placement of the remaining pillars. Thus, the parties agreed to submit the dispute to arbitration, in accordance with the 1979 Treaty.

The Tribunal consisted of five members, one national of each state nominated by the respective parties and three non-nationals acceptable to both sides. The Tribunal's task was extremely limited: it was to decide the location of fourteen boundary pillars, but it was not authorized to establish a location of a boundary pillar other than at a location advanced by Israel or by Egypt. "At stake were several hundred meters of shoreline, corresponding territorial water rights and a resort hotel complex."

2.   Issues and Arguments

Israel maintained that the Tribunal should refer to the boundary defined by the 1906 Agreement because Great Britain, as mandatory power, and Egypt had explicitly recognized this as the boundary between Egypt and Palestine in declarations in 1926. The Tribunal refused, stating that the 1979 Treaty of Peace referred to the "recognized international boundary between Egypt and the former mandated territory of Palestine" and not to the 1906 Agreement. The Tribunal thus established the period of the Palestinian Mandate as the critical period and relied on the location of the boundary pillars as they were understood during this period as the basis for its decision.

In support of their respective claims, the parties introduced maps, surveys, and photographs of the area indicating the erection, wear, removal, or replacement of the pillars at issue. With regard to the nine northernmost pillars, situated in an uninhabited desert region involving "apparently no essential interests of the Parties," the Tribunal found the arguments of both sides unpersuasive. It therefore decided in favor of the proposed locations of the pillars that came closest to establishing a straight line connecting adjacent agreed pillar locations. The Tribunal thus awarded five of these pillar locations to Egypt and four to Israel. With regard to the location of four other pillars, the Tribunal concluded, based on the factual evidence before it, that the locations advanced by Egypt established the recognized boundary during the critical period.

In reaching its decision regarding the final and most contested pillar location, the Tribunal relied primarily on photographs introduced by Egypt indicating the existence of a marker known as the "Parker pillar," which was erected by commissioners implementing the 1906 Agreement. The Tribunal rejected Israel's argument that the Parker pillar was not intervisible with the agreed location of the adjacent pillar to the north, and that this lack of intervisibility contradicted the 1906 Agreement. The Tribunal relied on evidence that Egypt and Turkey may have ignored the intervisibility requirement of the 1906 agreement when constructing the pillars in the area of the Parker pillar. The Tribunal also rejected Israel's argument that the pillar had been erroneously erected. The Tribunal concluded that the Parker pillar existed at the location advanced by Egypt, and that the Parties had recognized this pillar as a boundary throughout the critical period. Thus, Israel could not at this point challenge its location on the basis of an alleged error.

In its Award, the Tribunal commended the parties for the "spirit of cooperation and courtesy which permeated the proceedings in general and which thereby rendered the hearing a constructive experience." On March 15, 1989, following negotiations and the conclusion of an agreement, Israel transferred to Egypt sovereignty over the Taba area in its entirety, including the resort facilities located there.

3.   Preliminary Analysis

Like the Rann of Kutch arbitration, the Taba Area Arbitration successfully resolved a territorial dispute between nations that had a history of violent conflict. The two proceedings attest to the value of international arbitration as a procedure to demarcate boundaries between states. They also have other important similarities. For example, the dispute to be resolved by the Tribunal in the Taba Area Arbitration, like that in the Rann of Kutch Arbitration, was well-defined. The Tribunal had limited authority, authorized only to establish the pillar locations in accordance with one or the other of the party's claims. Furthermore, the two disputes, although complex, were primarily factual in nature. Thus, after determining the critical period, the Tribunal relied almost exclusively on testimony and documentary evidence in rendering its decision as opposed to relying on international legal theories.

Unlike the Rann of Kutch, however, the Taba area was economically valuable. The area included a multi-million dollar hotel complex and accompanying tourist village. In addition, after the award was issued, the Israeli government faced fierce and emotional opposition to the decision from citizens who worked in Taba. In agreeing to arbitration, however, the parties had already decided that control of the Taba was not worth undermining the 1979 peace treaty, which had officially terminated the thirty-one year old state of war between the two nations. In other words, "[o]nce the prospect of a meaningful agreement became real, both parties appreciated that the issue was strategically meaningless and that under no circumstances could it be permitted to disrupt the peace relationship that was, by then, seen as serving their common interests."

Notes and Questions

1. In the two successful international arbitrations over disputed territory, the Rann of Kutch and the Taba area conflict, the dispute was well-defined and both disputes were primarily factual in nature. How do these characteristic make a difference in the arbitration process?

2. Why is the arbitration process not widely used to resolve territorial disputes between ethnic groups? Why has it not been used to resolve the hotly disputed disputes over territory in Israel or in the Kashmir–Jammu dispute between Pakistan and India?

3. Assume that the parties had agreed to mediation, rather than arbitration in this case. What are some of the challenges that a mediator must address in this case? Describe the ideal mediator and mediation approach.

4. Besides mediation, what other processes might be appropriate for resolving the territorial dispute in this case?

Chapter 9

THE ROLE OF INTERNATION-
AL ORGANIZATIONS IN RE-
SOLVING CONFLICTS

A. INTRODUCTION

The influence of international organizations in global conflict resolution has expanded significantly since World War II as the world community is increasingly plagued by violent conflicts that threaten international peace and security. International organizations seek to facilitate the resolution of inter-State conflict as well as ethnic conflict within States. Conflicts between religious and ethnic groups during the post-Cold War era, such as those occurring in Bosnia, Liberia, Cambodia, Somalia, Ethiopia, Zaire, Georgia, and the former Yugoslavia, have proliferated. While the United Nations has been the principal force behind peace and security efforts, regional, non-governmental, and transnational organizations are acquiring a greater presence in this field.

This chapter begins with materials on the predominant international organization, the United Nations, exploring its organization and structure as well as its peace and security activities. It then focuses attention on the work of regional and non-governmental organizations that participate in conflict resolution activities and considers their strengths as well as their limitations.

The final part of the chapter considers transitional justice institutions and retributive and restorative justice approaches to conflict resolution efforts in the wake of egregious human rights violations. The final set of materials describes the tensions between mediative and human rights approaches to conflict resolution.

As you read through these materials, you should consider the extent to which cultural contexts affect the conflict resolution work of international, regional and non-governmental organizations. You should also think about the relevance of concepts such as neutrality that are often associated with forms of mediation activity. Finally, you should be concerned with questions of accountability. To whom are international organizations accountable, and why does it matter?

B.　THE ROLE OF THE UNITED NATIONS

1.　INTRODUCTION

The United Nations was established in 1945 as the successor organization to the League of Nations. Its foundational principle was to develop "faith in fundamental human rights" and to promote international peace and security.[1] It, therefore, has a critical role in the management and resolution of international conflict.

With the shift from inter-state to intra-state conflicts, the U.N. has had recourse to mediation more frequently than any other process for conflict management. There are, however, substantial constraints on the U.N.'s ability to engage effectively in mediation. In addition to the limitations imposed by traditional principles of sovereignty, mediators in the international context face challenges with respect to the availability of resources and decision-making—especially in regard to steering the parties toward prompt action.[2]

2.　ORGANIZATION AND STRUCTURE

The U.N. is a multi-lateral political organization composed of sovereign Member States and governed by a Charter. Member States possess exclusive governance rights; collective authorization is necessary to pursue action. The U.N. depends upon the ability of its members to cooperate and achieve consensus. Member support is instrumental to its legitimacy and activities.[3]

There are six principal organs of the United Nations: the (1) General Assembly; (2) Security Council; (3) Economic and Social Council, (4) Trusteeship Council, (5) International Court of Justice; and (6) Secretariat. The Security Council, General Assembly, and the Secretariat are the most significant organs for decisions regarding the maintenance of international peace and security.

Security Council

The Security Council has primary responsibility for carrying out the U.N.'s activities in regard to international peace and security. There are fifteen member countries, five of which are permanent (China, France, Russia, the United Kingdom, and the United States) and ten rotating member countries, periodically elected by the General Assembly. The U.N., however, cannot take action if one of the Security Council's five permanent members exercises its veto power. Scholarly commentators have been critical of the veto power because, in their view, it represents a significant obstacle to the management of international conflict.[4]

1. Oscar Schachter, *United Nations Law*, 88 Am. J. Int'l L. 1 (1994).

2. Judith Fretter, *International Organizations and Conflict Management: The United Nations and the Mediation of International Conflicts, in* Studies in International Mediation 98–100 (Jacob Bercovitch ed.,

2002) [hereinafter Bercovitch, International Mediation].

3. *Id.*

4. William R. Slomanson, Fundamental Perspectives on International Law 126 (4th ed. 2003).

Chapter VI of the Charter, which addresses primarily the peaceful settlement of disputes, gives the Security Council powers to investigate disputes that might threaten international peace and security and to recommend appropriate methods of settlement.[5] Chapter VII of the Charter empowers the Security Council to engage in a variety of measures, including force, to respond to and eliminate actual threats to international peace and security.

General Assembly

All U.N. Member States belong to the General Assembly. Some international organizations enjoy observer status and are permitted to attend General Assembly meetings. According to Chapter VI of the Charter, the role of the General Assembly in terms of conflict prevention and dispute settlement is: to (a) discuss questions related to the maintenance of international peace and security which have been brought before it by Member States or by the Security Council; (b) make recommendations on such questions; (c) bring to the attention of the Security Council situations which are likely to endanger international peace and security; (d) consider general principles of cooperation in the maintenance of international peace and security; (e) initiate studies; and (f) recommend measures for the peaceful resolution of situations that are likely to affect friendly relations between nations.[6]

Secretariat

The Secretariat office, headed by the U.N. Secretary General, is the primary administrator of U.N. programs. Under the U.N. Charter, the Secretary–General is authorized to gather and evaluate information concerning conflict prevention and inform the Security Council of situations that threaten international peace and security.[7] A growing number of U.N. mediation efforts have been undertaken under the aegis of the Secretary–General's good offices. Recent U.N. Secretary Generals, including Boutros Boutros–Ghali and Kofi Annan, have emphasized the preventive diplomacy aspect of their office.

The following excerpt reports on an interview with Alvaro de Soto, a U.N. mediator and under-secretary General. He elaborates in some detail upon the role played by the Secretary–General in the exercise of his good offices.

ROBERT KIRSCH, THE PEACEMAKER: AN INTERVIEW WITH UN UNDER–SECRETARY–GENERAL ALVARO DE SOTO

26 Fletcher Forum of World Affairs 83 (2002).

Alvaro de Soto, an under-secretary-general at the United Nations, has seen conflict in a way that few others ever will, having served as good officer for the United Nations in the peace negotiations on El Salvador

---

5. Handbook on the Peaceful Settlement of Disputes Between States 111–22 (1992).

6. *Id.* at 123–26.

7. *Id.* at 28.

and currently on Cyprus. As Secretary–General Javier Perez de Cuellar's personal representative for the Central American Peace Process, Mr. De Soto helped transform a raging civil war between the Government of El Salvador and the FMLN (Frente Farabundo Marti para la Liberacion Nacional) into a durable peace—a feat often viewed as the prototype for UN peacemaking efforts. In his 20 years at the United Nations, Mr. de Soto has worked under three successive secretaries-general, holding a variety of posts throughout his career. Today, he serves as Secretary–General Kofi Annan's special adviser on Cyprus, a position he has held since late 1999.

On October 23, 2001, Mr. de Soto sat down with The Fletcher Forum's *Robert Kirsch to discuss his career and experience in dealing with international conflict. In the course of a conversation, sometimes humorous and often sobering, he described the role of the mediator, the UN selection process, and the strategies used to bring two sides to an agreement.*

* * *

FORUM: When one opens the newspaper or turns on the news, one is increasingly exposed to the concept of mediation, be it in the Middle East, Northern Ireland, or even the current federal proceedings involving Microsoft. Despite this fact, little effort has been made to explain what mediation is and how the process actually works. Having now served as a mediator for the United Nations in both El Salvador and Cyprus, how do you define mediation and your role in international conflict?

DE SOTO: At the United Nations we are rarely entrusted with a mediation task as such. Mediation in our parlance has a rather precise meaning in which the person in the middle is actually able to submit proposals. We refer to ourselves as "good officers," with a good officer being a person who, acting on behalf of the secretary-general of the United Nations, is there to assist parties to a dispute within a wide range of possibilities. This can be as simple as conveying a message from one side to another or bringing about quiet and confidential meetings. The good-officer role can likewise range from shuttling between the parties to a conflict with a view to finding out the facts of the dispute, all the way up to convening direct face-to-face meetings, even submitting proposals, in writing or orally, for the two sides to consider. It is a broad term that covers a spectrum of possible activities ranging from facilitation to mediation as such.

FORUM: To touch on the one extreme you just mentioned about possibly offering options in written form to the parties, you have obviously been successful doing this over the years, but how have you managed to navigate the turbulent waters of Article 2(7) and "matters essentially within the domestic jurisdiction of states?"

DE SOTO: The rule of thumb at the United Nations in the case of an internal conflict is that the organization can be involved if two requirements are met: one is that the government or governmental party involved in a state—presumably a member of the organization—gives its consent to this involvement by the United Nations. With regard to the second requirement, the secretary-general should have the backing of a mandate. While this mandate need not be specific, it should come from an intergovernmental body of the organization authorized to confer such a mandate, usually the Security Council.

FORUM: How does the mediator selection process in the United Nations work? Is there specialized training or an emphasis on regional expertise?

DE SOTO: There is no specialized training. We keep in the Secretariat a confidential list, which we nickname the "List of the Great and the Good." We do consider various candidates when the need arises, but ultimately, it is the choice of the secretary-general. In selecting a mediator or a good officer, you have to combine a number of virtues and possibly even some faults. What you need is exactly the right person for the particular job in terms of personal qualifications, as well as his nationality, the connections that he has, and his knowledge, or lack thereof, but we do not have any specific training.

FORUM: There are obviously examples of the Security Council calling on the secretary-general to play an active role in the settlement of an international dispute. In the case of Resolution 186 in Cyprus and Resolution 637 in El Salvador, the Security Council appears to have opened the door to mediation efforts. However, these two cases are part of a much larger issue. Where does the mediator's role come from in terms of the UN Charter and international law?

DE SOTO: Well, I would think that international law is largely agnostic on the subject. Successful good offices are conducted necessarily with the consent of the parties. They are under no legal obligation to submit to talks within a UN framework. In terms of politics, what we would like to create at the United Nations is an ethos under which it would be considered bad form to reject the secretary-general's good offices without valid and arguable reasons for doing so. By and large, states involved in disputes and conflicts should accept a willingness by the secretary-general to find out the facts and to make a few suggestions without this being seen as undue intervention.

FORUM: Is there a particular part of the Charter from which this role of the secretary-general and his special representatives emerges?

DE SOTO: None. The Charter is notoriously silent on the subjects. There is a general duty on the part of states to resolve their disputes by a variety of means as outlined in Article 33—facilitation, conciliation, and mediation, to name a few—but there is no role provided for the secretary-general. The development of the secretary-general's good offices is a matter of practice, rather than a matter of law.

FORUM: Returning to the case of El Salvador, could you walk me through the process? Having been named the secretary-general's personal representative for the Central American Peace Process, what kind of preparations did you and your staff go through before entering talks with the parties?

DE SOTO: I was appointed to that position in early 1987, and by that time, certain of my colleagues and I had already spent a fair amount of time studying the conflict. It was difficult for me to do so, because I was in a rather visible position in the secretary-general's office, but one of my colleagues in particular, Francesc Vendrell, trail-blazer that he is, engaged in discreet discussions with all those who were in a position to provide us with insights and factual information. We spoke with members of the FMLN's roving political-diplomatic commission, who usually turned up on the margins of non-aligned conferences.

In the early years—1986, '87, and '88—our actions were not taken with the view that our role as a third party would evolve as it eventually did, though I will not hide from you that Vendrell and I certainly entertained the possibility. We were convinced that we could approach the conflict in a more calibrated way than was being done by others. At that time, however, we saw that a number of obstacles needed to be overcome before we could play a more active role in the dispute.

FORUM: It is my understanding that your efforts in El Salvador centered on the "single negotiating text" approach to mediation, an approach also used to some extent by President Carter during Camp David I and by George Mitchell in the Northern Ireland peace talks. What can you tell us abut this approach and your reasons for using it in this particular case?

DE SOTO: It is a matter of method. The "single negotiating text" lends itself best to addressing a dispute where the parties are not on speaking terms, or where the suspicion between them is of such a degree and the positions so entrenched that anything one side proposes is rejected by the other simply because it comes from the other side. In those circumstances, there is really no alternative to a third party helping them along by providing ideas, because there is little basis to hope that they themselves will work out formulas for moving the process forward. In addition, there are solutions which neither side would contemplate if proposed by the other. However, if a third party proposed these same solutions, they maybe more palatable.

You have mentioned two cases in which this method was used, and actually, this is the way the U.N. Law of the Sea Convention was negotiated, though in that case the method was chosen for another reason. At the UN Law of the Sea Conference there were just too many parties, almost 150 countries. It was impossible to have a processing system for individual proposals.

FORUM: And how does this process actually work?

DE SOTO: One listens very carefully to the positions of the two sides, trying to expurgate what is the position, that is, the public posture or the negotiating position, and getting down to the real interests, concerns, fears, and aspirations that have to be addressed. Once you have a clearer idea of those issues as they apply to both sides, it becomes possible to draw up a compromise which is not necessarily the middle point between the positions of the two sides, but which is fair and viable nevertheless. Then, as good officers, we put the text to the parties as a working paper rather than as a proposal, which is what a mediator would do, at least according to classical definitions.

At this point, we give the parties a bit of time to reflect on the document and to present their comments. We prefer comments to amendments. Then we go back and consider their comments and see how we can accommodate them in a way that is compatible with the comments of the other side, always having in mind interests rather than positions. Eventually, we revise the original working paper and submit a new one, which is identical for both sides. This is all done in the expectation of getting more comments. It may take 20 revisions, it may take 50, and it seems like a very slow way to proceed, but it is remarkable as you go along in a negotiation how the parties' more extreme negotiating positions can gradually fall by the way-side, a little bit like peeling an onion.

FORUM: Have you used this same approach in Cyprus?

DE SOTO: I would rather not get into discussing the efforts that are ongoing just now, but clearly in the case of Cyprus, the positions of the two sides are deeply entrenched, and there exist some of the characteristics that I described earlier, thus making it almost unavoidable that there be a third party to assist the two sides in reconciling their interests.

FORUM: Secretary–General Kofi Annan once remarked, "Impartiality does not—and must not—mean neutrality in the face of evil. It means strict and unbiased adherence to the principles of the Charter—nothing more, and nothing less." What are your views on the issue of neutrality versus impartiality? Has it ever been difficult for you to be impartial in a mediation?

DE SOTO: Obviously, I would cease to be a human being if I didn't have views and place value judgments on the conduct of the sides to a conflict. I try to keep those out of my thinking in approaching a negotiation. What I can say, however, is that the United Nations acts within a given framework defined by the Charter and the body of laws, particularly in the area of human rights, drawn up over the years. One cannot pretend that this framework does not exist. In fact, United Nations representatives of the secretary-general involved in good offices on his behalf have guidelines, which they are expected to follow. These guidelines do allow for flexibility, because no two negotiations are alike, but we do expect the parties to a dispute to adhere to these ideals in any agreements that they reach.

For a number of reasons, these guidelines are not made public, but to give you an example, the United Nations cannot be associated with an amnesty that would leave war crimes, crimes against humanity, or genocide in a state of impunity. We could not go along with something like that. Obviously, we cannot prevent the sides to a dispute from reaching an agreement on their own, but they will not have our blessing.

FORUM: What has been the most difficult lesson for you to learn in your work over the years?

DE SOTO: Patience

* * *

FORUM: And finally, you have obviously had some incredible experiences throughout your career, experiences that few individuals will ever be fortunate enough to have. If you could identify the three most important lessons that one could take away from the work you have done so far, what would those lessons be?

DE SOTO: Never try to trick anyone. You will usually be found out, and whatever you achieve from the trick will not be durable. Second, do not try to sweeten the state of play just to ingratiate yourself with one of the parties. Another way of saying that is, don't tell a party to a dispute or a conflict what he wants to hear, but rather what the situation really is. Third, don't negotiate side deals. The end result should be transparent, as distinct from the negotiations themselves, which should be confidential. Just as there exists the fog of war in which the first victim is the truth, there should exist the fog of diplomacy or the fog of good offices in which the truth should only come out in the end result.

---

3. PEACE AND SECURITY ACTIVITIES OF THE UNITED NATIONS

The U.N. engages in multiple peace and security activities including preventive diplomacy, peacemaking, peacekeeping, and post-conflict peace building. In its broadest sense, *preventive diplomacy* comprises the bulk of U.N. peacemaking activities, including active involvement in the search for peaceful settlements through various forms of humanitarian and economic assistance, supervised self-determination in the former colonies, and *peacemaking* activities through the use of mediation and the good offices of the Secretary General.[8] Sovereignty can hamper the prevention of conflict because it limits intervention until an international conflict has actually arisen.[9] It could be argued that effec-

8. Lily R. Sucharipa–Behrmann & Thomas M. Frank, *Preventive Measures*, 30 N.Y.U. J. INT'L L. & POL'Y 485, 486–93 (1998).

9. *Id.*

tive preventive diplomacy requires strengthening U.N. conflict prevention capabilities, rather than resorting to mechanisms that simply react to circumstances.

Chapter VII of the U.N. Charter, which permits the use of force to secure the peace, is understood as the source of the U.N.'s power to engage in *peacekeeping* operations. The traditional understanding of peacekeeping required the consent of the implicated States to the presence of the peacekeepers, lightly armed forces, and adherence to the principle of neutrality between the parties. In the aftermath of the Cold War, increased religious and ethnic conflicts have led to an expansion of the traditional range of activities by peacekeeping forces. The U.N. had been criticized for deploying under-resourced operations in many of the civil conflicts. In his 1992 *Agenda for Peace*, Secretary–General Boutros–Ghali asserted that the United Nations should confront the contemporary challenges facing the institution and its activities. To restore civil society, he argued for more heavily armed "peace-enforcement units" that would be capable of ensuring compliance with cease-fires.[10]

With the publication in 2001 of U.N. Secretary–General Kofi Annan's report, *Prevention of Armed Conflict*,[11] the U.N. renewed its commitment to preventive diplomacy. The report emphasized that the international community must move from a "culture of reaction" to a "culture of prevention."[12] In recent years, the U.N. has recognized that peacekeeping activities should not be used as a substitute for addressing the core causes of conflict, and it has acknowledged the importance of peacebuilding and economic recovery in war-torn societies. To this end, scholars have called for greater collaboration between governments and the private sector in peacebuilding after violent conflict.[13] Recent scholarship emphasizes the importance of strategic development in moving beyond cease-fire regimes to a durable peace. This requires developing legal, social, and political processes that can authoritatively resolve conflict.[14] As noted by Elizabeth Cousens, " . . . the most effective means to self-enforcing peace is to cultivate political processes and institutions that can manage group conflict without violence but with authority, and ultimately with legitimacy."[15]

In the following article, Professor Ruth Wedgwood reviews the historical development of U.N. peacekeeping activities and takes a criti-

10. *An Agenda for Peace: Preventive Diplomacy, Peacemaking and Peace-keeping*, UN Doc. A/47/277–S24111, at 22 (1992), UN Sales No. E.95.I.15 (1995).

11. *Prevention of Armed Conflict: Report of the Secretary–General*, U.N. GAOR/SCOR 55th Sess. Agenda Item 10, U.N. Docs A/55/985–S/2001/574 (2001).

12. *See generally* Owen Philip Lefkon, *Culture Shock: Obstacles to Bringing Conflict Prevention under the Wing of U.N. Development . . . and Vice Versa*, 35 N.Y.U. J. INT'L L. & POL'Y 671 (2003).

13. Ruth Wedgwood, Harold K. Jacobson & Allan Gerson, *Peace Building: The Private Sector's Role*, 95 AM. J. INT'L L. 102 (2001).

14. ELIZABETH M. COUSENS, *Introduction*, in PEACEBUILDING AS POLITICS: CULTIVATING PEACE IN FRAGILE SOCIETIES (Elizabeth M. Cousens & Chetan Kumar eds., with Karin Wermester 2001).

15. *Id.* at 12.

cal view of its progress. She advocates for the adoption of a new paradigm in the face of non-State, ethnic aggressors and unconventional war tactics.

RUTH WEDGWOOD, UNITED NATIONS PEACEKEEPING OPERATIONS AND THE USE OF FORCE

5 Washington University Journal of Law & Policy 69 (2001).

The question of United Nations peacekeeping and the use of force might seem to be a specialized topic. However, it is at the root of much of the dissatisfaction with the performance of the United Nations (UN)—both inside and outside the organization. When one views the UN up close, in the field and in New York, much of the unsteadiness in discharging its missions stems from the organization's deep ambivalence about the proper use of force in international conflict resolution and its hobbled ability to muster efficacious force.

Originally, in the midst of World War II, the UN was not a building on First Avenue, but the anti-fascist alliance itself. The UN included America's major allies in the war, namely Great Britain, the Soviet Union, China, and France. The major enemy states were Nazi Germany, fascist Italy, and—though later for the Soviet Union—an imperial Japan. So if provenance is any guide, the UN anticipated a future as a robust organization. Indeed, if you look at the UN Charter of 1945 in its closing paragraphs, Article 106 posits what the alliance should do in the interim period before a UN security council was established. It supposes that the world war allies would continue to consult and take such action as they thought necessary for international peace and security, including action against any resurgence of fascism.

The original scheme was to endow the security council with designated military forces under agreements with member states pursuant to Article 43 of the Charter. There was even supposed to be a UN air force, as stated in Article 45 of the Charter, with committed air assets from member states. However, the only air power now used by the UN is commercially leased surplus planes and helicopters from the former Soviet bloc and the occasional U–2 deployed by the Special Commission on Iraq to look for weapons of mass destruction hidden by Baghdad. So any association between the UN and a tepid response to aggression was not part of the original conception. However, after World War II, the confrontation with Communist countries began. With the Cold War underway, things fell apart and the UN's political machinery no longer operated as smoothly as intended. The Security Council froze-up in the ideological schism of the Cold War. With veto power guaranteed by the Charter to the permanent members, including the Soviet Union, very little could be accomplished through the Chapter 7 mechanism to muster armed forces in collective military action. The Security Council was given no committed forces under Article 43, and even now, a half century later, no country is willing to precommit its forces to UN deployment.

Peacekeeping was born in the interstices of the UN Charter. The famous joke is that peacekeeping is authorized under chapter "6 ½" of the Charter-halfway between the Security Council's procedures for conciliation and its procedures for deploying force. Peacekeeping was supposed to be limited and was intended as an interpositional buffer, an armed observation force designed to discourage adversaries from violating a ceasefire or peace agreement. Yet in reality it was a minimal show of force, almost a form of bird watching, by men who happened to wear uniforms. Peacekeepers kept apart parties to a truce and discouraged nighttime forays and border encounters. Having neutral observers on the border gave a bit of dignity to the fact of separation. It gave the parties a reason why they were not obliged to "have at" each other every foggy night.

Prime Minister Lester Pearson of Canada, Under–Secretary–General Ralph Bunche, and Secretary–General Dag Hammarskjold invented the institution of peacekeeping for situations such as Sinai and Cyprus, and, with less success, for the Congo. Initially, its funding was quite problematic. France and Russia were unhappy with the operations in Sinai and the Congo and refused to pay their dues. This led to the famous advisory opinion of the International Court of Justice (ICJ), holding that peacekeeping was not an ultra vires occupation for the UN. In the course of the decision, however, at least one judge on the ICJ cautioned that the UN should not become so expensive that its members could not afford membership. Perhaps in response to that problem, the United States and the other permanent members of the Security Council have traditionally paid an extra amount for the expenses of peacekeeping, which rose to almost four times the UN regular budget in the mid 1990s.

The classical account of peacekeeping states that at least three conditions must be met for peacekeeping to work: first, consent of parties to the peacekeepers' presence, upon entry and throughout the mission; second, the minimal use of force, mustering arms only in self-defense; and third, neutrality between the parties principally because peacekeeping was not an attempt to change the outcome of a war or conflict. This is the view of older UN hands such as Sir Marrack Goulding and Sir Brian Urquhart, and the reason why some people in the UN firmly believed that the organization should not go into Bosnia. The moral adequacy of "neutrality" has been contested when the UN deploys in circumstances where one side is the aggressor or abuses the laws of war.

Peacekeeping was also shaped by the Cold War. It was assumed that superpowers should not take part in peacekeeping because they were not neutral. Smaller countries, often the neutrals of Scandinavia or developing nations, were the stalwart troop contributors for peacekeeping. The deployment of peacekeepers was a method of preventing small conflicts from becoming occasions for major confrontation.

Peacekeeping had its disappointments even in the early, classical phase. It worked reasonably well in Cyprus during the 1960s, but the UN was powerless to prevent *enosis*, the attempt of Athens to integrate the island into Greece, or to resist the Turkish military intervention in 1974. There were also complaints that the blue line of peacekeepers permanently divided the island, thus freezing the conflict and giving each side an excuse not to negotiate.

The Congo intervention was a bloody mess, as shown by Sir Brian Urquhart's wonderful memoir. Sir Brian's recollections, entitled *A Life in Peace and War*, limn the larger-than-life quality of some of the early UN figures. He notes drolly that on one troop transport, a blue UN flag was draped across the train engine. The entourage was greeted by the question of a Congolese official: "L'ONU? C'est quel tribu?" or "what tribe is the UN?" Even in the 1960s the UN lacked credibility on the ground.

Yet after the end of the Cold War, the Security Council returned to work, and there was great anticipation of its potential in the 1990s. Many supposed that the UN would be able to act vigorously and with unity. This optimism was fueled by the unity of response in 1991 against Iraq's invasion of Kuwait and also by the rather unique period when a series of local conflicts diminished because there were no longer major patrons from the east-west struggle. Further, a peace agreement was reached in Cambodia, with cooperation from China and the ASEAN countries. The civil conflicts in Nicaragua, El Salvador, Guatemala, Mozambique, and Angola were no longer freighted with east-west rivalry, although the world soon learned that ethnic rivalry could be equally contentious. There was astronomical growth in the number of peacekeepers deployed on the ground-up to 70,000 in the mid 1990s. The UN's peacekeeping operations department was not equipped to handle the logistics of so many operations, and was often unable to find properly trained or disciplined troops, or to marry-up third-world brigades with modern equipment. Of course, as the numbers increased, the cost increased as well. It was largely the soaring cost of peacekeeping that provoked the United State's refusal to pay its assessments.

The peacekeeping of the 1990s was a new kind of operation. It was not just interpositional observation, or monitoring a peace accord. It often involved attempts to scale back a conflict and demobilize opposing forces even before there was any assurance of a binding ceasefire. Peacekeeping was attempted where there was no peace to keep—so the saying went. UN forces were asked to provide security for a host of new tasks in civil reconstruction such as the demobilization of guerrilla and government forces, the collection and caching of arms, emergency assistance to refugees and internally displaced persons, and organizing democratic elections for post-conflict governments. The UN attempted to become a full service provider for broken societies, in awkward coordination with regional agencies and frameworks such as the Organization for Security and Cooperation in Europe and the Organization of American States. Multifunctional peacekeeping was not just the work of soldiers but of many other UN agencies, including many that depend on voluntary contributions rather than mandatory dues. The High Commissioner for Refugees, for example, proved to be a key figure in this period.

UN Secretary–General Boutros Boutros–Ghali had high expectations for peacekeeping in the 1990s, as outlined in *An Agenda for Peace*. He even supposed that the UN might finally obtain assigned troops, deployable at will, under Article 43 agreements. That did not come to pass. Even the hope for standby troops earmarked for UN operations by member states fell prey to the realities of local politics and reluctant publics. Willingness to intervene with national contingents depended on the sympathies of a particular conflict, as well as the likelihood of success. The standby list was often a dance card for countries' right to say "no." Eighty or more countries would happily field telephone calls from the thirty-eighth floor of the UN Secretariat building, and then say it was not the right struggle for them. Yet there was a mood of anticipation in the early 1990s about what the UN and the accepted warrant of its authority for intervention might mean.

Disillusionment followed shortly thereafter. First, these conflicts involved a different kind of warfare. Ethnic wars engaged nonstate actors—singled minded groups lacking the full panoply of interests and linkages that often moderate the behavior of governments. Conflicts were fueled by opportunistic mercantile warlords such as those currently in Sierra Leone, Liberia, and the Congo, where diamonds and timber keep insurgencies going. These all-terrain conflicts do not lend themselves to interpositional peacekeeping. Indeed, there often are no organized command structures with which to negotiate. Intermingled populations, unconventional warfare, the deliberate targeting of civilians, the strategy of threatening peacekeepers and even taking them hostage, make this unconventional warfare; often the UN has not known how to cope. Blue berets were exchanged for blue helmets. The sense of vulnerability reached an apex in missions such as Rwanda, where the Hutu Interehamwe deliberately killed Belgian peacekeepers and propelled their withdrawal, and Somalia, where the urban forces of Mohammed Aidid—later shown to have been trained by Osama bin Laden—killed eighteen United States Rangers. This was not the tactically simpler task of interpositional peacekeeping, but rather an attempt to counter forces that know how to exploit the concerns of western democracies regarding the safety of their citizen-soldiers.

The apparent incapacity of UN troops to provide protection to the civilian populations they were sent to aid was equally troublesome. The deadly attrition of the Bosnian war killed 200,000 civilians out of a population of four million, and also displaced 800,000 people as refugees or internally displaced persons. The siege of Sarajevo saw Serb forces on the surrounding hills, heartlessly sniping at civilians and bombarding the town. The Sarajevo government was suspected by some, even inside the UN, of enhancing the visuals for a CNN war by setting up their own civilians as targets. Ultimately, observers witnessed the tragedy of Srebrenica in the Drina Valley where lightly armed Dutch peacekeeping forces did not, and perhaps could not, protect the civilian population, and 7,000 combat-age Muslim men and boys were summarily executed by the Bosnian Serbs.

Similarly, in Rwanda the UN and its member states disappointed many observers by failing to act in the face of the Hutu genocide against the Tutsi. The Secretariat disregarded warnings early in 1994 that genocidal plans might be in preparation. When the killing began, the UN forces of the "UNAMIR" mission were pulled out by their national commands, including the Belgians, Ghanaians, and Bangladeshi, and no other intervention force was mounted by the Security Council.

The heart of the failure was minimalism in the use of force. Whether a matter of philosophy or political skittishness, the UN and its members have often proved unwilling to use armed force in circumstances where a robust deployment might be effective. Observers often ascribed this to member states' reluctance to jeopardize their forces. Failure to deploy robustly may also signal an implicit sympathy with one of the sides in the conflict. However, it is also engendered by an ethos of nonviolence within the United Nations itself—a lingering doubt about the necessary use of defensive force in the international community, and perhaps a belief that the thin personality of a multilateral organization cannot sustain the morally contentious choices that are made by nation states in defense of their own existence. As a result, UN forces were put on the ground in Bosnia with the very limited mandate of delivering food and humanitarian assistance. To some, this seemed to be a replay of the moral indifference that characterized Europe during the rise of fascism; peacekeepers standing by as terrible things were done because it was not their department to stop it. Ultimately, when Boutros–Ghali went to the Security Council and asked for the creation of internal safe areas within Bosnia for the protection of civilians, he was not given the troops he wanted. Seven thousand troops were allocated, instead of the 34,000 recommended by his military advisors. At that point, many thought that the Secretary–General should have resigned, or at least have said that he could not be party to a deception and refused to implement the safe area mandate.

With great melancholy, I recall my visit to the Hague in July 1995. The International Criminal Tribunal for the former Yugoslavia was in its early months of operation. We had a pleasant dinner with prosecutor Richard Goldstone and then listened with horror to the television on the fall of Srebrenica. The Dutch contingent was placed inside the safe zone with deliberately scaled down equipment. The armored personnel carriers were stripped of the twenty millimeter cannons that are standard NATO equipment. This, after all, was peacekeeping. As with the Canadian troops who preceded them, the Dutch had also been helpless to prevent the Muslim forces in Srebrenica from taking up positions behind UN observation posts and firing out to draw incoming Serb fire. This was a debacle of peacekeeping in its classical mode with minimal use of force, the pretense of consent, neutrality between the parties, and above all, the attempt to avoid antagonizing the local combatants in a way that might endanger UN personnel. After Srebrenica, "neutrality" was understandably seen as a hollow word, and some began to entertain the idea of peacekeepers' right—or even duty—to use force for mission accomplishment, including the mission of protecting civilians.

The experience in Somalia was, of course, a major source of American anxiety over peacekeeping. The peacekeeping mission began with famine relief, but devolved into an attempt to restore a democratic structure to Somalia, without understanding the great depth of the clan structure. Secretary–General Boutros–Ghali's past career in the Egyptian foreign ministry, with responsibility for Egypt's policy towards Africa, ultimately thwarted the UN's acceptance of him as a local mediator, because Egypt had had distinct sympathies for Siad Barre, a prominent rival of Aidid. Somalia became a cataclysmic event for American involvement with peacekeeping. Pakistani peacekeepers were ambushed while on a food delivery mission in Mogadushi in June, 1993, and twenty-four peacekeepers were killed. Then in October, 1993, American Rangers attempted to raid an arms cache and were ambushed in a shootout in downtown Mogadishu. Eighteen Americans were killed and seventy-five wounded. The news was punctuated by a terrible photograph of a slain American GI whose body was degraded in the streets. As a result, Somalia became a watershed event, diminishing American support of UN peacekeeping.

The trauma of Somalia was largely responsible for the subsequent hesitation of support for intervention to stop the Hutu genocide in Rwanda. The United States declined to support any follow-on force to UNAMIR, and the genocide rolled on unabated until the Tutsi military advance succeeded. When the Hutu fled to the southwest, the French mounted a unilateral mission that gave them shelter as they crossed the border into Zaire. Yet, even as the Hutu fled from refugee camps besieged by the Tutsi, there were scenes of needless violence, marked with the same UN passivity. A memoir by an Australian aid worker recounts how Australian peacekeepers were instructed to hold their fire when Tutsi forces began to shoot into an encampment of Hutu civilians at Kibeho. Witnesses reported that 2,000 to 4,000 civilians were killed, though the official UN figure is much lower.

The UN is sometimes inclined to airbrush its disasters, thus avoiding the repercussions and lessons of traumatic or embarrassing events. In doing so, the organization does itself a disservice. In *An Agenda for Peace*, Boutros–Ghali had hoped that regional organizations might take on much of the burden of peacekeeping. There was a period in the mid–1990s when many thought that existing regional organizations were up to the task. Nigeria and Ghana intervened in the civil conflict in Liberia under the aegis of a subregional organization called the Economic Organization of West African States (ECOWAS), and its military arm called ECOMOG. The Security Council ultimately commended the intervention, despite the creditable argument that the exercise prolonged the conflict. However, it was not immediately recognized that the peacekeepers themselves could be a source of disorder. The ECOMOG forces were poorly disciplined and, too often, abused local civilians.

The real peacekeeping lesson of the last ten years is that the idea of separating Chapter 6 ½ from Chapter 7 is not realistic. Peacekeeping is not segregable from robust peace enforcement. Too many situations quickly turn sour, and one cannot always predict the course of events in advance.

* * *

There are several hard questions for the UN. First, there needs to be a philosophical discussion on the use of force. Inadequate force structures are often ascribed to the reluctance of member countries to contribute troops. However, the problem is deeper than that. It amounts to an unwillingness to admit that collective security requires robust action, that the United Nations cannot substitute itself for nation states and hope to eschew the modalities found necessary by nation states. The tradition of nonviolence and neutrality in peacekeeping might, in honor of some of its founders, be called a "Nordic minimalism." It is a Kantian ideal that words should be sufficient, but they are often not. It also betrays an ambivalence about the moral personality of multilateral organizations and a doubt as to whether they are competent to use the tools of military force because violence is an instrumental evil. It means that peacekeeping has become a temporizing tactic, in lieu of more effective action.

Second, there is a question of competence. In practice, the national contingents that take part in peacekeeping do not answer to the UN force commander. If the UN commander wants to move a battalion ten miles down the road in a disputed area, he must wait for the head of the national contingent to get permission. There really is no such thing as an integrated UN military force. The absence of effective logistics, transport, and on-the-ground intelligence means that peacekeepers are often vulnerable targets justifiably worried about unit safety and hardly able to focus on mission accomplishment. If peacekeeping cannot be done well, perhaps its should not be done it at all. Certainly when the UN thrusts itself into situations and promises people protection, there needs to be a realistic assessment of the capacity to muster defensive force.

In the mid–1990s, there was a passing discussion about having a standing army for the UN, a multinational rapid reaction force of perhaps 5,000 soldiers. The idea was tabled on grounds of budget and difficulty, as well as concern about political control. It would not be easy to take volunteer soldiers from different military backgrounds and form a coherent unit, even after joint training. A unit's coercive force also depends on the composition of its backup, and that again leaves the UN in the position of "dialing for doughboys." Even the numbers were not persuasive; 5,000 slots do not go as far as one might suppose. There is a rotational system, usually with a three-to-one ratio, in military deployments. This means one soldier is on the ground in the mission, one is training to replace him, and one is returning from service. The operational limits of a 5,000 man force are also shown by another divisor, the so-called "tooth to tail" ratio. To field a soldier at the sharp end of the stick requires numerous support and logistical personnel. The accepted ratio is between 3–1 and 6–1, depending on whether the European view or the American view is used. Thus, a stand-alone base force of 5,000 would yield a quite modest number of infantry peacekeepers on the ground—no more than 600. Further, military deployments cannot safely be mounted in an ad hoc fashion, like a "pick-up" basketball team. Participants must be trained together over a long period of time. A standing force would have to be some sort of foreign legion, not just an occasional gathering of retired military personnel. With these daunting problems, it is not surprising the idea was tabled.

Since that time, no one has known quite what to do. The UN has relied on "coalitions of the willing" made up of national military units, but even here there are real problems of competence because there is no occasion to have practice deployments. The UN recently inquired into what went wrong in Sierra Leone. In particular, it questioned how the Zambian contingent was taken hostage by an insurgent group known as the West Side Boys, stripped of their uniforms and weapons, and threatened with the death of their unit commander. As a result, the UN uncovered the following information. The Zambians deployed into Sierra Leone and were directed to enter an area where their Nigerian predecessors had not dared to tread. They were inadequately briefed about the nature of the threat. They had one radio and an out-of-date map. The force commander, along with a small contingent, was proceeding in advance of the rest of the Zambian column. The West Side Boys, comprised of child soldiers, confronted the Zambian commander at a roadblock, took him to see their own commander, and informed him that his soldiers must surrender to avoid a Salomé-like decapitation. Because the commander had the only radio, he could not warn the rest of his troops. Consequently, several hundred Zambian soldiers were forced to lay down their arms and surrender their uniforms. The West Side Boys used the Zambian uniforms as camouflage in later attacks against Nigerian peacekeepers elsewhere in the back country.

The UN hoped that fielding a large force in Sierra Leone would be sufficient to restore order, but the Indian force commander did not get along with the Nigerian contingent. The Jordanian and Indian contingents ultimately were withdrawn, and the British chose to remain entirely outside the UN command structure. These examples indicate that the problem of multinational cacophony is hard to solve by means other than the use of prior existing military organizations such as NATO or Partnership for Peace brigades that have practiced together and developed a common ethos.

Why did UN forces not go into Rwanda? In part it was due to American objections following the events of Somalia. These objectors were wary of an adversary that had already murdered Belgian peacekeepers for political effect. In addition, there was still no viable combination of troops and equipment. Some African countries were willing to supply troops, but had no vehicles or armored personnel carriers. Even if equipment had been immediately supplied, unfamiliar troops still needed to be trained in its operation. One practical longterm response is to train regional forces, and the United States is now doing that in Senegal and elsewhere.

The third problem is a version of the Hippocratic oath, "first do no harm." There must be a moral self-consciousness about the UN's duty to avoid damaging the areas in which it intervenes. The troubling reports of peacekeeper misconduct are anecdotal, they are not written down. How were troops recruited for Cambodia? At least one UN member state took men out of jail, gave them blue berets, and sent them off. Some contingents were eventually sent home because they were not helping anyone and were looting the countryside. The problems of corruption among UNPROFOR contingents in Bosnia were well-known; some Eastern European troops used their armored personnel carriers to smuggle consumer appliances into the city for resale. Equally disturbing is the politically difficult issue of HIV-positive troops. Some years ago, even before the AIDS crisis was so acute, the UN inadvertently obtained the full medical files of a national peacekeeping contingent and discovered that 65% of the blue berets were HIV-positive. The Secretariat sent the contingent home quietly by redesigning the areas of operation. However, the UN declined to institute any policy of testing, or even asking, for the voluntary disclosure of medical information from troop-donating countries. There are some good reasons for this decision. What if the consequence of testing is to force a military man into unemployment, with no treatment for him or his wife? Why HIV testing and not liver function testing? Yet, there is still the real problem of men with guns, far from home. Certainly in the choice among national contingents, the epidemiological hazard is a reasonable consideration.

Another part of the Hippocratic oath is the duty not to abandon people who have relied on a promise of protection. Michael Hourigan, an Atlanta lawyer, has been arguing this point. He brought a claim against the UN stemming from the Rwanda massacres, on behalf of two families. One was the family of the former Chief Justice of Rwanda and the other was the family of the former minister of labor and social affairs. UNAMIR troops had been assigned to guard the homes and safety of these two families, but when the Hutu militia came up, the troops allegedly left and the families were killed. Hourigan's claim is that if an organization promises protection, it has a moral and perhaps a legal duty to make good on the promise. The UN initially answered that such a claim was grounded in public law, not in private law, and therefore lacked an available claims procedure. Hourigan quickly recast the claim within the private law language of wrongful death. Regardless of the resolution of this particular claim, the larger point is that the UN too often has been satisfied with the appearance of peacekeeping, a charade of protection, instead of effective protection of civilian populations. The lack of credibility in UN deployments undermines its every other function, including post-conflict reconstruction. Refugees will not return to the areas from which minorities are "cleansed" when there is no real assurance of safety. The arrest of war criminals in Bosnia and the control of organized crime in East Timor and Kosovo depend on a willingness to use force in policing. Even thwarting corruption, which has throttled the economy of Bosnia, requires a force strong enough to suppress possible retaliation. Several international corporations have tried to go into Bosnia to revive industrial work and provide employment but they have been frustrated by the tangle of political control of the economy by the nationalist political parties and the rank and repetitive corruption. Why can't the international community confront this more directly or even arrest people for corruption? Part of the reason is diffidence, but part of it is danger. One does not dare step-up confrontations or make arrests because security on the ground is ineffective.

There is now a serious conversation about international policing, and how to restore a minimum degree of law and order in post-conflict arenas. President Bush's foreign affairs adviser, Condoleezza Rice, has noted her concern about the mid-level security gap in post-conflict areas. If peacekeepers eschew the tasks of policing and CIVPOL personnel assigned to the UN's volunteer international police force limit their functions to giving advice on "principles of democratic policing" and lack unit-wide training, then we will continue to have situations of tenuous stability such as in Bosnia today. We must address how to develop a more robust police capability. We need international personnel who are trained in the use of fire power and in the special competencies needed for policing, including investigative experience and language capability. One may wish to have specialized constabulary forces within NATO. Yet, it is time to get beyond the fiction that a thrown-together CIVPOL force is sufficient for all challenging situations.

On the American role in peacekeeping ... Washington's dissatisfaction with peacekeeping stems in part from the challenges of our military demobilization since the end of the Cold War. Tempted by the crumbling of the Soviet Union, both the United States and its NATO allies have scaled back their forces, responding to domestic constituencies that prefer to cut budgets. Yet in facing a belligerent North Korea and Iraq, there is still a need for an army that can effectively fight land battles. There is rightful concern about wasting training and overtaxing American military personnel. If we take combat recruits and train them to operate Bradley fighting vehicles and Abrams tanks in an integrated land-air campaign, and then take them off their equipment and turn them into peacekeepers, and then after their Bosnia rotation, try to recoup their combat skills, we will waste a lot of time and manpower. In addition, the Executive Branch has generally not been willing to ask Congress for money up-front for peacekeeping missions. Instead the White House has often found it more convenient to raid readiness and training money, and then ask Congress to restore these essential funds. Admittedly the White House may have feared that Congress would just say no if asked to appropriate peacekeeping money as such. However, the consequence has been an unhappy cycle of robbing Peter and underpaying Paul, thus putting pressure on United State's military readiness. We need to recognize that these missions are expensive, that they do take manpower, that they do have an operations tempo which wearies military personnel, burdens their family life, and causes them to leave the armed forces to join the private economy. To sustain these missions, in the configuration of our democracy, one needs to muster public support so that Congress can be persuaded to fund peacekeeping in a planned way that does not deride our other military needs. We cannot keep doing it through the backdoor. Though Congress is appropriately concerned about the safety of American personnel, the sensible provision of funds is necessary even where the United States is involved in supportive functions such as logistics, airlift, and intelligence.

We also need to consider what local political solutions are viable, given the constraints of UN peacekeeping capacity. Should we accept solutions such as the soft partition of Bosnia, where the so-called "inter entity boundary line" separates the Bosnian Serbs from the Muslims and Croats, because that allows a military mission much closer to the low-impact interpositional peacekeeping of yore? Can the political culture of a post-conflict society change through a top-down Fabian solution, as we are attempting in Bosnia, where the new state structure and constitution were implemented as part of the Dayton Plan but never endorsed in any popular ballot? There is a real challenge for political scientists and sociologists to assess how you can craft a solution that allows civic reeducation to take root.

Finally, there is concern that the international community may have been naive in supposing that elections are the answer to everything. Premature parliamentary and municipal elections may in fact reify the power of the nationalist political parties, such as the SDS and HDZ in Bosnia. Indeed, a popular mandate allows these parties to wrap their obstruction in the flag of sovereignty. If we had been a bit more bloody-minded in Bosnia and entertained a transitional structure more akin to a protectorate, we may have begun to displace the role of organized crime and organized ethnic thuggery.

The people who work inside the United Nations are often extremely talented. They work for very little money in dangerous places. Yet the most gallant of UN officials are among the most frustrated critics of the obstinacy of the institution and its failure to come to grips with its deficiencies. There is little close newspaper coverage of the UN as an institution, and thus no feedback loop to improve agency performance. Too few people know enough about the organization to point fingers and name names, or even make workable suggestions. There is no room for romantic multilateralism if we want the UN to be able to do its job.

Notes and Questions

1. The single negotiating text (SNT) discussed by former U.N. Under–Secretary Alvaro de Soto was used in the Camp David Negotiations in 1978 and is particularly helpful when dealing with multilateral negotiations. In this process the negotiator or mediator gathers information from the parties, drafts the initial agreement, and presents it to the parties separately for their input and criticism. Based on the parties' responses, the proposal is redrafted several times. A final proposal is submitted to the parties that incorporates their responses to earlier drafts and reflects their underlying preferences. The benefit of the SNT, according to Fisher & Ury, is that it "not only shifts the game away from positional bargaining, it greatly simplifies the process both of inventing options and of deciding jointly on one...."[16] Can you imagine some situations in which the single negotiating text would be unworkable?

2. Assume that you have been hired by the International Red Cross to conduct a skills training course for mediators dealing with intractable conflict in deeply-divided societies. How would Secretary–General Kofi Annan's remark that "impartiality does not—and must not—mean neutrality in the face of evil" inform your training program? How would you distinguish between the requirements of impartiality and neutrality for mediators?

3. If you had conducted the interview with former U.N. Under–Secretary–General Alvaro de Soto, what other questions would you have asked?

4. Modern peacekeeping operations involve conflict resolution, civil reconstruction, emergency assistance, democratic election organizations, and other activities. It transcends mere monitoring of the peace accord. What strategic and tactical problems posed by Professor Wedgwood would be resolved if the U.N. received an anonymous, no-strings-attached cash infusion large enough to employ a robust military force? What strategic and tactical problems would remain?

5. Professor Wedgwood contends that the U.N. must engage in a philosophical discussion concerning its use of force. What different levels of force are available to the UN and what consequences would result if the UN chose one over the others?

6. How would you reform the transparency problem described by Professor Wedgwood? Do you agree with her contention that peacekeeping is not separable from robust peace enforcement?

7. Professor Wedgwood argues against the limitations imposed on the functions of peacekeepers as an international police force. Can you think of any current U.N. peacekeeping operations where similar criticism exists?

C. THE ROLE OF REGIONAL ORGANIZATIONS

Regional organizations consist of individual sovereign States united together for peace and security reasons. Unlike a global organization like the U.N., regional organizations look inward and have the ability to

16. R. Fisher & W. Ury, Getting to Yes 118–22 (1981).

harness the resources of their common cultural background. They, therefore, have the potential to play a significant role in local peacemaking and conflict resolution.

Regional organizations—such as the European Union (EU), the African Union, the successor to the Organization of African Unity (OAU), the Organization for Security and Cooperation in Europe (OSCE), the Organization of the Islamic Conference (OIC), and the Arab League—have engaged in conflict resolution efforts that emphasized negotiation and mediation techniques.[17] OSCE, for example, one of the largest regional security organizations in the world with fifty-five Member States, focuses primarily on conflict prevention and early warning systems as a way to promote peace, security, and respect for human rights.[18] The African Union has been actively involved in peacekeeping efforts in a number of African countries.[19] It gives conflict resolution a central standing in its mission. The Association of Southeast Asian Nations (ASEAN) is committed to a program of preventive diplomacy to eliminate conflicts that could pose a threat to regional peace and stability and to prevent disputes from escalating into armed conflict.[20] The OIC has been involved in negotiating a resolution of armed conflict in a long-standing dispute between the Moro National Liberation Front and the government of the Philippines.[21]

Sovereignty and the principle of non-interference in a co-equal State's internal affairs hamper the peacemaking potential of regional organizations. Professor I. William Zartman has observed the paradox of regional organizations:

> They have the regional salience to intervene in regional conflicts, but lack the requisite, broad-based political will to sustain conflict management endeavors because they are not a corporate actor.... Their members are interest-driven parties to the very conflicts the organization is asked to resolve. And they can only be effective where they operate on a clear and firm normative base, which is still absent in the area of domestic conflict into which they are increasingly drawn.[22]

The following excerpt discusses the Organization of African Unity, the predecessor organization to the African Union. It illustrates how the OAU Charter's principle of non-interference in the internal affairs of Member States prevented it from resolving several internal conflicts in Africa.

17. Bercovitch, International Mediation, *supra* note 2, at 12.

18. Max van der Stoel, *The Role of the OSCE High Commissioner in Conflict Prevention*, in Herding Cats: Multiparty Mediation in a Complex World 65 (Chester A. Crocker, Fen Osler Hampson & Pamela Aall eds., 1999) [hereinafter Herding Cats].

19. *See* www.africa-union.org.

20. *See* www.aseansec.org.

21. Soliman M. Santos Jr., *The Muslim Dispute in the Southern Philippines: A Case of Islamic Conference Mediation*, [2001] Aus. Int'l L.J. 35.

22. I. William Zartman, *Mediation by Regional Organizations: The OAU in Chad and Congo*, in Bercovitch, International Mediation, *supra* note 2, at 95.

P. MWETI MUNYA, THE ORGANIZATION OF AFRICAN UNITY AND ITS ROLE IN REGIONAL CONFLICT RESOLUTION AND DISPUTE SETTLEMENT: A CRITICAL EVALUATION

19 Boston College Third World Law Journal 537, 572–81 (1999).

* * *

The Nigerian civil war is a microcosm of internal contradictions within the African nation-state. Nigeria was a country of promise when it gained independence from the British in 1960. It was a showcase of liberal democratic experimentation. If what a newly independent country required was a democratic institutional base, Nigeria had just that—the federal constitution adopted after independence contained an elaborate and generous bill of rights. Furthermore, the principles of separation of powers and the rule of law were deeply ingrained in the federal constitutional order.

Yet, behind this constitutional facade of democracy and rule of law, seeds of civil strife were slowly germinating in the political arena; the tribal inclination of Nigeria's political parties illustrated the precarious political balance that could be tilted at the slightest push. For example, the National Council of Nigerian Citizens (NCNC) was dominated by the Igbo of Eastern Nigeria; the Northern People's Congress of Nigeria (NPC), by the Hausa people of Northern Nigeria; and the Action Group (AG), by the Yoruba of the Western region. Nigeria's federal government was a quasi-national loose coalition of the Igbo and Hausa. Like other newly independent countries, allegiance to the tribe was the norm. Indeed, Nigeria was an amalgamation of tribes and not a nation per se.

In January, 1966, a military coup d'etat engineered by Igbo officers occurred, and Prime Minister Tafawa Balewa was assassinated. Later, Major General J.T.U. Aguiyi–Ironsi, the Igbo leader of that coup, was executed in a counter-coup that catapulted General Gowon to power. This retaliation was unacceptable to the Igbo. The Military Governor of Eastern Nigeria, Lieutenant–Colonel Odumegwu Ojukwu, declared the eastern region an independent state called Biafra. A bloody civil war ensued, pitting the federal government against the secessionist Biafra. The war claimed the lives of an estimated one million people.

What role did the OAU play in ending this unfortunate conflict? The OAU's capacity to resolve the Nigerian conflict was inhibited by the Charter's principle of non-interference in the internal affairs of member states, which prevented the OAU from getting fully involved in the crisis. Although the OAU was aware of its impotence, it did not want to appear to be doing nothing while a devastating civil war raged on in an African country. Therefore, the crisis was discussed at the Assembly of Heads of State and Government's summit meeting in Kinshasa, Zaire in September, 1967. The resolution passed at the end of the conference recognized that the conflict was Nigeria's internal affair, but placed the "services of the Assembly at the disposal of the Federal Government of Nigeria." The conference also decided to send a consultative mission to the head of Nigeria's federal government to "assure him of the Assembly's desire for the territorial integrity, unity and peace of Nigeria."

One wonders why the head of Nigeria's government needed this assurance from the OAU's Assembly. The Assembly was not fighting to dismember, nor was it violating the territorial integrity of, Nigeria. In any case, why did the OAU send a mission to convey such an assurance when sending one head of state or dispatching a letter to the federal government would have served the purpose? Whatever logic lay behind the Assembly's confused response to the Nigerian civil war, several issues are apparent. The tension between the desire to resolve the conflict and to remain faithful to the OAU Charter explains the Assembly's confused state of mind and unmitigated diplomatic blunder. However, by sending the mission to the federal government, the OAU did what it had all along pledged never to do—interfere in the internal affairs of a member state. Unfortunately, the OAU interfered not as an impartial umpire bent on genuinely mediating between the parties and ending the conflict, but as a supporter of the federal government.

5. Internal Conflicts Resulting from Challenges to the Legitimacy of the Authority in Power

Most of the previously examined cases are also manifestations of internal conflicts resulting from challenges to the legitimacy of power. Revisiting the Congo crisis case study illustrates this point. The Congo problem started as a conflict between the secessionist movement of Moise Tshombe and the government of Prime Minister Patrice Lumumba and President Joseph Kasavubu. At that point, there was no regional body within which the African states could launch an initiative. The African states, therefore, endorsed a United Nations peacekeeping operation. However, when internal conflicts grew between Lumumba and Kasavubu, the African states became deeply divided. The radical Casablanca group saw the ouster of Lumumba as an unacceptable challenge to the legitimate authority of the Congo, while the conservative Monrovia group viewed any overt support to a specific group in the Congo as interference with the internal affairs of the Congo. Because of this polarization, the African states could not act in concert within the United Nations.

When Cyrille Aduola was installed as the successor to Lumumba in 1961, the situation seemed to improve. However, his government proved ineffective and the conflict was renewed when Tshombe, supported by the Americans, Belgians, and other foreign mercenaries, invaded from the Kivu and Kwilu provinces.

In reaction to this externally supported offensive, CNL forces loyal to the late Lumumba received direct support from the neighboring states of Congo (Brazzaville), Burundi, Uganda, and the Sudan, while the United Arab Republic (UAR), Algeria, and Ghana supplied the CNL with arms. A majority of African state leaders questioned the legitimacy of

Tshombe's rule over the Congo and viewed him as a "neo-colonialist puppet."

Other conflicts like the Sudanese civil war, the Rhodesian crisis, and the Namibian civil war similarly resulted from challenges to the legitimacy of the government in power, although they have other distinct characteristics mentioned elsewhere.

6. Conflicts Involving External Intervention

A number of intra-state conflicts in Africa have involved external intervention from nations either within or outside of Africa. Some African countries in the early years of independence were accused of interfering in the internal conflicts of neighboring states. In fact, it was Ghana's alleged involvement in a coup in Togo that prompted the Addis Ababa conference to incorporate Article III, clause five into the OAU Charter. Probably the most famous unilateral intervention by an African state into another was the 1979 Tanzanian intervention and ousting of dictator Idi Amin in Uganda. The OAU, through its Liberation Committee indirectly gave aid to rebel groups who were fighting the last colonial regimes in the former Portugese colonies of Mozambique and Angola, as well as the racist white minority regimes in Rhodesia, Namibia, and South Africa.

A more recent unilateral involvement by African states in an internal conflict was the military support by Uganda, Angola, Burundi, and Rwanda of the rebels of Laurent Kabila in Zaire, which helped him gain the presidency. Mobutu's attempts to maintain power did not change the situation this time; he was eventually ousted by Kabila's forces.

The Cold War manifested itself in Africa through superpower intervention in African internal conflicts. External support of the Stanleyville operation and the Russian and Chinese involvement in the Congo crisis have already been discussed. The Angolan civil war was likewise sustained by Cuban and Russian support of the incumbent government and the sponsorship of the rebel movement by the former South African government and the United States. This article has already described the United States and Russian involvement in the conflict between Somalia and Ethiopia. France also has unilaterally intervened in its former colonies numerous times to save incumbent governments threatened by civil war or mutiny.

7. Conflicts with Strong Religious and Ethnic Underpinnings

The Hutu–Tutsi conflict within Rwanda and Burundi is an example of an ethnic conflict exacerbated by the colonial divide-and-rule policy of playing ethnic groups against each other. Another example of a conflict with both religious and ethnic undercurrents is the Sudanese civil war. Sudan is a country that is ethnically and religiously divided between the North and the South. Shortly after Sudanese independence from joint Egyptian and British rule in 1956, the predominantly black, Christian South took arms to fight for autonomy from the Khartoum government, which was controlled by the Muslim and Arabic North. A settlement of the bloody war was reached in 1972, whereby the South assumed greater autonomy within a federal system of government. The war resumed in 1983, when the increasingly fundamentalist government in Khartoum reneged on the 1972 agreement by adopting Islamic policies like Sharia law and imposing them on the southerners.

The Sudanese People's Liberation Movement and other liberation movements in the South have continued to fight what they perceive as internal colonization by the North, while the Khartoum government has attempted to crush what it views as an insurgency by infidels against Islam. Given this degree of polarization, a negotiated settlement in the near future is inconceivable. The OAU, in affiliation with the Intergovernmental Authority on Development (IGAD), a sub-regional body in the Horn of Africa, has attempted to mediate an end to the Sudanese conflict, but has avoided direct involvement for fear of precipitating a fallout between the Islamic states in North Africa and sub-Saharan states that could destroy the unity within the continental body.

VI.   ASSESSMENT OF THE ROLE OF THE OAU IN CONFLICT RESOLUTION
AND DISPUTE SETTLEMENT

The performance of the OAU in conflict resolution can be characterized by modest success in a few cases and dismal failure in most others. It is important to identify inroads that the OAU has made and the challenges it has faced in its endeavors to establish a lasting peace in Africa.

Internal conflicts have presented the most daunting challenges to the OAU for two reasons. First, where outside powers have been involved, the capacity of the OAU to deal with them was substantially eroded. This is explained by the fact that extraterritorial forces, as part of the United Nations, have more resources and authority than the OAU. For instance, the superpower interventions in the Congo crisis were so pervasive and overwhelming that the OAU efforts to nullify them proved fruitless. Secondly, the OAU lacks the power to intervene in internal conflicts. Article III, clause two of the OAU Charter explicitly prohibits member states from interfering with the internal affairs of other member states. This provision has been conservatively interpreted and applied so that conflicts within a state are placed beyond the purview and jurisdiction of the OAU. The result is an artificial and conceptually unrealistic dichotomy between interstate and intra-state conflicts, with the OAU having jurisdiction only to deal with the former. As is evident to any casual observer of the African scene, this distinction is unrealistic. All intra-state conflicts have a trans-border "spillover" effect that cannot be ignored by other states.

As the above case studies show, it is impossible for the OAU to be faithful to this distinction. The OAU intervened in one way or another in each of the conflicts that could be viewed as internal. In the case of Nigeria, for example, the OAU was unable to stay aloof, but because the Nigerian federal government insisted that the conflict was an internal affair, the OAU intervened in support of the federal government. Perhaps with its hesitant support of the federal government, the OAU thought that it had insulated itself from being accused of undermining the sovereign integrity of Nigeria.

However, the OAU has registered some success in the sphere of border conflicts, although this was the area that originally presented the OAU with the biggest challenge. While the colonial boundaries established in Africa are arbitrary and unsatisfactory, writers and observers of the African scene have nonetheless conceded that attempts to redraw the map of Africa will invite unprecedented problems and even more conflicts. The maintenance of the status quo has proven more prudent than attempting to revise borders. The OAU has consistently conformed to this rule. The rule has found juridical expression in the legal doctrine of uti possidetis. Although some scholars feel otherwise, the stability with which the colonial borders have been maintained in Africa is astounding, especially when compared to "the three major wars in Latin America fought over frontier issues, the three wars between India and Pakistan, the 1962 Sino–Indian war, and the extraordinary carnage of the 1980–88 Iran–Iraq war, which originated over disputed territory."

Moreover, the role played by the OAU in decolonization cannot be overemphasized. Many conflicts in Africa have been initiated by the African independent states and liberation movements within the colonial regimes. From its inception, the OAU dedicated itself to the eradication of all vestiges of colonialism from the continent. Through its Liberation Committee, the OAU gave material and military support to various liberation movements and also put diplomatic pressure on the United Nations to act. For instance, many anti-apartheid resolutions, sanctions against South Africa, and resolutions establishing steps towards independence for Namibia were drafted at the prodding of OAU members at the United Nations. The OAU has contributed to the independence movements of Angola, Mozambique, and Zimbabwe. Now that apartheid in South Africa has ended, it can be argued that Africa is finally free from any form of colonial rule.

Another significant effort by the OAU to contribute generally to peace and stability in the world has been through disarmament. It cannot be denied that the presence of highly sophisticated weaponry in the world increases insecurity, especially in Africa. The OAU has adopted a convention making Africa a denuclearized zone. Through this, it has saved Africa from the costs of an arms race. The OAU has also charted a new path in the ongoing search for peace and stability based on trust instead of militarism.

All conflicts have a human rights dimension. Conflicts may be caused by human rights violations or triggered by attempts to stop human rights violations, and they certainly entail human rights violations. The adoption of the African Charter on Human and Peoples'

Rights is a milestone on the long road towards establishing a culture of human rights in Africa, a prerequisite for peace and stability. The regionalization of human rights through the adoption of the Charter is a significant step in African human rights movements in that it marks a radical departure from the OAU policy of the 1970s whereby issues pertaining to human rights were seen as internal affairs of member states. This policy allowed the OAU to close its eyes to the massacres of tens of thousands of Hutu in Burundi in 1972–73 as well as mass violations of human rights by the notorious regimes of Jean–Bedel Bokassa in the Central African Republic, Marcias Nguema in Equitorial Guinea, and Idi Amin in Uganda.

Notes and Questions

1. Discuss some of the reasons for the OAU's failures in conflict resolution and dispute settlement in recent African conflicts. Do you agree with the author's contention that the intervention of superpowers prevented the OAU from intervening successfully in these conflicts?

2. Discuss the challenges the OAU faces with respect to the internal conflicts of its members. How realistic is the distinction between inter-state and intra-state conflicts in the OAU?

3. Do you think that if the African Charter on Human and Peoples' Rights had been in place, the OAU could have been more successful in the Nigerian conflict?

4. If you were the U.N. Secretary General, how would you respond to the paradox facing regional organizations that is described by Zartman?

D. THE LIMITATIONS OF INTERNATIONAL AND REGIONAL ORGANIZATIONS

1. IGNORANCE OF CULTURAL CONTEXTS

Notwithstanding their growing involvement in peace and security activities, the failure of international and regional organizations to manage and resolve armed conflicts in the post-Cold War era is of considerable concern to the international community. A major critique of international and regional organizations is their failure to appreciate the cultural context in which conflict arises. Too frequently, the international community has engaged in a "one-size-fits-all" approach to promoting democratic development without really considering the significance of a communist or colonialist past. In the following excerpt, Professor Dianne Orentlicher examines the deficiencies in the international community's efforts to mediate the conflicting territorial claims that ultimately led to the break-up of Yugoslavia.

DIANE F. ORENTLICHER, SEPARATION ANXIETY: INTERNATIONAL RESPONSES TO ETHNO– SEPARATIST CLAIMS

23 Yale Journal of International Law 1, 70–78 (1998).

* * *

4.   The Dayton Peace Agreement

The conflict finally came to an end in December 1995 as a result of peace negotiations brokered by the U.S. government in Dayton, Ohio. Although the Dayton Peace Agreement proximately caused the cessation of hostilities, it took military action and economic sanctions to bring the warring parties to the peace table. In particular, the combined effect of air attacks on Serb targets near Sarajevo by the North Atlantic Treaty Organization (NATO), a rout of Croatian Serbs by the Croatian army in August 1995, and economic sanctions against Serbia brought Serb leaders to the point where they were willing to negotiate seriously.

Although a general assessment of the Dayton Agreement is beyond the scope of this Article, one aspect of the peace plan has special pertinence here. Pursuant to Annex 3 of the peace accord, the Organization for Security and Cooperation in Europe (OSCE) was given the mandate to organize elections in Bosnia. The OSCE was to "certify whether elections can be effective under current social conditions ... and, if necessary, to provide assistance ... in creating these conditions." Pursuant to this authority, the OSCE held national elections on September 14, 1996, despite the fact that independent monitors called for postponement, arguing that conditions were not amenable to a free and fair election.

The poll stands as a cautionary tale of how ill-conceived elections can exacerbate divisions in an ethnically riven society like postwar Bosnia. Among other abuses, Bosnian Serb leader Radovan Karadzic—by then twice indicted by the U.N. Tribunal in The Hague—abused the registration process to secure Serb victories in the key areas. For example, humanitarian aid programs administered in Serb-held areas of Bosnia by Karadzic's wife were flagrantly manipulated to secure results that would ratify the result of "ethnic cleansing." Not surprisingly, the elections did just that, bringing into office hardline nationalists who openly opposed interethnic cooperation.

Conditions prevailing in the lead-up to these elections were so clearly inauspicious that the OSCE decided to postpone municipal elections, which initially had been scheduled to take place along with national elections in September 1996. Local elections, held September 13–14, 1997, after a second postponement, were marred by serious allegations of fraud and coercion by nationalist political leaders and resulted in the election of nationalist politicians in most municipalities. By virtue of its role in organizing the poll, the international community legitimized the nationalist leaders whose election was all but inevitable.

B.   Assessing International Responses

Neither the European Community nor any other international actor bears principal responsibility for the explosive nature of Yugoslavia's breakup; that belongs to political leaders in the former Yugoslavia who cynically played the national card to further their political ambitions. Even so, international actors made crucial blunders in their response to the challenge presented by Yugoslavia's violent implosion unwittingly abetting the violent dismemberment of a state they had pushed towards independence.

1.   Utilizing Electoral Processes to Ameliorate Ethnic Divisions

Among these mistakes were several instances of imprudent insistence on democratic processes during periods of intense ethnic polarization. As noted in the preceding Section, international actors such as the European Community and OSCE pressed for elections as a means of resolving such highly charged disputes as whether Bosnia would remain part of the rump Yugoslavia or seek independence, and insisted on holding elections when they were more likely to exacerbate than ameliorate ethnic insecurities.

This is not to say that the European Community, OSCE, and others were wrong to promote democratic principles and process in responding to the challenge presented by the SFRY's dissolution. Rather, the fault lies in these actors' ill conceived insistence on utilizing democratic polls as a principal vehicle for resolving ethnically charged disputes under conditions in which elections were likely to inflame tensions and legitimize hardline nationalist. In such conditions, it may be more constructive to emphasize programs that promote the flourishing of civil society, the sinews of a vibrant democracy.

2.   Reliable Engagement by the International Community

Deficiencies in the international community's efforts to mediate the conflicting claims that led to Yugoslavia's implosion highlight the lack of institutional mechanisms with established and acknowledged authority to resolve such claims. Over the course of the Yugoslav crisis, principal responsibility for attempting to reach a mediated solution shifted from the European community to a joint U.N.-EC conference to a five state Contact Group and finally to the United States.

Among other costs, this ad hoc improvising meant that mediators were perpetually behind the curve in their efforts to address the Yugoslav crisis. If, as some believed, the breakup of Yugoslavia was likely to be violent, efforts to avert this outcome should have begun before the logic of separation became inexorable. Yet the European community did not become seriously engaged until tensions had escalated to the point of armed conflict. It adopted its common recognition policy six months after armed conflict had erupted in Slovenia and seven months after one of the worst massacres in Croatia took place. If the European community hoped to use its recognition policy to advance a peaceful resolution of the disputes among Yugoslav republics, it waited too long.

Of course the European Community's failure to intervene earlier is a policy failure only if timely intervention can affect the outcome of intrastate disputes over territorial status. Is there any support for this proposition? While the answer must depend on the circumstances of each case, there can be no doubt that timely intervention can at times make a contribution to the peaceful resolution of contested separatist claims. For example, the OSCE has played a constructive part in mediating disputes between Ukraine and its separatist semiautonomous Crimean peninsula, and, despite periodic setbacks in its mediation efforts, was at times the most constructive outside actor with respect to Russia's recent confrontation with separatist Chechens.

Knowledgeable observers believe that as late as 1990 it might have been possible to devise a new constitutional order that would have addressed the respective concerns of Slovene, Croat, and Serb nationalists while avoiding the bloody breakup of Yugoslavia. In fact the presidents of the six constituent republics of the SFRY attempted to do just that during a series of meetings in the spring and summer of 1991. But to meet the enormous challenges presented at that time, statesmanship and good faith were in order, and neither Milosevic nor Tudjman was up to the job. A credible, impartial mediator was needed if negotiations were to forestall Yugoslavia's violent dismemberment.

But if earlier engagement by outside mediators might have averted Yugoslavia's breakup, the European Community and other critical actors also erred by insisting on preserving Yugoslav unity long after the inevitability of its breakup should have been apparent, again minimizing their ability to promote a peaceful process of territorial change. Some eight months after Slovenia made its first formal move toward secession, the states whose recognition policies would matter most to the contesting parties the Unites States and the EC member states were voicing strong support for Yugoslav unity, as was the CSCE.

In April 1991, the European Community asserted its commitment to the "unity and territorial integrity of Yugoslavia"; in June, the CSCE adopted a similar declaration, which U.S. Secretary of State James Baker endorsed during a visit to Belgrade two days later. The breakup of Yugoslavia, Baker warned, "could have some very tragic consequences." Nor, he added, would the United States recognize the independence of Slovenia and Croatia "under any circumstances."

To many observers, the message this transmitted was that the U.S. government would blame the breakaway republics, not Serbia, if the former persisted in seeking independence and were opposed by force. At a time when Milosevic was calculating the potential cost of aggressive force, that message was precisely the wrong one. In larger perspective, the position voiced by the CSCE and Secretary Baker had the effect of disabling the CSCE and the United States, respectively, from helping to assure a peaceful evolution of the political status of the territories of the former Yugoslavia. If secession was, in their view, nonnegotiable, they could hardly play a constructive part in mediating the contested claims.

Finally, for international institutions to be effective in inducing parties to the territorial disputes to submit to, and accept the results of, third-party mediation or arbitration procedures, it is incumbent on members of the sponsoring institution to observe its ground rules. When Germany broke ranks with its EC partners by announcing its unilateral intention to recognize Slovenia and Croatia, it fairly doomed the EC mediation process to irrelevance.

C. Authoritative Resolution

As noted above, recent initiatives by the OSCE have played a constructive part in addressing post-Yugoslavia separatist rebellion in Europe, and provide a paradigm for more effective international engagement in addressing destabilizing assertions of ethno-nationalism. But while the success of various OSCE mediators suggests the potentially constructive contribution of emerging mechanisms in resolving separatist claims peacefully, the more sobering record of early mediation efforts in respect of the former Yugoslavia highlights an important gap in international institutional competence.

In contrast to the period following World War I, no international institution exists that can authoritatively resolve separatist claims. The succession of ad hoc efforts to mediate the Yugoslav crisis highlights the uncertain competence of existing institutions and the uncertainty that any would respond in a timely and effective fashion. Further, while various international organizations have arbitration institutions that can impose binding judgements, these mechanisms generally cannot be invoked by non-state entities wishing to resolve a territorial claim.

This gap could be filled by establishing binding arbitration procedures, attached to both regional organizations and the United Nations, that have authority to resolve territorial disputes and can be invoked both by states and non-state entities. At the United Nations, an arbitration body with such competence could be established as a subsidiary organ of either the Security Council or the General Assembly, both of which play a role in admitting new members to the organization.

While such bodies would fill major institutional lacuna, they could not resolve every disputed secessionist claim, at least in the absence of additional measures aimed at inducing recalcitrant parties to accede to arbitration and accept the results. As the Yugoslav experience teaches, parties willing to use unbridled force to secure territorial aspirations are unlikely to submit to international mediation processes unless meaningful sanctions—perhaps even military force—provide the requisite incentive.

D. Membership in International Organizations

Apart from institutionalized arbitration procedures of the sort outlined above, international and regional organization can more effectively utilize their existing procedures for admitting new members to promote a peaceful resolution of conflicting territorial claims. In fact, the Europe-an organizations with respect to which membership is most coveted require, as a condition of membership, a demonstrated commitment to democracy and human rights. The historical record makes clear that these criteria can help advance human rights within established states, however slow the progress. By establishing that a condition of member-ship is commitment to pluralism and civic equality, such institutions can help dispel any hope on the part of political leaders that they will profit by resorting to national mobilization. At the same time, however, the tragic implications of the Badinter Commission's suggestion that Bosnia hold a plebiscite as a precondition by EC member states underscores the need for caution in pressing applicants to pursue shortcuts to democracy during periods of volatile transition.

In the interim period before a state gains entry into such organiza-tions, economic benefits and forms of association short of full member-ship should, within principled limits, be used as an inducement toward peaceful resolution of ethnic conflicts. While some practices may so offend core values that economic and other sanctions may be warrant-ed—"ethnic cleansing" surely falls in this category—using human rights criteria as a condition of economic aid may ironically exacerbate the problems that such conditionality is meant to address. In particular, withholding financial aid may foster the very conditions of disaffection in which political elites are most tempted to resort to ethnic mobilization.

To the extent that international organizations may be disposed to judge qualifications for membership in part by an applicant's demon-strated commitment to democratic principles, they must be prepared to assume the demanding challenge of applying this criterion responsibly. For while a liberal democratic culture may be the surest long-term guarantor of interethnic harmony, democratic processes are all too readily susceptible to ethnic mobilization, with potentially tragic results. The harsh lessons of Yugoslavia admonish us to support the emerging right to democratic government not only with active engagement, but also with prudent care.

2. THE DOCTRINE OF HUMANITARIAN INTERVENTION

Humanitarian intervention involves the use of force in order to prevent the wholesale massacre or mutilation of populations. Such interventions can be conducted by a group of states or by a single state. The Security Council authorizes humanitarian interventions under Arti-cle 42, after a determination that there exists a "threat to the peace, breach of the peace, or act of aggression." (Art. 39).

Whether, and to what extent, humanitarian intervention is permit-ted under customary international law is a matter of long-standing debate. The principle of sovereignty strengthens the non-interventionist arguments. Although the U.N. has engaged in humanitarian interventions on occasion, there is no universal consensus on whether state practice is now distanced from the norms of sovereign equality of states and non-interference with the internal affairs of a member state.

Regional organizations have been criticized for their failure to intervene and prevent atrocities. The following excerpts present competing arguments for and against humanitarian intervention in the face of human atrocities.

T. MODIBO OCRAN, THE DOCTRINE OF HUMANITARIAN INTERVENTION IN LIGHT OF ROBUST PEACEKEEPING

25 Boston College International and Comparative Law Review 1, 57–58 (2002).

* * *

From the 1860's onwards, philosophers and legal scholars seemed increasingly receptive to the suggested legal validity of humanitarian intervention by individual states or group of states, acting outside the auspices of any international organization. In the period immediately preceding World War I, the majority of writers had apparently accepted the legality of humanitarian intervention, even though there were still strong opponents of this position. It seems fair to assert that immediately prior to the adoption of the U.N. Charter in 1945, humanitarian intervention was a fairly settled practice under customary international law, even if there was never unanimity on its legal status.

By the end of World War II, and certainly after the formation of the U.N. in 1945, Sir Harley Shawcross could confidently declare, at the Nuremberg Trials in 1946, that, "the right of humanitarian intervention, in the name of the rights of man trampled upon by the state in a manner offensive to the feelings of humanity, has been recognized long ago as an integral part of the Law of Nations." However, some scholars still raise the uncomfortable but legitimate question whether this right of intervention survived the U.N. Charter, in view of the well established principle of non-intervention codified in Articles 2(4) and 2(7) of the Charter.

Over the past two decades, there have been quite a few dramatic cases of unilateral military interventions, some of which have been castigated as self-serving and thus not motivated primarily by humanitarian goals. There have also been various U.N. peacekeeping operations, including those in former Yugoslavia and Rwanda, which had strong elements of humanitarian intervention.

Whatever the strengths of some of the doctrinal objections to humanitarian intervention, it is the view of this writer that the world cannot sit by in the name of a single doctrine of international law, i.e., non-intervention, while human beings are being butchered and tortured on a wide and persistent scale by their own governments, or by factions in a civil war; or when human populations are subjected to starvation and epidemic diseases as a result of political conflicts. There are other international law doctrines that will justify humanitarian intervention, especially if they are embarked upon by U.N. sanctioned regional and multilateral forces. The minimization of conflict is not an absolute virtues, including the promotion of respect for certain fundamental human rights.

Further, so long as we insist on the need for a well-defined set of criteria, it might be advisable, given the inability or unwillingness of international bodies to react to all cases of grave human rights abuses, to legally recognize that in these extreme situations a state may be temporarily relieved from its Article 2(4) restraints in order to take unilateral action to enforce critical rights. As Lillich stated thirty-four years ago, "to require a state to sit back and watch the slaughter of innocent people in order to avoid violating blanket prohibitions against the use of force is to stress black letter at the expense of far more fundamental values."

When humanitarian interventions are undertaken not just in accordance with the U.N. Charter, but by U.N. peacekeepers or regional groups ratified by the U.N., the case for humanitarian intervention rests on even more solid ground. Even so, the multinational mode of intervention poses its own special problems, including the matter of command and control and the difficulty of implementing the generally agreed concept of unity of command. States contributing to U.N. robust peacekeeping operations should strive to downplay their parochial military professionalism and eschew narrow foreign policy agendas in the theaters of conflict. Only from this unified perspective and modus operandi can robust peacekeeping deliver a devastating blow to the forces of darkness that make humanitarian intervention a necessary part of our moral and legal duty.

In the following excerpt foreign policy and military strategist, Edward Luttwak, offers a view of war as a means of resolving political conflict. As you read this material, consider how his discussion of peacekeeping connects to that of Professor Wedgwood.

EDWARD N. LUTTWAK, GIVE WAR A CHANCE

78 Foreign Affairs 36 (1999).

* * *

An unpleasant truth often overlooked is that although war is a great evil, it does have a great virtue: it can resolve political conflicts and lead to peace. This can happen when all belligerents become exhausted or when one wins decisively. Either way the key is that the fighting must continue until a resolution is reached. War brings peace only after passing a culminating phase of violence. Hopes of military success must fade for accommodation to become more attractive than further combat.

Since the establishment to the United Nations and the enshrinement of great-power politics in its Security Council, however, wars among lesser powers have rarely been allowed to run their natural course. Instead, they have typically been interrupted early on, before they could burn themselves out and establish the preconditions for a lasting settlement. Cease-fires and armistices have frequently been imposed under the aegis of the Security Council in order to halt fighting. NATO'S intervention in the Kosovo crisis follows this pattern.

But a cease-fire tends to arrest war-induced exhaustion and lets belligerents reconstitute and rearm their forces. It intensifies and prolongs the struggle once the cease-fire ends—and it does usually end. This was true of the Arab–Israeli war of 1948–49, which might have come to closure in a matter of weeks if two cease-fires ordained by the Security Council had not let the combatants recuperate. It has recently been true in the Balkans. Imposed cease-fires frequently interrupted the fighting between Serbs and Croats in Krajina, between the forces of the rump Yugoslav federation and the Croat army, and between the Serbs, Croats, and Muslims in Bosnia. Each time, the opponents used the pause to recruit, train, and equip additional forces for further combat, prolonging the war and widening the scope of its killing and destruction. Imposed armistices, meanwhile—again, unless followed by negotiated peace accords—artificially freeze conflict and perpetuate a state of war indefinitely by shielding the weaker side from the consequences of refusing to make concessions for peace.

The Cold War provided compelling justification for such behavior by the two superpowers, which sometimes collaborated in coercing less-powerful belligerents to avoid being drawn into their conflicts and clashing directly. Although imposed cease-fires ultimately did increase the total quantity of warfare among the lesser powers, and armistices did perpetuate states of war, both outcomes were clearly lesser evils (from a global point of view) the possibility of nuclear war. But today, neither Americans nor Russians are inclined to intervene *competitively* in the wars of lesser powers, so the unfortunate consequences of interrupting war persist while no greater danger is averted. It might be best for all parties to let minor wars burn themselves out.

The Problems of Peacekeepers

Today cease-fires and armistices are imposed on lesser powers by multilateral agreement—not to avoid great-power competition but for essentially disinterested and indeed frivolous motives, such as television audiences' revulsion at harrowing scenes of war. But this, perversely, can *systematically* prevent the transformation of war into peace. The Dayton accords are typical of the genre: they have condemned Bosnia to remain divided into three rival armed camps, with combat suspended momentarily but a state of hostility prolonged indefinitely. Since no side is threatened by defeat and loss, none has a sufficient incentive to negotiate a lasting settlement; because no path to peace is even visible, the dominant priority is to prepare for future war rather than to reconstruct devastated economies and ravaged societies. Uninterrupted war would certainly have caused further suffering and led to an unjust outcome from one perspective or another, but it would also have led to a more stable situation that would have let the postwar era truly begin. Peace takes hold only when war is truly over.

A variety of multilateral organizations now make it their business to intervene in other peoples' wars. The defining characteristic of these entities is that they insert themselves in war situations while refusing to engage in combat. In the long run this only adds to the damage. If the United Nations helped the strong defeat the weak faster and more decisively, it would actually enhance the peacemaking potential of war. But the first priority of U.N. peacekeeping contingents is to avoid casualties among their own personnel. Unit commanders therefore habitually appease the *locally* stronger force, accepting its dictates and tolerating its abuses. This appeasement is not strategically purposeful, as siding with the stronger power overall would be; rather, it merely reflects the determination of each U.N. unit to avoid confrontation. The final result is to prevent the emergence of a coherent outcome, which requires an imbalance of strength sufficient to end the fighting.

Peacekeepers chary of violence are also unable to effectively protect civilians who are caught up in the fighting or deliberately attacked. At best, U.N. peacekeeping forces have been passive spectators to outrages and massacres, as in Bosnia and Rwanda; at worst, they collaborate with it, as Dutch U.N. troops did in the fall of Srebenica by helping the Bosnian Serbs separate the men of military age from the rest of the population.

The very presence of U.N. forces, meanwhile, inhibits the normal remedy of endangered civilians, which is to escape from the combat zone. Deluded into thinking that they will be protected, civilians in danger remain in place until it is too late to flee. During the 1992–94 siege of Sarajevo, appeasement interacted with the pretense of protection in an especially perverse manner: U.N. personnel inspected outgoing flights to prevent the escape of Sarajevo civilians in obedience to a cease-fire agreement negotiated with the locally dominant Bosnian Serbs—who habitually violated that deal. The more sensible, realistic response to a raging war would have been for the Muslims to either flee the city or drive the Serbs out.

Institutions such as the European Union, the Western European Union, and the Organization for Security and Cooperation in Europe lack even the U.N.'s rudimentary command structure and personnel, yet they too now seek to intervene in warlike situations, with predictable consequences. Bereft of forces even theoretically capable of combat, they satisfy the interventionist urges of member states (or their own institutional ambitions) by sending unarmed or lightly armed "observer" missions, which have the same problems as U.N. peacekeeping missions, only more so.

Military organizations such as NATO or the West African Peacekeeping Force (ECOMOG, recently at work in Sierra Leone) are capable of stopping warfare. Their interventions will have the destructive consequence of prolonging the state of war, but they can at least protect civilians from its consequences. Even that often fails to happen, however, because multinational military commands engaged in disinterested interventions tend to avoid any risk of combat, thereby limiting their effectiveness. U.S. troops in Bosnia, for example, repeatedly failed to arrest known war criminals passing through their checkpoints lest this provoke confrontation.

Multinational commands, moreover, find it difficult to control the quality and conduct of member states' troops, which can reduce the performance of all forces involved to the lowest common denominator. This was true of otherwise fine British troops in Bosnia and of the Nigerian marines in Sierra Leone. The phenomenon of troop degradation can rarely be detected by external observers, although its consequences are abundantly visible in the litter of dead, mutilated, raped, and tortured victims that attends such interventions. The true state of affairs is illuminated by the rare exception, such as the vigorous Danish tank battalion in Bosnia that replied to any attack on it by firing back in full force, quickly stopping the fighting.

The First "Post-Heroic" War

All prior examples of disinterested warfare and its crippling limitations, however, have been cast into shadow by NATO's current intervention against Serbia for the sake of Kosovo. The alliance has relied on air power alone to minimize the risk of NATO casualties, bombing targets in Serbia, Montenegro, and Kosovo for weeks without losing a single pilot. This seemingly miraculous immunity from Yugoslav anti-aircraft guns and missiles was achieved by multiple layers of precautions. First, for all the noise and imagery suggestive of a massive operation, very few strike sorties were actually flown during the first few weeks. That reduced the risks to pilots and aircraft but of course also limited the scope of the bombing to a mere fraction of NATO's potential. Second, the air campaign targeted air-defense systems first and foremost, minimizing present and future allied casualties, though at the price of very limited destruction and the loss of any shock effect. Third, NATO avoided most anti-aircraft weapons by releasing munitions not from optimal altitudes but from an ultra-safe 15,000 feet or more. Fourth, the alliance greatly restricted its operations in less-than-perfect weather conditions. NATO officials complained that dense clouds were impeding the bombing campaign, often limiting nightly operations to a few cruise-missile strikes against fixed targets of known location. In truth, what the cloud ceiling prohibited was not all bombing—low altitude attacks could easily have taken place—but rather perfectly safe bombing.

On the ground far beneath the high-flying planes, small groups of Serb soldiers and police in armored vehicles were terrorizing hundreds of thousands of Albanian Kosovars. NATO has a panoply of aircraft designed for finding and destroying such vehicles. All its major powers have antitank helicopters, some equipped to operate without base support. But no country offered to send them into Kosovo when the ethnic cleansing began—after all, they might have been shot down. When U.S. Apache helicopters based in Germany were finally ordered to Albania, in spite of the vast expenditure devoted to their instantaneous "readiness" over the years, they required more than three weeks of "predeployment preparations" to make the journey. Six weeks into the war, the Apaches had yet to fly their first mission although two had already crashed during training. More than mere bureaucratic foot dragging was responsible for this inordinate delay: the U.S. Army insisted that the Apaches could not operate on their own, but would need the support of heavy rocket barrages to suppress Serb anti-aircraft weapons. This created a much larger logistical load than the Apaches alone, and an additional, evidently welcome delay.

Even before the Apache saga began, NATO already had aircraft deployed on Italian bases that could have done the job just as well: U.S. A–10 "Warthogs" built around their powerful 30 mm antitank guns and British Royal Air Force Harriers ideal for low-altitude bombing at close range. Neither was employed, again because it could not be done in perfect safety. In the calculus of the NATO democracies, the immediate possibility of saving thousands of Albanians from massacre and hundreds of thousands from deportation was obviously not worth the lives of a few pilots. That may reflect unavoidable political reality, but it demonstrates how even a large-scale disinterested intervention can fail to achieve its ostensibly humanitarian aim. It is worth wondering whether the Kosovars would have been better off had NATO simply done nothing.

REFUGEE NATIONS

The most disinterested of all interventions in war—and the most destructive—are humanitarian relief activities. The largest and most protracted is the United Nations Relief and Works Agency (UNRWA). It was built on the model of its predecessor, the United Nations Relief and Rehabilitation Agency (UNRRA), which operated displaced persons' camps in Europe immediately after World War II. The UNRWA was established immediately after the 1948–49 Arab–Israeli war to feed, shelter, educate, and provide health services for Arab refugees who had fled Israeli zones in the former territory of Palestine.

By keeping refugees alive in spartan conditions that encouraged their rapid emigration or local resettlement, the UNRRA's camps in Europe had assuaged postwar resentments and helped disperse revanchist concentrations of national groups. But UNRWA camps in Lebanon, Syria, Jordan, the West Bank, and the Gaza Strip provided on the whole a higher standard of living than most Arab villagers had previously enjoyed, with a more varied diet, organized schooling, superior medical care, and no backbreaking labor in stony fields. They had, therefore, the opposite effect, becoming desirable homes rather than eagerly abandoned transit camps. With the encouragement of several Arab countries, the UNRWA turned escaping civilians into lifelong refugees who gave birth to refugee children, who have in turn had refugee children of their own.

During it half-century of operation, the UNRWA has thus perpetuated a Palestinian refugee nation, preserving its resentments in as fresh a condition as they were in 1948 and keeping the first bloom of revanchist emotion intact. By its very existence, the UNRWA dissuades integration into local society and inhibits emigration. The concentration of Palestinians in the camps, moreover, has facilitated the voluntary or forced enlistment of refugee youths by armed organizations that fight both Israel and each other. The UNRWA has contributed to a half-century of Arab–Israeli violence and still retards the advent of peace.

If each European war had been attended by its own postwar UNRWA, today's Europe would be filled with giant camps for millions of descendants of uprooted Gallo–Romans, abandoned Vandals, defeated Burgundians, and misplaced Visigoths—not to speak of more recent refugee nations such as post–1945 Sudeten Germans (three million of whom were expelled from Czechoslovakia in 1945). Such a Europe would have remained a mosaic of warring tribes, undigested and unreconciled in their separate feeding camps. It might have assuaged consciences to help each one at each remove, but it would have led to permanent instability and violence.

The UNRWA has counterparts elsewhere, such as the Cambodian camps along the Thai border, which incidentally provided safe havens for the mass-murdering Khmer Rouge. But because the United Nations is limited by stingy national contributions, these camps' sabotage of peace is at least localized.

That is not true of the proliferating, feverishly competitive non-governmental organizations (NGOS) that now aid war refugees. Like any other institution, these NGOS are interested in perpetuating themselves, which means that their first priority is to attract charitable contributions by being seen to be active in high-visibility situations. Only the most dramatic natural disasters attract any significant mass-media attention, and then only briefly; soon after an earthquake or flood, the cameras depart. War refugees, by contrast, can win sustained press coverage if kept concentrated in reasonably accessible camps. Regular warfare among well-developed countries is rare and offers few opportunities for such NGOS, so they focus their efforts on aiding refugees in the poorest parts of the world. This ensures that the food, shelter, and health care offered—although abysmal by Western standards—exceeds what is locally available to non-refugees. The consequences are entirely predictable. Among many examples, the huge refugee camps along the Democratic Republic of Congo's border with Rwanda stand out. They sustain a Hut nation that would otherwise have been dispersed, making the consolidation of Rwanda impossible and providing a base for radicals to launch more Tutsi-killing raids across the border. Humanitarian intervention has worsened the chances of a stable, long-term resolution of the tensions in Rwanda.

To keep refugee nations intact and preserve their resentments forever is bad enough, but inserting material aid into ongoing conflicts is even worse. Many NGOS that operate in an odor of sanctity routinely supply active combatants. Defenseless, they cannot exclude armed warriors from their feeding stations, clinics, and shelters. Since refugees are presumptively on the losing side, the warriors among them are usually in retreat. By intervening to help, NGOS systematically impede the progress of their enemies toward a decisive victory that could end the war. Sometimes NGOS, impartial to a fault, even help both sides, thus preventing mutual exhaustion and a resulting settlement. And in some extreme cases, such as Somalia, NGOS even pay protection money to local war bands, which use those funds to by arms. Those NGOS are therefore helping prolong the warfare whose consequences they ostensibly seek to mitigate.

MAKE WAR TO MAKE PEACE

Too many wars nowadays become endemic conflicts that never end because the transformative effects of both decisive victory and exhaustion are blocked by outside intervention. Unlike the ancient problem of war, however, the compounding of its evils by disinterested interventions is a new malpractice that could be curtailed. Policy elites should actively resist the emotional impulse to intervene in other peoples' wars—not because they are indifferent to human suffering but precisely because they care about it and want to facilitate the advent of peace. The United States should dissuade multilateral interventions instead of leading them. New rules should be established for U.N. refugee relief activities to ensure that immediate succor is swiftly followed by repatriation, local absorption, or emigration, ruling out the establishment of permanent refugee camps. And although it may not be possible to constrain interventionist NGOS, they should at least be neither officially encouraged nor funded. Underlying these seemingly perverse measures would be a true appreciation of war's paradoxical logic and a commitment to let it serve its sole useful function.

Notes and Questions

1. Did the introduction of democratic-style elections exacerbate ethnic tension in Bosnia and the former Yugoslavia or did it simply "legitimize" the *status quo* under the guise of a democratic election? Would the implementation of, for example, economic sanctions have been more effective? If the root of the problem in the former Yugoslavia is the intensity of ethnic conflict, how can international organizations effectively intervene to dispel that tension (aside from intervening in a more timely fashion)?

2. Orentlicher suggests that democracy can reduce the violence of inter-ethnic hostility and that civic culture is a strong component of democracy. How can international organizations play a role in creating or contributing to those factors that are conducive to democracy? That is, how can international organizations nurture civic culture to ensure democracy in the

long run? What lessons can be learned from the former Yugoslavia to prevent similar situations from recurring in the future?

3. Orentlicher argues that the European Community's earlier intervention might have prevented Yugoslavia's break-up. How does this position resonate with the claims of Professor I. William Zartman in *Cowardly Lion: Missed Opportunities*, discussed earlier?

4. Orentlicher argues for the use of force to require parties' participation in mediation. How does this conform to the understanding of mediation as a voluntary process?

5. How does the regionalization of human rights, adopted by the African Charter on Human Rights and Peoples' Rights discussed earlier in *The Organization of African Unity and its Role in Regional Conflict Resolution and Dispute Settlement*, resonate with the arguments advanced by the author in the *Doctrine of Humanitarian Intervention in Light of Robust Peacekeeping*?

6. Do you agree with Orentlicher's proposal for a binding arbitration procedure, attached to both regional organizations and the United Nations, that would have authority to resolve territorial disputes and that could be invoked both by States and non-State entities? What problems do you anticipate?

7. Luttwak's strong endorsement of a non-intervention principle is at odds with the other readings in this section. Is his argument persuasive?

8. Does Luttwak's argument against peacekeeping relate to the failure of doing it effectively or does it relate to something fatal in the nature of the peacekeeping enterprise?

9. In reflecting on Luttwak's article, would you consider war a type of adjudication with enforcement? Is it a pre-mediation process? How do you respond to Luttwak's proposal to let internal wars run their course? Is this approach consistent with general principles of conflict resolution?

10. Responding to what they describe as Luttwak's "let it burn" argument, some conflict resolution scholars argue:

> This argument ignores an increasingly important characteristic of contemporary warfare. The battlefield itself does not necessarily lead to a durable peace except in fairly unusual—and, arguably, increasingly unobtainable—circumstances: when the victor wins overwhelmingly and then rigorously assimilates (or annihilates) the loser, who gets little support from any quarter * * * Losers and victims in an era of globablization are less isolated and have more friends, enabling their causes to be sustained and reopened.

[CHESTER A. CROCKER, FEN OSLER HAMPSON & PAMELA AALL, TAMING INTRACTABLE CONFLICT 10, 11 (2004).]

Which argument do you find more persuasive?

E. THE ROLE OF NON–GOVERNMENTAL ORGANIZATIONS

1. INTRODUCTION

Non-governmental organizations (NGOs), also known as transnational organizations, play a significant role in contemporary global conflict resolution. Private individuals or corporations organize NGOs to highlight and address issues that they believe are not receiving the full or proper attention of national governments. NGOs operate unofficially at both the domestic and international level, and there are no specific international standards that govern the establishment of NGOs. These organizations are governed by the law of the State in which they are based.[23]

NGOs are becoming more significant in the decision-making activities of international organizations, particularly the U.N. In accordance with Article 71 of the U.N. Charter, the Economic and Social Council (ECOSOC) grants "consultative status" to NGOs that satisfy specific requirements. This status enhances the credibility of NGOs and enables them to attend ECOSOC proceedings and conduct a variety of advocacy and lobbying activities.

2. ROLE OF NGOs IN CONFLICT RESOLUTION

Increased ethnic violence since World War II has resulted in a proliferation of NGOs involved in humanitarian relief work and peacebuilding. Frequently, NGOs establish the groundwork for future mediation and conflict resolution activities by developing relationships with parties through humanitarian aid work. Once they become familiar with specific conflicts, NGOs are better able to engage in conflict resolution efforts and develop infrastructures to support peacebuilding.[24]

NGOs can exert a powerful influence in peace negotiations through advocacy and lobbying efforts. In some contexts, they may even be better situated than diplomats to resolve deadly conflict. For example, the Catholic NGO, the Community of Saint Egidio, furthered the Arusha peace process and mediated the deadly conflict in Mozambique.[25]

Nevertheless, NGO involvement in conflict resolution can be problematic. Their ability to perform a mediating role may be compromised by the very humanitarian activities they pursue. NGOs make decisions about the distribution of the resources they provide (food, water, farming equipment, and the like). Therefore, they, like governments, make

---

23. PETER MALANCZUK, AKEHURST'S MODERN INTRODUCTION TO INTERNATIONAL LAW 96 (7th rev. ed. 1997).

24. Pamela Aall, *Nongovernmental Organizations and Peacemaking*, in MANAGING GLOBAL CHAOS: SOURCES OF AND RESPONSES TO INTERNATIONAL CONFLICT 433, 438 (Chester A. Crocker & Fen Osler Hampson with Pamela

Aall eds., 1996) [hereinafter MANAGING GLOBAL CHAOS].

25. Andrea Bartoli, *Mediating Peace in Mozambique: The Role of the Community of Sant' Egidio*, in HERDING CATS, *supra* note 18, at 247–73.

decisions that have an impact.[26] The ability of NGOs to bring external resources into a conflict situation may affect the balance of power and decrease their chances of successful peacebuilding.[27]

The following excerpt describes the moral influence and advocacy role of several NGOs during the 1999 Rambouillet/Paris negotiations regarding the Kosovo conflict. Although the negotiations themselves were unsuccessful, they paved the way for the Dayton Accords.

PAUL R. WILLIAMS, THE ROLE OF JUSTICE IN PEACE NEGOTIATIONS

in POST-CONFLICT JUSTICE 122–23 (M. Cherif Bassiouni ed., 2002).

* * *

During the Dayton negotiations, non-state actors interested in the norms and institutions of justice, such as human rights NGOs, editorial boards, and individual representatives, generally observed and commented on the process, but did not engage in any organized campaign to influence the extent to which the norm of justice was incorporated within the Accords. During the Rambouillet/Paris negotiations, however, non-state actors were significantly more involved and sought to employ a number of means to ensure the adequate representation of the norms and institutions of justice.

During the opening days of the conference, Human Rights Watch issued a number of important documents, including a detailed report on atrocities recently committed by Serbian forces in Drenica against Kosovar civilians, and an accompanying press release calling upon the negotiators to ensure that justice was not traded for peace during the negotiations. Upon the suggestion of international experts advising the Kosovo delegation, Human Rights Watch issued a second press statement on February 9, 1999 calling for the inclusion of specific language relating to the obligation to arrest and extradite war criminals and a rejection of the sufficiency of language merely calling upon the Serbian regime to "cooperate" with the Yugoslav Tribunal.

To buttress the efforts of Human Rights Watch, the Italian based NGO, No Peace Without Justice, created by former EU Commissioner Emma Bonito, issued a lengthy report detailing the responsibility of Mr. Milosevic for war crimes and crimes against humanity committed against the people of Kosovo through 1998. These efforts were matched by the editorial board of the *New York Times* which tried to buttress those opposed to a grant of immunity by stating, "Mr. Milosevic senses that NATO countries are unenthusiastic about using air strikes. He expects he can divide the West and win concessions, among them the assurance

---

26. Pamela Aall, *Nongovernmental Organization and Peacemaking, in* MANAGING GLOBAL CHAOS, *supra* note 24, at 433, 440.

27. Mary B. Anderson, *Humanitarian NGOs in Conflict Intervention*, in MANAGING GLOBAL CHAOS, *supra* note 24, at 343; Larry A. Dunn & Louis Kriesberg, *Mediating Intermediaries: Expanding Roles of Transnational Organizations, in* BERCOVITCH, INTERNATIONAL MEDIATION, *supra* note 2, at 194, 201, 204, 206.

that he cannot be prosecuted by the war crimes tribunal. The [Contact Group] should not let him dictate the terms of settlement for [the] conflict."

A collection of NGOs in Washington, D.C. forming the Kosovo Action Coalition also prepared a steady stream of coalition letters to members of Congress, President Clinton and other executive branch officials in an attempt to explain the practical benefits of incorporating the norm of justice and adopting provisions similar to those proposed by the Kosovo delegation and supported by the European Union Co-chair. These efforts were supported by a letter to President Clinton from Senators Mitch McConnell and Gordon Smith advising that "there must be an immediate and complete withdrawal of all Serb police, security, army and paramilitary forces from Kosovo prior to any US deployment ... a level of zero simplifies the monitoring task, reduces the threat of violence to US troops and Kosovo's civilians, removes obstacles to the delivery of humanitarian relief, and opens access for ... Tribunal investigations."

While it is difficult to measure the actual impact of these efforts, they did have the effect of encouraging the Kosovo delegation to continue to strongly push for the inclusion of the norm of justice, and undercut the ability of the Contact Group to entirely dismiss the norm of justice, or to engage in any *de jure* grant of immunity. These efforts may also have enhanced the ability of certain Contact Group members to advocate for the inclusion of the norm of justice and against immunity.

---

3. ACCOUNTABILITY AND NEUTRALITY CONCERNS

Critics have called for caution in giving private actors diplomatic roles. Instead of supporting a regime of parallel diplomacy, they argue that regional and international organizations should work with NGOs to develop a coherent, strategic, long-term peacebuilding policy.[28] Others have called for more coordination of NGO efforts in conflict resolution and peacebuilding as well as greater accountability. For example, when NGOs move into collapsed States as they did in Rwanda and take over vital government functions, accountability is difficult to establish.

In the following reading, Gillian Sorenson, former Assistant Secretary General for External Relations at the United Nations, raises critical questions about accountability and neutrality of NGOs in the resolution of international conflict. [Author's note: Ms. Sorenson is now Senior Advisor at the United Nations Foundation.]

28. Fabienne Hara, *Burundi: A Case of Parallel Diplomacy, in* Herding Cats, *supra* note 18, at 139, 152.

GILLIAN MARTIN SORENSON, THE ROLES A CIVIL SOCIETY CAN PLAY IN INTERNATIONAL DISPUTE RESOLUTION

18 Negotiation Journal 355–58 (October 2002).

* * *

There are historic photographs of the United Nations Charter being drafted in 1945, in which you will see—at the far edges of the room—representatives of about 50 NGOs sitting discreetly. Among those NGOs were representatives of such groups as Rotary International, the Red Cross, and the Quakers. They observed throughout, but never spoke up; they certainly did not criticize. They were there, in a sense, to be supporters of the process and to respectfully watch and observe.

Those 51 original NGOs now number in the thousands. They are, of course, self appointed, self-organized, and many have acquired a level of activity and expertise that is extraordinary. They are the new "players" in international conflict resolution.

Governments have mixed feelings about this development. Some nations welcome NGO involvement. Most democratic governments have a long history of working with NGOs and its diplomats feel comfortable with them. But other governments, particularly the more repressive ones, have seen NGOs as the rabble, the opposition, the unruly and unwelcome upstarts. And they really do not welcome them. (They may say they do, but they may take discreet steps to see that they are not active, not present at key moments.)

Nonetheless, the whole dynamic of civil society, I believe, is absolutely unstoppable. It is the wave of the future. Governments, ready or not, like it or not, must recognize this. And with luck, they will increasingly recognize the value in partnerships with the wider civil society.

Some civil society representatives style themselves as "the players who can do what diplomats cannot do." I have, in fact, heard one of them say that diplomacy is far too important to leave to diplomats. What do they bring to this work that diplomats do not have?

Civil society representatives, or NGOs, bring a certain flexibility, an agility to the processes of international dispute resolution. They can move quickly because they are not tied to bureaucracies or protocol. They also can bring expertise and an ability to mobilize. In addition, they bring resources, financial and otherwise. They also bring numbers: Some NGOs represent thousands of people, while others have a membership of five or six persons. They bring the ability to go where governments do not: that is, when major powers do not see it in their interests to take action, it may be that some NGOs do, and are willing to move in ways that can be helpful, particularly in smaller conflicts.

The involvement of NGOs always presents interesting questions, often legitimately raised by governments. Who are these NGOs? Who do they represent? Who names or appoints them? Especially, who funds them? And can the information they offer be trusted—is it accurate?

When one asks, "to whom are NGOs accountable?" the answer—for the most part—turns out to be their donors. That accountability is frequently loose, and the lessons they learn can be pretty loose. I note this because I have spent most of my life working with NGO representatives. NGOs can be known for brief enthusiasms, they will be in and out. They will move on to the next crisis, the *crise du jour*. They want to be on the front line.

I do not in any way mean to be disrespectful by making such observations about NGOs. In general, the NGO representatives I have encountered are people who are moved by real passion for their work, and they want to be there when they are needed. But the learning process is different in civil society from what is learned or heard or understood among governments.

Some NGOs have clear-cut agendas. One such organization is the International Red Cross, which sponsors a huge, complex, and highly beneficial program of humanitarian aid, but does so with neutrality as its fundamental tenet. But one result of never wavering on this basic principle is that the Red Cross, in some situations, has been accused of complicity in genocide, because it cannot shed its neutrality. There are some other agendas among this vast community of NGOs that deserve looking at.

Some criticize NGOs for sometimes doing actual harm—by intruding into ongoing peace processes by government expert negotiators and mediators. As NGOs have tried to work around the margins, to go into side doors, to bring in underground information, they may possibly have caused harm, done damage, set the process back. That concern is why the relationship between the civil society and the state actors—diplomats and politicians—is fraught with tension. Efforts are made to communicate, to express mutual respect and support, to open the doors; but there is always the tension about who is doing what, and about "who is in charge here, after all?"

On funding, I am stunned sometimes by the resources NGOs have. The World Wildlife Fund, for instance, has roughly 200 times the budget of the small office on the Environment and Sustainable Development of the U.N. The World Wildlife Fund thus is way beyond what the U.N. can do; and that can sometimes make for an uncomfortable situation in conflict resolution matters.

With civil society there are some other problems. Often there are internal competitions among NGOs that can become pretty fierce: competition for leadership; competition for publicity; and certainly competition for funding. You may recall the dispute that broke into the press between the groups working on the land-mine issue. They were practically at blows when one of the NGOs received the Nobel Peace Prize a couple of years ago, because of who was getting the credit for the work to eliminate land mines. Such internal competitions can make NGOs a difficult community to work with.

Inside the U.N., the question often comes up as to how the organization is dealing with or working with civil society. The answer varies greatly. I would say that every department or program at the U.N. has an NGO liaison, a designated outreach person. Everyone in the U.N. Secretariat recognizes that there is a community of NGOs or civil society that shares a common interest, and they want to work together.

In more recent years, NGOs have been actively involved in conflict resolution and disarmament issues. Obviously, these areas involve life-or-death issues that are bound to generate controversies. The level of expertise brought to the table by many long-time diplomats is very high, and they may undervalue the contributions of NGOs, whom they may feel are not sufficiently informed.

I have no conclusions to offer about NGOs, except to observe that it is absolutely clear that, one way or another, relationships with them are going to continue and grow. We at the U.N. believe such relationships will deepen and strengthen to the benefit of all.

So although the civil society movement has been around not just since the founding of the U.N. but forever, we are in a position in the 21st century to make the most of this: to strengthen, to reinforce these relationships. To find where and how they can be productive. To listen carefully to what is being said by the NGOs. Above all, to deal with them with respect. We, the diplomats and the formal apparatus, must see where and when the NGOs can be given "a seat at the table."

Notes and Questions

1.   What is the value added of NGOs in conflict management efforts? In what ways do NGOs present potential threats to the work of diplomats?

2.   Assume that you have been invited to convene an international peace conference on the developing role of NGOs in conflict management. What topics would be covered in the conference, and what NGOs would be invited to make presentations?

3.   In both private and public disputes, you must consider who should participate in the negotiations in order for any negotiated result to take hold. This issue was raised when the Contact Group (which consisted of Germany, France, United States, United Kingdom, Russia and Italy) was constituted in the Rambouillet/Paris negotiations. Parties to the peace conference included a Kosovo delegation, a Serbian delegation, members of the non-Serbian ethnic minority in Albania and legal experts, representatives of the Contact Group, and representatives of the European Union and the OSCE. The negotiators decided that it was permissible for individuals suspected of war crimes to be included in the negotiation process. What

arguments would you advance in favor of including or excluding such individuals from the negotiation?

4. Draft a protocol for a new organization that will govern all international NGOs involved in conflict resolution projects around the world. Include ethical norms and standards that address the following topics: (1) relationships with official diplomats, (2) relationships with other NGOs, (3) funding, (4) accountability, and (5) neutrality.

5. How would you respond to Edward Luttwak's claim (*Give War A Chance*) that, "Many NGOs that operate in an odor of sanctity routinely support active combatants.... By intervening to help, NGOs systematically impede the progress of their enemies toward a decisive victory that could end the war...."?

F. TRANSITIONAL JUSTICE INSTITUTIONS

1. INTRODUCTION

Transitional justice refers to the reconstruction of a society in the aftermath of oppression and violent conflict. One of the major challenges facing transitional societies, such as South Africa, East Timor, and Sierra Leone, is addressing past human rights abuses while acknowledging the pragmatic reality of a transitional process. Complex questions abound. In the political negotiations that seek to end violent conflicts, to what extent should the perpetrators of atrocities be granted immunity?[29] How should transitional societies deal with the gross human rights violations that occurred in the past? How should transitional communities restore shattered infrastrucures and return to a sense of normalcy? Should newly democratic governments prosecute the crimes of the former regime? Whether transitional justice is "ordinary justice,"[30] or whether it is different, is a subject of debate.

In the following excerpt, Judge Richard Goldstone, former Justice of the Constitutional Court of South Africa and former Prosecutor for the Yugoslav and Rwanda Tribunals, describes how achieving justice can contribute to an enduring peace in transitional societies.

RICHARD J. GOLDSTONE, JUSTICE AS A TOOL FOR PEACE–MAKING: TRUTH COMMISSIONS AND INTERNATIONAL CRIMINAL TRIBUNALS

28 New York University Journal of International
Law and Policy 485, 488–89 (1996).

* * *

I have no doubt that in countries or regions where there have been egregious human rights violations, it is less likely that there will be an

---

29. M. Cherif Bassiouni, *Accountability for Violations of International Humanitarian Law and Other Serious Violations of Human Rights, in* Post-Conflict Justice 4 (M. Cherif Bassiouni ed., 2002).

30. Eric A. Posner & Adrian Vermeule, *Transitional Justice As Ordinary Justice,* 117 Harv. L. Rev. 761 (2004).

enduring peace without some attempt to bring justice to the victims. In particular, there are the following five positive contributions which justice can achieve.

First, exposure of the truth can help to individualize guilt and thus avoid the imposition of collective guilt on an ethnic, religious, or other group. During my visits to the former Yugoslavia, and particularly Belgrade, I was astounded at the manner in which Serbs I met were consumed by their historical hatred of Croats. Most meetings I attended began with a history lesson—if I was lucky the history began during the Second World War, but on less happy occasions it began with the Battle of Kosovo in the fourteenth century. It was no different in Zagreb or Sarajevo where collective guilt was ascribed to Serbs or Muslims, as the case may be. In the Balkans, violence has been erupting periodically over a span of six hundred years. Very seldom have the perpetrators of that violence been brought to account. Victims were denied justice.

The result is that blame has been ascribed not to the leaders who sponsored the violence, but to the communities or people represented by those leaders. In one respect, perhaps, the most important beneficiaries of the Nuremberg Trials were the German people. Credible evidence presented at those trials established the guilt of the Nazi leaders beyond a doubt. Through the criminal trial process, focus was placed upon the accused as individual criminals or leaders and not as Germans. So the group of men standing in the dock at Nuremberg were seen as the criminals they were, and not as representatives of the German people. I have no doubt that Germany would have had far more difficulty in coming to grips with its sordid World War II history but for the fact that those leaders were brought to trial.

Second, justice brings public and official acknowledgment to the victims. This usually is the first step in their healing process.

Third, public exposure of the truth is the only effective way of ensuring that history is recorded more accurately and more faithfully than otherwise would have been the case. The Nuremberg Trials have made the work of Holocaust deniers far more difficult. Without the exhumation of mass graves in Bosnia, the fabrications of some Bosnian Serb spokespersons would have had some credibility. The first Yugoslav war criminal to be sentenced, Drazan Erdemovic, confessed to having murdered over seventy innocent Muslim men outside Srebrenica in July, 1995. His evidence helped to verify the occurrence of mass murders at Srebrenica. This evidence was confirmed later by photographic material taken by the U.S. government which showed bodies lying in the vicinity of a grave on the day of the shooting. Further photographs taken the following day showed the grave freshly covered with earth. According to a Bosnian Serb Army spokesperson, the grave contained the bodies of soldiers killed during battle.

The exhumations conducted by the Office of the Prosecutor in the summer of 1996, however, exposed the lie in such claims. The persons buried in the grave had been killed with a single bullet shot in the back of the head, most of them while their arms were bound behind their backs—certainly not the way in which people die in the course of battle! Through the establishment of the Yugoslav Tribunal, the massacre of thousands of innocent Muslims who sought safety in the U.N. "safe haven" of Srebrenica has been established with a degree of certainty that otherwise would have been absent.

Fourth, in my experience, there is only one way to curb criminal conduct and that is through good policing and the implementation of efficient criminal justice. In any country there is a direct relationship between the effectiveness of policing and the crime rate. If would-be criminals believe that there is a good prospect of their being apprehended and punished, they will think twice before embarking upon criminal conduct. It is no different in the case of international crimes. If political and military leaders believe they are likely to be brought to account by the international community for committing war crimes, that belief in most cases will have a deterrent effect. Between the Nuremberg and Tokyo war crimes trials and the establishment of the Yugoslav Tribunal, there was not a single international attempt to enforce humanitarian law. Leaders of countries bent on fighting wars in blatant disregard of the laws of war could be confident that the international community would make no attempt to bring them to account. If they were safe in their own countries, they had nothing to fear from any external agency. An international deterrent can come only from the enforcement of international law.

Fifth, exposure of the nature and extent of human rights violations frequently will reveal a systematic and institutional pattern of gross human rights violations. It will assist in the identification and dismantling of institutions responsible therefor and deter future recurrences. That already has been the experience of the Yugoslav Tribunal in relation to the conduct of the Bosnian–Serb administration, and patterns may well emerge in the case of other parties to the Balkans conflict. It already is the experience of the South African Truth and Reconciliation Commission [TRC].

2. RETRIBUTIVE JUSTICE APPROACHES: TRIBUNALS

Retributive justice involves prosecution and punishment for past offenses. The international community's commitment to the protection of human rights has generated concern about accountability for human rights violations during transitional justice regimes. With respect to atrocities, such as genocide, crimes against humanity, and war crimes, several *ad hoc* criminal tribunals have been established to prosecute and punish perpetrators. States have united under the aegis of international treaty-making to develop specialized international tribunals for the enforcement of international criminal law. Beginning with the International Military Tribunal at Nuremberg in 1945, and more recently with the International Criminal Tribunal for the Former Yugoslavia (ICTY), the International Criminal Tribunal for Rwanda (ICTR), and the International Criminal Court (ICC), accountability mechanisms exist at the supranational level. Scholars have argued that more regionalized tribunals have a greater impact on post-conflict reconstruction,[31] and there are efforts in that direction as well.[32]

The tribunals apply international law principles and tend to expand the scope of legal rules applicable to individuals during armed conflicts. The policy justification for such tribunals is that they generate closure for victims, defendants, and internal and external observers. Whether they have achieved this objective is considered in the following excerpt.

JOSE E. ALVAREZ, RUSH TO CLOSURE: LESSONS OF THE TADIC JUDGMENT

96 Michigan Law Review 2031 (1998).

"Courts try cases, but cases also try courts."

In 1993 and 1994, following allegations of mass atrocities, including systematic killings, rapes, and other horrific forms of violence in Rwanda and the territories of the former Yugoslavia, two ad hoc international war crimes tribunals were established to prosecute individuals for grave violations of international humanitarian law, including genocide. As might be expected, advocates for the creation of these entities—the first international courts to prosecute individuals under international law since the trials at Nuremberg and Tokyo after World War II—aspired to grand goals inspired by, but extending far beyond, the pedestrian aims of ordinary criminal prosecutions. Those who pushed for the creation of these tribunals argued that, as with earlier trials of major Nazi and Japanese wartime leaders, properly conducted international criminal trials, brought by and on behalf of the international community, would: threaten those in positions of power to deter further violence; make possible atonement for the perpetrators and honor the dead; provide a mechanism to enable victims and their families to receive needed psychological relief, identify remains, restore lost property, and otherwise help heal wounds; channel victims' thirst for revenge toward peaceful dispute settlement; affirm the Nuremberg Principles at the international level while restoring faith in the rule of law generally; tell the truth of what occurred, thereby preserving an accurate historical account of barbarism that would help prevent its recurrence; and, perhaps most important, restore the lost civility of torn societies to achieve national reconciliation.

* * *

31. William W. Burke–White, *Regionalization of International Criminal Law Enforcement: A Preliminary Exploration*, 38 Tex. Int'l L.J. 729 (2003).

32. Carsten Stahn, *Accommodating Individual Criminal Responsibility and National Reconcilation: The UN Truth Commission for East Timor*, 95 Am. J. Int'l L. 952 (2001).

With respect to the Balkans and Rwanda, advocates of these prosecutions start from the premise that such trials "assign guilt for war crimes to the individual perpetrators ... rather than allowing blame to fall on entire groups and nations." Tribunal advocates, commonly members of the "invisible college" of international lawyers, generally assume that only individual, not collective, attribution of responsibility can terminate historical cycles of inter-group bloodletting; that only by bringing individuals to the dock will victims and survivors cease to "cry out for justice against the group" and find closure. In the words of a former prosecutor at the Yugoslav tribunal, Minna Schrag, by finding identifiable individuals accountable, the rest of the community is not "associated with collective guilt ... ," and generations do not grow up saying "it's the Serbs or the Croats or any other group that did this to my father ..." It is also assumed that, by punishing the guilty—and only the guilty—all of the other Nuremberg-inspired goals enumerated above will thereby be advanced.

The recipe for emotionally cathartic closure as the mechanism by which all these diverse goals are achieved is commonly grounded in a victim-centered approach that blurs the lines between criminal punishment and civil redress and between utilitarian and retributivist rationales for punishment. It is argued that international investigations and criminal prosecutions will permit victims' families and survivors to put the past to rest; that victims will channel their anger and vent their frustrations through their testimony at trial because, through participation as witnesses, they will be able to "reassert their sense of control and autonomy," enhance their dignity, "lessen their isolation, and increase their feeling of belonging to a community," and even "find some meaning in their victimization." The goal of using such trials to preserve an accurate collective memory is also based on the model of closure. It is said that war crimes trials permit entire societies to "draw[] a clear line between past and future, allowing the beginning of a healing process."

* * *

I. Closure and the New Ad Hoc Tribunals

International lawyers have advanced many reasons why the international polity, or at least its most reputable representative, the United Nations, should punish basic affronts to human dignity. They claim that the legal, political, and even moral choices have been, to a considerable degree, settled by international law as "shaped by the requirements of the international community." They argue that such a result is anticipated by the U.N. Charter and its provisions for handling threats to and breaches of the international peace, and that the U.N., or at least its post-cold war Security Council, now seems politically willing to establish such judicial fora when the failure to prosecute presents a sufficient threat to the international order. These arguments have been premised on the goal of generating "closure" for victims, defendants, and observers both inside and outside the regions affected. The model of closure, considered as a kind of Weberian "ideal type," has provided the single, coherent rubric to justify ad hoc international tribunals.

The policy justifications offered for international war crimes tribunals build from the premise, discussed above, that public criminal trials absolve those who are not in the dock. Given the impracticality of national venues for such trials as well as the comparative merits of U.N. fora, advocates for these tribunals conclude that international criminal proceedings are best able to unite spectators—whether or not involved in the conflict—in collective revulsion against the barbarism of a few and in support of the civilized nature of the trials themselves. International convictions, in short, are viewed as best able to provide the cathartic group therapy necessary to reestablish lost national and international consensus and, therefore, peace. It is assumed that everyone will find the judgments and verdicts of an international bench legitimate and that such universal forums, issuing verdicts with universal legitimacy, will restore lost civility—at least for the war-torn countries directly at issue and, over the longer term, for the entire international community.

Yet to be successful, the model of closure requires fulfilling the promise of the Nuremberg Principles while avoiding those characteristics of the Nuremberg and Tokyo trials that have been the target of fifty years of criticism. These critiques, adequately surveyed elsewhere, require only short summary here.

Prominent critics complain that the Nuremberg and Tokyo processes were tainted by "victor's justice," including procedures and verdicts that were unfair to the defendants. Critics also question the premise that World War II trials did much to preserve collective memory in the service of history. To at least some, the Nuremberg and Tokyo trial records make for a fundamentally flawed, even false, historical account that is grossly unfair to the victims of the Holocaust and to the actual conduct of World War II. With respect to Nuremberg's treatment of the Holocaust, some attribute the problem to the Allies' decision to make the waging of "aggressive" war the linchpin of all the major trials at Nuremberg, an approach that made the Holocaust incidental to the war instead of making its horrors at least the equal focus of attention. By, for example, arguing that Nazi concentration camps were effectively tools of the German war effort and by failing to bring charges or present evidence of Nazi crimes committed before the official onset of interstate aggression, such as under German pre–1939 racial purity laws, the trials of the major Nuremberg defendants obscured the real scope and depth of the Holocaust while providing a fundamentally misconceived account of German military strategy. By encouraging the theory that Nazi war criminals were merely an especially evil collection of gangsters bent solely on aggressive conquest, the major Nuremberg trials glossed over the ethnic, religious, and racial underpinnings of the Holocaust. In part because the testimonies of victims were deemed unnecessary, these proceedings obscured the discriminatory animus that motivated the Nazis, rendering their anti-Semitism and homophobia, for example, less prominent. By contrast, the Tokyo proceedings, along with the more notorious proceeding against General Tomoyuki Yamashita that reached the U.S. Supreme Court, have been criticized for presenting a racially charged, unnuanced account of atrocities committed by Japanese troops in the Pacific theater.

For the creators of the new ad hoc international tribunals, the flaws suggested by these criticisms needed to be avoided if the grand goals along the model of closure were to be achieved. To avoid the accusation of "victor's justice," they took a number of steps. They created denationalized entities established by the world community, namely the U.N. Security Council, its General Assembly, and Secretary–General. To deflect charges of double standards, they attempted to ensure that all those who committed crimes in the former Yugoslavia and in Rwanda, regardless of national origin, ethnicity, or religion, would be subject to prosecution—and by an international bench and prosecution teams that would not include persons from the region—presumptively tainted by national bias—but would reflect, as does the International Court of Justice, the full diversity of the world's legal systems.

To avoid related accusations of unfairness, they incorporated modern international human rights standards on behalf of criminal defendants into the tribunals' respective statutes and rules of procedure and evidence. To level the playing field between prosecution and defense, the tribunals borrowed considerably from the adversarial, oral nature of common law courtroom proceedings—including its procedures for cross examination—incorporated the possibility of appeals, and even anticipated the need to train lawyers in this novel synthesis of common law and continental procedures. In response to the perceived illegitimacy of ex post facto imposition of criminal liability, the creators of the Yugoslav tribunal restricted that body's jurisdiction to crimes based on "rules of international humanitarian law which are beyond any doubt part of customary law," thereby limiting the tribunal's reach to international crimes that, while arguably novel at the time of Nuremberg or Tokyo, now have a fifty-year-old pedigree.

Gone from both tribunals were the aspects of the World War II prosecutions most criticized from a modern human rights perspective: the death penalty, liability for membership in a criminal organization, and the possibility of trials in absentia. On the other hand, measures for the counseling of victims, the protection of witnesses and court-ordered restoration of stolen property responded to modern sensitivities favoring the rights of victims. Presumably this new sensitivity to victims also responded to the criticism that Nuremberg had dishonored the memory of victims of the Holocaust.

But closure demands not merely a demonstrable commitment to impartiality and procedural and substantive fairness: it requires certainty of results, such that the tribunals' orders are enforced no less than those of any court, and all perpetrators face a realistic prospect of becoming defendants. Accordingly, those who established the new ad hoc tribunals tried to replicate, despite the absence of victor's justice, conditions prevailing among national criminal courts in liberal states. While, ideally, closure demands an Austinian sovereign authority capable of enforcing the law against all, a precondition that is of course impossible to duplicate within the present international system, tribunal creators achieved the next best thing: tribunals backed by the power and resources of the Security Council, with jurisdictional primacy over national courts.

Consistent with the needs of closure, it is also argued—with some success—that multilateral forces need to use force as necessary to arrest those whom local authorities refuse to give up, that prosecutors courageously must indict at least the highest leaders responsible regardless of the political repercussions, since the conviction of only inconsequential small fry will delegitimize the entire process, and that tribunal orders need to be enforced directly on recalcitrant government officials through renewed Security Council sanctions if necessary. Proponents of closure argue further that international criminal prosecutions need to reach deeply into all regions of Rwanda and the Balkans to identify and punish all those who have been complicit with evil—even if such a thoroughgoing search for the truth requires expensive trials far into the future, politically treacherous manhunts by international forces, and innovative adaptations to established extradition practices.

Today, many international lawyers argue that the two ad hoc international war crimes tribunals now in place "have genuinely addressed many of the problems associated with their Nuremberg and Tokyo predecessors."

II. Closure Applied: The Tadic Judgment

After a trial that lasted nearly seven months, on May 7, 1997, a trial chamber of the Yugoslav tribunal found Dusko Tadic guilty on eleven of thirty-one counts charged in the original indictment. Tadic, who had not been charged with genocide, was convicted of "persecution" and fourteen beatings, designated as six crimes against humanity and five violations of the laws or customs of war. On July 14, 1997, Tadic was sentenced to twenty years in prison. Observers predict that Tadic will probably serve at most ten years.

As the following sections demonstrate, in judging and sentencing Tadic, the judges attempt to provide an account of the history of the region, the facts in the case, and the application of the law to these facts in a way that closely adheres to the model of closure's demands in four critical respects. First, they try to fulfill the demand for a definitive historical account that preserves the history of barbarism. Second, they resort to the law's apolitical neutrality and rely on its objectivity to make both factual and legal determinations, the better to highlight the contrast between the court's politically neutral treatment of the defendant as compared to the defendant's actions of persecution. Third, they repeatedly rely on concepts like the presumption of innocence to illustrate how closely and scrupulously they respect the defendant's rights to a "level playing field." Finally, the judges acknowledge the innocence of victims in both their historical accounts as well as in their application of the rules of humanitarian law.

A.   Preserving Collective Memory

The judgment's initial background and preliminary findings chronicle the historical and geographic background of Bosnia's multi-ethnic milieu, the disintegration of the Socialist Federal Republic of Yugoslavia, political developments in Bosnia and Herzegovina and the rise of a propaganda campaign in favor of ethnic cleansing for the good of "Greater Serbia," the formation of Serb autonomous regions, the transformation of the Yugoslav National Army (JNA) into the instrument of Serbia and Montenegro, the rise of the army of the Republika Srpska (VRS) in the face of the JNA's withdrawal from Bosnia and Herzegovina, and the effects within Bosnia, along ethnic lines, of the JNA's incursion into Croatia. These sections present an equally detailed account of the immediate history of the region in which Tadic's actions occurred, Opstina Prijedor, including the breakdown in ethnic relations there in the face of the "polarizing effect" of "propaganda and political manoeuvres" intended "to shift the balance of power in the former Yugoslavia to Serbia." The judgment also provides an account of the Serbian takeover of the town of Prijedor and its grim consequences.

This historical account, common to judgments involving administrative massacres, aspires to be the common history judged by common standards that the model of closure demands with respect to the preservation of "collective memory." It is a painstaking attempt to provide a definitive, historically accurate account not merely of Tadic's actions but of the immediate context in which these occurred. This historical section of the judgment appears to be intended to stand on its own, as a testament to how hate was permitted to consume a particular region. While it does not directly relate to the crimes charged, it seems intended to be a chronicle of the past that seeks to put the past to rest. The judges assume that their unflinching account of Serbian aggression against non-Serbs, replete with graphic descriptions of the severe torture, executions, sexual assaults, and beatings endemic to camps holding mostly Muslim and Croat civilians, along with the nearly ceaseless ethnic and religious epithets that encouraged and accompanied these horrific conditions, will repel ordinary readers.

The judges' historical chronicle is also intended to lend credibility to their subsequent findings with respect to the defendant. After all, if Serbs in this region were being encouraged to treat non-Serbs as sub-human and were in fact doing so, would it be particularly surprising if Tadic, a vitriolic supporter of "Greater Serbia," engaged in the same? At the same time, these preliminary findings imply that Serbian actions in 1991–92 and, by inference, Tadic's as well, were extreme in both cruelty and motivation, especially within the context of the formerly harmonious interethnic relations in the former Yugoslavia. The judges contrast the state of affairs in 1991–92 in Prijedor before the Serbian takeover— portrayed as a town where various ethnic groups lived in apparent harmony amidst significant intermarriages and friendships across ethnic lines with limited signs of division—with its post-invasion state in stark terms, drawing sharp black-and-white distinctions between good and evil, aggressor and victim. Readers are discouraged from seeing the underlying events as in any sense a continuation or exacerbation of older conflicts, but, at the same time, no one except the defendant is assigned specific blame.

The judges' findings, only nominally preliminary, are presented in a matter-of-fact tone that acknowledges little self-doubt or possibility of partiality. The judges tell a simple, linear story, presented as if it were an objective press account that would presumably be found credible by anyone, regardless of ethnicity or political sympathies. Their account relies on only those adverse inferences about Serbian motivations that, in the Chamber's view, any reasonable observer would draw. The judges do not render any outwardly valuative judgments with respect to Serbian nationalist goals, and they are careful to avoid any suggestion that all Serbs, even in Prijedor, are complicit in the mass atrocities they describe. This is strongly confirmed by the rest of the judgment which is devoted to showing, in elaborate detail, why Tadic, as an individual, is guilty of certain specific offenses.

B. The Factual Case Against the Defendant

* * *

With respect to every charge, Tadic relied on what his defense team characterized—misleadingly—as an alibi defense. Defense witnesses testified that Tadic was living in Banja Luka, some forty-five kilometers from Kozarac and further from Prijedor, from May 23 through June 15, 1992; that he made only four trips from Banja Luka; and that, thereafter, he lived in Prijedor while working as a reserve traffic policeman. According to the defense, Tadic was simply not present at Kozarac or in the relevant prison camps at the time of each of the alleged offenses.

* * *

The Chamber's sensitive handling of evidence seeks to elicit confidence that the judges are being apolitical and are not being drawn into local ethnic or religious tensions. At the same time, the judges emphasize that, under the applicable law, they are obliged to find evidence that Tadic was personally motivated by and acted upon the systematic nationalist ethno-religious hatreds canvassed in the judges' preliminary findings. The tribunal links Tadic's intent to those of the Serbian society at large in three steps. First, the judges cite their preliminary findings, along with other evidence, to conclude that Tadic's acts were taken within a "general context of discrimination." Second, they rely on specific examples of victimization of non-Serbs to conclude that "[a] policy to terrorize the non-Serb civilian population of opstina Prijedor on discriminatory grounds is evident[,] . . . that its implementation was widespread and systematic throughout," and that this was apparent "at the minimum" in Opstina Prijedor. Finally, the Chamber links these general policies to Tadic's own actions to conclude that Tadic was "aware of the policy of ... discrimination against non-Serbs, and acted on the basis of religious and political grounds."

C. The Legal Case Against the Defendant

In the final section of the judgment, the Chamber applies the applicable humanitarian law to its factual findings. The judges confirm that, as a matter of law, a showing of discriminatory animus on the part of Tadic individually and by advocates of "Greater Serbia" generally is needed to convict Tadic of either persecution as a crime against humanity or violations of the laws and customs of war. Affirming that convictions for violations of the laws or customs of war and for crimes against humanity require, apart from a demonstration that the acts allegedly committed are within those enumerated under those laws, that they be committed within the context of "armed conflict," the judges find that these requisites are met since Tadic's actions relating to the take-over of Kozarac and other villages were directly connected to this "ethnic war and the strategic aims of the Republika Srpska to create a purely Serbian State." Similarly, they conclude that Tadic's actions in the prison camps were also directly connected to the ongoing armed conflict, since they "clearly occurred with the connivance or permission of the authorities running these camps" and "effected the objective of the Republika Srpska to ethnically cleanse, by means of terror, killings or otherwise, the areas of the Republic of Bosnia and Herzegovina controlled by Bosnian Serb forces."

* * *

[T]he Tadic judgment as well as his sentencing wholeheartedly embrace the closure model. The purportedly authoritative and lengthy historical account that the judges supply in their preliminary factual findings, extending to facts and situations far removed from the charges directly at issue, presents a wealth of detail intended to evoke shared revulsion in court observers—the better to prevent barbarism's recurrence, to promote sympathy and solidarity with victims, and to strengthen the court's moral and legal legitimacy vis-à-vis Tadic and defendants generally. Those findings are also intended to lend credibility to the court's later factual and legal conclusions, and not merely because the court's version of history helps it to determine that the law's demand for a demonstration of discriminatory animus has been fulfilled. The black-and-white lines drawn by the court between perpetrator and victim and between the region's harmonious past and its recent decline into ethnic cleansing are intended to buttress the court's findings of guilt, to strengthen social solidarity on behalf of the universal values reflected in humanitarian law, and to support as well Tadic's sentence. At the same time, the apolitical tone adopted in those preliminary factual findings—as in the court's scrupulous attempt to avoid explicit condemnation of Serbian political goals, Serbian political or cultural institutions or Serbs generally—keeps the focus on Tadic's individual culpability, the better to avoid destabilizing implications of collective guilt. Finally, the court's careful delineation of evidence relative to particular charges, along with its effort to reduce reliance on credibility or other comparable "subjective" findings, seeks to promote closure with respect to the judges' adherence to the neutral application of law. In all these respects, Tadic's trial and judgment seem, as intended, at least the equal of the Nuremberg trials that inspired them.

* * *

Both proponents and critics of ad hoc international tribunals have it too easy. So far proponents have been content to enumerate objectives for these tribunals largely without acknowledging the tensions among their lofty goals. They have been content to stress the need for international criminal prosecutions only where most practical; that is, where both the U.N. seems inclined to act and alternatives to ad hoc international tribunals seem even more difficult. Proponents have generally assumed that when international tribunals become available, they need to take precedence over alternatives, including prosecutions in national courts. They have mistakenly relied on a model of closure that seeks to replicate the strengths of domestic criminal processes while correcting the flaws of Nuremberg, and have not tried to provide a coherent account of how international prosecutions are supposed to work in unison with other fora, including simultaneous attempts at national prosecutions or truth commissions. In response, critics have needed only to point to how many of Nuremberg's flaws are shared by these tribunals and how little agreement truly exists concerning values that are solemnly touted, but routinely ignored, under international humanitarian law. In short, tribunal advocates have been permitted to postulate mythical criminal processes and opponents have needed only to recycle revisionist critiques of the Nuremberg and Tokyo trials.

It is time to get off the merry-go-round. Both the proponents and critics of international criminal prosecutions need to address seriously the possibility that from Nuremberg to The Hague and Arusha, war crimes prosecutions do not produce closure but, at least when effectively conducted, lead to civil dissensus. This implies that both proponents and opponents of international criminal prosecutions need to address difficult questions, including whether international judges should give priority to the goal of preserving collective memory or whether at least some of the goals we now seek to pursue through international ad hoc tribunals are better accomplished through, for example, national prosecutions, truth commissions, civil suits, or other processes. A frank appraisal of what we can realistically expect international criminal prosecutions to achieve also appears necessary to respond effectively to complaints about financial and other costs. Tadic's trial cost the international community some twenty million dollars. Without knowing whether we ought to be comparing this effort to the astronomical costs of a full-scale military occupation of Bosnia or to the relatively modest costs of organizing a truth commission, it is difficult to say whether such expenditures were worthwhile and ought to continue.

At this juncture, the definitive case for the Yugoslav and Rwanda tribunals—and for international trials elsewhere—remains to be made. It may be that, over time, neither tribunal will successfully promote civil dissensus; if, for example, judgments stifle rather than encourage reasoned debates or if future trials or indictments receive dwindling public notice. It may be that alternative approaches, including truth commissions or adjudications in national courts, might be better at promoting civil dissensus, at least with respect to some issues, especially if the internalization of norms is best pursued through forums with democratic participation and legitimacy and not through authoritarian norms imposed from without. Contrary to what is argued here, some might contend that civil dissensus reflects a misguided or naive trust in the virtues of discourse and is an inappropriate construct except with respect to societies that are already committed to discursive democratic pluralism. Or perhaps we may ultimately decide that the models of closure and civil dissensus need not be seen as wholly incompatible and that aspects of both can be usefully adapted, depending on the circumstances in the societies most directly affected, to promote all or most of the goals we have in mind. It may be that aspects of both visions need to be pursued through a multi-pronged strategy, involving legal and nonlegal fora, that assigns particular goals to the most suitable entity or set of procedures.

The question of how we justify these or other ad hoc criminal tribunals is not purely of academic interest. We have, as yet, no consistent vision of when, if ever, it is appropriate to pursue international criminal trials as opposed to national prosecutions, truth commissions, general amnesties, pardons, or other measures. While some have suggested that international criminal trials must be pursued once offenses in a region cross a certain threshold of gravity, the argument seems to be premised, tenuously, on unexamined assumptions about the superiority of international fora and does not contain reliable criteria for choosing among options. And even if we had such criteria, difficult issues of consistency arise given the distinct audiences to which we seek to appeal. From a victim's perspective, for example, it is not clear why a person who tortures civilian prisoners in the Balkans merits an international criminal trial while someone who does the same in South Africa does not.

Notes and Questions

1. Justice Goldstone argues for the importance of securing justice for victims in countries or regions where there have been egregious human rights violations. How does he interpret justice for victims? Do you find his arguments persuasive?

2. Can you think of any additions to Justice Goldsone's list of positive contributions that justice can bring to the victims of human rights abuses?

3. The author of *Rush to Closure* argues that international tribunals have not been properly assessed by either proponents or critics. What are the

arguments in support of and critical of ad hoc international tribunals? How does the author respond to them?

4.   Evaluate how well the International Tribunal satisfied the demands of closure in the trial of Tadic in terms of:

  a.   Preserving a collective memory and an accurate historical account

  b.   Creating a neutral apolitical environment

  c.   Mollifying victims

  d.   Respecting the rights of defendants

  e.   Restoring order in civil society

  f.   Achieving reconciliation

3.   RESTORATIVE JUSTICE APPROACHES: TRUTH COMMISSIONS

Restorative justice approaches reject retribution and emphasize the importance of healing between victims, offenders, and the community.[33] Its goals are to restore human dignity to victims, hold perpetrators accountable for their crimes, and create new social infrastructures that honor human rights.[34] In reflecting on restorative justice, Professor Martha Minnow speaks of a "repair of social connections and peace rather than retribution against the offenders."[35]

Since the mid–1980s, there has been an expansive growth of truth commissions,[36] *ad hoc* institutions that deal with gross human rights abuses committed by prior governments during a period of violent conflict. They can be an important vehicle for developing accountability for violations of international and domestic law. Truth Commissions also help individuals to come to terms with the reality of what happened during the conflict.[37] Consider the reflections of an international lawyer from Belgrade on the atrocities committed in the former Yugoslavia:

> For many years now I have hardly spoken to one of my uncles. We parted ways after a series of heated discussions on the causes and course of the tragedy that was, at the time, unfolding in the former Yugoslavia. No amount of facts could convince him: he simply denied any Serbian responsibility for the bloodshed and de-

33.   Carrie J. Niebur Eisnaugle, *An International "Truth Commission": Utilizing Restorative Justice as an Alternative to Retribution*, 36 VAND. J. TRANSNAT'L L. 209 (2003).

34.   Elizabeth Kiss, *Moral Ambition Within and Beyond Political Constraints: Reflections on Restorative Justice, in* TRUTH v. JUSTICE 68, 79 (2000).

35.   MARTHA MINOW, BETWEEN VENGEANCE AND FOREGIVENESS: FACING HISTORY AFTER GENOCICDE AND MASS VIOLENCE 92 (1998).

36.   Jennifer J. Llewellyn & Robert Howse, *Institutions for Restorative Justice: The South African Truth and Reconciliation Commission*, 49 U. TORONTO L.J. 355, 372 (1999).

37.   *See* Audrey R. Chapman, *Truth Commissions as Instruments of Forgiveness and Reconciliation, in* FORGIVENESS AND RECONCILIATION: RELIGION, PUBLIC POLICY AND CONFLICT TRANSFORMATION 247–67 (Raymond G. Helmick, S.J. & Rodney L. Petersen eds., 2001).

struction visited by Serbian or Serbian-sponsored forces outside their borders and refused to believe that crimes were being committed. When I asked him once to pick up an opposition newspaper as proof of my arguments, he waved me down saying he did not need to read "Western propaganda." Time and again in our discussions I felt I was hitting a brick wall. When, several months ago, I learned that Yugoslav President Vojislav Kostunica had established a Yugoslav Truth and Reconciliation Commission ("Commission"), my uncle immediately came to mind. Finally, I thought, he will have to hear what really happened. Finally, he will have to come to terms with the magnitude of the atrocities committed in "his" name and will have to share the shame that I, and others like myself, have been living with.[38]

The following article describes the goals and characteristics of truth commissions as well as the critiques.

JASON S. ABRAMS & PRISCILLA HAYNER, DOCUMENTING, ACKNOWLEDGING AND PUBLICIZING THE TRUTH

in POST-CONFLICT JUSTICE 283 (M. Cherif Bassiouni ed., 2002).

Introduction

Although they are not yet as developed as international legal obligations concerning the prosecution of serious human rights abuses, emerging principles of international law have recognized a right of victims and their families to be apprised of the truth concerning human rights abuses and a corresponding duty upon States to investigate and disseminate the truth. These principles proceed from the dual notions that the truth is essential both to respecting and restoring the individual victim's human dignity and to the community's collective interest in understanding its history so that it may achieve reconciliation and prevent recurrence of the abuses.

Certainly, trials of offenders, whether before a national or international tribunal, can make an important contribution to ascertaining and disseminating the truth concerning an episode of human right violations. However, the 1980s and 1990s have seen the development of a novel mechanism for pursuing accountability and reconciliation, one that has evolved primarily with the goal of investigating and revealing the truth in mind—the truth commission. Referred to by a variety of names, such as investigatory commissions or commissions of inquiry, these are official or quasi-official bodies set up, usually for a limited period of time, to

---

38. Jelena Pejic, *The Yugoslav Truth and Reconciliation Commission: A Shaky Start*, 25 FORDHAM INTL L.J. 1 (2001).

investigate a period of human rights abuses and to report publicly on their findings. While commissions have been established in a wide variety of countries, they have been particularly popular in Latin America. The most widely known are those which operated in Chile, Argentina, El Salvador, and South Africa.

Characteristics

In contrast to criminal trials, where a fairly developed corpus of international law and practice has established certain minimum structural and procedural attributes, established international principles for truth commissions do not exist. While this lack of binding international standards can complicate the establishment and operation of commissions, it also offers flexibility that constitutes one of the most important advantages of this approach to accountability and reconciliation.

Despite the lack of international standards, virtually all truth commissions have shared certain general characteristics. First, they examine a record of abuses over a period of time in the past. While their task is not to focus on individual cases, they will frequently examine certain representative cases as illustrative of larger patterns. Truth commissions operate temporarily, with their work generally concluding with the submission of a report. Finally, they are officially sanctioned, usually by government, though sometimes by opposition elements or international organizations as well. This official sanction imparts authority to the commission that is crucial to its ability to carry out its work and to the efficacy of the findings and recommendations it issues.

Apart from the common elements noted above, commissions have varied widely in their structure, mandate, and procedures. The historical, political, cultural, and security context in which a commission operates plays a central role in determining these and other attributes of the commission.

Sponsorship and Composition

Although most commissions have been established by the executive branch of national governments, legislatures, inter-governmental organizations, and non-governmental organizations have also set up commissions. International sponsorship can be crucial to promoting the impartiality and credibility of a commission, particularly where a society is too polarized or traumatized by a period of abuses for a commission to emerge from domestic processes. Such was the case in El Salvador, where the UN-sponsored that country's well-regarded truth commission. However, in cases where domestic forces regard foreign involvement with suspicion or where an international organization or the international community as a whole has become associated with one side of a conflict, international sponsorship may be infeasible. Where a non-governmental organization sponsors a commission, some form of sanction by governmental authorities may be desirable to impart greater legitimacy and authority to the commission.

The success of a commission will inevitably hinge in part on the credibility and competence of the commission's members. The head of the commission must be a capable and strong administrator, able to lead, raise funds where necessary, and withstand intense public and political pressure. Commissioners must be perceived as independent and of high moral caliber, and, in some cases, this may require that commissioners be drawn from a wide variety of societal groups. Failure to abide by this principle can destroy the authority of a commission's work and even cause it to become yet another front on which the conflict underlying the abuses to be examined is fought, perhaps thereby exacerbating that conflict rather than helping the society move beyond it. Participation by a cross-section of the society in the selection of commissioners, as took place in South Africa, can help contribute to the goal of a credible commission.

The nationality of the commissioners will sometimes be a key issue, as well. The nature of the abuses being examined and the political and security situation in the country will determine the appropriate nationality of the commissioners. In some cases, foreign participation may be necessary to instill confidence in witnesses, provide useful expertise or perspectives and impart impartiality and credibility to the commission's work. Experience has also shown that the security situation in some countries may be so tense that domestic commissioners would face threats and reprisals, making their work difficult, if not impossible. For several of these reasons, the staffing of El Salvador's commission, for example, was exclusively foreign. On the other hand, domestic participation may be useful in offering the commission a better understanding of conditions in the country, and the continued presence of commissioners in the country after the commission has completed its work can provide useful follow-up attention and advocacy to promote implementation of the commission's work.

The composition of the commission's staff will depend on the commission's mandate and the circumstances under which it operates. A commission will almost inevitably require lawyers, human rights specialists, and investigators on its staff. In addition, the commission's tasks and conditions in the country may necessitate inclusion of forensic experts, therapists, social workers, historians, and security personnel.

Mandate and Activities

At the time of a commission's establishment, the sponsoring entity provides it with a mandate usually setting forth its goals, powers, and procedures. The types of abuses commissions are usually mandated to investigate have included political killings, torture, disappearances, and other serious acts of violence. In some cases, for example, Uruguay and Chile, mandates have limited commissions to examining only a certain segment of the abuses endured by the country. Political and resource constraints may also limit the scope of a commission's activities. Thus, while the Chilean and Argentine panels were able to examine a relatively large portion of the total number of cases falling under their mandates,

El Salvador's commission examined only a small portion of the total cases. Although most panels have examined only abuses committed by governmental officials, in light of international law's increasing focus on non-state actors and the interest in ensuring that the commission's inquiry is balanced and comprehensive, commissions may be advised to include an examination of serious abuses by opposition groups in their mandates as well.

In most cases, the goals of achieving justice and reconciliation militate in favor of providing commissions with the necessary mandate and resources to examine as wide a variety of serious abuses as possible. At the same time, however, advocates of truth commissions must recognize that it is unrealistic to expect a commission, with its limited resources and duration, to investigate every single atrocity that may have occurred. Rather, the commission's primary goal should be to convey an overall picture of the abuses inflicted on the society, and a form of selective truth will thus usually be the proper approach. Under this approach, the commission examines in depth the most important or representative cases and addressed the bulk of the incidents more generally by outlining patterns of abuse.

Most commission reports have included recommendations for reforms and other measures aimed at remedying past abuses and preventing their repetition. These have included recommendations for legal, judicial, and other institutional reforms, as well as for compensation and rehabilitation of victims and their families. However, the disappointing record of implementation in many countries suggests the need to devote greater attention to inducements and incentives to encourage implementation of recommendations.

Among the more sensitive issues that have confronted commissions is the question of whether to identify the perpetrators of the abuses examined by the commission. Commission mandates have usually not addressed this issue, and only recently have commissions begun to name perpetrators. Although commission reports which do not identify perpetrators have shown that they can still play a useful and potent role, identifying perpetrators seems appropriate to the accountability goals of a commission, especially where no judicial mechanism is available to prosecute offenders. Moreover, identification in a commission report does not itself result in a, loss of liberty. At the same time, due process concerns are clearly implicated, insofar as naming offenders may expose individuals to public condemnation, perception of guilt, and possible security risks. Accordingly, where a commission will name perpetrators, appropriate due process protections should be incorporated into the commission's procedures, including affording targets of the commission's inquiries an opportunity to respond to the allegations made against them.

Relationship to Judicial Proceedings

Although commissions have sometimes operated as the sole mechanism for pursuing accountability, they ideally operate as a supplement or precursor to judicial proceedings. Thus, for example, the Argentine, Chilean, and Ugandan commissions all submitted information they had developed to judicial authorities, in some cases allowing authorities to launch prosecutions more quickly and easily. Nevertheless, commission findings have only rarely become the subject of later criminal prosecutions, due to the weakness of the political or judicial system. Indeed, such weakness may have motivated resort to a commission in the first place, out of a recognition that prosecutions would be unlikely. Amnesties, such as those in Chile and El Salvador, have also prevented the work of commissions from leading to prosecutions.

In those cases where judicial proceedings are anticipated either during or after the commission's work, the relationship between the commission's activities and the judicial proceedings assumes critical importance, and the commission must endeavor to ensure that its activities will support the work of the courts and not hinder it. In particular, commissions must be careful to prevent their evidence-gathering activities from tainting evidence on which prosecutors will need to rely.

South Africa's recent commission, which has the power to issue an amnesty for politically-motivated offenses to individuals who acknowledge their offenses, has garnered much international attention for its novel approach to the relationship between the work of the commission and prosecutions. This acknowledgment-for-amnesty scheme offers victims and the country as a whole some closure on the abuses suffered, without a full-fledged trial. South Africa's approach, under which over 7,000 perpetrators submitted applications for amnesty, succeeded in eliciting some dramatic admissions concerning the apartheid regime's abuses, though at the same time ignited a wrenching national debate over whether such confessions are worth the price of impunity for some unbearably awful deeds. On balance, the South African approach appears to have been a success and may offer a useful model for other commissions. Of course, such an amnesty program can only be effective if the country is able and willing to carry out effective prosecutions of those who do not apply for amnesty.

Resources and Duration

A panel's resources are crucial to its effectiveness and credibility. A commission which is not afforded sufficient resources may not only fail to accomplish its mandate, but in dashing expectations, may even exacerbate the underlying conflict. Ideally, full funding for the commission's work should be appropriated at inception. While national governments finance most commissions, many commissions have relied on substantial assistance, both in cash and in kind, from foreign sources, including governments, international organizations, NGOs, foundations, and even private companies. El Salvador's UN-sponsored commission was entirely financed by international sources, a factor that helped to protect the panel's independence and credibility. The South African commission, the largest and best financed commission to date, had a staff of more than 150 and a total budget of approximately $40 million.

Those contemplating the creation of a commission must also bear in mind the enormous logistical preparations required to establish a commission, and a number of commissions have suffered from delays arising from a failure to address such needs early and adequately. These experiences highlight the importance of addressing, at as early a stage as possible, such administrative requirements as office space and equipment, personnel recruitment, and budgeting arrangements.

The duration of a commission should be fixed, as a commission with an unlimited duration runs the risk of losing its focus and is less likely to provide the closure a traumatized society needs. The duration of commission mandates ranges considerably, though in most cases they have operated for less than two years. Duration and quality are not, however, necessarily correlated. The scope of the abuses under examination should largely determine the appropriate duration, though resource constraints may limit a commission's period of operation.

Procedures and Methodologies

A commission's mandate or the panel itself determines the nature of its procedures. The rigor of a commission's methodology is important to its credibility, and, certainly, the greater the potential impact of its work on the rights of suspected perpetrators, the higher the procedural standards required. The extent to which a panel's inquiry resembles judicial proceedings assumes great importance where the commission intends to identify perpetrators. Some commissions have addressed these concerns by adopting quasi-judicial procedures, such as explaining to suspected perpetrators the accusations made against them, according them an opportunity to defend themselves, providing the accused legal representation, and permitting them to question witnesses. Security concerns may force a commission to restrict a suspected perpetrator's access to the identity of witnesses and the suspect's ability to cross-examine them.

As for transparency, closed proceedings may lead to accusations of partiality and abuse, yet public proceedings may pose risks to the security of commissioners and witnesses. In the end, the country's political and security situation will determine the necessary balance between public and non-public proceedings, and past practice has, therefore, varied. While the security situation in El Salvador and other Latin American countries led their commissions to operate relatively confidentially, South Africa's commission held many hearings in public. The closer a commission's work can be brought physically and psychologically to the victims and the public at large, the more potent the commission's cathartic and educational effects will be. In this regard, the South African commission, which received public testimony from over 2,000 witnesses and conducted hearings across the country, was successful in bringing its work close to the people.

A panel's resources and mandate, as well as the political and security conditions in the country, will also dictate its methodologies. Usually, commissions rely on testimony from individuals and information from governmental and non-governmental sources. Often, security conditions will require reliance on confidential information. In such cases the commission must remain especially mindful of the potential threat to due process for the targets of its inquiries and of the need to maintain strict impartiality in order to preserve the commission's credibility. A commission operating while armed conflict is still on-going may face the added obstacle of being unable to obtain full access to parts of the country.

Most commissions have not enjoyed the power to subpoena witnesses or evidence. In a rare and dramatic exception, South Africa's truth commission had search and seizure powers, as well as the authority to compel witnesses to testify. A number of panels, such as El Salvador's and Argentina's, have encountered difficulties in obtaining cooperation from certain elements that felt threatened by their work (usually the armed forces and security services). However, even where a commission enjoys subpoena power, compliance may be a problem. In a defiant challenge to the legitimacy and even-handedness of the South African commission, former President P.W. Botha refused to comply with the commission's order that he testify, forcing recourse to the courts. In some cases, evidence and information will be in the custody of foreign governments or international organizations, in which case the cooperation of such governments and organizations may be crucial.

In cases where fear and suspicion linger and the targets of a commission's inquiries remain in positions of power, such as in El Salvador, a panel may find that even those with the greatest incentive to cooperate—the victims of the abuses and their loved ones—may be reluctant to step forward. In such cases, a commission should have at its disposal the capability to protect witnesses to the extent consistent with the due process rights of suspected perpetrators. Thus, for example, South Africa's commission established a sophisticated witness protection program, including a network of safehouses, to protect witnesses at risk. In light of the special stigma attached to victims of sexual crimes, special procedures to facilitate the reporting and investigation of such offenses may often be necessary.

Reports

The dissemination of commission reports correlates closely with their impact, as wide dissemination allows a larger audience to benefit from the commission's work. In addition, broad and timely distribution indicates that the country's political climate is respectful of the commission and its work, increasing the likelihood that those in positions of power will respect its findings and implement its conclusions. Accordingly, commission reports should be released soon after completion and should be disseminated as broadly as possible and in a manner that will maximize the report's positive impact. Restricting access to the commission's report may inject further suspicion into an already tense post-conflict situation. In an especially potent gesture, the Chilean president presented the report of Chile's panel on national television, publicly apologized to victims ... and sent a copy of the report to each victim's family with a letter indicating on what page information on the victim could be found. In those countries where illiteracy is relatively high and media penetration is limited, special measures should be taken to maximize dissemination of a truth commission's findings.

Assessment and Conclusions

While truth commissions have varied in their success, experience has demonstrated that they can make a significant contribution to accountability, reconciliation, and the transition from an authoritarian past. First, an effective commission can establish an official, authoritative record of abuses in a country, thereby helping to educate the public, strengthen the rule of law, and possibly deter future abuses. Indeed, the notion that an understanding of the past is necessary to prevent its recurrence is, by now, axiomatic. While this role may be most potent and important in societies where official denial was a central aspect of the abuses at issue, this function can still yield benefits where this was not the case by assembling a detailed, comprehensive, and authoritative accounting and by combating attempts at fallacious revisionism. This may explain, at least in part, why commissions have made significant contributions even in cases where the general facts concerning the past were widely known.

Second, by acknowledging the suffering of victims and their families, helping to resolve uncertain cases, and involving ordinary citizens it its work, a commission can contribute to the psychological healing of the victims of human rights abuses and their families. This helps impart to the citizenry a sense of dignity and empowerment that can help them move beyond the pain of the past. The effect will be especially potent if the commission provides a forum where perpetrators actually acknowledge their abuses.

Third, a commission can promote justice by imposing moral condemnation and laying the groundwork for other sanctions, especially if it assigns responsibility for abuses. Fourth, it can demonstrate that human rights are a priority for a successor government, build the legitimacy of national institutions by holding them accountable and outlining needed reforms, and further discredit the perpetrators of abuses. Of course, commissions have sometimes been set up to serve, not as a genuine endeavor to reckon with the past, but rather as a mechanism for whitewashing it is an effort to appease the international community. This phenomenon, exemplified by the 1974 commission set up by Idi Amin in Uganda, must obviously be resisted by international negotiators at all costs. Fifth, while a judicial model is limited to the establishment of guilt or innocence, a truth commission can more readily go beyond such confines to explore the historical and political context of the abuses and make recommendations to deal with past abuses and prevent future ones. Indeed, its most important role may lie these advisory functions.

Although many of the goals described above can be achieved through judicial proceedings, a truth commission is especially suited to achieving them in countries where limited resources, the absence of a strong and impartial legal system, and other circumstances make a judicial approach infeasible. Moreover, while trials can reveal or confirm details about specific cases, they are less able to outline a broader pattern of events over a period of time or to conduct an analysis of institutional responsibility, general practices of the state or rebel elements, or the root causes of a conflict. Trials also tend to examine episodes of human rights abuses more narrowly than do truth commissions, and their adversarial nature often reinforces and perpetuates habits of denial. And, while creating a commission is never a simple endeavor, in most cases a truth commission can be created and carry out its functions relatively quickly and easily compared to the task of building a judicial system where a fair and effective one does not exist.

Nevertheless, like the goal of accountability generally, truth commissions may not be appropriate for every post-conflict situation. There are some societies where cultural outlook, the devastation of war, and political and security instability suggest that even this relatively mild and flexible mechanism for pursuing accountability and reconciliation may be unnecessary or even dangerous. In other cases, societies may need the truth-seeking palliatives of a truth commission, but conditions and institutional capacities may require that this process occur sometime later down the road. Chief among the factors bearing on the propriety of embarking on a truth-seeking endeavor is the degree to which elements of the society are demanding such an enterprise as essential to their sense of justice or as a necessary concession to their willingness to participate peacefully in civil society. These demands will almost inevitably be made well known. Furthermore, where the abuses were, and perhaps continue to be, denied by the perpetrators and official institutions, the need for the truth-seeking benefits of a commission is most profound. Of course, while the victimized society's own priorities and needs must remain paramount, the decision of whether to pursue the truth must also take account of the fact that many of the abuses at issue may constitute offenses in which international law and morality recognize that all humanity has an interest.

Even where a truth commission is an appropriate alternative, one must recognize that such commissions are not a perfect mechanism for pursuing accountability. They do not make a true judicial determination of responsibility and cannot directly punish perpetrators, beyond stigmatizing them or recommending non-criminal measures such as removal from positions in the government or armed forces. Such sanctions seem a paltry substitute for trial punishment where a person is personally responsible for atrocities of the highest magnitude. Moreover, commissions confront an enormously difficult task in developing an accurate and impartial accounting of the past, often in a politically charged environment where access to the facts is not readily available. Indeed, the record of these commissions is mixed, marked by several instances where excessively restricted mandates, political constraints, limited resources, or inadequate access to information prevented a commission from producing a full accounting of the past.

Significantly, the record suggests that commissions—even those operating in the most tense environments—have almost invariably improved, and not worsened, the human rights climate. However, where a society is unable to pursue a genuine process for reconciliation or a commission is not properly designed and administered[,] [t]heir activities may become little more than political fodder for manipulation by competing elements, create unrealistic expectations of further accountability, or, perhaps worst of all, whet a hunger for vengeance and exacerbate a society's already seething divisions. For these reasons, those involved in the process of setting up a commission must carefully examine the political and social context in which the commission would operate and tailor the commission's attributes to that environment. Likewise, the panel itself must manage its activities with the utmost sensitivity to such considerations.

The work of truth commissions is made more difficult by the lack of institutional history and credibility from which well-functioning judicial mechanisms benefit. Although their architects now have a variety of precedents from which to study, commissions remain ad hoc institutions that must build their credibility and modus operandi almost from the ground up and that are likely to be greeted with a combination of hope and distrust. Compounding these challenges, the societies not in need of a truth commission are often the ones least able to provide sufficient resources for it to conduct its work. States emerging from an episode of massive human rights violations may be desperately poor, devastated by violence, and depleted of their most talented and uncorrupted citizens. Such shattered states are unlikely to have the economic or human resources necessary to create a viable commission, making engagement by the international community imperative.

In conclusion, the experience of past truth commission[s] suggest[s] that there are certain factors, many of them inter-related, which contribute significantly to the success of a commission:

(1) The commission must operate in a political atmosphere that is supportive of its work. This suggests the need for the participation of a broad cross-section of political and societal actors in shaping the commission.

(2) The commissioners must be competent, respected, and credible.

(3) The mandate should be strong and flexible.

(4) The commission must enjoy full operational independence in interpreting and carrying out its mandate.

(5) The commission's procedures must be fair and credible. To the extent security and other constraints permit, the commission should consider holding some hearings in public and other measures for encouraging public involvement.

(6) The commission must have access to evidence and witnesses.

(7) The commission must have adequate resources.

(8) The commission should receive support from the international community as necessary.

(9) The commission's report should receive broad and timely dissemination.

[Bracketed material supplied by author.]

Notes and Questions

1. In what cases are truth commissions inappropriate in post-conflict societies?

2. What do you think of truth commissions offering amnesty? Can there ever be justice for the victims when the perpetrators receive amnesty after their infliction of cruelty? Why would victims view a process that offers amnesty as legitimate? Are there some cases where truth commissions should never offer amnesty?

3. Does offering amnesty hinder the ability of a community to move forward into a post conflict society?

4. What is the meaning of justice and what purpose does it serve in post-conflict societies that are moving from repressive regimes to some form of democratic rule? To what extent is there a connection between peace and justice? Give examples.

5. Is public exposure of the truth the only effective way to insure that history is recorded faithfully? In addition to truth commissions and tribunals, what other models might be constructed as part of the post-conflict justice project?

4. TENSIONS BETWEEN HUMAN RIGHTS AND MEDIATION APPROACHES

Scholars differ on the relative merits of mediative and human rights approaches to resolving contemporary conflicts. Whether these approaches are compatible or even complementary responses to conflict is a matter of debate.

Writing in the context of parade disputes in Northern Ireland, Professor Dominic Bryan equates group rights with human rights approaches and suggests some weaknesses in the human rights approach.

DOMINIC BRYAN, PARADING PROTESTANTS AND CONSENTING CATHOLICS IN NORTHERN IRELAND: COMMUNAL CONFLICT, CONTESTED PUBLIC SPACE, AND GROUP RIGHTS

5 Chicago Journal of International Law 233 (2004).

* * *

Returning to the original communal problem: do [these] human rights approaches offer us any likely resolution over the conflict between the rights of Protestant Orangemen to follow their "traditional" route and the rights of Catholic, Nationalist residents who feel threatened by what they argue is the intolerance and bigotry of the Orangemen? The answer seems to be that it does not. By the Northern Ireland Human Rights Commission's own argument, we are not dealing with minorities but rather with communities. And whilst Northern Ireland is certainly dealing with the legacy of discrimination and well-entrenched sectarianism, the relationships of power between local communities all over Northern Ireland vary widely. Management of this area of communal conflict will not be found using group rights. The evidence also suggests that whilst human rights approaches are important in managing conflict, their utility is often limited.

Looking at the parades disputes, what human rights approaches have been good at is holding the state accountable for the activities of the police and of its commissions and officials. In no small part thanks to human rights NGOs such as the CAJ, who had legal observers at Drumcree and other disputes, the RUC (now the PSNI) have improved their policing in a number of significant ways, such as in the use of force and the display of identifying numbers on vehicles and police officers. Equally, the Parades Commission has couched its determinations with at least some thought to the language of rights. But human rights instruments are not nearly so effective in providing guidance for inter-communal disputes. They can provide a basis upon which the representatives of the state can behave, but they do not solve the communal conflict itself. Whatever views one might have of the attempts by the UK government to deal with parade disputes, it is unlikely that courts in Europe or in the UK would strike down the broad approach.

* * *

There is a growing body of literature that looks at the tension between meditative approaches to conflict management and human rights approaches. Few people would deny the necessity of both but their relationship can be difficult. The conflict in Northern Ireland takes place within a number of spheres, ranging from a fundamental dispute between states and peoples over the political status of six counties to antagonisms born out of cultural identity politics, to religious and political differences as well as challenges to the sense of localized territory. What has been called the peace process has, in actuality, been an attempt to manage the conflict with a desire to overcome political differences and create a new political entity. This paper has attempted to explore the way in which human rights have been used as part of that process of conflict management surrounding disputes over parades.

The disputes over parades encapsulate many of the elements of the wider cultural conflict. It has demanded a military response to deal with a developing conflict. It has required reform of the state institutions and the development of new institutions better in a position to manage the conflict. And it has demanded that basic fundamental rights are made explicit and protected by the state. Up to this point, some regulation of the conflict has taken place. But so far it is similar to the building of peace walls around Belfast in that it is simply managing difference, not overcoming the divisions that underlie the conflict. That can only be done through the creation of social bonds that create interdependence between the communities. The notions of basic human rights may provide a basis for that society, but if they are to provide more than that, a much more sophisticated notion of the relationship between human rights and peace building is demanded.

There seem to me to be aspects of conflict that rights approaches deal with well, and aspects of conflict that need to be managed in other ways. Bell has shown the use and limitations of international human rights instruments through a range of recent peace agreements. Human rights approaches are good at dealing with the state but they have been less successful at providing ways of managing conflicting communities or giving clear guidance on the regulation of disputes between groups. So, for instance, in the parades disputes they have offered guidance on policing but less so on making determinations. Group rights may have some utility in protecting small minorities, but in contemporary Northern Ireland they simply provide competing groups with more weapons with which to fight one another. What we need to do is lower our expectations of the utility of human rights approaches, both individualistic approaches and those protecting groups. They may only provide broad parameters for managing and resolving the conflict. Indeed, we need to be aware that whilst legislation protecting minorities is vital in all societies, the enshrining of group rights in certain circumstances will provide another avenue for ethnic entrepreneurs and communal struggles to replicate.

In the following article, the authors discuss the core principles, goals and values of human rights practitioners that distinguish them from conflict resolution practitioners. As you read through this material, consider the extent to which human rights and conflict resolution practitioners share similar values.

ELLEN L. LUTZ, EILEEN F. BABBITT & HURST HANNUM, HUMAN RIGHTS AND CONFLICT RESOLUTION FROM THE PRACTITIONER'S PERSPECTIVE

27 Fletcher Forum of World Affairs 173 (2003).

* * *

When responding to conflict, human rights advocates and conflict resolvers share similar goals. In the short run, both sets of practitioners seek to end violence, limit loss of life, and minimize other suffering as quickly as possible. In the long run, both sets of practitioners try to assist societies in taking steps to ensure that the violence does not recur and that the rights of every human being are respected. However, to achieve these goals, each set of practitioners uses different methods based on different underlying assumptions. As a result, both groups occasionally adopt contradictory or even mutually exclusive approaches to the same problem. For example, conflict resolvers, eager to achieve a negotiated settlement to a conflict with minimum loss of life, may fail to give sufficient weight to the relevance of human rights to the long-term success of their work. Human rights advocates, on the other hand, may undervalue the pressures under which mediators operate to bring about an immediate end to loss of life. If they limit their activities to shaming, negative publicity, and judicial condemnation of criminals, human rights activists may miss opportunities for improvements in the human rights situation that could be achieved through the use of the negotiation and diplomatic techniques upon which conflict resolvers rely.

Preventing wars and massive human rights violations, and rebuilding societies in their aftermath, requires an approach that incorporates the perspectives of both human rights advocates and conflict resolution practitioners. This is easier to assert than to achieve. These two groups make different assumptions, apply different methodologies, and have different goals, values, and institutional constraints. As a result, they tend to be wary of one another. In the words of Barbara Frey, former executive director of the Minnesota Advocates for Human Rights:

> In general, human rights people and conflict resolution people don't speak the same language. They come from different backgrounds and there is a lot of suspicion between them. Human rights people are judgmental and tend to come from a legal background, whereas conflict resolution people are more interested in stopping hot conflict and are willing to rub hands with bad actors.

* * *

Human Rights

Modern international human rights advocacy is founded on international human rights norms that are embedded in international law, widely ratified by states and incorporated into domestic law (if not practice), and embraced by people of all cultures and all walks of life. International momentum to establish a legal order that would prohibit state-sponsored human rights abuses surged during World War II, as the scope of Nazi atrocities became known. The UN Charter, adopted in 1945, declares that the highest purposes of the organization are "to save succeeding generations from the scourge of war . . . , to reaffirm faith in fundamental human rights . . . , to establish conditions under which justice and respect for . . . international law can be maintained, . . . and to promote social progress and better standards of life in larger freedom."

Three years after the organization's founding, the UN General Assembly adopted the Universal Declaration of Human Rights (UDHR) to explicate the human rights expressed in the Charter. The UDHR's preamble declares that human rights are the foundation of freedom, justice, and peace. Its opening articles provide that every individual is entitled to all the rights and freedoms set forth without distinction with respect to race, color, sex, language, religion, political or other opinion, national or social origin, property, birth, or other status. It then enumerates a list of fundamental rights to security of the person, equality before the law, nationality, the means to escape from state abuse, political rights, and the rights to food, health care, education, work, family, ownership of property, and participation in cultural life.

Since 1948, intergovernmental organizations have codified most of the norms in the UDHR in international treaties, including two by the UN General Assembly itself: the International Covenant on Civil and Political Rights and the International Covenant on Economic, Social, and Cultural Rights. These two fundamental treaties have been ratified by over 140 states.

While reaching agreement on international human rights law was not easy, enforcement has proven even more problematic. It is one thing for a state to pledge to uphold human rights and another for it to tolerate policing of its compliance. Effective formal international enforcement mechanisms have been nonexistent for much of the last half of the twentieth century.

Partially in response to this enforcement vacuum, international human rights advocates, many of them lawyers, formed organizations to promote human rights and developed an array of strategies for pressuring governments to conform their behavior to international human rights law. International human rights investigators seek out the facts wherever rights abuses are alleged and publish their findings, whether countries are at war, suffering from varying degrees of political tension and/or repression, or are peaceful and generally rights-respecting. International human rights organizations hope that their reports will bring about a change in the behavior of the government or other entity whose abuses they spotlight, but their principal targets are the policy makers who are in a position to put pressure on rights violators.

International human rights NGOs see themselves as advocates for victims and supportive partners of their domestic human rights NGO counterparts. International human rights organizations lobby other governments to take human rights into account in their foreign aid appropriations and press the UN and other intergovernmental organizations to put pressure on rights abusers. In addition, they demand that governments establish domestic enforcement mechanisms, such as independent judiciaries. To ensure accountability when national courts do not exist or cannot act, international human rights NGOs support institutions like the recently formed International Criminal Court.

International human rights NGOs try to adapt their advocacy to ensure that it has the greatest possible impact. For example, organizations such as Human Rights Watch (HRW) devoted minimal resources to lobbying the United Nations during the Cold War, when the UN Security Council was frequently deadlocked and other human rights mechanisms were used by states primarily as platforms to express purely political views. Following the collapse of the Berlin Wall, the United Nations has become more creative and interventionist in seeking solutions to human rights problems, and has thus become a higher priority in HRW's advocacy.

In the 1980s, international human rights NGOs realized that international human rights law was inadequate to address conflict-related crimes, and they began to rely more heavily on international humanitarian law. This body of law, which predates international human rights law, was crafted to regulate conduct in armed conflict. It includes the four Geneva Conventions of 1949 and numerous other widely ratified international treaties, many of which contain provisions regarding the treatment of civilians and others not actively participating in the conflict. International humanitarian law also encompasses legal norms against genocide and crimes against humanity.

Domestic human rights NGO activists operate in a different milieu. They serve as the consciences of their societies and speak out to press their governments to protect the human rights of their citizens. In repressive societies or those seized by conflict, domestic human rights groups are invariably squeezed into a narrow operating space or are shut down by those in power. Any activities they do carry out, such as collecting information about ongoing abuses and passing it on to their international counterparts or aiding displaced persons, are undertaken at great personal risk.

Post-conflict societies often turn to human rights experts as advisors during peace-building. Survivors of human rights abuses trust them and seek them out as their advocates. Truth commissions and courts look to them as accurate sources of information about what occurred and as trusted go-betweens to victims whose trauma or other circumstances impede them from coming forward on their own. Sometimes, when democratic governments are in place, leading figures in the domestic human rights movement are called upon to take an unaccustomed governing role.

Conflict Resolution

International conflict resolvers come from a multiplicity of fields. They are scholars and practitioners from many of the social sciences (e.g., psychology, sociology, political science), law, public policy, and even the health sciences. Unlike human rights, there is no codified set of norms that govern the field and bind conflict resolution practitioners together. However, there is an implicit set of principles that frame their practice.

The first principle is participation. The most effective negotiation and decision-making processes are those in which the parties who have direct stakes in the outcome are actively engaged. The most basic goal of conflict resolution is to bring stakeholders into some kind of ad hoc or institutionalized forum and assure them of an opportunity for meaningful input.

The second principle is inclusion. This differs from participation in that it addresses not the manner of participating, but who participates. In the conflict resolution field, the preferred approach is to include as many stakeholders as possible, even those that might be potentially disruptive, on the grounds that those left on the sidelines will have a greater incentive to undermine any agreement that is reached.

The third principle is empowerment. The effectiveness of multi-party dialogue can be compromised by one or more parties' lack of experience, lack of resources, or both. To help balance the sides, conflict resolvers may incorporate teaching, training, and coaching into the process to maximize the effectiveness of all of the parties and provide a stronger basis on which genuine negotiations can proceed.

The fourth principle is cultural sensitivity. Most cultures have existing methods for handling conflict. Culturally familiar and appropriate practices and solutions will be sustainable long after an outside intervener has departed. Thus, it is very important to know what those practices are and, insofar as possible, to build upon and enhance indigenous methods.

The fifth principle is equity. Equity, as opposed to equality, is the notion that a mediator should treat all parties at the table with equal respect, giving each equal time and attention, even though there are differences in power. This respect and acknowledgment contribute to making the forum more suitable to constructive discussion and problem-solving.

Conflict resolvers operate on multiple levels: Track 1, Track 1½, and Track 2. At the Track 1½ level, official interveners representing a government or intergovernmental body such as the United Nations work with designated representatives or decision-makers of the parties to a conflict to assist them in reaching a resolution. Sometimes these interveners are neutral facilitators, but often they use the influence or power vested in them by the government or organization they represent to press the parties to reach agreement.

At the Track 1 level, non-official interveners such as NGOs, religious leaders, scholars, or internationally respected political figures meet together with, or shuttle between, official representatives of parties to a conflict to find a solution. While Track 1½ interveners may have little to offer in the way of incentives or sanctions to compel the parties to reach agreement, their personal qualities, mediation skills, or reputations for neutrality and high ethical standards may be enough to move the parties towards a peaceful resolution.

At the Track 2 level, non-official interveners facilitate dialogue among non-official but influential members of each of the communities that are in conflict. The theory behind Track 2 processes is that influential individuals, operating in an unofficial capacity, have fewer constraints than their official counterparts to engage in dialogue with their opponents and explore creative ideas for conflict resolution or transformation. At the same time, because Track 2 participants are influential, they have the ear of decision makers or may themselves someday serve in official decision-making positions.

International conflict resolution NGOs have emerged over the past two decades to complement the work of Track 1 governmental or intergovernmental interveners. These groups have developed a well-stocked toolbox of techniques that they adapt to the phase of conflict, the cultural and political context, and the role the conflict resolver is invited to play. International conflict resolution NGOs are involved in many traditional conflict resolution activities such as shuttle diplomacy, back channel negotiations between disputing parties, and Track 2–type dialogue activities among key actors. Many also engage in a variety of educational activities, including teaching conflict resolution skills and providing capacity building and conflict resolution training to disputants and other stakeholders.

Some international conflict resolution NGOs work independently, while others prefer to collaborate with other types of international NGOs or intergovernmental organizations, or with domestic conflict resolution NGOs that better understand the cultural nuances that need to be incorporated into an effective process. However, because the conflict resolution field is so young, there is often no established domestic NGO with which international NGOs can collaborate. In such circumstances, international NGOs sometimes turn their attention to developing post-conflict domestic NGO capacity. In doing so, they may encounter obstacles such as lack of training and education, inefficiency, bureaucracy, and corruption. These obstacles mirror the larger problems the post-conflict society faces in developing a strong and healthy civil society.

* * *

Protection vs. Assistance

During armed conflict, human rights NGOs use their fact-finding and advocacy skills to protect the lives and other rights of civilians. By contrast, conflict resolution NGOs assist key stakeholders to engage in a process directed at ending the violence. These differences can create tensions between practitioners in the two fields. For example, one concern when sensitive conflict resolution initiatives are contemplated or ongoing is the impact human rights reports have on efforts to bring parties to or keep them at the negotiating table. Human Rights Watch researcher Jemera Rone recalled, "I worked on a report on the FMLN's abductions and killings [in EI Salvador], and I released it at the moment they were going into negotiations; they accused me of being biased and trying to harm their cause. The truth is I wasn't even aware they were going into negotiations." According to Rone, the release date was chosen with only internal HRW editing and publication concerns in mind. Alvaro de Soto, the UN mediator in EI Salvador, admitted that while at first human rights reports like the one written by Rone were a hindrance, he later developed channels that enabled him to anticipate and use the pending release of such reports to urge the parties toward an accord that included significant human rights protections.

Even where peace negotiations are not in progress, human rights reporting can have unintended effects. Human rights reports may be used by one side of the conflict or the other to promote support for their position. Conversely, accusations of abuses are likely to provoke anger or hostility in those against whom they are directed. For example, Sarah Broughton, deputy director of Search for Common Ground in Macedonia, asserts that international human rights reports, while "morally necessary, . . . have in some ways negatively impacted the situation in Macedonia. Reporting of human rights abuses by the security forces inflames emotions in the Albanian community, while reports of abuses by the NLA (the Albanian fighters) have the same effect on Macedonians."

These are risks that international human rights groups are aware of and seek to minimize by maintaining a reputation for accuracy, even-handed reporting, and measuring abuses against widely accepted international legal norms. In their view, disseminating accurate reports so that influential external actors know what is happening and can take steps to lessen the suffering of innocent civilians outweighs the danger that the parties to the conflict will use the reports for propaganda purposes. Conflict resolvers, who are trying to persuade the parties to come to the table, may be frustrated when human rights reporting seems to contribute to the parties' unwillingness to engage in dialogue or hardens their demands once negotiations begin.

To reduce this tension, practitioners in both fields need to follow the lead of Ambassador de Soto and his human rights counterparts in EI Salvador. With greater communication about what each is doing or planning to do, and about what challenges each faces, human rights advocates and mediators not only can do their own jobs but can also enhance the work of the other.

Neutrality with Respect to Human Rights vs. Expressing Human Rights Values

Although not direct participants in conflicts, human rights NGOs see themselves and are seen by conflict resolvers as "parties," in that during conflict they adopt an explicit stance against human rights abuses and war crimes. Conflict resolvers often keep their distance from human rights practitioners during conflicts, because they want to be able to talk with everyone involved in the conflict. They are concerned that, if they associate with human rights advocates, their neutrality will be compromised.

This does not mean that international conflict resolvers are neutral about human rights. While most take the view that reaching an agreement that stops violence is the first priority, many also question whether it is acceptable to focus only on achieving a settlement when massive human rights abuses are occurring. The latter group would support raising human rights issues with the participants during the negotiation process and making explicit the belief that sustainable peace and the protection of human rights are intertwined. Some conflict resolution NGOs include human rights training in their post-conflict education or institution-building activities. For example, International Alert was founded on the premise that human rights abuses often stem from violent conflict, and it thus believes that concern with human rights must be part of any resolution of such conflicts. Another group, the South African-based Center for Conflict Resolution, has evolved into an educational organization that teaches both human rights norms and conflict resolution techniques to local NGOs in Africa.

In recent years, the United Nations also has moved towards a rights-oriented approach to its conflict resolution activities. The Brahimi Commission Report, for example, asserts: Impartiality for United Nations operations must mean adherence to the principles of the Charter: where one party to a peace agreement clearly and incontrovertibly is violating its terms, continued equal treatment of all parties by the United Nations can in the best case result in ineffectiveness and in the worst may amount to complicity with evil.

In April 2001, UN Secretary–General Kofi Annan took a major step toward clarifying the non-severability of human rights in UN efforts to broker peace negotiations. In a report submitted to the Security Council on the Protection of Civilians in Armed Conflict, Secretary–General Annan drew attention to the near debacle of the UN endorsing amnesty for crimes against humanity committed in the conflict in Sierra Leone. He declared, "The use of amnesties to provide impunity to those who committed serious violations of international humanitarian and criminal law, including genocide, crimes against humanity, war crimes and torture, is not acceptable." In his recommendations, he urged the "Security Council, Member States, and other actors involved in peace mediation to respect the prohibition of amnesty for genocide, crimes against humanity and war crimes during their negotiations and deliberations."

Researchers and practitioners seeking to understand and strengthen the capacity of human rights advocates and conflict resolvers to achieve their goals cannot avoid the ethical issues raised by the tension between neutrality and advocacy of human rights values. Research and reflection are needed on questions such as: Are there some issues that should never be open to negotiation? Are there circumstances under which attention to accountability can be momentarily suspended to allow peace efforts to proceed? What should be the role of conflict resolution in circumstances where one party to a conflict is responsible for genocide?

Justice vs. Reconciliation

The greatest tension in the two fields lies between human rights advocates' post-conflict focus on justice for past crimes and conflict resolvers' post-conflict desire to promote reconciliation, or at least peaceful coexistence, among previously warring parties. Sometimes the tension is so pointed that it is manipulated by the parties to the conflict in a way that undermines the post-settlement aims of both fields.

According to Hizkeas Assifa of the Nairobi Peace Initiative, issues of justice and reconciliation in Rwanda became polarized as a result of ethnic group distortion of NGO priorities. Because the primary victims of the genocide were Tutsi, justice came to be viewed as a "Tutsi issue." Hutus found they had more in common with international NGOs working on conflict resolution concerns, since these groups were prone to emphasize reconciliation or coexistence. This resulted in the Hutus becoming identified with the latter issue. Similarly, Ndubisi Obiorah, senior legal officer with the Human Rights Law Service in Nigeria, reported that the conflict resolver in Nigeria "tends to think that the human rights community's 'no peace without justice' sloganeering just messes things up ... The conflict resolution community appears to approach questions of impunity for human rights violations from the standpoint that dealing with 'the bad guys' is critical to resolving conflicts."

While both sides are convinced that their focus is the right one, almost no interdisciplinary research has been done on the impact of justice or reconciliation efforts on the shared long-term goal of building a peace-sustaining and rights-respecting society. More research is needed on what contributions to peace-building have been made by truth commissions, trials, and other domestic processes aimed at coming to terms with past abuses; whether such processes adequately address the grievances of those who suffered severe human rights violations under previous regimes; whether they strengthen civil society and encourage democratic participation; whether they help to inoculate a country against future experiences with rights-violating governments or factions; and whether they contribute to reconciliation and trust-building between previously warring groups.

A more forward-looking agenda that addresses the full range of post-settlement societal needs (including political restructuring, economic development, institution-building, physical reconstruction, education and health care, as well as truth, justice, and reconciliation) can enable both human rights and conflict resolution professionals to contribute synergistically to the nation-building process. At the same time, the adoption of a shared forward-looking approach diminishes the potential for either field to become identified with an issue that gives succor to only one party to the conflict, and, as a consequence, reduces the possibility of feeding into societal divisions that could flair into violence.

Notes and Questions

1. Within the context of Northern Ireland, what are some of the weakness of human rights approaches to resolving conflict in that country?

2. Can you think of any current conflicts where human rights approaches to conflict resolution would be helpful?

3. How does Professor Dominic Bryan suggest that the underlying divisions in the Northern Ireland conflict be overcome?

4. Discus the recurring areas of tension in both fields. Do the remedies suggested by Lutz, Babbitt, and Hannum to relieve these strains hold any reasonable hope?

5. How might Lutz, Babbitt, and Hannum respond to Professor Dominic Bryan's skepticism about the utility of human rights approaches with respect to group rights?

6. How can NGOs dealing with human rights violations in post-conflict societies avoid the perception that they are partisan advocates? Include in your discussion the relevance of Edward Luttwak's critique of NGOs.

7. If the new International Criminal Court commenced a proceeding regarding a complaint of genocide, might the proceeding impede the ongoing work of mediators and negotiators who are trying to stop the genocide?

*

Appendix 1

CONVENTION ON THE RECOGNITION AND ENFORCEMENT OF FOREIGN ARBITRAL AWARDS

[The New York Convention]

June, 1958

Article I

1. This Convention shall apply to the recognition and enforcement of arbitral awards made in the territory of a State other than the State where the recognition and enforcement of such awards are sought, and arising out of differences between persons, whether physical or legal. It shall also apply to arbitral awards not considered as domestic awards in the State where their recognition and enforcement are sought.

2. The term "arbitral awards" shall include not only awards made by arbitrators appointed for each case but also those made by permanent arbitral bodies to which the parties have submitted.

3. When signing, ratifying or acceding to this Convention, or notifying extension under article X hereof, any State may on the basis of reciprocity declare that it will apply the Convention to the recognition and enforcement of awards made only in the territory of another Contracting State. It may also declare that it will apply the Convention only to differences arising out of legal relationships, whether contractual or not, which are considered as commercial under the national law of the State making such declaration.

Article II

1. Each Contracting State shall recognize an agreement in writing under which the parties undertake to submit to arbitration all or any differences which have arisen or which may arise between them in respect of a defined legal relationship, whether contractual or not, concerning a subject matter capable of settlement by arbitration.

2. The term "agreement in writing" shall include an arbitral clause in a contract or an arbitration agreement, signed by the parties or contained in an exchange of letters or telegrams.

3. The court of a Contracting State, when seized of an action in a matter in respect of which the parties have made an agreement within the meaning of this article, shall, at the request of one of the parties, refer the parties to arbitration, unless it finds that the said agreement is null and void, inoperative or incapable of being performed.

Article III

Each Contracting State shall recognize arbitral awards as binding and enforce them in accordance with the rules of procedure of the territory where the award is relied upon, under the conditions laid down in the following articles. There shall not be imposed substantially more onerous conditions or higher fees or charges on the recognition or enforcement of arbitral awards to which this Convention applies than are imposed on the recognition or enforcement of domestic arbitral awards.

Article IV

1. To obtain the recognition and enforcement mentioned in the preceding article, the party applying for recognition and enforcement shall, at the time of the application, supply:

    (a) The duly authenticated original award or a duly certified copy thereof;

    (b) The original agreement referred to in article II or a duly certified copy thereof.

2. If the said award or agreement is not made in an official language of the country in which the award is relied upon, the party applying for recognition and enforcement of the award shall produce a translation of these documents into such language. The translation shall be certified by an official or sworn translator or by a diplomatic or consular agent.

Article V

1. Recognition and enforcement of the award may be refused, at the request of the party against whom it is invoked, only if that party furnishes to the competent authority where the recognition and enforcement is sought, proof that:

    (a) The parties to the agreement referred to in article II were, under the law applicable to them, under some incapacity, or the said agreement is not valid under the law to which the parties have subjected it or, failing any indication thereon, under the law of the country where the award was made; or

    (b) The party against whom the award is invoked was not given proper notice of the appointment of the arbitrator or of the arbitration proceedings or was otherwise unable to present his case; or

(c) The award deals with a difference not contemplated by or not falling within the terms of the submission to arbitration, or it contains decisions on matters beyond the scope of the submission to arbitration, provided that, if the decisions on matters submitted to arbitration can be separated from those not so submitted, that part of the award which contains decisions on matters submitted to arbitration may be recognized and enforced; or

(d) The composition of the arbitral authority or the arbitral procedure was not in accordance with the agreement of the parties, or, failing such agreement, was not in accordance with the law of the country where the arbitration took place; or

(e) The award has not yet become binding, on the parties, or has been set aside or suspended by a competent authority of the country in which, or under the law of which, that award was made.

2.   Recognition and enforcement of an arbitral award may also be refused if the competent authority in the country where recognition and enforcement is sought finds that:

(a) The subject matter of the difference is not capable of settlement by arbitration under the law of that country; or

(b) The recognition or enforcement of the award would be contrary to the public policy of that country.

Article VI

If an application for the setting, aside or suspension of the award has been made to a competent authority referred to in article V (1) *(e)*, the authority before which the award is sought to be relied upon may, if it considers it proper, adjourn the decision on the enforcement of the award and may also, on the application of the party claiming enforcement of the award, order the other party to give suitable security.

Article VII

1.   The provisions of the present Convention shall not affect the validity of multilateral or bilateral agreements concerning the recognition and enforcement of arbitral awards entered into by the Contracting States nor deprive any interested party of any right he may have to avail himself of an arbitral award in the manner and to the extent allowed by the law or the treaties of the country where such award is sought to be relied upon.

2.   The Geneva Protocol on Arbitration Clauses of 1923 and the Geneva Convention on the Execution of Foreign Arbitral Awards of 1927 shall cease to have effect between Contracting States on their becoming bound and to the extent that they become bound, by this Convention.

Article VIII

1. This Convention shall be open until 31 December 1958 for signature on behalf of any Member of the United Nations and also on behalf of any other State which is or hereafter becomes a member of any specialized agency of the United Nations, or which is or hereafter becomes a party to the Statute of the International Court of Justice, or any other State to which an invitation has been addressed by the General Assembly of the United Nations.

2. This Convention shall be ratified and the instrument of ratification shall be deposited with the Secretary–General of the United Nations.

Article IX

1. This Convention shall be open for accession to all States referred to in article VIII.

2. Accession shall be effected by the deposit of an instrument of accession with the Secretary–General of the United Nations.

Article X

1. Any State may, at the time of signature, ratification or accession, declare that this Convention shall extend to all or any of the territories for the international relations of which it is responsible. Such a declaration shall take effect when the Convention enters into force for the State concerned.

2. At any time thereafter any such extension shall be made by notification addressed to the Secretary–General of the United Nations and shall take effect as from the ninetieth day after the day of receipt by the Secretary–General of the United Nations of this notification, or as from the date of entry into force of the Convention for the State concerned, whichever is the later.

3. With respect to those territories to which this Convention is not extended at the time of signature, ratification or accession, each State concerned shall consider the possibility of taking the necessary steps in order to extend the application of this Convention to such territories, subject, where necessary for constitutional reasons, to the consent of the Governments of such territories.

Article XI

In the case of a federal or non-unitary State, the following provisions shall apply:

   (a) With respect to those articles of this Convention that come within the legislative jurisdiction of the federal authority, the obligations of the federal Government shall to this extent be the same as those of Contracting States which are not federal States;

(b) With respect to those articles of this Convention that come within the legislative jurisdiction of constituent states or provinces which are not, under the constitutional system of the federation, bound to take legislative action, the federal Government shall bring such articles with a favourable recommendation to the notice of the appropriate authorities of constituent states or provinces at the earliest possible moment;

(c) A federal State Party to this Convention shall, at the request of any other Contracting State transmitted through the Secretary–General of the United Nations, supply a statement of the law and practice of the federation and its constituent units in regard to any particular provision of this Convention, showing the extent to which effect has been given to that provision by legislative or other action.

Article XII

1. This Convention shall come into force on the ninetieth day following the date of deposit of the third instrument of ratification or accession.

2. For each State ratifying or acceeding to this Convention after the deposit of the third instrument of ratification or accession, this Convention shall enter into force on the ninetieth day after deposit by such State of its instrument of ratification or accession.

Article XIII

1. Any Contracting State may denounce this Convention by a written notification to the Secretary–General of the United Nations. Denunciation shall take effect one year after the date of receipt of the notification by the Secretary–General.

2. Any State which has made a declaration or notification under article X may, at any time thereafter, by notification to the Secretary–General of the United Nations, declare that this Convention shall cease to extend to the territory concerned one year after the date of the receipt of the notification by the Secretary–General.

3. This Convention shall continue to be applicable to arbitral awards in respect of which recognition or enforcement proceedings have been instituted before the denunciation takes effect.

Article XIV

A Contracting State shall not be entitled to avail itself of the present Convention against other Contracting States except to the extent that it is itself bound to apply the Convention.

Article XV

The Secretary–General of the United Nations shall notify the States contemplated in article VIII of the following:

(a) Signatures and ratifications in accordance with article VIII;

(b) Accessions in accordance with article IX;

(c) Declarations and notifications under articles I, X and XI;

(d) The date upon which this Convention enters into force in accordance with article XII;

(e) Denunciations and notifications in accordance with article XIII.

Article XVI

1. This Convention, of which the Chinese, English, French, Russian and Spanish texts shall be equally authentic, shall be deposited in the archives of the United Nations.

2. The Secretary–General of the United Nations shall transmit a certified copy of this Convention to the States contemplated in article VIII.

Note

The United States became a party to the New York convention in 1970. The United States ratified the Convention with the reservation that it would be applied "on the basis of reciprocity, to the recognition and enforcement of only those awards made in the territory of another Contracting State." See Art. I (3). The United States also ratified the Convention with the reservation that it would be applied "only to differences arising out of legal relationships, whether contractual or not, which are considered as commercial under the national law of the United States." See Art. I (3).

Index

References are to Pages